1001 ESSENTIAL FAMILY FAVORITES

CLASSIC RECIPES AND ESSENTIAL TECHNIQUES FOR THE FAMILY

ESSENTIAL 1001 FAMILY FAVORITES

CLASSIC RECIPES AND ESSENTIAL TECHNIQUES FOR THE FAMILY

bay books

Published by Bay Books, an imprint of Murdoch Magazines Pty Ltd.

GPO Box 1203
Sydney NSW 2001
Phone: + 61 (0) 2 4352 7000
Fax: + 61 (0) 2 4352 7026

Murdoch Books UK Limited
Ferry House
51–57 Lacy Road
Putney, London SW15 1PR
Phone: + 44 (0) 20 8355 1480
Fax: + 44 (0) 20 8355 1499

Project Manager: Zoë Harpham Editorial Director: Diana Hill
Designer: Michelle Cutler Creative Director: Marylouise Brammer
Indexer: Russell Brooks
Production: Janis Barbi

Chief Executive: Juliet Rogers
Publisher: Kay Scarlett

The Publisher gratefully acknowledges the contribution of the recipe writers, chefs,
photographers and stylists who worked on the material appearing in this publication.

ISBN 1 74045 330 1

PRINTED IN CHINA by Toppan Printing Co. (HK) Ltd.
First published 2003.

IMPORTANT: Those who might be at risk from the effects of salmonella food poisoning
(the elderly, pregnant women, young children and those suffering from immune deficiency
diseases) should consult their GP with any concerns about eating raw eggs.

OUR STAR RATING: When we test recipes, we rate them for ease of preparation.
The following cookery ratings are used in this book:
★ A single star indicates a recipe that is simple and generally quick to make—perfect for beginners.
★★ Two stars indicate the need for just a little more care, or perhaps a little more time.
★★★ Three stars indicate special dishes that need more investment in time,
care and patience—but the results are worth it. Even beginners can make these
dishes as long as the recipe is followed carefully.

1001 ESSENTIAL RECIPES

Cooking for the family day after day can really test your imagination. That's where this book comes in. It's packed full of recipes for every occasion, from the simple to the sublime. There are warming soups, easy pastas, hearty roasts, comforting bakes, spicy curries and tasty stir-fries that are perfect for dinner during the week. Top them off with one of the delicious desserts that will have you clamouring for more. Then there are all those special occasions. Choose from the array of antipasto picnic fare for long summer days to delicate sweet treats for afternoon tea and elaborate feasts for important holidays. There are also plenty of simple recipe ideas for things you've always wanted to try, like your own sun-dried tomatoes, as well as variations on many of the recipes.

CONTENTS

SPECIAL FEATURES

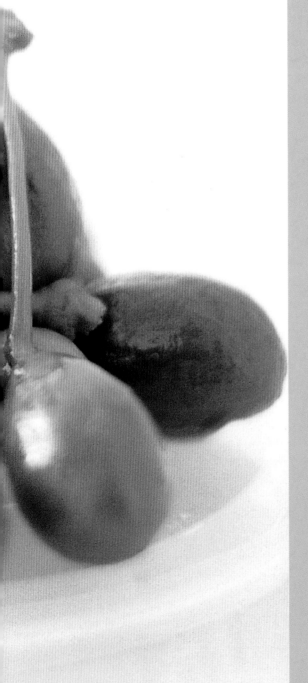

APPETIZERS

DEVILS AND ANGELS ON HORSEBACK

Preparation time: 10 minutes
  + 30 minutes soaking
Total cooking time: 10 minutes
Makes 24

4–6 bacon rashers

12 pitted prunes

12 oysters, fresh or bottled

2 tablespoons Worcestershire sauce

Tabasco sauce, to taste

1 Soak 24 toothpicks in cold water for 30 minutes to prevent them burning. Cut each bacon rasher into thin strips.
2 Wrap a piece of bacon around each prune and secure with a skewer.
3 Remove the oysters from their shells, or drain from the bottling liquid. Sprinkle lightly with Worcestershire sauce and black pepper, to taste. Wrap each oyster in bacon, securing with a toothpick. Preheat a lightly greased grill or barbecue flatplate. Cook the savouries, turning occasionally, until the bacon is crisp. Serve sprinkled with a dash of Tabasco sauce.

STEAMED PRAWN NORI ROLLS

Preparation time: 30 minutes
  + 1 hour refrigeration
Total cooking time: 5 minutes
Makes 24

500 g (1 lb) peeled raw prawns (shrimp)

1½ tablespoons fish sauce

1 tablespoon sake (Japanese rice wine)

2 tablespoons chopped fresh coriander (cilantro)

1 large makrut (kaffir) lime leaf, shredded

1 tablespoon lime juice

2 teaspoons sweet chilli sauce

1 egg white, lightly beaten

5 sheets nori (dried seaweed)

Dipping sauce

1/3 cup (80 ml/2¾ fl oz) sweet chilli sauce

1 tablespoon lime juice

1 Put the prawns, fish sauce, sake, coriander, lime leaf, lime juice and sweet chilli sauce into a food processor or blender and process until smooth. Add the egg white and pulse for a few seconds, or until just combined.
2 Lay the nori sheets on a work surface and spread prawn mixture over each, leaving a 2 cm (¾ inch) border at one end. Roll up tightly, cover and refrigerate for 1 hour. Trim the ends and with a very sharp knife cut into 2 cm (¾ inch) lengths.
3 Place the nori rolls in a paper-lined bamboo steamer, cover the steamer and place over a wok of simmering water. Steam for 5 minutes. Serve with the dipping sauce.
4 Make the dipping sauce by combining the sweet chilli sauce and lime juice in a bowl.

MINI EGGS FLORENTINE

Preparation time: 20 minutes
Total cooking time: 25 minutes
Makes 24

8 slices white bread

1–2 tablespoons olive oil

12 quail eggs

2 teaspoons lemon juice

85 g (3 oz) butter, melted, cooled

2 teaspoons finely chopped fresh basil

20 g (¾ oz) butter, extra

50 g (1¾ oz) baby English spinach leaves

1 Preheat the oven to moderate 180°C (350°F/ Gas 4). Cut 24 rounds from the bread with a 4 cm (1½ inch) cutter. Brush both sides of the rounds with the oil and bake for 10–15 minutes, or until golden brown.
2 Add the quail eggs to a small pan of cold water, bring to the boil, stirring gently (to centre the yolk) and simmer for 4 minutes. Drain, then soak in cold water until cool. Peel, then cut in half, remove the yolks and reserve the whites.
3 Process the quail egg yolks and lemon juice together in a food processor for 10 seconds. With the motor running, add the cooled melted butter in a thin stream. Add the chopped basil and process until combined.
4 Melt the extra butter in a pan, add the spinach leaves and toss until just wilted. Place a little on each bread round, top each with half a quail egg white and fill the cavity with basil mixture.

DEVILS OR ANGELS?
There are two versions of this popular party piece. They consist of either a prune (devil) or an oyster (angel) wrapped in bacon before being cooked. However, in some parts of the world both versions are angels and are turned into devils when enlivened by the addition of a hot sauce such as Tabasco. Just to add to the confusion, some people use scallops instead of oysters, while others cook the prunes in wine and stuff them with chicken livers, mango chutney or an almond.

OPPOSITE PAGE, CLOCKWISE FROM TOP LEFT: Devils and angels on horseback; Steamed prawn nori rolls; Mini eggs florentine

PRAWN TOASTS

Preparation time: 50 minutes
Total cooking time: 8 minutes
Makes 25

✩ ✩ ✩

Mayonnaise

1/2 cup (125 g/4 oz) whole-egg mayonnaise
1 teaspoon wasabi paste
2 teaspoons Japanese soy sauce

25 small raw prawns (shrimp)
1 loaf stale unsliced white bread
3 sheets nori (dried seaweed)
1/2 cup (80 g/2 3/4 oz) sesame seeds
3 eggs, lightly beaten
oil, for deep-frying

1 Mix the mayonnaise, wasabi paste and soy in a small bowl, then cover and refrigerate until ready to use.
2 Peel the prawns leaving the tails intact. Gently pull out the dark vein from each prawn back starting at the head end.
3 Cut the crust off the bread and cut the bread into twenty-five 3 cm (1 1/4 inch) cubes. With a sharp knife, make an incision in the top of the bread three-quarters of the way through. Gently ease a prawn into the cut in each bread cube, leaving the tail sticking out. Cut 25 strips from the nori measuring 1 x 15 cm (1/2 x 6 inches). Wrap a strip around the outside of each bread cube and secure with a toothpick.
4 Measure the sesame seeds into a bowl. Put the eggs in a small bowl and dip the bread in, draining off the excess. Coat the bread in the sesame seeds.
5 Fill a wok or a deep heavy-based saucepan one third full of oil and heat until a cube of bread browns in 15 seconds. Cook the prepared cubes in batches for 1–2 minutes, or until the bread is golden and the prawns cooked through. Drain on crumpled paper towels, remove the toothpicks and season with salt. Serve topped with a teaspoon of the mayonnaise.
IN ADVANCE: Cook this recipe close to serving time to ensure the bread cubes stay crisp. The wasabi mayonnaise can be made several hours ahead, then covered and refrigerated until you are ready to use it.

PUFF PASTRY TWISTS

Preparation time: 10 minutes
Total cooking time: 10 minutes per batch
Makes 96

✩

2 sheets ready-rolled puff pastry, thawed
1 egg, lightly beaten
1/2 cup (80 g/2 3/4 oz) sesame seeds, poppy seeds or caraway seeds

1 Preheat the oven to moderately hot 200°C (400°F/Gas 6). Lightly grease two baking trays. Brush the pastry with the egg and sprinkle with the sesame seeds.
2 Cut in half crossways and then into 1 cm (1/2 inch) wide strips. Twist the strips and put on greased baking trays. Bake for 10 minutes, or until golden. Store in an airtight container for up to 1 week. Refresh in a moderate 180°C (350°F/Gas 4) oven for 2–3 minutes, then cool.

ABOVE: Prawn toasts

PESTO PALMIERS

Preparation time: 20 minutes
Total cooking time: 15–20 minutes per batch
Makes 60

✫

1 cup (50 g/1¾ oz) fresh basil leaves
1 clove garlic, crushed
¼ cup (25 g/¾ oz) grated Parmesan
1 tablespoon pine nuts, toasted
2 tablespoons olive oil
4 sheets ready-rolled puff pastry, thawed

1 Preheat the oven to hot 220°C (425°F/Gas 7). Roughly chop the basil leaves in a food processor with the garlic, Parmesan and pine nuts. With the motor running, gradually add the oil in a thin stream and process until smooth.
2 Spread each pastry sheet with a quarter of the basil mixture. Roll up one side until you reach the middle then repeat with the other side. Place on a baking tray. Repeat with the remaining pastry and basil mixture. Freeze for 30 minutes.
3 Slice each roll into 1.5 cm (⅝ inch) slices. Curl each slice into a semi-circle and place on a lightly greased baking tray. Allow room for the palmiers to expand during cooking. Bake in batches for 15–20 minutes, or until golden brown.

VARIATIONS: Palmiers are delicious bite-sized specially shaped pastry snacks which traditionally were sweet. They were made by sprinkling sugar between the pastry folds and then cutting into slices before baking until crisp and golden. Sometimes they were dusted with icing (confectioners') sugar and served as a petit four with coffee. Other savoury variations include spreading with a prepared tapenade paste made with olives, capers, anchovies, oil and garlic, or with tahini, a sesame seed paste. Another simple version is to sprinkle just the grated Parmesan between the pastry layers.

PINE NUTS
These small, elongated, creamy kernels are sold shelled and blanched. The kernels are taken from the nuts of umbrella-shaped pine trees, sometimes called parasol pines, which are native to the Mediterranean. Recipes often suggest toasting or roasting them before use because this enhances their flavour. The easiest way to do this is to bake on a tray in a moderate 180°C (350°F/Gas 4) oven for 5 minutes, watching carefully that they don't burn. They can also be toasted in a dry frying pan over low heat, tossing constantly until golden.

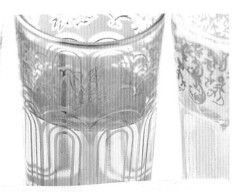

LEFT: Pesto palmiers

PATES
No occasion would be quite complete without a stylish pâté. Simply provide a knife and some crunchy toast and let your guests spread one of these pâtés as thickly as they like.

GRAND MARNIER PATE

Melt 90 g (3 oz) butter in a pan and cook 1 chopped onion and 1 crushed clove of garlic until the onion is tender. Add 250 g (4 oz) trimmed duck or chicken livers and cook for 5–10 minutes. Spoon into a food processor or blender with 2 tablespoons orange juice, 1 tablespoon Grand Marnier (or port or liqueur of your choice), 1 tablespoon sour cream and freshly ground pepper, to taste.

Process until smooth. To prepare the topping, arrange 2 orange slices (cut into quarters if you wish), and fresh chives or parsley in the base of a 2-cup (500 ml/ 16 fl oz) capacity serving dish. Sprinkle 1½ teaspoons gelatine over ½ cup (125 ml/4 fl oz) hot chicken stock and whisk vigorously with a fork to dissolve. Pour over the oranges to a depth of 1 cm (½ inch). Refrigerate until set. Spoon the pâté over the gelatine layer, tap gently

and smooth the top. Refrigerate until set. Unmould onto a serving plate. Serve with crackers or Melba toast. (Pâté can also be made without the gelatine topping, and served on cracker biscuits.) Serves 12–15.

SMOKED TROUT PATE

Mix 250 g (8 oz) skinned and boned smoked trout, 125 g (4 oz) softened butter and 125 g (4 oz) softened cream

cheese in a food processor for 20 seconds, or until smooth. Add 1 tablespoon lemon juice, 1 teaspoon horseradish cream, 15 g (1/2 oz) each of finely chopped fresh parsley and fresh chives and process for 10 seconds. Add salt and freshly ground black pepper, to taste, and more lemon juice, if liked. Transfer to a small serving dish. Serve with hot toasted brown bread. Serves 8–10.

LEMON PRAWN PATE

Melt 100 g (3 1/2 oz) butter in a frying pan. When it sizzles, add 3 crushed cloves garlic and 750 g (1 1/2 lb) peeled and deveined raw prawns (shrimp) and stir for 4 minutes, or until the prawns are pink and cooked through. Cool. Transfer to a food processor, add 1 teaspoon grated lemon rind, 3 tablespoons lemon juice and 1/4 teaspoon grated nutmeg and process for 20 seconds, or until roughly

puréed. Season and add 2 tablespoons each of mayonnaise and finely chopped fresh chives, then process for 20 seconds, or until combined. Spoon into a dish and chill for at least 1 hour, or until firm. Serves 6–8.

MUSHROOM PATE

Melt 40 g (1 1/4 oz) butter and 1 tablespoon oil in a large frying pan. Add 400 g (13 oz) chopped field mushrooms and 2 crushed cloves garlic. Cook until the mushrooms have softened and the mushroom liquid has evaporated. Stir in 3 chopped spring onions (scallions). Allow to cool, then process with 1 tablespoon lemon juice, 100 g (3 1/2 oz) ricotta cheese, 100 g (3 1/2 oz) soft cream cheese and 2 tablespoons chopped fresh coriander (cilantro) leaves. Process until smooth. Season, then spoon into a serving dish, cover and chill for 2 hours. Serves 8–10.

SOFT CHEESE PATE

Roughly chop 150 g (5 oz) toasted pine nuts in a food processor, add 500 g (1 lb) crumbled feta cheese, 3/4 cup (185 ml/6 fl oz) cream and 2 teaspoons coarsely ground pepper and mix until smooth. Add 30 g (1 oz) each of chopped fresh mint, dill and parsley and process until just combined. Line a 3-cup (750 ml/24 fl oz) capacity bowl with plastic wrap. Transfer the mixture to the bowl and press in firmly. Refrigerate, covered, for at least 1 hour, or until firm. Turn out onto a plate and smooth the surface with a knife. Serve with toast triangles. Serves 12–15.

CLOKWISE, FROM LEFT: Grand Marnier pâté; Smoked trout pâté; Lemon prawn pâté; Soft cheese pâté; Mushroom pâté

DIPS
These are a favourite at any gathering. Serve them up with crudités, crackers or crusty bread and watch your guests hovering around the bowl trying not to look too greedy.

CREAMY SALMON DIP
Combine 200 g (6½ oz) cream cheese with 100 g (3½ oz) chopped smoked salmon and 5 tablespoons cream in a food processor and mix until smooth. Season with pepper and sprinkle with a few chopped chives. Keep refrigerated until ready to use.
Makes about 1½ cups.

HOT APPLE CHUTNEY
Beat ¼ cup (60 g/2 oz) sour cream, ½ cup (125 g/4 oz) natural yoghurt, ¼ cup (70 g/2¼ oz) ready-made hot apple chutney and 1 teaspoon maple syrup together until smooth. Season to taste with salt and pepper and refrigerate until ready to serve.
Makes about 1½ cups.

BLUE CHEESE AND CREAM DIP
Mix 250 g (8 oz) blue cheese in a food processor with ½ cup (125 ml/4 fl oz) cream until smooth. Transfer to a bowl, stir in another ½ cup (125 ml/4 fl oz) cream and 2 teaspoons apple cider vinegar and mix well. Season with salt and pepper, cover and refrigerate until ready to use. Makes about 1½ cups.

SWEET AND SOUR DIP

Beat 1 cup (250 g/4 oz) natural yoghurt and ⅓ cup (80 ml/2¾ fl oz) bottled sweet and sour sauce together until smooth. Add 1 tablespoon finely chopped fresh chives and season to taste with salt and pepper. Cover and keep refrigerated until ready to use. Makes about 1½ cups.

CUCUMBER AND PEAR DIP

Beat 2 tablespoons whole-egg mayonnaise, 2 tablespoons natural yoghurt, 1 tablespoon sour cream and 1 teaspoon Dijon mustard together until well combined and smooth. Finely dice half a pear and ¼ of a small cucumber and stir into the mixture with 1 teaspoon of lemon juice. Season to taste with salt and freshly ground black pepper. Cover and keep refrigerated until ready to use. Makes about 1 cup.

REFRIED BEANS

Combine a 460 g (14 oz) can refried beans and ¼ cup (60 g/2 oz) sour cream in a food processor and mix until smooth, adding salt and pepper, to taste. Cover and keep at room temperature until ready to use. Makes about 1½ cups.

AVOCADO AND HERB DIP

Place 1 avocado, 1 tablespoon each of sour cream, lemon juice and light olive oil, 1 small seeded tomato and ¾ cup (25 g/¾ oz) coriander (cilantro) leaves in a food processor and mix until smooth. Season with salt and pepper. Transfer to a glass bowl, lay plastic wrap directly onto the surface of the dip (to prevent a skin forming) and keep refrigerated until ready to use. Try to make this dip close to serving time, so it doesn't discolour. Makes about 2 cups.

CORN AND BACON DIP

Cut the corn kernels from 2 cobs of corn and cook in boiling water, covered, for about 10 minutes, then drain. Meanwhile cook 250 g (8 oz) lean finely chopped bacon in a non-stick pan until very crispy and drain on paper towels. Put the corn in a food processor with 1 crushed clove garlic and mix until quite smooth. Add 250 g (8 oz) spreadable cream cheese and process until well combined. Spoon into a serving dish, cool to room temperature and sprinkle the bacon and some chopped chives over the top. Makes about 2 cups.

CLOKWISE, FROM TOP LEFT: Creamy salmon dip; Blue cheese and cream dip; Cucumber and pear dip; Avocado and herb dip; Corn and bacon dip; Refried beans; Sweet and sour dip; Hot apple chutney

in a small bowl. Peel the eggs, and toss lightly in the flour.

3 Divide the chicken mixture into 24 even portions. Using damp hands, wrap each portion around an egg. Brush each wrapped egg with the beaten egg, and then roll in breadcrumbs, shaking off any excess.

4 Fill a deep heavy-based pan one third full of oil and heat the oil to 180°C (350°F). The oil is ready when a cube of bread dropped in the oil turns golden brown in 15 seconds. Deep-fry the coated eggs until golden brown, then drain on crumpled paper towels. Serve hot, either whole or cut in half.

IN ADVANCE: The eggs can be assembled up to 4 hours ahead and refrigerated, covered, until required. Deep-fry just before serving and garnish with fresh herb sprigs.

RATATOUILLE TRIANGLES

Preparation time: 45 minutes + chilling
Total cooking time: 40 minutes
Makes 18

3 tablespoons oil
1 spring onion (scallion), finely chopped
1–2 cloves garlic, crushed
1 eggplant (aubergine), diced
1 red pepper (capsicum), diced
2 zucchini (courgettes), diced
6 button mushrooms, diced
1 tomato, peeled, seeded and chopped
1 tablespoon chopped capers
2 tablespoons chopped fresh parsley
50 g (1¾ oz) Parmesan, grated
2 sheets ready-rolled puff pastry

1 Heat the oil in a heavy-based frying pan, add the spring onion and garlic and stir for 2 minutes. Add the eggplant, red pepper, zucchini and mushrooms and cook, stirring, for 10 minutes, or until softened.

2 Remove from the heat and add the tomato, capers and parsley. Cool and add the Parmesan. Cut each sheet of pastry into 3 equal strips and each strip into 3 triangles. Roll up a thin border on each side of the triangle and twist the corners to seal. Place on a greased baking tray and prick all over with a fork. Cover and chill for 10–15 minutes.

3 Preheat the oven to moderately hot 190°C (375°F/Gas 5) and bake the triangles for

SCOTCH QUAIL EGGS

Preparation time: 30 minutes
Total cooking time: 20 minutes
Makes 24 whole eggs or 48 halves

24 quail eggs
600 g (1¼ lb) minced (ground) chicken
2 teaspoons grated fresh ginger
2 tablespoons chopped fresh chives
2 teaspoons Dijon mustard
½ cup (60 g/2 oz) plain (all-purpose) flour
2 eggs, lightly beaten
1 cup (100 g/3½ oz) dry breadcrumbs
oil, for deep-frying

1 Place the eggs in a pan and cover with water. Place over medium heat, stirring the eggs gently until the water boils (this centres the yolks). Cook for 5 minutes once boiling. Drain, place in a bowl of cold water and set aside to cool.

ABOVE: Scotch quail eggs

2 Mix the chicken, ginger, chives and mustard

15 minutes, or until crisp. Place a tablespoon of filling into each pastry triangle and reheat for 5–10 minutes.

IN ADVANCE: These ratatouille triangles can be made up to 2 days ahead. Store the pastry triangles and ratatouille separately, covered, in the refrigerator. When required, fill the triangles and reheat briefly on greased baking trays in a moderate 180°C (350°F/Gas 4) oven.

POTATO NOODLE NIBBLES

Preparation time: 30 minutes + cooling
Total cooking time: 40 minutes
Serves 6

 ☆ ☆

450 g (14 oz) floury potatoes, peeled and chopped

40 g (1¼ oz) butter, softened

2 tablespoons grated Parmesan or Pecorino cheese

100 g (3½ oz) besan (chickpea flour)

2 teaspoons ground cumin

2 teaspoons garam masala

1 teaspoon ground coriander

1 teaspoon chilli powder

1 teaspoon cayenne pepper

1½ teaspoons ground turmeric

oil, for deep-frying

1 Boil or steam the potato until tender. Drain and cool for 15–20 minutes, then mash with the butter and cheese. Add the besan, cumin, garam masala, coriander, chilli powder, cayenne, turmeric and ¾ teaspoon of salt and mix with a wooden spoon until a soft, light dough forms. Turn out and knead lightly 10–12 times, until quite smooth.

2 Fill a deep heavy-based pan one third full of oil and heat to 180°C (350°F). Test the temperature by dropping a small ball of dough into the oil. The oil is ready if the dough rises immediately to the surface.

3 Using a piping bag with a 1 cm (½ inch) star nozzle, pipe short lengths of dough into the oil, cutting the dough off with a knife. Cook in manageable batches. They will rise to the surface and turn golden quickly. Remove with a slotted spoon and drain on crumpled paper towels. Serve the nibbles within 2 hours of cooking.

SMOKED SALMON AND ROCKET ROLLS

Preparation time: 20 minutes
Total cooking time: Nil
Makes 36

 ☆

200 g (6½ oz) ricotta cheese

¼ cup (60 g/2 oz) crème fraîche or sour cream

2 teaspoons wasabi paste

1 tablespoon lime juice

12 slices brown bread, crusts removed

300 g (10 oz) smoked salmon

100 g (3½ oz) baby rocket (arugula), trimmed

rocket (arugula) leaves, extra, to garnish

1 Mix together the ricotta, crème fraîche, wasabi and lime juice.

2 Roll the bread out with a rolling pin to flatten.

3 Spread the ricotta over the bread, then top with the smoked salmon and rocket leaves, leaving a border. Roll up lengthways, wrap tightly in plastic wrap to hold the shape, then refrigerate for 30 minutes.

4 Unwrap, trim the ends and cut into 2 cm (¾ inch) slices. Garnish with rocket leaves.

POTATO NOODLE NIBBLES

Spoon the mixture into a piping bag with a star nozzle and pipe short lengths of dough into the oil, in small batches. Cut the dough off with a knife.

ABOVE: Potato noodle nibbles

1 Combine the flour and seasoning in a plastic bag and toss with the chicken strips to coat; remove and shake off excess.

2 Beat the eggs lightly in a shallow bowl, and put the breadcrumbs in a plastic bag.

3 Working with a few chicken strips at a time, dip into the beaten egg, then toss in the breadcrumbs. Transfer to a baking tray covered with baking paper and refrigerate for 30 minutes.

4 Heat 3 cm (1¼ inches) oil in a large frying pan to 180°C (350°F/Gas 4), or until a cube of bread dropped into the oil turns golden brown in 15 seconds. Fry the strips in batches for 3–5 minutes, or until golden brown. Drain on crumpled paper towels. Serve with the sauce.

5 For the sauce, combine the juice, vinegar, soy sauce, sugar and tomato sauce in a small pan. Stir over low heat until the sugar has dissolved. Blend the cornflour with 1 tablespoon water, add to the pan and stir constantly, until the mixture boils and thickens. Reduce the heat and simmer for 2 minutes.

BASIC SAUSAGE ROLLS

Preparation time: 30 minutes
Total cooking time: 15 minutes
Makes 36

3 sheets ready-rolled puff pastry
2 eggs, lightly beaten
750 g (1½ lb) minced (ground) sausage
1 onion, finely chopped
1 clove garlic, crushed
1 cup (80 g/2¾ oz) fresh breadcrumbs
3 tablespoons chopped fresh parsley
3 tablespoons chopped fresh thyme
½ teaspoon each ground sage, nutmeg, black pepper and cloves

1 Preheat the oven to 200°C (400°F/Gas 6). Cut the pastry sheets in half and lightly brush the edges with some of the beaten egg.

2 Mix half the remaining egg with the remaining ingredients in a large bowl, then divide into six even portions. Pipe or spoon the filling down the centre of each piece of pastry, then brush the edges with some of the egg. Fold the pastry over the filling, overlapping the edges and placing the join underneath. Brush the rolls with more egg, then cut each into 6 short pieces.

3 Cut two small slashes on top of each roll and

CHICKEN STRIPS WITH SWEET AND SOUR SAUCE

Preparation time: 30 minutes + chilling
Total cooking time: 30 minutes
Makes 35–40

½ cup (60 g/2 oz) plain (all-purpose) flour
1 tablespoon chicken seasoning salt
4 chicken breast fillets, cut into 2 cm (¾ inch) wide strips
2 eggs
1½ cups (150 g/5 oz) dry breadcrumbs
oil, for shallow-frying

Sweet and sour sauce

1 cup (250 ml/8 fl oz) pineapple juice
3 tablespoons white wine vinegar
2 teaspoons soy sauce
2 tablespoons soft brown sugar
2 tablespoons tomato sauce
1 tablespoon cornflour (cornstarch)

ABOVE: Chicken strips with sweet and sour sauce

place on lightly greased baking trays and bake for 15 minutes, then reduce the oven temperature to moderate 180°C (350°F/Gas 4) and bake for another 15 minutes, or until puffed and golden.

For a different flavour, select a filling from the recipes below and follow the method outlined for the basic sausage roll.

CURRIED PORK AND VEAL

Soak 3 dried Chinese mushrooms in hot water for 30 minutes, squeeze dry and chop finely. Cook 4 finely chopped spring onions (scallions), 1 crushed clove garlic, 1 finely chopped small red chilli and 2–3 teaspoons curry powder in 1 tablespoon oil. Transfer to a bowl and mix with 750 g (1½ lb) minced (ground) pork and veal, 1 cup (90 g/3 oz) fresh breadcrumbs, the dried mushrooms, 1 lightly beaten egg, 3 tablespoons chopped fresh coriander (cilantro) and 1 tablespoon each of soy and oyster sauce.

SPICY LAMB

Mix 750 g (1½ lb) minced (ground) lamb, 1 cup (90 g/3 oz) fresh breadcrumbs, 1 small grated onion, 1 tablespoon soy sauce, 2 teaspoons each of grated fresh ginger and soft brown sugar, 1 teaspoon ground coriander, ½ teaspoon each of ground cumin and sambal oelek. Sprinkle the rolls with poppy seeds after glazing and before baking.

SAUCY BEEF

Cook 1 finely chopped onion and 1–2 crushed cloves garlic in 20 g (¾ oz) butter until the onion is softened. Mix 750 g (1½ lb) minced (ground) lean beef the sautéed onion and garlic, 3 tablespoons finely chopped fresh parsley, 3 tablespoons plain (all-purpose) flour, 3 tablespoons tomato sauce, 1 tablespoon each of Worcestershire and soy sauces and 2 teaspoons ground allspice until well combined.

CHUTNEY CHICKEN

Mix 750 g (1½ lb) minced (ground) chicken, 4 finely chopped spring onions (scallions), 1 cup (80 g/2¾ oz) fresh breadcrumbs, 1 finely grated carrot, 2 tablespoons fruit chutney and 1 tablespoon each of sweet chilli sauce and grated ginger. Sprinkle the pastry with sesame seeds after glazing, before baking.

BELOW, FROM LEFT:
Basic sausage rolls;
Sausage rolls with
chutney chicken filling

OLIVES
All these recipes will keep in the fridge for 3 months if stored in properly sterilized jars. Wash jars and lids thoroughly in boiling water, rinse in boiling water and dry in a slow 150°C (300°F/Gas 2) oven for 30 minutes.

OLIVES WITH HERBS DE PROVENCE

Rinse and drain 500 g (1 lb) Niçoise or Ligurian olives. Put 1 crushed clove garlic, 2 teaspoons chopped fresh basil, 1 teaspoon each chopped fresh thyme, rosemary, marjoram, oregano and mint, 1 teaspoon fennel seeds, 2 tablespoons lemon juice and ½ cup (125 ml/4 fl oz) olive oil in a bowl and mix together. Layer the olives and marinade in a wide-necked, 3-cup (750 ml/24 fl oz) sterilized jar, adding extra olive oil to cover the olives. Seal and marinate in the refrigerator for at least 1 week before using. Serve at room temperature.

HONEY CITRUS OLIVES

Mix together the rind of 1 lemon, lime and orange, 2 tablespoons lime juice, 4 tablespoons lemon juice, 1 tablespoon orange juice, 1 tablespoon honey, 2 teaspoons wholegrain mustard, ½ cup (125 ml/4 fl oz) extra virgin olive oil, 2 thinly sliced cloves garlic, ¼ teaspoon dried oregano or 1 tablespoon chopped fresh oregano leaves and 6 thin slices of lemon and lime. Add 1½ cups (265 g/ 8½ oz) drained unpitted black olives, 1½ cups (265 g/8½ oz) drained unpitted green olives and 2 tablespoons chopped fresh parsley. Place in a wide-necked, 3-cup (750 ml/24 fl oz) sterilized jar, then seal and marinate in the refrigerator for at least 1 week before using. Serve at room temperature.

LEMON OLIVES WITH VERMOUTH

Combine 3 tablespoons dry vermouth, 1 tablespoon lemon juice, 2 teaspoons shredded lemon rind and 2 tablespoons extra virgin olive oil. Rinse 1 cup (170 g/5½ oz) of Spanish green or stuffed olives and pat dry. Add to the marinade and toss well. Cover and refrigerate overnight. Serve at room temperature.

DILL, GARLIC AND ORANGE OLIVES

Combine 500 g (1 lb) Kalamata olives with 3 tablespoons coarsely chopped fresh dill, 1 bruised clove garlic, 4 thin slices of orange cut into eighths and 2 torn bay leaves. Spoon into a 1 litre (32 fl oz) sterilized jar and pour in about 1¾ cups (440 ml/14 fl oz) olive oil or enough to cover the olives completely. Seal and marinate in the refrigerator for at least 2 days. Serve at room temperature.

CHILLI AND LEMON OLIVES

Combine 500 g (1 lb) cured black olives (olives with wrinkled skin) with 2 teaspoons finely grated lemon rind, 2 teaspoons chopped fresh oregano and 3 teaspoons dried chilli flakes. Transfer to a 3-cup (750 ml/24 fl oz) sterilized jar; cover with olive oil. Seal; chill for at least 2 days. Serve at room temperature.

SUN-DRIED TOMATO OLIVES

Rinse 500 g (1 lb) Spanish black olives; pat dry. Score or crack the olives. Layer in a 3-cup (750 ml/24 fl oz) sterilized jar, with 100 g (3½ oz) drained and chopped sun-dried tomatoes (reserve the oil), 2 crushed cloves garlic, 2 bay leaves, 3 teaspoons fresh thyme leaves and 2 teaspoons red wine vinegar. Pour over the reserved oil and 1 cup (250 ml/ 8 fl oz) extra virgin olive oil, or enough to cover. Seal and refrigerate overnight. Serve at room temperature.

MIXED OLIVE PICKLES

Combine 200 g (6½ oz) jumbo green olives, 4 gherkins, thickly sliced diagonally, 1 tablespoon capers, 2 brown pickling onions, quartered, 2 teaspoons mustard seeds and 1 tablespoon fresh dill sprigs in a bowl. Spoon into a 2-cup (500 ml/16 fl oz) sterilized jar and pour in ½ cup (125 ml/4 fl oz) tarragon vinegar. Top with about ½ cup (125 ml/4 fl oz) olive oil, or enough to cover completely. Seal and refrigerate for at least 2 days. Shake the jar occasionally. Serve at room temperature.

CLOKWISE, FROM TOP LEFT: Olives with herbs de provence; Honey citrus olives; Lemon olives with vermouth; Dill, garlic and orange olives; Chilli and lemon olives; Sun-dried tomato olives; Mixed olive pickles

1 Preheat the oven to hot 210°C (415°F/ Gas 6–7). Line two large baking trays with baking paper. Mix the cream cheese, mustards, lemon juice and dill in a bowl, then cover and refrigerate.

2 Cut four 9.5 cm (3¾ inch) rounds from each sheet of puff pastry, using a fluted cutter, and place on the baking trays. Prick the pastries all over. Cover and refrigerate for 10 minutes.

3 Bake the pastries in batches for 7 minutes, then remove from the oven and use a spoon to flatten the centre of each pastry. Return to the oven and bake for another 5 minutes, or until the pastry is golden. Cool, then spread some of the cream cheese mixture over each pastry, leaving a 1 cm (½ inch) border. Arrange the salmon over the top. Decorate with a few capers and a sprig of fresh dill. Serve immediately.

TURKEY MEATBALLS WITH MINT YOGHURT

Preparation time: 15 minutes
Total cooking time: 10 minutes
Makes 30

600 g (1¼ lb) minced (ground) turkey
2 cloves garlic, crushed
2 tablespoons finely chopped fresh mint
2 teaspoons finely chopped fresh rosemary
2 tablespoons mango-lime chutney
2 tablespoons oil

Mint yoghurt

200 g (6½ oz) natural yoghurt
2 tablespoons finely chopped fresh mint
2 teaspoons mango and lime chutney

1 Mix the turkey, garlic, mint, rosemary and chutney in a bowl. With wet hands, roll tablespoons of the mixture into balls. Heat half the oil in a large frying pan over medium heat and cook the balls, turning often, for 5 minutes, or until cooked through. Drain on crumpled paper towels. Repeat with the remaining oil and meatballs.

2 Put the mint yoghurt ingredients together in a small bowl and stir until well combined. Serve with the turkey balls.

NOTE: You may need to order the minced (ground) turkey from a poultry specialist or you can use chicken instead.

SMOKED SALMON TARTLETS

Preparation time: 30 minutes
  + 10 minutes refrigeration
Total cooking time: 30 minutes
Makes 24

250 g (8 oz) cream cheese, at room temperature
1½ tablespoons wholegrain mustard
2 teaspoons Dijon mustard
2 tablespoons lemon juice
2 tablespoons chopped fresh dill
6 sheets ready-rolled puff pastry
300 g (10 oz) smoked salmon, cut into
   thin strips
2 tablespoons bottled tiny capers, drained
fresh dill sprigs, to garnish

ABOVE: Smoked salmon tartlets

BLACK SESAME SEED TARTS WITH MARINATED FETA

Preparation time: 25 minutes
  + 10 minutes refrigeration
Total cooking time: 20 minutes
Makes 30

300 g (10 oz) tomatoes

200 g (6¹/2 oz) feta, diced

¹/2 cup (75 g/2¹/2 oz) black olives, pitted
  and diced

1 teaspoon finely chopped
  fresh thyme

2 cloves garlic, crushed

1 tablespoon extra virgin olive oil

2 cups (250 g/8 oz) plain (all-purpose) flour

125 g (4 oz) butter, chopped

60 g (2 oz) Parmesan, finely grated

1 tablespoon black sesame seeds

1 egg

fresh thyme, optional, to garnish

1 Preheat the oven to moderately hot 200°C (400°F/Gas 6). Lightly grease two 12-hole mini-muffin tins. Score a cross in the base of each tomato, place in a heatproof bowl and cover with boiling water. Leave for 30 seconds, then plunge in cold water. Peel away from the cross. Cut in half and scoop out the seeds with a teaspoon. Dice the flesh and combine in a bowl with the feta, black olives, thyme, garlic and oil. Set aside.

2 Sift the flour into a large bowl and add the butter. Rub together with your fingertips until the mixture resembles fine breadcrumbs. Stir in the Parmesan and black sesame seeds. Make a well, add the egg and mix with a flat-bladed knife, using a cutting action until the mixture comes together in beads (add a little cold water if too dry). On a lightly floured surface, press together into a ball, then wrap in plastic wrap and refrigerate for 10 minutes. Roll out to 2 mm (¹/8 inch) thick between two sheets of baking paper. Remove the paper and cut out 30 rounds with a 6 cm (2¹/2 inch) cutter. Gently press into the tins and bake for 10 minutes, or until dry and golden. Repeat with the remaining pastry rounds. Cool and place 1 heaped teaspoon feta filling into each pastry shell. Garnish and serve.

ABOVE: Black sesame seed tarts with marinated feta

CORIANDER
Also known as cilantro.
All parts of this plant, the
leaves, stems, roots and
dried seeds (whole or
ground) can be used in
cookery. The leaves are
usually added at the end
of cooking, either as a
flavouring or a garnish.
The stems are added if
a strong flavour is required
and the roots are chopped
and used in curry pastes.
Coriander is used quite
extensively in Chinese,
Middle Eastern, South
American, Mexican, Asian
and Mediterranean cookery.

THAI CHICKEN BALLS

Preparation time: 20 minutes
Total cooking time: 40 minutes
Makes about 50 balls

★ ★

1 kg (2 lb) minced (ground) chicken
1 cup (80 g/2³⁄₄ oz) fresh breadcrumbs
4 spring onions (scallions), sliced
1 tablespoon ground coriander
1 cup (50 g/1³⁄₄ oz) chopped fresh coriander
 (cilantro)
¹⁄₄ cup (60 ml/2 fl oz) sweet chilli sauce
1–2 tablespoons lemon juice
oil, for shallow-frying

1 Mix the chicken and breadcrumbs together. Add the spring onion, ground and fresh coriander, chilli sauce and lemon juice, and mix. With wet hands, form into evenly shaped walnut-sized balls. Preheat the oven to moderately hot 200°C (400°F/Gas 6).
2 Heat 3 cm (1¹⁄₄ inches) oil in a deep frying pan to 180°C (350°F), or until a cube of bread browns in 15 seconds. Cook the balls in batches until golden. Bake on a baking tray for 5 minutes, or until cooked through.

ABOVE: Thai chicken balls

SEAFOOD PYRAMIDS

Preparation time: 30 minutes
Total cooking time: 15 minutes
Makes 24

★ ★

200 g (6¹⁄₂ oz) scallops, without roe, chopped
8 spring onions (scallions), finely chopped
¹⁄₃ cup (35 g/1¹⁄₄ oz) Japanese breadcrumbs
4 tablespoons chopped fresh coriander (cilantro)
2 cloves garlic, crushed
1 makrut (kaffir) lime leaf, finely chopped
¹⁄₂ teaspoon sesame oil
24 won ton wrappers
oil, for deep-frying

Dipping sauce

2 tablespoons lime juice
1 tablespoon sake
2 teaspoons soy sauce
¹⁄₄ teaspoon sesame oil
1 teaspoon grated fresh ginger

1 Combine the scallops, spring onion, Japanese breadcrumbs, coriander, garlic, lime leaf and

sesame oil. Place 2 teaspoons of the mixture in the centre of each won ton wrapper. Brush the edges with water and bring the corners up to meet, pushing the edges together to form a pyramid shape.

2 Fill a heavy-based saucepan one third full of oil and heat the oil to 180°C (350°F), or until a cube of bread browns in 15 seconds. Deep-fry the pyramids in batches, until crisp and golden. Drain on crumpled paper towels.

3 Stir together all the dipping sauce ingredients and serve with the pyramids.

NOTE: Japanese breadcrumbs are readily available in Asian food speciality stores. They are white, quite big and crisp.

STEAMED PRAWN WON TONS

Preparation time: 30 minutes
Total cooking time: 15 minutes
Makes 24

3/4 cup (15 g/1/2 oz) dried Chinese
    mushrooms, sliced
24 raw prawns (shrimp)
1 tablespoon sake
1 tablespoon grated fresh ginger
1 teaspoon sesame oil
2 teaspoons sweet chilli sauce
24 gow gee wrappers

Dipping sauce

1/4 cup (60 ml/2 fl oz) soy sauce
1 tablespoon fish sauce
1 tablespoon lime juice
1/4 cup (60 ml/2 fl oz) sweet
    chilli sauce

1 Put the Chinese mushrooms in a heatproof bowl, cover with boiling water and soak for 10 minutes. Drain well and finely chop. Meanwhile, peel the prawns, leaving the tails intact. Gently pull out the dark vein from each prawn back, starting at the head end. Cut the prawns in half and set aside the ends with the tails. Finely chop the remaining prawns.

2 Combine the mushrooms and chopped prawns with the sake, ginger, sesame oil and chilli sauce. Put a heaped teaspoon of the mixture in the centre of each gow gee wrapper. Place a reserved prawn tail in the centre of each, standing up. Brush the edges of the wrappers with water and gather up to form parcels, leaving the prawn tails exposed. Steam in batches, in a bamboo steamer for 5 minutes, or until the prawns turn pink.

3 Stir together all the dipping sauce ingredients in a bowl and serve with the pyramids.

VARIATION: As an alternative, you can make coriander (cilantro) dipping sauce. Combine 1/4 cup (60 ml/2 fl oz) fish sauce, 1 tablespoon white vinegar, 1–2 finely chopped, seeded red chillies, 1 teaspoon sugar and 3 teaspoons chopped fresh coriander in a small bowl. Add 1–2 teaspoons of lime juice, to taste, and mix well. This sauce can also be served with fresh cooked peeled prawns, or drizzled on fresh oysters.

ABOVE: Steamed prawn won tons

HAM AND PINEAPPLE PIZZA WHEELS

Rub the chopped butter into the flour with your fingertips until the mixture resembles breadcrumbs.

Roll the dough into a rectangle and use a flat-bladed knife to spread all over with tomato paste.

Use the baking paper as a guide as you roll up the dough from the long side.

ABOVE: Ham and pineapple pizza wheels

HAM AND PINEAPPLE PIZZA WHEELS

Preparation time: 25 minutes
Total cooking time: 20 minutes
Makes 16

★★

2 cups (250 g/8 oz) self-raising flour
40 g (1 1/4 oz) butter, chopped
1/2 cup (125 ml/4 fl oz) milk
4 tablespoons tomato paste
   (tomato purée)
2 small onions, finely chopped
4 pineapple slices, finely chopped
200 g (6 1/2 oz) sliced ham, shredded
80 g (2 3/4 oz) Cheddar, grated
2 tablespoons finely chopped fresh parsley

1 Preheat the oven to moderate 180°C (350°F/ Gas 4). Brush 2 baking trays with oil. Sift the flour into a bowl, add the butter and rub into the flour with your fingertips until the mixture resembles fine breadcrumbs. Make a well and add almost all the milk. With a flat-bladed knife, mix with a cutting action until the mixture comes together in beads. Gather into a ball and turn onto a lightly floured surface. Divide the dough in half. Roll out each half on baking paper to a 20 x 30 cm (8 x 12 inch) rectangle, about 5 mm (1/4 inch) thick. Spread the tomato paste over each rectangle, leaving a 1 cm (1/2 inch) border.
2 Mix the onion, pineapple, ham, Cheddar and parsley. Spread evenly over the tomato paste, leaving a 2 cm (3/4 inch) border. Using the paper as a guide, roll up the dough from the long side.
3 Cut each roll into 8 even slices. Place on the tray and bake for 20 minutes, or until golden. Serve warm.
IN ADVANCE: The wheels can be made in advance and gently reheated.

CAVIAR POTATOES

Cook some unpeeled baby potatoes (enough for your gathering) in a large pan of boiling water until tender. Allow to cool slightly. While still warm, carefully cut off the top and scoop out a little of the centre. Fill the hole with sour cream and top with caviar. You can mix finely chopped herbs or spring onion (scallion) into the sour cream if you wish. Garnish with tiny sprigs of fresh dill. Serve warm.

PESTO AND TOMATO TOASTS

Preparation time: 15 minutes
Total cooking time: 5 minutes
Makes about 30

Pesto

1 cup (50 g/1³/₄ oz) fresh basil leaves
¹/₂ cup (50 g/1³/₄ oz) pecan nuts
¹/₄ cup (60 ml/2 fl oz) olive oil
3 cloves garlic

1 French bread stick, thinly sliced
10 large sun-dried tomatoes, cut into thin strips
150 g (5 oz) Parmesan, thinly shaved

1 To make the pesto, mix the basil leaves, pecans, oil and garlic in a food processor until the mixture is smooth.
2 Toast the bread slices under a grill until brown on both sides.
3 Spread the pesto evenly over the pieces of toast. Top each slice with sun-dried tomatoes and some of the Parmesan.
IN ADVANCE: The pesto can be made several days ahead and stored in a jar. Pour a thin layer of olive oil over the top of the pesto to just cover. Pesto can also be frozen in ice cube trays and thawed when required.

MINI VEAL SALTIMBOCCA

Preparation time: 20 minutes + soaking
Total cooking time: 15 minutes
Makes about 40

40 small wooden skewers (about 10 cm/
    4 inches) long
500 g (1 lb) piece veal fillet
8–10 slices prosciutto
60 g (2 oz) fresh sage leaves
30 g (1 oz) butter
2 teaspoons oil
2 tablespoons dry sherry

1 Soak the wooden skewers in warm water for about 20 minutes to prevent them burning while the meat is cooking. Cut the veal fillet into 40 thin slices, each measuring roughly 3 x 6 cm (1¹/₄ x 2¹/₂ inches). Cut the prosciutto slices slightly smaller than the veal. Top each piece of veal with a piece of prosciutto, then a fresh sage leaf. Weave a skewer through all the layers to secure.
2 Heat half the butter and oil in a large frying pan, add half the skewers and cook over high heat until the veal is brown, then turn and brown other side.
3 Drizzle half the dry sherry over the cooked meat and gently shake the pan. Remove the skewers from the pan, pouring any juices over the skewers. Keep warm while you repeat with the remaining skewers. Serve soon after cooking, drizzled with any juices.
IN ADVANCE: The skewers can be prepared a day ahead. Keep covered in the refrigerator.

ABOVE: Pesto and tomato toasts

29

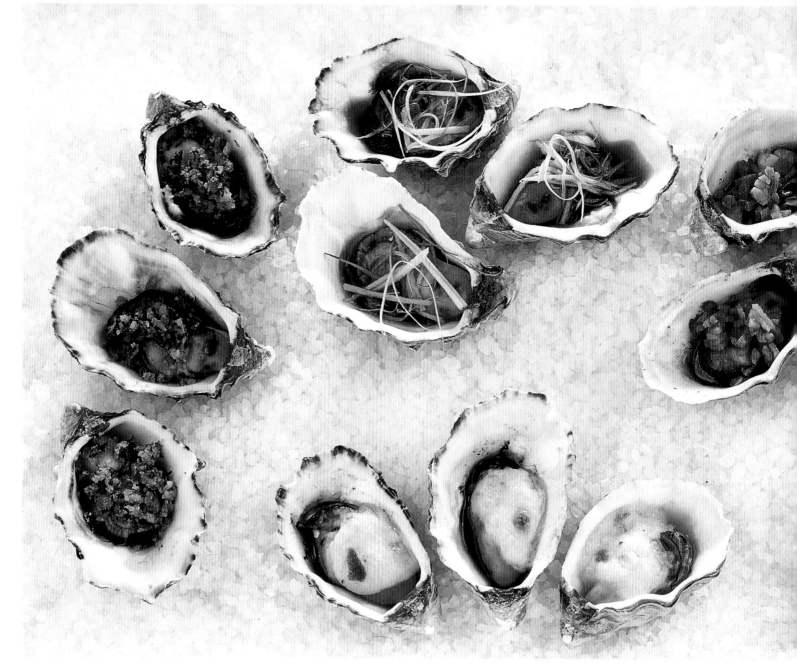

OYSTERS

Fresh oysters served in the shell are one of nature's works of art. It is impossible to improve on perfection... but these recipes certainly come close.

OYSTERS ROCKEFELLER

Arrange 24 oysters in their shells on a bed of rock salt on a baking tray. Cover and refrigerate. Melt 60 g (2 oz) butter in a pan. Add 2 finely chopped bacon rashers and cook until browned. Add 8 finely chopped English spinach leaves, 2 finely chopped spring onions (scallions), 2 tablespoons finely chopped fresh parsley, 4 tablespoons dry breadcrumbs and a drop of Tabasco sauce. Cook over medium heat until the spinach wilts. Spoon onto the oysters and grill until golden. Makes 24.

OYSTERS MORNAY

Melt 30 g (1 oz) butter in a small pan. Stir in 1 tablespoon plain (all-purpose) flour and cook for 2 minutes. Remove from the heat. Gradually add 2/3 cup (170 ml/ 5½ fl oz) hot milk. Return to medium heat and stir until the mixture boils and thickens. Add salt and pepper, to taste, and a pinch of cayenne pepper. Simmer for 2 minutes, stirring occasionally. Remove. Drain the juice from 24 oysters. Arrange the oysters in the shells on a bed of rock salt on a baking tray. Top each with a teaspoon of the sauce and sprinkle with grated Cheddar. Grill for a few minutes, or until golden. Makes 24.

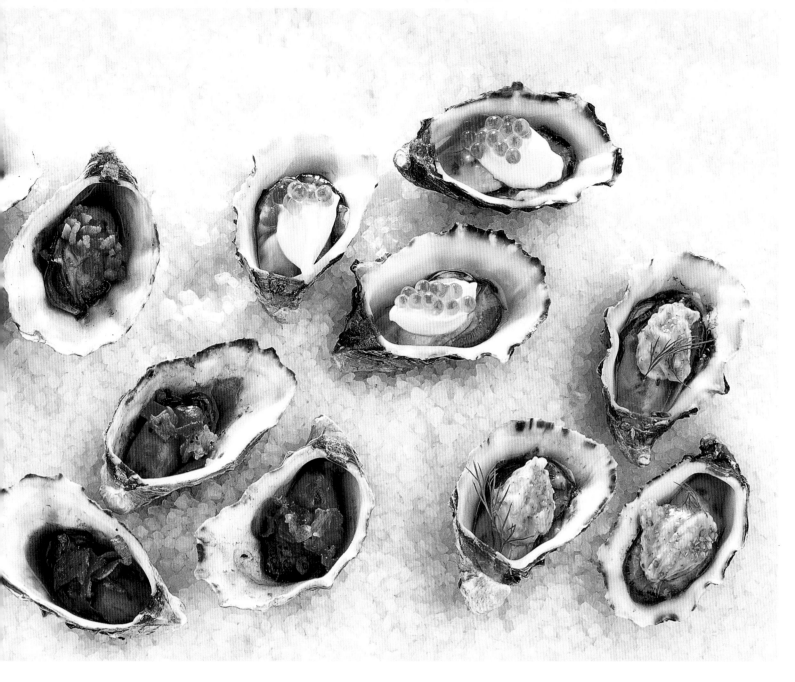

GINGER AND SOY OYSTERS

Arrange 24 oysters in their shells on a bed of rock salt on a baking tray. Combine in a bowl 2 tablespoons each of soy sauce and sweet sherry, 3 teaspoons sesame oil, 1 tablespoon finely shredded fresh ginger, 1 spring onion (scallion) cut into long shreds, and ground pepper. Divide evenly among the oysters. Bake in a preheated moderate 180°C (350°F/Gas 4) oven for 5–10 minutes, or until the oysters are just cooked. Makes 24.

OYSTERS KILPATRICK

Arrange 24 oysters in their shells on a bed of rock salt on a baking tray. Sprinkle lightly with Worcestershire. Sprinkle with 3 finely chopped bacon rashers and ground black pepper. Grill for 3–4 minutes. Makes 24.

MEDITERRANEAN OYSTERS

Arrange 24 oysters in their shells on a bed of rock salt on a baking tray. Sprinkle the oysters lightly with balsamic vinegar. Chop 6 slices of prosciutto and divide among the oysters. Sprinkle with black pepper. Grill for 1 minute, or until the prosciutto is crisp. Makes 24.

OYSTERS WITH SALMON ROE AND CREME FRAICHE

Spread rock salt over a large serving platter. Arrange 24 shucked oysters on the rock salt (the salt helps to steady the oysters). Spoon 1 teaspoon crème fraîche onto each oyster and top with 1/2 teaspoon salmon roe (you will need about 120 g/4 oz altogether). Season with freshly ground black pepper. Serve with lime wedges. Makes 24.

OYSTERS WITH SESAME SEED MAYONNAISE

Remove 24 oysters from their shells and pat dry. Wash the shells, replace the oysters and cover with a damp cloth. Refrigerate. Stir 1 tablespoon sesame oil, 1 clove crushed garlic and 2 tablespoons toasted sesame seeds into 1/3 cup (80 g/2 3/4 oz) whole-egg mayonnaise. Season and spoon a teaspoonful onto each oyster. Garnish each with a sprig of fresh dill. Makes 24.

CLOKWISE, FROM LEFT: Oysters Rockefeller; Ginger and soy oysters; Oysters Kilpatrick; Oysters with salmon roe and crème fraîche; Oysters with sesame seed mayonnaise; Mediterranean oysters; Oysters mornay

DEEP-FRIED ZUCCHINI FLOWERS
Zucchini (courgettes) are baby marrows, usually dark green in colour, but there are also light green and yellow varieties. The flowers are edible too, and deep-fried zucchini flowers make a great snack. To make them, whisk 2 eggs with 55 g (2 oz) plain (all-purpose) flour and some seasoning. To make the stuffing for the flowers, mix 125 g (4 oz) ricotta with 1 tablespoon shredded basil, 2 tablespoons each of grated Parmesan and breadcrumbs and 1 egg yolk. Season. Stuff the mixture into 10 zucchini flowers. Dip each flower in the batter and deep-fry until golden.

RIGHT, FROM LEFT:
Spicy sausage roll-ups;
Glazed chicken wings;
Zucchini boats

SPICY SAUSAGE ROLL-UPS

Preparation time: 20 minutes
Total cooking time: 20 minutes
Makes about 25

2 sheets frozen shortcrust pastry
2 tablespoons French mustard
5 sticks cabanossi
1 egg yolk, beaten

1 Preheat the oven to hot 200°C (400°F/Gas 6). Cut each pastry sheet in half. Cut triangles with bases of 6 cm (2½ inches). Place a small dob of mustard at the base of each pastry piece. Cut the cabanossi into 7 cm (2¾ inch) lengths and place across the mustard on the pastry triangles.
2 Dampen the tips of the triangles with a little water. Working from the base, roll each pastry triangle around the pieces of cabanossi. Press lightly to secure the tip to the rest of the pastry.
3 Place the roll-ups on a lightly greased baking tray and brush with a mixture of egg yolk and 2 teaspoons cold water. Bake for 15–20 minutes, or until the roll-ups are golden brown.
IN ADVANCE: These can be made up to 2 days ahead, refrigerated, then gently reheated in the oven when required.

GLAZED CHICKEN WINGS

Preparation time: 30 minutes + marinating
Total cooking time: 45 minutes
Makes about 40

2 kg (4 lb) chicken wings
½ cup (125 ml/4 fl oz) barbecue sauce
½ cup (160 g/5½ oz) apricot jam
2 tablespoons white vinegar
2 tablespoons soy sauce
2 tablespoons tomato sauce
1 tablespoon sesame oil
2 cloves garlic, crushed

1 Trim excess fat from the wings. Stir the barbecue sauce, jam, vinegar, soy sauce, tomato sauce, oil and garlic in a small pan over low heat until just combined. Cool slightly, pour over the chicken wings and mix well. Cover and marinate in the refrigerator for at least 2 hours.
2 Preheat the oven to moderate 180°C (350°F/Gas 4). Drain the excess marinade from the wings and reserve. Bake the wings in a lightly greased baking dish for 45 minutes. To prevent sticking, you can add a little water. Turn halfway through the cooking time, brushing occasionally with the reserved marinade.

ZUCCHINI BOATS

Preparation time: 20 minutes
Total cooking time: 10 minutes
Makes 30

5 large zucchini (courgettes)
1 large tomato, finely chopped
2 spring onions (scallions), finely chopped
1 tablespoon chopped fresh parsley
2 slices salami, finely chopped
1/2 cup (60 g/2 oz) grated Cheddar

1 Cut each zucchini into three equal pieces, about 4 cm (1 1/2 inches) long. Cut each piece in half lengthways.
2 Using a teaspoon, scoop a small hollow from each piece. Add the zucchini to a pan of simmering water for about 3 minutes, or until tender; drain. Refresh under cold water, then pat dry with paper towels.
3 Combine the tomato, onion, parsley, salami and Cheddar in a small bowl. Spoon the filling into the zucchini boats. Cook under a preheated grill until the Cheddar has melted and the boats are warmed through. Serve immediately.

CHILLI PRAWNS WITH SHREDDED COCONUT

Preparation time: 40 minutes + marinating
Total cooking time: 8–10 minutes
Makes about 48

1 cup (250 ml/8 fl oz) tomato sauce
3 cloves garlic, crushed
1 teaspoon ground chilli
1/4 cup (60 ml/2 fl oz) lemon juice
2 teaspoons finely grated lemon rind
2 tablespoons soy sauce
2 tablespoons honey
1 tablespoon oil
2 kg (4 lb) raw king prawns (shrimp), peeled and deveined
1 cup (60 g/2 oz) shredded coconut

1 In a large bowl, mix the tomato sauce, garlic, chilli, lemon juice, rind, soy sauce and honey. Add the prawns and marinate in the refrigerator for at least 2 hours. Drain. Reserve the marinade.
2 Heat the oil in a large frying pan. Add the prawns and coconut and cook until the prawns turn pink. Stir in the marinade and cook for until heated through. Stir in the coconut. Serve.

COCONUT
Grated and shredded coconut is best when fresh. Drain a coconut by punching a hole in two of the dark, coloured eyes. Drain out the liquid and use it as a refreshing drink. Holding the coconut in one hand, tap around the circumference firmly with a hammer or pestle. This should cause the coconut to split open evenly. (If the coconut doesn't crack easily, put it in a slow 150°C (300°F/Gas 2) oven for 15 minutes. This may cause it to crack as it cools. If it doesn't, it will crack easily when hit with a hammer.) If you don't have a coconut grater, prise the flesh out of the shell, trim off the hard, brown, outer skin and grate either by hand on a box grater or chop in a food processor. Freeze in small portions until needed.

ABOVE: Chilli prawns with shredded coconut

GRAVLAX

Remove any bones from the salmon with tweezers.

Rub the remaining sugar mixture into the second salmon fillet.

Whisk all the ingredients of the mustard sauce together.

For serving, the salmon can be sliced thinly on an angle towards the tail.

OPPOSITE PAGE, FROM TOP: Potted prawns; Gravlax

POTTED PRAWNS

Preparation time: 12 minutes + overnight chilling
Total cooking time: 3 minutes
Makes 1 1/3 cups (350 g/11 oz)

250 g (8 oz) small cooked prawns (shrimp)
100 g (3 1/2 oz) butter
1/4 teaspoon ground nutmeg
1/4 teaspoon ground ginger
pinch of cayenne pepper

1 Peel the prawns and gently pull out the dark vein from each prawn back, starting at the head end. Chop the prawns very finely. Melt 60 g (2 oz) of the butter over low heat in a small saucepan. Add the prawns, nutmeg, ginger, cayenne pepper and salt and pepper, to taste.
2 Stir over low heat for 2 minutes, or until all the butter has been absorbed into the mixture. Spoon into a 1 1/3 cup (350 ml/11 fl oz) capacity ramekin, press down, then smooth the surface.
3 Melt the remaining butter in a small pan and pour over the surface (leaving the white sediment behind in the pan) to cover completely. Refrigerate overnight to allow the flavours to develop. Bring back to room temperature and serve with toast.

GRAVLAX

Preparation time: 10 minutes + 24 hours chilling
Total cooking time: 5 minutes
Serves 12

1/4 cup (60 g/2 oz) sugar
2 tablespoons sea salt
1 teaspoon crushed black peppercorns
2.5 kg (5 lb) salmon, filleted, skin on
1 tablespoon vodka or brandy
4 tablespoons very finely chopped fresh dill

Mustard sauce

1 1/2 tablespoons cider vinegar
1 teaspoon caster (superfine) sugar
1/2 cup (125 ml/4 fl oz) olive oil
2 teaspoons chopped fresh dill
2 tablespoons Dijon mustard

1 Combine the sugar, salt and peppercorns in a small dish. Remove any bones from the salmon with tweezers. Pat dry with paper towels and lay a fillet skin-side-down in a shallow tray or baking dish. Sprinkle the fillet with half the vodka, rub half the sugar mixture into the flesh, then sprinkle with half the dill. Sprinkle the remaining vodka over the second salmon fillet and rub the remaining sugar mixture into the flesh. Lay it flesh-side-down on top of the other fillet. Cover with plastic wrap, place a heavy board on top and then weigh the board down with 3 heavy cans or a foil-covered brick. Refrigerate for 24 hours, turning it over after 12 hours.
2 For the mustard sauce, whisk all the ingredients together, then cover until needed.
3 Uncover the salmon and lay both fillets on a wooden board. Brush off all the dill and seasoning with a stiff pastry brush. Sprinkle with the remaining fresh dill and press it onto the salmon flesh, shaking off any excess. Serve whole on the serving board, or thinly sliced on an angle towards the tail, with the sauce.
NOTE: Gravlax can be refrigerated, covered, for up to a week.

SCOTCH WOODCOCK

Preparation time: 10 minutes
Total cooking time: 5 minutes
Serves 4

2 eggs
4 egg yolks
150 ml (5 fl oz) cream
2 tablespoons finely chopped fresh parsley
pinch of cayenne pepper
45 g (1 1/2 oz) can anchovy fillets, drained
20 g (3/4 oz) softened butter
4 thick slices bread, toasted

1 Whisk together the whole eggs, egg yolks, cream, half the parsley and the cayenne in a bowl until smooth. Add a little salt and pepper. Pour the mixture into a small heavy-based pan and cook over low heat, stirring frequently, until the egg has set and forms soft curds. Do not overheat or overmix.
2 Mash the anchovies and butter with a fork to form a smooth paste. Spread over the toast.
3 Spoon the egg over the anchovy toasts, sprinkle with the remaining parsley and serve. The toasts can be cut into small triangles.

TEMPURA PRAWNS

Score the underside of the prawns a few times.

Mix the flour into the batter with chopsticks—the batter should be lumpy.

Drizzle the prawns with a little of the remaining batter, but beware of oil spitting up at you.

ABOVE: Tempura prawns

TEMPURA PRAWNS

Preparation time: 25 minutes
Total cooking time: 10 minutes
Serves 4

★★

12 raw large prawns (shrimp)
oil, for deep-frying
1 egg
1 cup (250 ml/8 fl oz) iced water
1 cup (125 g/4 oz) tempura flour, sifted
2 ice cubes
1 sheet roasted nori, shredded

1 Peel and devein the prawns, keeping the tails intact. Using a sharp knife, make three or four diagonal cuts in the underside of each prawn one-third of the way through. Pat the prawns dry with paper towels.
2 Fill a wok one-third full of oil and heat to 180°C (350°F), or until a cube of bread browns in 15 seconds. While the oil is heating, put the egg in a large bowl and, using chopsticks or a fork, break it up. Add the iced water and mix well with chopsticks. Add the sifted flour all at once and mix with chopsticks until just combined, then add the ice cubes—the mixture should be lumpy. Dip the prawns in the batter and deep-fry in batches, four at a time, drizzling

with some of the remaining batter to give a spiky effect. Cook for 1 minute, or until crisp.
3 Drain the prawns on crumpled paper towels, sprinkle with the nori and serve immediately.

AGEDASHI TOFU

Preparation time: 15 minutes + 1 hour soaking
Total cooking time: 15 minutes
Serves 4

★★

40 g (1¼ oz) konbu (kelp)
1–2 tablespoons soy sauce
2–3 teaspoons sugar
2 × 300 g (10 oz) packets silken firm tofu
oil, for deep-frying
potato flour, to dust
4 spring onions (scallions), thinly sliced on the diagonal
20 g (¾ oz) daikon, grated
1 teaspoon grated fresh ginger

1 Wipe the konbu clean with a damp cloth (do not wash). Put it in a large bowl, cover with 1 litre (32 fl oz) water and leave for 1 hour. Transfer to a saucepan, bring to the boil, but remove from the heat just before boiling point. Discard the konbu. Stir in the soy sauce and

sugar, cover and keep hot.

2 Cut the silken firm tofu into 3 cm (1¼ inch) cubes and drain.

3 Fill a wok one-third full of oil and heat to 190°C (375°F), or until a cube of bread dropped into the oil browns in 10 seconds. Gently dust the flour over the tofu, shaking off any excess. Deep-fry the tofu cubes in three batches for 2–3 minutes each batch, or until lightly golden, turning halfway through if needed. Drain on paper towels, then sprinkle generously with salt.

4 Ladle ½ cup (125 ml/4 fl oz) broth into each serving bowl and top with the tofu. Sprinkle with the spring onion, daikon and ginger.

VEGETABLE TEMPURA PATTIES

Preparation time: 25 minutes
Total cooking time: 15 minutes
Serves 4

Wasabi mayonnaise
½ cup (125 g/4 oz) whole-egg mayonnaise
2 teaspoons wasabi paste
1 teaspoon Japanese soy sauce
1 teaspoon sake

1 small zucchini (courgette), grated
1 small potato, julienned
½ carrot, julienned
½ onion, thinly sliced
100 g (3½ oz) orange sweet potato, grated
4 spring onions (scallions), green part included, cut into 2 cm (¾ inch) lengths
4 nori sheets, shredded
2 cups (250 g/8 oz) tempura flour, sifted
2 cups (500 ml/16 fl oz) chilled soda water
oil, for deep-frying
2 tablespoons shredded pickled ginger

1 To make the wasabi mayonnaise, combine all the ingredients in a small bowl. Set aside until ready to serve.

2 To make the patties, put the zucchini, potato, carrot, onion, orange sweet potato, spring onion and nori in a bowl. Toss together.

3 Sift the tempura flour into a large bowl and make a well in the centre. Add the soda water and loosely mix together with chopsticks or a fork until just combined—the batter should still be lumpy. Add the vegetables and quickly fold through until just combined.

4 Fill a wok one-third full of oil and heat to 180°C (350°F), or until a cube of bread dropped into the oil browns in 15 seconds. Gently drop ¼ cup (60 ml/2 fl oz) of the vegetable mixture into the oil, making sure that the patty is not too compact, and cook for 1–2 minutes, or until golden and crisp. Drain on crumpled paper towels and season with sea salt. Repeat with the remaining mixture to make 11 more patties. Serve immediately, topped with the wasabi mayonnaise and the pickled ginger.

WASABI
The edible root of the *wasabia japonica* plant, which grows in Japan, when skinned has a fiery, fierce flavour like horseradish, hence the tag 'Japanese horseradish'. Fresh wasabi is grated or made into a paste, but the dried powder or ready-made paste are more easily available in the West. Beneath the searing heat of wasabi is a refreshing cleansing taste that lifts food.

LEFT: Vegetable tempura patties

SATAYS & KEBABS

If you are using wooden skewers, soak them in water for 30 minutes beforehand so that they don't burn before the food is cooked. The ends can be wrapped in foil.

LIME PRAWN SKEWERS

Using 12 canned sugar canes, cut into 5 mm (¼ inch) thick strips 10 cm (4 inches) long. Peel and devein 48 raw king prawns (shrimp). Thread 2 prawns onto each sugar cane skewer. You may need to make small cuts in the prawns to make it easier. Brush lightly with some lime juice and cook on a lightly oiled preheated chargrill pan for 2–3 minutes each side, or until cooked through. Makes 24.

BEEF SKEWERS WITH BLACK BEAN SAUCE

Cut 1 kg (2 lb) rump steak into 2 cm (¾ inch) cubes and make small slits in the meat with a sharp knife. Trim bay leaf stems of leaves and thread the meat onto the stems. Brush lightly with ⅓ cup (80 ml/2¾ fl oz) black bean sauce. Cook on a preheated oiled chargrill pan for 2–3 minutes on each side, brushing with any remaining black bean sauce during cooking. Makes 28.

GARLIC LAMB SKEWERS

Cut 600 g (1¼ lb) trimmed lamb steaks into 2 cm (¾ inch) cubes and 6 cloves of garlic into thick slices. Thread 2 pieces of lamb and 2 slices of garlic alternately onto 35 small metal skewers. Mix together 1 chopped red chilli, 2 crushed cloves garlic and 3 tablespoons oil. Heat a chargrill pan and lightly brush with oil. Cook the skewers for 2–5 minutes, brushing occasionally with the garlic and chilli marinade. Makes 35.

CHILLI VEGETABLE KEBABS

Halve 12 shiitake mushrooms, 12 baby corn cobs and 12 snow peas (mangetout). Thread alternately onto 24 small wooden skewers. Combine 2 tablespoons oil with 1 crushed clove garlic and 1 tablespoon sweet chilli sauce in a bowl and mix well. Brush over the skewers and cook the skewers in a preheated chargrill pan for 1–2 minutes, brushing with the sauce during cooking. Makes 24.

SALMON AND TUNA KEBABS

Cut 600 g (1¼ lb) salmon fillet and 500 g (1 lb) fresh tuna into 2 cm (¾ inch) cubes and season with salt and pepper. Thread alternately onto small wooden skewers, using 3 pieces on each. Heat a chargrill or frying pan and brush lightly with oil. Cook the skewers for 3–4 minutes, turning frequently and squeezing with a little lime or lemon juice as they cook. Makes 18–20.

CHICKEN AND LEMON GRASS SKEWERS

Cut 1 kg (2 lb) chicken thigh fillets into 2 cm (¾ inch) cubes. Trim the leaves off 6 lemon grass stems. Cut the thicker ends of the stems into 10 cm (4 inch) lengths, then into quarters lengthways. Cut 12 spring onion (scallion) bulbs into quarters. Make a slit in the centre of each chicken cube and through the onion pieces. Thread pieces of chicken and onion onto the lemon grass stems alternately, using 2 pieces of each for each stem. Mix together 3 tablespoons soy sauce, 3 tablespoons mirin and 2 tablespoons sugar. Heat a chargrill or frying pan and cook the skewers for 3–5 minutes. Brush with half the soy mixture as they cook, turning frequently. Add 1 thinly sliced stem lemon grass (white part only) and 1 seeded and finely chopped red chilli to the remaining soy mixture and serve with the skewers, for dipping. Makes 24.

MUSHROOM AND PROSCIUTTO SKEWERS

Wipe 48 Swiss brown mushrooms (sometimes called chestnut mushrooms) with a damp cloth, then cut them in half. Melt 80 g (2¾ oz) butter in a frying pan and add the mushrooms and a pinch of salt. Cook, stirring, over medium heat for 1 minute. Add ½ cup (125 ml/4 fl oz) port and cook, stirring, until it evaporates completely. Remove from the heat and set aside. Cut 18 slices of prosciutto into 4 pieces each. Thread 4 pieces of mushroom and 3 rolled pieces of prosciutto alternately onto wooden skewers and serve. Makes 24.

FROM LEFT: Lime prawn skewers; Centre plate: Beef skewers with black bean sauce; Chilli vegetable kebabs; Garlic lamb skewers; Right-hand plate: Chicken and lemon grass skewers; Mushroom and prosciutto skewers; Salmon and tuna kebabs

39

CRISPY CHICKEN AND FISH WRAPS WITH SWEET AND SOUR SAUCE

Preparation time: 30 minutes
Total cooking time: 4 minutes per batch
Makes 30

Sweet and sour sauce
1/2 cup (125 g/4 oz) sugar
1/2 cup (125 ml/4 fl oz) white vinegar
1 tablespoon tomato sauce
1 tablespoon cornflour (cornstarch)

30 won ton wrappers
oil, for deep-frying

Filling
100 g (3 1/2 oz) chicken, finely chopped
100 g (3 1/2 oz) fish fillets, finely chopped
1/2 stick celery, finely chopped
1 small spring onion (scallion), finely chopped
2 teaspoons light soy sauce

1 To make the sauce, combine the sugar, vinegar and tomato sauce with 3/4 cup (185 ml/ 6 fl oz) water in a small saucepan. Blend the cornflour with 1 tablespoon of water in a small bowl. Add to the saucepan and stir over low heat until the mixture boils and thickens and the sugar has dissolved.
2 Combine the filling ingredients with 1/4 teaspoon salt. Place 1 teaspoon of mixture onto each won ton wrapper. Brush the edges lightly with water. Fold to form a triangle. Dab water onto the left front corner of the triangle. Fold the two bottom corners across, one on top of the other, and press together lightly with your finger.
3 Fill a deep heavy-based pan one third full of oil. Heat the oil to 180°C (350°F). The oil is hot enough when a cube of bread dropped into the oil turns golden brown in 15 seconds. Deep-fry in batches until crisp and golden brown. Shake off the excess oil and drain on crumpled paper towel. Serve with the sauce.

PORK DUMPLINGS

Preparation time: 30 minutes
Total cooking time: 45 minutes
Makes 50

250 g (4 oz) minced (ground) pork
125 g (4 oz) raw prawn (shrimp) meat, finely chopped
60 g (2 oz) bamboo shoots, chopped
3 spring onions (scallions), finely chopped
3 mushrooms, finely chopped
1 stick celery, finely chopped
1/2 pepper (capsicum), finely chopped
1 tablespoon dry sherry
1 tablespoon soy sauce
1 teaspoon sesame oil
1/2 teaspoon chopped chilli
50 won ton wrappers
soy sauce, for dipping

1 Put the pork, prawn, bamboo shoots, spring onion, mushrooms, celery, pepper, dry sherry, soy sauce, sesame oil and chilli in a bowl and mix well. Put a heaped teaspoon of the filling in the centre of each wrapper. Brush the edges with a little water, then gather the wrapper around the filling to form a pouch, slightly open at the top.
2 Steam in a bamboo or metal steamer over a pan of simmering water for 15 minutes, or until cooked through. Serve with soy sauce.

CHICKEN DUMPLINGS

Preparation time: 30 minutes
Total cooking time: 45 minutes
Makes 50

375 g (12 oz) minced (ground) chicken
90 g (3 oz) ham, finely chopped
4 spring onions (scallions), finely chopped
1 stick celery, finely chopped
3 tablespoons bamboo shoots, chopped
1 tablespoon soy sauce
1 clove garlic, crushed
1 teaspoon grated fresh ginger

1 Combine all the ingredients in a bowl, then use to fill 50 won ton wrappers as above.

Lightly brush the edges of the won ton with water, then fold it over the filling to form a triangle.

Fold the two bottom corners across, one on top of the other, and press together lightly.

OPPOSITE PAGE, FROM TOP: Crispy chicken and fish wraps with sweet and sour sauce; Dumplings

GINGER

If ginger is fresh when you buy it, the flesh should be juicy, not shrivelled or dried out. To prepare it for cooking, just peel with a vegetable peeler or sharp knife and cut. You can rub the skin off some very fresh ginger with your fingers. For grating, don't fuss about the irregular-shaped knob, just peel as much as you need from any part, grate on a ginger grater and return the rest to the crisper in the refrigerator. Ceramic ginger graters have little sharp teeth that grate the ginger off as you rub it up and down. Bamboo graters look like small versions of old-fashioned washboards, made with angled strips of bamboo for rubbing the ginger against.

ABOVE: Yakitori

YAKITORI
(Skewered chicken)

Preparation time: 20 minutes + soaking
Total cooking time: 10 minutes
Makes about 25 skewers

1 kg (2 lb) chicken thigh fillets
1/2 cup (125 ml/4 fl oz) sake
3/4 cup (185 ml/6 fl oz) Japanese soy sauce
1/2 cup (125 ml/4 fl oz) mirin
2 tablespoons sugar
1 cup (65 g/2 1/4 oz) spring onions (scallions), cut diagonally into 2 cm (3/4 inch) pieces

1 Soak 25 wooden skewers for about 30 minutes in water, then drain and set aside.
2 Cut the chicken fillets into bite-sized pieces. Combine the sake, soy sauce, mirin and sugar in a small pan, bring to the boil, then remove the pan and set aside.
3 Thread 3 chicken pieces onto wooden skewers, alternating with pieces of spring onion. Place the skewers on a foil-lined tray and cook under a preheated grill or barbecue, turning and brushing frequently with the sauce for about 7–8 minutes, or until the chicken is cooked through. Serve.
NOTE: The yakitori can be served with a bottled Asian dipping sauce.

THAI NOODLE BALLS WITH ASIAN DIPPING SAUCE

Preparation time: 20 minutes + soaking
Total cooking time: 20 minutes
Makes 40

Asian dipping sauce
1/4 cup (60 ml/2 fl oz) sweet chilli sauce
1/4 cup (60 ml/2 fl oz) lime juice
2 tablespoons fish sauce
1 teaspoon soft brown sugar
2 teaspoons kecap manis
4 cm (1 1/2 inch) piece fresh ginger, cut into julienne strips

500 g (1 lb) Hokkien (egg) noodles

75 g (2 1/2 oz) snake beans, finely chopped

3 spring onions (scallions), finely chopped

2 cloves garlic, crushed

50 g (1 3/4 oz) fresh coriander (cilantro) leaves, chopped

1/4 cup (60 ml/2 fl oz) sweet chilli sauce

2 tablespoons fish sauce

2 tablespoons fresh lime juice

250 g (8 oz) minced (ground) pork

3 eggs, lightly beaten

1 cup (125 g/4 oz) plain (all-purpose) flour

oil, for deep-frying

1 Mix the dipping sauce ingredients in a bowl.
2 Break up the noodles and cut with scissors into short lengths. Soak in a bowl of boiling water for 2 minutes, then drain well. Combine with the beans, spring onion, garlic, coriander, sauces, lime juice, pork, eggs and flour and mix well.
3 Fill a deep heavy-based pan one third full of oil and heat the oil to 180°C (350°F). The oil is ready when a cube of bread dropped into the oil turns golden brown in 15 seconds. Roll heaped tablespoons of mixture into balls and deep-fry in batches for 2 minutes, or until deep golden. Drain on crumpled paper towels. Serve with sauce.

PRAWN PARCELS

Preparation time: 30 minutes
Total cooking time: 20 minutes
Makes 24

★ ★

1 tablespoon oil

2 cloves garlic, crushed

1 tablespoon grated fresh ginger

2 spring onions (scallions), chopped

500 g (1 lb) raw prawns (shrimp), peeled and chopped

1/2 teaspoon fish sauce

1/2 teaspoon sugar

1 tablespoon lemon juice

2 tablespoons chopped fresh coriander (cilantro)

6 large spring roll wrappers, cut into quarters

oil, for deep-frying

fresh chives, to serve

sweet chilli sauce, to serve

1 Heat the oil in a frying pan, add the garlic and ginger and cook over low heat for 2 minutes. Add the spring onion and cook for 2 minutes. Increase the heat to high, add the prawns and stir-fry for 2 minutes, or until the colour just changes. Be careful not to overcook the prawns or they will become tough once deep-fried.
2 Add the fish sauce, sugar, lemon juice and coriander to the pan. Toss with the prawns for 1 minute. Remove from the heat; cool slightly.
3 Divide the cooled mixture into 24 portions. Place one portion in the centre of each piece of spring roll wrapper. Brush the edges with water and fold to form a parcel.
4 Fill a deep heavy-based pan one third full of oil. Heat the oil to 180°C (350°F). The oil is hot enough when a cube of bread dropped into the oil turns golden brown in 15 seconds. Deep-fry the parcels one at a time, holding them with tongs for the first few seconds to keep them intact. Cook until golden brown. Drain on crumpled paper towels. Tie with lengths of chives. Serve with sweet chilli sauce.
NOTE: If the spring roll wrappers are very thin, you may need to use two together.

ABOVE: Prawn parcels

QUESADILLAS Use flour tortillas from

the bread section of your supermarket to make these Mexican snacks. And stun

your guests with your authentic pronunciation... 'kay-sah-dee-yah'.

GUACAMOLE ROLLS

Mix a 450 g (14 oz) can of refried beans with 90 g (3 oz) grated Cheddar. Cut 7 flour tortillas into rounds, using an 8 cm (3 inch) cutter. Wrap in foil and cook in a moderate 180°F (350°F/Gas 4) oven for 2–3 minutes, until warmed through. To make the guacamole, mash 2 avocados and mix with 1 small chopped red onion, 1 tablespoon mayonnaise, 1 chopped red chilli, 1 tablespoon lime juice and 1 tablespoon chopped fresh coriander (cilantro). Spread a little bean mixture over the base of each tortilla and roll up like a horn. Place, seam-side-down, on a baking tray and bake for another 5 minutes, or until crisp. Spoon a teaspoon of guacamole into the open end and serve. Makes 42.

CHEESE QUESADILLAS

Roast 2 jalapeno chillies by holding with tongs over a flame until blackened and blistered. You can also roast chillies under a hot grill. Put in a plastic bag and when cool, you will find the skin peels away easily. Finely chop the chilli flesh and mix with 250 g (8 oz) grated Cheddar and 75 g (2½ oz) grated mozzarella cheese. Spread evenly over 3 flour tortillas, then top with another 3 tortillas. Cut out rounds with a 6 cm (2½ inch) cutter, then fry in a little oil for 1–2 minutes, or until golden brown on each side. Serve with home-made salsa. Makes about 25–30.

TACO CHICKEN QUESADILLAS

In a large frying pan, heat 1 tablespoon oil, add 1 finely chopped red onion and 1 finely diced red pepper (capsicum). Cook until the onion has softened. Add 2 crushed cloves garlic, 1/4 teaspoon paprika, 1 teaspoon ground cumin and 1 teaspoon ground coriander and cook for 2 minutes. Add 400 g (13 oz) minced (ground) chicken and cook for about 7 minutes, or until brown, breaking up any lumps. Add a 400 g (13 oz) can chopped tomatoes and simmer for 20 minutes, or until thick. Cut 7 flour tortillas into rounds with an 8 cm (3 inch) cutter. Place a teaspoon of the mixture on one half of each round. Sprinkle with 220 g (7 oz) grated Cheddar. Bake in a moderate 180°C (350°F/Gas 4) oven for 1 minute, or until the cheese has melted. Fold over and hold for a few seconds to stick. Garnish with sliced spring onion (scallion). Makes 42.

CORN, TOMATO AND BEAN QUESADILLAS

Combine 1 finely chopped red onion, 2 chopped tomatoes, a 310 g (10 oz) can drained and rinsed corn kernels and 1 diced red pepper (capsicum). Drain and rinse a 425 g (14 oz) can pinto beans and mash with a fork. Place 3 flour tortillas on a work surface, spread the pinto beans evenly over the tortillas, top with the corn and tomato mixture and sprinkle with 90 g (3 oz) grated Cheddar. Top with 3 more flour tortillas. Heat 2 teaspoons oil in a 25 cm (10 inch) frying pan and cook the stacks for 3–4 minutes each side, until golden brown. Remove from the pan and cut into 12 triangles. Makes 36.

CHILLI BEEF QUESADILLAS

Heat 1 tablespoon oil in a frying pan and cook 1 chopped onion and 2 crushed cloves garlic for 2–3 minutes. Add 400 g (13 oz) minced (ground) beef and cook for 5–7 minutes until brown, breaking up any lumps. Stir in a 325 g (11 oz) bottle of Mexican black bean salsa. Bring to the boil, reduce the heat and simmer for 3–4 minutes, or until the mixture reduces and thickens. Season. Place 3 flour tortillas on a work surface and sprinkle with 125 g (4 oz) grated Cheddar. Spoon the beef evenly over the cheese, then top with another 3 tortillas. Heat 2 teaspoons oil in a 25 cm (10 inch) frying pan and cook the stacks for 3–4 minutes each side, or until golden brown. Remove from the pan, trim off the sides and cut into 5 cm (2 inch) squares. Makes about 36.

FROM LEFT: Guacamole rolls; Cheese quesadillas; Taco chicken quesadillas; Corn, tomato and bean quesadillas; Chilli beef quesadillas

CORNMEAL CHILLIES

Preparation time: 40 minutes + chilling
Total cooking time: 2–3 minutes each batch
Makes 24

2 x 330 g (11 oz) jars mild whole chillies
125 g (4 oz) Cheddar, grated
200 g (6½ oz) cream cheese, softened
⅔ cup (85 g/3 oz) plain (all-purpose) flour
4 eggs, lightly beaten
1¼ cups (185 g/6 oz) cornmeal
1¼ cups (125 g/4 oz) dry breadcrumbs
oil, for deep-frying
sour cream, to serve

1 Select 24 large, uniform chillies. Drain well and dry with paper towels. With a sharp knife, cut a slit down the length of one side of each chilli. Remove the seeds and membrane.

2 Combine the Cheddar and cream cheese and spoon some into each chilli. Put the flour on a large plate and the beaten egg in a small bowl. Combine the cornmeal and breadcrumbs on a flat dish. Roll each chilli in the flour, shake off the excess, dip in the egg and roll in the crumb mixture to coat thoroughly. Refrigerate for 1 hour. Re-dip in egg and re-roll in breadcrumbs. Refrigerate for another hour.

3 Fill a deep heavy-based pan one third full of oil and heat the oil to 180°C (350°F). The oil is ready when a cube of bread dropped into the oil turns golden brown in 15 seconds. Deep-fry the chillies in small batches until golden brown. Drain on crumpled paper towels. Serve with sour cream.

IN ADVANCE: These can be prepared up to 3 hours ahead.

ABOVE: Cornmeal chillies

STARS AND STRIPES BARBECUED RIBS

Preparation time: 30 minutes + overnight marinating
Total cooking time: 15 minutes
Makes about 30

1/2 teaspoon dry mustard, or prepared English mustard

1/2 teaspoon ground sweet paprika

1/4 teaspoon ground oregano

1/4 teaspoon ground cumin

1 1/2 tablespoons peanut oil

1 teaspoon Tabasco sauce

1 clove garlic, crushed

1/2 cup (125 ml/4 fl oz) tomato sauce

2 tablespoons tomato paste (tomato purée)

2 tablespoons soft brown sugar

1 tablespoon Worcestershire sauce

2 teaspoons brown vinegar

1.5 kg (3 lb) American-style pork spare ribs

1 For the sauce, combine the mustard, paprika, oregano, cumin and oil in a pan. Add the remaining ingredients, except the ribs. Cook, stirring, over medium heat for 3 minutes, or until combined. Allow to cool.

2 Coat the ribs with sauce and marinate overnight. Cook on a hot barbecue grill, turning frequently, until firm and well done. Cut into individual ribs before serving.

NOTE: Get very lean pork spare ribs as fatty ones tend to flare up and burn. You can use beef spare ribs if you prefer but first simmer until tender, then drain.

FRIED CHICKEN

Mix 1 kg (2 lb) chicken drumettes in a bowl with 2 cups (500 ml/16 fl oz) buttermilk. Cover and refrigerate for 2 hours, turning occasionally. Half fill a large, deep heavy-based pan with oil and heat to 180°C (350°F). The oil is ready when a cube of bread dropped into the oil turns golden brown in 15 seconds. Place 1 1/2 cups (185 g/6 oz) plain (all-purpose) flour in a shallow dish and season. Drain the chicken and shake off any excess buttermilk, then coat in the flour. Deep-fry in batches for about 7 minutes, making sure the oil is not too hot or the chicken won't cook through. Drain on paper towels. Makes about 20.

TOMATOES
Tomatoes are sold fresh, in cans, or processed and sold as sauces and pastes with various consistencies, sometimes with flavourings added. Tomato paste, known in the U.K. as tomato purée, is strained concentrated tomatoes which have been cooked for several hours until they form a very thick, dark paste. Salt is added, and sometimes sugar. The intense flavour is used sparingly to flavour stews, stocks, sauces and soups. Some are slightly more concentrated than others so experiment to find which you prefer. Tomato sauce is a much thinner consistency than the paste and is often blended with sugar, salt, spices and other flavourings.

LEFT: Stars and stripes barbecued ribs

47

BABY POTATOES

Preparation time: 10 minutes
Total cooking time: 40 minutes
Makes 30

30 baby new potatoes (see Note)
1 cup (250 g/8 oz) sour cream
2 tablespoons caviar

1 Preheat the oven to moderately hot 200°C (400°F/Gas 6). Prick the potatoes with a fork and place on a baking tray. Bake for 40 minutes, or until tender. Cool to room temperature.
2 Cut a large cross in the top of each potato, squeeze open, and top with a small dollop of sour cream and a little caviar.
IN ADVANCE: Cook the potatoes up to 4 hours ahead. Prepare up to 30 minutes before serving.
NOTE: Choose very small potatoes of the same size, so they take the same time to cook and are easy to eat. Use red or black caviar, or a combination. Caviar comes in different varieties and you may like to try various ones.

BEEF ROLLS

Preparation time: 30 minutes
Total cooking time: 30 minutes
Makes about 20

500 g (1 lb) beef fillet, 8 cm (3 inch) in diameter
3 tablespoons olive oil
1 1/2 tablespoons horseradish cream
1 1/2 tablespoons wholegrain mustard
1 zucchini (courgette), cut into fine strips
1 small carrot, cut into fine strips
1 small red pepper (capsicum), cut into thin strips
60 g (2 oz) snow peas (mangetout), cut into thin strips

1 Preheat the oven to moderately hot 200°C (400°F/Gas 6). Trim the beef of excess fat and sinew and brush with a little of the oil. Heat a heavy-based frying pan over high heat and brown each side of the beef fillet quickly, to seal in the juices. Transfer to a baking dish and bake for 20 minutes. Remove and set aside to cool.
2 Slice the cooled beef very thinly. Combine the horseradish cream and the mustard, then spread a little over each slice of beef.
3 Heat the remaining oil in a pan and cook the zucchini, carrot, pepper and snow peas quickly over high heat, and then allow to cool. Place a small bunch of the cooked vegetable strips on the end of each beef slice and roll up. Arrange on a platter and serve.

CORN MINI MUFFINS WITH PRAWNS AND DILL MAYONNAISE

Preparation time: 15 minutes
Total cooking time: 40 minutes
Makes about 50

2 cups (250 g/8 oz) plain (all-purpose) flour, sifted
3/4 cup (110 g/3 1/2 oz) cornmeal
1 tablespoon baking powder
1/4 cup (60 g/2 oz) sugar
2 eggs, lightly beaten
125 g (4 oz) butter, melted
1 cup (250 ml/8 fl oz) milk
300 g (10 oz) small cooked prawns (shrimp)

Dill mayonnaise
3 tablespoons finely chopped fresh dill
1 tablespoon lemon juice
1 teaspoon horseradish cream
1 1/2 cups (375 g /12 oz) whole-egg mayonnaise

1 Preheat the oven to moderately hot 200°C (400°F/Gas 6) and oil or spray two 12-hole mini muffin pans. Sift the flour into a large bowl and mix with the cornmeal, baking powder, sugar and 1/2 teaspoon salt. Add the eggs, butter and milk. Stir until just combined. Spoon small amounts into the muffin tins, filling the holes three-quarters full. Cook for 15–20 minutes, or until lightly browned. Turn onto a cake rack to cool. Repeat until you have used all the mixture.
2 Mix the dill, lemon juice and horseradish cream into the mayonnaise and add plenty of salt and black pepper.
3 When the muffins are cool, cut a circle from the top, as you would with a butterfly cake, and spoon a little dill mayonnaise into the cavity. Top with a prawn and some freshly ground black pepper.

DILL AND LEMON BUTTER
Dill is a tall annual herb with delicate, long, thin leaves which have an intense aroma and distinctive taste. The leaves are chopped and served with fish, potatoes and other vegetables, or added to butters and sauces. To make a quick Dill and lemon butter to serve with fish or over baby potatoes, put 100 g (3 1/2 oz) chopped, slightly softened unsalted butter in a bowl and beat smooth with electric beaters. Add 2 tablespoons chopped fresh dill, 1/2 teaspoon grated lemon rind and 2 tablespoons lemon juice and beat well. Spoon onto a piece of baking paper and shape into a 4–5 cm (1 1/2–2 inches) wide log, then roll up and twist the ends to seal. Refrigerate for at least 30 minutes, or until firm, then cut into thin slices.

OPPOSITE PAGE, FROM TOP: Beef rolls; Baby potatoes

STARTERS

SALMON AND FENNEL
FRITTATA

Pour the wine over the
onion and fennel and cook,
stirring frequently, until the
vegetables are tender.

Pour half the egg mixture
into the tin and sprinkle
with some smoked salmon.

SALMON AND FENNEL FRITTATA

Preparation time: 35 minutes
Total cooking time: 1 hour 15 minutes
Serves 8

1½ tablespoons olive oil

1 onion, finely chopped

1 fennel bulb (about 280 g/9 oz),
   finely chopped

¼ cup (60 ml/2 fl oz) white wine

2 cups (60 g/2 oz) watercress sprigs

12 eggs

1¾ cups (440 ml/14 fl oz) cream

3 tablespoons chopped fresh dill

½ cup (50 g/1¾ oz) grated Parmesan

300 g (10 oz) smoked salmon, cut into strips

1 Preheat the oven to moderate 180°C (350°F/
Gas 4). Lightly grease a 22 cm (9 inch)
springform tin and line the base and side with
baking paper, making sure you have a tight seal
all the way around the tin. Place the tin on a
baking tray in case it leaks.

2 Heat the olive oil in a heavy-based saucepan
and add the onion, fennel and a pinch of salt.
Cook over low heat for 5 minutes, stirring
occasionally. Add the white wine and cook for
another 5 minutes, or until the vegetables are
tender. Remove from the heat and leave to cool.

3 Finely chop half the watercress and divide the
remainder into small sprigs. Beat the eggs lightly
in a bowl, then add the cream, dill, grated
Parmesan, chopped watercress, and onion and
fennel mixture. Season to taste with salt and
black pepper.

4 Pour half the egg mixture into the prepared
tin, sprinkle with 200 g (6½ oz) smoked salmon
and pour in the remaining egg mixture. Bake for

*ABOVE: Salmon
and fennel frittata*

1 hour, or until the frittata is set in the centre and golden on the surface. Remove from the pan and peel off the baking paper from the side. Flip over onto a plate and remove the paper from the base. Flip over again onto a serving dish and arrange the remaining salmon and watercress on top. Cut into wedges and serve warm.

PRAWN COCKTAILS

Preparation time: 20 minutes
Total cooking time: Nil
Serves 4

¹/₄ cup (60 g/2 oz) whole-egg mayonnaise
2 teaspoons tomato sauce
dash of Tabasco sauce
¹/₄ teaspoon Worcestershire sauce
2 teaspoons thick (double) cream
¹/₄ teaspoon lemon juice
24 cooked large prawns (shrimp)
4 lettuce leaves, shredded
lemon wedges, to serve

1 Mix the mayonnaise, sauces, cream and juice together in a small bowl.
2 Peel the prawns, leaving the tails intact on eight of them. Gently pull out the dark vein from the back of each prawn, starting at the head end.
3 Divide the lettuce among 4 glasses. Arrange the prawns without the tails in the glasses and drizzle with the sauce. Hang 2 of the remaining prawns over the edge of each glass and serve with lemon wedges.

CHEESY PROSCIUTTO TWISTS

Brush a thawed sheet of puff pastry with a little beaten egg and cut into 1.5 cm (⁵/₈ inch) wide strips. Holding both ends, twist the strips in opposite directions to create twists. Place the twists on lightly greased baking trays and bake in a hot 210°C (415°F/Gas 6–7) oven for 10 minutes or until lightly browned and puffed. Remove from the trays and cool on a wire rack. Cut about 8 slices prosciutto into half lengthways, twist the prosciutto around the puff twists and serve. Makes 16.

PRAWNS
Also called shrimp. Dishes using prawns are a delicious addition to the table. Fresh prawns should look shiny and have a pleasant sea smell. Don't buy prawns if they show any signs of dark discolouration around the head and legs or if they smell like ammonia. Prawns come in a variety of sizes so choose the size that best suits your dish.

LEFT: Prawn cocktails

ANTIPASTO

A selection of antipasto (literally, before the meal) is a fabulous way to begin a meal, with a little of this and a little of that to whet the appetite.

GRILLED EGGPLANT AND PEPPERS

Cut 1 large eggplant (aubergine) into 1 cm (½ inch) thick slices. Cut 2 large red peppers (capsicums) in half and remove the seeds and membrane. Put the red pepper, skin-side-up, under a hot grill and cook for 8 minutes, or until the skins blister and blacken. Remove from the heat and cover with a damp tea towel. When cool enough to handle, peel away the skin and cut the pepper flesh into thick strips. Brush the eggplant slices liberally with olive oil and cook under a medium grill until deep golden brown. Carefully turn the slices over, brush the other sides with oil and grill again until golden. Do not rush this process by having the grill too hot, as slow cooking allows the sugar in the eggplant to caramelize. Combine the eggplant and peppers in a bowl with 2 crushed cloves of garlic, 2 tablespoons of extra virgin olive oil, a pinch of sugar and about 2 tablespoons of chopped fresh parsley. Cover and marinate in the refrigerator overnight. Bring to room temperature before serving. Serves 4–6.

PESTO BOCCONCINI BALLS

Blend 1 cup (50 g/1¾ oz) fresh basil leaves, 3 tablespoons each of pine nuts and freshly grated Parmesan with 2 cloves of garlic, in a food processor until finely chopped. With the motor running, gradually add ⅓ cup (80 ml/2¾ fl oz) olive oil and process until a paste is formed. Transfer the pesto to a bowl and add 300 g (10 oz) baby bocconcini. Mix very gently, cover and marinate in the refrigerator for 2 hours. Serves 4–6.

SLOW-ROASTED BALSAMIC TOMATOES

Preheat the oven to warm 160°C (315°F/Gas 2). Cut 500 g (1 lb) Roma (plum) tomatoes in half. Put them on a non-stick baking tray and brush lightly with extra virgin olive oil. Sprinkle with salt and drizzle with 2 tablespoons of balsamic vinegar. Roast for 1 hour, basting every 15 minutes with 2 tablespoons balsamic vinegar. Serves 6–8.

BRUSCHETTA

Cut 1 loaf of Italian bread into thick slices. Chop 500 g (1 lb) ripe tomatoes into very small cubes. Finely dice 1 red onion. Combine the tomato and onion in a bowl with 2 tablespoons olive oil. Season to taste with salt and freshly ground pepper. Lightly toast the bread and, while still hot, rub both sides with a whole garlic clove. Top each piece with some of the tomato mixture and serve warm, topped with strips of finely shredded fresh basil leaves (shred them just before serving). Serves 6–8.

CRISPY CAULIFLOWER BITES

Cut 300 g (10 oz) of cauliflower into large florets. Cook in a large pan of salted boiling water until just tender. Be careful that you do not overcook them. Drain thoroughly and set aside to cool slightly. Cut 200 g (6½ oz) of fontina cheese into small cubes and carefully tuck the cheese inside the florets. Beat 3 eggs together in a bowl and dip each floret in the egg. Next, roll the florets in ½ cup (40 g/1¼ oz) of fresh breadcrumbs. When they are all crumbed, deep-fry them in hot oil, in batches, until they are crisp and golden. Serve hot. Serves 4–6.

FROM LEFT: Grilled eggplant and peppers; Pesto bocconcini balls; Slow-roasted balsamic tomatoes; Bruschetta; Crispy cauliflower bites

CAULIFLOWER FRITTERS

Preparation time: 15 minutes + standing
Total cooking time: 15 minutes
Makes about 40 pieces

600 g (1 1/4 lb) cauliflower
1/2 cup (55 g/2 oz) besan flour
2 teaspoons ground cumin
1 teaspoon ground coriander
1 teaspoon ground turmeric
pinch of cayenne pepper
1 egg, lightly beaten
1 egg yolk
oil, for deep-frying

1 Cut the cauliflower into bite-sized florets. Sift the flour and spices into a bowl, then stir in 1/2 teaspoon salt and make a well in the centre.
2 Combine 1/4 cup (60 ml/2 fl oz) water with the egg and egg yolk and gradually pour into the well, whisking to make a smooth lump-free batter. Cover and leave for 30 minutes.
3 Fill a deep heavy-based pan one third full of oil and heat to 180°C (350°F), or until a cube of bread dropped into the oil browns in 15 seconds. Holding the florets by the stem, dip into the batter, draining the excess back into the bowl. Deep-fry in batches for 3–4 minutes, or until puffed and brown. Drain, season and serve hot.

CHEESY ZUCCHINI FLOWERS

Preparation time: 1 hour 20 minutes + standing
Total cooking time: 10 minutes
Makes 24

1 1/2 cups (185 g/6 oz) plain (all-purpose) flour
7 g (1/4 oz) dry yeast or 15 g (1/2 oz) compressed fresh yeast
24 zucchini (courgettes) with flowers
50 g (1 3/4 oz) kefalotyri cheese or Parmesan
8 anchovy fillets in oil, drained
oil, for deep-frying

1 Sift the flour and 1 1/4 teaspoons salt into a bowl and make a well. Whisk the yeast and 1 1/4 cups (315 ml/10 fl oz) warm water in a bowl until dissolved and pour into the well. Gradually stir with the whisk to form a thick batter. Cover with plastic wrap and leave in a warm place for 1 hour, or until frothy. Do not stir.
2 Gently open the zucchini flowers and remove the centre stamens. Wash and drain. Cut the cheese into 1 cm (1/2 inch) cubes. Cut the anchovies into 1.5 cm (5/8 inch) pieces.
3 Put a cube of cheese and a piece of anchovy into the centre of each flower. Fold the petals around them. Fill a deep pan one third full of oil and heat to 180°C (350°F), or until a cube of bread dropped into the oil browns in 15 seconds. Dip the flowers into the batter, turning to coat and drain off the excess. Deep-fry in batches for 1–2 minutes, or until puffed and lightly brown. Drain on crumpled paper towel. Serve hot.

SPANISH TORTILLA

Preparation time: 20 minutes
Total cooking time: 30 minutes
Makes 16 wedges

1/2 cup (125 ml/4 fl oz) olive oil
2 large potatoes (600 g/1 1/4 lb), peeled and cut into 5 mm (1/4 inch) slices
2 large onions, sliced
3 eggs

1 Heat the oil in a 20 cm (8 inch) diameter, 5 cm (2 inch) deep non-stick frying pan. Place alternate layers of potato and onion in the pan, cover and cook for 8 minutes over low heat. Using tongs, turn the layers in sections (it doesn't matter if they break up). Cover and cook for 8 minutes, without allowing the potato to colour.
2 Place a strainer over a bowl and drain the potato mixture, reserving 1 tablespoon of the oil. (The rest can be used for cooking another time, it will have a delicately sweet onion flavour.)
3 Place the eggs and 1/2 teaspoon each salt and pepper in a bowl and whisk to combine. Add the potato mixture, pressing down with the back of a spoon to completely cover with the egg.
4 Heat the reserved oil in the same frying pan over high heat. Pour in the egg mixture, pressing down to even it out. Reduce the heat to low, cover with a lid or foil and cook for 12 minutes, or until set. Gently shake the pan to ensure the tortilla is not sticking. Leave for 5 minutes, then invert onto a plate. Cut into wedges. Serve hot.

ANCHOVY SPREADS
To make anchoïade, a Provençal spread or paste, blend 160 g (5 1/2 oz) anchovy fillets, 2 cloves garlic, 1 teaspoon thyme, 3 teaspoons chopped parsley and enough olive oil to make a thick paste. Season with pepper and lemon juice and serve with toasted bread.

To make Anchovy bread, make diagonal cuts along a baguette, cutting only two thirds of the way through. Spread each cut with some butter and some gentleman's relish (a paste made from a mixture of anchovies, butter, herbs and spices), then wrap the loaf tightly in foil. Bake in a moderately hot 200°C (400°F/Gas 6) oven for 10 minutes, or until heated through.

OPPOSITE PAGE, FROM TOP: Cauliflower fritters; Cheesy zucchini flowers

FLAT-LEAF PARSLEY
Also known as continental or Italian parsley, flat-leaf parsley has a slightly stronger flavour than curly-leafed parsley and is available all year round. Both the stems and leaves are used in French cooking, whereas in Italy they normally just use the leaves. Buy parsley with firm stems and bright leaves, not yellowing. To store, stand the stalks in a jar of water in the refrigerator or wrap in paper towels and keep in the vegetable crisper.

ABOVE: Whitebait fritters

WHITEBAIT FRITTERS

Preparation time: 20 minutes + resting
Total cooking time: 15 minutes
Makes 12–15

★ ★

1/4 cup (30 g/1 oz) self-raising flour

1/4 cup (30 g/1 oz) plain (all-purpose) flour

1/2 teaspoon bicarbonate of soda

1 egg, lightly beaten

3 tablespoons dry white wine

2 teaspoons chopped fresh flat-leaf (Italian) parsley

1 clove garlic, crushed

1/2 small onion, grated

200 g (6 1/2 oz) whitebait (see Note)

olive oil, for shallow-frying

lemon wedges, to serve

1 Sift the flours, bicarbonate of soda, 1/2 teaspoon salt and some freshly ground black pepper into a bowl. Stir in the egg and wine, whisk until smooth, then add the parsley, garlic, onion and whitebait. Cover and refrigerate for 20 minutes.

2 Heat about 2 cm (3/4 inch) of the oil in a deep frying pan to 180°C (350°F). The oil is ready when a cube of bread dropped into the oil turns golden brown in 15 seconds. Drop in level tablespoons of batter and, when the batter is puffed and bubbles appear on the surface, carefully turn to cook the other side.
3 Drain on paper towels and serve immediately with lemon wedges.
NOTE: The whitebait is very small and fine and is available fresh or frozen. There is no need to gut or scale them as they are so small.

WRAPPED PRAWNS WITH MANGO DIP

Blanch some snow peas (mangetout) and wrap around peeled cooked prawns (shrimp). Secure each with a toothpick. Make a dip by mixing 1/2 cup (125 ml/ 4 fl oz) mayonnaise with 2 tablespoons mango chutney, 1 teaspoon curry paste and 1 tablespoon lime juice. Vary the amount of snow peas and prawns according to your needs and double the dip if you need more.

CHARGRILLED OCTOPUS

Preparation time: 15 minutes + marinating
Total cooking time: 10 minutes
Serves 6

²/₃ cup (170 ml/5¹/₂ fl oz) olive oil
¹/₃ cup (10 g/¹/₄ oz) chopped fresh oregano
¹/₃ cup (10 g/¹/₄ oz) chopped fresh parsley
1 tablespoon lemon juice
3 small red chillies, seeded, finely chopped
3 cloves garlic, crushed
1 kg (2 lb) baby octopus

1 Combine the oil, herbs, lemon juice, chilli and garlic in a large bowl and mix well.
2 Use a small sharp knife to remove the octopus heads. Grasp the bodies and push the beaks out from the centre with your index finger; remove and discard. Slit the heads and remove the gut. If the octopus are too large, cut them into smaller portions.
3 Mix the octopus with the herb marinade. Cover and refrigerate for 3–4 hours, or overnight. Drain, reserving the marinade. Cook on a very hot lightly oiled barbecue or in a very hot pan for 3–5 minutes, or until the flesh turns white. Turn frequently and brush generously with the marinade during cooking.

MARINATED SEAFOOD

Preparation time: 40 minutes + chilling
Total cooking time: 10 minutes
Serves 8

500 g (1 lb) mussels, scrubbed, beards removed
¹/₂ cup (125 ml/4 fl oz) white wine vinegar
3 bay leaves
500 g (1 lb) small squid hoods, sliced
500 g (1 lb) scallops
500 g (1 lb) raw prawns (shrimp), peeled and deveined
2 cloves garlic, crushed
¹/₂ cup (125 ml/4 fl oz) extra virgin olive oil
3 tablespoons lemon juice
1 tablespoon white wine vinegar
1 teaspoon Dijon mustard
1 tablespoon chopped fresh parsley

1 Discard any mussels that are already open. Put the vinegar, bay leaves, 3 cups (750 ml/24 fl oz) water and ¹/₂ teaspoon of salt in a large pan and bring to the boil. Add the squid and scallops, then reduce the heat to low and simmer for 2–3 minutes, or until the seafood has turned white. Remove the squid and scallops with a slotted spoon and place in a bowl.
2 Repeat the process with the prawns, cooking until just pink, then removing with a slotted spoon. Return the liquid to the boil and add the mussels. Cover, reduce the heat and simmer for 3 minutes, or until all the shells are open. Stir occasionally and discard any unopened mussels. Cool, remove the meat and add to the bowl.
3 Whisk the garlic and oil together with the lemon juice, vinegar, mustard and parsley. Pour over the seafood and toss well. Refrigerate for 1–2 hours before serving.
NOTE: Seafood should never be overcooked or it will become tough.

ABOVE: Chargrilled octopus (top); Marinated seafood

59

GARLIC

One of the smallest members of the onion family, garlic is also the most pungent. Indispensable, its essence imparts a crucial depth of flavour to many dishes such as skordalia. As well as its unique flavour, garlic has the advantage of being rich in minerals and vitamins. As a general rule, the finer that garlic is crushed, the more of its pungent oil is released, hence the popularity of garlic presses. When choosing garlic look for hard, large, round bulbs and always check underneath for any signs of unwanted mould.

ABOVE: Tzatziki

TZATZIKI
(Cucumber and yoghurt dip)

Preparation time: 10 minutes
+ 15 minutes standing
Total cooking time: Nil
Makes 2 cups

★

2 Lebanese (short) cucumbers (300 g/13 oz)
400 g (13 oz) Greek-style natural yoghurt
4 cloves garlic, crushed
3 tablespoons finely chopped fresh mint
1 tablespoon lemon juice
chopped fresh mint, extra, to garnish

1 Cut the cucumbers in half lengthways, scoop out the seeds with a teaspoon and discard. Leave the skin on and coarsely grate the cucumber into a small colander. Sprinkle with a little salt and leave to stand over a large bowl for 15 minutes to drain off any bitter juices.
2 Meanwhile, stir together the yoghurt, garlic, mint and lemon juice in a bowl.
3 Rinse the cucumber under cold water then, taking small handfuls, squeeze out any excess moisture. Combine the cucumber with the yoghurt mixture and season to taste. Serve immediately or refrigerate until ready to serve.

Garnish with mint. Can be served as a dip with flatbread or as a sauce for seafood and meat.

SKORDALIA
(Garlic sauce)

Preparation time: 15 minutes
Total cooking time: 10 minutes
Makes 2 cups

★

500 g (1 lb) floury potatoes (desiree, King Edward), cut into 2 cm (3/4 inch) cubes
5 cloves garlic, crushed
3/4 cup (185 ml/6 fl oz) olive oil
2 tablespoons white vinegar

1 Bring a large saucepan of water to the boil, add the potato and cook for 10 minutes, or until very soft. Drain thoroughly and mash until quite smooth.
2 Stir the garlic, 1 teaspoon salt and a pinch of ground white pepper into the potato, then gradually pour in the olive oil, mixing well with a wooden spoon. Stir in the vinegar and season to taste. Serve warm or cold with crusty bread or crackers as a dip, or with grilled meat, fish or chicken.

DOLMADES
(Stuffed vine leaves)

Preparation time: 40 minutes
  + 15 minutes soaking
Total cooking time: 45 minutes
Makes 24

200 g (6¹/₂ oz) packet vine leaves in brine
1 cup (250 g/8 oz) medium-grain rice
1 small onion, finely chopped
1 tablespoon olive oil
60 g (2 oz) pine nuts, toasted
2 tablespoons currants
2 tablespoons chopped fresh dill
1 tablespoon finely chopped fresh mint
1 tablespoon finely chopped fresh flat-leaf
  (Italian) parsley
¹/₃ cup (80 ml/2³/₄ fl oz) olive oil, extra
2 tablespoons lemon juice
2 cups (500 ml/16 fl oz) chicken stock

1 Soak the vine leaves in cold water for
15 minutes, then remove and pat dry. Cut off
any stems. Reserve some leaves to line the
saucepan and discard any that have holes or
look poor. Meanwhile, soak the rice in boiling
water for 10 minutes to soften, then drain.
2 Place the rice, onion, olive oil, pine nuts,
currants, herbs and salt and pepper in a large
bowl and mix well.
3 Lay some leaves vein-side-down on a flat
surface. Place 1 tablespoon of filling in the
centre of each, fold the stalk end over the filling,
then the left and right sides into the centre, and
finally roll firmly towards the tip. The dolmades
should resemble a small cigar. Repeat with the
remaining filling and leaves.
4 Use the reserved vine leaves to line the base
of a large, heavy-based saucepan. Drizzle with
1 tablespoon olive oil. Add the dolmades,
packing them tightly in one layer, then pour the
remaining oil and the lemon juice over them.
5 Pour the stock over the dolmades and cover
with an inverted plate to stop the dolmades moving
around while cooking. Bring to the boil, then
reduce the heat and simmer, covered, for
45 minutes. Remove with a slotted spoon. Serve
warm or cold.
NOTE: Unused vine leaves can be stored in
brine in an airtight container in the fridge for
up to a week.

DOLMADES

Fold the sides of the vine
leaf into the middle and roll
up towards the tip.

Pack the dolmades tightly
into the pan and pour on
the oil and lemon juice.

When the dolmades are
cooked, remove from the
pan with a slotted spoon.

LEFT: Dolmades

61

CHEESE TRIANGLES

Mix the Gruyére, egg and pepper into the feta.

Fold the pastry over the filling to form a triangle and continue folding.

OPPOSITE PAGE, FROM TOP: Meatballs; Quail in vine leaves; Cheese triangles

MEATBALLS

Preparation time: 15 minutes
+ 1 hour refrigeration
Total cooking time: 15 minutes
Serves 4

1 egg, lightly beaten
1/2 cup (40 g/1 1/4 oz) fresh breadcrumbs
1 brown onion, finely chopped
2 tablespoons chopped fresh flat-leaf (Italian) parsley
3 tablespoons chopped fresh mint
500 g (1 lb) minced (ground) beef or lamb
2 tablespoons lemon juice
plain (all-purpose) flour, for coating
vegetable oil, for shallow-frying
lemon wedges, to serve

1 In a large bowl, mix the egg, breadcrumbs, onion, herbs, mince and lemon juice until well combined. Season well, then with wet hands, shape the mixture into large walnut-sized balls and flatten slightly. Place on a tray, cover and refrigerate for 1 hour.
2 Roll the balls in flour, shaking off any excess. In a large frying pan, heat the oil until very hot. Fry the meatballs for 3–4 minutes on each side, or until crisp and brown, being careful not to overcrowd the pan. Drain on crumpled paper towels and serve with lemon wedges.

QUAIL IN VINE LEAVES

Preparation time: 15 minutes
Total cooking time: 25 minutes
Serves 4

12 black grapes
1 tablespoon olive oil
1 clove garlic, crushed
4 large quail
8 fresh or preserved vine leaves
4 slices prosciutto
black grapes, extra, for garnish

1 Preheat the oven to moderate 180°C (350°F/ Gas 4). Cut each grape in half and toss them all with the oil and crushed garlic. Place 6 grape halves in the cavity of each quail.

2 If you are using fresh vine leaves, blanch them for 1 minute in boiling water, then remove the central stem. If using preserved vine leaves, wash them under running water to remove any excess preserving liquid.
3 Wrap each quail in a piece of prosciutto and place each on top of a vine leaf. Place another vine leaf over the top of each quail and wrap into parcels, tying with string to secure. Bake on a baking tray for 20–25 minutes, depending on the size of the quail. Serve garnished with the whole grapes.
NOTE: Vine leaves are available from speciality food stores.

CHEESE TRIANGLES

Preparation time: 35 minutes
Total cooking time: 20 minutes
Makes 30

250 g (4 oz) Greek feta
180 g (6 oz) Gruyère cheese, grated
2 eggs, lightly beaten
15 sheets filo pastry
1/2 cup (125 ml/4 fl oz) olive oil
125 g (4 oz) butter, melted

1 Preheat the oven to moderate 180°C (350°F/ Gas 4). Place the feta in a bowl and mash with a fork. Add the Gruyère, egg and pepper and mix.
2 Cut the filo sheets in halves widthways. Keep the unused pastry covered with a damp tea towel to prevent it drying out. Place one half of one sheet lengthways on a work surface. Brush with the combined oil and butter, then fold into thirds lengthways. Brush with the oil and butter.
3 Place 1 tablespoon of the cheese mixture on the corner of the pastry strip. Fold this corner over the filling to edge of pastry to form a triangle. Continue to fold until the filling is enclosed and the end of pastry is reached. Repeat with the remaining pastry and filling.
4 Place the triangles on a lightly greased baking tray and brush them with the oil and butter mixture. Bake for 20 minutes, or until crisp.
VARIATIONS: You can easily adapt these pastries to suit your personal taste. Try using ricotta instead of gruyère and adding your favourite fresh herbs, finely chopped. Flat-leaf (Italian) parsley, mint or thyme are all suitable.

TARTLETS

These savoury tartlet recipes are simplicity itself and will provide you with ideas for very quick lunch or first course dishes. Most can be ready in under half an hour.

These delicious tartlets can be made with either home-made or bought puff pastry. They can be made as four individual serves or shaped into two rectangles to serve 4 people as a light meal.

You will need 500 g (1 lb) of home-made (see page 488) or bought puff pastry. The pastry should be divided into two and each portion rolled between two sheets of baking paper. If making four tartlets, cut out two 12 cm (5 inch)

circles of pastry from each portion, or for two long tartlets roll each portion of pastry into a rectangle 12 x 25 cm (5 x 10 inches). The topping variations are placed on the pastry shapes, leaving a 1.5 cm (½ inch) border. The tartlets are then baked in the top half of a preheated moderately hot 200°C (400°F/Gas 6) oven. These tartlets are best served warm or hot. They are delicious accompanied by some dressed green salad leaves.

TOPPINGS

Tapenade and anchovy Spread ½ cup (125 g/4 oz) tapenade evenly over the pastry, leaving a 1.5 cm (½ inch) border. Drain a 45 g (1½ oz) can of anchovies, cut them into thin strips and arrange them over the top of the tapenade. Sprinkle ⅓ cup (35 g/1¼ oz) grated Parmesan and ½ cup (75 g/2½ oz) grated mozzarella over the top and bake for 10 minutes, or until risen and golden.

Mushroom, asparagus and feta Heat 2 tablespoons oil in a frying pan, add 400 g (13 oz) sliced, small button mushrooms and 100 g (3½ oz) thin asparagus spears and stir until softened. Remove from the heat, add 2 tablespoons chopped fresh parsley and 200 g (6½ oz) chopped feta. Stir and season. Spoon onto the pastry bases, leaving a 1.5 cm (½ inch) border. Bake for 10–15 minutes, until risen and brown.

Fried green tomato Thinly slice 2 green tomatoes. Heat 1 tablespoon oil in a frying pan, add ½ teaspoon cumin and 1 crushed clove garlic and cook for 1 minute. Add the tomatoes in two batches and cook for 2–3 minutes each batch, adding more oil and garlic if needed, until slightly softened. Drain on paper towels. Combine ⅓ cup (90 g/3 oz) sour cream, 2 tablespoons

chopped fresh basil and 2 tablespoons chopped fresh parsley and set aside. Using 1 cup (120 g/4 oz) grated Cheddar, sprinkle over the centre of the pastry bases, leaving a 1.5 cm (½ inch) border. Arrange the tomato over the cheese and bake for 10 minutes. Place a dollop of cream mixture in the middle and sprinkle the tarts with another tablespoon of shredded fresh basil.

Italian summer Heat 2 tablespoons olive oil in a saucepan over low heat, add 2 sliced red onions and cook, stirring occasionally, for 10 minutes. Add 1 tablespoon each of balsamic vinegar and soft brown sugar and cook for 10 minutes, or until soft and lightly browned. Remove from the heat, stir in 1 tablespoon chopped fresh thyme, then leave to cool. Spread evenly over the pastry, leaving a 1.5 cm (½ inch) border.

Bake for 10 minutes. Drain a 170 g (5½ oz) jar of quartered, marinated artichokes and arrange over the onion. Fill the spaces with 24 pitted black olives and 6 quartered slices of lightly rolled prosciutto. Drizzle with extra virgin olive oil and garnish with thyme.

Cherry tomato and pesto Spread ½ cup (125 g/4 oz) pesto over the pastry shapes, leaving a 1.5 cm (½ inch) border. Top with cherry tomatoes (you will need about 375 g/12 oz) and 2 thinly sliced spring onions (scallions). Season and bake for 10 minutes, or until golden. Drizzle with extra virgin olive oil and garnish with sliced spring onion.

FROM LEFT: Tapenade and anchovy (top);
Mushroom, asparagus and feta (2);
Fried green tomato (2); Italian summer (2);
Cherry tomato and pesto (2)

65

BLACK OLIVES

Olives are indispensable as a savoury nibble to accompany drinks and are an attractive addition to an antipasto platter. They also add a distinctive flavour to many Mediterranean dishes. Some varieties are larger, some rounder than others. When olives are unripe, they are green, hard and bitter. Black olives have been left on the tree to darken and mature. Olives can either be preserved in oil, sometimes flavoured with herbs, or in brine. Italian and Greek olives are considered the best.

ABOVE, FROM LEFT:
Carpaccio; Pasta frittata;
Stuffed cherry tomatoes

CARPACCIO

Preparation time: 15 minutes + freezing
Total cooking time: Nil
Serves 8

400 g (13 oz) beef eye fillet
1 tablespoon extra virgin olive oil
rocket (arugula) leaves, torn
60 g (2 oz) Parmesan, shaved
black olives, cut into slivers

1 Remove all the visible fat and sinew from the beef, then freeze for 1–2 hours, until firm but not solid. This makes the meat easier to slice thinly.
2 Cut paper-thin slices of beef with a large, sharp knife. Arrange on a serving platter and allow to return to room temperature.
3 Just before serving, drizzle with oil, then scatter with rocket, Parmesan and olives.
IN ADVANCE: The beef can be cut into slices a few hours in advance, covered and refrigerated. Drizzle with oil and garnish with the other ingredients just before serving.

PASTA FRITTATA

Preparation time: 15 minutes
Total cooking time: 25 minutes
Makes 8 wedges

300 g (10 oz) spaghetti
4 eggs
50 g (1 3/4 oz) Parmesan, grated
2 tablespoons chopped fresh parsley
60 g (2 oz) butter

1 Cook the spaghetti in a large pan of boiling water for about 10 minutes, until just tender but still retaining a little bite, then drain well.
2 Whisk the eggs in a large bowl, then add the Parmesan, parsley and some salt and freshly ground black pepper. Toss with the spaghetti.
3 Melt half the butter in a 23 cm (9 inch) frying pan and add the spaghetti mixture. Cover and cook over low heat until the base is crisp and golden. Slide onto a plate, melt the remaining butter in the pan and flip the frittata back in to cook the other side (do not cover). Serve warm, cut into wedges.

STUFFED CHERRY TOMATOES

Preparation time: 15 minutes
Total cooking time: Nil
Makes 16

16 cherry tomatoes
50 g (1³/4 oz) goat's cheese
50 g (1³/4 oz) ricotta
2 slices prosciutto, finely chopped

1 Slice the tops from the tomatoes, hollow out and discard the seeds. Turn them upside-down on paper towel and drain for a few minutes.
2 Beat together the goat's cheese and ricotta until smooth. Mix in the prosciutto, then season. Spoon into the tomatoes and refrigerate until required.

PROSCIUTTO WITH MELON

Preparation time: 20 minutes
Total cooking time: Nil
Makes 16

1 rockmelon or honeydew melon
16 slices prosciutto
extra virgin olive oil

1 Remove the seeds from the melon, cut into thin wedges and wrap a slice of prosciutto around each. Drizzle with oil and grind black pepper over each. Refrigerate until required.

MARINATED EGGPLANT

Preparation time: 15 minutes +
   salting + marinating
Total cooking time: 15 minutes
Serves 6–8

750 g (1¹/2 lb) slender eggplant (aubergine)
¹/4 cup (60 ml/2 fl oz) olive oil
2 tablespoons balsamic vinegar
2 cloves garlic, crushed
1 anchovy fillet, finely chopped
2 tablespoons chopped fresh parsley

1 Cut the eggplant into thick diagonal slices, place in a colander and sprinkle well with salt. After 30 minutes, rinse and pat dry.
2 Whisk the oil, vinegar, garlic and anchovy until smooth. Season to taste.
3 Heat a little oil in a frying pan and brown the eggplant in batches. Transfer to a bowl, toss with the dressing and parsley and marinate for 4 hours. Serve at room temperature.

CHERRY TOMATOES
There are many different types and sizes of cherry tomato, all low in acid and quite sweet. Most are an ideal size for stuffing with a filling, but some are as tiny as small grapes and are sold in clusters. Although these can't be stuffed, they can be used to add colour or to garnish a dish.

LEFT, FROM LEFT:
Prosciutto with melon;
Marinated eggplant

HUMMUS

Preparation time: 20 minutes + overnight soaking
Total cooking time: 1 hour 15 minutes
Makes 3 cups

1 cup (220 g/6¹/₂ oz) dried chickpeas
2 tablespoons tahini
4 cloves garlic, crushed
2 teaspoons ground cumin
¹/₃ cup (80 ml/2³/₄ fl oz) lemon juice
3 tablespoons olive oil
large pinch of cayenne pepper
extra lemon juice, optional
extra virgin olive oil, to garnish
paprika, to garnish
chopped fresh flat-leaf (Italian) parsley,
    to garnish

BELOW: Hummus

1 Put the chickpeas in a bowl, add 1 litre (32 fl oz) water, then soak overnight. Drain and place in a large saucepan with 2 litres (64 fl oz) water, or enough to cover the chickpeas by 5 cm (2 inches). Bring to the boil, then reduce the heat and simmer for 1 hour 15 minutes, or until the chickpeas are very tender. Skim any scum from the surface. Drain well, reserving the cooking liquid and leave until cool enough to handle. Pick through for any loose skins and discard them.
2 Combine the chickpeas, tahini, garlic, cumin, lemon juice, olive oil, cayenne pepper and 1¹/₂ teaspoons salt in a food processor until thick and smooth. With the motor running, gradually add enough of the reserved cooking liquid, about ³/₄ cup (185 ml/6 fl oz), to form a smooth creamy purée. Season with salt or some extra lemon juice.
3 Spread onto flat bowls or plates, drizzle with the extra virgin olive oil, sprinkle with paprika and scatter parsley over the top. Delicious served with warm pita bread or pide.

WALNUT TARATOOR

Preparation time: 5 minutes
Total cooking time: Nil
Serves 8

250 g (8 oz) shelled walnuts
1 cup (80 g/2³/₄ oz) soft white breadcrumbs
3 cloves garlic
¹/₄ cup (60 ml/2 fl oz) white wine vinegar
1 cup (250 ml/8 fl oz) olive oil
chopped fresh parsley, to garnish

1 Finely chop the walnuts in a blender or food processor. Set aside ¹/₂ teaspoon of the walnuts for a garnish. Add the breadcrumbs, garlic, vinegar and 3 tablespoons water to the rest and blend well.
2 With the motor running, gradually add the olive oil in a thin steady stream until smooth. Add a little more water if the sauce appears to be too thick. Season to taste, then transfer to a serving bowl and refrigerate.
3 Combine the reserved walnuts and parsley and sprinkle on top before serving.
NOTE: This is suitable for serving with seafood, salads, fried vegetables or bread. It can be made with almonds, hazelnuts or pine nuts instead of the walnuts. Lemon juice can be used as a substitute for the vinegar.

BOREK
(Turkish filo parcels)

Preparation time: I hour
Total cooking time: 20 minutes
Makes 24

 ✷ ✷

400 g (13 oz) feta
2 eggs, lightly beaten
3/4 cup (25 g/3/4 oz) chopped fresh flat-leaf
   (Italian) parsley
375 g (12 oz) filo pastry
1/3 cup (80 ml/23/4 fl oz) good-quality olive oil

I Preheat the oven to moderate 180°C (350°F/ Gas 4). Lightly grease a baking tray. Crumble the feta into a large bowl using a fork or your fingers. Mix in the eggs and parsley and season with freshly ground black pepper.
2 Cover the filo pastry with a damp tea towel so it doesn't dry out. Remove one sheet at a time. Brushing each sheet lightly with olive oil, layer 4 sheets on top of one another. Cut the pastry into four 7 cm (23/4 inch) strips.
3 Place 2 rounded teaspoons of the feta mixture in one corner of each strip and fold diagonally, creating a triangle pillow. Place on the baking tray, seam-side-down, and brush with olive oil. Repeat with the remaining pastry and filling to make 24 parcels. Bake for 20 minutes, or until golden. Serve these as part of a large meze plate.
VARIATION: Fillings for borek are versatile and can be adapted to include your favourite cheeses such as haloumi, Gruyère, Cheddar or mozzarella.

CUCUMBER AND YOGHURT SALAD

Unlike the Greek cucumber and yoghurt dip, tzatziki (page 60), this cucumber and yoghurt salad has only a small amount of garlic and is flavoured with dill instead of mint. It is very popular in Turkey.
Coarsely grate or chop 1 large unpeeled cucumber into a colander, sprinkle with salt and set aside for 15–20 minutes. In a bowl, combine 2 cups (500 g/1 lb) thick, creamy yoghurt with 1 crushed clove of garlic, 2 tablespoons chopped fresh dill and 1 tablespoon of white wine vinegar. Add the cucumber and season with some salt and white pepper. Cover and refrigerate. If you are making this salad just before serving you don't need to salt the cucumber. Serve drizzled with olive oil. Serves 6–8.

OLIVE OIL
Like wine, the flavour, colour and taste of olive oil varies according to the type of fruit used and the climate, soil and area of cultivation. Unique among oils due to its great diversity, olive oil connoisseurs identify four categories along the taste spectrum. Fine, gentle-flavoured oil with a hint of olive taste is considered light; delicate, buttery-flavoured oil is mild; oils with a stronger, more distinct olive taste are semi–fruity; and the fully fledged, strongest olive-flavoured oils are regarded as fruity or peppery.

ABOVE: Borek

TAPENADE

This Provençal paste takes its name from the 'tapeno', or capers, which are its key ingredient. Although only invented in Marseilles in the nineteenth century, this timeless liaison between anchovies, olives and capers quickly established itself as a classic appetizer. It is delicious served with fresh or toasted bread and makes an excellent stuffing for hard-boiled eggs.

TAPENADE
(Provençal olive, anchovy and caper paste)

Preparation time: 10 minutes
Total cooking time: Nil
Makes 1 1/2 cups

400 g (13 oz) Kalamata olives, pitted
2 cloves garlic, crushed
2 anchovy fillets in oil, drained
2 tablespoons capers in brine, rinsed, squeezed dry
2 teaspoons chopped fresh thyme
2 teaspoons Dijon mustard
1 tablespoon lemon juice
1/4 cup (60 ml/2 fl oz) olive oil
1 tablespoon brandy, optional

1 Process all the ingredients together in a food processor until they form a smooth consistency. Season with freshly ground black pepper. Spoon into a sterilized, warm jar (see Notes), seal and refrigerate for up to 2 weeks.

NOTES: To prepare a sterilized storage jar, preheat the oven to very slow 120°C (250°F/ Gas 1/2). Wash the jar and lid in hot soapy water and rinse with hot water. Put the jar in the oven for 20 minutes, or until fully dry. Do not dry with a tea towel.

If refrigerated, the olive oil may solidify, making it white. This will not affect the flavour of the dish. Bring to room temperature before serving and the oil will return to a liquid state.

BAGNA CAUDA

Preparation time: 5 minutes
Total cooking time: 8 minutes
Makes about 1 cup

1 1/4 cups (315 ml/10 fl oz) cream
45 g (1 1/2 oz) can anchovy fillets, drained
10 g (1/4 oz) butter
2 cloves garlic, crushed

1 Bring the cream slowly to the boil in a small heavy-based saucepan. Boil for 8 minutes, stirring frequently and taking care that the cream doesn't boil over. This cooking time reduces and thickens the cream.
2 Meanwhile, finely chop the anchovies. Melt the butter in a small saucepan, add the anchovies and garlic and cook, stirring, over low heat for 1 minute without allowing to brown.
3 Pour in the cream and mix thoroughly, then add salt and pepper, if necessary. Pour into a serving bowl. Serve warm as a dipping sauce, with vegetable crudités. The mixture will thicken on standing.

RIGHT: Tapenade

AIOLI WITH CRUDITES

Preparation time: 15 minutes
Total cooking time: 1 minute
Serves 4

Aïoli

4 cloves garlic, crushed

2 egg yolks

1¼ cups (315 ml/10 fl oz) light olive or
 vegetable oil

1 tablespoon lemon juice

pinch of ground white pepper

12 asparagus spears, trimmed

12 radishes, trimmed

½ telegraph cucumber, deseeded, halved
 lengthways and cut into batons

1 head of witlof (chicory/Belgian endive), leaves
 separated

1 For the aïoli, place the garlic, egg yolks and a
pinch of salt in a food processor and process for
10 seconds. With the motor running, add the
oil in a thin, slow stream. The mixture will
start to thicken. When this happens you can
add the oil a little faster. Process until all the
oil is incorporated and the mayonnaise is thick
and creamy. Stir in the lemon juice and pepper.
2 Bring a saucepan of water to the boil, add
the asparagus and cook for 1 minute. Remove
and plunge into a bowl of iced water.
3 Arrange the asparagus, radish, cucumber and
witlof decoratively on a platter and place the
aïoli in a bowl on the platter. The aïoli can also
be used as a sandwich spread or as a sauce for
chicken or fish.
NOTE: It is important that all the ingredients are
at room temperature when making this recipe.
Should the mayonnaise start to curdle, beat in
1–2 teaspoons boiling water. If this fails, put
another egg yolk in a clean bowl and very
slowly whisk into the curdled mixture, one
drop at a time, then continue as above.
VARIATION: Many other vegetables, including
green beans, baby carrots, broccoli and
cauliflower florets, sliced peppers (capsicums)
and cherry tomatoes are suitable for making
crudités. Choose vegetables in season when they
are at their best.

AIOLI
Referred to as 'the butter
of Provence', aïoli holds
such an important place
in the region's cuisine that
local villagers honour it in
annual festivals, or 'fête de
la grande aïoli'. It is the
name of both the garlic
mayonnaise and the
Provençal feast where
it accompanies cooked
and raw vegetables, salt
cod, seafood and snails.
Aïoli is the traditional
and indispensable
accompaniment to
bourride, the French
Riviera's fish soup.

ABOVE: Aioli with crudités

Empanadas are traditional Spanish and Central American individual pastry turnovers. They usually have a savoury meat and vegetable filling, although they can also be filled with fruit and served as a dessert. They range from tiny, canapé size, to those large enough to feed a family.

ABOVE: Empanadas

EMPANADAS
(Spanish turnovers)

Preparation time: 45 minutes
Total cooking time: 25 minutes
Makes about 15

★ ★

2 eggs
40 g (1 1/4 oz) stuffed green olives, chopped
95 g (3 oz) ham, finely chopped
1/4 cup (30 g/1 oz) grated Cheddar
3 sheets ready-rolled puff pastry, thawed
1 egg yolk, lightly beaten

1 Place the eggs in a small saucepan, cover with water and bring to the boil. Boil for 10 minutes, then drain and cool for 5 minutes in cold water. Peel and chop.
2 Preheat the oven to hot 220°C (425°F/Gas 7). Lightly grease two baking trays. Combine the egg, olives, ham and Cheddar in a large bowl.
3 Cut about five 10 cm (4 inch) rounds from each pastry sheet. Spoon a tablespoon of the filling into the centre of each round, fold the pastry over and crimp the edges to seal.
4 Place the pastries on the trays, about 2 cm (3/4 inches) apart. Brush with the egg yolk and

bake in the centre or top half of the oven for 15 minutes, or until well browned and puffed. Swap the trays around after 10 minutes and cover loosely with foil if the empanadas start to brown too much. Serve hot.

CHILLI GARLIC PRAWNS

Preparation time: 30 minutes
   + 30 minutes refrigeration
Total cooking time: 10 minutes
Serves 4–6

★

1 kg (2 lb) raw prawns (shrimp)
60 g (2 oz) butter
1/3 cup (80 ml/2 3/4 fl oz) olive oil
3 cloves garlic, roughly chopped
1/4 teaspoon chilli flakes
1/2 teaspoon paprika

1 Peel the prawns, leaving the tails intact. Gently pull out the dark vein from each prawn back, starting at the head end. Mix the prawns with 1/2 teaspoon salt in a large bowl, cover and refrigerate for about 30 minutes.
2 Heat the butter and oil in a flameproof dish

over medium heat. When foaming, add the garlic and chilli and stir for 1 minute, or until golden. Add the prawns, cook for 3–6 minutes, or until they change colour, then sprinkle with paprika. Serve hot with bread for dipping.

NOTE: Traditionally, Chilli garlic prawns (*Gambas al pil pil* in Spanish) is made and served in small earthenware dishes, with one small dish serving two people. You can make this recipe in two small dishes but remember that it will cook more quickly.

BARBECUED SQUID WITH PICADA DRESSING

Preparation time: 40 minutes +
    30 minutes refrigeration
Total cooking time: 15 minutes
Serves 6

★★

500 g (1 lb) small squid (see Note)

Picada dressing
2 tablespoons extra virgin olive oil
2 tablespoons finely chopped fresh
    flat-leaf (Italian) parsley
1 clove garlic, crushed

1 To clean the squid, gently pull the tentacles away from the hood (the intestines should come away at the same time). Remove the intestines from the tentacles by cutting under the eyes, then remove the beak if it remains in the centre of the tentacles by using your fingers to push up the centre. Pull away the soft bone from the hood.

2 Rub the hoods under cold running water. The skin should come away easily. Wash the hoods and tentacles and drain well. Place in a bowl, add ¼ teaspoon salt and mix well. Cover and refrigerate for 30 minutes.

3 Heat a lightly oiled barbecue hotplate or preheat a grill to its highest setting.

4 Close to serving time, whisk the picada dressing ingredients with ¼ teaspoon ground black pepper and some salt in a jug or bowl.

5 Cook the squid hoods in small batches on the barbecue or under the grill for 2–3 minutes, or until the hoods turn white and are tender. Barbecue or grill the squid tentacles, turning to brown them all over, for 1 minute, or until they curl up. Serve hot, drizzled with the dressing.

NOTE: Bottleneck squid is the name given to the small variety of squid used in this recipe. If unavailable, choose the smallest squid you can find.

VARIATIONS: You can also use cuttlefish, octopus, prawns (shrimp) or even chunks of firm white fish fillet.

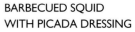
BARBECUED SQUID
WITH PICADA DRESSING

Gently pull the tentacles away from the squid hood.

Cut under the eyes, removing the intestines.

Remove the beak if it remains in the centre of the tentacles.

Pull away the soft bone, rinse the hoods and remove the skin.

LEFT: Barbecued squid with picada dressing

73

MARINATED RED PEPPERS

Preparation time: 20 minutes
  + overnight marinating
Total cooking time: 5 minutes
Serves 6

3 red peppers (capsicums)
3 sprigs of fresh thyme
1 clove garlic, thinly sliced
2 teaspoons coarsely chopped fresh
  flat-leaf (Italian) parsley
1 bay leaf
1 spring onion (scallion), sliced
1 teaspoon paprika
1/4 cup (60 ml/2 fl oz) extra virgin olive oil
2 tablespoons red wine vinegar

1 Preheat the grill. Cut the red peppers into quarters and grill, skin-side-up, until the skin blackens and blisters. Cool in a plastic bag, then peel. Slice thinly, then place in a bowl with the thyme, garlic, parsley, bay leaf and spring onion. Mix well.
2 Whisk together the paprika, oil, vinegar and some salt and pepper. Pour over the red pepper mixture and toss to combine. Cover and refrigerate for at least 3 hours, or preferably overnight. Remove from the refrigerator about 30 minutes before serving.
NOTE: These peppers can be refrigerated for up to 3 days.

TUNA SKEWERS WITH CAPERBERRIES

Soak 8 wooden skewers in cold water for 1 hour to prevent them burning during cooking. Cut 250 g (4 oz) raw tuna into 24 even-sized cubes. Remove the rind from a lemon, avoiding the bitter white pith, and cut the rind into thin strips. Combine the tuna, rind and 1 tablespoon each of lemon juice and olive oil in a bowl. Thread 3 pieces of tuna, 2 caperberries and a green olive, stuffed with anchovy fillet, onto each skewer, alternating each ingredient. Place in a non-metallic dish and pour the marinade over them. Grill under a hot grill for 4 minutes, turning to cook each side, or until done to your liking. Makes 8.

CHICKPEAS WITH CHORIZO SAUSAGE

Preparation time: 15 minutes
  + overnight soaking
Total cooking time: 1 hour 10 minutes
Serves 6

3/4 cup (165 g/5 1/2 oz) dried chickpeas
1 bay leaf
4 cloves
1 cinnamon stick
1 litre (32 fl oz) chicken stock
2 tablespoons olive oil
1 onion, finely chopped
1 clove garlic, crushed
pinch of dried thyme
375 g (12 oz) chorizo sausages, chopped
1 tablespoon chopped fresh flat-leaf
  (Italian) parsley

1 Put the chickpeas in a large bowl, cover well with water and soak overnight. Drain well, then combine in a large saucepan with the bay leaf, cloves, cinnamon stick and stock. Cover well with water, bring to the boil, then reduce the heat and simmer for 1 hour, or until the chickpeas are tender. If they need more time, add a little more water. There should be just a little liquid left in the saucepan. Drain and remove the bay leaf, cloves and cinnamon stick.
2 Heat the oil in a large frying pan, add the onion and cook over medium heat for 3 minutes, or until translucent. Add the garlic and thyme and cook, stirring, for 1 minute. Increase the heat to medium-high, add the chorizo sausage and cook for 3 minutes.
3 Add the chickpeas to the frying pan, mix well, then stir over medium heat until they are heated through. Remove from the heat and mix in the parsley. Season to taste with salt and freshly ground black pepper. This dish is equally delicious served hot or at room temperature.

CINNAMON STICKS
Cinnamon sticks are the curled, thin pieces of bark of a tropical evergreen tree. The bark is removed during the rainy season when it is pliable and easy to work with. When it dries, it curls into quills which are then cut to size or ground to a powder. It is a much-prized spice in Spanish cooking, widely used in both sweet and savoury dishes. Cinnamon keeps its flavour best when whole; however, if the recipe calls for ground cinnamon, buy a small quantity.

OPPOSITE PAGE, FROM TOP: Marinated red peppers; Chickpeas with chorizo sausage

BARBECUED PRAWNS
WITH ROMESCO SAUCE

Squeeze the garlic and
scrape the tomato flesh
into a blender or processor.

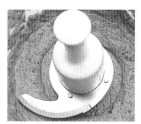

Blend the mixture together
until quite smooth.

BARBECUED PRAWNS WITH ROMESCO SAUCE

Preparation time: 30 minutes
  + 30 minutes refrigeration
  + 15 minutes cooling
Total cooking time: 25 minutes
Serves 6–8

30 raw large prawns (shrimp)

Romesco sauce
4 cloves garlic, unpeeled
1 Roma (plum) tomato, halved and seeded
2 long fresh red chillies
1/4 cup (35 g/1 1/4 oz) blanched almonds
60 g (2 oz) sun-dried peppers (capsicums) in oil
1 tablespoon olive oil
1 tablespoon red wine vinegar

1 Peel the prawns, leaving the tails intact. Gently pull out the dark vein from each prawn back, starting at the head end. Mix with 1/4 teaspoon salt and refrigerate for 30 minutes.

2 For the Romesco sauce, preheat the oven to moderately hot 200°C (400°F/Gas 6). Wrap the garlic in foil, place on a baking tray with the tomato and chillies and bake for 12 minutes. Spread the almonds on the tray and bake for another 3–5 minutes. Leave to cool for 15 minutes.

3 Transfer the almonds to a small blender or food processor and blend until finely ground. Squeeze the garlic and scrape the tomato flesh into the blender, discarding the skins. Split the chillies and remove the seeds. Scrape the flesh into the blender, discarding the skins. Pat the peppers dry with paper towels, then chop them and add to the blender with the oil, vinegar, some salt and 2 tablespoons water. Blend until smooth, adding more water, if necessary, to form a soft dipping consistency. Preheat a grill or lightly oiled barbecue.

4 Brush the prawns with a little oil and cook for 3 minutes, or until curled up and changed colour. Serve with the sauce.

NOTE: Romesco sauce is traditionally served with seafood.

IN ADVANCE: The Romesco sauce can be made up to 5 days in advance and stored in the refrigerator.

*RIGHT: Barbecued
prawns with Romesco
sauce*

STUFFED MUSSELS

Preparation time: 40 minutes + cooling
Total cooking time: 20 minutes
Makes 18

18 black mussels

2 teaspoons olive oil

2 spring onions (scallions), finely chopped

1 clove garlic, crushed

1 tablespoon tomato paste (tomato purée)

2 teaspoons lemon juice

3 tablespoons chopped fresh flat-leaf (Italian)
   parsley

1/3 cup (35 g/1 1/4 oz) dry breadcrumbs

2 eggs, beaten

oil, for deep-frying

White sauce
40 g (1 1/4 oz) butter
1/4 cup (30 g/1 oz) plain (all-purpose) flour
1/3 cup (80 ml/2 3/4 fl oz) milk

1 Scrub the mussels and remove the hairy beards. Discard any open mussels or those that don't close when tapped on the bench. Bring 1 cup (250 ml/4 fl oz) water to the boil in a saucepan, add the mussels, cover and cook for 3–4 minutes, shaking the pan occasionally, until the mussels have just opened. Remove them as soon as they open or they will be tough. Strain the liquid into a jug until you have 1/3 cup (80 ml/2 3/4 fl oz). Discard any unopened mussels. Remove the other mussels from their shells and discard one half shell from each. Finely chop the mussel meat.

2 Heat the oil in a pan, add the spring onion and cook for 1 minute. Add the garlic and cook for 1 minute. Stir in the mussels, tomato paste, lemon juice, 2 tablespoons of the parsley, salt and pepper, then set aside to cool.

3 For the white sauce, melt the butter in a saucepan over low heat. Stir in the flour and cook for 1 minute, or until pale and foaming. Remove from the heat and gradually whisk in the reserved mussel liquid, milk and some pepper. Return to the heat and boil, stirring, for 1 minute, or until the sauce boils and thickens. Reduce the heat and simmer for 2 minutes. Set aside to cool.

4 Spoon the mussel mixture into the shells. Top each with some of the sauce and smooth the surface, making the mixture heaped.

5 Combine the crumbs and remaining parsley.

Dip the mussels in the egg, then press in the crumbs to cover the top. Fill a deep, heavy-based saucepan one third full of oil and heat to 180°C (350°F), or until a cube of bread dropped in the oil browns in 15 seconds. Cook the mussels in batches for 2 minutes each batch. Remove with a slotted spoon and drain well. Serve hot.

PAN CON TOMATE

Slice a baguette diagonally and toast the slices very lightly. Rub them on one side with a cut garlic clove, then with half a tomato, squeezing the juice onto the bread. Season with a little salt and drizzle with extra virgin olive oil. Serve as part of a tapas, or as a simple snack.

ABOVE: Stuffed mussels

CHORIZO

Chorizo is a popular sausage in Spanish cuisine and most regions have their own special variety. They are a pork sausage with a coarse texture, highly seasoned with paprika and garlic, and are either mild or made spicy with the addition of chillies. In Spain they are generally sold cured or smoked, and are indispensable in many traditional recipes. They can also be grilled, then cut into chunks and served as part of a tapas spread.

OPPOSITE PAGE, FROM TOP: Meatballs in spicy tomato sauce; Chorizo in cider

MEATBALLS IN SPICY TOMATO SAUCE

Preparation time: 40 minutes
+ 30 minutes refrigeration
Total cooking time: 30 minutes
Serves 6

★ ★

175 g (6 oz) minced (ground) pork
175 g (6 oz) minced (ground) veal
3 cloves garlic, crushed
1/3 cup (35 g/1 1/4 oz) dry breadcrumbs
1 teaspoon ground coriander
1 teaspoon ground nutmeg
1 teaspoon ground cumin
pinch of ground cinnamon
1 egg
2 tablespoons olive oil

Spicy tomato sauce
1 tablespoon olive oil
1 onion, chopped
2 cloves garlic, crushed
1/2 cup (125 ml/4 fl oz) dry white wine
400 g (13 oz) can crushed good-quality
   tomatoes
1 tablespoon tomato paste (tomato purée)
1/2 cup (125 ml/4 fl oz) chicken stock
1/2 teaspoon cayenne pepper
1/2 cup (80 g/2 3/4 oz) frozen peas

1 Combine the meat, garlic, breadcrumbs, spices, egg and some salt and pepper in a bowl. Mix by hand until smooth and leaving the side of the bowl. Refrigerate, covered, for 30 minutes.
2 Roll tablespoons of mixture into balls. Heat 1 tablespoon of the oil in a frying pan and toss half the meatballs over medium–high heat for 2–3 minutes, until browned. Drain on paper towels. Add the remaining oil, if necessary, and brown the rest of the balls. Drain on paper towels.
3 For the sauce, heat the oil in a frying pan over medium heat and cook the onion, stirring occasionally, for 3 minutes, or until transparent. Add the garlic and cook for 1 minute. Increase the heat to high, add the wine and boil for 1 minute. Add the tomato, tomato paste and stock and simmer for 10 minutes. Add the cayenne, peas and meatballs. Simmer for 5–10 minutes, or until the sauce is thick. Serve hot.

CHORIZO IN CIDER

Preparation time: 5 minutes
Total cooking time: 15 minutes
Serves 4

★ ★

3 teaspoons olive oil
1 small onion, finely chopped
1 1/2 teaspoons paprika
1/2 cup (125 ml/4 fl oz) dry alcoholic
   apple cider
1/4 cup (60 ml/2 fl oz) chicken stock
1 bay leaf
280 g (9 oz) chorizo, sliced diagonally
2 teaspoons sherry vinegar, or to taste
2 teaspoons chopped fresh flat-leaf (Italian)
   parsley

1 Heat the oil in a saucepan over low heat, add the onion and cook for 3 minutes, stirring occasionally, or until soft. Add the paprika and cook for 1 minute.
2 Increase the heat to medium, add the apple cider, stock and bay leaf to the pan and bring to the boil. Reduce the heat and simmer for 5 minutes. Add the sliced chorizo and simmer for 5 minutes, or until the sauce has reduced slightly. Stir in the sherry vinegar and parsley. Serve hot.

SALTED ALMONDS

Preheat the oven to very slow 120°C (250°F/Gas 1/2). In a large bowl, lightly whip an egg white and 1/4 teaspoon sweet paprika with a fork until the mixture starts to froth. Add 500 g (1 lb) blanched almonds and toss to coat evenly. Divide the nuts between two non-stick baking trays. Sprinkle with 1 1/2 tablespoons coarse sea salt grains (not flakes), turning the nuts several times so that the salt adheres to them. Spread over the trays. Bake for 30 minutes, turning the nuts over occasionally to prevent them sticking. Turn off the heat and leave the almonds in the oven for 30 minutes. When completely cooled, store in airtight jars. Serves 6–8.

SALT COD
FRITTERS

Remove the skin and any bones from the cooked salt cod.

Fold the whisked egg white into the potato and cod mixture.

Deep-fry the fritters in hot oil until puffed and golden.

SALT COD FRITTERS

Preparation time: 15 minutes + 24 hours soaking
Total cooking time: 1 hour
Makes 35

★★

500 g (1 lb) salt cod

1 large potato (200 g/6½ oz), unpeeled

2 tablespoons milk

3 tablespoons olive oil

1 small onion, finely chopped

2 cloves garlic, crushed

¼ cup (30 g/1 oz) self-raising flour

2 eggs, separated

1 tablespoon chopped fresh flat-leaf (Italian)
  parsley

olive oil, extra, for deep-frying

1 Soak the cod in cold water for 24 hours, changing the water regularly to remove as much salt as possible. Cook the potato in a pan of boiling water for 20 minutes, or until soft. When cool, peel and mash with the milk and 2 tablespoons of the olive oil.
2 Drain the cod, cut into large pieces and place in a saucepan. Cover with water, bring to the boil over high heat, then reduce the heat to medium and cook for 10 minutes, or until soft and there is a froth on the surface. Drain. When cool enough to handle, remove the skin and any

bones, then mash well with a fork until flaky.
3 Heat the remaining oil in a small frying pan and cook the onion over medium heat for 5 minutes, or until softened and starting to brown. Add the garlic and cook for 1 minute. Remove from the heat.
4 Combine the potato, cod, onion, flour, egg yolks and parsley in a bowl and season. Whisk the egg whites until stiff, then fold into the mixture. Fill a large heavy-based saucepan one third full of olive oil and heat to 190°C (375°F), or until a cube of bread dropped into the oil browns in 10 seconds. Drop heaped tablespoons of mixture into the oil and cook for 2 minutes, or until puffed and golden. Drain and serve.

KIDNEYS IN SHERRY

Preparation time: 15 minutes
Total cooking time: 20 minutes
Serves 4

★

2 tablespoons olive oil

1 large onion, finely chopped

2 cloves garlic, crushed

1 tablespoon plain (all-purpose) flour

1¼ cups (315 ml/10 fl oz) chicken stock

1 tablespoon tomato paste (tomato purée)

1 bay leaf

ABOVE: Salt cod fritters

1 kg (2 lb) lambs' kidneys, cut into halves

40 g (1¼ oz) butter

150 ml (5 fl oz) dry sherry

1 tablespoon chopped fresh flat-leaf (Italian) parsley

1 Heat the oil in a frying pan and cook the onion and garlic over moderate heat for about 5 minutes, until the onion softens. Add the flour and cook, stirring, for 1 minute. Add the stock, tomato paste and bay leaf. Bring to the boil and cook, stirring, until thickened. Season with salt and ground black pepper and simmer for 3–4 minutes. Keep warm.

2 Cut out the white cores from the kidneys. Slice each half into three. Melt the butter in a large frying pan and add half the kidneys. Cook over high heat, stirring often, until they brown on all sides. Remove from the pan and cook the rest. Remove, pour the sherry into the pan and cook over high heat, stirring to deglaze, until reduced by half. Return the kidneys to the pan, add the sauce and stir the parsley through. Taste for seasoning and simmer for another 2 minutes before serving. Delicious with rice.

PATATAS BRAVAS
(Crisp potatoes in spicy tomato sauce)

Preparation time: 15 minutes
Total cooking time: 1 hour
Serves 6

★★

1 kg (2 lb) desiree potatoes

oil, for deep-frying

500 g (1 lb) ripe Roma (plum) tomatoes

2 tablespoons olive oil

¼ red onion, finely chopped

2 cloves garlic, crushed

3 teaspoons paprika

¼ teaspoon cayenne pepper

1 bay leaf

1 teaspoon sugar

1 tablespoon chopped fresh flat-leaf (Italian) parsley, to garnish

1 Cut the potatoes into 2 cm (¾ inch) cubes. Rinse, then drain well and pat completely dry. Fill a deepfryer or large heavy-based saucepan one third full of oil and heat to 180°C (350°F), or until a cube of bread dropped into the oil browns in 15 seconds. Cook the potato in batches for 10 minutes, or until golden. Drain well on paper towels. Do not discard the oil.

2 Score a cross in the base of each tomato. Place in a bowl of boiling water for 10 seconds, then plunge into cold water and peel the skin away from the cross. Chop the flesh.

3 Heat the olive oil in a saucepan over medium heat and cook the onion for 3 minutes, or until softened. Add the garlic, paprika and cayenne, and cook for 1–2 minutes, until fragrant.

4 Add the tomato, bay leaf, sugar and 90 ml (3 fl oz) water, and cook, stirring occasionally, for 20 minutes, or until thick and pulpy. Cool slightly and remove the bay leaf. Blend in a food processor until smooth, adding a little water if necessary. Before serving, return the sauce to the saucepan and simmer over low heat for 2 minutes, or until heated though. Season well.

5 Reheat the oil to 180°C (350°F) and cook the potato again, in batches, for 2 minutes, or until very crisp and golden. Drain on paper towels. This second frying makes the potato extra crispy and stops the sauce soaking in immediately. Place on a platter and cover with sauce. Garnish with parsley and serve.

BELOW: Patatas bravas

HAM AND MUSHROOM
CROQUETTES

Roll portions of the mixture
into croquette shapes.

Use two forks to lower
each floured croquette into
the beaten egg.

*RIGHT: Ham and
mushroom croquettes*

HAM AND MUSHROOM CROQUETTES

Preparation time: 35 minutes
  + 2 hours cooling
  + 30 minutes refrigeration
Total cooking time: 20 minutes
Makes 18

★ ★

90 g (3 oz) butter
1 small onion, finely chopped
110 g (3½ oz) cap mushrooms, finely chopped
¾ cup (90 g/3 oz) plain (all-purpose) flour
1 cup (250 ml/4 fl oz) milk
¾ cup (185 ml/6 fl oz) chicken stock
110 g (3½ oz) ham, finely chopped
½ cup (60 g/2 oz) plain (all-purpose) flour,
  extra
2 eggs, lightly beaten
½ cup (50 g/1¾ oz) dry breadcrumbs
oil, for deep-frying

1 Melt the butter in a saucepan over low heat,
add the onion and cook for 5 minutes, or until
translucent. Add the mushrooms and cook over
low heat, stirring occasionally, for 5 minutes.
Add the flour and stir over medium-low heat
for 1 minute, or until the mixture is dry and
crumbly and begins to change colour. Remove
from the heat and gradually add the milk, stirring
until smooth. Stir in the stock and return to
the heat, stirring until the mixture boils and
thickens. Stir in the ham and some black pepper,
then transfer to a bowl to cool for about 2 hours.

2 Roll 2 tablespoons of mixture at a time into
croquette shapes 6 cm (2½ inches) long. Place
the extra flour, beaten egg and breadcrumbs
in three shallow bowls. Toss the croquettes
in the flour, dip in the egg, allowing the excess
to drain away, then roll in the breadcrumbs.
Place on a baking tray and refrigerate for about
30 minutes.

3 Fill a deep, heavy-based saucepan one third
full of oil and heat to 180°C (350°F), or until
a cube of bread dropped into the oil browns in
15 seconds. Deep-fry the croquettes, in batches,
for 3 minutes, turning, until brown. Drain well.
VARIATION: You can vary these croquettes very
easily to suit your taste. For example, they are
delicious if you replace the ham with finely
chopped chicken or flaked cooked fish and add
your favourite finely chopped fresh herb.

GARLIC PRAWNS

Preparation time: 20 minutes
Total cooking time: 15 minutes
Serves 4

1.25 kg (2¹/2 lb) raw prawns (shrimp)
80 g (2³/4 oz) butter, melted
³/4 cup (185 ml/6 fl oz) olive oil
8 cloves garlic, crushed
2 spring onions (scallions), thinly sliced

1 Preheat the oven to very hot 250°C (500°F/ Gas 10). Peel the prawns, leaving the tails intact. Pull out the vein from each back, starting at the head end. Cut a slit down the back of each prawn.
2 Combine the butter and oil and divide among four 500 ml (16 fl oz) cast iron pots. Divide half the crushed garlic among the pots.
3 Place the pots on a baking tray and heat in the oven for 10 minutes, or until the mixture is bubbling. Remove and divide the prawns and remaining garlic among the pots. Return to the oven for 5 minutes, or until the prawns are cooked. Stir in the spring onion. Season to taste. Serve with bread to mop up the juices.
NOTE: Garlic prawns can also be made in a cast iron frying pan in the oven or on the stovetop.

GARLIC MUSHROOMS

Preparation time: 10 minutes
Total cooking time: 15 minutes
Serves 4

6 cloves garlic
1¹/2 tablespoons lemon juice
650 g (1 lb 5 oz) button mushrooms, sliced
¹/4 cup (60 ml/2 fl oz) olive oil
¹/4 small fresh red chilli, finely chopped
2 teaspoons chopped fresh flat-leaf
  (Italian) parsley

1 Crush four of the garlic cloves and thinly slice the rest. Sprinkle the lemon juice over the sliced mushrooms.
2 Heat the oil in a large frying pan and add the crushed garlic and chopped chilli. Stir over medium-high heat for 10 seconds, then add the mushrooms. Season and cook, stirring often, for 8–10 minutes. Stir in the sliced garlic and parsley and cook for another minute. Serve hot.
VARIATION: You can also use field, Swiss brown or any wild mushrooms for this recipe, but take care to reduce the cooking times if you use the more fragile wild mushrooms.

GARLIC PRAWNS
In Spain, this is one of the most popular tapas dishes served in bars and restaurants all around the coastal regions. It is traditional for them to be served in the dish that they have been cooked in, and this is usually a small cast iron or glazed terracotta pot. It is served with crusty bread so that all the juices and crispy flavours can be mopped up and savoured.

ABOVE: Garlic prawns

SPANISH-STYLE BEEF KEBABS WITH PAPRIKA DRESSING

Preparation time: 15 minutes + marinating
Total cooking time: 5 minutes
Makes 18–20

1 kg (2 lb) rump steak, trimmed and cut into
   2 cm (3/4 inch) pieces
3 cloves garlic, chopped
1 tablespoon chopped fresh flat-leaf (Italian)
   parsley
1/3 cup (80 ml/2 3/4 fl oz) lemon juice
18–20 small wooden skewers

Paprika dressing

2 teaspoons paprika
large pinch of cayenne pepper
2 tablespoons red wine vinegar
1/3 cup (80 ml/2 3/4 fl oz) olive oil

1 Combine the steak, garlic, parsley, lemon juice and 1/2 teaspoon pepper in a bowl, cover with plastic wrap and marinate for 2 hours in the refrigerator. Meanwhile, soak the skewers in water for 30 minutes.
2 To make the paprika dressing, whisk the paprika, cayenne pepper, vinegar, oil and 1/2 teaspoon salt together until well blended.
3 Preheat a lightly oiled barbecue hotplate or grill. Thread the pieces of marinated meat onto the skewers, then cook the kebabs, turning occasionally for about 4–5 minutes, or until cooked through. Drizzle with the paprika dressing and serve hot with wedges of lemon.

HALOUMI

This is a firm, stretched-curd cheese that is matured in brine (salt water). It has a salty, sharp taste, similar to feta. Haloumi can be served as part of a cheese platter, together with fresh fruit. It can also be pan-fried in olive oil, or brushed with oil before grilling. It has a smooth and creamy texture when melted.

ABOVE: Spanish-style beef kebabs with paprika dressing

BARBECUED HALOUMI

Lightly brush 10 slices of French bread on both sides with olive oil and barbecue until brown. Cut 250 g (8 oz) haloumi cheese into 5 mm (1/4 inch) slices. Combine a little oil and crushed garlic and brush over the cheese. Barbecue on a hotplate for 1 minute, or until soft and golden underneath. Use a spatula to remove the cheese and place some on each piece of toast. Drizzle with a little olive oil and sprinkle with chopped mint and ground black pepper. Makes 10.

BABA GANOUJ
(Eggplant dip)

Preparation time: 15 minutes + standing
Total cooking time: 35 minutes
Makes about 1 cup (250 ml/8 fl oz)

2 eggplants (aubergines)
3–4 cloves garlic, crushed
2 tablespoons lemon juice
2 tablespoons tahini
1 tablespoon olive oil
sprinkle of paprika, to garnish

1 Halve the eggplants (aubergines) lengthways, sprinkle with salt and leave to stand for 15–20 minutes. Rinse and pat dry with paper towels. Preheat the oven to moderate 180°C (350°F/Gas 4).
2 Place the eggplants on a baking tray and bake for 35 minutes, or until soft. Peel away the skin and discard. Place the flesh in a food processor with the garlic, lemon juice, tahini and olive oil and season to taste with salt and pepper. Process for 20–30 seconds. Sprinkle with paprika and serve with pieces of Lebanese bread.
NOTES: The reason eggplants are sprinkled with salt and left to stand before using is that they can have a bitter taste. The salt draws out the bitter liquid from the eggplant. Slender eggplants do not need to be treated in this way before you use them. Tahini is a paste made from crushed sesame seeds and is available at the supermarket.

TARAMASALATA

Remove the crusts from 4 slices of white bread. Put in a bowl, cover with water, drain and squeeze out as much water as possible. Put in a bowl. Finely grate a small onion into the bowl, add 100 g (3½ oz) tarama (cod roe), 2 tablespoons lemon juice, 3 tablespoons olive oil and a pinch of freshly ground black pepper. Mix well with a fork until well combined. Makes 1 cup.

BELOW: Baba ganouj

BRUSCHETTA
Crusty bread—whether it's an Italian loaf, French stick or sourdough—lightly toasted and topped with colourful fresh ingredients will satisfy the hungriest of guests.

SMOKED SALMON AND CAPERS
Cut 2 small French bread sticks into 1 cm (½ inch) slices and lightly grill until golden on both sides. Mix 250 g (8 oz) cream cheese with 2 tablespoons lemon juice and 15 g (½ oz) chopped chives. Spread over the toast and top with small slices of smoked salmon and a few baby capers. Garnish with sprigs of fresh dill before serving. Makes about 24.

GRILLED PEPPERS
Cut 2 yellow, 2 green and 2 red peppers (capsicums) in half lengthways. Remove the seeds and membrane, place skin-side-up under a hot grill and cook until the skins have blackened. Cool in a plastic bag, then peel off the skins. Thinly slice the peppers and place in a large bowl. Add 1 small red onion, sliced into thin wedges, 1½ tablespoons olive oil, 1½ tablespoons balsamic vinegar and

2 crushed cloves of garlic. Slice 2 small sourdough bread sticks into 1 cm (½ inch) slices. Lightly grill until golden on both sides. Top with the pepper mixture. Makes about 24.

ROCKET AND FETA
Cut a large French bread stick or an Italian loaf into 1 cm (½ inch) slices, brush with olive oil and grill until golden on both sides. Arrange rocket (arugula)

leaves over each piece, using about 90 g (3 oz) altogether. Toss 200 g (6½ oz) crumbled feta with 2 teaspoons finely grated orange rind and 2 tablespoons olive oil. Spoon 2 teaspoons of the mixture over the rocket on each bruschetta. Grill 6 slices prosciutto until crispy, then crumble over the bruschetta. Makes about 30.

CAPRESSE

Mix 150 g (5 oz) finely diced bocconcini, with 3 tablespoons shredded fresh basil and 3 tablespoons warm extra virgin olive oil in a glass bowl. Season to taste. Cover and leave in a warm place for 1 hour to allow the flavours to develop. Cut a large French bread stick or an Italian loaf into 1 cm (½ inch) slices, brush with olive oil and grill until golden on both sides. Spread the bocconcini mixture over the toast. Makes about 30.

MUSHROOM AND PARSLEY

Cut a large French bread stick or Italian loaf into 1 cm (½ inch) slices, brush with olive oil and grill until golden on both sides. Heat 1 tablespoon of olive oil in a small frying pan, and fry 200 g (6½ oz) quartered small button mushrooms until just tender. Stir in 1 tablespoon lemon juice, 50 g (1¾ oz) crumbled goat's cheese, a tablespoon of chopped fresh flat-leaf (Italian) parsley and season to taste. Spread over the toast. Makes about 30.

TOMATO AND BASIL

Cut a large French bread stick or Italian loaf into 1 cm (½ inch) slices, brush with olive oil and grill until golden on both sides. Finely chop 4 ripe tomatoes and mix with ½ cup (30 g/1 oz) finely shredded fresh basil and 2 tablespoons extra virgin olive oil. Spread over the toast. Makes about 30.

PASTRAMI AND HERBS

Cut a large French bread stick or Italian loaf into 1 cm (½ inch) slices, brush with olive oil and grill until golden on both sides. Combine 200 ml (6½ fl oz) of crème fraîche with 1 teaspoon each of chopped fresh parsley, chives and basil. Spread 1 teaspoon over each slice of toast. Halve 30 slices of pastrami, fold in half again and place 2 pieces over the crème fraîche. Mix 2 chopped tomatoes with ½ finely chopped red onion and 2 teaspoons each of balsamic vinegar and olive oil. Spoon over the top and garnish with small fresh basil leaves. Makes about 30.

FROM LEFT: Smoked salmon and capers; Grilled peppers; Rocket and feta; Capresse; Mushroom and parsley; Tomato and basil; Pastrami and herbs

SCALLOPS CEVICHE

Pull away the dark vein and white muscle from each scallop.

Stir the scallops to coat in the marinade.

TORTILLA

Preparation time: 25 minutes
Total cooking time: 20 minutes
Serves 6–8

★ ★

500 g (1 lb) potatoes, cut into 1 cm
   (½ inch) slices
¼ cup (60 ml/2 fl oz) olive oil
1 brown onion, thinly sliced
4 cloves garlic, thinly sliced
2 tablespoons finely chopped fresh flat-leaf
   (Italian) parsley
6 eggs

1 Place the potato slices in a large pan, cover with cold water and bring to the boil over high heat. Boil for 5 minutes, then drain and set aside.
2 Heat the oil in a deep-sided non-stick frying pan over medium heat. Add the onion and garlic and cook for 5 minutes, or until the onion softens.
3 Add the potato and parsley to the pan and stir to combine. Cook over medium heat for 5 mintues, gently pressing down into the pan.
4 Whisk the eggs with 1 teaspoon each of salt and freshly ground black pepper and pour evenly over the potato. Cover and cook for about 20 minutes, on low–medium heat until the eggs are just set. Slide onto a serving plate or serve directly from the pan.

SCALLOPS CEVICHE

Preparation time: 20 minutes + 2 hours marinating
Total cooking time: Nil
Makes 15

★ ★

15 scallops on the half shell
1 teaspoon finely grated lime rind
¼ cup (60 ml/2 fl oz) lime juice
2 cloves garlic, chopped
2 red chillies, seeded and chopped
1 tablespoon chopped fresh parsley
1 tablespoon olive oil

1 Take the scallops off their half shell. If they need to be cut off the shell, use a small, sharp paring knife to slice the attached part from the shell, being careful to leave as little scallop meat on the shell as possible. Remove the dark vein and white muscle from each and wash the shells.
2 In a non-metallic bowl, mix the lime rind and juice, garlic, chilli, parsley and oil and season with salt and ground black pepper. Add the scallops and stir to coat. Cover with plastic wrap and refrigerate for 2 hours to 'cook' the scallop meat.
3 To serve, slide the scallops onto the half shells and spoon the dressing over them. Serve cold.
IN ADVANCE: These scallops will keep for up to 2 days in the dressing.

RIGHT: Tortilla

OCTOPUS IN GARLIC ALMOND SAUCE

Preparation time: 25 minutes + cooling
Total cooking time: 50 minutes
Serves 4

1 kg (2 lb) baby octopus
1/2 small red pepper (capsicum), seeded
125 g (4 oz) flaked almonds
3 cloves garlic, crushed
1/3 cup (80 ml/2³/4 fl oz) red wine vinegar
3/4 cup (185 ml/6 fl oz) olive oil
2 tablespoons chopped fresh flat-leaf (Italian)
   parsley

1 Using a small knife, carefully cut between the head and tentacles of the octopus and push the beak out and up through the centre of the tentacles with your finger. Cut the eyes from the head of the octopus by slicing off a small disc with a sharp knife. Discard the eye section. To clean the octopus head, carefully slit through one side and rinse out the gut. Drop the octopus into a large pan of boiling water and simmer for 20–40 minutes, depending on size, until tender. After 15 minutes cooking, start pricking them with a skewer to test for tenderness. When ready, remove from the heat and cool in the pan for 15 minutes.

2 For the sauce, heat the griller to high. Grill the red pepper skin-side-up until charred and blistered. Cool in a plastic bag, then peel and place in a food processor with the almonds and garlic, then purée. With the motor running, gradually pour in the vinegar followed by the oil. Stir in 1/2 cup (125 ml/4 fl oz) boiling water and parsley and season to taste.

3 To serve, cut the tentacles into pieces. Place in a serving bowl with the sauce and toss to coat. Serve warm, or chill and serve as a salad.

ALMONDS
Almonds are the kernel from the fruit of the almond tree, and although Mediterranean in origin, are now grown extensively throughout California, Australia and South Africa. There are two varieties available, the sweet almond, which is readily available, and should be used in recipes where no variety is specified. The other type is a bitter almond, primarily used to flavour extracts and liqueurs.

ABOVE: Octopus in garlic almond sauce

89

PRAWN CROUSTADE

Preparation time: 45 minutes
Total cooking time: 25 minutes
Serves 6

✮ ✮

¹/₂ loaf unsliced white bread
¹/₂ cup (125 ml/4 fl oz) olive oil
1 clove garlic, crushed

Filling

500 g (1 lb) raw prawns (shrimp)
1¹/₂ cups (375 ml/12 fl oz) fish stock
2 slices lemon
50 g (1³/₄ oz) butter
6 spring onions (scallions), chopped
¹/₄ cup (30 g/1 oz) plain (all-purpose) flour
1 tablespoon lemon juice
¹/₂–1 teaspoon chopped fresh dill
¹/₄ cup (60 ml/2 fl oz) cream

BELOW: Prawn croustade

1 Preheat the oven to hot 210°C (415°F/Gas 6–7). Remove the crust from the bread and cut the bread into slices about 5 cm (2 inches) thick. Cut each slice diagonally to form triangles. Cut triangles 1 cm (¹/₂ inch) inside the others, leaving a base on each, then scoop out the centres to create cavities for the filling. Heat the oil and garlic in a small pan, brush all over the bread cases, then place on a baking tray and bake for 10 minutes, or until golden brown.
2 For the filling, peel the prawns and gently pull out the dark vein from each prawn back, starting at the head end. Roughly chop the prawns, place in a small pan and cover with stock. Add the lemon slices, simmer for 15 minutes, strain and reserve the liquid and prawns separately.
3 Melt the butter in a small pan, add the spring onion and stir over medium heat until soft. Stir in the flour and some pepper and cook for 2 minutes. Remove from the heat and gradually stir in the reserved prawn liquid. Return to the heat and stir constantly over medium heat for 5 minutes, or until the sauce boils and thickens. Add the lemon juice, dill, cream and reserved prawns, and stir until heated through.
4 To serve, spoon the filling into the warm bread cases.

SEAFOOD VOL-AU-VENTS

Preparation time: 30 minutes
Total cooking time: 20 minutes
Serves 4

✮

250 g (8 oz) raw prawns (shrimp)
250 g (8 oz) black mussels
125 g (4 oz) scallops
4 large cooked vol-au-vent cases
1 cup (250 ml/8 fl oz) fish stock
60 g (2 oz) butter
1¹/₂ tablespoons plain (all-purpose) flour
1 tablespoon white wine
1 tablespoon cream
60 g (2 oz) button mushrooms, diced
1 tablespoon fresh lemon juice
1–2 tablespoons chopped fresh parsley

1 Peel the prawns and gently pull out the dark vein from each prawn back, starting at the head end. Scrub the mussels with a stiff brush and pull out the hairy beards. Discard any broken mussels, or open ones that don't close when

tapped on the bench. Rinse well. Slice or pull off any vein, membrane or hard white muscle from the scallops, leaving any roe attached.

2 Preheat the oven to 160°C (315°F/Gas 2–3). Place the vol-au-vent cases on a baking tray and heat in the oven while preparing the filling.

3 Heat the fish stock in a small pan, add the prawns and mussels and simmer for 4–5 minutes. Add the scallops and cook for 1 minute, or until tender. Drain and cool, reserving the stock. Remove the meat from the mussels, discarding any unopened mussels.

4 Melt half the butter in a small pan over low heat. Stir in the flour and cook for 2 minutes, or until pale and foaming. Remove from the heat and gradually stir in the reserved stock and wine. Return to the heat and stir constantly until the sauce boils and thickens. Simmer for 5 minutes. Remove from the heat and stir in the cream.

5 Melt the remaining butter in a pan and cook the mushrooms for 2–3 minutes, or until soft. Add the seafood, sauce, lemon juice, parsley, and salt and pepper, to taste. Stir until heated through.

6 Spoon the seafood mixture into the warm vol-au-vent cases and serve immediately.

PRAWN FRITTERS

Preparation time: 25 minutes
Total cooking time: 15 minutes
Serves 4-6

50 g (1¾ oz) dried rice vermicelli
300 g (10 oz) raw prawns (shrimp)
1 egg
1 tablespoon fish sauce
1 cup (125 g/4 oz) plain (all-purpose) flour
¼ teaspoon shrimp paste
3 spring onions (scallions), sliced
1 small fresh red chilli, finely chopped
oil, for deep-frying
sweet chilli sauce, to serve

1 Soak the rice vermicelli in a bowl of boiling water for 5 minutes, then drain, pat dry and cut into short lengths.

2 Peel the prawns and gently pull out the dark vein from each prawn back, starting at the head end. Process half the prawns in a food processor until smooth, then transfer to a bowl. Chop the remaining prawns and add to the bowl.

3 Beat the egg, fish sauce and ¾ cup (185 ml/ 6 fl oz) water in a small jug. Sift the flour into a

bowl, make a well in the centre and gradually add the egg mixture, whisking to make a smooth lump-free batter.

4 Add the prawns, shrimp paste, spring onion, red chilli and rice vermicelli to the bowl, then mix until well combined.

5 Fill a deep, heavy-based pan one third full of oil and heat to 180°C (350°F), or until a cube of bread browns in 15 seconds. Drop tablespoons of mixture into the oil and deep-fry in batches for 3 minutes, or until crisp and golden. Drain on crumpled paper towels. Repeat until all the mixture is used. Serve hot, with sweet chilli sauce.

ABOVE: Prawn fritters

SOUPS

MAKING YOUR OWN STOCK
Flavoursome home-made stock can make the difference between a good soup and a fabulous one.

FISH STOCK
To prepare the fish trimmings, discard the eyes and gills, then roughly chop the bones, heads and tails. Remove the eyes from any fish heads with a teaspoon and put all the bones and trimmings in a bowl of salted water for 10 minutes. Drain and rinse under cold water. Place 2 kg (4 lb) of chopped fish trimmings, 1 chopped onion, 1 chopped leek, 1 chopped celery stick, 6 peppercorns, 1 bay leaf and the juice of 1 lemon in a large pan or stock pot with the remaining ingredients and 2 litres (64 fl oz) cold water. Bring the mixture to the boil, skimming off any scum that rises to the surface. Reduce the heat and simmer for 20 minutes, skimming when necessary. Strain through a fine sieve and place in the refrigerator to cool. Makes about 1.5 litres (48 fl oz).

VEGETABLE STOCK
Heat a tablespoon of oil in a large heavy-based pan. Add a chopped onion, 2 chopped leeks, 4 chopped carrots, 2 chopped parsnips and 4 chopped celery sticks and toss to coat in the oil. Cover

and cook for 5 minutes without browning. Add 3 litres (96 fl oz) water and bring to the boil. Skim the surface if required and add 2 bay leaves, 4 unpeeled garlic cloves, 8 peppercorns and a few parsley stalks. Reduce the heat and simmer for 1 hour. Ladle the stock in batches into a fine sieve sitting over a bowl. Gently press the solids to extract all the liquid. Cool in the fridge. Makes about 2.5 litres (80 fl oz).

BEEF STOCK

Preheat the oven to hot 220°C (425°F/ Gas 7). Put 2 kg (4 lb) beef bones (ask your butcher to chop them up) on an oven tray and roast for 20 minutes. Add 1 quartered onion, 2 chopped carrots, 1 chopped leek and 1 chopped celery stick and roast for 20 minutes. Transfer it all to a large pan or stock pot, discarding any excess fat left in the roasting tray. Add a bay leaf, 6 peppercorns, a sprig of thyme, a few parsley stalks and 6 litres (192 fl oz) cold water and bring to the boil, skimming off any scum that rises to the surface. Reduce the heat and simmer for 3–4 hours, skimming when necessary. Strain the stock through a fine sieve over a bowl. Gently press the solids to extract all the liquid. Leave overnight in the refrigerator. Remove the fat from the surface. Makes about 3 litres (96 fl oz).

CHICKEN STOCK

Put 2 kg (4 lb) chicken bones, 1 chopped carrot, 1 chopped leek, 1 chopped onion, 1 chopped celery stick, 8 peppercorns, 1 bay leaf, a few parsley stalks and a sprig of thyme in a large pan or stock pot and add 6 litres (192 fl oz) cold water. Bring to the boil and skim off any scum from the surface. Reduce the heat and simmer for 2–3 hours, skimming as necessary. Strain the stock through a fine sieve and refrigerate overnight. Remove the fat from the surface. Makes about 3.5 litres (112 fl oz).

FREEZING STOCK

Cool the stock, then line a measuring jug with a plastic bag and ladle the amount you want to freeze into the bag. Remove the bag from the jug, label the bag, seal securely and freeze. Repeat until all the stock is used.

PASTA AND BEANS
Combining pasta and beans
may seem strange, but they
have an affinity recognised
in a number of cuisines. In
Italy, each region seems to
have its own version of
pasta e fagioli, with the local
pasta and favourite beans
matched with vegetables,
sausage, or perhaps just
Parmesan. Pasta combined
with beans creates a
complete protein, making
it a good vegetarian meal.

*BELOW: Pasta
and bean soup*

PASTA AND BEAN SOUP

Preparation time: 20 minutes
   + overnight soaking
Total cooking time: 1 hour 25 minutes
Serves 4–6

250 g (8 oz) borlotti beans, soaked
   in water overnight
1 ham hock
1 onion, chopped
pinch of ground cinnamon
pinch of cayenne pepper
2 teaspoons olive oil
2 cups (500 ml/16 fl oz) chicken stock
125 g (4 oz) tagliatelle (plain or spinach),
   broken into short lengths

1 Drain and rinse the borlotti beans, then put
in a saucepan, cover with cold water and bring
to the boil. Stir, reduce the heat and simmer for
15 minutes.

2 Drain the beans and transfer to a large
saucepan, with a tight-fitting lid. Add the ham
hock, onion, cinnamon, cayenne, olive oil and
stock, and enough cold water to cover. Cover
the pan with a lid and simmer over low heat for
1 hour, or until the beans are cooked and have
begun to thicken the stock. Remove the hock
and cut off any meat. Chop the meat and return
to the pan, discarding the bone.

3 Season to taste, then bring the soup back to
the boil, toss in the tagliatelle and cook until
al dente. Remove the pan from the heat and set
aside for 1–2 minutes before serving. Can be
garnished with fresh herbs.

CHICKEN AND PASTA SOUP

Preparation time: 20 minutes
Total cooking time: 20 minutes
Serves 4

2 chicken breast fillets
90 g (3 oz) mushrooms
2 tablespoons olive oil
1 onion, finely diced
180 g (6 oz) spaghetti, broken into
　short lengths
1.5 litres (48 fl oz) chicken stock
1 cup (35 g/1¼ oz) torn fresh basil leaves

1 Finely dice the chicken breast fillets and roughly chop the mushrooms. Heat the olive oil in a pan and cook the onion until soft and golden. Add the chicken, mushrooms, spaghetti pieces and chicken stock. Bring to the boil.
2 Reduce the heat and simmer for 10 minutes. Stir in the fresh basil leaves. Season to taste with salt and freshly ground black pepper.

GARLIC, PASTA AND FISH SOUP

Preparation time: 30 minutes
Total cooking time: 40 minutes
Serves 4–6

4 tablespoons olive oil
1 leek, sliced
20–30 cloves garlic, thinly sliced
2 potatoes, chopped
2 litres (64 fl oz) fish stock
½ cup (75 g/2½ oz) miniature pasta shapes
10 baby yellow squash, halved
2 zucchini (courgettes), cut into thick slices
300 g (10 oz) ling fillets, cut into
　large pieces
1–2 tablespoons lemon juice
2 tablespoons shredded fresh basil

1 Heat the oil in a large pan, add the leek, garlic and potato and cook over medium heat for 10 minutes. Add 500 ml (16 fl oz) of the stock and cook for 10 minutes.
2 Allow to cool slightly before puréeing, in batches, in a food processor or blender.

3 Pour the remaining stock into the pan and bring to the boil. Add the pasta, squash and zucchini, along with the purée, and simmer for 15 minutes.
4 When the pasta is soft, add the fish and cook for 5 minutes, or until tender. Add the lemon juice and basil, and season to taste with salt and freshly ground black pepper.

PARMESAN CROUTONS

Remove the crusts from 2 slices of day-old white bread and cut the bread into 1 cm (½ inch) squares. Heat 2 tablespoons oil in a frying pan and when it is very hot add the bread and fry, tossing continuously until the croutons are browned all over. Remove the croutons from the pan and toss them while they are still very hot with 1 tablespoon finely grated Parmesan. Sprinkle over soups. Serves 4.

ABOVE: Chicken and pasta soup

MINESTRONE
Just about every region
of Italy has its own
minestrone. This version
has a spoonful of pesto
stirred through at the end.
To make the Milanese
version of minestrone,
Minestrone alla Milanese,
add 100 g (3 1/2 oz) of
arborio rice instead of
the pasta.

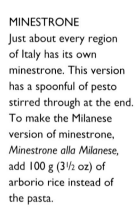

*ABOVE: Minestrone
with pesto*

MINESTRONE WITH PESTO

Preparation time: 25 minutes + overnight soaking
Total cooking time: 2 hours
Serves 6

125 g (4 oz) dried borlotti beans
1/4 cup (60 ml/2 fl oz) olive oil
1 large onion, finely chopped
2 cloves garlic, crushed
60 g (3 oz) pancetta, finely chopped
1 stick celery, halved lengthways, then cut
    into 1 cm (1/2 inch) slices
1 carrot, halved lengthways, then cut into
    1 cm (1/2 inch) slices
1 potato, diced
2 teaspoons tomato paste (tomato purée)
400 g (13 oz) can good-quality crushed tomatoes
6 fresh basil leaves, roughly torn
2 litres (64 fl oz) chicken or vegetable stock
2 thin zucchini (courgettes), cut into
    1.5 cm (5/8 inch) slices
3/4 cup (115 g/4 oz) shelled fresh peas
60 g (2 oz) green beans, cut into short lengths
80 g (2 3/4 oz) silverbeet (Swiss chard) leaves,
    shredded
3 tablespoons chopped fresh flat-leaf (Italian) parsley
75 g (2 1/2 oz) ditalini or other small pasta

Pesto

1 cup (30 g/1 oz) fresh basil leaves
20 g (3/4 oz) lightly toasted pine nuts
2 cloves garlic
100 ml (3 1/2 fl oz) olive oil
1/4 cup (25 g/3/4 oz) grated Parmesan

1 Soak the borlotti beans in plenty of cold water overnight. Drain and rinse thoroughly under cold water.
2 Heat the oil in a large deep saucepan, add the onion, garlic and pancetta and cook over low heat, stirring occasionally, for 8–10 minutes, until softened.
3 Add the celery, carrot and potato to the saucepan and cook for 5 minutes. Stir in the tomato paste, tomato, basil and drained borlotti beans. Season to taste with freshly ground black pepper. Add the stock and bring slowly to the boil. Cover and simmer, stirring occasionally, for 1 hour 30 minutes.
4 Add the remaining vegetables, parsley and the pasta. Simmer for 8–10 minutes, or until the vegetables and pasta are *al dente*. Check for seasoning and adjust if necessary.
5 For the pesto, combine the fresh basil, pine nuts and garlic with a pinch of salt in a food processor. Process until finely chopped. With the motor running, slowing add the olive oil. Transfer to a bowl and stir in the Parmesan and a little freshly ground black pepper. Spoon on top of the soup.

TOMATO BREAD SOUP

Preparation time: 25 minutes
Total cooking time: 25 minutes
Serves 4

750 g (1 1/2 lb) vine-ripened tomatoes
1 loaf (450 g/14 oz) day-old crusty Italian bread
1 tablespoon olive oil
3 cloves garlic, crushed
1 tablespoon tomato paste (tomato purée)
1.25 litres (40 fl oz) hot vegetable stock or
    water
1/3 cup (20 g/3/4 oz) torn fresh basil leaves
2–3 tablespoons extra virgin olive oil
extra virgin olive oil, extra, to serve

1 Score a cross in the base of each tomato. Place the tomatoes in a bowl of boiling water for 10 seconds, then plunge into cold water and peel the skin away from the cross. Cut the tomatoes in half and scoop out the seeds with a teaspoon. Roughly chop the tomato flesh.
2 Discard most of the crust from the bread and tear the bread into 3 cm (1 1/4 inch) pieces.

3 Heat the oil in a large saucepan. Add the garlic, tomato and tomato paste, then reduce the heat and simmer, stirring occasionally, for 10–15 minutes, or until reduced. Add the stock and bring to the boil, stirring for 2–3 minutes. Reduce the heat to medium, add the bread pieces and cook, stirring, for 5 minutes, or until the bread softens and absorbs most of the liquid. Add more stock or water if the soup is too thick. Remove the saucepan from the heat.
4 Stir in the basil leaves and extra virgin olive oil, and leave for 5 minutes so the flavours have time to develop. Serve drizzled with a little extra virgin olive oil.

BOUQUET GARNI

To make a bouquet garni, bunch together a bay leaf, sprig of thyme and a few stalks of parsley, then wrap the green part of a leek loosely around the herbs. Tie together with kitchen string, leaving one long end. When you are cooking, tie the long end of the string to the handle of the saucepan so you can remove it easily at the end of the cooking time.

LEFT: Tomato bread soup

99

KAKAVIA

Although bouillabaise is the most famous of a large number of Mediterranean fish stew or soup dishes, there are many others, including the Greek version, Kakavia. It is named after the kakavi, a three-legged cooking pot taken by ancient Ionians on their fishing expeditions. This version was always filled with the smallest fish from the catch, olive oil, onions and saffron. Today, it is still made with whatever small fish are available but tomatoes, rather than saffron, are used for colour.

RIGHT: Kakavia

KAKAVIA

Preparation time: 20 minutes
Total cooking time: 20 minutes
Serves 6

2 onions, thinly sliced
400 g (13 oz) can good-quality chopped tomatoes
750 g (1 1/2 lb) potatoes, cut into 5 mm (1/4 inch) slices
1 teaspoon chopped fresh oregano
150 ml (5 fl oz) olive oil
2 litres (64 fl oz) fish or vegetable stock
1.5 kg (3 lb) white fish fillets, such as cod, jewfish or snapper, cut into chunks
500 g (1 lb) raw prawn (shrimp) meat
1/2 cup (125 ml/4 fl oz) lemon juice
chopped fresh flat-leaf (Italian) parsley, to garnish

1 Layer the onion, tomato and potato in a large heavy-based saucepan, seasoning with salt, pepper and oregano between each layer. Add the oil and stock and bring the mixture to the boil. Reduce the heat and simmer for 10 minutes, or until the potato is cooked through and tender.
2 Add the fish and prawn meat and cook for 5 minutes, or until the seafood is cooked. Add the juice, spoon into bowls and top with parsley.

CANNELLINI BEAN SOUP

Preparation time: 20 minutes + overnight soaking
Total cooking time: 1 hour 15 minutes
Serves 8

500 g (1 lb 2 oz) dried cannellini beans
2 tablespoons olive oil
2 onions, chopped
2 cloves garlic, crushed
450 g (1 lb) ripe tomatoes, peeled and chopped
3 tablespoons tomato passata
2 large carrots (400 g/13 oz), diced
2 sticks celery, (200 g/7 oz), trimmed and diced
1.75 litres (56 fl oz) vegetable or chicken stock
2 bay leaves
2 tablespoons lemon juice
1/2 cup (30 g/1 oz) chopped fresh flat-leaf (Italian) parsley

1 Place the beans in a bowl, cover with cold water and leave to soak overnight.
2 Drain the beans and rinse under cold water. Heat the oil in a large saucepan. Add the onion, reduce the heat and cook gently for 10 minutes, stirring occasionally. Stir in the garlic and cook for 1 minute.
3 Add the cannellini beans, chopped tomato,

passata, carrot, celery and stock. Stir and add the bay leaves. Bring to the boil, then reduce the heat to medium-low and simmer, covered, for 45–60 minutes, or until the beans are tender.

4 Stir in the lemon juice and season to taste with salt and pepper. Stir in some of the parsley and use the rest as a garnish.

IN ADVANCE: This soup can be made a day ahead as the flavour improves with time. Reheat over low heat and if too thick, add a little water.

AVGOLEMONO SOUP WITH CHICKEN

Preparation time: 20 minutes
Total cooking time: 30 minutes
Serves 4

1 onion, halved

2 cloves

1 carrot, cut into chunks

1 bay leaf

500 g (1 lb) chicken breast fillets

1/3 cup (75 g/2½ oz) short-grain rice

3 eggs, separated

3 tablespoons lemon juice

2 tablespoons chopped fresh flat-leaf (Italian) parsley

4 thin lemon slices, to garnish

1 Stud the onion with the cloves and place in a large saucepan with 1.5 litres (48 fl oz) water. Add the carrot, bay leaf and chicken and season with salt and black pepper. Slowly bring to the boil, then reduce the heat and simmer for 10 minutes, or until the chicken is cooked.

2 Strain the stock into a clean saucepan, reserving the chicken and discarding the vegetables. Add the rice to the stock, bring to the boil, then reduce the heat and simmer for 15 minutes, or until the rice is tender. Meanwhile, tear the chicken into shreds.

3 Whisk the egg whites in a clean dry bowl until stiff peaks form, then beat in the yolks. Slowly beat in the lemon juice. Gently stir in about 150 ml (5 fl oz) of the hot (not boiling) stock and beat thoroughly. Add the egg mixture to the stock and heat gently, but do not let it boil otherwise the eggs may scramble. Add the chicken and season with salt and black pepper. Set aside for 2–3 minutes to allow the flavours to develop, then sprinkle with parsley. Garnish with lemon.

AVGOLEMONO SAUCE

Bring 1½ cups (375 ml/12 fl oz) chicken stock to the boil in a small saucepan. Mix 1 tablespoon cornflour (cornstarch) with enough cold water to make a thick paste. Add to the stock and stir until the mixture thickens. Simmer for 2–3 minutes, then remove from the heat and allow to cool slightly. Separate 3 eggs and beat the whites in a large bowl until stiff peaks form. Add the egg yolks and beat until light and fluffy. Mix in 2–3 tablespoons lemon juice. Gradually pour in the thickened stock, beating constantly. Return the sauce to the pan and cook over low heat, stirring constantly for 1–2 minutes. Season to taste with salt and pepper, then remove from the heat and stir for 1 minute. Pour immediately over the dish it is to dress. Serve with Dolmades (page 61), poached fish or steamed vegetables. Serves 4.

ABOVE: Avgolemono soup with chicken

STILTON CHEESE

This cheese is made exclusively in three parts of England: Leicestershire, Nottinghamshire and Derbyshire. The most commonly used is blue-veined Stilton. It has a creamy consistency and distinct tangy flavour and is regarded as the best of all English blue cheeses. It is made in large cylindrical shapes. White Stilton, which does not have the mould, is younger and has a milder flavour. Stilton cheese is traditional fare at Christmas time in England.

ABOVE: Stilton soup

STILTON SOUP

Preparation time: 20 minutes
Total cooking time: 30 minutes
Serves 4–6

Thyme pitta croutons

2 large Lebanese breads
1 1/2 tablespoons fresh thyme leaves
1/2 cup (50 g/1 1/2 oz) grated Parmesan

30 g (1 oz) butter
2 leeks, white part only, chopped
1 kg (2 lb) potatoes, chopped
  into chunks
1.25 litres (40 fl oz) chicken stock
1/2 cup (125 ml/4 fl oz) cream
100 g (3 1/2 oz) Stilton cheese
fresh thyme sprigs, to garnish

1 Preheat the oven to moderate 180°C (350°F/Gas 4). Split each Lebanese bread into two, then cut each half into 8 wedges. Put on baking trays, sprinkle with the combined thyme and Parmesan and bake in batches for 5–8 minutes each batch, or until golden and crisp.
2 Melt the butter in a large saucepan, add the leek and cook until softened. Add the potato and chicken stock and bring to the boil. Simmer, covered, for 15 minutes, or until the potato is tender (pierce with the point of a knife—if the potato comes away easily, it is cooked).
3 Transfer the mixture, in batches if necessary, to a blender or food processor and blend until smooth. Return to the saucepan and add the cream and cheese. Stir over low heat until the cheese has melted, being careful not to let the mixture boil. Ladle into individual dishes and garnish with sprigs of fresh thyme. Serve with the thyme pitta croutons.
IN ADVANCE: The croutons can be made up to a week ahead and stored in an airtight container. If they soften, spread on a baking tray and bake in a warm 160°C (315°F/Gas 2–3) oven for 3 minutes.

WATERCRESS SOUP

Preparation time: 15 minutes
Total cooking time: 15–20 minutes
Serves 4–6

1 onion
4 spring onions (scallions)
450 g (14 oz) watercress
100 g (3¹/₂ oz) butter
¹/₃ cup (40 g/1¹/₄ oz) plain (all-purpose) flour
3 cups (750 ml/24 fl oz) vegetable stock
1¹/₄ cups (315 ml/10 fl oz) water
sour cream or cream, to serve

1 Roughly chop the onion, spring onions and watercress. Heat the butter in a large pan and add the onion, spring onions and watercress. Stir over low heat for 3 minutes or until the vegetables have softened.
2 Add flour and stir until combined. Gradually add the stock and water to the pan, stirring until smooth. Stir until mixture boils and thickens. Simmer, covered, over low heat for 10 minutes, or until the watercress is tender. Cool slightly.
3 Transfer the mixture to a food processor or blender and process in batches until smooth. Before serving, gently heat through and season with salt and pepper. Serve with a dollop of sour cream or cream and garnish with fresh watercress, if desired.

QUICK FRENCH ONION SOUP

Slice 1 kg (2 lb) onions into rings. Heat 1 tablespoon oil and 40 g (1¹/₄ oz) butter in a large frying pan. Add the onion rings and 1 teaspoon soft brown sugar, and cook, stirring frequently, over medium heat for 10–15 minutes, or until the onion is golden brown and softened. Add 2 tablespoons plain (all-purpose) flour and cook for 1–2 minutes over medium heat. Remove from the heat and gradually stir in a 410 g (13 oz) can of beef consommé and 2 cups (500 ml/16 fl oz) water. Return to the heat, stirring constantly, until the soup boils and thickens. Season to taste with salt and freshly ground black pepper and serve topped with croutons and grated Cheddar. Serves 4.

CORN CHOWDER

Preparation time: 15 minutes
Total cooking time: 30 minutes
Serves 8

90 g (3 oz) butter
2 large onions, finely chopped
1 clove garlic, crushed
2 teaspoons cumin seeds
1 litre (32 fl oz) vegetable stock
2 potatoes, peeled and chopped
1 cup (250 g/8 oz) canned creamed-style corn
2 cups (400 g/13 oz) fresh corn kernels
3 tablespoons chopped fresh parsley
1 cup (125 g/4 oz) grated Cheddar cheese
3 tablespoons cream (optional)
2 tablespoons chopped fresh chives, to garnish

1 Heat the butter in large heavy-based pan. Add the onions and cook over medium–high heat for 5 minutes or until golden. Add the garlic and cumin seeds, cook 1 minute, stirring constantly. Add the stock, then bring to the boil. Add the potatoes and reduce the heat. Simmer, uncovered, for 10 minutes.
2 Add the creamed corn, corn kernels and parsley. Bring to the boil, reduce the heat, then simmer for 10 minutes. Stir in the cheese and cream and season. Heat gently until the cheese melts. Serve immediately, sprinkled with chopped chives.

CHOWDERS
A chowder is a thick soup, usually milk-based, made with vegetables, fish or chicken. The name comes from the French *chaudière*, the copper pot in which fishermen's wives cooked a communal soup from a share of each man's catch to celebrate the safe return of the fishing fleet.

ABOVE: Corn chowder

GAZPACHO
(Spanish cold tomato and cucumber soup)

Preparation time: 20 minutes
Total cooking time: 10–15 minutes
Serves 6-8

1 red onion

3 tomatoes

½ cucumber

½ green pepper (capsicum), seeded

½ red pepper (capsicum), seeded

1 clove garlic, crushed

3½ cups (875 ml/28 fl oz) tomato juice

½ teaspoon sugar

¼ cup (60 ml/2 fl oz) olive oil

¼ cup (60 ml/2 fl oz) white wine vinegar

Garlic croutons

6 slices white bread

¼ cup (60 ml/2 fl oz) olive oil

1 clove garlic, crushed

1 Finely chop the onion, tomatoes, cucumber and peppers. Place in a large bowl with the crushed garlic.
2 Stir in the juice, sugar, a little salt and pepper, and combined oil and vinegar and mix well. Refrigerate. Serve cold, with the croutons.
3 To make the garlic croutons, preheat the oven to moderate 180°C (350°F/Gas 4). Trim the crusts from the bread and cut the bread into 1 cm (½ inch) cubes. Drizzle with the combined oil and garlic and mix well. Spread on a baking tray. Bake for 10–15 minutes, turning twice, or until golden brown.

FAST ZUCCHINI SOUP

Fry a finely chopped onion in about 30 g (1 oz) of butter in a frying pan. Add 4 grated zucchinis (courgettes) and 2 crushed cloves of garlic and stir-fry for 2–3 minutes, until the vegetables are soft. Add 1 litre (32 fl oz) vegetable stock, bring to the boil, then reduce the heat slightly and simmer, uncovered, for 10 minutes. Stir in ¼ cup (60 ml/2 fl oz) fresh cream and season to taste with salt and freshly ground black pepper. Serve immediately. Serves 4.

FAST SPICY BEAN SOUP

Fry a chopped onion in a little oil in a medium pan until soft. Add 2 crushed cloves of garlic and ½ teaspoon of chilli powder, stir-fry for 1 minute, then add two 425 g (14 oz) cans mixed beans, rinsed and drained. Stir in 2 cups (500 ml/16 fl oz) of vegetable stock and 400 g (13 oz) canned tomato purée; cook until heated through. Season to taste with salt and pepper. Garnish with a combination of finely chopped boiled egg and finely chopped parsley, and serve. Serves 4.
NOTE: Combinations of beans such as red kidney, cannellini and haricot, are available in cans. If you prefer, you can use just one kind of bean.

SPINACH AND LENTIL SOUP

Preparation time: 10 minutes
Total cooking time: 1 hour 25 minutes
Serves 4-6

2 cups (370 g/12 oz) brown lentils

2 teaspoons olive oil

1 onion, finely chopped

2 cloves garlic, crushed

20 English spinach leaves, stalks removed and leaves finely shredded

1 teaspoon ground cumin

1 teaspoon finely grated lemon rind

2 cups (500 ml/16 fl oz) vegetable stock

2 tablespoons finely chopped fresh coriander (cilantro)

1 Place the lentils in a large pan with 1.25 litres (40 fl oz) water. Bring to the boil and then simmer, uncovered, for 1 hour. Rinse and drain, then set aside. In a separate pan heat the oil; add the onion and garlic. Cook over medium heat until golden. Add the spinach and cook for another 2 minutes.
2 Add the lentils, cumin, lemon rind, stock and 2 cups (500 ml/16 fl oz) water to the pan. Simmer, uncovered, for 15 minutes. Add the coriander and stir through. Serve immediately.

PREPARING DRIED BEANS OR SPLIT PEAS

Place the beans in a large bowl and cover with plenty of water (they will expand). Soak for 4 hours or time stated on the packet; drain.

Place beans in a pan, cover with fresh water, bring to boil, simmer over low heat. Skim any froth that gathers on the surface during cooking.

If the water reduces too much, top up with boiling water. When the beans are tender, drain in a colander, use as needed. Use for Fast Spicy Bean Soup, if you like.

OPPOSITE PAGE:
Gazpacho

RED PEPPER SOUP

Preparation time: 20 minutes
Total cooking time: 30 minutes
Serves 6

★ ★

4 red peppers (capsicums)
4 tomatoes
1/4 cup (60 ml/2 fl oz) oil
1/2 teaspoon dried marjoram
1/2 teaspoon dried mixed herbs
2 cloves garlic, crushed
I teaspoon mild curry paste
I red onion, sliced
I leek, sliced (white part only)
250 g (8 oz) green cabbage, chopped
I litre (32 fl oz) water
I teaspoon sweet chilli sauce

I Cut the red peppers into quarters. Remove the seeds and membrane. Grill until the skin blackens and blisters. Place on a cutting board, cover with a tea towel and allow to cool before peeling. Mark a small cross on the top of each tomato. Place in a bowl and cover with boiling water for about 2 minutes. Drain and cool. Peel the skin off downwards from the cross and discard. Cut the tomatoes in half and gently scoop out the seeds using a small spoon.
2 Heat the oil in a large pan; add the herbs, garlic and curry paste. Stir over low heat for 1 minute, or until aromatic. Add the onion and leek and cook for 3 minutes or until golden. Add the cabbage, tomatoes, red peppers and water. Bring to the boil, reduce the heat and simmer for 20 minutes. Remove from the heat; allow to cool slightly.
3 Place the soup in small batches in a food processor bowl. Process for 30 seconds or until smooth. Return the soup to a clean pan, stir in the chilli sauce and season with salt and pepper. Reheat gently and serve hot.

FAST MUSHROOM SOUP

Fry 2 chopped onions in 60 g (2 oz) butter until they are lightly golden. Add 500 g (1 lb) of chopped button mushrooms and cook for another 5 minutes, stirring. Add 1/4 cup (30 g/1 oz) plain (all-purpose) flour and stir for 1 more minute. Stir in 2 cups (500 ml/16 fl oz) milk and 1 1/2 cups (375 ml/ 12 fl oz) of vegetable stock. Reduce the heat and simmer, uncovered, for about 15 minutes, until the soup has thickened and the mushrooms are tender. Serve topped with a dollop of sour cream and some chopped parsley. Serves 4.

ABOVE: Red pepper soup

PIE-CRUST MUSHROOM SOUP

Preparation time: 25 minutes
Total cooking time: 35 minutes
Serves 4

400 g (13 oz) large field mushrooms
60 g (2 oz) butter
1 onion, finely chopped
1 clove garlic, crushed
1/4 cup (30 g/1 oz) plain (all-purpose) flour
3 cups (750 ml/24 fl oz) chicken stock
2 tablespoons fresh thyme leaves
2 tablespoons sherry
1 cup (250 ml/8 fl oz) cream
1 sheet frozen puff pastry, thawed
1 egg, lightly beaten

1 Preheat the oven to moderately hot 200°C (400°F/Gas 6). Peel and roughly chop the mushrooms, including the stems. Melt the butter in a large saucepan, add the onion and cook over medium heat for 3 minutes, or until soft. Add the garlic and cook for another minute. Add the mushrooms and cook until soft. Sprinkle with the flour and stir for 1 minute.
2 Stir in the stock and thyme and bring to the boil. Reduce the heat and simmer, covered, for 10 minutes. Cool before processing in batches. Return the soup to the pan, stir in the sherry and cream, then pour into four ovenproof bowls (use small deep bowls rather than wide shallow ones, or the pastry may sag into the soup).
3 Cut rounds of pastry slightly larger than the bowl tops and cover each bowl with pastry. Seal the pastry edges and brush lightly with the egg. Place the bowls on a baking tray and bake for 15 minutes, or until golden and puffed.

ROAST PUMPKIN SOUP

Preparation time: 20 minutes
Total cooking time: 55 minutes
Serves 6

1.25 kg (2 1/2 lb) pumpkin, cut into chunks
2 tablespoons olive oil
1 onion, chopped
2 teaspoons ground cumin
1 carrot, chopped
1 stick celery, chopped
1 litre (32 fl oz) chicken or vegetable stock
sour cream, to serve
finely chopped fresh parsley, to serve
ground nutmeg, to garnish

1 Preheat the oven to moderate 180°C (350°F/Gas 4). Put the pumpkin on a greased baking tray and lightly brush with half the olive oil. Bake for 25 minutes, or until softened and slightly browned around the edges.
2 Heat the remaining oil in a large pan. Cook the onion and cumin for 2 minutes over medium heat, then add the carrot and celery and cook for 3 minutes, stirring frequently. Add the pumpkin and stock. Bring to the boil, then reduce the heat and simmer for 20 minutes.
3 Cool a little then purée in batches in a blender or food processor until smooth. Return the soup to the pan and gently reheat without boiling. Season to taste with salt and freshly ground black pepper. Top with sour cream and sprinkle with parsley and ground nutmeg before serving.
NOTE: Butternut pumpkin (squash) and jap pumpkin is often used in soups for a sweeter flavour.

ABOVE: Pie-crust mushroom soup

SMOKED HADDOCK CHOWDER

Preparation time: 20 minutes
Total cooking time: 35 minutes
Serves 4-6

500 g (1 lb) smoked haddock or cod
1 potato, diced
1 stick celery, chopped
1 onion, finely chopped
50 g (1¾ oz) butter
1 rasher bacon, finely chopped
2 tablespoons plain (all-purpose) flour
½ teaspoon dried mustard
½ teaspoon Worcestershire sauce
1 cup (250 ml/8 fl oz) milk
3 tablespoons chopped fresh parsley
¼ cup (60 ml/2 fl oz) cream, optional

BELOW: Smoked haddock chowder

1 To make the fish stock, put the fish in a deep frying pan, add 1.25 litres (40 fl oz) water and bring to the boil. Reduce the heat and simmer for 8 minutes, or until the fish flakes easily. Drain; reserve the stock. Discard the skin and bones and flake the fish. Set aside.

2 Put the potato, celery and onion in a pan with 3 cups (750 ml/24 fl oz) reserved stock. Bring to the boil, reduce the heat and simmer for 8 minutes, or until the vegetables are tender. Set aside.

3 Melt the butter in a large pan over low heat, add the bacon and stir for 3 minutes. Stir in the flour, mustard and Worcestershire sauce and cook for 1 minute, or until pale and foaming. Remove from the heat and gradually stir in the milk. Return to the heat and stir until the chowder boils and thickens. Reduce the heat and simmer for 2 minutes. Stir in the vegetables and stock mixture, then add the parsley and fish. Simmer over low heat for 5 minutes, or until heated through. Season and serve with cream.

CREAMY MUSSEL SOUP

Preparation time: 30 minutes
Total cooking time: 40 minutes
Serves 4

750 g (1½ lb) black mussels
1 stick celery, chopped
1 carrot, chopped
1 onion, chopped
10 black peppercorns
4 fresh parsley stalks
100 g (3½ oz) butter, softened
3 spring onions (scallions), chopped
2 cloves garlic, crushed
1 large potato, cut into small dice
¾ cup (185 ml/6 fl oz) white wine
⅓ cup (40 g/1¼ oz) plain (all-purpose) flour
1 cup (250 ml/8 fl oz) cream
2 tablespoons chopped fresh parsley

1 Scrub the mussels and pull out the hairy beards. Place in a large saucepan with the celery, carrot, onion, peppercorns, parsley and 1.5 litres (48 fl oz) water. Bring to the boil, reduce the heat and simmer, covered, for 4–5 minutes.

2 Strain the stock through a fine sieve and discard any unopened mussels. Remove the meat from the remaining mussels and set aside. Discard the shells and vegetables. Return the

stock to the pan and simmer for 15 minutes. Remove from the heat.

3 Melt half the butter in a large saucepan, add the spring onion, garlic and potato and stir over medium heat for 3 minutes, or until the onion is soft. Add the wine, bring to the boil, then reduce the heat and simmer for 1 minute.

4 Blend the flour and remaining butter in a bowl to form a paste. Pour 3½ cups (875 ml/28 fl oz) of the stock into the saucepan with the garlic and potato. Gradually add the butter mixture, whisking until the mixture boils and thickens. Reduce the heat and simmer for 15 minutes, or until the potato is cooked. Stir in the mussel meat and cream until heated through. Stir in the parsley.

NEW ENGLAND CLAM CHOWDER

Preparation time: 35 minutes + soaking
Total cooking time: 45 minutes
Serves 4

1.5 kg (3 lb) clams (vongole) or pipis, in shell
2 teaspoons oil
3 rashers bacon, chopped
1 onion, chopped

1 clove garlic, crushed
750 g (1½ lb) potatoes, cut into small dice
1¼ cups (315 ml/10 fl oz) fish stock
2 cups (500 ml/16 fl oz) milk
½ cup (125 ml/4 fl oz) cream
3 tablespoons chopped fresh parsley

1 Discard any clams that are broken, already open or do not close when tapped on the bench. If necessary, soak in cold water for 1–2 hours to remove sand. Drain and put in a large heavy-based pan with 1 cup (250 ml/8 fl oz) water. Cover and simmer over low heat for 5 minutes, or until open. Discard any that do not open. Strain and reserve the liquid. Remove the clam meat from the shells.

2 Heat the oil in the cleaned pan. Add the bacon, onion and garlic and cook, stirring, over medium heat until the onion is soft and the bacon golden. Add the potato and stir well.

3 Measure the reserved liquid and add water to make 1¼ cups (315 ml/10 fl oz). Add to the pan with the stock and milk. Bring to the boil, reduce the heat, cover and simmer 20 minutes, or until the potato is tender. Uncover and simmer for 10 minutes, or until slightly thickened.

4 Add the cream, clam meat and parsley and season to taste with salt and pepper. Heat through gently before serving, but do not allow to boil or the liquid may curdle.

ABOVE: New England clam chowder

109

PEELING TOMATOES

To peel tomatoes, score a cross in the base of the tomatoes. Place in a heatproof bowl and cover with boiling water. Leave for 30 seconds then transfer to a bowl of cold water and peel the skin away from the cross. To de-seed, cut the tomato in half and scoop out the seeds with a teaspoon.

ABOVE: Bouillabaisse with rouille

BOUILLABAISSE WITH ROUILLE

Preparation time: 40 minutes
Total cooking time: 30 minutes
Serves 4

300 g (10 oz) raw prawns (shrimp)
16–18 black mussels
200 g (6 1/2 oz) scallops
1.5 kg (3 lb) assorted white fish fillets (eg. red rock cod, snapper, red mullet, monkfish)
2 tablespoons oil
1 fennel bulb, thinly sliced
1 onion, chopped
5 ripe tomatoes, peeled, seeded and chopped
1.25 litres (40 fl oz) fish stock
pinch of saffron threads
1 bay leaf
1 bouquet garni
5 cm (2 inch) strip of orange rind
1 tablespoon chopped fresh parsley, to garnish

Rouille

1 small red pepper (capsicum)
1 red chilli
1 slice white bread, crusts removed
2 cloves garlic
1 egg yolk
1/3 cup (80 ml/2 3/4 fl oz) olive oil

1 Peel the prawns and gently pull out the dark vein from each prawn back, starting at the head end. Scrub the mussels with a stiff brush and pull out the hairy beards. Discard any broken mussels, or open ones that don't close when tapped on the bench. Slice or pull off any vein, membrane or hard white muscle from the scallops, leaving any roe attached. Cut the fish into large bite-sized pieces. Refrigerate the seafood, covered.
2 Heat the oil in a large saucepan over medium heat and cook the fennel and onion for 5 minutes, or until golden. Add the tomato and cook for 3 minutes. Stir in the stock, saffron, bay leaf, bouquet garni and orange rind. Bring to the boil and boil for 10 minutes. Reduce the heat to simmer and add the scallops, prawns, mussels and

fish. Simmer for 4–5 minutes, or until the mussels open. Discard any unopened mussels. Remove the bouquet garni and orange rind.

3 For the rouille, cut the red pepper and chilli into large flattish pieces. Remove the seeds and membrane and cook, skin-side-up, under a hot grill until the skin blackens and blisters. Place in a plastic bag and leave to cool, then peel.

4 Soak the bread in 3 tablespoons water, then squeeze out any excess. Process the pepper, chilli, bread, garlic and egg yolk in a food processor. With the motor running, add the oil in a thin stream, until the mixture is thick and smooth.

5 Ladle the bouillabaisse into bowls, sprinkle with parsley and serve with the rouille.

MANHATTAN-STYLE SEAFOOD CHOWDER

Preparation time: 30 minutes
Total cooking time: 30 minutes
Serves 4–6

60 g (2 oz) butter
3 rashers bacon, chopped
2 onions, chopped
2 cloves garlic, finely chopped
2 sticks celery, sliced
3 potatoes, diced
1.25 litres (40 fl oz) fish or chicken stock
3 teaspoons chopped fresh thyme
12 raw large prawns (shrimp)
1 tablespoon tomato paste (tomato purée)
425 g (14 oz) can chopped tomatoes
375 g (12 oz) skinless white fish fillets (eg. ling, cod, flake, hake), cut into bite-sized pieces
310 g (10 oz) can baby clams (vongole), undrained
2 tablespoons chopped fresh parsley
grated orange rind, to garnish

1 Melt the butter in a large pan and cook the bacon, onion, garlic and celery over low heat, stirring occasionally, for 5 minutes, or until soft but not brown.

2 Add the potato, stock and thyme to the pan and bring to the boil. Reduce the heat and simmer, covered, for 15 minutes.

3 Meanwhile, peel the prawns and pull out the dark vein from each prawn back, starting at the head end. Add the tomato paste and tomato to the pan, stir through and bring back to the boil. Add the fish pieces, prawns and clams with juice and simmer over low heat for 3 minutes. Season to taste and stir in the parsley. Serve garnished with the grated orange rind.

BELOW: Manhattan-style seafood chowder

JAPANESE VEGETABLE RAMEN NOODLE SOUP

Preparation time: 15 minutes
Total cooking time: 15 minutes
Serves 6

250 g (8 oz) fresh ramen noodles
1 tablespoon vegetable oil
1 tablespoon finely chopped fresh ginger
2 cloves garlic, crushed
150 g (5 oz) oyster mushrooms, halved
1 small zucchini (courgette), thinly sliced
1 leek, halved lengthways and thinly sliced
100 g (3 1/2 oz) snow peas (mangetout), halved
  on the diagonal
100 g (3 1/2 oz) fried tofu puffs, cut into julienne
  strips
1/3 cup (80 g/2 3/4 oz) white miso paste
1/3 cup (80 ml/2 3/4 fl oz) light soy sauce
1/4 cup (60 ml/2 fl oz) mirin
1 cup (90 g/3 oz) bean sprouts, tailed
1/2 teaspoon sesame oil
4 spring onions (scallions), thinly sliced
100 g (3 1/2 oz) enoki mushrooms

1 Bring a large saucepan of lightly salted water
to the boil. Add the noodles and cook, stirring
to prevent them sticking together, for 2 minutes,
or until just tender. Drain, rinse under cold
running water, then drain again.
2 Heat a wok over medium heat, add the
vegetable oil and swirl to coat. Add the ginger
and garlic and stir-fry for 30 seconds, then add
the oyster mushrooms, zucchini, leek, snow peas
and sliced tofu puffs and stir-fry for 4 minutes.
Pour in 1.5 litres (48 fl oz) water and bring to
the boil, then reduce the heat and simmer. Stir
in the miso paste, soy sauce and mirin until
heated through, but don't let it boil. Just before
serving, stir in the bean sprouts and sesame oil.
3 Place the noodles in the bottom of six serving
bowls, then pour the broth over the top.
Sprinkle with the sliced spring onion and
enoki mushrooms.

*RIGHT: Japanese
vegetable ramen
noodle soup*

COCONUT PRAWN SOUP

Preparation time: 20 minutes +
   20 minutes soaking
Total cooking time: 45 minutes
Serves 4

Curry paste

6 long dried red chillies
2 teaspoons coriander seeds
1 teaspoon cumin seeds
1 teaspoon ground turmeric
1/2 teaspoon paprika
1/2 teaspoon black peppercorns
4 red Asian shallots, chopped
4 cloves garlic, roughly chopped
1 tablespoon sliced fresh ginger
4 fresh coriander (cilantro) roots, well rinsed
2 tablespoons chopped fresh coriander
   (cilantro) stems
1 teaspoon grated lime rind
2 stems lemon grass, white part only, sliced
   (reserve the stems for the stock)
2 fresh makrut (kaffir) lime leaves, thinly
   shredded
1 teaspoon shrimp paste
2 tablespoons vegetable oil

Stock

700 g (1 lb 7 oz) raw prawns (shrimp)
4 red Asian shallots, chopped
1 clove garlic
reserved grassy ends of lemon grass stems
6 black peppercorns

2 tablespoons vegetable oil
800 ml (26 fl oz) coconut milk
1/4 cup (60 ml/2 fl oz) fish sauce
fresh coriander (cilantro) leaves, to garnish
thinly sliced lime rind, to garnish

1 To make the curry paste, soak the chillies in boiling water for 20 minutes, then drain. Toss the spices and peppercorns in a dry frying pan over medium heat for 1 minute, or until fragrant. Grind to a powder, then transfer to a food processor and add the remaining paste ingredients and 1 teaspoon salt. Process until smooth, adding a little water, if necessary.
2 Peel and devein the prawns, leaving the tails intact. Cover with plastic wrap and refrigerate. Reserve the heads and shells.
3 To make the stock, dry-fry the prawn heads and shells in a wok over high heat for 5 minutes, or until orange. Add the remaining stock ingredients and 1.5 litres (48 fl oz) water and bring to the boil. Reduce the heat, simmer for 15–20 minutes, then strain into a bowl.
4 Heat a clean, dry wok over medium heat, add the oil and swirl to coat the side. Add 3 tablespoons of the curry paste and stir constantly over medium heat for 1–2 minutes, or until fragrant. Stir in the stock and coconut milk and bring to the boil, then reduce the heat and simmer for 10 minutes. Add the prawns and cook, stirring, for 2 minutes, or until they are cooked. Stir in the fish sauce and garnish with coriander leaves and lime rind.
NOTES: Spoon the leftover curry paste into an airtight container. You can use this stock as a base for other seafood soups. Store it in the freezer, and bring to the boil before you use it.

ABOVE: Coconut prawn soup

reserving the soaking liquid. Discard the woody stalks and thinly slice the caps.

2 Bring 2 litres (64 fl oz) water to the boil in a large saucepan and cook the noodles for 1–2 minutes, or until tender. Drain immediately and rinse under cold water. Set aside.

3 Pour the stock and 1 litre (32 fl oz) water into a wok and bring to the boil, then reduce the heat and simmer. Add the chicken and cook for 2–3 minutes, or until almost cooked through.

4 Add the mushrooms and cook for 1 minute. Add the bok choy halves and simmer for a further minute, or until beginning to wilt, then add the miso paste, dashi granules, wakame and reserved mushroom liquid. Stir to dissolve the dashi and miso paste. Do not allow to boil.

5 Gently stir in the tofu. Distribute the noodles among the serving bowls, then ladle the hot soup over them. Sprinkle with the spring onion.

CHINESE COMBINATION SHORT SOUP

Preparation time: 20 minutes +
 2 hours refrigeration
Total cooking time: 2 hours 20 minutes
Serves 4-6

Stock

1.5 kg (3 lb) whole chicken

1/4 cup (60 ml/2 fl oz) Chinese rice wine

1/2 star anise

8 spring onions (scallions), chopped

2 leafy celery tops

1/2 teaspoon white peppercorns

4 cloves garlic, bruised

2 x 10 cm (3/4 x 4 inch) piece fresh ginger,
 thinly sliced

24 won tons

12 raw prawns, (shrimp) peeled and deveined

200 g (6 1/2 oz) Chinese barbecued pork, thinly
 sliced

1/3 cup (60 g/2 oz) Chinese straw mushrooms

70 g (2 1/4 oz) sliced bamboo shoots

500 g (1 lb) baby bok choy (pak choi), thinly sliced

2 spring onions (scallions), sliced

2 1/2 tablespoons light soy sauce

1 tablespoon oyster sauce

1/2 teaspoon sesame oil

JAPANESE UDON MISO SOUP WITH CHICKEN

Preparation time: 15 minutes + 20 minutes soaking
Total cooking time: 15 minutes
Serves 4-6

8 dried shiitake mushrooms

400 g (13 oz) fresh udon noodles

1 litre (32 fl oz) good-quality chicken stock

600 g (1 1/4 lb) chicken breast fillets, cut into
 1.5 cm (5/8 inch) thick strips

300 g (10 oz) baby bok choy (pak choi), halved
 lengthways

1/4 cup (60 g/2 oz) white miso paste

2 teaspoons dashi granules

1 tablespoon wakame flakes or other seaweed

150 g (5 oz) silken firm tofu, cut into 1 cm
 (1/2 inch) cubes

3 spring onions (scallions), sliced on the diagonal

ABOVE: Japanese udon miso soup with chicken

1 Soak the mushrooms in 1 cup (250 ml/8 fl oz) boiling water for 20 minutes. Squeeze dry,

I Put all the stock ingredients in a stockpot and cover with 4 litres (128 fl oz) water. Bring to the boil over high heat and skim off any scum that forms on the surface. Reduce the heat and simmer for 2 hours. Cool slightly, then remove the chicken and strain the stock into a bowl. Cover and refrigerate the meat and stock separately until chilled. Skim off the fat from the top of the stock.

2 Pour 2 litres (64 fl oz) of the stock into a large wok and bring to the boil. Meanwhile, remove one breast from the chicken, then discard the skin and thinly slice the flesh.

3 Add the won tons to the boiling stock and cook for 2–3 minutes, or until they have risen to the surface and are cooked. Remove with a slotted spoon and divide among serving bowls. Reduce the stock to a simmer, add the prawns, pork, mushrooms and bamboo shoots and cook for 30 seconds, or until the prawns are just curled, then add the bok choy, spring onion, chicken and the combined soy sauce, oyster sauce and sesame oil and cook for 2 minutes, or until the prawns are completely cooked. Ladle the soup over the won tons and serve.

EIGHT TREASURE SOUP

Preparation time: 15 minutes + 20 minutes soaking
Total cooking time: 1 hour
Serves 4-6

4 dried shiitake mushrooms

1 tablespoon vegetable oil

1 teaspoon sesame oil

2 teaspoons finely chopped fresh ginger

1 tablespoon finely chopped spring onion
  (scallion)

60 g (2 oz) Chinese bacon or ham, cut into
  thin strips (see Note)

1 litre (32 fl oz) good-quality chicken stock

1 tablespoon soy sauce

1 tablespoon rice wine

250 g (8 oz) chicken breast fillet

1 carrot, cut into 1 cm (1/2 inch) slices

12 small raw prawns (shrimp), peeled and
  deveined

200 g (6 1/2 oz) firm tofu, cut into 2 cm
  (3/4 inch) cubes

50 g (1 3/4 oz) sliced bamboo shoots

100 g (3 1/2 oz) English spinach, chopped

2 spring onions (scallions), thinly sliced, extra

I Soak the mushrooms in 1/2 cup (125 ml/ 4 fl oz) boiling water for 20 minutes. Squeeze dry, reserving the soaking liquid. Discard the woody stalks and cut the caps into quarters.

2 Heat a wok over high heat. Add the oils and swirl to coat the side of the wok, then add the ginger, spring onion and bacon. Cook for about 10 seconds before adding the stock, soy sauce, rice wine, mushroom liquid and 1/2 teaspoon salt. Bring to the boil, then add the chicken. Reduce the heat to low, cover with a lid and poach the chicken for 40 minutes. Remove the chicken from the stock and, when cool enough to handle, shred the meat.

3 Return the stock to the boil, add the carrot and cook for 5 minutes. Add the prawns, tofu, bamboo shoots, spinach and chicken meat to the wok and cook over low heat for a further 5 minutes. Serve with the extra spring onion.

NOTE: Chinese bacon has a dryish flesh with a strong flavour very much like prosciutto. You can substitute prosciutto.

BELOW: Eight treasure soup

TOM YUM GOONG

Preparation time: 25 minutes
Total cooking time: 45 minutes
Serves 4-6

★★

500 g (1 lb) raw prawns (shrimp)
1 tablespoon oil
2 tablespoons Thai red curry paste or
    tom yum paste
2 tablespoons tamarind purée
2 teaspoons ground turmeric
1 teaspoon chopped red chillies
4 makrut (kaffir) lime leaves, shredded
2 tablespoons fish sauce
2 tablespoons lime juice
2 teaspoons grated palm sugar or brown sugar
2 tablespoons fresh coriander (cilantro) leaves,
    to serve

1 Peel the prawns, leaving the tails intact. Pull out the dark vein from each prawn back, starting at the head end. Reserve the shells and heads. Cover and refrigerate the prawn meat. Heat the oil in a large pan or wok and cook the shells and heads for 10 minutes over medium-high heat, stirring frequently, until the heads are deep orange.
2 Add 1 cup (250 ml/8 fl oz) water and the curry paste to the pan. Bring to the boil and cook for 5 minutes, or until reduced slightly. Add another 2 litres (64 fl oz) water and simmer for 20 minutes. Strain, discarding the shells and heads, and return the stock to the pan.
3 Add the tamarind, turmeric, chilli and lime leaves to the pan, bring to the boil and cook for 2 minutes. Add the prawns and cook for 5 minutes, or until pink. Stir in the fish sauce, lime juice and sugar. Serve sprinkled with coriander leaves.

WON TON SOUP

Preparation time: 40 minutes +
    30 minutes soaking
Total cooking time: 5 minutes
Serves 4-6

★★

4 dried Chinese mushrooms
250 g (8 oz) raw prawns (shrimp)
250 g (8 oz) minced (ground) pork
1 tablespoon soy sauce

BELOW: Tom yum goong

1 teaspoon sesame oil

2 spring onions (scallions), finely chopped

1 teaspoon grated fresh ginger

2 tablespoons chopped canned water chestnuts

250 g (8 oz) packet won ton wrappers

cornflour (cornstarch), to dust

1.5 litres (48 fl oz) chicken or beef stock

thinly sliced spring onions (scallions), to garnish

1 Soak the mushrooms in a bowl of hot water for 30 minutes. Drain, then squeeze to remove any excess liquid. Discard the stems and chop the caps finely. Peel the prawns and pull out the dark vein from each prawn back, starting at the head end. Finely chop the prawn meat and mix with the mushrooms, pork, soy sauce, sesame oil, spring onion, ginger and water chestnuts in a bowl.

2 Cover the won ton wrappers with a damp tea towel to prevent them drying out. Working with one wrapper at a time, place a heaped teaspoon of mixture on the centre of each.

3 Moisten the pastry edges with water, fold in half diagonally and bring the two points together. Place on a tray dusted with cornflour.

4 Cook the won tons in rapidly boiling water for 4–5 minutes. Bring the stock to the boil in another pan. Remove the won tons with a slotted spoon and place in serving bowls. Top with spring onion. Ladle the stock over the won tons.

PUMPKIN, PRAWN AND COCONUT SOUP

Preparation time: 15 minutes

Total cooking time: 20 minutes

Serves 4-6

500 g (1 lb) pumpkin, diced

4 tablespoons lime juice

1 kg (2 lb) raw large prawns (shrimp)

2 onions, chopped

1 small fresh red chilli, finely chopped

1 stem lemon grass, white part only, chopped

1 teaspoon shrimp paste

1 teaspoon sugar

1 1/2 cups (375 ml/12 fl oz) coconut milk

1 teaspoon tamarind purée

1/2 cup (125 ml/4 fl oz) coconut cream

1 tablespoon fish sauce

2 tablespoons fresh Thai basil leaves

1 Combine the pumpkin with half the lime juice in a bowl. Peel the prawns and pull out the dark vein from each back, starting at the head end.

2 Process the onion, chilli, lemon grass, shrimp paste, sugar and 3 tablespoons of the coconut milk in a food processor until a paste forms.

3 Combine the paste with the remaining coconut milk, tamarind purée and 1 cup (250 ml/8 fl oz) water in a large pan and stir until smooth. Add the pumpkin with the lime juice to the pan and bring to the boil. Reduce the heat and simmer, covered, for about 10 minutes or until the pumpkin is just tender.

4 Add the raw prawns and coconut cream, then simmer for 3 minutes, or until the prawns are just pink and cooked through. Stir in the fish sauce, the remaining lime juice and the Thai basil leaves. Serve garnished with Thai basil leaves or sprigs.

ABOVE: Pumpkin, prawn and coconut soup

PHO

Noodle soups are a way of life in Vietnam and pho (pronounced fur) is the most well known of these soups. Vietnamese people eat pho at any time of the day—breakfast, lunch or dinner. The aromatic accompaniment of fresh herbs gives the pho a fragrance that typifies Vietnamese cuisine, while the extra seasonings on the side allow each diner to create a tailor-made pho. The soup is originally from the North but is now a classic throughout Vietnam.

ABOVE: Beef pho

BEEF PHO

Preparation time: 15 minutes + 15 minutes soaking
Total cooking time: 35 minutes
Serves 4

★ ★

2 litres (64 fl oz) good-quality beef stock
1 star anise
1 x 4 cm (¹/₂ x 1¹/₂ inch) piece fresh ginger, sliced
2 pigs' trotters (ask your butcher to cut in half)
¹/₂ onion, studded with 2 cloves
2 stems lemon grass, bruised
2 cloves garlic, crushed
¹/₄ teaspoon ground white pepper
1 tablespoon fish sauce, plus extra to serve
200 g (6¹/₂ oz) fresh thin round rice noodles
300 g (10 oz) beef fillet, partially frozen, thinly sliced
1 cup (90 g/3 oz) bean sprouts, tailed
2 spring onions (scallions), thinly sliced on the diagonal

¹/₂ cup (25 g/³/₄ oz) chopped fresh coriander (cilantro) leaves, plus extra to serve
4 tablespoons chopped fresh Vietnamese mint, plus extra to serve
1 fresh red chilli, thinly sliced, plus extra to serve
2 limes, cut into quarters

1 Put the beef stock, star anise, ginger, pigs' trotters, onion, lemon grass, garlic and white pepper in a wok and bring to the boil. Reduce the heat to very low and simmer, covered, for 30 minutes. Strain, return to the wok and stir in the fish sauce.
2 Meanwhile, put the noodles in a heatproof bowl, cover with boiling water and gently separate. Drain well, then refresh under cold running water.
3 Divide the noodles among four deep soup bowls, then top with beef strips, bean sprouts, spring onion, coriander, mint and chilli. Ladle on the broth.
4 Place the extra chilli, mint, coriander, lime quarters and fish sauce in small bowls on a platter, serve with the soup and allow your guests to help themselves.

CLEAR CHINESE PORK BALL AND NOODLE SOUP

Preparation time: 20 minutes +
  1 hour refrigeration
Total cooking time: 30 minutes
Serves 4-6

1 tablespoon peanut oil

2 teaspoons sesame oil

4 cloves garlic, crushed

2 teaspoons grated fresh ginger

150 g (5 oz) wom bok (Chinese cabbage),
  shredded

300 g (10 oz) minced (ground) pork

1 egg white

1¹/₂ tablespoons cornflour (cornstarch)

¹/₄ teaspoon ground white pepper

¹/₃ cup (80 ml/2³/₄ fl oz) light soy sauce

2 tablespoons Chinese rice wine

6 spring onions (scallions), thinly sliced

¹/₂ cup (15 g/¹/₂ oz) fresh coriander (cilantro)
  leaves, finely chopped

1.5 litres (48 fl oz) home-made chicken stock
  (page 95) or 1.25 litres (40 fl oz) purchased
  stock diluted with 1 cup (250 ml/8 fl oz)
  water (see Note)

3 teaspoons grated fresh ginger, extra

200 g (6¹/₂ oz) fresh thin egg noodles

finely chopped fresh red chilli, to garnish
  (optional)

1 Heat a wok over high heat, add the peanut oil and 1 teaspoon of the sesame oil, then swirl to coat the side of the wok. Add the garlic, ginger and wom bok and stir-fry for 1 minute, or until the garlic begins to brown. As soon as this happens, remove the wok from the heat and allow to cool.

2 Transfer the cooled wom bok mixture to a large bowl and add the pork, egg white, cornflour, white pepper, 2 tablespoons of the soy sauce, 1 tablespoon of the rice wine, half the spring onion and 3 tablespoons of the coriander. Mix thoroughly, then cover with plastic wrap and refrigerate for 1 hour. Shape 1 tablespoon of the mixture into a ball using wet hands. Repeat with the remaining mixture.

3 Clean and dry the wok, then pour in the stock. Bring the stock to the boil, then reduce the heat and simmer for 1–2 minutes. Add the extra ginger, remaining soy sauce and rice wine and cook, covered, for 5 minutes before adding the pork balls. Cook, uncovered, for a further 8–10 minutes, or until the balls rise to the top and are cooked through.

4 Meanwhile, cook the noodles in a large saucepan of boiling water for 1 minute, or until they separate. Drain, then rinse well. Divide the noodles among serving bowls, then ladle on the soup. Sprinkle with the remaining spring onion and coriander, then add a couple of drops of the remaining sesame oil. Serve with chilli and extra soy sauce, if desired.

NOTE: Because many purchased stocks are very salty, when used in large quantities, they need to be diluted with water. Home-made stocks tend to be less salty, so they do not require dilution.

*ABOVE: Clear Chinese
pork ball and noodle soup*

PRAWN LAKSA

Preparation time: 30 minutes
Total cooking time: 35 minutes
Serves 4-6

★ ★

1½ tablespoons coriander seeds

1 tablespoon cumin seeds

1 teaspoon ground turmeric

1 onion, roughly chopped

2 teaspoons roughly chopped fresh ginger

3 cloves garlic

3 stems lemon grass, white part only, sliced

6 candlenuts or macadamias, roughly chopped

4–6 small fresh red chillies, roughly chopped

2–3 teaspoons shrimp paste

1 litre (32 fl oz) good-quality chicken stock

¼ cup (60 ml/2 fl oz) vegetable oil

3 cups (750 ml/24 fl oz) coconut milk

4 fresh makrut (kaffir) lime leaves

2½ tablespoons lime juice

2 tablespoons fish sauce

2 tablespoons grated palm sugar or
    soft brown sugar

750 g (1½ lb) raw prawns (shrimp), peeled
    and deveined, with tails intact

250 g (8 oz) dried rice vermicelli

1 cup (90 g/3 oz) bean sprouts, tailed

4 fried tofu puffs, cut into julienne strips

3 tablespoons roughly chopped fresh
    Vietnamese mint

⅔ cup (20 g/¾ oz) fresh coriander (cilantro)

lime wedges, to serve

1 Dry-fry the coriander seeds in a small frying pan over medium heat for 1–2 minutes, or until fragrant, tossing constantly. Grind finely. Repeat the process with the cumin seeds.
2 Place the ground coriander and cumin, turmeric, onion, ginger, garlic, lemon grass, candlenuts, chilli and shrimp paste in a food processor or blender. Add about ½ cup (125 ml/4 fl oz) of the stock and blend to a fine paste.
3 Heat a wok over low heat, add the oil and swirl. Cook the paste for 3–5 minutes, stirring constantly. Pour in the remaining stock and bring to the boil, then reduce the heat and simmer for 15 minutes, or until reduced slightly.
4 Add the coconut milk, lime leaves, lime juice, fish sauce and sugar and simmer for 5 minutes. Add the prawns and simmer for 2 minutes, or until pink and cooked. Do not boil or cover.
5 Meanwhile, soak the vermicelli in boiling water for 6–7 minutes, or until soft. Drain and divide among serving bowls along with most of the sprouts. Ladle on the hot soup, then top with the tofu, mint, coriander and the remaining sprouts. Serve with lime wedges.

LAKSA

There are several versions of the popular noodle soup, laksa. The best known is a dish of rice noodles and prawn or chicken in a broth enriched with coconut milk, as featured on this page. Another type is the thin, fragrant sour Penang laksa which is a fish soup based on a broth flavoured with tamarind instead of coconut milk (see recipe page 121). Finally, there is the lesser known Johore laksa which combines puréed fish with noodles and coconut milk. Each version has its faithful adherents.

RIGHT: Prawn laksa

PENANG FISH LAKSA

Preparation time: 20 minutes +
  20 minutes soaking
Total cooking time: 40 minutes
Serves 4

★ ★

1 whole snapper (750 g/1 1/2 lb), scaled
  and cleaned

3 cups (750 ml/24 fl oz) good-quality
  chicken stock

6 fresh Vietnamese mint stalks

4 dried red chillies

2 x 3 cm (3/4 x 1 1/4 inch) piece fresh
  galangal, finely chopped

4 red Asian shallots, finely chopped

2 stems lemon grass, white part only,
  finely chopped

1 teaspoon ground turmeric

1 teaspoon shrimp paste

4 tablespoons tamarind purée

1 tablespoon sugar

500 g (1 lb) fresh round rice noodles

1 small Lebanese (short) cucumber, seeded and
  cut into strips

1/2 cup (10 g/1/4 oz) fresh Vietnamese mint

1 large fresh green chilli, sliced

1 Trim the fins and tail off the fish with kitchen scissors. Make several deep cuts through the thickest part of the fish on both sides.
2 Pour the stock and 3 cups (750 ml/24 fl oz) water into a non-stick wok. Add the mint stalks and bring to the boil over high heat. Place the fish in the wok and simmer for 10 minutes, or until cooked. The fish should remain submerged during cooking; add more water if necessary. Remove the fish and allow to cool.
3 Soak the chillies in 1 cup (250 ml/8 fl oz) boiling water for 20 minutes. Drain and chop. To make the laksa paste, place the chilli, galangal, shallots, lemon grass, turmeric and shrimp paste in a food processor or blender and blend to a smooth paste, adding a little water if needed.
4 Flake the flesh off the fish and remove all the bones, reserving both. Add the bones and tamarind to the stock in the wok and bring to the boil. Simmer for 10 minutes, then strain and return the liquid to a clean wok—make sure no bones slip through. Stir the laksa paste into the liquid and simmer over medium heat for 10 minutes. Stir in the sugar, add the fish flesh and simmer for 1–2 minutes, or until the fish is heated through.
5 Place the noodles in a heatproof bowl, cover with boiling water, then gently separate. Drain immediately and refresh under cold water. Divide the noodles among four bowls. Ladle on the fish pieces and broth, then sprinkle with cucumber, mint and chilli and serve.

SHRIMP PASTE
There are two types of shrimp paste. The most common type in Malaysia and Indonesia is a compressed block made from partially fermented shrimps that have been dried and ground. The Chinese version is softer and more sauce-like and is sold in jars rather than blocks. In both cases, the paste should be used very sparingly as it can easily overpower other elements in the dish.

ABOVE: Penang fish laksa

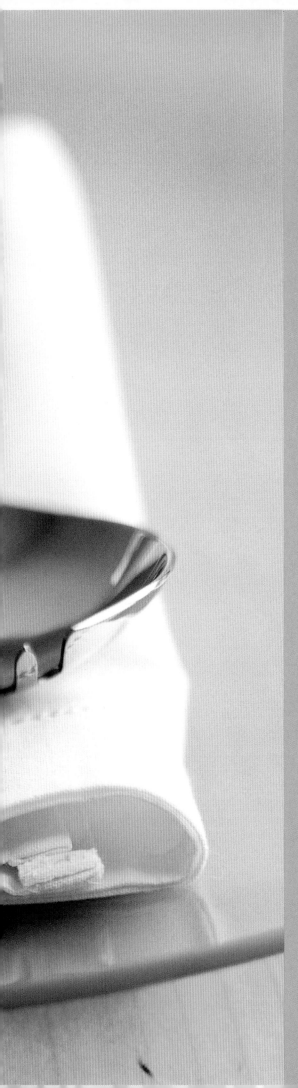

SALADS

DRESSINGS AND SAUCES

To transform a salad into something sublime, choose one of these classic French

dressings and sauces.

SAUCE RAVIGOTE

This sauce teams well with cold chicken, turkey, prawns (shrimp) or vegetables. Dissolve a pinch of salt in 2 tablespoons red wine vinegar. Stir in 6 tablespoons olive oil, 3 tablespoons chopped fresh parsley, tarragon or chives, 1 small finely chopped onion, 2 tablespoons finely chopped gherkins or cornichons and 2 tablespoons capers. Season to taste with salt and freshly ground black pepper. Makes ¾ cup (185 ml/6 fl oz).

BASIC VINAIGRETTE

Dissolve a pinch of salt in 2 tablespoons of red wine vinegar and very slowly beat in 6 tablespoons of extra virgin olive oil. Season with pepper and stir. To vary this recipe you can add any of the following: 1 clove crushed garlic, 1 teaspoon Dijon mustard, 2 tablespoons chopped fresh chives, parsley or mint. You can use lemon juice or any type of wine vinegar instead of the red wine vinegar. Makes ⅔ cup (170 ml/5½ fl oz).

CLASSIC MAYONNAISE

Home-made mayonnaise is very good and easy to prepare. Whether making it by hand or in a food processor, all the ingredients should be at room temperature and the oil must be added very slowly. To make a simple mayonnaise, beat 2 egg yolks and 1 teaspoon of Dijon mustard with a whisk for 1 minute. Slowly add 1¾ cups (450 ml/14 fl oz) olive oil in a thin stream while continuing to beat.

When the mayonnaise begins to thicken, you can add the oil more rapidly, still beating well after each addition. When all the oil has been added, beat in 2 tablespoons lemon juice and some salt and freshly ground black pepper. If the mayonnaise separates, place a fresh yolk in a clean bowl and start adding the curdled mixture very slowly, whisking continuously until the mixture is silky and firm. Makes 1¾ cups (450 ml/ 14 fl oz).

FRESH TOMATO DRESSING

Peel, seed and finely dice 900 g (1 lb 13 oz) ripe tomatoes. Place in a bowl and mix with 1 tablespoon each of chopped fresh basil and flat-leaf (Italian) parsley, 2 finely chopped French shallots and 3 tablespoons extra virgin olive oil. Season and stir well to combine. Serve at room temperature. Makes 625 ml (20 fl oz).

SAUCE VERTE

This sauce is delicious on poached or grilled fish and cold meats. It will keep, refrigerated, covered, for up to 3 days. Blanch and then drain 280 g (9 oz) English spinach and when cool enough to handle, squeeze with your hands to remove the excess moisture. Alternatively, you can use 140 g (4½ oz) frozen spinach, thawed and drained well. Put the spinach in a blender or food processor. Add 1 slice of bread that has been moistened with a little water, 1 chopped hard-boiled egg, 6 anchovy fillets, 2 tablespoons red wine vinegar and ½ cup (125 ml/4 fl oz) olive oil. Process until you have a smooth sauce. Stir in 1 tablespoon finely chopped cornichons and 1 teaspoon finely chopped capers. Season to taste with salt and freshly ground black pepper. Makes 220 ml (7 fl oz).

SAUCE VIERGE

This raw tomato sauce is excellent with grilled tuna and swordfish. In a bowl, combine 700 g (1 lb 7 oz) peeled, seeded and chopped tomatoes, ⅔ cup (170 ml/ 5 fl oz) extra virgin olive oil, 3 tablespoons lemon juice, 2 cloves crushed garlic and salt and pepper. Set aside for 2 hours. Just before serving, stir in 6 pitted, finely chopped black olives and 1 tablespoon each of finely chopped fresh chives, parsley and tarragon. Makes 1¾ cups (450 ml/15 fl oz).

FROM LEFT: Sauce ravigote; Basic vinaigrette; Classic mayonnaise; Fresh tomato dressing; Sauce verte; Sauce vierge

RADISHES
Radishes vary considerably in shape, size and even their external colour, which ranges from white to red to black. The white internal flesh is crisp with a slightly peppery taste which can be weak or strong, They are often used raw in salads and in many cuisines they are sculpted into interesting shapes to be used as a decoration on the plate.

OPPOSITE PAGE, CLOCKWISE FROM TOP: Coleslaw; Hot potato salad; Cold potato salad

COLESLAW

Preparation time: 20 minutes
Total cooking time: Nil
Serves 10

1/2 green (savoy) cabbage
1/4 red cabbage
3 carrots, coarsely grated
6 radishes, coarsely grated
1 red pepper (capsicum), chopped
4 spring onions (scallions), sliced
3 tablespoons chopped fresh flat-leaf (Italian) parsley
1 cup (250 g/8 oz) good-quality mayonnaise

1 Remove the hard cores from the cabbages and thinly shred the leaves with a sharp knife. Place in a large bowl and add the carrot, radish, red pepper, spring onion and parsley.
2 Add the mayonnaise, season and toss well.
IN ADVANCE: The vegetables can be chopped and refrigerated for up to 3 hours before serving. Add the mayonnaise just before serving.

COLD POTATO SALAD

Preparation time: 30 minutes
Total cooking time: 10 minutes
Serves 8

1.2 kg (2 lb 6 1/2 oz) waxy white or red potatoes, unpeeled and cut in bite-sized pieces
2 onions, finely chopped
2 green peppers (capsicums), chopped
4–5 celery sticks, chopped
6 tablespoons finely chopped fresh parsley

Dressing
1 1/2 cups (375 g/12 oz) whole-egg mayonnaise
3–4 tablespoons white wine vinegar or lemon juice
1/3 cup (90 g/3 oz) sour cream

1 Steam or boil the potatoes for 5–10 minutes, or until just tender (pierce with the point of a small sharp knife—if the potato comes away easily it is ready). Don't let the skins break away. Drain and cool completely.

2 Combine the onion, green pepper, celery and parsley with the potato in a large bowl, reserving some parsley for garnish.
3 For the dressing, mix together all the ingredients in a bowl and season with salt and black pepper. Pour over the salad and toss gently. Garnish with the reserved parsley.
NOTE: If you accidentally overcook the potatoes, drain them carefully and spread out on a large flat dish or tray and cool completely. Most of the potatoes will firm up if you do this. In this case, you should also take a little extra care when stirring in the mayonnaise.

HOT POTATO SALAD

Preparation time: 15 minutes
Total cooking time: 25 minutes
Serves 8

4 rashers bacon, rind removed
1.5 kg (3 lb) small waxy red potatoes, unpeeled
4 spring onions (scallions), sliced
3 tablespoons chopped fresh flat-leaf (Italian) parsley

Dressing
2/3 cup (170 ml/5 1/2 fl oz) extra virgin olive oil
1 tablespoon Dijon mustard
1/3 cup (80 ml/2 3/4 fl oz) white wine vinegar

1 Cook the bacon under a hot grill until crisp. Chop into small pieces.
2 Steam or boil the potatoes for 10–15 minutes, or until just tender (pierce with the point of a small sharp knife—if the potato comes away easily it is ready). Don't let the skins break away. Drain and cool slightly.
3 For the dressing, whisk all the ingredients together in a jug.
4 Cut the potatoes into quarters and place in a bowl with half the bacon, the spring onion, parsley and some salt and freshly ground black pepper. Pour in half the dressing and toss to coat the potatoes thoroughly. Transfer to a serving bowl, drizzle with the remaining dressing and sprinkle the remaining bacon over the top.
NOTE: The cooking time will depend on the size of the potatoes. The potatoes can be diced instead of quartered if you prefer.

TOMATO AND BOCCONCINI SALAD

Cut the Roma tomatoes lengthways into three or four thick slices. Discard the outside slices because they won't sit flat.

Use a sharp knife to cut each bocconcini lengthways into three or four thick slices.

Whisk the olive oil and balsamic vinegar together in a small jug.

TOMATO AND BOCCONCINI SALAD

Preparation time: 15 minutes
Total cooking time: Nil
Serves 6–8

12 ripe Roma (plum) tomatoes
10 bocconcini
1 1/3 cups (40 g/1 1/2 oz) fresh basil leaves

Dressing

1/2 cup (125 ml/4 fl oz) extra virgin olive oil
1/3 cup (80 ml/2 3/4 fl oz) balsamic vinegar

1 Cut the tomatoes lengthways into 3–4 slices (discard the outside slices, which won't lie flat). Slice each bocconcini lengthways into 3–4 slices.
2 Arrange some tomato slices on a serving plate, place a bocconcini slice on top of each and scatter with some basil leaves. Repeat until all the tomato, bocconcini and basil have been used. Season with salt and pepper.

3 For the dressing, whisk the oil and vinegar together. Drizzle over the salad.
VARIATION: This salad can also be served with a pesto dressing. Finely chop 1 cup (50 g/1 3/4 oz) fresh basil leaves, 2 tablespoons pine nuts, 1/2 cup (50 g/1 3/4 oz) grated Parmesan and 2 crushed garlic cloves in a food processor. With the motor running, add 1/2 cup (125 ml/4 fl oz) olive oil and 2 tablespoons lemon juice in a steady stream.

ASPARAGUS AND HAZELNUT SALAD

Toast 2/3 cup (95 g/3 oz) hazelnuts in a frying pan over medium heat for 3 minutes, shaking the pan to prevent the nuts burning. Lightly crush the nuts in a mortar and pestle. Trim the woody ends from 300 g (10 oz) asparagus spears and cook the spears in a large pan of boiling water for 1 minute. Drain and plunge into iced water. Drain. Mix 3 tablespoons olive oil and 3 teaspoons white wine vinegar in a screw top jar. Season and drizzle over the asparagus. Sprinkle with the nuts. Serves 4.

ABOVE: Tomato and bocconcini salad

WALDORF SALAD

Preparation time: 20 minutes
Total cooking time: Nil
Serves 4–6

2 green apples, cut into small pieces
2 red apples, cut into small pieces
2 tablespoons lemon juice
4 celery sticks, sliced
1/4 cup (30 g/1 oz) walnut pieces
1 cup (250 g/8 oz) whole-egg mayonnaise
chopped fresh parsley, to garnish, optional

1 Put the apple in a large bowl, drizzle with the lemon juice and toss to coat (this prevents the apples discolouring). Mix in the celery and most of the walnut pieces.
2 Add the mayonnaise to the bowl and toss until well coated. Season to taste. Spoon the salad into a serving bowl, sprinkle with the remaining walnut pieces and serve. Garnish with parsley.
IN ADVANCE: This salad is convenient as it can be made up to 2 hours in advance and stored, covered, in the refrigerator.

QUICK PESTO PASTA SALAD

Preparation time: 25 minutes
Total cooking time: 15 minutes
Serves 6–8

2 cups (100 g/3 1/2 oz) fresh basil leaves
2 cloves garlic, crushed
1/2 cup (50 g/1 3/4 oz) grated Parmesan
2 tablespoons pine nuts, toasted
1/3 cup (80 ml/2 3/4 fl oz) olive oil
500 g (1 lb) penne pasta, cooked
250 g (8 oz) cherry tomatoes, halved
1 small red onion, sliced into thin wedges
150 g (5 oz) black olives
Parmesan shavings, to garnish

1 Process the basil in a food processor with the garlic, Parmesan and pine nuts until roughly chopped. With the motor running, gradually add the olive oil in a thin stream until well combined.
2 Place the pasta in a large bowl, stir in the pesto and mix well. Add the tomatoes, onion and olives and stir gently. Spoon into a serving dish and garnish with Parmesan. Serve while the pasta is still warm or, if you prefer, leave until cold.

WALNUTS

Walnuts have been eaten since prehistoric times and have been cultivated as long ago as in ancient Greece. There are many species of walnut tree but the most important originated in Persia. The shelled nut is used mostly in cakes, desserts, ice cream, confectionery and, of course, the popular Middle Eastern pastry, baklava. It is also used in savoury dishes such as salads, soups, sauces and dressings for pasta. Oil has been yielded from walnuts since antiquity.

ABOVE: Waldorf salad

Dressing

¹/₂ cup (125 ml/4 fl oz) extra virgin olive oil

2 tablespoons white wine vinegar

I teaspoon sugar

I tablespoon Dijon mustard

I clove garlic, crushed

I Cut the green beans into short lengths. Bring a small pan of water to the boil and cook the beans for 2 minutes. Drain and rinse, then leave in a bowl of iced water until cold. Drain well.
2 Drain and rinse the chickpeas, kidney beans, cannellini beans and corn kernels. Mix them in a large bowl with the green beans, spring onion, red pepper, celery, gherkin, mint and parsley. Season with salt and freshly ground black pepper.
3 To make the dressing, whisk together the oil, white wine vinegar and sugar in a small jug. Season with salt and black pepper. Whisk in the mustard and garlic. Drizzle over the salad and toss gently.

RICE SALAD

Preparation time: 30 minutes
  + I hour refrigeration
Total cooking time: 20 minutes
Serves 6–8

☆

I¹/₂ cups (300 g/10 oz) long-grain rice

¹/₂ cup (80 g/2³/₄ oz) fresh or frozen peas

3 spring onions (scallions), sliced

I green pepper (capsicum), finely diced

I red pepper (capsicum), finely diced

310 g (10 oz) can corn kernels, drained, rinsed

¹/₄ cup (15 g/¹/₂ oz) chopped fresh mint

Dressing

¹/₂ cup (125 ml/4 fl oz) extra virgin olive oil

2 tablespoons lemon juice

I clove garlic, crushed

I teaspoon sugar

I Bring a large pan of water to the boil and stir in the rice. Return to the boil and cook for 12–15 minutes, or until tender. Drain and cool.
2 Cook the peas in a small pan of boiling water for about 2 minutes. Rinse under cold water and drain well.
3 For the dressing, whisk together the oil, juice, garlic and sugar in a small jug, then season.

BEAN SALAD

Preparation time: 30 minutes
Total cooking time: 2 minutes
Serves 8–10

250 g (8 oz) green beans, topped and tailed

400 g (12³/₄ oz) can chickpeas

425 g (13¹/₂ oz) can red kidney beans

400 g (12³/₄ oz) can cannellini beans

270 g (8³/₄ oz) can corn kernels

3 spring onions (scallions), sliced

I red pepper (capsicum), finely chopped

3 celery sticks, chopped

4–6 bottled gherkins, chopped, optional

3 tablespoons chopped fresh mint

ABOVE: Bean salad 3 tablespoons chopped fresh parsley

4 Combine the rice, peas, spring onion, peppers, corn and mint in a large bowl. Add the dressing and mix well. Cover and refrigerate for 1 hour. Transfer to a serving dish.

CARAMELIZED ONION AND POTATO SALAD

Preparation time: 20 minutes
Total cooking time: 50 minutes
Serves 10–12

2 tablespoons oil
6 red onions, thinly sliced
1 kg (2 lb) kipfler, desiree or pontiac potatoes
4 rashers bacon
6 tablespoons chopped fresh chives

Dressing

1 cup (250 g/8 oz) whole-egg mayonnaise
1 tablespoon Dijon mustard
2–3 tablespoons lemon juice
2 tablespoons sour cream

1 Heat the oil in a large heavy-based frying pan, add the onion and cook over low-medium heat for 40 minutes, or until caramelized.
2 Cut the potatoes into large chunks (if small, leave them whole) and steam or boil for 5–10 minutes until just tender (pierce with the point of a small knife—if the potato comes away easily, it is ready). Drain and cool slightly.
3 Remove the rind from the bacon and grill until crisp. Drain on crumpled paper towels and cool slightly before roughly chopping.
4 Put the potato, onion and chives in a large bowl, reserving a few chives for garnish, and toss to combine.
5 To make the dressing, whisk the ingredients together in a bowl. Pour over the salad and toss to coat. Sprinkle with the bacon and garnish with the reserved chives.
NOTE: Ideal boiling potatoes are waxy in texture with a high moisture content and low starch content. Examples other than those given in the recipe are sebago, coliban, pink fir apple and jersey royals.

BELOW: Caramelized onion and potato salad

131

MIXED SEAFOOD SALAD

Preparation time: 1 hour + 1 hour chilling
Total cooking time: 20 minutes
Serves 8

1.25 kg (2½ lb) large cooked prawns (shrimp)
12 cooked yabbies or crayfish
500 g (1 lb) scallops
½ cup (125 ml/4 fl oz) white wine
pinch of dried thyme
pinch of dried tarragon or a bay leaf
400 g (13 oz) salmon, trout or firm white
  fish fillets (eg. flake, hake, ling)
6 hard-boiled eggs
150 g (5 oz) mixed lettuce leaves
2 tablespoons chopped fresh parsley
2 ripe avocados, sliced
2 tablespoons lemon juice
2 cups Green goddess dressing (see page 194)

Vinaigrette

½ cup (125 ml/4 fl oz) extra virgin olive oil
2 tablespoons white wine vinegar
1 teaspoon sugar
2 teaspoons Dijon mustard
1 tablespoon chopped fresh dill

1 Peel the prawns and pull out the dark vein from each prawn back, starting at the head end.
2 Cut down each side of the shell on the underside of each yabby with scissors, starting at the head end. Pull back the flap and remove the meat from each shell. Gently pull out the vein from each back and discard each shell.
3 Slice or pull off any vein, membrane or hard white muscle from the scallops.
4 Put 1 cup (250 ml/8 fl oz) water with the wine, herbs, and a pinch each of salt and pepper, in a pan. Bring to the boil, then reduce the heat and simmer for 5 minutes. Add the scallops and poach for a few minutes, or until they have just turned white, then remove with a slotted spoon and drain on a wire rack. Add the fish fillets to the liquid. Poach until cooked and just tender, remove with a slotted spoon and drain. Break into large pieces.
5 Combine the prawns, yabbies, scallops and fish in a bowl. Whisk together the oil, vinegar, sugar, mustard and dill, and season. Pour over the seafood, cover and refrigerate for 1 hour.
6 Peel and slice the eggs, reserving 2 yolks. Put half the lettuce leaves in a deep serving bowl.

Arrange half the seafood over the lettuce, reserving the vinaigrette. Sprinkle with half the parsley, top with half the avocado, drizzle with half the lemon juice, then finish with half the sliced eggs, including the extra whites. Season. Repeat the layers. Drizzle with the reserved vinaigrette. Crumble the reserved egg yolks over the top. Serve with the green goddess dressing.

CURRIED PRAWNS

Preparation time: 20 minutes
Total cooking time: 10 minutes
Serves 4

30 g (1 oz) butter
1 onion, chopped
1 clove garlic, crushed
1 tablespoon curry powder
¼ cup (60 g/2 oz) plain (all-purpose) flour
2 cups (500 ml/16 fl oz) milk
¼ teaspoon ground nutmeg
¼ teaspoon paprika
1 kg (2 lb) raw prawns (shrimp), peeled and
  deveined, with the tails intact

1 Melt the butter in a pan over low heat, add the onion and cook until soft. Stir in the garlic, curry powder and flour and cook for 1 minute.
2 Remove from the heat and gradually stir in the milk, nutmeg, and paprika. Return to the heat and stir until the sauce boils and thickens.
3 Add the prawns and stir over medium heat for 2–3 minutes, or until the prawns are pink and cooked through.

PUMPKIN AND PRAWN SALAD WITH ROCKET

Cut 800 g (1 lb 10 oz) pumpkin into small cubes and 2 small red onions into wedges. Toss with 1 tablespoon oil and 2 crushed garlic cloves and put in a single layer on a baking tray. Bake in a moderately hot (200°C/400°F/Gas 6) oven for 35 minutes, or until tender. Toss in a bowl with 300 g (10 oz) cooked, peeled and deveined prawns (shrimp) and 200 g (6½ oz) torn rocket (arugula). Whisk 1 tablespoon balsamic vinegar, 1 tablespoon olive oil and salt and pepper. Drizzle over the salad. Serves 4–6.

YABBIES
Yabbies are also known as lobby, crawbob and freshwater crayfish. They have a delicious, sweet moist flesh and are available alive and cooked. Ensure live yabbies are active and have all their claws intact. If sluggish, it means the yabbies are either immobilized by the cold, or dying and not as fresh as they could be. They should have a pleasant sea smell. Cooked yabbies should have a firm shell, all the claws intact and no discolouration on the underside.

OPPOSITE PAGE: Mixed seafood salad

OILS & VINEGARS

Most oils and vinegars will keep for up to 6 months if you sterilize the storage jars

by washing, rinsing with boiling water and drying in a warm oven.

RASPBERRY VINEGAR

Put 2⅓ cups (290 g/10 oz) fresh or thawed frozen raspberries in a non-metallic bowl and crush gently with the back of a spoon. Warm 2 cups (500 ml/16 fl oz) white wine vinegar in a saucepan over low heat. Add the vinegar to the berries and mix well. Pour into a 2 cup (500 ml/16 fl oz) sterilized glass bottle and leave in a warm place for about 2 weeks, shaking regularly. Strain through a muslin-lined

sieve into a small pan. Add 2 teaspoons caster (superfine) sugar and stir over medium heat until dissolved. Pour into the clean, warm sterilized bottle. Add 2–3 raspberries, if desired, then seal, label and date. Store in a cool, dark place. Makes 2 cups (500 ml/16 fl oz).

TARRAGON VINEGAR

Warm 2 cups (500 ml/16 fl oz) white wine vinegar in a saucepan over low

heat. Gently bruise 25 g (¾ oz) fresh tarragon leaves in your hands and put into a 2 cup (500 ml/16 fl oz) sterilized glass bottle. Pour in the vinegar, seal with a non-metallic lid and shake well. Leave to infuse in a warm place for about 2 weeks. Strain and return to the clean, warm sterilized bottle. Add a fresh sprig of tarragon, then seal, label and date. Store in a cool, dark place. Makes 2 cups (500 ml/16 fl oz).

CHILLI OIL

Place 6 dried chillies and 1 teaspoon chilli powder in a heavy-based saucepan. Add 3 cups (750 ml/24 fl oz) olive oil and stir over medium heat for 5 minutes (if it gets too hot the oil will change flavour). Remove from the heat. Cover with plastic wrap and leave in a cool, dark place for 3 days. Strain into a 3 cup (750 ml/24 fl oz) sterilized bottle. Discard the chillies and add new chillies. Seal, label and date, then store in a cool, dark place. Makes 3 cups (750 ml/24 fl oz).

SPICED MALT VINEGAR

Pour 2 cups (500 ml/16 fl oz) malt vinegar into a saucepan. Add a 1 cm (1/2 inch) piece fresh ginger, quartered, 10 whole cloves, 1 cinnamon stick, 2 teaspoons allspice berries, 1/2 teaspoon black peppercorns, 1 teaspoon brown mustard seeds and warm over low heat.

Pour into a warm, sterilized 2 cup (500 ml/16 fl oz) glass bottle and seal with a non-metallic lid. Leave in a warm place for 2 weeks. Strain the vinegar and return to the clean, warm bottle with some black peppercorns. Seal, label and date, then store in a cool, dark place. Makes 2 cups (500 ml/16 fl oz).

PARMESAN OIL

Combine 2 cups (500 ml/16 fl oz) olive oil and 100 g (3 1/2 oz) finely grated Reggiano Parmesan in a small pan. Stir the oil mixture over low heat for 10–15 minutes, or until the Parmesan starts to melt and clump together. Remove from the heat and allow to cool. Strain into a sterilized 2 cup (500 ml/16 fl oz) bottle and add 20 g (3/4 oz) shaved Parmesan. Seal, label and date, then store in a cool, dark place. Makes 2 cups (500 ml/16 fl oz).

SPICED APPLE AND CINNAMON VINEGAR

Combine 2 cups (500 ml/16 fl oz) white wine vinegar, 1/3 cup (30 g/1 oz) finely chopped dried apple slices, 1/4 teaspoon black peppercorns, 2 bay leaves, 1/4 teaspoon yellow mustard seeds, 2 cinnamon sticks, 2 sprigs fresh thyme or a sprig of fresh tarragon and 1 peeled garlic clove in a sterilized 2 cup (500 ml/16 fl oz) bottle. Seal and leave in a cool, dark place for 2 weeks. Strain the vinegar and return to the warm sterilized bottle. Seal, label and date, then store in a cool, dark place. Makes 2 cups (500 ml/16 fl oz).

FROM LEFT: Raspberry vinegar (2); Tarragon vinegar (2); Chilli oil; Spiced malt vinegar; Parmesan oil (2); Spiced apple and cinnamon vinegar (with tarragon); Spiced apple and cinnamon vinegar (with thyme)

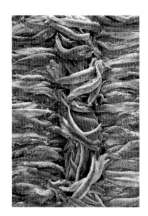

CAESAR SALAD

Preparation time: 25 minutes
Total cooking time: 20 minutes
Serves 6

1 small French bread stick

2 tablespoons olive oil

2 cloves garlic, halved

4 rashers bacon (trimmed of fat)

2 cos (romaine) lettuces

10 anchovy fillets, halved lengthways

1 cup (100 g/3¹/₂ oz) shaved Parmesan

Parmesan shavings, extra, for serving

Dressing

1 egg yolk

2 cloves garlic, crushed

2 teaspoons Dijon mustard

2 anchovy fillets

2 tablespoons white wine vinegar

1 tablespoon Worcestershire sauce

³/4 cup (185 ml/6 fl oz) olive oil

1 Preheat the oven to moderate 180°C (350°F/ Gas 4). To make the croutons, cut the bread stick into 15 thin slices and brush both sides of each slice with oil. Spread them all on a baking tray and bake for 10–15 minutes, or until golden brown. Leave to cool slightly, then rub each side of each slice with the cut edge of a garlic clove. The baked bread can then be broken roughly into pieces or cut into small cubes.

2 Cook the bacon under a hot grill until crisp. Drain on paper towels until cooled, then break into chunky pieces.

3 Tear the lettuce into pieces and put in a large serving bowl with the bacon, anchovies, croutons and Parmesan.

4 For the dressing, place the egg yolks, garlic, mustard, anchovies, vinegar and Worcestershire sauce in a food processor or blender. Season and process for 20 seconds, or until smooth. With the motor running, add enough oil in a thin stream to make the dressing thick and creamy.

5 Drizzle the dressing over the salad and toss very gently until well distributed. Sprinkle the Parmesan shavings over the top and serve immediately.

CAESAR SALAD
This classic American dish is named after its inventor, Caesar Cardini, who served it in his Tijuana, Mexico, restaurant in the 1920s. It became very popular with people in Hollywood and soon appeared in menus in restaurants in Los Angeles, from where it gradually spread elsewhere.
A great variation is to add some slices of cooked chicken breast.

RIGHT: Caesar salad

CHICKPEA AND OLIVE SALAD

Preparation time: 20 minutes
  + overnight soaking
Total cooking time: 25 minutes
Serves 6

1 1/2 cups (330 g/11 oz) dried chickpeas

1 small Lebanese (short) cucumber

2 tomatoes

1 small red onion

3 tablespoons chopped fresh parsley

1/2 cup (60 g/2 oz) pitted black olives

1 tablespoon lemon juice

3 tablespoons olive oil

1 clove garlic, crushed

1 teaspoon honey

1 Place the chickpeas in a large bowl and cover with cold water. Leave to soak overnight. Drain the chickpeas, place in a pan, cover with fresh water and cook for 25 minutes or until just tender. Drain and allow to cool.
2 Cut the cucumber in half lengthways, scoop out seeds and cut into 1 cm (1/2 inch) slices. Cut the tomatoes into cubes roughly the same size as the chickpeas, and chop onion finely. Combine the chickpeas, cucumber, tomato, onion, parsley and olives in a serving bowl.
3 Place the lemon juice, oil, garlic and honey in a small screw-top jar and shake well. Pour the dressing over the salad and toss lightly to combine. Serve at room temperature.

TOFU SALAD

Preparation time: 20 minutes
  + 1 hour marinating
Total cooking time: Nil
Serves 4

2 teaspoons sweet chilli sauce

1/2 teaspoon grated fresh ginger

1 clove garlic, crushed

2 teaspoons soy sauce

2 tablespoons oil

250 g (8 oz) firm tofu

105 g (3 1/2 oz) snow peas (mangetout), cut
  into 3 cm (1 1/4 inch) lengths

2 small carrots, cut into matchsticks

105 g (3 1/2 oz) red cabbage, finely shredded

2 tablespoons chopped peanuts

1 Place the chilli sauce, ginger, garlic, soy sauce and oil in a small screw-top jar and shake well. Cut the tofu into 2 cm (3/4 inch) cubes. Place the tofu in a medium bowl, pour the marinade over and stir. Cover with plastic wrap and refrigerate for 1 hour.
2 Place the snow peas in a small pan, pour boiling water over and leave to stand for 1 minute, then drain and plunge into iced water. Drain well.
3 Add the snow peas, carrots and cabbage to tofu and toss lightly to combine. Transfer to a serving bowl or individual plates, sprinkle with peanuts and serve immediately.

*BELOW, FROM TOP:
Chickpea and olive salad;
Tofu salad*

SALAD NICOISE
This dish literally has dozens of interpretations. Many modern versions now use fresh tuna. Heat a frying pan over very high heat. Add 1 tablespoon olive oil and allow to heat. Season 600 g (1 1/4 lb) tuna steaks on both sides, then cook them for 1 1/2–2 minutes on each side, or until cooked, but still rare in the middle. Allow the tuna to cool for a few minutes, then thinly slice it. Add to the salad.

ABOVE: Salad Niçoise

SALAD NICOISE

Preparation time: 30 minutes
Total cooking time: 15 minutes
Serves 4

3 eggs
2 vine-ripened tomatoes
175 g (6 oz) baby green beans, trimmed
1/2 cup (125 ml/4 fl oz) olive oil
2 tablespoons white wine vinegar
1 large clove garlic, halved
325 g (11 oz) iceberg lettuce heart, cut into 8 wedges
1 small red pepper (capsicum), seeded and sliced thinly
1 Lebanese (short) cucumber, cut into thin 5 cm (2 inch) lengths
1 stick celery, cut into thin 5 cm (2 inch) lengths
1/4 large red onion, thinly sliced
2 x 185 g (6 oz) cans tuna, drained, broken into chunks
12 Kalamata olives
45 g (1 1/2 oz) can anchovy fillets, drained
2 teaspoons baby capers
12 small fresh basil leaves

1 Place the eggs in a saucepan of cold water. Bring to the boil, then reduce the heat and simmer for 10 minutes. Stir during the first few minutes to centre the yolks. Cool under cold water, then peel and cut into quarters. Meanwhile, score a cross in the base of each tomato and place in a bowl of boiling water for 10 seconds. Plunge into cold water and peel away from the cross. Cut each tomato into eight.
2 Cook the beans in a saucepan of boiling water for 2 minutes, rinse under cold water, then drain.
3 For the dressing, place the oil and vinegar in a jar and shake to combine.
4 Rub the garlic over the base and sides of a platter. Arrange the lettuce over the base. Layer the egg, tomato, beans, red pepper, cucumber and celery over the lettuce. Scatter the onion and tuna over them, then the olives, anchovies, capers and basil. Drizzle with dressing and serve.

FAST PASTA SALAD

Cook 250 g (8 oz) pasta spirals in a large pan of boiling water until *al dente*. Drain well and return to the pan. Stir through a little olive oil, then add 4 tablespoons of ready-made pesto and toss well. Transfer to a serving bowl to cool, then add 150 g (4 3/4 oz) quartered cherry tomatoes and 1/2 cup (75 g/2 1/2 oz) chopped black olives. Serve at room temperature. Serves 4.

POTATO AND ANCHOVY SALAD

Preparation time: 20 minutes
Total cooking time: 25 minutes
Serves 6

1 kg (2 lb) waxy potatoes (such as pink
   fir apple, binji, kipfler), unpeeled
1/4 cup (60 ml/2 fl oz) dry white wine
1 tablespoon cider vinegar
1/4 cup (60 ml/2 fl oz) olive oil
4 spring onions (scallions), finely chopped
35 g (1 1/4 oz) drained anchovy fillets
1 tablespoon chopped parsley
1 tablespoon chopped fresh chives

1 Cook the potatoes in their skins in boiling salted water for about 20 minutes, until just tender. Drain and then peel away the skins while the potatoes are still hot. Cut into 1 cm (1/2 inch) thick slices.
2 Place the wine, vinegar, olive oil and spring onion in a large heavy-based frying pan over low heat and add the potato slices. Shake the pan to coat the potatoes, then reheat gently.
3 When hot, remove from the heat and season to taste. Coarsely chop half the anchovies and toss them through the potatoes with the parsley and chives. Transfer to a platter and put the remaining anchovies on top. Serve warm or at room temperature.

FRESH BEETROOT AND GOAT'S CHEESE SALAD

Preparation time: 20 minutes
Total cooking time: 30 minutes
Serves 4

1 kg (2 lb) fresh beetroot (4 bulbs with leaves)
200 g (6 1/2 oz) green beans
1 tablespoon red wine vinegar
2 tablespoons extra virgin olive oil
1 clove garlic, crushed
1 tablespoon drained capers, coarsely chopped
100 g (3 1/2 oz) goat's cheese

1 Trim the leaves from the beetroot. Scrub the bulbs and wash the leaves well. Add the whole bulbs to a large saucepan of salted water, bring to the boil, then reduce the heat and simmer, covered, for 30 minutes, or until tender when pierced with the point of a knife.
2 Meanwhile, bring a saucepan of water to the boil, add the beans and cook for 3 minutes, or until just tender. Remove with a slotted spoon and plunge into a bowl of cold water. Drain well. Add the beetroot leaves to the same saucepan of water and cook for 3–5 minutes, or until the leaves and stems are tender. Drain, plunge into a bowl of cold water, then drain well.
3 Drain and cool the beetroots, then peel the skins off and cut the bulbs into thin wedges.
4 For the dressing, put the red wine vinegar, oil, garlic, capers, 1/2 teaspoon each of salt and pepper in a screw top jar and shake.
5 To serve, divide the beans, beetroot leaves and bulbs among four serving plates. Crumble goat's cheese over the top of each and drizzle with dressing. Delicious served with fresh crusty bread.

BELOW: Fresh beetroot and goat's cheese salad

GREEK SALAD

What is widely known as Greek salad is but one of the numerous salads served in Greece. Its Greek name, *salata horiatiki*, translates as Greek country or village salad. It is a rustic salad with tomato, cucumber, feta cheese, olives and peppers (capsicums) as its staple ingredients, although cos (romaine) lettuce, anchovy fillets, flat-leaf (Italian) parsley, capers and a sprinkle of oregano are not unusual additions.

ABOVE: Greek salad

GREEK SALAD

Preparation time: 20 minutes
Total cooking time: Nil
Serves 4

1 telegraph cucumber, peeled
2 green peppers (capsicums)
4 vine-ripened tomatoes, cut into wedges
1 red onion, thinly sliced
16 Kalamata olives
250 g (8 oz) Greek feta, cubed
24 fresh flat-leaf (Italian) parsley leaves
12 whole fresh mint leaves
1/2 cup (125 ml/4 fl oz) good-quality olive oil
2 tablespoons lemon juice
1 clove garlic, crushed

1 Cut the cucumber in half lengthways and discard the seeds. Cut into bite-sized pieces. Cut each pepper in half lengthways, remove the membrane and seeds and cut the flesh into 1 cm (1/2 inch) wide strips. Gently mix the cucumber, green pepper, tomato, onion, olives, feta, parsley and mint leaves in a large salad bowl.
2 Place the oil, lemon juice and garlic in a screw top jar, season and shake well. Pour over the salad and serve.

EGGPLANT SALAD

Preparation time: 20 minutes + 30 minutes draining
Total cooking time: 1 hour 35 minutes
Serves 6

1 kg (2 lb) large eggplants (aubergines)
1/2 cup (125 ml/4 fl oz) olive oil
1 brown onion, finely chopped
1/2 teaspoon ground cinnamon
4 cloves garlic, crushed
2 x 400 g (13 oz) cans crushed tomatoes
2 tablespoons chopped fresh coriander (cilantro)
3 tablespoons chopped fresh parsley
1 tablespoon lemon juice
2 tablespoons chopped fresh mint
150 g (5 oz) Greek-style natural yoghurt
25 g (3/4 oz) pine nuts, toasted

1 Cut the eggplants into 2 cm (3/4 inch) cubes, place in a colander over a bowl and sprinkle generously with salt. Leave for 30 minutes, rinse under cold water, then pat dry with a tea towel.
2 Heat 2 tablespoons oil in a large frying pan and fry batches of eggplant until golden, adding more oil if necessary. Drain on paper towels.
3 Heat another 2 tablespoons oil in the pan and fry the onion for 1 minute. Add the cinnamon and half the garlic, cook for 1 minute, then

add the tomato. Add the eggplant and simmer, uncovered, for 1 hour, or until the mixture is quite dry. Add half of each of the coriander and parsley. Stir and leave to cool.

4 Mix 2 tablespoons of oil with the lemon juice and add the remaining crushed garlic and all the mint, then stir into the yoghurt.

5 Gently toss the pine nuts through the salad and garnish with the remaining fresh herbs. Serve at room temperature with the dressing.

HALOUMI WITH SALAD AND GARLIC BREAD

Preparation time: 20 minutes
Total cooking time: 5 minutes
Serves 4

Garlic bread
1 loaf crusty unsliced white bread
5 tablespoons olive oil
1 large clove garlic, cut in half

4 firm, ripe tomatoes
1 Lebanese (short) cucumber
140 g (4 1/2 oz) rocket (arugula)
1/2 cup (80 g/2 3/4 oz) Kalamata olives
400 g (13 oz) haloumi cheese
1 tablespoon lemon juice
1 tablespoon chopped fresh oregano

1 Preheat the oven to moderate 180°C (350°F/Gas 4). Heat the grill to high.

2 To make the garlic bread, slice the bread into eight 1.5 cm (5/8 inch) slices, drizzle 1 1/2 tablespoons of the olive oil over the bread and season. Grill until lightly golden, then rub each slice thoroughly with a cut side of the garlic. Wrap loosely in foil and keep warm in the oven.

3 Cut the tomatoes and cucumber into bite-sized chunks and place in a serving dish with the rocket and olives. Mix well.

4 Cut the haloumi into 8 slices. Heat 1/2 tablespoon of the oil in a shallow frying pan and fry the haloumi slices for 1–2 minutes on each side, until crisp and golden brown.

5 Whisk together the lemon juice, oregano and remaining olive oil to use as a dressing. Season to taste. Pour half the dressing over the salad and toss well. Arrange the haloumi on top and drizzle with dressing. Serve immediately with the warm garlic bread.

KALAMATA OLIVES
Hailing from Kalamata in the southern Peloponnese, these almond-shaped olives are considered to be Greece's best due to the fruity, rich flavour and firm flesh. Packed in either olive oil or wine vinegar to accentuate their robust taste, they are often found on a meze plate, and in salads, sauces and breads.

LEFT: Haloumi with salad and garlic bread

1 Wash and dry the salad greens thoroughly, then tear into bite-size pieces. Combine the salad greens, green pepper and lemon zest in a large serving bowl.

2 To make the dressing, whisk all the ingredients in a small mixing bowl for 2 minutes, or until well combined. Pour the dressing over the salad and toss to combine. Serve chilled.

NOTE: Make the dressing and salad just before serving. Choose a selection of your favourite salad greens for this recipe. This is delicious served in summer with a chilled frascati or a light red wine.

WARM LENTIL AND RICE SALAD

Preparation time: 15 minutes
Total cooking time: 40 minutes
Serves 6

★ ★

1 cup (185 g/6 oz) green lentils
1 cup (200 g/6½ oz) basmati rice
4 large red onions, thinly sliced
4 cloves garlic, crushed
1 cup (250 ml/8 fl oz) olive oil
45 g (1½ oz) butter
2 teaspoons ground cinnamon
2 teaspoons ground sweet paprika
2 teaspoons ground cumin
2 teaspoons ground coriander
3 spring onions (scallions), chopped

1 Cook the lentils and rice in separate pans of water until the grains are just tender; drain.

2 Meanwhile, cook the onions and garlic in oil and butter for 30 minutes, over low heat, until very soft.

3 Stir in the cinnamon, paprika, cumin and coriander and cook for a few minutes longer.

4 Combine the onion and spice mixture with the well-drained rice and lentils. Stir in the chopped spring onions until combined and season to taste with freshly ground black pepper. Serve warm.

NOTE: Do not use red lentils for this recipe as they become mushy very quickly and do not retain their shape. It is not necessary to soak the lentils prior to cooking, but they need to be rinsed thoroughly.

BASMATI RICE
Basmati rice is a narrow long-grain rice with a silky texture, grown in the foothills of the Himalayas. Before basmati rice is cooked, it should always be washed to remove any dust and grit. Its delicate flavour makes it the ideal accompaniment for spicy Indian dishes.

GARDEN SALAD

Preparation time: 15 minutes
Total cooking time: Nil
Serves 4-6

★

1 green oak-leaf lettuce
150 g (5 oz) rocket (arugula)
1 small radicchio lettuce
1 large green pepper (capsicum), cut into thin strips
rind of 1 lemon

Dressing

2 tablespoons roughly chopped fresh coriander (cilantro)
¼ cup (60 ml/2 fl oz) lemon juice
2 teaspoons soft brown sugar
2 tablespoons olive oil
1 clove garlic, crushed (optional)

ABOVE: Garden salad

SOUTH-WESTERN BEAN SALAD

Preparation time: 20 minutes
 + overnight soaking
Total cooking time: 50 minutes
Serves 4-6

1 cup (220 g/7 oz) dried black beans

1 cup (200 g/6 1/2 oz) white cannellini beans

1 red onion

1 red pepper (capsicum)

270 g (9 oz) canned corn kernels, drained

3 tablespoons chopped fresh coriander
 (cilantro)

1 clove garlic, crushed

1/2 teaspoon ground cumin

1/2 teaspoon French mustard

2 tablespoons red wine vinegar

1/4 cup (60 ml/2 fl oz) olive oil

1 Soak the beans in separate bowls in cold water overnight. Drain the beans; place them in separate pans and cover with water. Bring both pans of water to the boil, reduce the heat and simmer for 45 minutes, or until tender. Drain, rinse and allow to cool.

2 Chop the onion and red pepper. Place in a bowl and add the beans, corn and coriander. Stir until well combined.

3 Combine the garlic, cumin, mustard and vinegar in a small jug, then gradually whisk in the oil. Season lightly with salt and pepper. Pour the dressing over the bean mixture and toss lightly to combine.

NOTE: Black beans are also known as turtle beans and are available at good delicatessens. They are not to be confused with Chinese black beans.

FAST MELON SALAD

Cut a large honeydew melon into slices and arrange on a large platter. Scatter 2 cups (60 g/4 oz) of thoroughly washed watercress sprigs (the leaves can harbour a lot of grit) over the top. Arrange on top 2 sliced avocados, 1 thinly sliced large red pepper (capsicum), 220 g (7 oz) of marinated feta cheese that has been broken into large chunks, and 90 g (3 oz) of marinated niçoise olives. Make a dressing by putting 1/4 cup (60 ml/2 fl oz) olive oil, 2 tablespoons of white wine vinegar and 1 teaspoon Dijon mustard in a screw-top jar. Shake until well combined and drizzle over the salad. Serves 4–6.

ABOVE: South-western bean salad

CURLY ENDIVE AND BLUE CHEESE SALAD

Preparation time: 15 minutes
Total cooking time: 5 minutes
Serves 6

3 slices bread
3 tablespoons oil
30 g (1 oz) butter
1 curly endive
125 g (4 oz) blue cheese
2 tablespoons olive oil
3 teaspoons white wine vinegar
2 tablespoons chopped fresh chives

1 To make the croutons, remove the crusts from the bread and cut the bread into small cubes. Heat the oil and butter in a frying pan until bubbling, then add the cubes of bread. Cook, tossing frequently, for 3 minutes, or until golden. Drain on paper towels.
2 Wash and dry the endive thoroughly. Place the leaves in a serving bowl and crumble cheese over the top.
3 Put the oil and vinegar in a small screw-top jar and shake well. Drizzle the dressing over the salad, add the chives and croutons and toss.

RED CABBAGE SALAD

Preparation time: 15 minutes
Total cooking time: Nil
Serves 6

155 g (5 oz) red cabbage, finely shredded
125 g (4 oz) green cabbage, finely shredded
2 spring onions (scallions), finely chopped
3 tablespoons olive oil
2 teaspoons white wine vinegar
1/2 teaspoon French mustard
1 teaspoon caraway seeds

1 Combine the red and green cabbage and spring onions in a serving bowl.
2 Place the oil, vinegar, mustard and caraway seeds in a small screw-top jar and shake well.
3 Pour the dressing over the salad, toss lightly to combine and serve immediately.

GREEN BEAN SALAD

Preparation time: 15 minutes
Total cooking time: 15 minutes
Serves 4

280 g (9 oz) green beans, trimmed
1 tablespoon olive oil
2 teaspoons lemon juice
1 tablespoon pine nuts
1/3 cup (80 ml/2 3/4 fl oz) tomato juice
1 clove garlic, crushed
few drops Tabasco sauce

1 Boil the beans for 1 minute, then drain and plunge into iced water. Drain well, then toss with oil and lemon juice. Preheat the oven to moderate 180°C (350°F/Gas 4). Spread the nuts on a baking tray and cook for 5 minutes.
2 Combine the tomato juice, garlic and Tabasco in a small pan. Bring to the boil, then simmer, uncovered, over low heat for 8 minutes, or until reduced by half. Allow to cool. Arrange the beans on a serving plate, then pour the tomato mixture over the top. Sprinkle with the pine nuts.

SPINACH AND NUT SALAD

Preparation time: 15 minutes
Total cooking time: 2 minutes
Serves 4

30 English spinach leaves
250 g (8 oz) young green beans, chopped
1/2 onion, thinly sliced
1/3 cup (90 g/3 oz) plain yoghurt
1 tablespoon lemon juice
1 tablespoon shredded fresh mint
4 tablespoons chopped walnuts, toasted
fresh mint leaves, to serve
red pepper (capsicum) curls, to serve

1 Rinse the spinach in cold water. Cover the beans with boiling water and leave for 2 minutes. Drain. Pat the spinach and beans dry, then cool.
2 Arrange the spinach, beans and onion on a serving plate. Mix the yoghurt, lemon juice and mint in a bowl. Pour over the salad, sprinkle with walnuts and garnish with mint and red pepper.

BLUE CHEESE
Blue cheeses happened first by accident, but the penicillin moulds that give cheese blue veins have since been identified and isolated, and blue varieties are now manufactured by most cheese-producing countries. Blue cheese can be anything from golden yellow to chalk white, but should be flecked with blue mould throughout. The only thing a blue cheese should never be is brown and clouded.

OPPOSITE PAGE, FROM TOP: Green bean salad; Red cabbage salad; Curly endive and blue cheese salad

and blistered. Remove from the heat and cover with a damp tea towel. When cool, peel away the skin and cut the flesh into thin strips.

3 In a large salad bowl, combine the pasta, pepper strips, onion, parsley, anchovies, oil, lemon juice, and salt and pepper, to taste. Toss until well combined and serve immediately.

NOTE: To prevent pasta sticking together, after rinsing, add a little oil to pasta and toss well.

WARM PASTA AND CRAB SALAD

Preparation time: 20 minutes
Total cooking time: 10 minutes
Serves 6

200 g (6½ oz) spaghetti

2 tablespoons olive oil

30 g (1 oz) butter

3 x 200 g (6½ oz) cans crab meat, drained

1 large red pepper (capsicum), cut into thin strips

2 teaspoons finely grated lemon rind

3 tablespoons grated fresh Parmesan

2 tablespoons chopped chives

3 tablespoons chopped fresh parsley

1 Break the spaghetti in half and cook it in a large pan of rapidly boiling salted water until *al dente*. Drain.

2 Place the spaghetti in a large serving bowl and toss with the oil and butter. Add all the remaining ingredients and toss to combine. Sprinkle with pepper and serve warm.

GRILLED PEPPERS AND ANCHOVY SALAD

Preparation time: 15 minutes
Total cooking time: 25 minutes
Serves 6

500 g (1 lb) penne or spiral pasta

2 large red peppers (capsicums)

1 small red onion, finely chopped

1 cup (20 g/¾ oz) fresh flat-leaf (Italian) parsley

2–3 anchovies, whole or chopped

¼ cup (60 ml/2 fl oz) olive oil

2 tablespoons lemon juice

1 Cook the pasta in a large pan of rapidly boiling salted water until *al dente*. Drain, rinse under cold water and drain again.

2 Cut the peppers in half and remove seeds and membrane. Place skin-side-up under a hot grill and cook for 8 minutes, or until the skin is black

ABOVE: Grilled peppers and anchovy salad

FAST PEPPER SALAD

Roast or chargrill 1 large red, 1 large green and 1 large yellow pepper (capsicum). Cover with a tea towel and allow the flesh to cool before peeling away the skin. Cut the peppers into thick strips. Place in a bowl with 1 tablespoon of olive oil, 2 tablespoons of green peppercorns and 155 g (5 oz) marinated Kalamata olives. Stir through 2 tablespoons of chopped fresh mint and 1 tablespoon of raspberry vinegar. Serve on a bed of rocket (arugula) leaves. Serves 4–6.

TUSCAN WARM PASTA SALAD

Preparation time: 15 minutes
Total cooking time: 15 minutes
Serves 6

500 g (1 lb) rigatoni

1/3 cup (80 ml/2³/4 fl oz) olive oil

1 clove garlic, crushed

1 tablespoon balsamic vinegar

425 g (14 oz) can artichoke hearts, drained
   and quartered

8 thin slices prosciutto, chopped

1/2 cup (80 g/2³/4 oz) sun-dried tomatoes in oil,
   drained and thinly sliced

1/4 cup (15 g/¹/2 oz) fresh basil leaves, shredded

2 cups (70 g/2¹/4 oz) rocket (arugula) leaves,
   washed and drained well

1/4 cup (40 g/1¹/4 oz) pine nuts, lightly toasted

1/4 cup (45 g/1¹/2 oz) small black Italian olives

1 Add the rigatoni to a large pan of rapidly boiling water and cook until *al dente*. Drain the pasta thoroughly and transfer to a large serving bowl.

2 While the pasta is cooking, whisk together the oil, garlic and balsamic vinegar.

3 Toss the dressing through the hot pasta. Allow the pasta to cool slightly. Add the artichoke hearts, prosciutto, sun-dried tomato, basil, rocket, pine nuts and olives.

4 Toss all the ingredients together until well combined. Season to taste with salt and freshly ground black pepper.

NOTE: To toast the pine nuts, cook in a dry frying pan over medium heat for 1–2 minutes, until lightly golden. Allow to cool.

*ABOVE: Tuscan
warm pasta salad*

FISH & SEAFOOD

SUSHI & SASHIMI Only the freshest ingredients

are used by the Japanese to prepare these traditional dishes. They are beautifully

presented to appeal to the eye as well as the taste buds.

WHAT'S THE DIFFERENCE?

Japanese *sashimi* is very thin slices of raw fish or other seafood, prepared in various delicate ways and usually served as an appetizer with dipping sauces.

Sushi consists of cold vinegar-flavoured rice topped with sashimi and a limitless variety of ingredients, including omelette or vegetables. Alternatively, for sushi the rice can be rolled, with fillings in the centre, in precooked nori (seaweed). Sushi is

served as a main meal with pickled ginger, soy and wasabi.

For making sushi, you will need a bamboo mat. They are not expensive and are available at Asian grocery stores. There isn't really a successful substitute.

TUNA/SALMON NORI ROLLS

You will need a bamboo mat, 5 sheets of nori, each cut in half lengthways, 4 cups (800 g/1 lb 10 oz) cooked sushi rice (see page 152), wasabi and 200 g (6½ oz)

sashimi tuna or salmon, cut into thin strips. Place a piece of nori on the mat, shiny-side-down, and spread 4 tablespoons rice over it, leaving a 2 cm (¾ inch) border along one end. Make a slight indentation along the centre to hold the fish in place, then dab a small amount of wasabi along the ridge. Top with the fish. Roll the mat over to enclose the filling, pressing gently to form a firm roll. Slice the roll in half and then each half into three. Makes 60.

SUSHI HAND ROLLS

You will need 10 sheets of nori, each cut in half diagonally, 2 cups (400 g/13 oz) cooked sushi rice (see page 152), wasabi, 20 peeled, deveined raw small prawns (shrimp), 1 thinly sliced avocado and 1 cup (125 g/4 oz) tempura flour. Prepare the tempura batter, following the instructions on the flour packet. Dip the prawns in the batter and deep-fry in hot oil, in batches, until crisp and golden. Drain on crumpled paper towel. Hold a sheet of nori shiny-side-down, flat in your hand, place 2 tablespoons rice on the left-hand side and spread over half of the nori sheet. Dab with wasabi. Place a prawn on the rice with a slice of avocado, then roll the nori to form a cone, enclosing the smaller end. Repeat to use all the remaining ingredients. Makes 20.

PRAWN AND TUNA NIGIRI

You will need 10 peeled, butterflied cooked prawns (shrimp), 250 g (8 oz) sashimi tuna, wasabi and 2 cups (400 g/ 13 oz) cooked sushi rice (see page 152). Trim the tuna into a rectangle, removing any connective tissue or blood. Cut thin slices, wiping the knife after each slice. Form a tablespoon of sushi rice into an oval the same length and width as the fish. Place one of the tuna slices flat on your hand, then spread a small dab of wasabi over the centre. Place the rice on the fish and cup your palm. Press the rice onto the fish, firmly pushing with a slight upward motion to make a neat shape. Turn over and repeat the shaping process, finishing with the fish on top. Repeat until you have used the remaining cooked sushi rice and prawns. Makes 16–20.

SASHIMI SALMON, CUCUMBER AND CHIVE ROLLS

Cut a 200 g (6½ oz) fillet of salmon into paper-thin slices, on an angle. Cut 1 small Lebanese (short) cucumber in half and discard the seeds. Cut the flesh into long thin strips. Place a salmon slice on a board, top with strips of cucumber, roll up and tie with trimmed chives. Serve with ginger, shoyu and wasabi. Makes 25.
NOTE: Shoyu is Japanese-style soy sauce, a much lighter and sweeter sauce than the Chinese one. It should be refrigerated after opening.

FROM LEFT: Tuna and salmon nori rolls; Sushi hand rolls; Prawn and tuna nigiri; Sashimi salmon, cucumber and chive rolls

SUSHI & SASHIMI

MAKING SUSHI RICE

Rinse 2½ cups (550 g/1 lb 2 oz) white short-grain rice under cold running water until the water runs clear; drain in the strainer for 1 hour. Transfer to a large saucepan with 3 cups (750 ml/24 fl oz) water, bring to the boil and cook for 5–10 minutes, without stirring, or until tunnels form on the surface. Reduce the heat to low, cover and cook for 12–15 minutes, or until tender. Remove from the heat, place a tea towel over the rice; leave for 15 minutes. Combine 5 tablespoons rice vinegar, 1 tablespoon mirin, 2 teaspoons salt and 2 tablespoons sugar in a bowl and stir until the sugar dissolves. Spread the rice over a flat non-metallic tray, top with the dressing and stir to mix through. Spread out and cool to body temperature. If the rice gets too cold, it will turn hard and be difficult to work with. Spread a damp tea towel over the rice and keep it covered as you work. To prevent rice sticking to your hands, dip your fingers in a bowl of warm water with a few drops of rice vinegar added. Makes 6 cups (1.2 kg/2 lb 6½ oz).

SASHIMI

Preparing sashimi is relatively simple. You will need a good, very sharp knife. There are four ways of cutting fish for sashimi, all used for different types of fish. The simplest is the straight down cut, about 2 cm (¾ inch) wide. For a cubed cut, the straight pieces are cut into cubes. There is also an angled cut and a paper-thin slice used for white fish.

CALIFORNIA ROLLS

To make these, you will need 4 sheets of nori, 3 cups (600 g/1¼ lb) cooked sushi rice, 10 g (¼ oz) flying fish roe, 1 sliced avocado, 10 cooked peeled, deveined prawns (shrimp), each halved lengthways, or 2 crab sticks, and 2 tablespoons Japanese mayonnaise (kyuupi). Lay 1 sheet of nori on a bamboo mat, shiny-side-down. Spread 2–3 tablespoons of rice in the middle of the nori, leaving a 2 cm (¾ inch) border along the end nearest you. Make a slight indentation along the centre of the rice to hold the filling in, then spread a small line of mayonnaise

along the ridge. Spread about
1 tablespoon of flying fish roe over
the centre of the rice and top with
some prawn and avocado. Roll the mat
over to enclose the filling, then roll the
mat, pressing gently to form a firm roll.
Slice the roll in half and then each half
into three. Makes 24.

INSIDE-OUT ROLLS

These have the rice on the outside. Use
8 sheets of nori and 6 cups (1.2 kg/
2 lb 6½ oz) cooked sushi rice. Place a
sheet of nori on a bamboo mat and spread
1 cm (½ inch) rice over the top, leaving a
1 cm (½ inch) border. Cover with a sheet
of plastic wrap, slightly larger than the nori.
In one quick motion, turn the whole
thing over, then place it back on the mat,
so the plastic is under the rice and the nori
on top. Spread a little wasabi on the nori,
along the short end, 4 cm (1½ inches)

from the edge. Lay strips of cucumber,
avocado and fresh crab on top of the
wasabi, then roll from this end, using the
plastic as a guide. Rewrap in plastic, then
roll up in the mat. Remove the plastic and
roll in flying fish roe or sesame seeds. Cut
in half, trim the ends, and cut each half
into three. Serve with shoyu. Makes 48.

CHIRASHI-ZUSHI

A Japanese sushi meal in a bowl, chirashi
means scattered, and that is how it is
prepared. A bed of cooked sushi rice is
placed in the bottom of a lacquered
bowl, then vegetables and seafood are
scattered over the top. The seafood can
be raw or cooked, but usually the fish
will be sashimi. Chirashi-zushi is
accompanied by pickled ginger, wasabi,
and soy sauce. To make chirashi-zushi,
you will need 4 cups (800 g/1 lb 10 oz)
cooked sushi rice, 3 tablespoons each

of toasted white sesame seeds, shredded
pickled daikon and shredded nori. Soak
6 dried shiitake mushrooms in boiling
water for 10 minutes, then drain. Cut the
mushrooms into thin strips and combine
in a saucepan with 3 tablespoons soy
sauce, 1 cup (250 ml/8 fl oz) dashi stock
and 1 tablespoon mirin, and simmer for
10 minutes, then drain. Spread the sushi
rice into a large bowl or four individual
bowls. Top with the sesame seeds,
pickled daikon, nori and mushrooms.
Over the top, decoratively arrange
1 thinly sliced cucumber, 16 blanched
snow peas (mangetout), 100 g (3½ oz)
each of sashimi tuna and salmon and
16 cooked, peeled, deveined and
butterflied prawns (shrimp). Serves 4–6.

*FROM LEFT: Sashimi tuna (top) and
salmon; California rolls; Inside-out rolls;
Chirashi-zushi*

GARLIC AND GINGER
PRAWNS

Gently cut a slit down the
back of each prawn.

Remove the dark vein from
the back of each prawn.

When the veins have been
removed, press the prawns
out flat.

GARLIC AND
GINGER PRAWNS

Preparation time: 25 minutes
Total cooking time: 10 minutes
Serves 4

1 kg (2 lb) raw large prawns (shrimp)
2 tablespoons oil
3–4 cloves garlic, finely chopped
5 cm (2 inch) piece fresh ginger, julienned
2–3 small red chillies, seeded and finely chopped
6 fresh coriander (cilantro) roots, finely chopped
8 spring onions (scallions), cut into short lengths
1/2 red pepper (capsicum), thinly sliced
2 tablespoons lemon juice
1/2 cup (125 ml/4 fl oz) white wine
2 teaspoons grated palm sugar or brown sugar
2 teaspoons fish sauce
1 tablespoon fresh coriander (cilantro) leaves,
    to garnish

1 Peel the prawns, leaving the tails intact. Gently
cut a slit down the back of each prawn and
remove the dark vein from each. Press each
prawn out flat.
2 Heat a wok until very hot, add the oil and
swirl it around to coat the side. Stir-fry half of
the prawns, garlic, ginger, chilli and coriander
root for 1–2 minutes over high heat, or until the
prawns have just turned pink, then remove from
the wok. Repeat with the remaining prawns,
garlic, ginger, chilli and coriander root. Remove
all of the prawns from the wok and set aside.
3 Add the spring onion and pepper to the wok.
Cook over high heat for 2–3 minutes. Add the
combined lemon juice, wine and palm sugar.
Boil until the liquid has reduced by two thirds.
4 Return the prawns to the wok and sprinkle
with the fish sauce, to taste. Toss until the
prawns are heated through. Remove from the
heat and serve sprinkled with coriander leaves.

*ABOVE: Garlic
and ginger prawns*

CRUNCHY FISH FILLETS

Preparation time: 10 minutes
Total cooking time: 6 minutes
Serves 4

1/2 cup (75 g/2 1/2 oz) cornmeal
4 firm white fish fillets (eg. snapper, perch,
   John dory, whiting, haddock, cod)
1/4 cup (60 ml/2 fl oz) oil
2/3 cup (170 g/5 1/2 oz) mayonnaise
2 tablespoons chopped fresh chives
1 tablespoon sweet chilli sauce

1 Place the cornmeal on a plate. Cut 4 shallow diagonal slashes in the skin side of each fish fillet, to prevent the fish curling during cooking.
2 Press the fillets into the cornmeal to coat thoroughly. Heat the oil in a frying pan over medium heat. Add the fish and cook skin-side-up for 3 minutes. Turn and cook for another 3 minutes, or until tender and the fish flakes easily when tested with a fork. Remove and drain on crumpled paper towels.
3 Combine the mayonnaise, chives and chilli sauce in a small bowl and serve with the fish.

SPANISH MACKEREL WITH GARLIC BUTTER

Preparation time: 10 minutes
Total cooking time: 15 minutes
Serves 4

2 tablespoons oil
80 g (2 3/4 oz) butter
4 cloves garlic, crushed
4 x 180 g (6 oz) Spanish mackerel cutlets
1/3 cup (30 g/1 oz) flaked almonds
2 tablespoons finely chopped fresh parsley

1 Heat the oil and butter in a pan. Add the garlic and stir over low heat for 2 minutes, or until light golden. Remove from the pan.
2 Add the fish to the pan and cook over high heat for 2–3 minutes, until golden brown on each side and cooked through (the flesh should flake easily when tested with a fork). Remove from the pan, cover and keep warm.
3 Add the almonds to the pan juices and stir until golden brown. Add the parsley and reserved garlic butter and stir for 1 minute.
4 Serve the hot cutlets with the almond and parsley mixture spooned evenly over the top.

JOHN DORY
The French name for this unattractive saltwater fish is Saint-Pierre (St Peter). The John dory has a large head, huge mouth and a deep, thin body. On either side of the body is a fingerprint-shaped impression, the subject of many fanciful legends. One such tale has St Peter leaving the print after throwing a John dory, which was making noises of distress, back into the Sea of Galilee. Another has him throwing it back because it was so ugly. Since this 'sea' is fresh water, the fish could not have been caught there. Despite its ugliness, the fillets yielded from John dory have a most delectable flavour.

LEFT: Crunchy fish fillets

PAN-FRIED FISH

Coat both sides of the fish cutlets with seasoned flour, shaking off any excess.

After 3 minutes cooking, turn the fish and brown the other side.

Reduce the heat and cook the fish until the flesh flakes easily with a fork.

PAN-FRIED FISH

Preparation time: 5 minutes
Total cooking time: 8 minutes
Serves 4

2–3 tablespoons plain (all-purpose) flour
4 firm white fish cutlets (eg. blue-eye, jewfish, warehou, snapper)
olive oil, for shallow-frying

1 Sift the flour together with a little salt and pepper onto a dinner plate. Pat the fish dry with paper towels, then coat both sides of the cutlets with seasoned flour, shaking off any excess.
2 Heat about 3 mm (1/8 inch) oil in a large frying pan until very hot. Put the fish into the hot oil immediately and cook for 3 minutes on one side, then turn and cook the other side for 2 minutes, or until the coating is crisp and well browned. Reduce the heat to low and cook for another 2–3 minutes, until the flesh flakes easily when tested with a fork.
3 Remove the fish from the pan and drain briefly on crumpled paper towels. If cooking in batches, keep warm while cooking the remaining cutlets. Serve immediately.
NOTE: This method is good for any fish cutlet, fillet or steak. However, the cooking time will vary depending on the thickness of the fish.

FISH CRUSTED WITH PARMESAN AND HERBS

Lightly dust 4 x 200 g (6½ oz) skinless white fillets of ling, snapper or perch with seasoned flour. Dip into a beaten egg whisked with 1 tablespoon of milk, then coat with a mixture of ½ cup (50 g/1¾ oz) dry breadcrumbs, 2 tablespoons each of chopped fresh dill and parsley, 4 tablespoons grated Parmesan and 4 tablespoons lightly crushed flaked almonds. Press on firmly. Heat 1 tablespoon oil and 30 g (1 oz) butter in a frying pan, add the fish and cook over medium heat on both sides until golden and cooked. Top with guacamole, or serve with tartare sauce (see page 194). Serves 4.

RIGHT: Pan-fried fish

WARM PRAWN AND SCALLOP STIR-FRY

Preparation time: 30 minutes +
10 minutes marinating
Total cooking time: 15 minutes
Serves 4

500 g (1 lb) raw small prawns (shrimp)

300 g (10 oz) scallops

2 teaspoons five-spice powder

1–2 small fresh red chillies, seeded and
finely chopped

2–3 cloves garlic, crushed

2 tablespoons oil

2 teaspoons sesame oil

200 g (6½ oz) fresh asparagus, cut into
short lengths

150 g (5 oz) snow peas (mangetout), trimmed

125 g (4 oz) rocket (arugula), torn into pieces

2 tablespoons light soy sauce

2 tablespoons lemon juice

1 tablespoon mirin

1 tablespoon oil, extra

1 tablespoon honey

6 spring onions (scallions), chopped

1 tablespoon chopped fresh coriander (cilantro)

1 tablespoon sesame seeds, lightly toasted

1 Peel the prawns, leaving the tails intact. Gently pull out the dark vein from each prawn back, starting at the head end. Slice or pull off any vein, membrane or hard white muscle from the scallops, leaving any roe attached.

2 Combine the five-spice powder, chilli, garlic and oils in a large glass or ceramic bowl. Add the prawns and scallops and toss to coat. Cover and refrigerate for at least 10 minutes.

3 Blanch the asparagus and snow peas briefly in a pan of boiling water. Drain and plunge into a bowl of iced water, then drain again. Arrange the asparagus, snow peas and rocket on 4 plates.

4 Put the soy sauce, lemon juice, mirin, extra oil and honey in a small bowl. Stir to combine.

5 Heat the wok, and stir-fry the prawns, scallops and spring onion over high heat, in batches, for 3–4 minutes, or until cooked through. Remove from the wok and set aside.

6 Add the sauce and coriander to the wok, and bring to the boil. Cook over high heat for 1–2 minutes. Return the seafood to the wok and toss. Divide among the serving plates and sprinkle with the sesame seeds.

ABOVE: Warm prawn and scallop stir-fry

FISH AND CHIPS

A cube of bread will brown in 30 seconds when the oil is ready.

Handle the fish with tongs, turning if necessary.

FISH AND CHIPS

Preparation time: 25 minutes + soaking
Total cooking time: 25 minutes
Serves 4

★ ★

1¼ cups (155 g/5 oz) plain (all-purpose) flour
1½ cups (375 ml/12 fl oz) beer
4 floury potatoes (desiree, spunta or russet)
oil, for deep-frying
4 firm white fish fillets (eg. bream, cod, coley, flake, flathead, pollack, snapper)
cornflour (cornstarch), for coating
lemon wedges, to serve

1 Sift the flour into a large bowl and make a well. Gradually add the beer, whisking to make a smooth lump-free batter. Cover and set aside.
2 Peel the potatoes and cut into chips 1 cm (³/4 inch) thick. Soak for 10 minutes in cold water. Drain and pat dry. Fill a deep heavy-based pan one third full of oil and heat to 160°C (315°F), or until a cube of bread browns in 30 seconds. Cook batches of chips for 4–5 minutes, or until pale golden. Remove with tongs or a slotted spoon. Drain on crumpled paper towels.
3 Just before serving, reheat the oil to moderate 180°C (350°F), or until a cube of bread browns in 15 seconds. Cook the chips again, in batches, until crisp and golden. Drain on crumpled paper towels. Keep hot in the oven. Serve with the fish.
4 Pat the fish dry with paper towels. Dust with cornflour, dip into the batter and drain off excess. Deep-fry in batches for 5–7 minutes, or until cooked. Turn with tongs if necessary. Drain on crumpled paper towels. Serve with lemon wedges.

CRUMBED CALAMARI WITH CHILLI PLUM SAUCE

Preparation time: 25 minutes
Total cooking time: 12 minutes
Serves 4

★ ★

500 g (1 lb) squid hoods
¼ cup (30 g/1 oz) plain (all-purpose) flour, seasoned
1–2 eggs, lightly beaten
3 cups (240 g/7½ oz) fresh white breadcrumbs
oil, for deep-frying

Chilli plum sauce
1 teaspoon oil
1 clove garlic, crushed
1 cup (315 g/10 oz) dark plum jam
¹/3 cup (80 ml/2³/4 fl oz) white vinegar
1–2 tablespoons sweet chilli sauce

1 Pat the squid with paper towels. Remove the quill and any skin. Cut into 1 cm (½ inch) rings.
2 Put the flour in a plastic bag, add the rings and toss. Dip each ring in beaten egg, drain off excess, then coat in breadcrumbs. Pat the crumbs lightly onto the rings and shake off any excess crumbs.
3 Fill a deep heavy-based pan one third full of oil and heat to 180°C (350°F), or until a cube of bread dropped into the oil turns golden brown in 15 seconds. Cook batches of rings for 3 minutes, or until golden. Drain on crumpled paper towels. Keep warm. Skim crumbs from the surface of the oil between batches. Serve hot, with the sauce.
4 For the sauce, heat the oil in a small pan over low heat and cook the garlic until softened. Stir in the jam, vinegar and chilli over medium heat until combined.

BREADED SCAMPI

Preparation time: 15 minutes
Total cooking time: 10 minutes
Serves 4 as a first course

★ ★

1 kg (2 lb) peeled raw scampi (scampi meat) or peeled raw large prawns (shrimp)
½ cup (60 g/2 oz) plain (all-purpose) flour
4 eggs, lightly beaten
2 cups (200 g/6½ oz) dry breadcrumbs
1 tablespoon finely chopped fresh parsley
oil, for deep-frying
tartare sauce (see page 194), to serve
lemon wedges, to serve

1 Pat the scampi or prawns dry with paper towel, then toss in the flour and shake off any excess. Dip into the egg, then the combined crumbs and parsley.
2 Fill a deep heavy-based pan one third full of oil and heat to 180°C (350°F), or until a cube of bread dropped into the oil browns in 15 seconds. Deep-fry the scampi in batches for 2 minutes, or until golden and cooked through. Drain. Serve with tartare sauce and lemon wedges.

FRIED WHITEBAIT

Preparation time: 10 minutes
Total cooking time: 10 minutes
Serves 6

500 g (1 lb) whitebait
2 teaspoons sea salt
1/3 cup (40 g/1 1/4 oz) plain (all-purpose) flour
1/4 cup (30 g/1 oz) cornflour (cornstarch)
2 teaspoons finely chopped fresh parsley
oil, for deep-frying
1 lemon, cut into wedges, to serve

1 Combine the whitebait and sea salt in a bowl and mix well. Cover and refrigerate.
2 Combine the sifted flours and parsley in a bowl and season well with freshly ground black pepper. Fill a deep heavy-based pan one third full of oil and heat to 180°C (350°F), or until a cube of bread dropped into the oil browns in 15 seconds. Toss a third of the whitebait in the flour mixture, shake off the excess flour, and deep-fry for 1 1/2 minutes, or until pale and crisp. Drain well on crumpled paper towels. Repeat with the remaining whitebait, cooking in batches.
3 Reheat the oil and fry the whitebait a second time, in batches, for 1 minute each batch, or until lightly browned. Drain on crumpled paper towels and serve hot with lemon wedges.

DEEP-FRIED SQUID

Preparation time: 30 minutes +
  30 minutes chilling
Total cooking time: 5 minutes
Serves 4

500 g (1 lb) small squid (about 20)
1/3 cup (40 g/1 1/4 oz) plain (all-purpose) flour
oil, for deep-frying
lemon wedges, to serve

1 To clean the squid, gently pull the tentacles away from the hood—the intestines should come away with them. Remove the intestines from the tentacles by cutting under the eyes and remove the beak if it remains in the centre of the tentacles. Pull away the soft bone 'quill' from the hood. Rub the hoods under running water and the skin should come away easily. Wash the hoods and tentacles and drain well. Place in a

bowl and season well with salt. Cover and refrigerate for about 30 minutes.
2 Combine the flour with a pinch each of salt and cracked pepper in a shallow dish. Fill a deep, heavy-based pan one third full of oil and heat to 180°C (350°F), or until a cube of bread browns in 15 seconds. Coat the squid hoods in flour and deep-fry in batches for about 30–60 seconds, or until light brown and tender. Toss the tentacles in the flour and deep-fry for 20–30 seconds, or until lightly browned and tender. Partially cover the deep-fryer while cooking as the squid tends to splatter. Drain on crumpled paper towels, then transfer to a serving platter and sprinkle with salt. Serve hot with lemon wedges.

FISH TEMPURA

Preparation time: 10 minutes
Total cooking time: 20 minutes
Makes 24

1 sheet nori (dried seaweed)
3 tablespoons tempura flour
500 g (1 lb) skinless fish fillets (eg. snapper,
  bream, haddock, John dory, mirror dory,
  silver dory, ling), cut into bite-sized pieces
1 cup (250 ml/8 oz) iced water
2 cups (250 g/8 oz) tempura flour
oil, for deep-frying

1 Using scissors, cut the nori into tiny squares and combine on a plate with the tempura flour.
2 To make the tempura batter, quickly mix the iced water with the tempura flour. It should still be slightly lumpy. If it is too thick, add more water. Fill a deep, heavy-based pan one third full of oil and heat to 180°C (350°F), or until a cube of bread browns in 15 seconds. The oil is ready when 1/4 teaspoon of batter dropped into the oil keeps its shape, sizzles and rises to the top. Make sure the oil stays at the same temperature and does not get too hot. The fish should cook through as well as browning.
3 Dip the fish, in batches, into the nori and flour, then in the batter. Fry until golden brown, then drain on crumpled paper towels. Season with salt, to taste, and keep warm in a single layer on a baking tray in a very slow 120°C (250°F/Gas 1/2) oven.
NOTE: Buy tempura flour at Asian supermarkets. If unavailable, use 1/2 cup (90 g/3 oz) rice flour and 1 1/2 cups (185 g/6 oz) plain (all-purpose) flour.

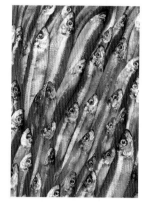

WHITEBAIT
Whitebait are tiny fish, the young of herrings and sprats. They are plentiful in spring and summer, but are also available frozen all year round. Because whitebait are so small, they are best eaten whole. Usually deep-fried, they can also be used in omelettes, fritters or patties. Refrigerate in a covered container that allows them to drain, for up to 2 days. Excess liquid will cause them to sweat. Avoid placing them in a bag. To freeze, drain them and place in a tightly sealed freezer bag for up to 6 months.

OPPOSITE PAGE, FROM TOP: Fried whitebait; Deep-fried squid

FROM THE SHELL Some

foods need little dressing up—they seem to have been born to party. Shellfish are a

wonderful example—drizzle with sauce and serve in the shells nature gave them.

OYSTERS WITH PROSCIUTTO AND BALSAMIC VINEGAR

Place 24 fresh oysters on a baking tray and sprinkle with 2–3 tablespoons of balsamic vinegar. Chop 6 slices of prosciutto and sprinkle over the oysters. Sprinkle with cracked black pepper and place under a hot grill for 1 minute, or until the prosciutto is starting to crisp. Makes 24.

OYSTERS WITH TARRAGON

Remove 24 fresh oysters from their shells. Wash the shells and set aside. Combine the oysters with 1 tablespoon chopped fresh tarragon, 1 small finely chopped spring onion (scallion), 2 teaspoons white wine vinegar, 1 tablespoon lemon juice and 2 tablespoons extra virgin olive oil, cover and refrigerate for 30 minutes. Place the

oyster shells on a plate and spoon an oyster back into each shell. Drizzle with any remaining viniagrette. Makes 24.

SCALLOPS WITH LIME HOLLANDAISE SAUCE

Using a sharp knife, carefully cut 24 scallops from their shells, as cleanly as possible, and remove the veins. Wash the shells in warm water and warm

through on a baking tray in a moderate 180°C (350°F/Gas 4) oven for 5 minutes. Chargrill or fry the scallops for 2–4 minutes, then return to their shells. For the sauce, mix 1 egg yolk and 1 tablespoon lime juice in a food processor for 30 seconds. With the motor running, add 45 g (1½ oz) melted butter in a thin stream. (Beat in a bowl if you prefer.) Transfer to a bowl, add 1 tablespoon snipped chives and season with salt and pepper. Spoon 1 teaspoon over each scallop and serve. Makes 24.

CITRUS SAUCY SCALLOPS

Using a sharp knife, carefully cut 24 scallops from their shells, as cleanly as possible, and remove the veins. Wash the shells in warm water and warm through on a baking tray in a moderate 180°C (350°F/Gas 4) oven for 5 minutes.

Chargrill or fry the scallops for 3 minutes and return to their shells. For the sauce, combine 3 tablespoons lime juice, 1 tablespoon lemon juice, 1 finely chopped red chilli, 1 tablespoon fish sauce, 2 teaspoons sugar, 3 teaspoons chopped fresh coriander (cilantro) and 2 teaspoons chopped fresh mint. Spoon 1 teaspoon over each scallop and serve. Makes 24.

MUSSELS WITH BLOODY MARY SAUCE

Scrub 24 black mussels and remove the beards (discard any mussels which are open and don't close when tapped). Place in a large heavy-based pan with the juice of a lemon and 1 tablespoon water. Cover and steam over medium–low heat for 2–3 minutes, removing them as they open. (Discard any which haven't opened in that time.) Remove and discard the

top shell. Run a small knife along the shell under the mussel to detach it from the shell. Place the mussels in their shells on a baking tray which has been spread with a layer of salt (to keep them level and stop the filling falling out). For the sauce, combine 2 tablespoons vodka, 2 tablespoons tomato juice, 1 tablespoon lemon juice, 2 teaspoons Worcestershire sauce, a dash of Tabasco and ¼ teaspoon celery salt. Spoon 1 teaspoon into each shell and grill for a few seconds, or until the sauce is warm. Serve with a sprinkle of freshly ground black pepper. Makes 24.

FROM LEFT: Oysters with prosciutto and balsamic vinegar; Oysters with tarragon; Scallops with lime hollandaise sauce; Citrus saucy scallops; Mussels with bloody Mary sauce

163

ABOVE: Blackened fish

BLACKENED FISH

Preparation time: 5 minutes
Total cooking time: 6–8 minutes
Serves 6

6 large white fish fillets (eg. blue-eye, snapper,
  ling, warehou, mahi mahi), 2 cm (³⁄₄ inch) thick
125 g (4 oz) unsalted butter, melted
2 tablespoons Cajun spices (see page 165)
2 teaspoons sweet paprika
lemon wedges or halves, to serve

1 Brush each fish fillet liberally with the butter.
2 Combine the Cajun spices and paprika, then
sprinkle thickly over the fish. Use your fingers to
rub the spice mix evenly over the fillets.
3 Heat a large frying pan over high heat. Place
two fillets in the pan and cook for 1–2 minutes.
Turn and cook for another few minutes, until
the fish is cooked and flakes easily. The surface
should be well charred on each side. Add extra
butter if necessary. Cook the remaining fillets.
4 Serve drizzled with any remaining melted
butter. The lemon can be served lightly charred.

NEW ORLEANS OYSTERS

Preparation time: 10 minutes
Total cooking time: 4–6 minutes
Serves 4

24 large fresh oysters, shelled
2 teaspoons Cajun spices (see page 165)
¹⁄₂ teaspoon hot paprika
¹⁄₄ teaspoon dried basil
¹⁄₂ cup (60 g/2 oz) plain (all-purpose) flour
¹⁄₂ cup (125 ml/4 fl oz) oil
45 g (1¹⁄₂ oz) unsalted butter
lemon wedges, to serve
mayonnaise, to serve

1 Dry the oysters on paper towels. In a shallow
dish, mix the Cajun spices, paprika and basil. Set
aside 2 teaspoons of the mixture. Add the flour
to the remaining spice mix and stir thoroughly.
2 Lightly oil 8 thin wooden or metal skewers
and thread 3 oysters onto each. Coat with the
spiced flour, then shake off any excess.
3 Heat the oil and butter in a large frying pan

wide enough to fit the skewers. Fry the oysters over medium heat until golden brown, turning several times, for about 3–4 minutes. Drain on crumpled paper towel. Sprinkle with the reserved spice mix and serve with the lemon wedges and a dish of mayonnaise.

CAJUN 'POPCORN'

Preparation time: 10 minutes +
  30 minutes standing
Total cooking time: 10 minutes
Serves 6

★ ★

750 g (1 1/2 lb) raw prawns (shrimp)
1 egg
1 cup (250 ml/8 fl oz) milk
1/4 cup (35 g/1 1/4 oz) fine cornmeal
3/4 cup (90 g/3 oz) plain (all-purpose) flour
1/2 teaspoon baking powder
1 1/2 teaspoons Cajun spices (see recipe on right)

1/4 teaspoon dried basil
1/2 teaspoon celery salt
oil, for deep-frying

1 Peel the prawns and gently pull out the dark vein from each back, starting at the head end. Pat dry with paper towels.
2 Beat the egg and milk together. In a large bowl, combine the cornmeal, flour, baking powder, Cajun spices, basil and celery salt. Make a well in the centre, gradually add half the beaten egg mixture and whisk to form a smooth paste. Add the remaining egg mixture, mix well and leave to stand for 30 minutes.
3 Fill a deep, heavy-based pan one third full of oil and heat to 180°C (350°F), or until a cube of bread dropped in the oil browns in 15 seconds.
4 Dip the prawns in the batter and allow excess to drain off. Cook in small batches in the oil until crisp and lightly golden. Remove with a slotted spoon or strainer and drain on crumpled paper towel. Serve hot with a sauce of your choice.

CAJUN SPICE MIX
Cajun cuisine originated in Louisiana in America. Its distinctive flavour has been influenced by the French, Spanish, Africans and American Indians. You can make your own Cajun spice mix by mixing together 1 tablespoon each of garlic powder and onion powder, 2 teaspoons each of white pepper and cracked black pepper, 1 1/2 teaspoons cayenne pepper, 2 teaspoons dried thyme and 1/2 teaspoon dried oregano. It can be stored in an airtight jar for up to 3 months.

LEFT: Cajun 'popcorn'

JOHN DORY WITH PRAWNS AND HOT CREAMY DILL SAUCE

Preparation time: 15 minutes
Total cooking time: 20 minutes
Serves 4

12 raw large prawns (shrimp)
4 x 200 g (6¹/₂ oz) John dory fillets

Creamy dill sauce

2¹/₂ cups (600 ml/20 fl oz) fish stock
30 g (1 oz) butter
1 clove garlic, finely chopped
2 tablespoons plain (all-purpose) flour
2 tablespoons cream
1 tablespoon chopped fresh chives
1 tablespoon chopped fresh dill

1 Peel the prawns and pull out the dark vein from each prawn back, starting at the head end.
2 Heat the stock in a saucepan and bring to the boil. Reduce the heat and simmer for 10 minutes, or until the liquid has reduced. You will need 1¹/₂ cups (375 ml/12 fl oz) fish stock.
3 Melt the butter in a small saucepan and add the garlic. Stir in the flour and cook for 1 minute, or until pale and foaming. Remove from the heat and gradually stir in the stock. Return to the heat and stir constantly until the sauce boils and thickens. Reduce the heat and simmer for 1 minute. Remove from the heat and stir in the cream. Season to taste. Keep warm while you cook the fish and prawns.
4 Heat a little oil in a frying pan and cook the fish fillets over medium heat for 2 minutes each side, or until the fish flakes easily when tested with a fork. Transfer to serving plates.
5 Add the prawns to the same pan and cook for 2–3 minutes, or until pink and cooked through.
6 To serve, stir the fresh chives and dill into the hot sauce, then arrange the prawns on top of the fillets and spoon sauce over the top.

RIGHT: John dory with prawns and hot creamy dill sauce

166

FISH MEUNIERE

Preparation time: 5 minutes
Total cooking time: 10 minutes
Serves 4

4 thick white fish fillets (eg. blue-eye, warehou,
   cod, jewfish)
plain (all-purpose) flour, to dust
125 g (4 oz) butter
1–2 tablespoons lemon juice
1 tablespoon chopped fresh parsley

1 Dust the fish lightly with flour and shake off
any excess. Heat a little oil in a pan and cook the
fish for 5–8 minutes each side, until lightly
golden. Transfer to serving plates. Wipe out the
pan with paper towel.
2 Heat the pan over high heat, add the butter
and swirl quickly to melt (the butter will start to
brown). Remove from the heat, immediately
add the lemon juice, parsley and some freshly
ground black pepper, then pour over the fish.
Serve with extra lemon wedges.

NOTE: The cooking time will depend on the
thickness of the fish. This recipe, with its simple
sauce, is suitable for most types and cuts of fish.

GRATED POTATO CAKES WITH SALMON

Coarsely grate 1.5 kg (3 lb) peeled waxy
potatoes, such as desiree, bintji or pontiac.
Rinse in cold water and drain well,
squeezing out any excess moisture. Combine
in a large bowl with a lightly beaten egg and
1 tablespoon of oil. Season with salt and
pepper and stir in 2 tablespoons of plain (all-
purpose) flour. With floured hands, form
into flat patty shapes using 2 tablespoons of
mixture for each. Shallow-fry on both sides,
in a large pan, until golden brown. Drain
on crumpled paper towel. Stack several
warm cakes on top of each other on a
serving plate, top with a small pile of
smoked salmon, a dollop of light sour
cream, a few red onion rings and a sprinkle
of chopped fresh chives. Serves 4–6.

ABOVE: Fish meunière

Pour in enough water to
cover the fish fillets, then
slowly heat the water.

Mix the flaked fish with the
herbs, potato, juice, capers,
gherkin and seasoning.

FISH BURGERS AND WEDGES

Preparation time: 30 minutes + 1 hour chilling
Total cooking time: 25 minutes
Serves 4

500 g (1 lb) skinless white fish fillets
  (eg. flake, ling, redfish, warehou)
2 tablespoons finely chopped fresh parsley
2 tablespoons finely chopped fresh dill
2 tablespoons lemon juice
1 tablespoon drained bottled capers, chopped
2 bottled gherkins, finely chopped
350 g (11 oz) potatoes, cooked and mashed
plain (all-purpose) flour, to dust
1 tablespoon olive oil
4 hamburger buns, split into halves
lettuce leaves
2 Roma (plum) tomatoes, sliced
tartare sauce (see page 194)

Crunchy potato wedges

6 potatoes, unpeeled, cut into wedges
1 tablespoon oil
1/2 teaspoon chicken or vegetable stock powder
1/4 cup (25 g/3/4 oz) dry breadcrumbs
2 teaspoons chopped fresh chives
1 teaspoon celery salt
1/4 teaspoon garlic powder
1/2 teaspoon chopped fresh rosemary

1 Place the fish in a frying pan and just cover
with water. Slowly heat, making sure the water
doesn't boil. Cover and cook over low heat until
just cooked. Drain the fish on paper towels,
transfer to a bowl and flake with a fork, removing
any bones. Add the parsley, dill, juice, capers,
gherkins and potato, season with pepper and salt
and mix well. Shape into 4 patties. Dust with
flour and refrigerate on a plate for 1 hour.
2 Heat the oil in a large non-stick frying pan,
add the patties and cook for 5–6 minutes on each
side, or until well browned and cooked through.
3 Grill the buns and butter if you wish. On each
base, put some lettuce, tomato, a patty and some
tartare sauce. Top and serve.
4 For the wedges, preheat the oven to moderately
hot 200°C (400°F/Gas 6). Pat the potato dry
with paper towels and toss with the oil.
Combine the remaining wedge ingredients and
toss with the wedges. Spread on greased baking
trays and bake for 40 minutes, or until golden.

PRAWN BURGERS WITH COCKTAIL SAUCE

Preparation time: 35 minutes + 10 minutes chilling
Total cooking time: 5–10 minutes
Serves 4

12 raw large prawns (shrimp)
2 tablespoons lemon juice
1 tablespoon sesame seeds
1 1/2 cups (120 g/4 oz) fresh white breadcrumbs
2 tablespoons chopped fresh coriander
  (cilantro)
1 egg, lightly beaten
2 teaspoons chilli sauce
plain (all-purpose) flour, to dust
olive oil, for frying
1/3 cup (80 g/2 3/4 oz) whole-egg mayonnaise
1 spring onion (scallion), finely chopped
1 tablespoon tomato sauce
1 teaspoon Worcestershire sauce
chilli sauce, to taste, extra
1 tablespoon lemon juice, extra
4 hamburger buns, split into halves
rocket (arugula) leaves
1 firm ripe avocado, thinly sliced

1 Peel the prawns and pull out the dark vein
from each prawn back, starting at the head end.
Flatten slightly to open out. Mix with the juice.
2 Combine the sesame seeds, breadcrumbs and
coriander on a sheet of greaseproof paper.
Combine the egg and chilli sauce in a bowl.
Dust the prawns in the flour and shake off the
excess. Dip in the egg mixture, then press firmly
in breadcrumbs. Place on a tray covered with
baking paper. Cover and chill for 10 minutes.
3 Heat a little oil in a frying pan. Cook the
prawns in batches over medium heat 2–3 minutes
each side, or until crisp and golden brown.
Remove and drain on crumpled paper towels.
4 Combine the mayonnaise, spring onion,
tomato and Worcestershire sauces, extra chilli
sauce and extra lemon juice in a bowl.
5 Grill the buns and butter if you wish. On each
base, put some rocket and avocado. Sprinkle
with freshly ground black pepper. Add the
prawns, a dollop of the cocktail sauce and finally,
the bun top.

*OPPOSITE PAGE: Fish
burgers and wedges*

SEAFOOD PLATTERS

Presentation is vital when serving seafood platters. Keep the hot and cold seafood separate. Serve with wedges of lemon or lime and the sauces of your choice.

PLANNING AND SERVING

We have suggested quantities of seafood required to assemble platters for 4 people. Most of the preparation can be done before your guests arrive. If it is a hot day, chill the platter you will be using for the cold seafood, or serve it on a bed of crushed ice. Serve the platters with bowls of tartare sauce (see page 194), sour cream mixed with sweet chilli sauce, or

soy sauce mixed with a little honey. And don't forget lime and lemon wedges, finger bowls and maybe wedges or chips.

COLD PLATTER

You will need 500 g (1 lb) cooked tiger prawns (shrimp), 2 quartered cooked crabs, 12 oysters and 100 g (3½ oz) smoked salmon. You could also add 2 halved cooked lobsters.

HOT PLATTER

A hot platter can be very simple, using prepared, ready to cook, deep-fried calamari rings, battered fish and crumbed prawn (shrimp) cutlets, found in the freezer at the fishmongers or supermarket. They don't need thawing before cooking. Or, you can stun your guests by combining some of the easy dishes with your choice of the following recipes. For

deep-frying, fill a deep heavy-based saucepan one third full of oil and heat to 180°C (350°F), or until a cube of bread browns in 15 seconds. Don't cook too many pieces at once or the oil temperature will lower and the batter will be soggy. Skim crumbs from the surface as you go.

PRAWNS AND SQUID

Combine 2 cups (120 g/4 oz) Japanese breadcrumbs and 1 tablespoon chopped fresh parsley. Lightly beat 2 eggs and stir in 1 teaspoon sesame oil and 1 crushed garlic clove. Season 1 cup (125 g/4 oz) plain (all-purpose) flour. Peel, devein and butterfly 1 kg (2 lb) raw prawns (shrimp) and cut 4 squid hoods into rings. Coat the prawns and rings in the flour. Dip, in

batches, into the egg, then coat in the breadcrumbs, shaking off any excess. Lower batches of prawns into the oil and deep-fry until golden. Drain on paper towels. Repeat with the squid.

JAPANESE OYSTERS

Place 12 fresh oysters in a bamboo steamer, top with thin slivers of spring onion (scallion) and grated fresh ginger. Drizzle with teriyaki marinade. Cover and steam for 4 minutes, or until heated through.

CRISPY LEMON FISH STRIPS

Sift ½ cup (60 g/2 oz) plain (all-purpose) flour into a bowl, make a well in the centre and whisk in ½ cup (125 ml/4 fl oz) soda water with the grated rind from 1 lemon. Cut 2 skinless snapper fillets into thin

strips. Dust lightly with seasoned flour and dip, in batches, into the batter, allowing any excess to drip off. Carefully lower into the oil and deep-fry until golden. Drain on crumpled paper towels.

PROSCIUTTO-WRAPPED SCALLOPS

Rinse 16 cleaned scallops (without roe) and pat dry. Cut 4 thin slices of prosciutto into quarters, each large enough to enclose a scallop. Wrap around the scallops and thread in pairs onto small wooden skewers. Grill under a preheated grill, or on a barbecue for 5 minutes, turning a couple of times during cooking.

FROM LEFT: Cold seafood platter; Hot seafood platter

171

SALT-AND-PEPPER SQUID

Preparation time: 30 minutes + marinating
Total cooking time: 10 minutes
Serves 6

★★

1 kg (2 lb) squid hoods, halved lengthways

1 cup (250 ml/8 fl oz) lemon juice

2 cups (250 g/8 oz) cornflour (cornstarch)

1 1/2 tablespoons salt

1 tablespoon ground white pepper

2 teaspoons caster (superfine) sugar

4 egg whites, lightly beaten

oil, for deep-frying

lemon wedges, to serve

fresh coriander (cilantro) leaves, to garnish

1 Open out the squid hoods, wash and pat dry. Lay on a chopping board with the inside facing upwards. Score a fine diamond pattern on the squid, being careful not to cut all the way through. Cut into pieces about 5 x 3 cm (2 x 1 1/4 inches). Place in a flat non-metallic dish and pour the lemon juice over. Cover and refrigerate for 15 minutes. Drain and pat dry.

2 Combine the cornflour, salt, white pepper and sugar in a bowl. Dip the squid into the egg white and dust with the flour mixture, shaking off any excess.

3 Fill a deep heavy-based pan one third full of oil and heat to 180°C (350°F), or until a cube of bread dropped into the oil turns golden brown in 15 seconds. Deep-fry the squid, in batches, for 1–2 minutes, or until the squid turns white and curls. Drain on crumpled paper towels. Serve immediately, with lemon wedges and garnish with coriander leaves or sprigs.

VARIATION: To make Salt and pepper prawns (shrimp), mix together an egg white and 2 crushed garlic cloves in a bowl and add 1 kg (2 lb) peeled and deveined (with the tails intact) raw prawns. Cover and refrigerate for 30 minutes. Put 1/2 cup (90 g/3 oz) rice flour, 1 tablespoon ground Sichuan peppercorns, 1 teaspoon ground white pepper, 2 teaspoons ground sea salt and 1 teaspoon caster (superfine) sugar in a bowl and combine well. Coat each prawn in the flour, then deep-fry as described above for 1 minute, or until lightly golden.

ABOVE: Salt-and-pepper squid

BACALAO CROQUETTES WITH SKORDALIA

Preparation time: 50 minutes +
   8–12 hours soaking
Total cooking time: 55 minutes
Makes 24

400 g (13 oz) dried salt cod (bacalao)
300 g (10 oz) floury potatoes, unpeeled
1 small brown pickling onion, grated
2 tablespoons chopped fresh flat-leaf
   (Italian) parsley
1 egg, lightly beaten
1/2 teaspoon cracked pepper
oil, for deep-frying

Skordalia

250 g (8 oz) floury potatoes, unpeeled
2 cloves garlic, crushed
1 tablespoon white wine vinegar
2 tablespoons olive oil

1 Put the cod in a large bowl, cover with cold water and soak for 8–12 hours, changing the water three times. This will remove the excess salt from the cod. Drain on paper towels.
2 To make the skordalia, boil or steam the potatoes until tender, remove the peel and mash in a large bowl. Cool and add the garlic, vinegar and oil. Season with salt and black pepper, then mix with a fork. Set aside.
3 Put the cod in a saucepan, cover with water, bring to the boil, then reduce the heat and simmer for 15 minutes. Drain on crumpled paper towels. When cool enough to handle, remove the skin and bones from the cod and flake with your fingers into a large bowl.
4 Meanwhile, boil or steam the potatoes until tender, then peel and mash. Add to the cod with the onion, parsley, egg and pepper. Mix well with a wooden spoon to form a thick mixture. Taste, then season with salt if necessary.
5 Fill a deep heavy-based pan one third full of oil and heat to 180°C (350°F), or until a cube of bread dropped into the oil browns in 15 seconds. Drop level tablespoons of the mixture into the oil and cook in batches for 2–3 minutes, or until well browned. Drain on crumpled paper towels. Serve hot with skordalia.

BELOW: Bacalao croquettes with skordalia

FRITTO MISTO DI MARE

Preparation time: 30 minutes
Total cooking time: 12 minutes
Serves 4

★★☆

1 cup (125 g/4 oz) self-raising flour

¹/₄ cup (30 g/1 oz) cornflour (cornstarch)

1 tablespoon oil

8 raw large prawns (shrimp)

8 scallops

12 fresh sardines

500 g (1 lb) skinless white fish fillets (eg. perch, snapper, ling, John dory), cut into short strips

1 squid hood, cut into rings

plain (all-purpose) flour, for coating

oil, for deep-frying

tartare sauce (see page 194), to serve

lemon wedges, to serve

ABOVE: Fritto
misto di mare

1 Sift the flour and cornflour, with some salt and pepper, into a bowl and make a well in the centre. Combine the tablespoon of oil with 1 cup (250 ml/8 fl oz) water and gradually whisk into the flour to make a smooth lump-free batter.

2 Peel the prawns and gently pull out the dark vein from each prawn back, starting at the head end. Slice or pull off any vein, membrane or hard white muscle from the scallops.

3 To prepare the sardines, split them open down the belly, remove the gut, then clean with salted water. Cut off the head. Place skin-side-up on a work surface, flatten with the palm of your hand, then turn over and pull out the backbone with your fingers and cut at the tail with scissors.

4 Dry the prepared seafood with paper towels, then dip in flour and shake off the excess.

5 Fill a deep heavy-based pan one third full of oil and heat to 180°C (350°F), or until a cube of bread dropped into the oil browns in 15 seconds. Coat a few pieces of seafood at a time with batter and deep-fry each batch for 2–3 minutes, or until golden brown and crisp. Remove with tongs or a slotted spoon, drain on crumpled paper towels and keep warm. Serve with tartare sauce and lemon wedges.

IN ADVANCE: The seafood can be prepared several hours ahead. Cover and refrigerate.

BARBECUED PRAWNS WITH SWEET CUCUMBER VINEGAR

Preparation time: 30 minutes
Total cooking time: 5 minutes
Serves 4

Sweet cucumber vinegar

1/4 cup (60 ml/2 fl oz) white wine vinegar

1/3 cup (90 g/3 oz) caster (superfine) sugar

2 tablespoons lime juice

2 tablespoons fish sauce

1 long red chilli, seeded, thinly sliced

1 long green chilli, seeded, thinly sliced

2 spring onions (scallions), diagonally sliced

1 Lebanese (short) cucumber, peeled, halved, seeded and thinly sliced

2 tablespoons chopped fresh coriander (cilantro)

24 raw prawns (shrimp)

1 Combine the vinegar and caster sugar in a pan and bring to the boil. Stir, remove from the heat and cool. Stir in the lime juice, fish sauce, chilli, spring onion, cucumber and coriander.
2 Cook the unpeeled prawns on a chargrill or barbecue plate over medium heat for 1–2 minutes each side, or until pink and cooked through. Pour the sauce over the prawns.

HERBED SCAMPI WITH CIDER SAUCE

Preparation time: 15 minutes +
   1 hour freezing + 1 hour marinating
Total cooking time: 5–10 minutes
Serves 4

12 raw scampi or Balmain bugs

1/4 cup (60 ml/2 fl oz) olive oil

1/2 cup (125 ml/4 fl oz) lemon juice

2 cloves garlic, crushed

5 tablespoons finely chopped fresh parsley

2 tablespoons finely chopped fresh dill

Cider sauce

1/4 cup (60 ml/2 fl oz) apple cider

30 g (1 oz) butter

1 Freeze live bugs for 1 hour to immobilize, then cut bugs or scampi in half lengthways. Place in a single layer in a shallow non-metallic dish. Combine the olive oil, lemon juice, garlic, parsley and dill, and pour over the seafood. Cover and refrigerate for at least 1 hour.
2 Cook the seafood on a chargrill or barbecue plate, shell-side-down, for 2 minutes. Turn and cook for another 2 minutes, or until tender. (Bugs may take longer to cook.) Transfer to a serving platter.
3 Simmer the apple cider in a small saucepan until reduced by two thirds. Reduce the heat and add the butter, stirring until melted. Remove from the heat, pour over the scampi and serve.

ABOVE: Barbecued prawns with sweet cucumber vinegar

POACHED WHOLE SNAPPER

Trim the fins off the fish with kitchen scissors.

After blanching the lettuce leaves, use to wrap the fish.

Put the wrapped fish into a deep-sided baking dish.

POACHED WHOLE SNAPPER

Preparation time: 15 minutes
Total cooking time: 40 minutes
Serves 4-6

10–15 cos (romaine) lettuce leaves
1.25 kg (2½ lb) whole snapper, gutted and scaled
2 onions, thinly sliced
1 lemon, thinly sliced
⅔ cup (170 ml/5½ fl oz) fish stock
⅔ cup (170ml/5½ fl oz) white wine
12 whole black peppercorns
1 bay leaf
155 g (5 oz) unsalted butter, chopped
1 tablespoon lime juice

1 Preheat the oven to moderate 180°C (350°F/Gas 4). Place the lettuce in a large bowl, cover with boiling water to soften, then drain well and refresh in cold water.
2 Trim the fins off the fish with kitchen scissors. Fill the cavity of the fish with one of the sliced onions and the lemon. Wrap the fish completely in the lettuce leaves and place into a deep-sided baking dish.
3 Pour the stock and wine over the fish. Add the remaining onion, peppercorns and bay leaf to the dish, then dot the lettuce with 30 g (1 oz) of the butter. Cover tightly with foil and bake for 30 minutes, or until the flesh flakes in the thickest part when tested with a fork.
4 Remove the fish from the dish, transfer to a serving dish and keep warm. Strain the liquid into a saucepan, then boil for about 10 minutes, or until reduced by half. Remove from the heat and whisk in the remaining butter a little at a time, whisking constantly until the mixture has thickened slightly. Stir in the lime juice and season to taste with salt and pepper. Serve on the side.
NOTE: You can substitute red emperor, coral trout or murray cod for the snapper.

POACHED SNAPPER WITH FRESH TOMATO SAUCE

Preparation time: 20 minutes
Total cooking time: 45 minutes
Serves 4

1 kg (2 lb) whole snapper, gutted and scaled
4 ripe tomatoes
1 onion, finely chopped
4 spring onions (scallions), thinly sliced
2 tablespoons chopped fresh parsley
1¼ cups (315 ml/10 fl oz) fish stock
60 g (2 oz) butter
1 tablespoon plain (all-purpose) flour

1 Preheat the oven to moderately hot 190°C (375°F/Gas 5). Wash the fish in cold water, pat dry inside and out with paper towels.
2 Score a cross in the base of each tomato. Place in a heatproof bowl and cover with boiling water. Leave for 30 seconds, then transfer to cold water. Peel, then cut each in half and remove the core. Scrape out the seeds with a teaspoon and roughly chop the flesh.
3 Lightly grease a baking dish, large enough to hold the fish, with butter. Spread half the tomato, onion and spring onion over the base. Place the fish over the top and cover with the remaining vegetables. Sprinkle with half the parsley, then pour in the stock. Dot the fish with half the butter.
4 Bake for 30 minutes, or until the fish is cooked and flakes easily when tested with a fork.
5 Carefully lift the fish out of the dish, drain well, place on a serving dish and keep warm. Transfer the cooking liquid and vegetables to a small pan. Taste and adjust the seasoning. Bring to the boil and simmer for 5 minutes, or until reduced by a quarter.
6 Make a paste with the remaining butter and the flour in a small bowl. Gradually add to the pan and simmer, whisking until the sauce has thickened. Add salt and pepper, to taste, and pour over the fish. Garnish with the remaining chopped parsley.
NOTE: You can also use red emperor, coral trout or murray cod for this recipe.

OPPOSITE PAGE, FROM TOP: Poached snapper with fresh tomato sauce; Poached whole snapper

MUSSELS WITH LEMON GRASS, BASIL AND WINE

Preparation time: 30 minutes
Total cooking time: 15 minutes
Serves 4-6

1 kg (2 lb) small black mussels
1 tablespoon oil
1 onion, chopped
4 cloves garlic, chopped
2 stems lemon grass, white part only, sliced
1–2 fresh red chillies, seeded, chopped
1 cup (250 ml/8 fl oz) white wine or water
1 tablespoon fish sauce
1 cup (50 g/1¾ oz) fresh Thai basil leaves, roughly chopped

1 Scrub the mussels with a stiff brush and pull out the hairy beards. Discard any broken mussels, or open ones that don't close when tapped on the bench. Rinse well.
2 Heat the oil in a large pan. Add the onion, garlic, lemon grass and chilli, and cook for 4 minutes over low heat, stirring occasionally.

Add the wine and fish sauce and continue to cook for 3 minutes.
3 Add the mussels to the pan and toss well. Cover, increase the heat and cook for 4–5 minutes, or until the mussels open. Discard any unopened mussels. Add the basil; toss and serve with rice.

FISH IN GINGER BROTH

Preparation time: 5 minutes
Total cooking time: 15 minutes
Serves 4

1 tablespoon oil
8 spring onions (scallions), sliced diagonally
2 tablespoons finely chopped fresh ginger
4 tablespoons fish sauce
4 tablespoons grated palm sugar or brown sugar
4 x 200 g (6½ oz) salmon or ocean trout cutlets or fillets
2 tablespoons lime juice
200 g (6½ oz) frozen baby green peas
fresh coriander (cilantro) leaves, to garnish

ABOVE: Mussels with lemon grass, basil and wine

1 Heat the oil in a large frying pan, add the spring onion and ginger and cook over low heat for 2 minutes, stirring occasionally. Add the fish sauce, sugar and 1.5 litres (48 fl oz) water and bring to the boil. Reduce the heat, add the fish and poach gently for 3–4 minutes, or until the fish is just cooked and flakes easily when tested with a fork. Lift the fish out with a slotted spatula and put in a warm shallow bowl. Cover with foil to keep warm.

2 Bring the liquid in the pan to the boil, reduce the heat and simmer until reduced by half. Add the lime juice.

3 Cook the baby peas in a pan of boiling water until tender.

4 For serving, put the fish on plates and ladle the broth over the top. Serve with the peas. Garnish the dish with the coriander leaves.

STEAMED FISH CUTLETS WITH GINGER AND CHILLI

Preparation time: 15 minutes
Total cooking time: 10 minutes
Serves 4

4 medium-sized firm white fish cutlets
5 cm (2 inch) piece fresh ginger, shredded
2 cloves garlic, chopped
2 teaspoons chopped fresh red chillies
2 tablespoons chopped fresh coriander (cilantro) stalks
3 spring onions (scallions), shredded
2 tablespoons lime juice

1 Line a bamboo steamer basket with banana leaves or baking paper to prevent sticking.

2 Arrange the fish in the basket and top with the ginger, garlic, chilli and coriander stalks. Cover and steam over a wok or pan of boiling water for 8–10 minutes. Sprinkle the spring onion and lime juice over the fish. Cover and steam for 30 seconds, or until the fish flakes easily. Serve.

STEAMING FISH
To prepare for steaming fish, fill a wok or large pan about one third full of water. Before you bring the water to the boil, stand the steamer over the water to check that you have the correct amount. The base of the steamer should not touch the water. If you have too much water, it will boil up into the food. If you have too little, it will boil dry. When the water is boiling, place the steamer with the food in it over the top, cover the wok or pan and maintain the heat so that the water continues to boil rapidly. Be careful when you lift the lid, that you don't get a blast of steam.

LEFT: Steamed fish cutlets with ginger and chilli

JAPANESE-STYLE
SALMON PARCELS

Cut the celery sticks into short lengths, then cut into thin strips.

Arrange celery and spring onion strips, then ginger slices, on top of the fish.

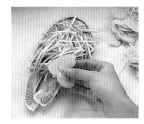

Wrap the salmon in baking paper, tightly folding the sides to seal in the juices.

JAPANESE-STYLE SALMON PARCELS

Preparation time: 40 minutes
Total cooking time: 20 minutes
Serves 4

2 teaspoons sesame seeds

4 x 150 g (5 oz) salmon cutlets or fillets

2.5 cm (1 inch) piece fresh ginger

2 sticks celery

4 spring onions (scallions)

1/4 teaspoon dashi granules

1/4 cup (60 ml/2 fl oz) mirin

2 tablespoons tamari

1 Cut baking paper into four squares large enough to enclose the salmon steaks. Preheat the oven to very hot 230°C (450°F/Gas 8). Stir the sesame seeds over low heat in a small pan until lightly browned, then remove from the pan.

2 Wash the salmon and pat dry with paper towels. Place a salmon cutlet in the centre of each paper square.

3 Cut the ginger into paper-thin slices. Slice the celery and spring onions into long thin strips. Arrange a bundle of the prepared strips and several slices of ginger on each salmon steak.

4 Combine the dashi granules, mirin and tamari in a small saucepan. Stir gently over low heat until the granules dissolve. Drizzle over each parcel, sprinkle with sesame seeds and carefully wrap the salmon, folding in the sides to seal in all the juices. Arrange the parcels in a bamboo steamer over a pan of simmering water and steam for about 15 minutes. (The paper will puff up when the fish is cooked.) Serve immediately with boiled rice.

NOTES: You can use ocean trout as a substitute for this recipe.

Dashi, mirin and tamari are all available from Japanese food stores.

ABOVE: Japanese-style salmon parcels

STEAMED SCALLOPS

Preparation time: 20 minutes
Total cooking time: 10 minutes
Serves 4

1 small red pepper (capsicum)
90 g (3 oz) butter
1 tablespoon chopped fresh chives
2 teaspoons Dijon mustard
1/4 teaspoon cracked black pepper
2 teaspoons lime juice
24 scallops on the shell
6 spring onions (scallions), cut into long thin strips

1 Cut the red pepper into quarters and remove the seeds and membrane. Cook, skin-side-up, under a hot grill until the skin blackens and blisters. Cool in a plastic bag, then peel. Purée the flesh until smooth.
2 Beat the butter in a small bowl until light, then beat in the chives, mustard, pepper, lime juice and red pepper purée. Set aside.
3 Remove the scallops and slice or pull off any vein, membrane or hard white mussel from each.

Place a few strips of spring onion over each shell and top with the scallop. Place the scallops in a single layer in a bamboo or metal steamer. Place over a large pan of simmering water and steam in batches for 2–3 minutes. Transfer to a warmed serving platter while cooking the remaining scallops. Top with a dollop of butter. The butter will melt from the heat of the scallops. Serve.

STEAMED PRAWN ROLLS

Unroll 4 fresh rice noodle rolls (available from Asian supermarkets) and use a sharp knife to cut each in half. Peel and devein 24 raw prawns (shrimp). Place 3 prawns, a sprinkle of finely chopped fresh ginger and garlic and some strips of spring onion (scallion) and shredded Chinese broccoli leaves on one long edge. Fold in the ends and roll up like a spring roll. Line a bamboo steamer with baking paper and steam a few rolls over simmering water for about 10 minutes, or until the prawns are pink and cooked through. Cover with foil while cooking the remaining rolls. Serve with a bowl of light soy sauce for dipping. Serves 4.

BELOW: Steamed scallops

MARINADES & BASTES

Add a little extra zest to your barbecued seafood by using one of these tangy

marinades or spicy bastes.

SPICED YOGHURT MARINADE
(For firm-fleshed skinless fish fillets—
snapper, bream, ocean perch, flake.)
Combine 400 g (13 oz) natural yoghurt,
1 tablespoon each of grated fresh ginger,
ground cumin, ground cinnamon,
ground coriander and ground mace, add
1–2 tablespoons each of grated lime rind
and juice and 2 tablespoons chopped
fresh mint. Add 1 kg (2 lb) fish fillets,

cover and refrigerate for 3 hours. Cook
on a preheated barbecue hotplate until
tender. Serves 4–6.

SWEET AND SPICY
BASTING SAUCE
(For yabbies, bugs and scampi.)
Combine 1 cup (250 ml/8 fl oz) sweet
chilli sauce, 2 crushed cloves garlic,
1–2 tablespoons lemon juice, 1 tablespoon

peanut oil, 50 g (1¾ oz) melted butter
and 2 tablespoons chopped fresh coriander
(cilantro) in a large jug. Toss 1 kg
(2 lb) yabby, bug or scampi meat in
1 tablespoon oil and cook in batches on a
preheated barbecue hotplate, turning and
basting frequently with the sauce. Serve
with any leftover sauce. Serves 4–6.

LIME AND PEPPERCORN MARINADE

(For prawns (shrimp), fish steaks and cutlets—tuna, swordfish, blue-eye, salmon.) Stir-fry 1 cup (60 g/2 oz) Szechwan or black peppercorns in a wok until fragrant. Transfer to a mortar and pestle or spice grinder, add 4 chopped Asian shallots and crush together. Transfer to a shallow glass dish and add 1/3 cup (80 ml/2 3/4 fl oz) lime juice, 1 tablespoon salt, 1 teaspoon sesame oil and 1/4 cup (60 ml/2 fl oz) peanut oil. Add 1 kg (2 lb) firm white fish fillets or 1 kg (2 lb) peeled, deveined prawns (shrimp) with tails intact. Cover; chill for 3 hours. Cook on a preheated barbecue hotplate in batches until the seafood is cooked through. If you are using tuna or salmon, don't overcook it or it will be dry. Serves 4–6.

GARLIC MARINADE

(For prawns (shrimp) and fish.) Combine 6 crushed cloves garlic, 1 cup (250 ml/8 fl oz) extra virgin olive oil, 1 tablespoon lemon juice and chopped fresh dill in a shallow dish. Add 1 kg (2 lb) cubed firm white fish or 1 kg (2 lb) peeled, deveined prawns (shrimp). Coat in the marinade, cover and chill overnight. Return to room temperature, thread onto skewers and cook on a hot barbecue grill or hotplate until cooked through. Serves 4–6.

THAI MARINADE

(For octopus.) Combine 1/2 cup (125 ml/4 fl oz) fish sauce, 4 finely shredded makrut (kaffir) lime leaves, 2–3 tablespoons grated palm sugar, juice and rind of 2 limes and 1 teaspoon sesame oil. Add 1 kg (2 lb) cleaned octopus and marinate overnight. Drain well. Cook over very high heat on a barbecue grill, turning frequently, for 3 minutes or until cooked. Serves 4–6.

TEXAN BARBECUE BASTING SAUCE

(For all shellfish.) Combine 1 cup (250 ml/8 fl oz) tomato sauce, 6 splashes of Tabasco, 3 chopped rehydrated chipotle chillies, 1 tablespoon each of vinegar and oil in a bowl. Use to baste while cooking 1 kg (2 lb) prawns (shrimp), bugs or yabbies. Serves 4–6.

CLOCKWISE, FROM TOP LEFT: Spiced yoghurt marinade; Lime and peppercorn marinade; Thai marinade; Texan barbecue basting sauce; Garlic marinade; Sweet and spicy basting sauce

INDIAN STEAMED FISH

Trim off the fins and tail with scissors.

Make several deep cuts through the thickest part of the fish on both sides.

INDIAN STEAMED FISH

Preparation time: 20 minutes
Total cooking time: 20 minutes
Serves 2–4

500 g (1 lb) whole white-fleshed fish (eg. bream, ocean perch, whiting, snapper), cleaned, scaled
15 g (1/2 oz) toasted almonds
2 bay leaves
1/2 green pepper (capsicum), sliced
1 tablespoon oil
1 1/4 cups (315 g/10 oz) natural yoghurt
1/2 teaspoon garam masala
1/2 teaspoon sugar

1 Wash the fish and pat dry inside and out with paper towels. Cut off the fins and tail. Make several deep diagonal cuts through the thickest part of the flesh on both sides, then put in a steamer lined with banana leaves or baking paper.
2 Combine the remaining ingredients and spoon over the fish. Steam the fish over a saucepan of simmering water for 20 minutes, or until the fish flakes easily when tested with a fork.

RED EMPEROR POACHED IN COCONUT MILK

Preparation time: 20 minutes
Total cooking time: 30–40 minutes
Serves 4

1 litre (32 fl oz) coconut milk
2 teaspoons grated fresh ginger
3 small red chillies, finely chopped
1 tablespoon chopped fresh coriander (cilantro) roots and stems
6 red Asian shallots, finely chopped
6 makrut (kaffir) lime leaves, shredded
2 stems lemon grass, white part only, sliced
2 teaspoons grated lime rind
2 cups (500 ml/16 fl oz) fish stock
1/3 cup (80 ml/2 3/4 fl oz) fish sauce
1/3 cup (80 ml/2 3/4 fl oz) lime juice, strained
4 x 250 g (8 oz) red emperor fillets, skin on
coriander (cilantro) leaves, to garnish
1 small red chilli, cut in long strips, to garnish
2 makrut (kaffir) lime leaves, shredded, to garnish

1 Bring the coconut milk to the boil in a saucepan and boil for 3 minutes. Add the ginger, chilli, coriander roots and stems, shallots, lime leaves, lemon grass and lime rind and bring back to the boil. Add the fish stock and fish sauce and simmer for 15 minutes. Pass through a fine strainer and add the lime juice. Taste and add extra fish sauce if necessary.
2 Heat the sauce in a wide-based frying pan and when it comes to the boil add the fish, then reduce the heat and simmer very gently for 10–15 minutes, or until just cooked through.
3 Carefully transfer the fish to a serving platter. Serve with some of the liquid and a sprinkling of coriander, chilli and shreds of lime leaf.
NOTE: You can also use coral trout, snapper or murray cod.

POACHED FILLETS IN DILL SAUCE

Preparation time: 15 minutes
Total cooking time: 20 minutes
Serves 4

500 g (1 lb) skinless fish fillets (eg. groper, ocean perch, snapper, blue-eye)
1 onion, sliced
1 small bay leaf
1 tablespoon butter
1 tablespoon plain (all-purpose) flour
1/2 cup (125 ml/4 fl oz) sour cream
2 tablespoons chopped fresh dill

1 Remove any bones from the fish. Combine 2 1/2 cups (625 ml/20 fl oz) water with the onion and bay leaf in a large frying pan. Bring to the boil and reduce the heat to low. Add the fish and poach over gentle heat for 5 minutes, or until cooked and the fish flakes easily when tested with a fork. Remove the fish with a fish slice and keep warm on a serving dish.
2 Strain the cooking liquid and reserve 1 cup (250 ml/8 fl oz). Melt the butter in a small pan over low heat. Stir in the flour and cook for 1 minute, or until pale and foaming. Remove from the heat and gradually stir in the reserved stock. Return to the heat and stir until the sauce boils and thickens. Reduce the heat and simmer for 2 minutes. Remove from the heat and stir in the sour cream and dill. Add salt and white pepper. Serve the sauce over fish, with extra dill.

OPPOSITE PAGE: Red emperor poached in coconut milk

ABOVE: Sole Veronique

SOLE VERONIQUE

Preparation time: 45 minutes
Total cooking time: 20 minutes
Serves 4

12 sole fillets or 3 whole sole, filleted
  and skinned
1 cup (250 ml/8 fl oz) fish stock
1/4 cup (60 ml/2 fl oz) white wine
1 French shallot, thinly sliced
1 bay leaf
6 black peppercorns
2 sprigs fresh parsley
3 teaspoons butter
3 teaspoons plain (all-purpose) flour
1/2 cup (125 ml/4 fl oz) milk
1/4 cup (60 ml/2 fl oz) cream
125 g (4 oz) seedless white grapes,
  peeled

1 Preheat the oven to moderate 180°C (350°F/ Gas 4). Roll the fillets into coils with the skin side on the inside. Secure the coils with toothpicks and place side-by-side in a well-greased shallow ovenproof dish.

2 Combine the stock, wine, shallot, bay leaf, peppercorns and parsley in a jug and pour over the fish. Cover with greased foil and bake for 15 minutes, or until the fish flakes when tested with a fork. Carefully lift the rolls out of the liquid with a slotted spoon and transfer to another dish. Cover and keep warm.

3 Pour the cooking liquid into a saucepan and boil for about 2 minutes, or until reduced by half, then strain through a fine strainer.

4 In a clean pan, melt the butter, add the flour and stir for 1 minute, or until pale and foaming. Remove from the heat and gradually stir in the combined milk, cream and reduced cooking liquid. Return to the heat and stir until the mixture boils and thickens. Season to taste, add the grapes, then stir until heated through. Serve the sauce over the fish.

NOTE: You can substitute flounder for the sole.

GLAZED GRILLED FISH FILLETS

Preparation time: 10 minutes +
   1 hour marinating
Total cooking time: 8 minutes
Serves 4

2 tablespoons olive oil

2 tablespoons lemon juice

2 tablespoons fruit chutney

1 tablespoon honey

1 tablespoon chopped fresh coriander (cilantro)

2 cloves garlic, crushed

4 firm-fleshed white fish fillets (eg. snapper, flounder, John dory, bream, leatherjacket)

1 Combine the olive oil, lemon juice, fruit chutney, honey, fresh coriander and garlic in a small bowl.
2 Place the fish fillets in a flat non-metallic dish and pour the oil mixture over the fish. Cover and refrigerate for 1 hour.
3 Preheat the grill to high and put the fish fillets on a lightly oiled grill tray. Cook the fish, brushing with the remaining marinade occasionally, for about 5 minutes each side, or until the flesh flakes easily when tested with a fork.

BARBECUED SALMON CUTLETS WITH SWEET CUCUMBER DRESSING

Preparation time: 15 minutes
Total cooking time: 5 minutes
Serves 4

Sweet cucumber dressing

2 small Lebanese (short) cucumbers, peeled, seeded and finely diced

1 red onion, finely chopped

1 fresh red chilli, finely chopped

2 tablespoons pickled ginger, shredded

2 tablespoons rice wine vinegar

1/2 teaspoon sesame oil

4 salmon cutlets

1 sheet toasted nori (dried seaweed), cut into thin strips

1 Combine the cucumber, onion, chilli, ginger, rice wine vinegar and sesame oil in a medium bowl, cover and stand at room temperature while cooking the salmon.
2 Preheat a barbecue flatplate and lightly brush with oil. Cook the salmon on the barbecue for about 2 minutes on each side, or until cooked as desired. Be careful you do not overcook the fish or it will be dry—it should be still just pink in the centre. Serve the salmon topped with the cucumber dressing. Sprinkle the top with strips of toasted nori.
NOTES: Ocean trout cutlets can also be used in this recipe.
   An easy way to cut the nori into thin strips is to cut it with clean, dry scissors.

ABOVE: Glazed grilled fish fillets

LOBSTER THERMIDOR

Use a sharp knife to cut the lobster in half lengthways through the shell.

Pull the meat out of the shell and wash the head and shell halves.

Cut the lobster meat into bite-sized pieces after patting dry.

Place the prepared lobster under the grill until lightly browned.

LOBSTER THERMIDOR

Preparation time: 25 minutes
Total cooking time: 5–10 minutes
Serves 2

⋆⋆

1 cooked medium lobster
80 g (2¾ oz) butter
4 spring onions (scallions), finely chopped
2 tablespoons plain (all-purpose) flour
½ teaspoon dry mustard
2 tablespoons white wine or sherry
1 cup (250 ml/8 fl oz) milk
¼ cup (60 ml/2 fl oz) cream
1 tablespoon chopped fresh parsley
60 g (2 oz) Gruyère cheese, grated

1 Using a sharp knife, cut the lobster in half lengthways through the shell. Lift the meat from the tail and body. Remove the cream-coloured vein and soft body matter and discard. Cut the meat into 2 cm (¾ inch) pieces, cover and refrigerate. Wash the head and shell halves, then drain and pat dry.
2 In a frying pan, heat 60 g (2 oz) of the butter, add the spring onion and stir for 2 minutes. Stir in the flour and mustard and cook for 1 minute, or until pale and foaming. Remove from the heat and gradually stir in the wine and milk. Return to the heat and stir constantly until the mixture boils and thickens. Reduce the heat and simmer for 1 minute. Stir in the cream, parsley and lobster meat, then season with salt and pepper, to taste. Stir over low heat until the lobster is heated through.
3 Heat the grill. Spoon the mixture into the lobster shells, sprinkle with cheese and dot with the remaining butter. Place under the grill for 2 minutes, or until lightly browned. Serve with mixed salad leaves and lemon slices.

LOBSTER MORNAY

Preparation time: 25 minutes +
  15 minutes standing
Total cooking time: 5–10 minutes
Serves 2

⋆⋆

1 cooked medium lobster
1¼ cups (315 ml/10 fl oz) milk
1 slice of onion
1 bay leaf
6 black peppercorns
30 g (1 oz) butter
2 tablespoons plain (all-purpose) flour
2 tablespoons cream
pinch of nutmeg
60 g (2 oz) Cheddar, grated
pinch of paprika, to garnish

1 Using a sharp knife, cut the lobster in half lengthways through the shell. Lift the meat from the tail and body. Remove the cream-coloured vein and soft body matter and discard. Cut the meat into 2 cm (¾ inch) pieces, cover and refrigerate. Wash the head and shell halves, then drain and pat dry. Set aside.
2 Heat the milk, onion, bay leaf and peppercorns in a small pan. Bring to the boil. Remove from the heat, cover and leave for 15 minutes. Strain.
3 Melt the butter in a large pan, stir in the flour and cook for 1 minute, or until pale and foaming. Remove from the heat and gradually stir in the milk. Return to the heat and stir constantly until the mixture boils and thickens. Reduce the heat and simmer for 1 minute. Stir in the cream. Season with the nutmeg and salt and pepper, to taste.
4 Fold the lobster meat through the sauce. Stir over low heat until the lobster is heated through. Spoon the mixture into the shells and sprinkle with cheese. Heat the grill and place the lobster under the grill for 2 minutes, or until the cheese is melted. Sprinkle with paprika. Can be served with thick potato chips.

OPPOSITE PAGE, FROM TOP: Lobster thermidor; Lobster mornay

FISH BAKED IN SALT

Preparation time: 20 minutes
Total cooking time: 30–40 minutes
Serves 6

1.8 kg (3 lb 10 oz) whole fish (eg. blue-eye,
    jewfish, sea bass, groper), scaled and cleaned
2 lemons, sliced
4 sprigs of fresh thyme
1 fennel bulb, thinly sliced
3 kg (6 lb) rock salt
100 g (3¹/2 oz) plain (all-purpose) flour

1 Preheat the oven to moderately hot 200°C
(400°F/Gas 6). Rinse the fish and pat dry inside
and out with paper towel. Place the lemon,
thyme and fennel inside the cavity.
2 Pack half the salt into a large baking dish and
place the fish on top.
3 Cover with the remaining salt, pressing down
until the salt is packed firmly around the fish.
4 Combine the flour with enough water to form
a smooth paste, then brush, spreading carefully
and evenly, over the surface of the salt. Be
careful not to disturb the salt.
5 Bake the fish for 30–40 minutes, or until a
skewer inserted into the centre of the fish comes
out hot. Carefully crack open the salt crust with
the back of a spoon and gently remove the skin
from the fish, ensuring that no salt remains on
the flesh. Serve with Montpellier butter (see
page 195).

CURRIED PRAWNS

Preparation time: 20 minutes
Total cooking time: 10 minutes
Serves 4

1 kg (2 lb) raw prawns (shrimp)
30 g (1 oz) butter
1 onion, chopped
1 clove garlic, crushed
1 tablespoon curry powder
1/4 cup (60 g/2 oz) plain (all-purpose) flour
2 cups (500 ml/16 fl oz) milk
1/4 teaspoon ground nutmeg
1/4 teaspoon paprika

1 Peel the prawns, leaving the tails intact. Gently
pull out the dark vein from each prawn back,
starting at the head end.
2 Melt the butter in a pan over low heat, add
the onion and cook until soft. Stir in the garlic,
curry powder and flour and cook for 1 minute,
until the onion is coated in flour.
3 Remove from the heat and gradually stir in
the milk, nutmeg, and paprika. Return to the
heat and stir until the sauce boils and thickens.
4 Add the prawns and stir over medium heat for
2–3 minutes, or until the prawns are pink and
cooked through.

STUFFED FISH

Preparation time: 30–40 minutes
Total cooking time: 45 minutes
Serves 4

1 kg (2 lb) whole fish (eg. snapper, murray cod,
    sea bass), scaled and cleaned
1/4 cup (60 ml/2 fl oz) lemon juice
30 g (1 oz) butter, chopped

Stuffing

2 tablespoons olive oil
1 small onion, finely chopped
3 tablespoons chopped celery leaves
2 tablespoons chopped fresh parsley
1 cup (80 g/2³/4 oz) fresh breadcrumbs
1¹/2 tablespoons lemon juice
1 egg, lightly beaten

1 Preheat the oven to moderate 180°C (350°F/
Gas 4). Pat the fish dry and sprinkle with salt and
the lemon juice. Set aside.
2 For the stuffing, heat the oil in a pan, add
the onion and cook over medium heat for
2 minutes, or until softened. Add the celery
leaves and parsley and cook, stirring, for another
2 minutes. Spoon into a bowl, add the
breadcrumbs, lemon juice and salt, to taste, then
mix well. Cool slightly, then stir in the egg.
3 Place the stuffing in the fish cavity and secure
the opening with skewers. Place the fish in a
large greased baking dish and dot with butter.
Bake for 30–35 minutes, or until the fish is
cooked and flakes easily when tested with a fork.
The thickness of the fish will determine the
cooking time. Transfer to a serving dish. Can be
garnished with lemon slices and fresh dill sprigs.

FISH BAKED IN SALT
When whole fish is baked
in layers of salt, the flesh
stays very moist, without
being too salty. When the
skin is peeled back, a
delightful, succulent flesh
is revealed. The salt helps
retain the moisture as well
as adding flavour. Since
ancient times, salt has
been used in food
preparation as both a
preservative and flavouring.

*OPPOSITE PAGE, FROM
TOP: Fish baked in salt;
Stuffed fish*

INTERNATIONAL BARBECUED SHELL PLATTER

Preparation time: 40 minutes + 1 hour freezing
Total cooking time: 30 minutes
Serves 6

★ ★ ★

6 raw Balmain bugs
30 g (1 oz) butter, melted
1 tablespoon oil
12 black mussels
12 scallops on their shells
12 oysters
18 raw large prawns (shrimp), unpeeled

Salsa verde, for scallops

1 tablespoon finely chopped preserved lemon
　(see Notes)
1 cup (20 g/³/4 oz) fresh parsley leaves
1 tablespoon drained bottled capers
1 tablespoon lemon juice
3 tablespoons oil, approximately

Vinegar and shallot dressing, for mussels

1/4 cup (60 ml/2 fl oz) white wine vinegar
4 French shallots, finely chopped
1 tablespoon chopped fresh chervil

Pickled ginger and wasabi sauce,
　for oysters

1 teaspoon soy sauce
1/4 cup (60 ml/2 fl oz) mirin
2 tablespoons rice wine vinegar
1/4 teaspoon wasabi paste
2 tablespoons thinly sliced pickled ginger

Sweet balsamic dressing, for
　Balmain bugs

1 tablespoon olive oil
1 tablespoon honey
1/2 cup (125 ml/4 fl oz) balsamic vinegar

Thai coriander sauce, for prawns (shrimp)

1/2 cup (125 ml/4 fl oz) sweet chilli sauce
1 tablespoon lime juice
2 tablespoons chopped fresh coriander
　(cilantro) leaves

1 Freeze the bugs for 1 hour to immobilize. Cut each bug in half with a sharp knife, then brush the flesh with the combined butter and oil. Set aside while you prepare the rest of the seafood.
2 Scrub the mussels with a stiff brush and pull out the hairy beards. Discard any broken mussels, or open ones that don't close when tapped on the bench. Rinse well.
3 Slice or pull off any vein, membrane or hard white muscle from the scallops, leaving any roe attached. Brush the scallops with the combined butter and oil.
4 Remove the oysters from the shells, then rinse the shells under cold water. Pat the shells dry and return the oysters to their shells. Cover and refrigerate all the seafood while you make the dressings.
5 For the salsa verde, combine all the ingredients in a food processor and process in short bursts until roughly chopped. Transfer to a bowl and add enough oil to moisten the mixture. Season with salt and pepper. Serve a small dollop on each cooked scallop.
6 For the vinegar and shallot dressing, whisk the vinegar, shallots and chervil in a bowl until combined. Pour over the cooked mussels.
7 For the pickled ginger and wasabi sauce, whisk all the ingredients in a bowl until combined. Spoon over the cooked oysters.
8 For the sweet balsamic dressing, heat the oil in a pan, add the honey and vinegar and bring to the boil, then boil until reduced by half. Drizzle over the cooked bugs.
9 For the Thai coriander sauce, combine all the ingredients in a jug or bowl and drizzle over the cooked prawns.
10 Cook the seafood in batches on a preheated barbecue grill and flatplate. If necessary, do this in batches, depending on the size of your barbecue. The Balmain bugs will take the longest time to cook, about 5 minutes—they are cooked when the flesh turns white and starts to come away from the shells. The mussels, scallops, oysters and prawns all take about 2–5 minutes to cook.
NOTES: To prepare the preserved lemon, remove the flesh and discard. Wash the skin to remove excess salt and then chop finely.

Mirin, rice wine vinegar and pickled ginger are all available from Asian food speciality stores.

OYSTERS
Oysters are sold freshly shucked on the half shell, in bottles of salted water, or alive and unshucked. Shucked oysters are also sold canned, dried and frozen. When buying fresh shucked oysters, look for a plump moist oyster. The flesh should be creamy with a clear liquid (oyster liquor) surrounding it. Oysters should smell like the fresh sea and have no traces of shell particles. If you prefer to shuck them yourself, look for tightly closed, unbroken shells.

OPPOSITE PAGE:
International barbecued
shell platter

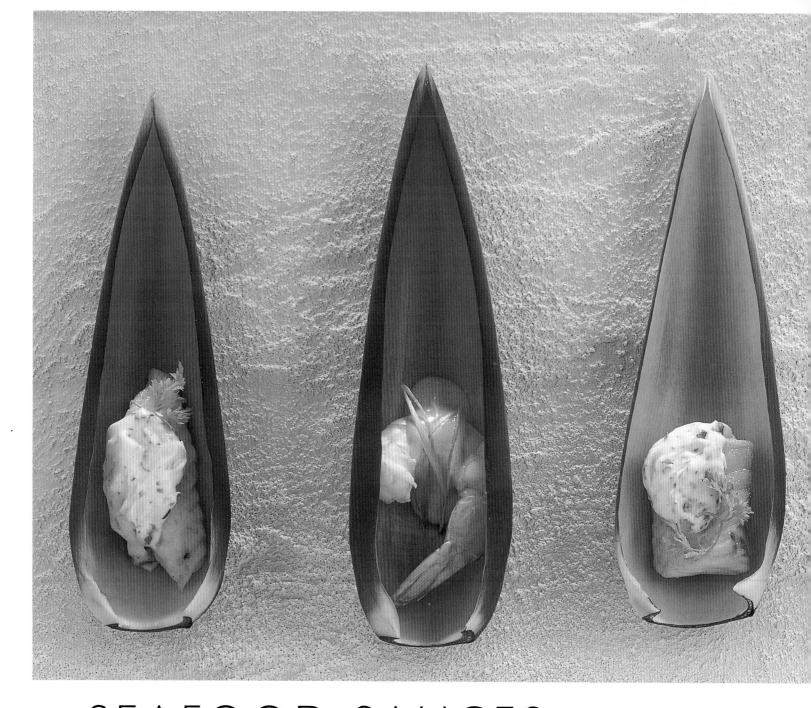

SEAFOOD SAUCES A piece of freshly

cooked seafood becomes simple perfection when topped with a good spoonful

of one of these favourite sauces.

TARTARE SAUCE

Mix 1 tablespoon finely chopped onion,
1 teaspoon lemon juice, 1 tablespoon
chopped gherkins, 1 teaspoon drained,
chopped capers, 1/4 teaspoon Dijon
mustard, 1 tablespoon finely chopped
fresh parsley and 1 1/2 cups (375 g/
12 oz) mayonnaise. Season to taste.
Cover and refrigerate for up to 1 month.
Makes about 2 cups.

COCKTAIL SAUCE

Mix 1 cup (250 g/8 oz) whole-egg
mayonnaise, 3 tablespoons tomato sauce,
2 teaspoons Worcestershire sauce,
1/2 teaspoon lemon juice and 1 drop
of Tabasco sauce. Season with salt and
pepper, to taste. Cover and refrigerate
for up to 1 month. Makes about 1 cup.

GREEN GODDESS DRESSING

Mix 1 1/2 cups (375 g/12 oz) whole-egg
mayonnaise, 4 mashed anchovy fillets,
4 finely chopped spring onions (scallions),
1 crushed clove garlic, 3 tablespoons
chopped fresh flat-leaf (Italian) parsley,
3 tablespoons finely chopped chives and
1 teaspoon tarragon vinegar. Cover and
refrigerate for up to 1 month. Makes
about 2 cups.

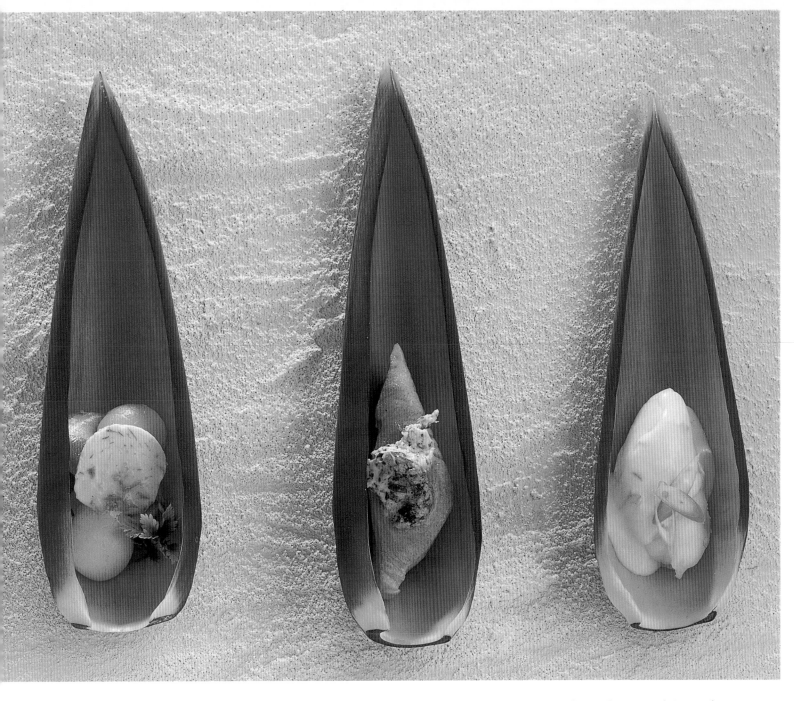

LEMON CAPER BUTTER

Combine 250 g (8 oz) soft butter in a bowl with 1 tablespoon each of finely grated lemon rind and juice, 1 crushed garlic clove and 1 tablespoon drained, chopped capers. Roll up firmly in foil to form a roll. Refrigerate for up to 1 month. Cut into rounds for serving. Serve at room temperature. Makes about 1 cup.

MONTPELLIER BUTTER

Beat 250 g (8 oz) softened butter in a bowl until creamy. Blanch 100 g (3½ oz) baby spinach leaves. Drain, refresh in cold water, then squeeze out as much water as possible. Chop roughly, then combine in a food processor with 2 tablespoons chopped fresh parsley leaves, 1 tablespoon chopped fresh tarragon, 2 small chopped gherkins, 1 tablespoon drained bottled capers, 2 drained anchovy fillets, 2 hard-boiled egg yolks, 1 teaspoon lemon juice and 2 tablespoons oil. Process until fine. Add to the butter, mix well, then season with freshly ground black pepper. Cover and refrigerate for up to 3 days, or freeze. Serve at room temperature. Portions of the butter are placed on top of hot seafood and allowed to melt. Makes about 1 cup.

WHITE WINE SAUCE

Melt 1 tablespoon butter in a medium pan, add 1 finely chopped spring onion (scallion) and cook, stirring over medium heat until the onion is soft. Add ½ cup (125 ml/4 fl oz) white wine, bring to the boil and simmer for 5 minutes, or until reduced by half. Add ½ cup (125 ml/ 4 fl oz) each of cream and milk and bring to the boil. Blend 3 teaspoons each of soft butter and plain (all-purpose) flour to form a paste, then whisk into the boiling liquid and boil until thick. Season to taste with salt and pepper. If too thick, thin with a little milk to reach a pouring consistency. Cover and refrigerate for up to 3 days. Makes about 1 cup.

FROM LEFT: Tartare sauce; Cocktail sauce; Green goddess dressing; Lemon caper butter; Montpellier butter; White wine sauce

ABOVE: Baked salmon

BAKED SALMON

Preparation time: 10 minutes +
 45 minutes standing
Total cooking time: 35 minutes
Serves 8

2 kg (4 lb) whole salmon, cleaned and gutted

2 spring onions (scallions), roughly chopped

3 sprigs of fresh dill

1/2 lemon, thinly sliced

6 black peppercorns

1/4 cup (60 ml/2 fl oz) dry white wine

3 bay leaves

1 Preheat the oven to moderate 180°C (350°F/ Gas 4). Rinse the salmon under cold running water and pat dry inside and out with paper towels. Stuff the cavity with the spring onion, dill, lemon and peppercorns.

2 Brush a large double-layered piece of foil with oil and lay the salmon on the foil. Sprinkle with wine and arrange the bay leaves over the top. Fold the foil over and wrap up, enclosing the salmon tightly.

3 Place in a shallow baking dish and bake for 30 minutes. Turn the oven off and leave the salmon in the oven for 45 minutes with the door closed.

4 Undo the foil and carefully peel away the skin of the salmon on the top side. Carefully flip the salmon onto the serving plate and remove the skin from the other side. Pull out the fins and any visible bones. Serve at room temperature. The baked salmon can be served with a sauce of your choice.

NOTES: Do not open the foil during the cooking or standing time. Remove the fish head if necessary.

SERVING SUGGESTION: A simple cucumber sauce for serving with the salmon can be made by mixing some chopped Lebanese (short) cucumbers with chopped fresh chives and 2 tablespoons of whole-egg mayonnaise and a little French mustard.

SNAPPER PIES

Preparation time: 25 minutes
Total cooking time: 1 hour 10 minutes
Serves 4

2 tablespoons olive oil

4 onions, thinly sliced

1¹/₂ cups (375 ml/12 fl oz) fish stock

3¹/₂ cups (875 ml/28 fl oz) cream

1 kg (2 lb) skinless snapper fillets,
   cut into large pieces

2 sheets ready-rolled puff pastry, thawed

1 egg, lightly beaten

1 Preheat the oven to hot 220°C (425°F/ Gas 7). Heat the oil in a large deep-sided frying pan, add the onion and stir over medium heat for 20 minutes, or until the onion is golden brown and slightly caramelized.

2 Add the fish stock, bring to the boil and cook for 10 minutes, or until the liquid is nearly evaporated. Stir in the cream and bring to the boil. Reduce the heat and simmer for about 20 minutes, until the liquid is reduced by half, or until it coats the back of a spoon.
3 Divide half the sauce among four 2-cup (500 ml/16 fl oz) capacity, deep ramekins. Put some fish in each ramekin, then top each with some of the remaining sauce.
4 Cut the pastry sheets into rounds slightly larger than the tops of the ramekins. Brush the edges of the pastry with a little of the egg. Press onto the ramekins. Brush lightly with the remaining beaten egg. Bake for 30 minutes, or until crisp, golden and puffed.
NOTE: You can substitute bream, sea perch or garfish for the snapper fillets.

ABOVE: Snapper pies

197

SEAFOOD QUICHE

Preparation time: 20 minutes +
20 minutes chilling
Total cooking time: 1 hour
Serves 4-6

2 sheets ready-rolled shortcrust pastry
100 g (3¹/₂ oz) scallops
30 g (1 oz) butter
100 g (3¹/₂ oz) raw prawn (shrimp) meat
100 g (3¹/₂ oz) canned, fresh or frozen
   crab meat
90 g (3 oz) Cheddar, grated
3 eggs
1 tablespoon plain (all-purpose) flour
¹/₂ cup (125 ml/4 fl oz) cream
¹/₂ cup (125 ml/4 fl oz) milk
1 small fennel bulb, thinly sliced
1 tablespoon grated Parmesan

1 Lightly grease a 22 cm (9 inch) diameter loose-based flan tin. Place the 2 sheets of pastry slightly overlapping, on a work bench, and roll out until large enough to fit the prepared tin. Press the pastry into the base and side of the tin and trim off any excess with a sharp knife. Refrigerate for 20 minutes.
2 Slice or pull off any vein, membrane or hard white muscle from the scallops, leaving any roe attached. Preheat the oven to moderately hot 190°C (375°F/Gas 5).
3 Cover the pastry with baking paper, fill evenly with baking beads or uncooked rice and bake for 10 minutes. Remove the paper and rice and bake for another 10 minutes, or until lightly golden. Cool on a wire rack. If the pastry puffs up, press down lightly with a tea towel.
4 Melt the butter in a frying pan and fry the prawns and scallops for 2–3 minutes, or until cooked. Allow to cool, then arrange all the seafood over the base of the pastry shell. Sprinkle with the Cheddar.
5 Beat the eggs in a small jug, whisk in the flour, cream and milk, and season with salt and pepper. Pour over the filling. Sprinkle with fennel and Parmesan. Bake for 30–35 minutes, or until set and golden brown. Cool slightly before serving.

RIGHT: Seafood quiche

COULIBIAC

Preparation time: 25 minutes +
  30 minutes chilling
Total cooking time: 40 minutes
Serves 4-6

60 g (2 oz) butter
I onion, finely chopped
200 g (6¹/2 oz) button mushrooms, sliced
2 tablespoons lemon juice
220 g (7 oz) salmon fillet, boned, skinned,
  cut into 2 cm (³/4 inch) pieces
2 hard-boiled eggs, chopped
2 tablespoons chopped fresh dill
2 tablespoons chopped fresh parsley
I cup (185 g/6 oz) cold, cooked rice
¹/4 cup (60 ml/2 fl oz) cream
375 g (12 oz) block frozen puff pastry, thawed
I egg, lightly beaten

1 Lightly grease a baking tray. Melt half the butter in a frying pan. Add the onion and cook over medium heat for 5 minutes or until soft but not browned. Add the mushrooms and cook for 5 minutes. Add the lemon juice to the pan and stir to combine. Transfer the mixture to a bowl.
2 Melt the remaining butter in a pan, add the salmon and cook for 2 minutes. Transfer to a bowl, cool slightly and add the egg, dill, parsley and salt and pepper, to taste. Combine gently and set aside. Combine the rice and cream in a small bowl and season with salt and pepper.
3 Roll out half the pastry to a rectangle measuring 18 x 30 cm (7 x 12 inches) and place on the prepared tray. Spread half the rice mixture onto the pastry, leaving a 3 cm (1¹/4 inch) border all the way around. Top with the salmon mixture, then the mushroom mixture, and finish with the remaining rice.
4 Roll out the remaining pastry to 20 x 32 cm (8 x 13 inches) and place over the filling. Press the edges together, then crimp to seal. Decorate with pastry cut-outs if you like. Refrigerate for 30 minutes. Meanwhile, preheat the oven to hot 210°C (415°F/Gas 6–7). Brush the pastry with the beaten egg and bake for 15 minutes. Reduce the heat to moderate 180°C (350°F/Gas 4) and bake for another 15–20 minutes, until the top is golden brown.
NOTES: You can substitute ocean trout for the salmon. A can of red salmon can also be used.
  You will need ¹/3 cup (65 g/2¹/4 oz) raw rice.

BAKED POTATOES WITH PRAWNS AND YOGHURT

Wash and dry 4 large potatoes, then prick all over with a fork. Place on a baking tray and brush with oil. Bake in a hot 220°C (425°F/Gas 7) oven for 1–1¹/2 hours, until cooked through when tested with a skewer. Meanwhile, heat 300 g (10 oz) cooked and peeled small prawns (shrimp) in a lightly oiled pan with a crushed garlic clove. Stir in some chopped fresh chives and ¹/2 cup (125 g/ 4 oz) natural yoghurt. Cut a deep cross in the top of each potato and fill with prawn mixture. Serve with lemon wedges. Makes 4.

ABOVE: Coulibiac

BRIK A L'OEUF

Carefully crack an egg into the centre of the tuna mixture.

Lay an extra 2 sheets of filo over the tuna and egg and fold in the sides.

Roll up the pastry into a neat firm package, keeping the egg intact.

RIGHT: Brik a l'oeuf

BRIK A L'OEUF

Preparation time: 30 minutes
Total cooking time: 15 minutes
Serves 2

★ ★

6 sheets filo pastry

30 g (1 oz) butter, melted

1 small onion, finely chopped

200 g (6½ oz) can tuna in oil, drained

6 black olives, pitted and chopped

1 tablespoon finely chopped fresh parsley

2 eggs

1 Preheat the oven to moderately hot 200°C (400°F/Gas 6). Cut the filo pastry sheets in half widthways. Layer 4 sheets together with melted butter. Keep the remaining pastry covered with a damp tea towel. Combine the onion, tuna, olives and parsley in a bowl and spoon half the mixture onto one end of the buttered pastry, leaving a border. Make a well in the centre of the tuna mixture and break an egg into the well, being careful to leave it whole. Season with salt and freshly ground black pepper.

2 Layer 2 more sheets of filo together with melted butter and place on top of the tuna and egg. Fold in the pastry sides, then roll into a firm parcel, keeping the egg whole. Place on a lightly greased baking tray and brush with melted butter. Repeat with the remaining pastry, filling and egg.

3 Bake for 15 minutes, or until the pastry is golden brown. Serve warm.

NOTE: The yolk is still soft after 15 minutes. If you prefer a firmer egg, bake a little longer.

HADDOCK DUGLESE

Preparation time: 20 minutes
Total cooking time: 30 minutes
Serves 4

★

500 g (1 lb) smoked haddock, or cod, fillets

1 cup (250 ml/4 fl oz) dry white wine

1 teaspoon whole black peppercorns

1 large onion, cut in 1 cm (½ inch) slices

30 g (1 oz) butter

2 tablespoons plain (all-purpose) flour

2 tomatoes, peeled and chopped, seeds removed

¼ cup (60 ml/2 fl oz) cream

1 tablespoon chopped fresh parsley, to garnish

1 Preheat the oven to moderate 180°C (350°F/ Gas 4). Thoroughly wash the haddock and place in a pan. Cover with water, bring slowly to the boil, reduce the heat and simmer, uncovered, for 5 minutes. Strain off the water.

2 Pour the wine and 1 cup (250 ml/8 fl oz) water over the haddock, scatter the peppercorns and onion on top. Cover and simmer gently for 5–8 minutes, or until just tender.

3 Remove the haddock with a slotted spoon and place in an ovenproof dish. Reserve 1 cup (250 ml/8 fl oz) of the liquid for the sauce.

4 For the sauce, melt the butter in a pan over low heat. Stir in the flour and cook for 1 minute, or until pale and foaming. Remove from the heat and gradually stir in the reserved stock. Return to the heat and stir until the sauce boils and thickens. Reduce the heat and simmer for 2 minutes. Add the tomato and the cream and stir until heated through.

5 Pour the sauce over the fish, sprinkle with parsley and bake for 15–20 minutes. Serve immediately with hot fluffy mashed potatoes and steamed vegetables.

FREEFORM PRAWN PIES

Preparation time: 30 minutes + 15 minutes chilling
Total cooking time: 30 minutes
Serves 4

★★

2 cups (250 g/8 oz) plain (all-purpose) flour

125 g (4 oz) chilled butter, cubed

1 kg (2 lb) raw medium prawns (shrimp)

1 tablespoon oil

5 cm (2 inch) piece fresh ginger, grated

3 cloves garlic, crushed

1/3 cup (80 ml/2³/4 fl oz) sweet chilli sauce

1/3 cup (80 ml/2³/4 fl oz) lime juice

1/3 cup (80 ml/2³/4 fl oz) thick (double) cream

25 g (³/4 oz) chopped fresh coriander (cilantro)

1 egg yolk, lightly beaten, to glaze

strips of lime rind, to garnish

 Sift the flour into a large bowl, add the butter and rub into the flour with your fingertips until the mixture resembles fine breadcrumbs. Make a well, add 3 tablespoons water and mix with a flat-bladed knife, using a cutting action, until the mixture comes together in beads. Gather the dough together and lift out onto a lightly floured surface. Press into a ball and flatten into a disc.

(Alternatively, make in a food processor.) Wrap in plastic wrap and chill for 15 minutes.

2 Preheat the oven to moderately hot 200°C (400°F/Gas 6). Peel the prawns and gently pull out the dark vein from each prawn back, starting at the head end.

3 Heat the oil in a large frying pan and fry the ginger, garlic and prawns for 2–3 minutes. Remove the prawns and set aside. Add the chilli sauce, lime juice and cream to the pan and simmer over medium heat, until the sauce has reduced by about one third. Return the prawns to the pan and add the coriander; cool.

4 Grease 2 baking trays. Divide the pastry into 4 and roll out each portion, between sheets of baking paper, into a 20 cm (8 inch) circle. Divide the filling into 4 and place a portion in the centre of each pastry, leaving a wide border. Fold the edges loosely over the filling. Brush the pastry with egg yolk. Bake for 25 minutes, or until golden. Serve garnished with lime rind.

ABOVE: Freeform prawn pies

201

SEAFOOD MORNAY

Preparation time: 35 minutes
Total cooking time: 35 minutes
Serves 8–10

80 g (2³/4 oz) butter
¹/2 cup (60 g/2 oz) plain (all-purpose) flour
¹/2 cup (125 ml/4 fl oz) dry white wine
1 cup (250 ml/8 fl oz) thick (double) cream
1 cup (250 ml/8 fl oz) milk
125 g (4 oz) Cheddar, grated
2 tablespoons wholegrain mustard
1 tablespoon horseradish cream
6 spring onions (scallions), chopped
1 cup (80 g/2³/4 oz) fresh breadcrumbs
1 kg (2 lb) skinless white fish fillets
   (eg. monkfish, coley, snapper, flathead),
   cut into cubes
450 g (14 oz) scallops, cleaned
400 g (13 oz) cooked peeled small prawns
   (shrimp)

Topping

3 cups (240 g/7¹/2 oz) fresh breadcrumbs
3 tablespoons chopped fresh parsley
60 g (2 oz) butter, melted
125 g (4 oz) Cheddar, grated

1 Preheat the oven to moderate 180°C (350°F/ Gas 4). Lightly grease a 2 litre (64 fl oz) capacity ovenproof dish.
2 Melt 60 g (2 oz) of the butter in a pan over low heat. Stir in the flour until pale and foaming. Remove from the heat and gradually stir in the wine, cream and milk. Return to the heat and stir over high heat until the sauce boils and thickens. Season with salt and pepper, to taste. Add the Cheddar, mustard, horseradish, spring onion and breadcrumbs. Mix well and set aside.
3 Melt the remaining butter in a large pan and add the fish and scallops in batches. Stir over low heat until the seafood starts to change colour. Drain the seafood, add to the sauce with the prawns, then transfer to the greased dish.
4 For the topping, mix all the ingredients and spread over the seafood. Bake for 35 minutes, or until the top is golden and the sauce bubbling.

ABOVE: Seafood mornay

CIOPPINO

Preparation time: 30 minutes +
30 minutes soaking
Total cooking time: 1 hour
Serves 4

2 dried Chinese mushrooms
1 kg (2 lb) skinless white fish fillets (eg. hake,
    snapper, ocean perch, red mullet)
375 g (12 oz) raw large prawns (shrimp)
1 raw lobster tail (about 400 g/13 oz)
12–15 black mussels
1/4 cup (60 ml/2 fl oz) olive oil
1 large onion, finely chopped
1 green pepper (capsicum), finely chopped
2–3 cloves garlic, crushed
425 g (14 oz) can crushed tomatoes
1 cup (250 ml/8 fl oz) white wine
1 cup (250 ml/8 fl oz) tomato juice
1 cup (250 ml/8 fl oz) fish stock
1 bay leaf
2 sprigs of fresh parsley
2 teaspoons chopped fresh basil
1 tablespoon chopped fresh parsley, extra

1 Place the mushrooms in a small bowl, cover with boiling water and soak for 20 minutes. Cut the fish into bite-size pieces, removing bones.
2 Peel the prawns, leaving the tails intact. Gently pull out the dark vein from each prawn back, starting at the head end.
3 Starting at the end where the head was, cut down the sides of the lobster shell on the underside of the lobster with kitchen scissors. Pull back the flap, remove the meat from the shell and cut into small pieces.
4 Scrub the mussels with a stiff brush and pull out the hairy beards. Discard any broken mussels, or open ones that don't close when tapped on the bench. Rinse well.
5 Drain the mushrooms, squeeze dry and chop finely. Heat the oil in a heavy-based pan, add the onion, pepper and garlic and stir over medium heat for about 5 minutes, or until the onion is soft. Add the mushrooms, tomato, wine, tomato juice, stock, bay leaf, parsley sprigs and basil. Bring to the boil, reduce the heat, then cover and simmer for 30 minutes.
6 Layer the fish and prawns in a large pan. Add the sauce, then cover and leave on low heat for 10 minutes, or until the prawns are pink and the fish is cooked. Add the lobster and mussels and simmer for another 4–5 minutes. Season. Discard any unopened mussels. Sprinkle with parsley.

SALMON CRUMBLE

Peel and quarter 1 kg (2 lb) floury potatoes, (russet or pontiac). Boil until tender, drain and mash. Melt 60 g (2 oz) butter in a pan and fry 10 finely chopped spring onions (scallions) and 2 cloves crushed garlic until soft. Stir into the potato with 4 tablespoons milk and a 415 g (13 oz) can of drained, flaked salmon. Spread into a shallow casserole dish. Combine 60 g (2 oz) melted butter, 2 cups (160 g/5^1/$_2$ oz) fresh breadcrumbs, 3 tablespoons grated Cheddar and some chopped parsley in a bowl. Sprinkle over the top. Bake in a moderately hot 200°C (400°F/Gas 6) oven for 20 minutes, or until golden and crisp. Serves 4–6.

BELOW: Cioppino

Dill and caper mayonnaise

3/4 cup (185 g/6 oz) whole-egg mayonnaise

2 tablespoons chopped fresh dill

1 1/2 tablespoons lemon juice

1 gherkin, finely chopped

1 teaspoon drained bottled capers, chopped

1 clove garlic, crushed

1 For the marinade, combine the olive oil, lemon juice, mustard, honey and fresh dill in a bowl, pour over the unpeeled prawns and coat well. Cover and refrigerate for at least 2 hours, turning occasionally.

2 For the dill mayonnaise, whisk together the mayonnaise, dill, lemon juice, gherkin, capers and garlic in a small bowl, then cover and chill.

3 Lightly oil a heated chargrill pan or barbecue grill or hotplate. Add the drained prawns and cook in batches over high heat for 4 minutes, turning frequently until pink and cooked through. Serve with the dill mayonnaise.

TUNA WITH SOY AND HONEY

Preparation time: 15 minutes +
   1 hour chilling
Total cooking time: 8–10 minutes
Serves 4

4 tuna steaks

10 cm (4 inch) piece of peeled fresh ginger,
   cut into julienne strips

2 spring onions (scallions), thinly sliced

2 tablespoons honey

2 tablespoons balsamic vinegar

1/2 cup (125 ml/4 fl oz) low-salt soy sauce

1 Place the tuna, ginger and spring onion in a shallow non-metallic dish.

2 Stir the honey, balsamic vinegar and soy sauce together in a small bowl. Pour over the tuna steaks and turn them to coat in the marinade. Cover and refrigerate for 1 hour.

3 Heat the barbecue grill. Cook on the barbecue for 3–4 minutes each side, or until cooked to your liking. The cooking time will depend on the thickness of the tuna.

NOTE: Swordfish, striped marlin and kingfish are all just as suitable as the tuna steaks for making this recipe.

PRAWNS WITH DILL AND CAPER MAYONNAISE

Preparation time: 15 minutes +
   2 hours marinating
Total cooking time: 10–15 minutes
Serves 4

Marinade

1/2 cup (125 ml/4 fl oz) olive oil

1/3 cup (80 ml/2 3/4 fl oz) lemon juice

2 tablespoons wholegrain mustard

2 tablespoons honey

2 tablespoons chopped fresh dill

20 raw large prawns (shrimp)

ABOVE: Prawns with dill and caper mayonnaise

SALMON WITH DILL CREAM

Preparation time: 25 minutes
Total cooking time: 25 minutes
Serves 4

4 baby salmon
4 cloves garlic, peeled
2 lemons, sliced
8 fresh bay leaves
8 sprigs fresh flat-leaf (Italian) parsley
8 sprigs fresh thyme
olive oil, for brushing

Dill cream

90 g (3 oz) butter
1 cup (250 ml/8 fl oz) fish stock
1 1/2 teaspoons wholegrain mustard
1 cup (250 ml/8 fl oz) cream
2 tablespoons lemon juice
3 tablespoons chopped fresh dill

1 Preheat a barbecue or chargrill pan to hot. Wash the fish and pat dry inside and out with paper towels. Place a clove of garlic, a few slices of lemon and a bay leaf in the cavity of each fish. Bundle together 1 sprig of parsley and thyme and tie a bundle with string onto each fish, near the tail. Reserve the other sprigs. Brush both sides of the fish with a little of the olive oil.

2 For the dill cream, melt the butter in a pan and add the fish stock, mustard and cream. Bring to the boil, then reduce the heat and simmer for 15 minutes, or until the sauce is slightly thickened. Stir in the lemon juice and dill. Set aside and keep warm. Season to taste with salt and pepper.

3 While the dill cream is cooking, barbecue or chargrill the fish for 3–6 minutes on each side, turning carefully, or until cooked through. Discard the herbs. For serving, bundle together a fresh parsley sprig, a thyme sprig and a bay leaf, and tie a bundle near each fish tail. Serve warm with the dill cream.
NOTE: Rainbow trout is also a suitable fish for this recipe.

BELOW: Salmon with dill cream

FISH COOKED IN PAPER

Put a teaspoon of butter and 3 slices of lemon over the leek and spring onion.

Fold the paper into a parcel around the fish, tucking the ends under.

FISH COOKED IN PAPER

Preparation time: 20 minutes
Total cooking time: 20 minutes
Serves 4

4 skinless fish fillets, 200 g/6½ oz each
    (e.g. John dory, orange roughy, snapper, bream)
1 leek, white part only, julienned
4 spring onions (scallions), julienned
30 g (1 oz) butter, softened
1 lemon, cut into 12 very thin slices
2–3 tablespoons lemon juice

1 Preheat the oven to moderate 180°C (350°F/ Gas 4). Place each fish fillet in the centre of a piece of baking paper large enough to enclose the fish. Season lightly.

2 Scatter with the leek and spring onion. Top each with a teaspoon of butter and 3 slices of lemon. Sprinkle with the extra lemon juice. Bring the paper together and fold over several times. Fold the ends under. Bake on a baking tray for 20 minutes (the steam will make the paper puff up). Check to see that the fish is cooked (it should be white and flake easily when tested with a fork) and then serve. Serve as parcels or lift the fish out and pour the juices over.

ABOVE: Fish cooked in paper

POACHED SALMON WITH DILL MAYONNAISE

Preparation time: 40 minutes
Total cooking time: 1 hour
Serves 8–10

2 litres (64 fl oz) good-quality white wine
¼ cup (60 ml/2 fl oz) white wine vinegar
2 onions
10 whole cloves
4 carrots, chopped
1 lemon, cut into quarters
2 bay leaves
1 teaspoon whole black peppercorns
4 sprigs fresh parsley
2.5 kg (5 lb) Atlantic salmon, cleaned and scaled
watercress and lemon slices, to garnish

Dill mayonnaise
1 egg, at room temperature
1 egg yolk, at room temperature, extra
1 tablespoon lemon juice
1 teaspoon white wine vinegar
1½ cups (375 ml/12 fl oz) light olive oil
1 tablespoon chopped fresh dill

1 Put the wine, wine vinegar and 2.5 litres (80 fl oz) water in a large heavy-based pan. Stud the onions with the cloves. Add to the pan with the carrot, lemon, bay leaves, peppercorns and parsley. Bring to the boil, reduce the heat and simmer for 30–35 minutes. Cool. Strain into a fish kettle that will hold the salmon.

2 Place the whole fish in the fish kettle and cover. Bring to the boil, reduce the heat and poach gently for 10–15 minutes, until the fish flakes when tested in the thickest part. Remove from the heat and cool the fish in the liquid.

3 Process the egg, extra yolk, juice and vinegar in a food processor for 10 seconds. With the motor running, add the oil in a thin, steady stream, blending until all the oil is added and the mayonnaise is thick and creamy. Stir in the dill, and salt and pepper, to taste.

4 Remove the fish from the liquid, place on a work surface or serving platter and peel back the skin. Garnish with watercress and lemon slices and serve with the dill mayonnaise.

NOTE: As a simple alternative, try this herb sauce. Mix together 1 tablespoon finely chopped parsley, 1 tablespoon finely chopped chervil, 1 tablespoon finely shredded basil, the finely grated zest of 1 small lemon and 300 g (10 oz) crème fraîche.

SCALLOPS PROVENCALE

Preparation time: 20 minutes
Total cooking time: 30 minutes
Serves 4 as a starter

600 g (1 ¼ lb) ripe tomatoes
3 tablespoons olive oil
1 onion, finely chopped
4 French shallots, finely chopped
¼ cup (60 ml/2 fl oz) dry white wine
60 g (2 oz) butter
20 fresh scallops, cleaned and dried, with shells
4 cloves garlic, crushed
2 tablespoons finely chopped fresh parsley
½ teaspoon fresh thyme leaves
2 tablespoons fresh breadcrumbs

1 Score a cross in the base of each tomato. Place the tomatoes in boiling water for 10 seconds, then plunge into cold water and peel. Cut each tomato in half and scoop out the seeds with a teaspoon and discard them.

Finely dice the tomato flesh.

2 Heat 2 tablespoons of the oil in a frying pan over medium heat, add the onion and shallots, then reduce the heat and cook for 5 minutes, or until soft. Add the wine and simmer for several minutes until reduced slightly, then add the tomato. Season and cook, stirring occasionally, for 20 minutes, or until thick and pulpy. Preheat the oven to moderate 180°F (350°F/Gas 4).

3 Heat the butter and remaining oil in a frying pan over high heat until foamy. Cook half the scallops for 1–2 minutes each side, or until lightly golden. Remove and repeat with the remaining scallops. Set aside.

4 Add the garlic to the hot scallop pan and stir for 1 minute. Remove from the heat and stir in the parsley, thyme and breadcrumbs.

5 To serve, warm the shells on a baking tray in the oven. Place a small amount of tomato mixture on each shell, top with a scallop and sprinkle with breadcrumb and parsley mixture.

NOTE: If the shells are not available, simply serve the scallops on a small plate. Place them on a bed of the tomato mixture and top with the breadcrumb mixture.

BELOW: Scallops Provençale

COATINGS & BATTERS Each of

these mixtures will coat four medium fish fillets (we used snapper). The egg white

batter is enough for six fillets. You can use the mixtures for other seafood as well.

To prepare for all the deep-fried recipes, fill a deep heavy-based saucepan one third full of oil and heat the oil to 180°C (350°F), or until a cube of bread dropped into the oil browns in 15 seconds. Fry the food in batches for even cooking.

BASIC BATTER

Sift 1 cup (125 g/4 oz) self-raising flour into a large bowl, then make a well in the centre. Beat an egg with 1 cup (250 ml/8 fl oz) milk and 1 tablespoon oil in a large jug. Gradually pour into the well, whisking to make a smooth batter. Cover and leave to stand for 10 minutes before using. The mixture should be the consistency of thick (double/heavy) cream. Thin with a little extra milk if necessary. Pat the fish dry with paper towel, dust lightly with flour, then dip in the batter, in batches, allowing the excess to drain off. Lower the fish in batches into the oil and deep-fry until golden brown. Drain on crumpled paper towels.

EGG WHITE BATTER

Sift 1 cup (125 g/4 oz) self-raising flour into a large bowl, make a well in the centre and gradually whisk in 1 cup (250 ml/8 fl oz) water to make a smooth batter. Leave to stand for 5 minutes. Beat 2 egg whites in a small clean bowl with electric beaters until stiff peaks form, then fold into the batter in two batches. Use immediately. Pat the fish dry with paper towel, dust lightly with flour, then dip into the batter in batches, allowing the excess batter to drain off. Lower the fish

in batches into the oil and deep-fry until golden brown. Drain well on crumpled paper towels.

BEER BATTER

Sift 1 cup (125 g/4 oz) plain (all-purpose) flour into a large bowl, make a well in the centre and gradually whisk in 1 cup (250 ml/8 fl oz) chilled beer. Pat the fish dry with paper towel, dust with flour, then dip into the batter in batches, allowing the excess to drain off. Lower into the oil in batches and deep-fry until golden. Drain on crumpled paper towels. (Soda water can be used instead of beer.)

SESAME SEED COATING

Season some flour with pepper and salt in a shallow bowl. Put 1 cup (155 g/5 oz) sesame seeds in another. Lightly beat an egg in a separate bowl. Pat the fish dry with paper towel, dust lightly with the flour, then dip in the egg, allowing the excess to drain off. Coat in sesame seeds. Heat 3 cm (1¼ inches) oil in a heavy-based frying pan to 180°C (350°F), or until a cube of bread dropped into the oil browns in 15 seconds. Shallow-fry the fish in batches until golden, turning once. Drain on crumpled paper towels.

NORI AND CRUMB COATING

Place 1½ cups (90 g/3 oz) Japanese breadcrumbs in a bowl. Tear or cut a sheet of nori into small pieces and stir into the crumbs. Season some flour with a little salt and pepper in a shallow bowl. Lightly beat an egg in a separate bowl. Pat the fish fillet dry with paper towel and dust lightly with flour. Dip in the egg, allowing the excess to drain off, then coat in the nori. Deep-fry the fish in batches until golden, then drain on crumpled paper towels.

CHIVE AND LEMON COATING

Combine 1¼ cups (100 g/3½ oz) fresh breadcrumbs with 6 tablespoons finely chopped fresh chives and 1 teaspoon finely grated lemon rind. Season some flour with salt and pepper in a shallow bowl. Lightly beat an egg in a separate bowl. Pat the fillet dry with paper towel and dust lightly with the flour. Dip in the egg, allowing the excess to drain off, then coat in the breadcrumbs. Melt 30 g (1 oz) butter and 2 tablespoons oil in a large frying pan, add the fish in batches and cook over medium heat until golden brown. Turn and cook the other side, adding butter and oil as required.

CLOCKWISE, FROM TOP LEFT:
Basic batter; Beer batter (with prawns/shrimp); Nori and crumb coating (with calamari); Chive and lemon coating; Sesame seed coating; Egg white batter

209

INDONESIAN SAMBAL SQUID

Preparation time: 20 minutes +
  10 minutes soaking
Total cooking time: 15 minutes
Serves 6

✷ ✷

1 kg (2 lb) cleaned squid hoods
1 tablespoon white vinegar
1 tablespoon tamarind pulp
4 red Asian shallots, finely chopped
8 small fresh red chillies, half of them seeded,
  chopped
6 cloves garlic
1 stem lemon grass, white part only, chopped
2 teaspoons grated fresh ginger
1/2 teaspoon shrimp paste
2 1/2 tablespoons peanut oil
1/2 teaspoon ground cumin
1 1/2 tablespoons brown sugar

1 Cut each squid hood in half lengthways and open out flat with the inside uppermost. Score a shallow diamond pattern all over the squid hoods, taking care not to cut all the way through. Cut the hoods into 5 cm (2 inch) squares. Put the pieces in a bowl with the vinegar and 1 litre (32 fl oz) water and soak for 10 minutes, then rinse and drain the squid and set aside.

2 Put the tamarind in a bowl and pour in 1/3 cup (80 ml/2 3/4 fl oz) boiling water. Allow to steep for 5 minutes, breaking up the pulp as it softens. Strain, then discard the solids.

3 Put the shallots, chilli, garlic, lemon grass, ginger, shrimp paste and 1 teaspoon of the oil in a small food processor or mortar and pestle and blend until a smooth paste is formed, then stir in the cumin.

4 Heat a non-stick wok over high heat, add 1 tablespoon of the oil and swirl to coat the side of the wok. Add the paste and cook for 5 minutes, or until it is fragrant, glossy and the liquid has evaporated. Remove from the wok.

5 Reheat the wok to very hot, add the remaining oil and swirl to coat. Add the squid pieces in small batches, stir-frying for 1–2 minutes each batch, or until cooked through. Remove from the wok.

6 Reduce the heat to medium, then add the spice paste, strained tamarind water and sugar. Stir-fry for 2 minutes, or until the sauce ingredients are well combined. Return the squid to the wok and stir-fry for 1 minute, or until the squid is well coated with the sauce and heated through. Serve with steamed rice.

NOTE: Use a non-stick or stainless steel wok to cook this recipe because the tamarind purée will react with the metal in a regular wok and badly taint the dish.

SAMBAL

Sambal gorengs, or chilli stir-fries, are a common feature of Indonesian cuisine. Their characteristic red colour is derived from the large numbers of chillies used in the spice paste that flavours the dishes.

RIGHT: Indonesian sambal squid

Pull back the apron and remove the top shell from the crab.

Remove the intestines and grey feathery gills and segment into 4 pieces.

Crack the claws open with a cracker to make the crab easier to eat.

CHILLI CRAB

Preparation time: 20 minutes
Total cooking time: 15 minutes
Serves 4

★ ★

1 kg (2 lb) raw blue swimmer crabs

2 tablespoons peanut oil

2 cloves garlic, finely chopped

2 teaspoons finely chopped fresh ginger

2 fresh red chillies, seeded and sliced

2 tablespoons hoisin sauce

$^{1}/_{2}$ cup (125 ml/4 fl oz) tomato sauce

$^{1}/_{4}$ cup (60 ml/2 fl oz) sweet chilli sauce

1 tablespoon fish sauce

$^{1}/_{2}$ teaspoon sesame oil

4 spring onions (scallions), sliced

fresh coriander (cilantro) sprigs, to garnish

1 Pull back the apron and remove the top shell from the crabs. Remove the intestines and grey feathery gills. Segment each crab into 4 pieces. Use a cracker to crack the claws open; this will make it easier to eat later and will also allow the flavours to get into the crab meat.

2 Heat a wok over high heat, add the oil and swirl to coat. Add the garlic, ginger and chilli, and stir-fry for 1–2 minutes.

3 Add the crab pieces and stir-fry for about 6 minutes, or until they turn orange.

4 Stir in the hoisin, tomato, sweet chilli and fish sauces, the sesame oil and $^{1}/_{4}$ cup (60 ml/2 fl oz) water. Bring to the boil, then reduce the heat and simmer, covered, for 6 minutes, or until the crab shell turns bright orange and the flesh turns white and flakes easily.

5 Sprinkle with the spring onion and serve on a platter, garnished with the coriander sprigs. Serve with steamed rice.

NOTES: You can use any variety of raw crab, or substitute raw prawns (shrimp) or Balmain bugs. To make Singapore pepper crab, follow the Chilli crab recipe up to the end of step 3. Then add 150 g (5 oz) butter, 2 tablespoons finely chopped garlic, 1 tablespoon finely chopped fresh ginger, 1 seeded and finely chopped small fresh red chilli and 1$^{1}/_{2}$ tablespoons ground black pepper to the wok and stir-fry for 30 seconds. Add a mixture of 2 tablespoons dark soy sauce, 2 tablespoons oyster sauce and 1 tablespoon grated palm sugar. Return the crab to the wok, cover with a lid and stir every minute for 4 minutes, or until the crab is cooked.

ABOVE: Chilli crab

211

1 Combine the oyster sauce, soy sauce, sesame oil and sugar in a small bowl and stir until the sugar dissolves.

2 Heat a wok over medium heat, add the oil and swirl to coat. Add the garlic and ginger and stir-fry for 30 seconds, or until fragrant. Add the peas and cook for 1 minute, then add the scallops and spring onion and cook for 1 minute, or until the spring onion is wilted. Stir in the sauce and heat for 1 minute, or until heated through and combined. Serve with rice.

GREEN CURRY PRAWN AND NOODLE STIR-FRY

Preparation time: 20 minutes
Total cooking time: 15 minutes
Serves 4

400 g (13 oz) Hokkien (egg) noodles
2 teaspoons grated palm sugar
1 tablespoon fish sauce
2 teaspoons lime juice
1 tablespoon peanut oil
1 onion, cut into thin wedges
1 1/2 tablespoons good-quality green curry paste
150 g (5 oz) baby corn, cut in half on the diagonal
125 g (4 oz) snake beans, cut into 4 cm
   (1 1/2 inch) lengths
1 cup (250 ml/8 fl oz) coconut milk
1/2 cup (125 ml/4 fl oz) chicken stock
800 g (1 lb 10 oz) raw king prawns (shrimp),
   peeled and deveined, with tails intact
3 tablespoons chopped fresh coriander
   (cilantro) leaves

1 Put the noodles in a heatproof bowl, cover with boiling water and soak for 1 minute, or until tender and separated. Drain well.

2 Combine the palm sugar, fish sauce and lime juice in a small bowl or jug.

3 Heat a wok over high heat, add the oil and swirl to coat. Stir-fry the onion for 1–2 minutes, or until soft. Add the curry paste and cook for 1 minute, or until fragrant. Add the baby corn, snake beans, coconut milk and stock to the wok and simmer for 3–4 minutes. Add the prawns and cook for 3–4 minutes, or until they are pink and cooked. Stir the sauce into the wok. Add the noodles and chopped coriander and toss well until the noodles are heated through. Serve.

STIR-FRIED SCALLOPS WITH SUGAR SNAP PEAS

Preparation time: 20 minutes
Total cooking time: 5 minutes
Serves 4

2 1/2 tablespoons oyster sauce
2 teaspoons soy sauce
1/2 teaspoon sesame oil
2 teaspoons sugar
2 tablespoons vegetable oil
2 large cloves garlic, crushed
3 teaspoons finely chopped fresh ginger
300 g (10 oz) sugar snap peas
500 g (1 lb) scallops, without roe, membrane
   removed
2 spring onions (scallions), cut into 2 cm
   (3/4 inch) lengths

ABOVE: Stir-fried scallops with sugar snap peas

PRAWN SAN CHOY BAU

Preparation time: 20 minutes
Total cooking time: 5 minutes
Serves 4-6

1 iceberg lettuce
2 tablespoons soy sauce
2 tablespoons oyster sauce
2 tablespoons lime juice
1 kg (2 lb) raw prawns (shrimp)
  (see Note)
1 tablespoon vegetable oil
1 teaspoon sesame oil
2 spring onions (scallions), finely chopped
2 cloves garlic, crushed
1 x 2 cm ($^1/_2$ x $^3/_4$ inches) piece fresh ginger, grated
120 g (4 oz) drained water chestnuts, chopped
1 tablespoon chopped fresh red chilli
1 cup (185 g/6 oz) cold, cooked white rice
1 cup (90 g/3 oz) bean sprouts, tailed
$^1/_2$ cup (25 g/$^3/_4$ oz) chopped fresh coriander
  (cilantro) leaves
$^1/_4$ cup (60 ml/2 fl oz) hoisin sauce

1 Wash the lettuce and separate the leaves. Shake off any excess water and dry thoroughly on paper towels.

2 Combine the soy sauce, oyster sauce and lime juice in a small bowl or jug. Set aside until needed.

3 Peel and devein the prawns, then, if they are large, cut them into smaller pieces.

4 Heat a wok over high heat, add the vegetable and sesame oils and swirl to coat the side of the wok. Add the spring onion, garlic and ginger and cook for 30 seconds. Add the prawn meat, water chestnuts and chilli, season with salt and freshly ground black pepper and continue stir-frying for 2 minutes. Add the rice, sprouts and coriander and stir until combined.

5 Pour in the stir-fry sauce, toss briefly, then remove the wok from the heat. Transfer the mixture to a serving bowl. Place the dry lettuce cups on a plate. Either fill the lettuce cups with the mixture yourself, or allow your guests to do so at the table. Serve with hoisin sauce, to be drizzled over the top.

NOTE: To save time, you can buy peeled prawns. You will only need 500 g (1 lb)—about half their weight comes from the shells.

WATER CHESTNUTS
Although the dark brown skin and shape of the water chestnut resemble those of the true chestnut, they are, in fact, not nuts at all. The first part of the name is more accurate, as they are actually the edible tuber of a plant grown in water, such as that found in rice paddies. Unlike rice, they are harvested when the paddies are dry. Used in stir-fries, stuffing, dumpling fillings and hotpots, water chestnuts add crispness and textural contrast to many dishes, which is particularly valued in Chinese cuisine.

LEFT: Prawn san choy bau

213

MALAYSIAN FISH CURRY

Preparation time: 25 minutes
Total cooking time: 25 minutes
Serves 4

★ ★

500 g (1 lb) skinless white fish fillets
   (eg. ling, flake, hake, coley)
3–6 medium-sized fresh red chillies
1 onion, chopped
4 cloves garlic
3 stems lemon grass, white part only,
   sliced
4 cm (1 1/2 inch) piece fresh ginger, sliced
2 teaspoons shrimp paste
1/4 cup (60 ml/2 fl oz) oil
1 tablespoon fish curry powder (see Note)
1 cup (250 ml/8 fl oz) coconut milk
1 tablespoon tamarind concentrate
1 tablespoon kecap manis
2 ripe tomatoes, chopped
1 tablespoon lemon juice

ABOVE: Malaysian
fish curry

1 Cut the fish into cubes. Combine the chillies, onion, garlic, lemon grass, ginger and shrimp paste in a small food processor and process until roughly chopped. Add 2 tablespoons of the oil, to assist the blending, and process until the mixture forms a smooth paste, regularly scraping down the sides of the bowl with a spatula.
2 Heat the remaining oil in a wok or deep, heavy-based frying pan and add the paste. Cook for 3–4 minutes over low heat, stirring constantly until very fragrant. Add the curry powder and stir for another 2 minutes. Add the coconut milk, tamarind, kecap manis and 1 cup (250 ml/8 fl oz) water to the wok. Bring to the boil, stirring occasionally, then reduce the heat and simmer for 10 minutes.
3 Add the fish, tomato and lemon juice. Season to taste with salt and pepper. Simmer for 5 minutes, or until the fish is just cooked. The flesh will flake easily when tested with a fork. Serve immediately with steamed rice.
NOTE: Fish curry powder is a special blend of spices suited to seafood flavours. It is available from Asian food stores. Use chillies according to your taste. If you leave the seeds in, the curry will have a hotter taste.

THAI GREEN FISH CURRY

Preparation time: 40 minutes
Total cooking time: 20 minutes
Serves 4

4 fresh green chillies, seeded and chopped

4 spring onions (scallions), chopped

I small onion, roughly chopped

2 cloves garlic, crushed

2 stems lemon grass, white part only, chopped

I tablespoon chopped coriander (cilantro) root

6 tablespoons fresh coriander (cilantro) leaves

6 whole black peppercorns

I teaspoon ground coriander

2 teaspoons ground cumin

2 teaspoons finely grated lime rind

2 teaspoons shrimp paste

I teaspoon ground turmeric

I teaspoon salt

3 tablespoons oil

2¹/₂ cups (600 ml/20 fl oz) coconut milk

2 dried makrut (kaffir) lime leaves

2 cm (³/4 inch) piece dried galangal root

I tablespoon fish sauce

750 g (1 ¹/₂ lb) skinless white fish fillet (eg. cod, coley, flake, ling), cut into cubes

1 Combine the chilli, spring onion, onion, garlic, lemon grass, coriander root and half the leaves, the peppercorns, ground coriander, cumin, lime rind, shrimp paste, turmeric, salt and 2 tablespoons of the oil in a small food processor. Blend to a smooth paste.

2 Heat the remaining oil in a pan, add half the curry paste and cook for 2 minutes, or until fragrant. Stir in the coconut milk, kaffir lime leaves, galangal and fish sauce and mix well.

3 Add the fish to the pan and simmer, uncovered, for 15 minutes, or until the fish is tender and the sauce has thickened slightly. Stir in the remaining coriander leaves. Serve with rice.

NOTES: This curry is even more delicious if made a day ahead. Refrigerate, covered. Leftover paste can be sealed in an airtight container and refrigerated for up to 2 weeks, or frozen for up to 2 months.

GALANGAL

Fresh galangal is a rhizome that looks like its close relative, ginger. It has a ginger-peppery flavour and is used as a seasoning. There are two types of galangal: white-fleshed *greater galangal* (also known as Siamese ginger, Laos ginger and Thai ginger) is the most common. *Lesser galangal*, which has orange-red flesh, is much hotter and stronger and is usually cooked as a vegetable.

ABOVE: Thai green fish curry

215

MEAT

GLAZED HAM

The size of ham we have used is enough for about 20 people. Choose your favourite glaze and follow the directions below. Carving is easier if you hold onto the unglazed shank end.

PREPARING, GLAZING AND HEATING LEG HAM

Preheat the oven to moderate 180°C (350°F/Gas 4). Cut a line through the thick rind of a 7 kg (14 lb) smoked, cooked leg ham, 6 cm (2½ inches) from the shank end so you can easily lift the rind. (For an uncooked leg of ham, refer to the note further on.) To remove the rind, run your thumb around the edge, under the rind and carefully pull back, easing your hand under the rind between the fat and the rind. With a sharp knife, lightly score the fat to form a diamond pattern. Do not cut all the way through to the ham or the fat will fall off during cooking. Spread half the glaze of your choice over the ham with a palette knife or the back of a spoon and press a clove into the centre of each diamond. Put the ham on a rack in a deep baking dish and pour 2 cups (500 ml/16 fl oz) water into the dish. Cover the ham and dish securely with greased foil and cook for

45 minutes. Remove from the oven and brush or spread the remaining glaze over the ham. Increase the heat to hot 210°C (415°F/Gas 6–7) and bake, uncovered, for 20 minutes, or until the surface is lightly caramelized. Set aside for 15 minutes before carving.

NOTE: If you are using an uncooked leg ham, for a 7 kg (14 lb) leg ham, soak the ham overnight in a large clean bucket or container of cold water, changing the water a couple of times. Preheat the oven to warm 160°C (315°F/Gas 2–3). Tip out the soaking water and rinse the ham thoroughly under cold running water. Pat dry with paper towels and place in a deep baking dish large enough to hold the ham (the end may stick out slightly). Chop an onion, carrot and stick of celery and place around the baking dish with a couple of bay leaves and a few peppercorns. Pour 2 cups (500 ml/ 16 fl oz) cold water into the dish and cover the dish completely with foil. Bake for 2 hours 40 minutes (20 minutes per kilo, plus 20 minutes). When cooked, remove the ham from the liquid and discard the liquid and vegetables. Allow the ham to cool (this can be done several days ahead if you wish). When ready to use, prepare, glaze and heat as described for the cooked leg of ham above.

HONEY GLAZE

Mix ⅔ cup (125 g/4 oz) soft brown sugar, 3 tablespoons honey and 1 tablespoon hot English mustard together in a bowl.

ORANGE GLAZE

Stir together 1 cup (250 ml/8 fl oz) orange juice, ¾ cup (140 g/4½ oz) soft brown sugar, 1 tablespoon French mustard, ½ cup (175 g/6 oz) honey, 2 teaspoons soy sauce and 2 tablespoons Grand Marnier in a bowl.

MUSTARD AND REDCURRANT GLAZE

Put ⅓ cup (90 g/3 oz) Dijon mustard, 1 cup (315 g/10 oz) redcurrant jelly, 4 crushed cloves of garlic and 2 tablespoons each of oil and soy sauce into a small saucepan. Stir and gently warm over medium heat for 2–3 minutes, or until the jelly has melted. Take care the glaze doesn't catch on the base of the pan.

219

ROAST BEEF WITH YORKSHIRE PUDDINGS

Preparation time: 15 minutes +
 1 hour refrigeration
Total cooking time: 1 hour 40 minutes
Serves 6

★ ★

2 kg (4 lb) piece roasting beef
  (Scotch fillet, rump or sirloin)
2 cloves garlic, crushed

Yorkshire puddings

3/4 cup (90 g/3 oz) plain (all-purpose) flour
1/2 cup (125 ml/4 fl oz) milk
2 eggs

Red wine gravy

2 tablespoons plain (all-purpose) flour
1/3 cup (80 ml/2 3/4 fl oz) red wine
2 1/2 cups (600 ml/20 fl oz) beef stock

1 Preheat the oven to very hot 240°C (475°F/ Gas 9). Rub the piece of beef with the crushed garlic and some freshly ground black pepper and drizzle with oil. Bake on a rack in a baking dish for 20 minutes.

2 Meanwhile, for the Yorkshire puddings, sift the flour and 1/2 teaspoon salt into a large bowl, then make a well in the centre and whisk in the milk. In a separate bowl, whisk the eggs together until fluffy, then add to the batter and mix well. Add 1/2 cup (125 ml/4 fl oz) water and whisk until large bubbles form on the surface. Cover the bowl with plastic wrap and refrigerate for 1 hour.

3 Reduce the oven to moderate 180°C (350°F/ Gas 4) and continue to roast the meat for 1 hour for a rare result, or longer for well done. Cover loosely with foil and leave in a warm place while making the Yorkshire puddings.

4 Increase the oven to hot 220°C (425°F/Gas 7). Pour off all the pan juices into a jug and spoon 1/2 teaspoon of the juices into twelve 1/3 cup (80 ml/2 3/4 fl oz) patty or muffin tins. (Reserve the remaining juice for the gravy.) Heat the muffin tins in the oven until the fat is almost

BELOW: Roast beef with Yorkshire puddings

smoking. Whisk the batter again until bubbles form on the surface. Pour into each muffin tin to three-quarters full. Bake for 20 minutes, or until puffed and lightly golden. Make the gravy while the Yorkshire puddings are baking.

5 To make the gravy, heat 2 tablespoons of the reserved pan juices in the baking dish on the stove over low heat. Add the flour and stir well, scraping the dish to incorporate all the sediment. Cook over medium heat for 1–2 minutes, stirring constantly, until the flour is well browned. Remove from the heat and gradually stir in the wine and stock. Return to the heat, stirring constantly, until the gravy boils and thickens. Simmer for 3 minutes, then season, to taste, with salt and freshly ground black pepper. Strain, if desired.

6 Serve the beef with the hot Yorkshire puddings and red wine gravy.

NOTE: Cooking times vary, but generally, for every 500 g (1 lb) beef, allow 20 minutes for rare, 30 minutes for medium, and 35 minutes for well done.

ROAST LEG OF LAMB WITH GARLIC AND ROSEMARY

Preparation time: 20 minutes
Total cooking time: 1 hour 30 minutes
Serves 6

2 kg (4 lb) leg of lamb
2 cloves garlic, cut into thin slivers
2 tablespoons fresh rosemary sprigs
2 teaspoons oil

1 Preheat the oven to moderate 180°C (350°F/ Gas 4). Using a small sharp knife, cut small slits all over the lamb. Insert the slivers of garlic and sprigs of rosemary into the slits.

2 Brush the lamb with the oil and sprinkle with salt and black pepper. Place on a rack in a baking dish. Add ½ cup (125 ml/4 fl oz) water to the dish. Bake for about 1 hour 30 minutes for medium, or until cooked as desired, basting often with the pan juices. Keep warm and leave for 10–15 minutes before carving. Serve with mint sauce (see page 231).

ABOVE: Roast leg of lamb with garlic and rosemary

PORK WITH APPLE
AND PRUNE STUFFING

Use a spoon to spread the stuffing over the meat side of the pork loin.

Roll up and secure the pork with string, then score the rind at regular intervals.

PORK WITH APPLE AND PRUNE STUFFING

Preparation time: 35 minutes
Total cooking time: 2 hours
Serves 8

★★

1 green apple, chopped
1/3 cup (90 g/3 oz) pitted prunes, chopped
2 tablespoons port
1 tablespoon chopped fresh parsley
2 kg (4 lb) piece boned pork loin
olive oil and salt, to rub on pork
gravy with wine (see page 230), to serve

1 Preheat the oven to very hot 240°C (475°F/ Gas 9). To make the stuffing, combine the apple, prunes, port and parsley. Lay the pork loin on a board with the rind underneath. Spread the stuffing over the meat side of the loin, roll up and secure with skewers or string at regular intervals. If some of the filling falls out while tying, carefully push it back in. Score the pork rind with a sharp knife at 1 cm (1/2 inch) intervals (if the butcher hasn't already done so) and rub generously with oil and salt.

2 Place on a rack in a baking dish. Bake for 15 minutes, then reduce the heat to moderate 180°C (350°F/Gas 4) and bake for 1 1/2–2 hours, or until the pork is cooked through. The juices will run clear when a skewer is inserted into the thickest part of the meat. Cover and stand for 15 minutes before removing the skewers or string and carving. Reserve any pan juices for making the gravy.

NOTE: If the rind fails to crackle, carefully remove it from the meat, cutting between the fat layer and the meat. Scrape off any excess fat and put the rind on a piece of foil. Place under a moderate grill, and grill until the rind has crackled. Alternatively, place between several sheets of paper towel and microwave on high in 1 minute bursts, for about 2–3 minutes altogether (depending on the thickness of the rind).

ABOVE: Pork with apple and prune stuffing

ROAST SIRLOIN WITH MUSTARD SAUCE

Preparation time: 15 minutes
Total cooking time: 1 hour 30 minutes
Serves 6

★ ★

1.5 kg (3 lb) beef sirloin
1/3 cup (90 g/3 oz) wholegrain mustard
1 tablespoon Dijon mustard
1 teaspoon honey
1 clove garlic, crushed
1 tablespoon oil

Mustard sauce

1 cup (250 ml/8 fl oz) white wine
1 tablespoon Dijon mustard
1/4 cup (60 g/2 oz) wholegrain mustard
2 tablespoons honey
200 g (6 1/2 oz) chilled butter, cubed

1 Preheat the oven to hot 220°C (425°F/Gas 7). Cut most of the fat from the piece of beef sirloin, leaving a thin layer.
2 Mix together the mustards and add the honey and garlic. Spread evenly over the sirloin in a thick layer.
3 Place the oil in a baking dish and heat it in the oven for 2 minutes. Place the meat in the hot dish and roast for 15 minutes.
4 Reduce the oven temperature to moderately hot 200°C (400°F/Gas 6) and cook for about 40 minutes for rare, 45–50 minutes for medium rare and 60–65 minutes for well done. Remove from the oven, cover the meat and set aside for 10–15 minutes before carving.
5 For the mustard sauce, pour the wine into a pan and cook over high heat for 5 minutes, or until reduced by half. Add the mustards and honey. Reduce the heat to a simmer and slowly whisk in the butter, without boiling. Remove from the heat and season to taste. Serve thin slices of the meat with the sauce and roast vegetables.

MUSTARD
Mustard seeds come from various species of mustard plant and have differing strengths, colours and sizes. The main types of mustard seeds are yellow, brown and black, the black ones being hotter. Dijon mustard is made from mustard flour mixed with grape must (unfermented juice pressed from the grape, also known as verjuice), vinegar, herbs and spices. Wholegrain mustard uses ground and half-ground seeds resulting in a grainy texture. In cookery, mustard is often added towards the end of the cooking process as it loses its aroma when subjected to heat.

ABOVE: Roast sirloin with mustard sauce

223

1 Preheat the oven to hot 210°C (415°F/ Gas 6–7). Trim the meat of any excess fat and sinew. Fold the thinner part of the tail end under and tie the meat securely with kitchen string at regular intervals to form an even shape.

2 Rub the meat with freshly ground black pepper. Heat the oil over high heat in a large frying pan. Add the meat and brown well all over. Remove from the heat and allow to cool. Remove the string.

3 Spread the pâté over the top and sides of the beef. Cover with the mushrooms, pressing them onto the pâté. Roll the block pastry out on a lightly floured surface to a rectangle large enough to completely enclose the beef.

4 Place the beef on the pastry, brush the edges with egg, and fold over to enclose the meat completely, brushing the edges of the pastry with the beaten egg to seal, and folding in the ends. Invert onto a greased baking tray so the seam is underneath. Cut leaf shapes from the sheet of puff pastry and use to decorate the Wellington. Use the egg to stick the shapes on. Cut a few slits in the top to allow the steam to escape. Brush the top and sides of the pastry with egg, and cook for 45 minutes for rare, 1 hour for medium or 1½ hours for well done. Leave in a warm place for 10 minutes before cutting into slices for serving.

NOTE: Use a firm pâté, discarding any jelly. Cover the pastry loosely with foil if it begins to darken too much.

BEEF WELLINGTON

Preparation time: 25 minutes
Total cooking time: 1 hour 30 minutes
Serves 6–8

★★

1.2 kg (2 lb 6½ oz) beef fillet or
  rib-eye in 1 piece
1 tablespoon oil
125 g (4 oz) pâté
60 g (2 oz) button mushrooms, sliced
375 g (12 oz) block puff pastry, thawed
1 egg, lightly beaten
1 sheet ready-rolled puff pastry, thawed

ABOVE: Beef Wellington

CHIPOLATAS WRAPPED IN BACON

Preheat the oven to moderate 180°C (350°/ Gas 4). Remove the rind from 6 thin bacon rashers, then halve the bacon widthways. Using 12 chipolatas, wrap a piece of the bacon around each one and secure with toothpicks. Line a baking tray with baking paper and place the chipolatas on the tray. Bake for 25–30 minutes, or until the chipolatas are thoroughly cooked through. Alternatively, the chipolatas can be placed around the base of a roast during the last 20–25 minutes of cooking time. Makes 12.

Spoon the pâté mixture into the meat pocket and press it in with the back of a teaspoon.

Tie thick kitchen string at regular intervals to hold the meat together.

STANDING RIB ROAST WITH PATE

Preparation time: 30 minutes
Total cooking time: 2 hours 20 minutes
Serves 6

★ ★

1 rasher bacon, chopped

1 onion, finely chopped

125 g (4 oz) mushrooms, finely chopped

1/2 cup (50 g/1 3/4 oz) dry breadcrumbs

125 g (4 oz) pâté (see Note)

2 tablespoons chopped fresh parsley

1 teaspoon chopped fresh oregano

1 egg, lightly beaten

4 kg (8 lb) standing rib roast (6 chops)

 Preheat the oven to very hot 240°C (475°F/ Gas 9). Place the bacon in a dry frying pan, and cook gently over medium heat until it begins to soften and release its fat. Add the onion and mushroom and cook, stirring, for 3 minutes. Transfer to a bowl and mix in the breadcrumbs, pâté, parsley, oregano and egg. Season to taste with salt and freshly ground black pepper.

2 Cut a slit in the meat, between the rib bones and the meat, to form a pocket. Spoon the pâté mixture into the pocket. Secure the meat firmly with string.

3 Place the meat in a baking dish fat-side-up (the bones form a natural rack). Bake for 15 minutes, then reduce the heat to moderate 180°C (350°F/Gas 4). Bake for another 1 1/2 hours for rare, or up to 2 hours for medium, or until cooked according to taste. Work out the cooking time based on 15–20 minutes per 500 g (1 lb) of meat. This will achieve a roast that is well done on the outside and rare inside.

4 Allow the meat to rest for 15 minutes before carving. Remove the string and cut the meat into thick slices, allowing 1 bone per person. Delicious served with gravy (see page 230) and roast vegetables.

NOTE: You can use any firm-textured pâté, such as peppercorn or Grand Marnier. Discard the jelly from the top of the pâté.

ABOVE: Standing rib roast with pâté

Remove from the heat and allow to cool.

2 Place the veal in a baking dish and rub with salt and white pepper. Pour the onion and wine mixture into the baking dish with the veal.

3 Mix the breadcrumbs and cheese, and press firmly on the veal to form a thick coating. (This will help stop the veal drying out.) Melt the remaining butter and pour over the cheese crust.

4 Roast the veal for 1¼–1½ hours, checking every 30 minutes and being careful not to disturb the crust. If the crust is browning too quickly, cover lightly with foil. Leave for 10 minutes before carving into 1 cm (½ inch) slices. Spoon pan juices over the top.

NOTE: Nut of veal is a piece from the leg.

LAMB CROWN ROAST WITH SAGE STUFFING

Preparation time: 30 minutes
Total cooking time: 50 minutes
Serves 4–6

✹ ✹

1 crown roast of lamb (minimum 12 cutlets)
20 g (¾ oz) butter
2 onions, chopped
1 green apple, peeled and chopped
2 cups (160 g/5½ oz) fresh breadcrumbs
2 tablespoons chopped fresh sage
1 tablespoon chopped fresh parsley
¼ cup (60 ml/2 fl oz) unsweetened apple juice
2 eggs, separated

1 Preheat the oven to hot 210°C (415°F/ Gas 6–7). Trim the meat of excess fat and sinew.

2 Melt the butter in a small pan. Add the onion and apple and cook over medium heat until soft. Remove from the heat and stir into the combined breadcrumbs, sage and parsley. Whisk the apple juice and egg yolks together, then lightly stir into the breadcrumb mixture.

3 Beat the egg whites in a small bowl with electric beaters until soft peaks form. Fold lightly into the stuffing mixture.

4 Place the roast on a sheet of greased foil in a baking dish. Wrap some foil around the tops of the bones to prevent burning. Spoon the stuffing into the cavity. Roast for 45 minutes for medium, or until cooked to your liking. Leave for 10 minutes before cutting between the cutlets.

NOTE: Excess stuffing can be moistened with apple juice, rolled in greased foil and baked.

VEAL FOYOT

Preparation time: 25 minutes
Total cooking time: 1 hour 35 minutes
Serves 6

✹ ✹

50 g (1¾ oz) butter
1 onion, chopped
¾ cup (185 ml/6 fl oz) white wine
¾ cup (185 ml/6 fl oz) beef stock
1.4–1.5 kg (2 lb 13 oz–3 lb) nut of veal
1 cup (80 g/2¾ oz) fresh breadcrumbs
125 g (4 oz) Gruyère cheese, grated

1 Preheat the oven to moderate 180°C (350°F/ Gas 4). Melt half the butter in a saucepan and fry the onion until soft. Add the wine and stock, bring to the boil and boil for 2 minutes. Add ¼ teaspoon each of salt and white pepper.

ABOVE: Veal foyot

ROAST PORK FILLET WITH APPLE AND MUSTARD SAUCE AND GLAZED APPLES

Preparation time: 30 minutes
Total cooking time: 25 minutes
Serves 4

750 g (1 1/2 lb) pork fillet

30 g (1 oz) butter

1 tablespoon oil

1 clove garlic, crushed

1/2 teaspoon grated fresh ginger

1 tablespoon seeded mustard

1/4 cup (60 ml/2 fl oz) apple sauce

2 tablespoons chicken stock

1/2 cup (125 ml/4 fl oz) cream

1 teaspoon cornflour (cornstarch)

Glazed apples

2 green apples

50 g (1 3/4 oz) butter

2 tablespoons soft brown sugar

1 Trim the pork fillet, removing any fat or sinew from the outside. Tie the fillet with kitchen string at 3 cm (1 1/4 inch) intervals to keep in shape.

2 Heat the butter and oil in a frying pan, add the pork fillet and cook until lightly browned all over. Remove and place on a rack in a baking dish. (Retain the cooking oils in the frying pan.) Add 1/2 cup (125 ml/4 fl oz) water to the baking dish and bake in a moderate 180°C (350°F/ Gas 4) oven for 15–20 minutes. Leave in a warm place for 10 minutes before removing the string and slicing.

3 For the sauce, reheat the oils in the frying pan, add the garlic and ginger and stir for 1 minute. Stir in the mustard, apple sauce and stock. Slowly stir in the combined cream and cornflour and stir until the mixture boils and thickens.

4 For the glazed apples, cut the apples into 1 cm (1/2 inch) slices. Melt the butter in the pan and add the sugar. Stir until the sugar dissolves. Add the apple slices and pan-fry, turning occasionally, until the apples are glazed and lightly browned.

5 Slice the pork and serve the apple and mustard sauce over it. Serve with the glazed apples.

NOTE: Pork fillets can be thick and short or long and thin and the time they take to cook will vary accordingly.

ABOVE: Roast pork fillet with apple and mustard sauce and glazed apples

DRYING SAGE

You can easily dry your own sage. Harvest the sage on a dry day and divide into small bunches. Strip a few leaves away from the base of the stem so that they can be tied in neat bunches without mould forming on the stems. Tie the stems firmly and hang the bunches in a warm, airy place away from direct sunlight.

PORK WITH SAGE AND CAPERS

Preparation time: 25 minutes
Total cooking time: 1 hour 15 minutes
Serves 4

★★

1/4 cup (60 ml/2 fl oz) extra virgin olive oil

25 g (3/4 oz) unsalted butter

1 onion, finely chopped

100 g (3 1/2 oz) fresh white breadcrumbs

2 teaspoons chopped fresh sage

1 tablespoon chopped fresh flat-leaf (Italian) parsley

2 teaspoons grated lemon rind

2 1/2 tablespoons salted baby capers, rinsed and drained

1 egg

2 large pork fillets (about 500 g/1 lb each)

8 large thin slices of streaky bacon or prosciutto

2 teaspoons plain (all-purpose) flour

100 ml (3 1/2 fl oz) dry vermouth

1 1/4 cups (315 ml/10 fl oz) chicken or vegetable stock

8 whole sage leaves, extra, to garnish

1 Preheat the oven to warm 170°C (325°F/ Gas 3). Heat 1 tablespoon of the oil and the butter in a frying pan, add the onion and cook for 5 minutes, or until lightly golden.
2 Place the breadcrumbs, chopped sage, parsley, lemon rind, 1/2 tablespoon capers and the cooked onion in a bowl. Add the egg and season well.
3 Split each pork fillet in half lengthways and open out. Spread the stuffing down the length of one and cover with the other fillet.
4 Stretch the bacon or prosciutto with the back of a knife and wrap each piece slightly overlapping around the pork to form a neat parcel. Tie with string at intervals.
5 Place the pork in a baking dish and drizzle with 1 tablespoon oil. Bake for 1 hour. To test if the meat is cooked, insert a skewer in the thickest part. The juices should run clear. Remove the meat from the tin, cover with foil and leave to rest. Place the baking dish on the stovetop, add the flour and stir in well. Add the vermouth and allow to bubble for 1 minute. Add the stock and stir while cooking to remove all the lumps. Simmer for 5 minutes. Add the remaining capers to the sauce.
6 In a small saucepan, heat the remaining oil and when very hot, fry the whole sage leaves until crisp. Drain on crumpled paper towels.
7 Slice the pork into 1 cm (1/2 inch) slices. Spoon a little sauce over the pork and serve each portion with fried sage leaves on top.

RIGHT: Pork with sage and capers

GASCONNADE

Preparation time: 25 minutes
Total cooking time: 1 hour 30 minutes
Serves 6

★ ★

1 large leg of lamb, about 2.5 kg (5 lb),
   partially boned (see Note)
1 carrot, coarsely chopped
1 stick celery, coarsely chopped
1 large onion, coarsely chopped
1 bay leaf
bouquet garni (see page 99)
2 cloves garlic, crushed
6 anchovy fillets, mashed
1/2 tablespoon finely chopped fresh parsley
1/2 tablespoon finely chopped fresh thyme
1/2 tablespoon finely chopped fresh rosemary
3 tablespoons olive oil
25 cloves garlic, unpeeled

 Preheat the oven to hot 220°C (425°F/Gas 7). Place the removed lamb bone in a stockpot with the carrot, celery, onion, bay leaf and bouquet garni, and add just enough cold water to cover. Bring to the boil and simmer uncovered for 1 hour. Strain and if necessary simmer until reduced to 2 cups (500 ml/16 fl oz).

2 Meanwhile, combine the crushed garlic, anchovies, chopped herbs and olive oil in a small bowl with some freshly ground black pepper. Rub the cavity of the lamb with most of the herb mixture. Roll the meat up and tie securely with kitchen string. Rub the lamb with the remaining herb mixture and place in a baking dish. Bake for 15 minutes, then reduce the temperature to moderate 180°C (350°F/Gas 4). Continue baking for about 45 minutes (for medium-rare), basting with the pan juices occasionally, until cooked to your liking.

3 Bring a saucepan of water to the boil and add the garlic cloves. Boil for 5 minutes. Drain and rinse under cold water. Peel the garlic and purée the pulp. Put it in the saucepan with the 2 cups (500 ml/16 fl oz) of stock and bring to the boil. Simmer for 10 minutes. Transfer the lamb to a carving tray and keep warm. Spoon off the fat from the pan juices. Add the garlic stock and place the dish over high heat. Bring to the boil and cook until reduced by half. Adjust the seasoning. Serve the lamb sliced, accompanied by the sauce.

NOTE: Ask your butcher to partially bone the leg of lamb, leaving the shank bone in place. Take home the removed bone to use when making the stock.

RESTING ROAST LAMB

A perennial French bistro favourite, roast leg of lamb has its origins as a one-pot dish that could be taken to the village baker to be cooked in the local baker's oven. It is important to rest roast lamb after it is cooked and before it is carved, as this ensures that the juices will permeate the meat evenly. If cut too early, the interior will be moist but the exterior will be dry, as the juices flow towards the centre when red meat is cooked.

ABOVE: Gasconnade

SAVOURY SAUCES

These delicious classic sauces and gravies can be quickly made while the roast is

cooking or resting. Mint sauce will develop in flavour if made a day in advance.

APPLE SAUCE

Peel and core 4 green apples, then roughly chop the flesh. Place the flesh in a pan with 1 tablespoon caster (superfine) sugar, ½ cup (125 ml/4 fl oz) water, 2 whole cloves and 1 cinnamon stick. Cover and simmer for 10 minutes, or until soft. Remove from the heat and discard the cloves and cinnamon stick. Mash or, for a finer sauce, press through a sieve. Stir in 1–2 teaspoons lemon juice, or to taste. Serve with roast pork or ham. Makes 1 cup (250 ml/8 fl oz).

GRAVY WITH WINE

Discard all but 2 tablespoons of the pan juices from the baking dish you cooked the roast in. Heat the dish on the stovetop over moderate heat, stir in 2 tablespoons plain (all-purpose) flour and cook, stirring, until well browned. Remove from the heat and gradually add 2 teaspoons Worcestershire sauce, 2 tablespoons red or white wine and 2¼ cups (560 ml/18 fl oz) beef or chicken stock. Return to the heat, stir until the mixture boils and thickens, then simmer for 2 minutes. Season with salt and pepper, to taste. Suitable for all roast meats. Makes 1½ cups (375 ml/12 fl oz).

MINT SAUCE

Sprinkle 1 tablespoon caster (superfine) sugar over ½ cup (10 g/¼ oz) fresh mint leaves on a chopping board, then finely chop the mint. Transfer to a bowl and add 2 tablespoons caster (superfine) sugar. Cover with ¼ cup (60 ml/2 fl oz) boiling water and stir until the sugar has dissolved. Stir in ¾ cup (185 ml/6 fl oz) malt vinegar, cover and chill overnight. Traditionally served with roast lamb. Makes 1½ cups (375 ml/12 fl oz).

CREAMY HORSERADISH

Combine 175 g (6 oz) horseradish cream, 1 finely chopped spring onion (scallion) and ¼ cup (60 g/2 oz) sour cream in a bowl. Fold in ½ cup (125 ml/ 4 fl oz) whipped cream. Season. Serve with roast beef or veal. Makes 1½ cups (375 ml/12 oz).

BREAD SAUCE

Slice 1 small onion and combine in a small pan with 1¼ cups (315 ml/10 fl oz) milk, 1 bay leaf, 4 black peppercorns and 2 whole cloves. Bring to the boil over medium heat, then lower the heat and simmer for 10 minutes. Strain into a large heatproof bowl and discard the onion and flavourings. Add 1¼ cups (100 g/3½ oz) fresh breadcrumbs to the bowl with a pinch of ground nutmeg and 20 g (¾ oz) butter. Stir until smooth, then season with salt and pepper, to taste. Bread sauce is traditionally served with roast goose, turkey or chicken.
Makes 1¼ cups (315 ml/10 fl oz).

RASPBERRY AND CRANBERRY SAUCE

Purée 150 g (5 oz) fresh or frozen raspberries, then press through a sieve to remove the seeds. Combine the purée in a small pan with ¼ cup (60 ml/2 fl oz) orange juice, ½ cup (160 g/5½ oz) cranberry sauce, 2 teaspoons Dijon mustard and 1 teaspoon finely grated orange rind. Stir over heat until smooth. Add ¼ cup (60 ml/2 fl oz) port and simmer for 5 minutes. Remove and allow to cool—the sauce will thicken slightly. Serve with roast turkey, goose, ham or duck.
Makes 1 cup (250 ml/8 fl oz).

FROM LEFT: Apple sauce; Gravy with wine; Mint sauce; Creamy horseradish; Bread sauce; Raspberry and cranberry sauce

231

ACCOMPANIMENTS

Apart from the old favourites on the previous page, the flavour of roasts and cold

cuts can be transformed by serving with one of these imaginative concoctions.

BEETROOT RELISH

Put 750 g (1½ lb) peeled and coarsely grated fresh beetroot in a large saucepan with 1 chopped onion, 400 g (13 oz) peeled, cored and chopped green apples, 1²/₃ cups (410 ml/13 fl oz) white wine vinegar, ½ cup (95 g/3 oz) soft brown sugar, ½ cup (125 g/4 oz) sugar, 2 tablespoons lemon juice and 2 teaspoons salt and stir over low heat, without boiling, until all the sugar has dissolved. Bring to the boil and simmer, stirring

often, for 20–30 minutes, or until the beetroot and onion are tender and the relish is reduced and thickened. Spoon into clean, warm jars and seal. Turn upside down for 2 minutes, invert and leave to cool. Label and date. Leave for a month before using. Store in a cool, dark place up to 12 months. Refrigerate after opening, for up to 6 weeks. Serve with ham, beef, turkey, duck or goose.
Makes 1 litre (32 fl oz).

MOSTARDA DI FRUTTA

Blend 1 teaspoon of cornflour (cornstarch) with 1 tablespoon water in a small bowl. Pour ¾ cup (185 ml/6 fl oz) water into a saucepan and pour in 1¼ cups (315 ml/10 fl oz) white wine. Add 1 tablespoon honey, 3 cloves, 1 tablespoon yellow mustard seeds, ¼ teaspoon ground nutmeg, ½ teaspoon grated nutmeg and 2 broken cinnamon sticks. Bring to the boil, then stir in the cornflour mixture, lower the heat and cook, stirring, for

5 minutes or until the mixture boils and thickens. Add 175 g (6 oz) chopped assorted glacé fruits and 1 tablespoon lemon juice and simmer for 15 minutes, or until the fruit is soft and the mixture is thick. Spoon into a warm clean jar and seal immediately. Delicious served with cold meats, especially ham, and poultry and game. Makes 1 cup (250 ml/8 fl oz).

GRAINY SWEET MUSTARD

Combine 30 g (1 oz) brown or black mustard seeds with 70 g (2¼ oz) yellow mustard seeds in a bowl. Add ½ cup (125 ml/4 fl oz) white wine vinegar, cover and leave overnight. Process three-quarters of the seeds, 2 teaspoons lemon juice, 1 teaspoon salt and 1 tablespoon honey in a food processor until roughly crushed. Transfer to a bowl and stir in the remaining seeds. Spoon into clean jars. Seal. Refrigerate after opening. Keeps for 2 months. Makes 1 cup (250 g/8 oz).

WASABI MAYONNAISE

Combine ½ cup (125 g/4 oz) each of whole-egg mayonnaise and thick natural yoghurt in a small bowl with 2 teaspoons wasabi paste and 1 tablespoon each of freshly squeezed lime juice and chopped fresh coriander (cilantro). Stir thoroughly until combined, then allow to stand for at least 20 minutes before serving. This mayonnaise is particularly suitable for serving with cold seafood such as oysters, prawns (shrimp) and fish. Makes 1 cup (250 g/8 oz).

RED PEPPER AND CORIANDER AIOLI

Drain the oil from 150 g (5 oz) char-grilled peppers (capsicums). Process the peppers in a food processor with 1 cup (250 g/8 oz) whole-egg mayonnaise for 2 minutes, or until smooth. Add 1 crushed clove of garlic and 1 tablespoon each of lemon juice and chopped fresh coriander (cilantro). Process until combined. Serve with hot and cold cuts of meat, or seafood such as prawns (shrimp), fish and scallops. Makes 1½ cups (375 ml/12 fl oz).

HONEY MUSTARD

Combine 8 tablespoons honey, 4 tablespoons each of yellow mustard and cider vinegar, and 2 tablespoons olive oil in a small pan. Stir constantly over medium heat for 5 minutes, or until thickened. Allow the mixture to cool completely, then spoon into clean jars. Seal the jars, then label and date them. Honey mustard is delicious served with beef, ham or veal. Makes ⅔ cup (170 g/5½ oz).

FROM LEFT: Beetroot relish; Mostarda di frutta; Grainy sweet mustard; Wasabi mayonnaise; Red pepper and coriander aïoli; Honey mustard

PORK SAUSAGES WITH WHITE BEANS

Twist each sausage tightly in opposite directions so that it forms two short fat sausages joined in the middle.

Cook until all the water in the pan has evaporated and the sausages are lightly browned.

ABOVE: Pork sausages with white beans

PORK SAUSAGES WITH WHITE BEANS

Preparation time: 25 minutes + overnight soaking
Total cooking time: 1 hour 40 minutes
Serves 4

✷ ✷

350 g (11 oz) dried white haricot beans
150 g (5 oz) tocino, speck or pancetta, unsliced
1/2 leek, thinly sliced
2 whole cloves garlic
1 bay leaf
1 small red chilli, split and seeds removed
1 small onion
2 cloves
1 sprig of fresh rosemary
3 sprigs of fresh thyme
1 sprig of fresh parsley
3 tablespoons olive oil
8 pork sausages
1/2 onion, finely chopped
1 green pepper (capsicum), finely chopped
1/2 teaspoon paprika
1/2 cup (125 ml/4 fl oz) puréed tomato
1 teaspoon cider vinegar

1 Soak the beans overnight in plenty of cold water. Drain and rinse the beans under cold water. Put them in a large saucepan with the tocino, leek, garlic, bay leaf and chilli. Stud the onion with the cloves and add to the saucepan. Tie the rosemary, thyme and parsley together and add to the saucepan. Pour in 3 cups (750 ml/24 fl oz) cold water and bring to the boil. Add 1 tablespoon oil, reduce the heat and simmer, covered, for about 1 hour, until the beans are tender. When necessary, add a little more boiling water to keep the beans covered.
2 Prick each sausage 5 or 6 times and twist tightly in opposite directions in the middle to give 2 short fat sausages joined in the middle. Put in a single layer in a large frying pan and add enough cold water to reach halfway up their sides. Bring to the boil and simmer, turning two or three times, until all the water has evaporated and the sausages brown lightly in the little fat that is left in the pan. Remove from the pan and cut the short sausages apart. Add the remaining 2 tablespoons oil, the chopped onion and green pepper to the pan and fry over medium heat for 5–6 minutes. Stir in the paprika, cook for 30 seconds then add the puréed tomato. Season to taste. Cook, stirring, for 1 minute.
3 Remove the tocino, herb sprigs and any loose large pieces of onion from the bean mixture. Leave in any loose leaves from the herbs, and any small pieces of onion. Add the sausages and sauce to the pan and stir the vinegar through. Bring to the boil. Adjust the seasoning.
IN ADVANCE: This dish improves if cooked in advance and left for up to 2 days before serving.

SPANISH BRAISED LAMB

Preparation time: 15 minutes
Total cooking time: 2 hours 15 minutes
Serves 4

1/3 cup (80 ml/2³/4 fl oz) olive oil
1 kg (2 lb) lamb shoulder, diced
1 large onion, finely chopped
4 cloves garlic, crushed
2 teaspoons paprika
5 tablespoons lemon juice
2 tablespoons chopped fresh flat-leaf
   (Italian) parsley

1 Heat the oil in a large, heavy-based deep frying pan over high heat. Sauté the lamb in two batches for 5 minutes each batch, until well browned. Remove all the lamb from the pan and set aside.
2 Add the onion and cook for 4–5 minutes, or until soft and golden. Add the garlic and paprika and stir for 1 minute. Return the meat to the pan with 4 tablespoons lemon juice and 1.75 litres (56 fl oz) water and simmer over low heat, stirring occasionally for 2 hours, until the liquid has almost evaporated and the oil starts to reappear. Stir in the remaining lemon juice and the parsley, season to taste, and serve.

SOUVLAKI

Preparation time: 20 minutes +
   overnight marinating + 30 minutes standing
Total cooking time: 10 minutes
Serves 4

1 kg (2 lb) boned leg lamb, trimmed, cut
   into 2 cm (³/4 inch) cubes
1/4 cup (60 ml/2 fl oz) olive oil
2 teaspoons finely grated lemon rind
1/3 cup (80 ml/2³/4 fl oz) lemon juice
1/2 cup (125 ml/4 fl oz) dry white wine
2 teaspoons dried oregano
2 fresh bay leaves
2 large cloves garlic, finely chopped
1 cup (250 g/8 oz) Greek-style natural yoghurt
2 cloves garlic, crushed, extra

1 Put the lamb in a non-metallic bowl with 2 tablespoons oil, the lemon rind and juice, wine, oregano, bay leaves, the garlic and some pepper. Toss, then cover and refrigerate overnight.
2 Combine the yoghurt and remaining garlic and leave for 30 minutes.
3 Drain the lamb. Thread onto 8 skewers and cook on a barbecue or chargrill plate, brushing with the remaining oil, for 7–8 minutes, or until done to your liking. Serve with the yoghurt, bread and a salad.

LAMB IN GREECE
The popularity of lamb in Greece is linked to the country's hilly, often barren landscape. This terrain is not naturally suitable for cattle so, instead, sheep and goats are usually reared, both for their meat and milk. As meat was historically scarce and expensive, it is a food traditionally associated with religious feast days and other special occasions. During Easter, the most important religious festival for Orthodox Greeks, it is customary to spit roast an entire lamb, including its entrails. As with all their meat, Greeks generally prefer lamb to be well done, so that it falls off the bone, but the recipes we have given can be cooked to your liking.

ABOVE: Souvlaki

2 large ripe tomatoes, peeled and chopped
2 tablespoons tomato paste (tomato purée)
$^1/_2$ cup (125 ml/4 fl oz) white wine
3 tablespoons chopped fresh parsley

Cheese sauce
60 g (2 oz) butter
$^1/_2$ cup (60 g/2 oz) plain (all-purpose) flour
$2^1/_2$ cups (625 ml/20 fl oz) milk
pinch of ground nutmeg
$^1/_3$ cup (35 g/1 $^1/_4$ oz) finely grated kefalotyri
  or Parmesan
2 eggs, lightly beaten

1 Lay the eggplant on a tray, sprinkle with salt and leave to stand for 30 minutes. Rinse under water and pat dry. Preheat the oven to moderate 180°C (350°F/Gas 4).
2 Heat 2 tablespoons olive oil in a frying pan, add the eggplant in batches and cook for 1–2 minutes each side, or until golden and soft. Add a little more oil when needed.
3 Heat 1 tablespoon olive oil in a large saucepan, add the onion and cook over medium heat for 5 minutes. Add the garlic, allspice and cinnamon and cook for 30 seconds. Add the lamb and cook for 5 minutes, or until browned, breaking up any lumps with the back of a spoon. Add the tomato, tomato paste and wine, and simmer over low heat for 30 minutes, or until the liquid has evaporated. Stir in the chopped parsley and season to taste.
4 For the cheese sauce, melt the butter in a saucepan over low heat. Stir in the flour and cook for 1 minute, or until pale and foaming. Remove the saucepan from the heat and gradually stir in the milk and nutmeg. Return the saucepan to the heat and stir constantly until the sauce boils and thickens. Reduce the heat and simmer for 2 minutes. Stir in 1 tablespoon of the cheese until well combined. Stir in the egg just before using.
5 Line the base of a 3 litre (96 fl oz) ovenproof dish measuring 25 x 30 cm (10 x 12 inches) with a third of the eggplant. Spoon half the meat sauce over it and cover with another layer of eggplant. Spoon the remaining meat sauce over the top and cover with the remaining eggplant. Spread the cheese sauce over the top and sprinkle with the remaining cheese. Bake for 1 hour. Leave to stand for 10 minutes before slicing.
VARIATION: You can substitute an equal quantity of sliced, shallow-fried zucchini (courgettes) or potatoes, or any combination of these vegetables for the eggplant (aubergine).

MOUSSAKA

Preparation time: 20 minutes
  + 30 minutes standing
Total cooking time: 2 hours
Serves 6

★ ★

1.5 kg (3 lb) eggplants (aubergines),
  cut into 5 mm ($^1/_4$ inch) slices
$^1/_2$ cup (125 ml/4 fl oz) olive oil
2 onions, finely chopped
2 large cloves garlic, crushed
$^1/_2$ teaspoon ground allspice
1 teaspoon ground cinnamon
750 g (1 $^1/_2$ lb) minced (ground) lamb

ABOVE: Moussaka

PASTITSIO
(Meat and pasta bake)

Preparation time: 40 minutes + standing
Total cooking time: 1 hour 30 minutes
Serves 6

150 g (5 oz) elbow macaroni
40 g (1¼ oz) butter
¼ teaspoon ground nutmeg
60 g (2 oz) kefalotyri or Parmesan, grated < ¾C
1 egg, lightly beaten

Meat sauce
2 tablespoons oil
1 onion, finely chopped
2 cloves garlic, crushed
500 g (1 lb) minced (ground) beef
½ cup (125 ml/4 fl oz) red wine
1 cup (250 ml/8 fl oz) beef stock
3 tablespoons tomato paste (tomato purée)
1 teaspoon chopped fresh oregano

Béchamel sauce
40 g (1¼ oz) butter
1½ tablespoons plain (all-purpose) flour
pinch of nutmeg
1½ cups (375 ml/12 fl oz) milk
1 egg, lightly beaten

1 Preheat the oven to moderate 180°C (350°F/Gas 4). Lightly grease a 1.5 litre (48 fl oz) ovenproof dish. Cook the macaroni in a large saucepan of boiling salted water for 10 minutes, or until *al dente*. Drain and return to the pan. Melt the butter in a small saucepan until golden, then pour it over the macaroni. Stir in the nutmeg and half the cheese and season to taste. Leave until cool, then mix in the egg and set aside.

2 For the meat sauce, heat the oil in a large frying pan, add the onion and garlic and cook over medium heat for 6 minutes, or until the onion is soft. Increase the heat, add the beef and cook, stirring, for 5 minutes or until the meat is browned. Add the wine and cook over high heat for 1 minute, or until evaporated. Add the stock, tomato paste, oregano, salt and pepper. Reduce the heat, cover and simmer for 20 minutes.

3 Meanwhile, to make the béchamel sauce, melt the butter in a small saucepan over low heat. Stir in the flour and cook for 1 minute, or until pale and foaming. Remove from the heat and gradually stir in the milk. Return to the heat and stir constantly until the sauce boils and thickens. Reduce the heat and simmer for 2 minutes. Add the nutmeg and some salt and pepper. Allow to cool a little before stirring in the beaten egg. Stir 3 tablespoons of the béchamel into the meat sauce.

4 Spread half the meat sauce in the dish, then layer half the pasta over it. Layer with the remaining meat sauce and then the remaining pasta. Press down firmly with the back of a spoon. Spread the béchamel sauce over the pasta and sprinkle the remaining cheese on top. Bake for 45–50 minutes, or until golden. Let it stand for 15 minutes before serving.

NOTE: Tubular bucatini, which is available in varying thicknesses, can be used as a substitute for the elbow macaroni. Choose one that is a little thicker than spaghetti.

BELOW: Pastitsio

MARINADES

Marinades not only tenderize meats, chicken and fish, but they add flavour and moisture. The length of time needed for the marinade to penetrate will depend on the size of the pieces of meat and the type of meat used. Often the marinade will be used as a basting paste during cooking to add even more flavour.

SHISH KEBABS WITH PEPPERS AND HERBS

Preparation time: 20 minutes
  + 4 hours marinating
Total cooking time: 5 minutes
Serves 4

1 kg (2 lb) boneless leg of lamb
1 red pepper (capsicum)
1 green pepper (capsicum)
3 red onions
olive oil, for brushing

Marinade

1 onion, thinly sliced
2 cloves garlic, crushed
1/4 cup (60 ml/2 fl oz) lemon juice
1/3 cup (80 ml/2 3/4 fl oz) olive oil
1 tablespoon chopped fresh thyme
1 tablespoon paprika
1/2 teaspoon chilli flakes
2 teaspoons ground cumin
1/2 cup (15 g/1/2 oz) chopped fresh
  flat-leaf (Italian) parsley
1/3 cup (20 g/3/4 oz) chopped fresh mint

1 Trim the sinew and most of the fat from the lamb and cut the meat into 3 cm (1 1/4 inch) cubes.
2 Mix all the ingredients for the marinade in a large bowl. Season well with salt and freshly ground black pepper, add the meat and mix

well. Cover and refrigerate for 4–6 hours, or overnight, if time permits.
3 Cut the peppers into 3 cm (1 1/4 inch) squares. Cut each red onion into 6 wedges.
4 Remove the lamb from the marinade and reserve the liquid. Thread the meat onto long skewers, alternating with onion and pepper pieces. Grill the skewers for 5–6 minutes, brushing frequently with the marinade for the first couple of minutes. Serve immediately. These are delicious served with bread or pilaf.

ROMAN LAMB

Preparation time: 15 minutes
Total cooking time: 1 hour 20 minutes
Serves 4–6

1/4 cup (60 ml/2 fl oz) olive oil
1 kg (2 lb) spring lamb, cut into 2 cm
  (3/4 inch) cubes
2 cloves garlic, crushed
6 fresh sage leaves
1 sprig fresh rosemary
1 tablespoon plain (all-purpose) flour
1/2 cup (125 ml/4 fl oz) white wine vinegar
6 anchovy fillets

1 Heat the oil in a heavy-based frying pan and cook the meat in batches over medium heat for 3–4 minutes, until browned on all sides.
2 Return all the meat to the pan and add the garlic, sage and rosemary. Season with salt and

RIGHT: Shish kebabs with peppers and herbs

pepper, combine well and cook for 1 minute.
3 Dust the meat with the flour using a fine sieve, then cook for another minute. Add the vinegar and simmer for 30 seconds, then add 1 cup (250 ml/8 fl oz) water. Bring to a gentle simmer, lower the heat and cover, leaving the lid partially askew. Cook for 50–60 minutes, or until the meat is tender, stirring occasionally and adding a little more water if necessary.
4 When the lamb is almost cooked, mash the anchovies in a mortar and pestle with 1 tablespoon of the cooking liquid, until a paste is formed. Add to the lamb and cook, uncovered, for another 2 minutes. Delicious served with Rosemary potatoes.
NOTES: This dish is best served immediately but can be prepared in advance up to the end of Step 3. The anchovies should be added at the last moment or they overpower the delicate flavour of the lamb.

The secret of success for this famous recipe depends very much on the quality of lamb used. Ideally, the lamb should be just one month old and entirely milk-fed, but anything no older than a spring lamb will still give tender results.

BEEF PROVENCALE

Preparation time: 20 minutes
  + overnight refrigeration
Total cooking time: 2 hours 25 minutes
Serves 6

 ★ ★

1.5 kg (3 lb) chuck steak, cut into
  3 cm (1¼ inch) cubes
2 tablespoons olive oil
1 small onion, sliced
1½ cups (375 ml/12 fl oz) red wine
2 tablespoons chopped fresh flat-leaf
  (Italian) parsley
1 tablespoon chopped fresh rosemary
1 tablespoon chopped fresh thyme
2 fresh bay leaves
250 g (8 oz) speck, rind removed, cut into
  1 x 2 cm (½ x ¾ inch) pieces
400 g (13 oz) can crushed good-quality
  tomatoes
1 cup (250 ml/8 fl oz) beef stock
500 g (1 lb) baby carrots
⅓ cup (45 g/1½ oz) pitted Niçoise olives

1 In a bowl, combine the cubed beef with 1 tablespoon of the oil, the onion, 1 cup (250 ml/8 fl oz) of wine and half the herbs. Cover with plastic wrap and marinate in the refrigerator overnight.
2 Drain the beef, reserving the marinade. Heat the remaining oil in a large heavy-based saucepan and brown the beef and onion in batches. Remove from the pan.
3 Add the speck to the saucepan and cook for 3–5 minutes, until crisp. Return the beef to the pan with the remaining wine and marinade and cook, scraping the residue from the base of the pan for 2 minutes, or until the wine has slightly reduced. Add the tomato and stock and bring the boil. Reduce the heat and add the remaining herbs. Season well, cover and simmer for 1½ hours.
4 Add the carrots and olives to the saucepan and cook, uncovered, for another 30 minutes, or until the meat and the carrots are tender. Before serving, check the seasoning and adjust if necessary.

ABOVE: Beef Provençale

HARICOT BEANS
These are a small white bean usually used in the dried form. They have a mild flavour and are best known as the bean used for baked beans. Like all dried beans, they need to be covered with cold water and soaked overnight, before draining and then cooking until tender.

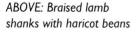
ABOVE: Braised lamb shanks with haricot beans

BRAISED LAMB SHANKS WITH HARICOT BEANS

Preparation time: 10 minutes + overnight soaking
Total cooking time: 2 hours 15 minutes
Serves 4

2 cups (400 g/13 oz) dried haricot beans

4 tablespoons oil

4 lamb shanks, trimmed

2 tablespoons butter

2 cloves garlic, crushed

2 brown onions, finely chopped

1 1/2 tablespoons thyme leaves

2 tablespoons tomato paste (tomato purée)

2 x 400 g (13 oz) cans good-quality crushed
 tomatoes

1 tablespoon paprika

1 dried jalapeño chilli, roughly chopped

1 cup (30 g/1 oz) roughly chopped fresh
 flat-leaf (Italian) parsley

1 Put the haricot beans in a bowl, cover well with water and soak overnight.
2 Heat 3 tablespoons of the oil in a large heavy-based frying pan over medium heat and brown the shanks on all sides. Remove and set aside. Drain the fat from the pan.
3 Heat the butter and the remaining oil in the pan and cook the garlic and onion over medium heat for 3–4 minutes, or until softened. Add the thyme, tomato paste, tomato and paprika and simmer for 5 minutes. Add the lamb shanks and 2 cups (500 ml/16 fl oz) hot water. Season well and bring to the boil. Cover the pan, reduce the heat and simmer gently for 30 minutes.
4 Drain the beans and add to the pan with the jalapeño chilli and another 2 cups (500 ml/16 fl oz) of hot water. Bring to the boil again, cover and simmer for another 1–1 1/2 hours or until both the beans and the meat are tender, adding more water, 1/2 cup (125 ml/4 fl oz) at a time, if necessary. Check the seasoning, adjust if necessary, and stir in half the parsley. Serve hot sprinkled with the remaining parsley.

PORK CHOPS IN MARSALA

Preparation time: 10 minutes
Total cooking time: 10 minutes
Serves 4

4 pork loin chops, about 2.5 cm (1 inch) thick
2 tablespoons olive oil
1/2 cup (125 ml/4 fl oz) Marsala
2 teaspoons grated orange rind
1/4 cup (60 ml/2 fl oz) orange juice
3 tablespoons chopped fresh flat-leaf
   (Italian) parsley

1 Pat dry the pork chops and season well with salt and freshly ground black pepper.
2 Heat the oil in a heavy-based frying pan over medium heat and cook the chops on both sides for 5 minutes on each side, or until browned all over and cooked through.
3 Add 1/2 cup (125 ml/4 fl oz) Marsala, 2 teaspoons grated orange rind and 1/4 cup (60 ml/2 fl oz) orange juice and cook for 4–5 minutes, or until the sauce has reduced and thickened. Add the parsley and serve.

GRILLED LAMB KOFTA

Preparation time: 20 minutes
   + 1 hour soaking
Total cooking time: 10 minutes
Makes 8

400 g (13 oz) lean minced (ground) lamb
1 tablespoon chopped fresh
   flat-leaf (Italian) parsley
1 teaspoon ground cumin
2 tablespoons chopped fresh coriander
   (cilantro)
pinch of cayenne pepper
2 cloves garlic, crushed
1/2 teaspoon dried mint
3/4 cup (185 g/6 oz) Greek-style
   natural yoghurt
lemon wedges, to serve

1 Soak eight 15 cm (6 inch) wooden skewers in water for 1 hour, or until they sink, to ensure that they don't burn during cooking.

2 Combine the lamb, chopped parsley, cumin, coriander, cayenne pepper, half the garlic and 1/2 teaspoon salt in a bowl, and knead the mixture by hand for a few minutes until the mixture is quite smooth and comes away from the side of the bowl.
3 Divide the mixture into 16 portions. Wet your hands with cold water and roll each portion into a ball. Thread 2 balls onto each prepared skewer, moulding each ball into an oval shape about 4–5 cm (1 1/2–2 inches) long.
4 To make the sauce, combine the dried mint, yoghurt and remaining clove of garlic in a bowl. Season with salt and pepper.
5 Heat a lightly oiled barbecue hotplate until hot, or heat a grill to its highest setting. Cook the kofta for about 6 minutes, turning once.
6 Serve the kofta hot with the sauce for dipping and some lemon wedges for sprinkling.

BELOW: Grilled lamb kofta

SPICED BEEF AND ONIONS

Preparation time: 15 minutes
Total cooking time: 1 hour 30 minutes
Serves 4

★

1 kg (2 lb) chuck steak
1/4 cup (60 ml/2 fl oz) olive oil
750 g (1 1/2 lb) whole baby onions
3 cloves garlic, cut in half lengthways
1/2 cup (125 ml/4 fl oz) red wine
1 cinnamon stick
4 whole cloves
1 bay leaf
1 tablespoon red wine vinegar
2 tablespoons tomato paste (tomato purée)
2 tablespoons currants

1 Trim the meat, then cut into bite-sized cubes. Heat the oil over medium heat in a large heavy-based saucepan. Add the onions and stir for 5 minutes, or until golden. Remove from the pan and drain on paper towels.

BELOW: Spiced beef with onions

2 Add the meat all at once to the pan and stir over high heat for 10 minutes, or until the meat is well browned and almost all the liquid has been absorbed.
3 Add the garlic, wine, spices, bay leaf, vinegar, tomato paste, 1/4 teaspoon ground black pepper, some salt and 1 1/2 cups (375 ml/12 fl oz) water to the pan and bring to the boil. Reduce the heat, cover and simmer for 1 hour, stirring occasionally.
4 Return the onions to the saucepan, add the currants and stir gently. Simmer, covered, for 15 minutes. Discard the cinnamon before serving. Serve with rice, bread or potatoes.
VARIATION: For a richer flavour, use 1 1/2 cups (375 ml/12 fl oz) beef or veal stock instead of water in this recipe.

VEAL COOKED WITH VINEGAR

Preparation time: 10 minutes
Total cooking time: 1 hour 50 minutes
Serves 6–8

★

1/2 cup (60 g/2 oz) plain (all-purpose) flour
large pinch of cayenne pepper
1 kg (2 lb) veal steaks
1/4 cup (60 ml/2 fl oz) olive oil
1 bay leaf
5 cloves garlic, crushed
2/3 cup (170 ml/5 1/2 fl oz) red wine vinegar
2 1/2 cups (625 ml/20 fl oz) beef stock
chopped flat-leaf (Italian) parsley, to serve

1 Combine the flour with the cayenne and season well with salt and pepper. Lightly coat the veal with the flour, shaking off any excess.
2 Heat the oil in a large, deep frying pan over high heat and cook the veal a few pieces at a time for 1 minute on each side, or until lightly browned. Remove from the pan and set aside.
3 Add the bay leaf, garlic, red wine vinegar and stock to the pan and bring to the boil, scraping up any residue from the base of the pan. Reduce the heat to low and return the veal and any juices back to the pan. Cover and cook, stirring gently occasionally, for 1 1/2 hours, or until the veal is very tender and sauce is thickened. If the sauce is too watery, carefully transfer the veal to a serving platter and boil the sauce until it is the consistency of a smooth gravy. Sprinkle with parsley before serving.

LAMB AND ARTICHOKE FRICASSEE

Preparation time: 50 minutes
Total cooking time: 1 hour 50 minutes
Serves 8

★★

6 fresh globe artichokes
1/4 cup (60 ml/2 fl oz) lemon juice
2 large, ripe tomatoes
1/3 cup (80 ml/2³/4 fl oz) olive oil
2 kg (4 lb) diced lamb
750 g (1 1/2 lb) brown onions, thinly sliced
1 tablespoon plain (all-purpose) flour
2 cloves garlic, crushed
3/4 cup (185 m/l6 fl oz) white wine
1 1/3 cups (350 ml/11 fl oz) chicken stock
1 bouquet garni (see page 99)
chopped fresh parsley, to garnish
lemon wedges, to serve

 To prepare the globe artichokes, bring a large saucepan of water to the boil and add the lemon juice. Trim the stems from the artichokes and remove the tough outer leaves. Cut off the hard tips of the remaining leaves using scissors. Blanch the artichokes for 5 minutes. Remove and turn upside-down to drain. When cool enough to handle, use a small spoon to remove the choke from the centre of each. Scrape the bases well to remove all the membrane. Cut the artichokes into quarters and set aside.

2 Score a cross in the base of each tomato and place in a bowl of boiling water for 10 seconds. Plunge into cold water and peel away from the cross. Cut each tomato in half and scoop out the seeds with a teaspoon. Chop the tomatoes.

3 Heat half the oil in a deep heatproof casserole and fry batches of the lamb until golden. Add the remaining oil and cook the onion for about 8 minutes, until soft and caramelized. Add the flour and cook for 1 minute. Add the garlic, tomato, wine and chicken stock. Return the lamb to the pan add the bouquet garni and simmer, covered, for 1 hour.

4 Place the artichokes in the casserole and simmer, uncovered, for another 15 minutes. Remove the meat and artichokes with a slotted spoon and place in a serving dish. Keep warm. Discard the bouquet garni. Cook the sauce over high heat until it thickens. Pour the sauce over the lamb and garnish with parsley. Serve with lemon wedges.

NOTE: If fresh artichokes are not available, you can use 1 cup (270 g/9 oz) marinated artichokes. Drain them well and pat dry with paper towels.

BOUQUET GARNI
This is a small bundle of herbs used to flavour casseroles, soups and fricassees. It usually includes a few stalks of parsley, a sprig of thyme and a bay leaf. See page 99 for a recipe for a traditional bouquet garni. The herbs can be tied together with string or in a knot of muslin. Other herbs can be added if you feel they are appropriate to the dish you are making. Ready-made bouquet garni are also available in the herb section of your supermarket.

ABOVE: Lamb and artichoke fricassee

500 g (1 lb) home-made or bought puff pastry
  (see page 488)
1 egg, lightly beaten

1 Lightly grease six metal pie tins measuring
9 cm (3½ inches) along the base and 3 cm
1¼ inches) deep.
2 Heat 2 tablespoons of the oil in a large frying
pan and brown the meat in batches. Remove
from the pan. Heat the remaining oil in the same
pan, add the onion and garlic and stir over
medium heat until golden brown. Add the flour
and stir over medium heat for 2 minutes, or until
well browned. Remove from the heat and
gradually stir in the combined wine and stock.
3 Return to the heat and stir until the mixture
boils and thickens. Return the meat to the pan,
add the bay leaves and thyme and simmer for
1 hour. Add the carrot and simmer for another
45 minutes, or until the meat and carrot are
tender and the sauce has thickened. Season, then
remove the bay leaves and thyme. Allow to cool.
4 Preheat the oven to moderately hot 200°C
(400°F/Gas 6). Divide the shortcrust into six
and roll out each piece between two sheets of
baking paper to a 25 cm (10 inch) square, 3 mm
(⅛ inch) thick. Cut a circle from each shortcrust
sheet big enough to line the base and side of a
pie tin. Place in the tins and trim the edges.
Line each pastry shell with baking paper and
fill with baking beads or uncooked rice. Place
on a baking tray and bake for 8 minutes.
Remove the paper and beads and bake for
another 8 minutes, or until the pastry is lightly
browned. Allow to cool.
5 Divide the puff pastry into six portions and
roll each piece between two sheets of baking
paper to a square. Cut circles from the squares
of dough, to fit the tops of the pie tins. Spoon
some of the filling into each pastry case and
brush the edge with some of the beaten egg.
Cover with a pastry round and trim any excess
pastry, pressing the edges with a fork to seal.
Cut a slit in the top of each pie. Brush the pie
tops with the remaining beaten egg and bake
for 20–25 minutes, or until the pastry is cooked
and golden brown.
NOTES: You can make a family-sized pie using
the same ingredients, but substituting a 23 cm
(9 inch) metal pie tin. Bake in a moderately hot
200°C (400°F/Gas 6) oven for 30–35 minutes.
Any remaining pastry can be rolled and used to
decorate the pie, or frozen for later use.
  The alcohol content of the red wine dissipates
on heating. While it adds a distinct flavour, you
can use all stock if you don't like to use wine.

BEEF AND RED WINE PIES

Preparation time: 50 minutes
Total cooking time: 2 hours 40 minutes
Makes 6

¼ cup (60 ml/2 fl oz) oil
1.5 kg (3 lb) chuck steak, cubed
2 onions, chopped
1 clove garlic, crushed
¼ cup (30 g/1 oz) plain (all-purpose) flour
1¼ cups (315 ml/10 fl oz) good-quality
  dry red wine
2 cups (500 ml/16 fl oz) beef stock
2 bay leaves
2 sprigs fresh thyme
2 carrots, chopped
500 g (1 lb) home-made or bought
  shortcrust pastry (see page 490)

*ABOVE: Beef
and red wine pies*

244

STEAK AND KIDNEY PIE

Preparation time: 20 minutes
Total cooking time: 1 hour 50 minutes
Serves 6

★★

750 g (1 1/2 lb) round steak

4 lamb kidneys

2 tablespoons plain (all-purpose) flour

1 tablespoon oil

1 onion, chopped

30 g (1 oz) butter

1 tablespoon Worcestershire sauce

1 tablespoon tomato paste (tomato purée)

1/2 cup (125 ml/4 fl oz) red wine

1 cup (250 ml/8 fl oz) beef stock

125 g (4 oz) button mushrooms,
    sliced

1/2 teaspoon dried thyme

4 tablespoons chopped fresh parsley

500 g (1 lb) home-made or bought
    puff pastry (see page 488)

1 egg, lightly beaten

1 Trim the meat of excess fat and sinew and cut into 2 cm (3/4 inch) cubes. Peel the skin from the kidneys. Quarter the kidneys and trim away any fat or sinew. Place the flour in a plastic bag with the meat and kidneys and toss gently.
2 Heat the oil in a frying pan, add the onion and cook for 5 minutes, or until soft. Remove from the pan with a slotted spoon. Add the butter to the pan, brown the meat and kidneys in batches and then return all the meat, kidneys and onion to the pan.
3 Add the Worcestershire sauce, tomato paste, wine, stock, mushrooms, thyme and parsley to the pan. Bring to the boil, reduce the heat and simmer, covered, for 1 hour or until the meat is tender. Season to taste and allow to cool. Spoon into a 1.5 litre (48 fl oz) pie plate.
4 Preheat the oven to hot 210°C (415°F/ Gas 6–7). Roll the puff pastry between two sheets of baking paper, so that it is 4 cm (1 1/2 inches) larger than the pie plate. Cut thin strips from the edge of the pastry and press onto the rim of the plate, sealing the joins. Place the pastry on the pie, trim the edges and cut two steam holes in the pastry. Decorate the pie with leftover pastry and brush the top with egg. Bake for 35–40 minutes or until the pastry is golden.

STEAK AND KIDNEY PIE
This is a traditional British pie. Sometimes oysters, boiled eggs and potatoes are added. The cooled mixture is placed in a casserole dish and topped with a pastry crust. If the pie dish is deep, a decorative funnel, often in the shape of a bird, is placed in the centre of the pie to support the pastry and act as a steam vent during the long cooking. Another traditional dish, known as steak and kidney pudding, uses the same ingredients but they are placed, uncooked, in a pudding basin that is lined with suet pastry. The pudding is then steamed or baked.

*ABOVE: Steak
and kidney pie*

245

BACON

Bacon is meat from the side and back of a pig. It is cured by dry-salting and then smoked to give the distinctive taste. Bacon is usually sold in thin slices called rashers. The middle cut, sometimes called the prime cut, contains the least fat and most meat. Streaky bacon is cut from the tail end of the loin and is streaked with more fat.

ABOVE: Bacon and egg pie

BACON AND EGG PIE

Preparation time: 20 minutes
  + 20 minutes refrigeration
Total cooking time: 1 hour
Serves 4–6

2 tablespoons oil

4 rashers bacon, chopped

250 g (8 oz) home-made or bought shortcrust pastry (see page 490)

250 g (8 oz) home-made or bought puff pastry (see page 488)

5 eggs, lightly beaten

¼ cup (60 ml/2 fl oz) cream

1 egg, extra, lightly beaten

1 Lightly grease a 20 cm (8 inch) loose-based pie tin. Heat the oil in a frying pan. Add the bacon and cook over medium heat for a few minutes, or until lightly browned. Drain on paper towels and allow to cool slightly.

2 Roll out the shortcrust pastry between two sheets of baking paper until slightly larger than the tin. Place in the tin and roll a rolling pin over the tin to trim off any excess pastry. Refrigerate for 20 minutes. Preheat the oven to hot 210°C (415°F/Gas 6–7).

3 Line the pastry shell with a piece of baking paper and pour in some baking beads or uncooked rice. Bake for 10 minutes, then remove the paper and beads and cook for another 10 minutes, or until the pastry is dry and golden. Allow to cool.

4 Roll out the puff pastry between two sheets of baking paper to a circle large enough to cover the top of the pie. Arrange the bacon over the cooled pastry base and pour the combined egg and cream over the top. Cover the pie with the puff pastry and press on firmly to seal. Trim the pastry edges and decorate the top with shapes cut from the pastry scraps. Brush with the extra egg and bake for 30–35 minutes, or until the pastry is puffed and golden. Serve warm or at room temperature.

NOTE: Bacon and egg pie is excellent for taking on picnics. It can be made a day ahead and refrigerated overnight. Allow to come to room temperature before serving.

CORNISH PASTIES

Preparation time: 35 minutes
+ 20 minutes refrigeration
Total cooking time: 45 minutes
Makes 6

Shortcrust pastry

2¹/₂ cups (310 g/10 oz) plain (all-purpose) flour
125 g (4 oz) butter, chilled and cubed
4–5 tablespoons iced water

160 g (5¹/₂ oz) round steak,
  finely chopped
I small potato, finely chopped
I small onion, finely chopped
I small carrot, finely chopped
I–2 teaspoons Worcestershire sauce
2 tablespoons beef stock
I egg, lightly beaten

I Lightly grease a baking tray. Sift the flour and a pinch of salt into a large bowl and rub in the butter with your fingertips until the mixture resembles fine breadcrumbs. Make a well in the centre and add almost all the water. Mix together with a flat-bladed knife, using a cutting action, until the mixture comes together in small beads, adding more water if the dough is too dry. Turn out onto a floured surface and form into a ball. Cover with plastic wrap and refrigerate for 20 minutes.
2 Preheat the oven to hot 210°C (415°F/Gas 6–7). Mix together the steak, potato, onion, carrot, Worcestershire sauce and stock in a bowl and season well.
3 Divide the dough into 6 portions. Roll out each portion to 3 mm (¹/₈ inch) thick. Using a 16 cm (6¹/₂ inch) diameter plate as a guide, cut six circles. Divide the filling among the circles.
4 Brush the edges with beaten egg and bring the pastry together to form a semi-circle. Pinch the edges into a frill and place on the tray. Brush the pastry with egg and bake for 15 minutes. Reduce the oven to moderate 180°C (350°F/Gas 4) and cook for 25–30 minutes, or until golden.

CORNISH PASTIES

Mix together the steak, potato, onion, carrot, Worcestershire sauce and beef stock.

Lift both sides of the pastry up to enclose the filling. Pinch the edges to seal.

LEFT: Cornish pasties

ABOVE: Herbed rack of veal

HERBED RACK OF VEAL

Preparation time: 45 minutes
Total cooking time: 1 hour 40 minutes
Serves 4–6

★★

1 cup (80 g/2³/4 oz) fresh breadcrumbs
1/2 cup (50 g/1³/4 oz) dry breadcrumbs
2 tablespoons chopped fresh parsley
2 egg whites, lightly beaten
2 cloves garlic, crushed
1 tablespoon oil
30 g (1 oz) butter, melted
1.2 kg (2 lb 6¹/2 oz) rack of veal, trimmed

Lemon sauce
1/3 cup (80 ml/2³/4 fl oz) dry white wine
2 tablespoons lemon juice
2 teaspoons sugar
1/2 cup (125 ml/4 fl oz) cream
60 g (2 oz) chilled butter, cubed
1 tablespoon chopped fresh parsley

1 Preheat the oven to warm 160°C (315°F/ Gas 2–3). Combine the breadcrumbs and parsley. Mix in the combined egg whites, garlic, oil and butter. Press firmly over the meat and put in a baking dish, crust-side-up. Bake for 1¹/4 hours for medium, or 1¹/2 hours for well done. Remove from the pan and rest for 10 minutes. Drain off all but 2 tablespoons of pan juices.
2 Put the baking dish on the stove. Add 1/2 cup (125 ml/4 fl oz) water with the wine, lemon juice, sugar and cream. Bring to the boil, then simmer for 5 minutes, or until reduced by about 1/2 cup (125 ml/4 fl oz). Remove from the heat and whisk in the butter, 1 cube at a time, then strain and stir in the parsley. Serve the veal with sauce.

SHEPHERD'S PIE

Preparation time: 30 minutes
Total cooking time: 1 hour 15 minutes
Serves 6

750 g (1½ lb) lean cooked roast lamb
25 g (¾ oz) butter
2 onions, finely chopped
¼ cup (30 g/1 oz) plain (all-purpose) flour
½ teaspoon dry mustard
1½ cups (375 ml/12 fl oz) chicken stock
2 tablespoons Worcestershire sauce

Potato topping

4 large potatoes
½ cup (125 ml/4 fl oz) hot milk
30 g (1 oz) butter

1 Brush a 2 litre (64 fl oz) casserole with melted butter or oil. Preheat the oven to hot 210°C (415°F/Gas 6–7). Trim the meat of excess fat, then mince (grind) or finely chop. Melt the butter in a large pan, add the onion and stir over medium heat for 5–10 minutes, until golden.
2 Add the flour and mustard to the pan and cook for 1 minute, or until pale and foaming. Remove from the heat and gradually stir in the stock. Return to the heat and stir constantly until the sauce boils and thickens. Reduce the heat and simmer for 2 minutes.
3 Add the meat and Worcestershire sauce to the pan and stir. Season to taste. Remove from the heat and spoon into the casserole dish.
4 For the potato topping, steam or boil the potatoes for 10–15 minutes, or until just tender (pierce with the point of a small sharp knife—if the potato comes away easily, it's ready). Drain and mash well. Add the milk, butter, and salt and pepper, to taste, to the mashed potato and mix until smooth and creamy. Spread evenly over the meat and rough up the surface with the back of a spoon. Bake for 40–45 minutes, or until the meat is heated through and the topping is golden.

ABOVE: Shepherd's pie

WORCESTERSHIRE
SAUCE
This condiment was
developed in India by an
Englishman. It was first
bottled by a company
called Lea and Perrins, in
the town of Worcester in
England, hence the name.
Today it is still made by
the same company. Widely
available the world over,
it is a piquant mixture of
onions, garlic, tamarind,
soy sauce, molasses, lime,
anchovies and vinegar. It is
used to add flavour to
stews, gravies and soups,
and is particularly famous
as an essential ingredient
in the cocktail called
Bloody Mary.

POTATO PIES

Preparation time: 25 minutes
Total cooking time: 1 hour 5 minutes
Makes 6

★

1 kg (2 lb) floury potatoes, chopped
1 tablespoon oil
1 onion, finely chopped
1 clove garlic, crushed
500 g (1 lb) minced (ground) beef
2 tablespoons plain (all-purpose) flour
2 cups (500 ml/16 fl oz) beef stock
2 tablespoons tomato paste (tomato purée)
1 tablespoon Worcestershire sauce
500 g (1 lb) home-made or bought shortcrust
    pastry (see page 490)
45 g (1 1/2 oz) butter, softened
1/4 cup (60 ml/2 fl oz) milk

1 Steam or boil the potatoes for 10 minutes, or until tender (pierce with the point of a small sharp knife and if the potato comes away easily it is ready). Drain thoroughly, then mash.

2 Preheat the oven to hot 210°C (415°F/ Gas 6–7). Heat the oil in a frying pan, add the onion and cook for 5 minutes, or until soft. Add the garlic and cook for another minute. Add the beef and cook over medium heat for 5 minutes, or until browned, breaking up any lumps with a fork.

3 Sprinkle the flour over the meat and stir to combine. Add the stock, tomato paste, sauce and some salt and pepper to the pan and stir for 2 minutes. Bring to the boil, then reduce the heat slightly and simmer for 5 minutes, or until the mixture has reduced and thickened. Allow to cool completely.

4 Lightly grease six 11 cm (4 1/2 inch) pie tins. Roll out the pastry between two sheets of baking paper and, using a plate as a guide, cut the pastry into 15 cm (6 inch) circles and line the pie tins. Cut baking paper to cover each tin, spread baking beads or uncooked rice over the paper and bake for 7 minutes. Remove the paper and beads and cook the pastry for another 5 minutes. Allow to cool.

5 Divide the meat filling among the pastry cases. Stir the butter and milk into the mashed potato and pipe or spread all over the top of the meat filling. Bake for 20 minutes, or until the potato is lightly golden.

RIGHT: Potato pies

LAMB AND FILO PIE

Preparation time: 20 minutes
Total cooking time: 55 minutes
Serves 6

★ ★

2 tablespoons oil
2 onions, chopped
1 clove garlic, chopped
1 teaspoon ground cumin
1 teaspoon ground coriander
1/2 teaspoon ground cinnamon
1 kg (2 lb) minced (ground) lamb
3 tablespoons chopped fresh parsley
2 tablespoons chopped fresh mint
1 tablespoon tomato paste (tomato purée)
10 sheets filo pastry
250 g (8 oz) butter, melted

 Heat the oil in a large frying pan. Add the onion and garlic and cook for 3 minutes, or until just soft. Add the cumin, coriander and cinnamon to the pan and cook, stirring constantly, for another minute.

2 Add the lamb to the pan and cook over medium heat for 10 minutes, or until the meat is brown and all the liquid has evaporated. Use a fork to break up any lumps as it cooks. Add the herbs, tomato paste and 1/4 teaspoon salt and mix well. Cool completely.

3 Preheat the oven to moderate 180°C (350°F/ Gas 4). Lightly grease a 33 x 23 cm (13 x 9 inch) ovenproof dish. Remove 3 sheets of filo. Cover the remainder with a damp tea towel to prevent them drying out. Brush the top sheet of filo with melted butter. Cover with another 2 sheets of filo and brush the top one with butter. Line the baking dish with these sheets, leaving the excess overhanging the dish.

4 Spread the lamb mixture over the pastry and fold the overhanging pastry over the filling. Butter 2 sheets of filo, place one on top of the other and fold in half. Place over the top of the filling and tuck in the edges. Butter the remaining sheets of filo, cut roughly into squares and then scrunch these over the top of the pie. Bake for 40 minutes, or until crisp and golden.

FILO PASTRY
This is a pastry commonly used in Middle Eastern, Turkish, Greek, Austrian and Hungarian cuisines. It is a very thin pastry that is layered and used to fill and wrap around both sweet and savoury foods. When baked, the flaky layers are light, crisp and golden. It is readily available in supermarkets. When working with filo, keep the unused sheets covered with a slightly damp tea towel. The pastry is so thin that it dries out very quickly and becomes unworkable. Brush the filo sheets lightly with oil or melted butter using a wide pastry brush so that the pastry is covered as quickly as possible and doesn't have time to dry out. Spray oil can also be used if preferred.

ABOVE: Lamb and filo pie

PARMESAN

Parmesan is a hard, crumbly cheese made from skimmed or partially skimmed cow's milk. The most superior Parmesan is Parmigiano Reggiano, produced in the Parma and Reggio provinces of Northern Italy using techniques that are seven centuries old. The name is stringently protected by law. Parmigiano Reggiano is aged for up to 4 years and is unrivalled in flavour and texture. Parmigiano Grana is, as its name implies, a grainy cheese and is suitable for grating or serving as a table cheese. Buy Parmesan in a wedge or if possible, ask that it be cut from the wheel. Grate it as you need it because when cut, the cheese becomes dry and the flavour is altered. For this reason, never buy pre-grated cheese as it bears little resemblance in flavour and texture to the real thing. Select Parmesan with the rind still attached and with no evidence of whitening at the rim. To store, wrap tightly in greaseproof paper, then in heavy-duty aluminium foil.

RIGHT: Parmesan and rosemary crusted veal chops

PARMESAN AND ROSEMARY CRUSTED VEAL CHOPS

Preparation time: 15 minutes
Total cooking time: 15 minutes
Serves 4

4 veal chops
150 g (5 oz) fresh white breadcrumbs
75 g (2½ oz) grated Parmesan
1 tablespoon fresh rosemary, finely chopped
2 eggs, lightly beaten, seasoned
3 tablespoons olive oil
60 g (2 oz) butter
4 cloves garlic

1 Trim the chops of excess fat and sinew and flatten to 1 cm (½ inch) thickness. Pat the meat dry with paper towels. Combine the breadcrumbs, Parmesan and rosemary in a shallow bowl.

2 Dip each chop in the beaten egg, draining off the excess. Press both sides of the chops firmly in the crumbs.

3 Heat the oil and butter in a heavy-based frying pan over low heat, add the garlic and cook until golden. Discard the garlic.

4 Increase the heat to medium, add the chops to the pan and cook for 4–5 minutes on each side, depending on the thickness of the chops, until golden and crisp. Transfer to a warm serving dish and season with salt and pepper.

HAM AND CIDER CASSEROLE

Preheat the oven to moderately hot 200°C (400°F/Gas 6). Melt 20 g (¾ oz) butter in a heavy-based frying pan, add 1 chopped onion and cook over low heat for 2–3 minutes, or until tender. Add 2 thinly sliced leeks (white part only) and stir until cooked through. Stir in 2 crushed garlic cloves. Transfer the onion mixture to an ovenproof dish. Scatter 8 chopped ham slices over the top and season with freshly ground black pepper. Pour in 100 ml (3½ fl oz) apple cider. Spoon a 300 g (10 oz) can of rinsed and drained butter beans over and around the ham and then sprinkle with ⅓ cup (25 g/¾ oz) fresh breadcrumbs and 1 tablespoon grated Parmesan. Dot with 20 g (¾ oz) butter and bake for 20 minutes, or until lightly golden on top.

SALTIMBOCCA
(Veal escalopes with prosciutto)

Preparation time: 15 minutes
Total cooking time: 20 minutes
Serves 4

4 thin veal steaks
2 cloves garlic, crushed
4 slices prosciutto
4 fresh sage leaves
30 g (1 oz) butter
2/3 cup (170 ml/5 1/2 fl oz) Marsala

1 Trim the meat of excess fat and sinew and flatten each steak to 5 mm (1/4 inch) thick. Nick the edges to prevent them from curling and pat the meat dry with paper towels. Combine the garlic with 1/4 teaspoon salt and 1/2 teaspoon ground black pepper and rub some of the mixture over one side of each veal steak. Place a slice of prosciutto on each and top with a sage leaf. The prosciutto should cover the veal completely but not overlap.

2 Melt the butter in a large heavy-based frying pan, add the veal, prosciutto-side-up, and cook over medium heat for 5 minutes, or until the underside is golden brown. Do not turn the veal. Add the Marsala, without wetting the top of the veal. Reduce the heat and simmer very slowly for 10 minutes. Transfer the veal to warm serving plates. Boil the sauce for 2–3 minutes, or until syrupy, then spoon it over the veal.

SWEET AND SOUR LIVER

Preparation time: 10 minutes
Total cooking time: 10 minutes
Serves 4

40 g (1 1/4 oz) butter
1/3 cup (80 ml/2 3/4 fl oz) olive oil
600 g (1 1/4 lb) calves' livers, cut into long
    thin slices
1 cup (80 g/2 3/4 oz) fresh white breadcrumbs
1 tablespoon sugar
2 cloves garlic, crushed
1/4 cup (60 ml/2 fl oz) red wine vinegar
1 tablespoon chopped fresh flat-leaf
    (Italian) parsley

1 Heat the butter and half the oil in a heavy-based frying pan over medium heat. Coat the liver in breadcrumbs, pressing them on firmly with your hands. Shake off the excess and place in the pan when the butter begins to foam. Cook on each side for 1 minute, or until the crust is brown and crisp. Remove from the pan and keep warm.

2 Add the remaining oil to the frying pan and cook the sugar and garlic over low heat until golden. Add the vinegar and cook for 30 seconds, or until almost evaporated. Add the parsley and pour over the liver. Serve hot or at room temperature.

ABOVE: Sweet and sour liver

MINTED RACKS OF LAMB

Trim any excess fat from the lamb and clean away any meat or sinew from the bones.

Place the racks, overlapping, on a rack in a baking dish.

Brush the mint glaze all over the back of the racks of lamb.

MINTED RACKS OF LAMB

Preparation time: 15 minutes
Total cooking time: 45 minutes
Serves 4

★

4 x 4-cutlet racks of lamb
1 cup (300 g/10 oz) mint jelly
2 tablespoons white wine
3 tablespoons finely chopped fresh chives

1 Preheat the oven to moderately hot 200°C (400°F/Gas 6). Trim any excess fat from the lamb, leaving a thin layer of fat, and clean any meat or sinew from the ends of the bones using a small sharp knife. Cover the bones with foil. Place on a rack in a baking dish.
2 Mix the mint jelly and white wine together in a small saucepan over high heat. Bring to the boil and boil for 4 minutes, or until the mixture is reduced and thickened. Cool slightly, then stir in the chives. Brush the glaze mixture over the racks of lamb. Bake for 15–20 minutes for rare, or 35 minutes if you prefer medium-rare, brushing with glaze every 10 minutes or so. Remove the foil from the bones and leave the lamb to stand for 5 minutes before serving with some steamed vegetables.

ROAST LAMB WITH LEMON AND POTATOES

Preparation time: 20 minutes
Total cooking time: 3 hours
Serves 6

★

2.5–3 kg (5–6 lb) leg of lamb
2 cloves garlic
1/2 cup (125 ml/4 fl oz) lemon juice
3 tablespoons dried oregano
1 brown onion, sliced
2 sticks celery, sliced
40 g (1 3/4 oz) butter, softened
1 kg (2 lb) potatoes, quartered

RIGHT: Minted racks of lamb

1 Preheat the oven to moderate 180°C (350°F/ Gas 4). Cut small slits in the lamb and cut the garlic into slivers. Insert the garlic into the slits. Rub the entire surface with half the lemon juice, sprinkle with salt, pepper and half the oregano. Place in a baking dish and bake for 1 hour.

2 Drain the fat from the pan and add the onion, celery and 1 cup (250 ml/8 fl oz) hot water. Spread the butter on the lamb, reduce the oven to warm 160°C (315°F/Gas 2–3) and cook for 1 hour. Turn during cooking to brown evenly.

3 Add the potatoes to the pan, sprinkle with the remaining oregano and lemon juice and some salt and pepper. Bake for another hour, adding more water if required and turning the potatoes halfway through cooking. Cut the lamb into chunks. Skim any excess fat from the pan and serve the juices with the potatoes and lamb.

PEPPERED BEEF FILLET WITH BEARNAISE SAUCE

Preparation time: 30 minutes
Total cooking time: 45 minutes
Serves 6

★★

1 kg (2 lb) beef eye fillet
1 tablespoon oil
2 cloves garlic, crushed
1 tablespoon cracked black peppercorns
2 teaspoons crushed coriander seeds

Béarnaise sauce

3 spring onions (scallions), chopped
1/2 cup (125 ml/4 fl oz) dry white wine
2 tablespoons tarragon vinegar
1 tablespoon chopped fresh tarragon
125 g (4 oz) butter
4 egg yolks
1 tablespoon lemon juice

1 Preheat the oven to hot 210°C (415°F/ Gas 6–7). Trim the fillet, removing any excess fat. Tie at regular intervals with kitchen string. Combine the oil and garlic, brush over the fillet, then roll the fillet in the combined peppercorns and coriander seeds.

2 Place the meat on a rack in a baking dish. Bake for 10 minutes, then reduce the oven to moderate 180°C (350°F/Gas 4) and cook for another 15–20 minutes for a rare result, or until cooked according to taste. Cover and leave for 10–15 minutes.

3 For the béarnaise sauce, put the spring onion, wine, vinegar and tarragon in a small saucepan. Boil the mixture rapidly until only 2 tablespoons of the liquid is left. Strain and set aside. Melt the butter in a small pan.

4 Place the wine mixture in a food processor with the egg yolks, and process for 30 seconds. With the motor running, add the hot butter in a thin stream, leaving the milky white sediment behind in the saucepan. Process until thickened. Add the lemon juice, to taste, and season with salt and white pepper.

5 Serve the beef with the béarnaise sauce, and some broccoli and potatoes.

ABOVE: Peppered beef fillet with béarnaise sauce

THAI CURRY PASTES

Curry pastes are great to make in advance and store. They are surprisingly easy to make and they are a great flavour starter for soups and curries, and will also spice up other dishes.

Curry pastes will keep in an airtight container for 2 weeks in the fridge or 2 months in the freezer. To ensure that your container is clean, preheat the oven to very slow 120°C (250°F/Gas ½). Thoroughly wash a glass jar and its lid in hot, soapy water (or preferably a dishwasher) and rinse well with hot water. Put the jar in the oven for 20 minutes, or until completely dried—don't dry it with a tea towel or germs can be transferred to the jar.

THAI RED CURRY PASTE

Preheat the oven to moderate 180°C (350°F/Gas 4). Put 15 large dried red chillies in a heatproof bowl, cover with boiling water and soak for 20 minutes. Drain, then remove the seeds and roughly chop the flesh.

Meanwhile, put 2 teaspoons shrimp paste (wrapped in foil), 2 teaspoons coriander seeds and 1 teaspoon each of white peppercorns and cumin seeds in a roasting tin and bake for 5–10 minutes, or until aromatic. Remove the foil.

Transfer the shrimp paste to a food processor or mortar and pestle with the chopped chilli, then add 5 chopped red Asian shallots, 10 chopped cloves garlic,

2 thinly sliced stems lemon grass (white part only), 1 tablespoon chopped fresh galangal, 2 tablespoons chopped fresh coriander (cilantro) root and 1 teaspoon finely grated makrut (kaffir) lime rind. Process or grind until it forms a smooth paste. Makes 1 cup.

THAI GREEN CURRY PASTE

Preheat the oven to moderate 180°C (350°F/Gas 4). Place 2 tablespoons coriander seeds, 2 teaspoons shrimp paste (wrapped in foil) and 1 teaspoon each of white peppercorns and cumin seeds in a roasting tin and bake for 5–10 minutes, or until aromatic. Remove the foil from the shrimp paste. Transfer to a food

processor or mortar and pestle and add 1 teaspoon sea salt, 4 finely chopped stems lemon grass (white part only), 2 teaspoons each of chopped fresh galangal and finely shredded fresh makrut (kaffir) lime leaves, 1 tablespoon chopped fresh coriander (cilantro) root, 5 chopped red Asian shallots, 10 chopped cloves garlic and 16 seeded and chopped large green chillies. Process or grind until it forms a smooth paste. Makes 1 cup.

CHU CHEE CURRY PASTE

Preheat the oven to moderate 180°C (350°F/Gas 4). Put 10 large dried red chillies in a heatproof bowl, cover with boiling water and soak for 20 minutes. Drain, then remove the seeds and roughly chop the flesh.

Meanwhile, put 1 teaspoon coriander seeds, 1 tablespoon shrimp paste (wrapped in foil) and 1 tablespoon white peppercorns in a roasting tin and bake for 5 minutes, or until aromatic. Remove the foil from the shrimp paste.

Transfer the toasted spices to a food processor or mortar and pestle with the chopped chilli and add 10 finely shredded fresh makrut (kaffir) lime leaves, 10 chopped red Asian shallots, 2 teaspoons finely grated makrut (kaffir) lime rind, 1 tablespoon chopped fresh coriander (cilantro) stem and root, 1 finely chopped stem lemon grass (white part only), 3 tablespoons chopped fresh galangal, 1 tablespoon chopped Krachai (see Note) and 6 chopped cloves garlic. Process or grind to a smooth paste. You may need to add a little lemon juice if the paste is too thick. Makes 1/2 cup.
NOTE: Krachai (bottled lesser galangal) is available from Asian grocery stores. It is an optional ingredient—you can omit it without detrimentally affecting the recipe.

THAI YELLOW CURRY PASTE

Put 8 small fresh green chillies, 5 roughly chopped red Asian shallots, 1 chopped stem lemon grass (white part only), 2 chopped cloves garlic, 2 tablespoons finely chopped fresh galangal, 1 tablespoon each of lime juice and finely chopped fresh coriander (cilantro) stem and root, 1 teaspoon each of ground coriander and cumin and 1/2 teaspoon each of ground turmeric and black peppercorns in a food processor or mortar and pestle. Process or grind to a smooth paste. Makes 1/2 cup.

FROM LEFT: Thai red curry paste; Thai green curry paste; Chu chee curry paste; Thai yellow curry paste

ASSORTED CURRY PASTES

BALTI CURRY PASTE

One at a time, dry-fry 4 tablespoons coriander seeds, 2 tablespoons cumin seeds, 2 crumbled cinnamon sticks, 2 teaspoons each of fennel seeds, black mustard seeds and cardamom seeds, 1 teaspoon fenugreek seeds and 6 whole cloves in a small frying pan over medium heat for 2–3 minutes, or until each spice starts to become aromatic.

Transfer the spices to a food processor or mortar and pestle, allow to cool and process or grind to a fine powder. Add

20 fresh curry leaves, 4 fresh bay leaves, 1 tablespoon ground turmeric, 2 crushed cloves garlic, 1 tablespoon grated fresh ginger, 1½ teaspoons chilli powder and ¾ cup (185 ml/6 fl oz) malt vinegar, and mix together well.

Heat ½ cup (125 ml/4 fl oz) vegetable oil in the frying pan, add the paste and cook, stirring, for 5 minutes. Add ¼ cup (60 ml/2 fl oz) malt vinegar and mix well. Makes 1 cup.

MADRAS CURRY PASTE

Dry-fry 2½ tablespoons coriander seeds and 1 tablespoon cumin seeds separately in a frying pan for 30 seconds–1 minute, or until aromatic, being careful not to burn them. Cool, then grind the seeds in a food processor or mortar and pestle.

Transfer to a small bowl and add 2 crushed cloves garlic, 2 teaspoons grated fresh ginger, 1 teaspoon each of brown mustard seeds, chilli powder, ground turmeric and salt, and ½ teaspoon cracked black peppercorns.

Mix together well. Add 3–4 tablespoons white vinegar and mix to a smooth paste. Makes 1/2 cup.

VINDALOO CURRY PASTE

Put 2 tablespoons grated fresh ginger, 4 chopped cloves garlic, 4 chopped fresh red chillies, 1 tablespoon each of ground coriander and cumin seeds, 2 teaspoons each of ground turmeric and ground cardamom, 1 teaspoon ground cinnamon, 4 whole cloves, 6 peppercorns and 1/2 cup (125 ml/4 fl oz) cider vinegar in a food processor and process for 20 seconds, or until well combined and smooth. Makes 1/2 cup.

MUSAMAN CURRY PASTE

Preheat the oven to moderate 180°C (350°F/Gas 4). Put 10 dried red chillies in a heatproof bowl and cover with boiling water. Soak for 20 minutes.

Drain, remove the seeds and roughly chop the flesh.

Meanwhile, put 5 chopped red Asian shallots, 1 finely chopped stem lemon grass (white part only), 1 tablespoon chopped fresh galangal, 10 chopped cloves garlic, 3 cardamom pods, 1 tablespoon coriander seeds, 1 teaspoon cumin seeds, 1 teaspoon shrimp paste (wrapped in foil) and 1/4 teaspoon black peppercorns in a roasting tin and bake for 5 minutes, or until aromatic. Remove the foil from the shrimp paste.

Transfer the roasted ingredients to a food processor or mortar and pestle, then add the chopped chilli, 1/2 teaspoon ground nutmeg and 1/4 teaspoon each of ground cinnamon and ground cloves. Process or grind to a smooth paste. If the mixture is too dry, add a little white vinegar. Makes 1/2 cup.

JUNGLE CURRY PASTE

Soak 12 large dried red chillies in boiling water for 20 minutes. Drain and chop.

Meanwhile, wrap 1 tablespoon shrimp paste in foil and heat under a hot grill for 1 minute, or until aromatic. Remove the foil from the shrimp paste.

Transfer the shrimp paste to a food processor, add the chopped chilli, 4 red Asian shallots, 4 sliced cloves garlic, 1 sliced stem lemon grass (white part only), 2 chopped small coriander (cilantro) roots, 1 tablespoon each of finely chopped fresh galangal and finely chopped fresh ginger and 1 teaspoon each of ground white pepper and salt, then blend until a smooth paste forms—add a little water, if necessary. Makes 1/2 cup.

FROM LEFT: Balti curry paste; Madras curry paste; Vindaloo curry paste; Musaman curry paste; Jungle curry paste

4 fl oz) boiling water in a bowl and set aside to cool. Mash the pulp with your fingertips to dissolve the pulp, then strain and reserve the liquid—discard the pulp.

2 Heat a non-stick wok over high heat, add the oil and swirl to coat. Add the beef in batches and cook over high heat for 5 minutes each batch, or until browned all over. Reduce the heat, add the coconut milk and cardamom pods, and simmer for 1 hour, or until the beef is tender. Remove the beef from the wok, then strain the cooking liquid into a bowl.

3 Heat the coconut cream in the wok and stir in the curry paste. Cook for 10 minutes, or until the oil starts to separate from the cream.

4 Add the fish sauce, onions, potatoes, beef mixture, palm sugar, peanuts, tamarind water and the reserved cooking liquid. Simmer for 25–30 minutes, or until thickened and the meat is tender.

NOTE: It is important to use a non-stick or stainless steel wok as the tamarind purée will react with the metal in a regular wok and badly taint the dish.

BALTI LAMB

Cut 1 kg (2 lb) lamb leg steaks into 3 cm (1¼ inch) cubes, then put in a wok with 1 tablespoon Balti curry paste (see page 258) and 1 litre (32 fl oz) boiling water. Bring to the boil over high heat, then reduce the heat to very low and cook, covered, for 40–50 minutes, or until the meat is almost cooked through. Drain, reserving the sauce. Wipe the wok clean. Heat 2 tablespoons ghee or oil in the clean wok over medium heat. Add 1 finely chopped large onion and cook for about 6 minutes, or until it is soft and golden brown. Add 3 crushed garlic cloves and 1 tablespoon garam masala and cook for a further 2–3 minutes. Increase the heat, add another 4 tablespoons of curry paste and return the lamb to the wok. Cook for 5 minutes, or until the meat has browned. Slowly add the reserved sauce and simmer over low heat, stirring occasionally, for 15 minutes. Add 2 tablespoons chopped coriander (cilantro) leaves and 1 cup (250 ml/ 8 fl oz) water and simmer for 15 minutes, or until the meat is tender and the sauce has thickened slightly. Season. Garnish with extra coriander (cilantro) and serve with poppadoms and steamed rice. Serves 4.

THAI MUSAMAN BEEF CURRY

Preparation time: 30 minutes + cooling
Total cooking time: 2 hours
Serves 4

★★

1 tablespoon tamarind pulp

2 tablespoons vegetable oil

750 g (1½ lb) lean stewing beef, cubed

2 cups (500 ml/16 fl oz) coconut milk

4 cardamom pods, bruised

2 cups (500 ml/16 fl oz) coconut cream

2 tablespoons Musaman curry paste
    (see page 259)

2 tablespoons fish sauce

8 pickling onions (see Notes)

8 baby potatoes (see Notes)

2 tablespoons grated palm sugar

½ cup (80 g/2¾ oz) unsalted peanuts, roasted
    and ground

*ABOVE: Thai Musaman
beef curry*

 Put the tamarind pulp and ½ cup (125 ml/

THAI BEEF AND PUMPKIN CURRY

Preparation time: 20 minutes
Total cooking time: 1 hour 30 minutes
Serves 6

2 tablespoons vegetable oil

750 g (1 1/2 lb) blade steak, thinly sliced

4 tablespoons Musaman curry paste
   (see page 259)

2 cloves garlic, finely chopped

1 onion, sliced lengthways

6 curry leaves, torn

3 cups (750 ml/24 fl oz) coconut milk

3 cups (450 g/14 oz) roughly diced
   butternut pumpkin (squash)

2 tablespoons chopped unsalted
   peanuts

1 tablespoon palm sugar

2 tablespoons tamarind purée

2 tablespoons fish sauce

curry leaves, to garnish

1 Heat a non-stick wok over high heat. Add the oil and swirl it around to coat the side of the wok. Add the meat in batches and cook for 5 minutes, or until browned. Remove the meat from the wok.

2 Add the curry paste, garlic, onion and curry leaves to the wok, and stir to coat. Return the meat to the wok and cook, stirring, over medium heat for 2 minutes.

3 Pour the coconut milk into the wok, then reduce the heat and simmer for 45 minutes. Add the diced pumpkin and simmer for a further 25–30 minutes, or until the meat and vegetables are tender and the sauce has thickened.

4 Stir in the peanuts, palm sugar, tamarind purée and fish sauce, and simmer for 1 minute. Garnish with curry leaves. Serve with rice.

NOTE: Use a non-stick or stainless steel wok because the acidity of the tamarind may cause the seasoning surface of a carbon-steel wok to lift off.

ABOVE: Thai beef and pumpkin curry

PANANG BEEF

Preparation time: 30 minutes +
 20 minutes soaking
Total cooking time: 1 hour
Serves 4–6

✯ ✯

Curry paste
8–10 large dried red chillies
6 red Asian shallots, chopped
6 cloves garlic, chopped
1 teaspoon ground coriander
1 tablespoon ground cumin
1 teaspoon white pepper
2 stems lemon grass, white part only,
 bruised, sliced
1 tablespoon chopped fresh galangal
6 fresh coriander (cilantro) roots
2 teaspoons shrimp paste
2 tablespoons roasted peanuts

BELOW: Panang beef

400 ml (13 fl oz) can coconut cream (do
 not shake)
1 kg (2 lb) round or blade steak, cut into
 1 cm (1/2 inch) slices
400 ml (13 fl oz) can coconut milk
1/3 cup (90 g/3 oz) crunchy peanut butter
4 fresh makrut (kaffir) lime leaves
1/4 cup (60 ml/2 fl oz) lime juice
21/2 tablespoons fish sauce
3–4 tablespoons grated palm sugar
chopped roasted peanuts, to garnish
fresh Thai basil, to garnish

1 To make the curry paste, put the chillies in
a bowl and cover with boiling water. Soak
them for 20 minutes, or until softened. Remove
the seeds and roughly chop the flesh. Put the
chopped chillies in a food processor along with
the shallots, garlic, ground coriander, ground
cumin, white pepper, lemon grass, galangal,
coriander roots, shrimp paste and roasted peanuts
and process until a smooth paste forms—you
might need to add a little water if the paste is
too thick.

2 Open the can of coconut cream and scoop
off the really thick cream from the top. Put this
thick cream in a wok and cook over medium
heat for 10 minutes, or until the oil starts to
separate from the cream. Stir in 8 tablespoons
of the curry paste and cook, stirring often, for
5–8 minutes, or until fragrant.

3 Add the beef, coconut milk, peanut butter,
lime leaves and the remaining coconut cream
to the wok and cook for 8 minutes, or until the
beef just starts to change colour. Reduce the
heat to low and simmer for 30 minutes, or until
the beef is tender, stirring every few minutes to
prevent it from catching on the bottom.

4 Stir in the lime juice, fish sauce and sugar until
they are mixed into the curry. Serve in bowls,
garnished with the roasted peanuts and basil.
NOTE: Store the rest of the curry paste in a small
jar in the refrigerator. You can use it to make a
curry on another occasion.

LION'S HEAD MEATBALLS

Preparation time: 20 minutes +
20 minutes soaking
Total cooking time: 45 minutes
Serves 4

★ ★

6 dried shiitake mushrooms

100 g (3¹/₂ oz) cellophane noodles

600 g (1¹/₄ lb) minced (ground) pork

1 egg white

4 cloves garlic, finely chopped

2 tablespoons finely grated fresh ginger

1 tablespoon cornflour (cornstarch)

1¹/₂ tablespoons Chinese rice wine

6 spring onions (scallions), thinly sliced

2 tablespoons peanut oil

2 litres (64 fl oz) home-made chicken stock
(see page 95) or 1.5 litres (48 fl oz) purchased
stock diluted with 2 cups (500 ml/16 fl oz)
water

¹/₄ cup (60 ml/2 fl oz) light soy sauce

1 teaspoon sugar

400 g (13 oz) bok choy (pak choi), cut in half
lengthways and leaves separated

 Soak the mushrooms in 1 cup (250 ml/8 fl oz) boiling water for 20 minutes. Squeeze dry,

reserving the soaking liquid. Discard the stems and thinly slice the caps. Meanwhile, put the noodles in a heatproof bowl, cover with boiling water and soak for 4–5 minutes, or until soft. Drain and rinse.

2 Put the pork, egg white, garlic, ginger, cornflour, rice wine, two-thirds of the spring onion, and a pinch of salt in a food processor. Using the pulse button, process until smooth and well combined. Divide the mixture into eight portions and shape into large balls using wet hands.

3 Heat a wok over high heat, add the peanut oil and swirl to coat. Cook the meatballs in batches for 2 minutes on each side, or until golden but not cooked through. Drain.

4 Clean and dry the wok, then pour the stock into the wok and bring to the boil. Add the meatballs, soy sauce, sugar and mushrooms with the soaking liquid, then cover and cook over low heat for 20–25 minutes, or until the meatballs are cooked through.

5 Add the bok choy and noodles, cover and cook for 5 minutes, or until the noodles are heated through. Sprinkle with the remaining spring onion, then serve.

LION'S HEAD MEATBALLS

This eastern Chinese speciality is traditionally made with wom bok (Chinese cabbage), but can also be made with bok choy (pak choi). It gained its name from the large meatballs, which are said to resemble a lion's head, with the leaves representing the mane. Legend has it that the dish was invented by a woman especially for her aged father-in-law, who had lost all his teeth and could only eat soft food. It is a rather wet-braised dish, but is eaten as a meal with noodles (as in the adjacent recipe) or with rice, rather than being eaten as a soup.

ABOVE: Lion's head meatballs

beef and toss well. Cover with plastic wrap and marinate in the fridge for 20 minutes.

2 Heat a wok over high heat, add the peanut oil and swirl around to coat the side of the wok. Add the meat in batches and cook each batch for 2–3 minutes, or until browned.

3 Arrange the beef on a serving platter, sprinkle with the chopped peanuts and fresh coriander, and serve with steamed rice.

GARLIC BEEF WITH RED PEPPER

Preparation time: 5 minutes +
  15 minutes marinating
Total cooking time: 15 minutes
Serves 4

1 tablespoon Chinese rice wine

2 teaspoons light soy sauce

1 clove garlic, finely chopped

1/4 teaspoon ground white pepper

2 tablespoons vegetable oil

500 g (1 lb) lean beef fillet, thinly sliced
  across the grain

1 small red pepper (capsicum), cut into
  4 cm (1 1/2 inch) batons

Garlic sauce

1 teaspoon cornflour (cornstarch)

2 teaspoons vegetable oil

4 cloves garlic, finely chopped

4 spring onions (scallions), finely chopped
  (white and green parts separated)

200 ml (6 1/2 fl oz) hot chicken stock

2 teaspoons vegetarian oyster sauce

2 teaspoons chilli garlic sauce

1/2–1 teaspoon chilli oil

1 Combine the rice wine, soy sauce, garlic, white pepper, 1 teaspoon of the oil and 1/4 teaspoon salt in a non-metallic bowl. Add the beef, cover and refrigerate for at least 15 minutes.

2 Heat a wok over high heat, add 2 teaspoons of the oil and swirl to coat. Add the red pepper strips and stir-fry for 1–2 minutes, or until the pepper is cooked. Remove from the wok.

3 Heat the remaining oil in the wok, add the beef in two batches and stir-fry for 2–3 minutes per batch, or until cooked through. Remove from the wok.

CHILLI BEEF

Preparation time: 10 minutes +
  20 minutes marinating
Total cooking time: 10 minutes
Serves 4

1/4 cup (60 ml/2 fl oz) kecap manis

2 1/2 teaspoons sambal oelek

2 cloves garlic, crushed

1/2 teaspoon ground coriander

1 tablespoon grated palm sugar

1 teaspoon sesame oil

400 g (13 oz) lean beef fillet, thinly sliced
  across the grain

1 tablespoon peanut oil

2 tablespoons chopped roasted peanuts

3 tablespoons chopped fresh coriander
  (cilantro) leaves

1 Combine the kecap manis, sambal oelek, garlic, ground coriander, palm sugar, sesame oil and 2 tablespoons water in a large bowl. Add the

ABOVE: Chilli beef

4 To make the garlic sauce, blend the cornflour with 1 tablespoon water and set aside. Add the oil to the wok and reduce the heat to low. Add the garlic and white part of the spring onions and cook for 30 seconds, or until fragrant. Pour in the stock and stir thoroughly. Increase the heat to high, bring the sauce to the boil and reduce slightly. Add the oyster sauce, chilli garlic sauce and chilli oil and stir together, before mixing in the cornflour paste. Cook for 1–2 minutes, or until the sauce thickens.
5 Return the red pepper and meat to the wok, quickly stir to coat and heat through, then serve, garnished with the spring onion (scallion) tops.

CHINESE BEEF AND ASPARAGUS WITH OYSTER SAUCE

Preparation time: 10 minutes + 15 minutes marinating
Total cooking time: 10 minutes
Serves 4

✶

1 tablespoon light soy sauce
1/2 teaspoon sesame oil
1 tablespoon Chinese rice wine
500 g (1 lb) lean beef fillet, thinly sliced
  across the grain
2 1/2 tablespoons vegetable oil
200 g (6 1/2 oz) fresh thin asparagus, cut into
  thirds on the diagonal
3 cloves garlic, crushed
2 teaspoons julienned fresh ginger
1/4 cup (60 ml/2 fl oz) chicken stock
2–3 tablespoons oyster sauce

1 Combine the soy sauce, sesame oil and 2 teaspoons of the rice wine in a large non-metallic bowl. Add the beef, cover with plastic wrap and marinate in the fridge for at least 15 minutes.
2 Heat a wok over high heat, add 1 tablespoon of the vegetable oil and swirl to coat the side of the wok. Add the asparagus and stir-fry for 1–2 minutes. Remove from the wok.
3 Heat another tablespoon of oil in the wok over high heat, then add the beef in two batches, stir-frying each batch for 1–2 minutes, or until cooked through. Remove the meat from the wok and add to the asparagus.
4 Add the remaining oil to wok, add the garlic and ginger before the oil becomes too hot and stir-fry for 1 minute, or until fragrant. Pour the stock, oyster sauce and remaining rice wine into the wok, bring to the boil and boil rapidly for 1–2 minutes, or until the sauce is slightly reduced. Return the beef and asparagus to the wok and stir-fry for a further minute, or until heated through and coated in the sauce. Serve immediately with steamed rice.

CHINESE ETIQUETTE
Chinese etiquette requires both hands to be held above the table during meals, with one hand holding the rice bowl and the other holding the chopsticks. The origins of this rule date back to the third century when a famous banquet disintegrated into a massacre when soldiers at the banquet, who had kept their daggers concealed under the table, turned upon their fellow diners.

LEFT: Chinese beef and asparagus with oyster sauce

Traditionally, teriyaki refers to any food (usually beef, chicken or fish) that is glazed with a special, sweet marinade in the final stages of being grilled or pan-fried. Teri means gloss and yaki refers to grilling or pan-frying in Japanese, its country of origin. As teriyaki has spread around the world, it has earnt a looser definition, referring more to the trio of favoured Japanese ingredients that go to make up teriyaki sauce (mirin, sake and soy sauce), than the cooking method (see the adjacent recipe). Teriyaki sauce can be easily made at home, but it is also commercially available.

ABOVE: Teriyaki beef and soy bean stir-fry

TERIYAKI BEEF AND SOY BEAN STIR-FRY

Preparation time: 15 minutes
Total cooking time: 20 minutes
Serves 4

⭐

1 tablespoon mirin

2 tablespoons sake

2 tablespoons Japanese soy sauce

2 teaspoons sugar

400 g (13 oz) frozen soy beans (see Note)

1 tablespoon peanut oil

700 g (1 lb 7 oz) lean beef fillet, thinly sliced across the grain

6 spring onions (scallions), thinly sliced

2 cloves garlic, chopped

2 teaspoons finely chopped fresh ginger

50 g (1 3/4 oz) soy bean sprouts, tailed

1 red pepper (capsicum), thinly sliced

1 To make the stir-fry sauce, combine the mirin, sake, Japanese soy sauce and sugar in a small bowl or jug and set aside until it is needed.
2 Cook the soy beans in a saucepan of boiling water for 2 minutes. Drain.
3 Heat a large wok over high heat. Add 2 teaspoons of the peanut oil and swirl it around to coat the side of the wok. Cook the beef in three batches for 3–4 minutes per batch, or until well browned. Remove from the wok. Add the spring onion and stir-fry for 30 seconds, or until it has wilted.
4 Return the beef to the wok, add the garlic, ginger, soy beans, soy bean sprouts and pepper, and stir-fry for 2 minutes. Add the stir-fry sauce to the wok and stir-fry until heated through. Serve hot with steamed rice.
NOTE: Frozen soy beans are available in packets, either in their pods or shelled. They are available from Asian food stores. This recipe uses the shelled variety.

LEMON GRASS BEEF

Preparation time: 15 minutes +
10 minutes marinating
Total cooking time: 25 minutes
Serves 4

3 cloves garlic, finely chopped

1 tablespoon grated fresh ginger

4 stems lemon grass (white part only),
    finely chopped

2¹/₂ tablespoons vegetable oil

600 g (1¹/₄ lb) lean beef fillet, thinly sliced
    across the grain

1 tablespoon lime juice

1–2 tablespoons fish sauce

2 tablespoons kecap manis

1 large red onion, cut into small wedges

200 g (6¹/₂ oz) green beans, sliced on the
    diagonal into 5 cm (2 inch) lengths

1 Combine the garlic, ginger, lemon grass and 2 teaspoons of the oil in a large non-metallic bowl. Add the beef, toss well until it is coated in the marinade, then cover with plastic wrap and marinate in the fridge for at least 10 minutes.
2 To make the stir-fry sauce, combine the lime juice, fish sauce and kecap manis in a small bowl or jug and set aside until needed.
3 Heat a wok over high heat, add 1 tablespoon oil and swirl to coat the side of the wok. Stir-fry the beef in batches for 2–3 minutes, or until browned. Remove from the wok.
4 Reheat the wok over high heat, heat the remaining oil, then add the onion and stir-fry for 2 minutes. Add the beans and cook for another 2 minutes, then return the beef to the wok. Pour in the stir-fry sauce and cook until heated through. Serve with steamed rice.

LEMON GRASS TEA
Lemon grass is common in the cuisines of Southeast Asia. The 'sweet-sour' lemony flavour of the leaves makes a great herbal tea. Tie a piece of lemon grass into a knot and infuse it in 1 cup (250 ml/8 fl oz) of boiling water.

LEFT: Lemon grass beef

STIR-FRIED BEEF WITH SNAKE BEANS AND BASIL

Preparation time: 10 minutes +
  2 hours marinating
Total cooking time: 10 minutes
Serves 4

3 fresh bird's eye chillies, seeded and
  finely chopped
3 cloves garlic, crushed
2 tablespoons fish sauce
1 teaspoon grated palm sugar
2 tablespoons peanut or vegetable oil
400 g (13 oz) lean beef fillet, thinly sliced
  across the grain
150 g (5 oz) snake beans, sliced into
  3 cm (1 1/4 inch) lengths
1 cup (30 g/1 oz) loosely packed fresh Thai basil
thinly sliced fresh bird's eye chilli, to garnish

1 Combine the chilli, garlic, fish sauce, palm
sugar and 1 tablespoon of the oil in a large
non-metallic bowl. Add the beef, toss well, then
cover and marinate in the fridge for 2 hours.
2 Heat a wok to hot, add 2 teaspoons of the oil
and swirl to coat. Stir-fry the beef in two batches
over high heat for 2 minutes each batch, or until
just browned. Remove from the wok.

3 Heat the remaining oil in the wok, then
add the snake beans and 1/4 cup (60 ml/2 fl oz)
water and cook over high heat for 3–4 minutes,
tossing regularly until tender. Return the beef
to the wok with the basil. Cook for a further
1–2 minutes, or until warmed through. Garnish
with chilli, then serve.

STIR-FRIED BEEF AND CHILLI BEAN PASTE

Preparation time: 20 minutes
Total cooking time: 15 minutes
Serves 4-6

2 tablespoons light soy sauce
1 tablespoon Chinese rice wine
1 tablespoon oyster sauce
1 tablespoon chilli bean paste
2 teaspoons brown bean sauce
1–2 tablespoons peanut oil
600 g (1 1/4 lb) lean beef fillet, thinly sliced
  across the grain
1 onion, sliced into thin wedges
2 cloves garlic, crushed
1 fresh red chilli
120 g (4 oz) green beans, trimmed and
  halved if long

RIGHT: Stir-fried beef with snake beans and basil

1 To make the stir-fry sauce, combine the soy sauce, rice wine, oyster sauce, chilli bean paste and brown bean sauce in a small, non-metallic bowl or jug. Set aside until needed.

2 Heat a wok with a lid over high heat, add 1 tablespoon of the oil and swirl to coat the side of the wok. Stir-fry the beef in batches over high heat for 2 minutes each batch, or until browned. Remove from the wok.

3 Reheat the wok to hot, add the onion and stir-fry for 3–5 minutes, or until browned, then add the garlic and chilli and cook for a further minute. Toss in the beans, pour in the stir-fry sauce, then cover with a lid and cook for 3 minutes.

4 Remove the lid, return the beef to the wok and stir-fry for 1–2 minutes, or until the meat is coated with the sauce and heated through. Serve with steamed rice.

GINGER BEEF STIR-FRY

Preparation time: 20 minutes +
   15 minutes marinating
Total cooking time: 15 minutes
Serves 4

1 clove garlic, crushed

1 teaspoon grated fresh ginger

1/4 cup (60 ml/2 fl oz) kecap manis

1/4 cup (60 ml/2 fl oz) Chinese rice wine

1 teaspoon sugar

pinch of five-spice powder

500 g (1 lb) lean beef fillet, thinly sliced across
   the grain

1/2 teaspoon cornflour (cornstarch)

1/4 cup (60 ml/2 fl oz) peanut oil

1 red onion, sliced into thin wedges

1 1/2 tablespoons julienned fresh ginger

400 g (13 oz) gai larn (Chinese broccoli),
   cut into 6 cm (2 1/2 inch) lengths

1 Combine the garlic, grated ginger, kecap manis, rice wine, sugar and five-spice powder in a large non-metallic bowl. Add the beef, toss together, then cover and marinate in the fridge for at least 15 minutes.

2 Mix together the cornflour with 1 tablespoon water to form a paste.

3 Heat a wok over high heat, add 1 tablespoon of the oil and swirl to coat the side of the wok. Remove half the meat from the marinade with

tongs or a slotted spoon, add to the wok and stir-fry for 2–3 minutes, or until browned and just cooked. Remove from the wok. Repeat with more oil and the rest of the beef, reserving the marinade.

4 Add the remaining oil to the wok and stir-fry the onion for 2–3 minutes, or until it starts to soften, then add the julienned ginger and stir-fry for another minute. Stir in the gai larn and cook for 2–3 minutes, or until wilted and tender.

5 Return the beef to the wok, along with the reserved marinade and any meat juices. Add the cornflour paste and stir until thoroughly combined. Continue to cook for 1–2 minutes, or until the sauce has thickened slightly and the meat is heated through. Serve with steamed rice or noodles.

ABOVE: Ginger beef stir-fry

Satay are short skewers
of beef, pork or chicken
marinated in coconut milk
and spices, then quickly
grilled over charcoal and
served with a spicy peanut
sauce. Satays are one of
a number of dishes often
prepared by street
vendors who find
themselves a spot near
markets and popular
restaurants to tempt
passers-by. In some areas,
waiters from nearby
restaurants pass orders
from customers in the
restaurant to the street
vendor, then fetch the
finished satay and include
it on the restaurant bill. In
Malaysia, Thailand and
Indonesia, there is an
entire culinary sub-culture
based around street
vendors. While some
tourists to these countries
have a perception that the
food from street vendors
is of lesser quality than
that served in restaurants,
in many cases the opposite
is true and large crowds
form around the most
popular venues.

ABOVE: Satay lamb

SATAY LAMB

Preparation time: 10 minutes
Total cooking time: 15 minutes
Serves 4

1/4 cup (60 ml/2 fl oz) peanut oil
750 g (1 1/2 lb) lamb loin fillets, thinly sliced
    across the grain
2 teaspoons ground cumin
1 teaspoon ground turmeric
1 red pepper (capsicum), sliced
1/4 cup (60 ml/2 fl oz) sweet chilli sauce
1/4 cup (60 g/2 oz) crunchy peanut butter
1 cup (250 ml/8 fl oz) coconut milk
2 teaspoons soft brown sugar
1–2 tablespoons lemon juice, to taste
4 tablespoons chopped fresh coriander
    (cilantro) leaves
1/4 cup (40 g/1 1/4 oz) unsalted peanuts, roasted,
    chopped, to serve

1 Heat a wok over high heat, add 1 tablespoon
oil and swirl. Add half the lamb and stir-fry for
3 minutes, or until browned. Remove. Repeat
with 1 tablespoon oil and the remaining lamb.
2 Reheat the wok, add the remaining oil and
cumin, turmeric and pepper, and stir-fry for
2 minutes, or until the pepper is tender.

3 Return the lamb to the wok. Stir in the chilli
sauce, peanut butter, coconut milk and sugar.
Bring to the boil, then reduce the heat and
simmer for 5 minutes, or until the meat is tender
and the sauce has thickened slightly. Remove
from the heat and add the lemon juice. Stir in the
coriander and sprinkle with the peanuts. Serve.

LAMB AND LETTUCE
LEAF PARCELS

Preparation time: 15 minutes +
    10 minutes marinating
Total cooking time: 10 minutes
Serves 4

2 teaspoons light soy sauce
2 teaspoons Chinese rice wine
300 g (10 oz) lean minced (ground) lamb
8 baby cos (romaine) lettuce leaves
2 tablespoons vegetable oil
2 cloves garlic, crushed
2 red Asian shallots, finely chopped
1 fresh bird's eye chilli, finely chopped
120 g (4 oz) water chestnuts, finely diced
5 fresh baby corn, finely diced
1 tablespoon vegetarian oyster sauce
1 tablespoon kecap manis

2–3 tablespoons chicken stock
pinch of white pepper
1 cup (90 g/3 oz) bean sprouts, tailed
2 tablespoons fresh mint, finely shredded
1 tablespoon fresh coriander (cilantro) leaves,
  chopped
crisp fried shallots, to garnish

1 Combine the light soy sauce and 1 teaspoon of
the rice wine in a large non-metallic bowl. Add
the lamb, toss together, then marinate for at least
10 minutes.
2 Meanwhile, wash and dry the baby
cos leaves, then place on a serving plate.
3 Heat a wok over high heat, add 1 tablespoon
of the oil and swirl to coat. Add the garlic, Asian
shallots and chilli and stir-fry for 30 seconds, or
until fragrant. Add the water chestnuts and corn
and continue to stir-fry for an extra minute, then
remove everything from the wok.
4 Wipe the wok clean, heat over high heat, then
add the remaining oil and swirl to coat. When
the oil is smoking, add the lamb, toss briskly
to break up any clumps, then stir-fry for
4–5 minutes, or until cooked through. Add the
oyster sauce, kecap manis, stock and remaining
rice wine, season with white pepper and stir
thoroughly. Return the water chestnut mixture
to the wok with the bean sprouts and mix well.
Remove from the heat, then stir in the mint.
5 Spoon equal portions of the lamb mixture
onto each of the cos leaves, garnish with
coriander and crisp fried shallots, then serve.

LAMB AND MINT STIR-FRY

Preparation time: 10 minutes
Total cooking time: 15 minutes
Serves 4

1/4 cup (60 ml/2 fl oz) lime juice
2 tablespoons sweet chilli sauce
2 tablespoons fish sauce
2 tablespoons vegetable oil
750 g (1 1/2 lb) lamb loin fillets, thinly sliced
  across the grain
2 cloves garlic, finely chopped
1 small red onion, cut into wedges
1 fresh bird's eye chilli, finely chopped
1/2 cup (10 g/1/4 oz) fresh mint

1 To make the stir-fry sauce, combine the lime
juice, chilli sauce and fish sauce in a small
non-metallic bowl.
2 Heat a wok over high heat, add 1 tablespoon
of the oil and swirl it around to coat the side of
the wok. Add the lamb in batches and cook for
2 minutes each batch, or until browned.
Remove from the wok.
3 Heat the remaining oil in the wok, add the
garlic and onion and stir-fry for 1 minute, then
add the chilli and cook for 30 seconds. Return
the lamb to the wok, pour in the stir-fry sauce
and cook for 2 minutes over high heat. Stir in
the mint, then serve with steamed jasmine rice.

*LEFT: Lamb and mint
stir-fry*

1 Combine the garlic, ginger, Chinese rice wine, soy sauce, hoisin sauce and sesame oil in a large non-metallic bowl. Add the lamb and toss until well coated. Cover with plastic wrap and marinate in the refrigerator overnight, tossing occasionally.

2 Heat a wok over high heat, add 1 tablespoon of the peanut oil and swirl to coat the wok. Add the spring onion and stir-fry for 1 minute, or until lightly golden. Remove, reserving the oil in the wok.

3 Lift the lamb out of the marinade with tongs, reserving the marinade. Add the meat in four batches and stir-fry for 1–2 minutes per batch, or until browned but not completely cooked through, adding more oil and making sure the wok is very hot before cooking each batch. Return all the meat and any juices to the wok with the spring onion and stir-fry for 1 minute, or until meat is cooked through.

4 Remove the meat and spring onion from the wok with a slotted spoon and place in a serving bowl, retaining the liquid in the wok. Add any reserved marinade to the wok along with the chilli sauce and extra hoisin sauce, then boil for 3–4 minutes, or until the sauce thickens and becomes slightly syrupy. Spoon the sauce over the lamb, toss together well, then serve with steamed rice.

CUMIN LAMB STIR-FRY

Preparation time: 15 minutes +
  10 minutes marinating
Total cooking time: 10 minutes
Serves 4

1 tablespoon dark soy sauce

1 tablespoon Chinese rice wine

1 tablespoon light soy sauce

500 g (1 lb) lean lamb loin fillets, thinly sliced across the grain

1/3 cup (80 ml/2³/4 fl oz) chicken or vegetable stock

2 teaspoons Chinese black vinegar

2 teaspoons chilli garlic sauce

2 tablespoons vegetable oil

1 red onion, cut into small wedges

1 teaspoon cumin seeds, lightly crushed

1 clove garlic, crushed

1 teaspoon fresh ginger, finely chopped

75 g (2¹/2 oz) garlic chives, trimmed and halved

MONGOLIAN LAMB

Preparation time: 25 minutes +
  overnight marinating
Total cooking time: 15 minutes
Serves 4-6

2 cloves garlic, crushed

2 teaspoons finely grated fresh ginger

1/4 cup (60 ml/2 fl oz) Chinese rice wine

1/4 cup (60 ml/2 fl oz) soy sauce

2 tablespoons hoisin sauce

1 teaspoon sesame oil

1 kg (2 lb) lamb loin fillets, thinly sliced across the grain

1/3 cup (80 ml/2³/4 fl oz) peanut oil

6 spring onions (scallions), cut into 3 cm (1¹/4 inch) lengths

2 teaspoons chilli sauce

1¹/2 tablespoons hoisin sauce, extra

ABOVE: Mongolian lamb

1 Combine the dark soy sauce, Chinese rice wine and 2 teaspoons of the light soy sauce in a large non-metallic bowl. Add the lamb and toss well. Cover with plastic wrap and marinate in the refrigerator for at least 10 minutes.

2 To make the stir-fry sauce, combine the stock, black vinegar, chilli garlic sauce and remaining light soy sauce in a small non-metallic jug.

3 Heat a wok over high heat, add 1 tablespoon of the oil and swirl to coat. Add the lamb in two batches and stir-fry for 1–2 minutes, or until browned. Remove from the wok.

4 Heat the remaining oil in the wok, add the onion wedges and stir-fry for 2 minutes. Add the cumin, garlic, ginger and garlic chives and cook for 30 seconds, or until fragrant. Pour in the stir-fry sauce, and bring to the boil until thickened slightly and combined with the other ingredients. Return the lamb to the wok, quickly stir to coat with the sauce then serve with steamed rice and Asian greens.

GREEN TEA NOODLE SALAD WITH LAMB AND TOMATO

Preparation time: 20 minutes + 2 hours marinating
Total cooking time: 20 minutes
Serves 4

★

1 teaspoon hot mustard
2 tablespoons vegetable oil
1/4 cup (60 ml/2 fl oz) balsamic vinegar
400 g (13 oz) lamb loin fillets, thinly sliced
  across the grain
250 g (8 oz) chasoba noodles (see Note)
1/4 cup (60 ml/2 fl oz) light soy sauce
2 tablespoons mirin
1–2 teaspoons sesame oil
1/2 teaspoon sugar
2 Lebanese (short) cucumbers, cut in half
  lengthways and thinly sliced on the diagonal
2 large tomatoes, cut into 1 cm (1/2 inch) cubes
1/2 cup (15 g/1/2 oz) fresh coriander (cilantro)
  leaves
2 spring onions (scallions), thinly sliced on
  the diagonal
1 tablespoon sesame seeds, lightly toasted

1 Combine the mustard, 1 tablespoon of the oil, 1 tablespoon of the vinegar and 1/2 teaspoon pepper in a large non-metallic bowl. Add the

lamb and toss. Cover, then refrigerate for 2 hours.

2 Add the noodles to a large saucepan of boiling water and stir to separate. Return to the boil, adding 1 cup (250 ml/8 fl oz) cold water and repeat this step three times, as it comes to the boil. Drain and rinse under cold water. Place in a large bowl.

3 Combine the soy sauce, mirin, sesame oil, sugar, the remaining balsamic vinegar and 1/2 teaspoon salt and stir until the sugar dissolves. Toss half of the dressing through the noodles.

4 Place the cucumber, tomato and 1/2 teaspoon salt in a bowl and toss well. Add to the noodles with the coriander and spring onion and toss well.

5 Heat a wok over high heat, add the remaining oil and swirl to coat. Drain the lamb, then, using tongs or a slotted spoon, add the lamb to the wok in two batches, and stir-fry each batch for 2–3 minutes, or until the lamb is seared and cooked to your liking. Divide among serving plates, then top with the lamb. Drizzle with dressing, sprinkle with sesame seeds and serve.

NOTE: Chasoba noodles are soba noodles that have had green tea powder added to them.

BELOW: Green tea noodle salad with lamb and tomato

273

PHAD THAI

Preparation time: 30 minutes + 20 minutes soaking
Total cooking time: 10 minutes
Serves 4-6

250 g (8 oz) dried rice stick noodles
1 small fresh red chilli, chopped
2 cloves garlic, chopped
2 spring onions (scallions), sliced
1 tablespoon tamarind purée, mixed
    with 1 tablespoon water
1 1/2 tablespoons sugar
2 tablespoons fish sauce
2 tablespoons lime juice
2 tablespoons vegetable oil
2 eggs, beaten
150 g (5 oz) pork fillet, thinly sliced

8 raw large prawns (shrimp), peeled and
    deveined, with tails intact
100 g (3 1/2 oz) fried tofu puffs, julienned
1 cup (90 g/3 oz) bean sprouts, tailed
1/4 cup (40 g/1 1/4 oz) chopped roasted peanuts
3 tablespoons fresh coriander (cilantro) leaves
1 lime, cut into wedges

1 Soak the noodles in warm water for
15–20 minutes, or until tender. Drain.
2 Pound together the chilli, garlic and spring
onion in a mortar and pestle. Gradually blend
in the tamarind mixture, sugar, fish sauce and
lime juice.
3 Heat a wok over high heat, add 1 tablespoon
of the oil and swirl to coat. Add the egg, swirl
to coat and cook for 1–2 minutes, or until set
and cooked. Remove and shred.
4 Heat the remaining oil, stir in the chilli
mixture, and stir-fry for 30 seconds. Add the
pork and stir-fry for 2 minutes, or until
tender. Add the prawns and stir-fry for a further
1 minute.
5 Stir in the noodles, egg, tofu and half the bean
sprouts, and toss to heat through.
6 Serve immediately, topped with the peanuts,
coriander, lime and remaining bean sprouts.
NOTE: Use a non-stick or stainless steel wok to
cook this dish as the tamarind purée will react
with the metal in a regular wok and badly taint
the dish.

BELOW: Phad Thai

CHINESE BARBECUED PORK WITH GAI LARN

Preparation time: 10 minutes
Total cooking time: 10 minutes
Serves 4

1/4 cup (60 ml/2 fl oz) chicken or vegetable
    stock
1/4 cup (60 ml/2 fl oz) oyster sauce
1 tablespoon kecap manis
1.6 kg (3 1/4 lb) gai larn (Chinese broccoli),
    cut into 5 cm (2 inch) lengths
1 tablespoon peanut oil
2 cm (3/4 inch) piece fresh ginger, julienned
2 cloves garlic, crushed
500 g (1 lb) Chinese barbecued pork, thinly
    sliced

Use a pair of scissors to trim the lettuce leaves into neat cups.

1 To make the stir-fry sauce, combine the stock, oyster sauce and kecap manis in a small bowl.
2 Put the gai larn in a steamer over a saucepan or wok of simmering water and cook for 5 minutes, or until just tender but still crisp.
3 Heat a wok over high heat, add the oil and swirl to coat. Add the ginger and garlic, and stir-fry for 30 seconds, or until fragrant. Add the gai larn and pork, and toss to coat. Pour in the stir-fry sauce and toss together until heated through. Serve with rice or noodles.

SAN CHOY BAU

Preparation time: 25 minutes
Total cooking time: 10 minutes
Makes 12 small or 4 large

 ✩✩

1/4 cup (60 ml/2 fl oz) oyster sauce
2 teaspoons soy sauce
1/4 cup (60 ml/2 fl oz) sherry
1 teaspoon sugar
1 1/2 tablespoons vegetable oil
1/4 teaspoon sesame oil
3 cloves garlic, crushed
3 teaspoons grated fresh ginger
6 spring onions (scallions), sliced on the diagonal
500 g (1 lb) minced (ground) pork
100 g (3 1/2 oz) bamboo shoots, finely chopped
100 g (3 1/2 oz) water chestnuts, drained and finely chopped
1 tablespoon pine nuts, toasted
12 small or 4 large whole lettuce leaves (e.g. iceberg), trimmed
oyster sauce, to serve (optional)

1 To make the stir-fry sauce, combine the oyster and soy sauces, sherry and sugar in a small bowl or jug and stir until the sugar dissolves.
2 Heat a wok over high heat, add the vegetable and sesame oils and swirl. Add the garlic, ginger and half the spring onion and stir-fry for 1 minute. Add the pork and cook for 3 minutes, or until just cooked, breaking up any lumps.
3 Add the bamboo shoots, water chestnuts and remaining spring onion, then pour in the stir-fry sauce. Cook for 2–3 minutes, or until the liquid thickens a little. Stir in the pine nuts.
4 Divide among the lettuce cups to make either 12 small portions or four very large ones. Drizzle with oyster sauce, if desired, then serve.

ABOVE: San choy bau

PORK AND BROWN BEAN SAUCE NOODLES

Preparation time: 10 minutes
Total cooking time: 15 minutes
Serves 4-6

★★

1/4 cup (60 ml/12 fl oz) brown bean sauce

2 tablespoons hoisin sauce

3/4 cup (185 ml/6 fl oz) chicken stock

1/2 teaspoon sugar

2 tablespoons peanut oil

3 cloves garlic, finely chopped

6 spring onions (scallions), sliced, white and
    green parts separated

650 g (1 lb 5 oz) minced (ground) pork

500 g (1 lb) fresh Shanghai noodles

1 telegraph cucumber, halved lengthways,
    seeded and sliced on the diagonal

1 cup (30 g/1 oz) fresh coriander (cilantro) leaves

1 cup (90 g/3 oz) bean sprouts, tailed

1 tablespoon lime juice

1 Combine the bean and hoisin sauces, stock and sugar and mix until smooth.
2 Heat a wok over high heat, add the oil and swirl. Add the garlic and spring onion (white part) and cook for 10–20 seconds. Add the pork and cook over high heat for 2–3 minutes, or until it has browned. Add the bean mixture, reduce the heat and simmer for 7–8 minutes.
3 Cook the noodles in a large saucepan of boiling water for 4–5 minutes, or until tender. Drain and rinse, then divide among bowls. Toss together the cucumber, coriander, sprouts, lime juice and remaining spring onion. Spoon the sauce over the noodles and top with the salad.

PORK FILLET IN BLACK BEAN SAUCE

Preparation time: 10 minutes + 1 hour marinating
Total cooking time: 15 minutes
Serves 4

★

2 cloves garlic, crushed

2 teaspoons finely grated fresh ginger

2 tablespoons vegetable oil

600 g (1 1/4 lb) pork loin fillet, thinly sliced
    across the grain

2–3 tablespoons black beans, rinsed

1/4 cup (60 ml/2 fl oz) chicken stock

1 1/2 tablespoons soy sauce

1 1/2 teaspoons cornflour (cornstarch)

1 teaspoon sugar

1/4 teaspoon sesame oil

1 small onion, thinly sliced

3 spring onions (scallions), thinly sliced

ABOVE: Pork and brown bean sauce noodles

1 Combine the garlic, ginger and 2 teaspoons of the vegetable oil in a large non-metallic bowl. Add the pork, cover and refrigerate for 1 hour.
2 Place the black beans in a small jug with the stock, soy sauce, cornflour and sugar. Mix well and mash the beans with a fork.
3 Heat a wok over high heat, add the sesame oil and 1 tablespoon of the vegetable oil and swirl. Stir-fry the meat in batches for 3 minutes, or until browned. Remove from the wok.
4 Add the remaining oil to the wok and stir-fry the onion for 2 minutes. Return the pork to the wok and add the black bean sauce and spring onion. Toss for 3 minutes, or until the sauce comes to the boil and thickens enough to coat the meat. Season. Serve as part of a banquet.

CARAMEL PORK AND PUMPKIN STIR-FRY

Preparation time: 15 minutes
Total cooking time: 20 minutes
Serves 4

500 g (1 lb) pork fillet, thinly sliced across
    the grain
2 cloves garlic, crushed
2–3 tablespoons peanut oil

300 g (10 oz) butternut pumpkin (squash),
    sliced into pieces about 2 x 4 cm
    ($^3/_4$ x 1$^1/_2$ inch) and 5 mm ($^1/_4$ inch) thick
$^1/_3$ cup (60 g/2 oz) soft brown sugar
$^1/_4$ cup (60 ml/2 fl oz) fish sauce
$^1/_4$ cup (60 ml/2 fl oz) rice vinegar
2 tablespoons chopped fresh coriander
    (cilantro) leaves

1 Put the pork in a bowl, add the garlic and about 2 teaspoons of the peanut oil, then season with salt and plenty of freshly ground pepper.
2 Heat a wok over high heat, add 1 tablespoon oil and swirl to coat the side of the wok. Stir-fry the pork in two batches for about 1 minute per batch, or until the meat changes colour. Transfer the meat to a plate.
3 Add the remaining oil to the wok and stir-fry the pumpkin for about 4 minutes, or until tender but not falling apart, then remove and add to the plate with the pork.
4 Put the sugar, fish sauce, rice vinegar and $^1/_2$ cup (125 ml/4 fl oz) water in the wok, stir thoroughly, then bring to the boil and boil for about 10 minutes, or until syrupy. Return the pork and pumpkin to the wok and stir for 1 minute, or until well coated with the syrup and heated through. Stir in the coriander and serve immediately with steamed rice and some steamed Asian greens, if desired.

BELOW: Caramel pork and pumpkin stir-fry

POULTRY & GAME

ROSEMARY

The Latin name for rosemary is *Rosmarinus officinalis* meaning 'dew of the sea', a reference probably to the fact that it grows near the sea. Dating back to Roman times, rosemary was used as much for its medicinal properties as for its aromatic flavour. It is a herb which should be used with discretion, as its distinctive flavour can easily overpower others. Rosemary is one of the most commonly used herbs in Italy, along with parsley, and is usually associated with roasts. If possible, use only fresh rosemary, snipping the tips off the younger, more fragrant branches.

ABOVE: Roasted rosemary chicken

ROASTED ROSEMARY CHICKEN

Preparation time: 15 minutes
  + 10 minutes standing
Total cooking time: 1 hour
Serves 4

★

1.5–1.8 kg (3 lb–3lb 10 oz) chicken
6 large sprigs fresh rosemary
4 cloves garlic
3 tablespoons olive oil

1 Preheat the oven to hot 220°C (425°F/Gas 7). Wipe the chicken inside and out and pat dry with paper towels. Season the chicken cavity and place 4 rosemary sprigs and the garlic cloves inside.
2 Rub the outside of the chicken with 1 tablespoon of the oil, season and place the chicken on its side in a roasting tin. Put the remaining rosemary sprigs in the tin and drizzle the remaining oil around the tin.
3 Place the tin on the middle shelf in the oven. After 20 minutes, turn the chicken onto the other side, baste with the juices and cook for another 20 minutes. Turn the chicken breast-side-up, baste again and cook for another 15 minutes, or until the juices between the body and thigh run clear when pierced with a knife. Transfer the chicken to a warm serving dish and set aside for at least 10 minutes before carving.
4 Meanwhile, pour most of the fat from the roasting tin and return the tin to the stovetop over high heat. Add 2 tablespoons water and, using a wooden spoon, scrape the base of the pan to loosen the residue. Check the seasoning and pour over the chicken to serve.

ROAST CHICKEN STUFFED WITH PINE NUTS AND RICE

Preparation time: 30 minutes
Total cooking time: 2 hours 30 minutes
Serves 4–6

Stuffing

60 g (2 oz) clarified butter (see Note)
  or ghee, melted
1 onion, chopped
1 teaspoon ground allspice
1/3 cup (60 g/2 oz) basmati rice
1/4 cup (30 g/1 oz) walnuts, chopped
1/3 cup (50 g/1 3/4 oz) pine nuts
1/3 cup (55 g/2 oz) sultanas
1/2 cup (125 ml/4 fl oz) chicken stock

1.6 kg (3 1/2 lb) chicken
2/3 cup (170 ml/5 1/2 fl oz) chicken stock

1 Preheat the oven to moderate 180°C (350°F/ Gas 4). Pour half the butter into a large frying pan, then add the onion and cook for 5 minutes over medium heat until the onion is transparent. Stir in the allspice.
2 Add the rice and nuts to the pan, then cook for 3–4 minutes over medium-high heat. Add the sultanas, stock and 1/4 cup (60 ml/2 fl oz) of water. Bring to boil, then reduce the heat and simmer for 8–10 minutes, until the water is absorbed. Allow to cool.
3 Rinse the cavity of the chicken with cold water and pat dry inside and out with paper towels.
4 When the stuffing is cool, spoon the stuffing into the cavity. Truss the chicken, using string, then place in a deep baking dish, then rub 1/2 teaspoon salt and 1/4 teaspoon freshly ground black pepper into the skin using your fingertips.
5 Pour the rest of the butter over the chicken, then add the stock to the pan. Roast for 2 hours 10 minutes, basting every 20–25 minutes with juices from the pan. Rest the chicken for 15 minutes before carving. Serve with the stuffing.
NOTE: To clarify butter, melt it in a saucepan over low heat, then remove from the heat and let the milk solids drop to the base. Only use the yellow liquid part of the butter. Discard the white milk solids at the base of the saucepan.

ABOVE: Roast chicken stuffed with pine nuts and rice

ROAST TURKEY WITH STUFFING

Preparation time: 45 minutes + making stuffing
Total cooking time: 2 hours
Serves 6–8

★★

3 kg (6 lb) turkey
1 quantity stuffing (see recipes on right)
2 tablespoons oil
2 cups (500 ml/16 fl oz) chicken stock
2 tablespoons plain (all-purpose) flour

1 Remove the neck and giblets from inside the turkey. Wash the turkey well and pat dry inside and out with paper towels. Preheat the oven to moderate 180°C (350°F/Gas 4).
2 Make the stuffing you prefer and loosely stuff into the turkey cavity. Tuck the wings underneath and join the cavity with a skewer. Tie the legs together. Place on a rack in a baking dish. Roast for 2 hours, basting with the combined oil and ½ cup (125 ml/4 fl oz) of the stock. Cover the breast and legs with foil after 1 hour if the turkey is overbrowning. Remove from the oven, cover and leave to rest for 15 minutes.
3 To make the gravy, drain off all except 2 tablespoons of pan juices from the baking dish. Place the dish on the stove over low heat, add the flour and stir well. Stir over medium heat until browned. Gradually add the remaining stock, stirring until the gravy boils and thickens. Serve the turkey with gravy and roast vegetables.
NOTE: Do not stuff the turkey until you are ready to cook it. Stuffing can be made ahead of time and frozen for up to a month in an airtight container. If you prefer to cook the stuffing separately, press it lightly into a lightly greased ovenproof dish and bake for about 30 minutes, or until golden brown. Small greased muffin tins can also be used (bake for 15–20 minutes). Alternatively, you can form the mixture into balls and fry in a little melted butter or oil, over medium heat, until golden brown all over.

CITRUS STUFFING

Heat 1 tablespoon oil in a small frying pan and cook 1 finely chopped onion until soft. Transfer to a large bowl and cool. Add 200 g (6½ oz) minced (ground) sausage meat, 2 crushed cloves of garlic, 2 cups (160 g/5½ oz) fresh white breadcrumbs, 2 teaspoons each of grated lemon and orange rinds and ½ cup (60 g/2 oz) finely chopped pecans and mix well. Season to taste with salt and pepper and mix.

COUNTRY SAGE STUFFING

Melt 45 g (1½ oz) butter in a small saucepan and cook 1 finely chopped onion and 1 sliced celery stick over medium heat for 3 minutes, or until the onion has softened. Transfer to a bowl and add 10 shredded large fresh sage leaves, 2 cups (160 g/5½ oz) fresh white breadcrumbs, 1½ teaspoons dried sage, 4 tablespoons finely chopped fresh parsley, 2 lightly beaten egg whites, 1 teaspoon salt and ½ teaspoon white pepper.

CASHEW STUFFING

Melt 60 g (2 oz) butter in a frying pan and cook 1 chopped onion until golden. Cool, then mix thoroughly with 2 cups (370 g/12 oz) cooked long-grain brown rice, 1 cup (185 g/6 oz) chopped dried apricots, ½ cup (80 g/2¾ oz) unsalted cashews, 3 tablespoons chopped fresh parsley, 2 tablespoons chopped fresh mint and 1 tablespoon lemon juice. Season to taste with salt and pepper. (You will need to cook 1 cup/200 g/6½ oz brown rice for this recipe.)

SPINACH AND RICOTTA STUFFING

Heat 2 tablespoons oil in a small saucepan, add 1 finely chopped onion and 2 crushed cloves of garlic and cook, stirring over medium heat for 5 minutes, or until soft. Squeeze as much liquid as possible from 2 thawed 250 g (8 oz) packets of frozen spinach and add the spinach to the pan. Cook, stirring for 2–3 minutes, or until as dry as possible. Remove from the heat and place in a large bowl to cool. Add ½ cup (80 g/2 oz) pine nuts, 1 cup (80 g/2¾ oz) stale white breadcrumbs, 400 g (13 oz) ricotta and 200 g (7½ oz) finely chopped semi-dried (sun-blushed) tomatoes. Season to taste with salt and pepper.

CHRISTMAS LEGENDS
Most people believe that the white, deep green and red colours we associate with Christmas come from the snowy fields in the northern hemisphere winter contrasting with the brilliant evergreens and crimson berries on the holly plant. However, there is a legend that tells of a lamb making its way to Bethlehem to see the Christ Child. Along the way, its fluffy white fleece was caught on a thorny holly plant and in the struggle to get free, the lamb pricked its skin and tiny droplets of blood oozed out and were frozen onto the branches.

OPPOSITE PAGE: Roast turkey with stuffing. Stuffings: In cavity, citrus; In bowls, Cashew (top left), Spinach and ricotta; Balls of stuffing, clockwise from top, Country sage, Spinach and ricotta (2), Country sage, Spinach and ricotta

ROAST DUCK WITH ORANGE SAUCE

Preparation time: 40 minutes
Total cooking time: 2 hours 15 minutes
Serves 4

★★

2 kg (4 lb) duck, with neck
2 chicken wings, chopped
1/2 cup (125 ml/4 fl oz) white wine
1 onion, chopped
1 carrot, sliced
1 ripe tomato, chopped
bouquet garni (see page 99)

Orange sauce

2 tablespoons shredded orange rind
2/3 cup (170 ml/5 1/2 fl oz) orange juice
1/3 cup (80 ml/2 3/4 fl oz) Cointreau
2 teaspoons cornflour (cornstarch)

1 Place the duck neck, chicken wings and wine in a pan. Boil over high heat for 5 minutes, or until the wine has reduced by half. Add the onion, carrot, tomato, bouquet garni and 2 cups (500 ml/16 fl oz) water. Bring to the boil and simmer gently for 40 minutes. Strain and set aside 1 cup (250 ml/8 fl oz) of the stock.

2 Preheat the oven to moderate 180°C (350°F/ Gas 4). Place the duck in a large saucepan, cover with boiling water, then drain. Dry with paper towels. With a fine skewer, prick all over the outside of the duck, piercing only the skin, not the flesh. Place the duck breast-side-down on a rack in a baking dish and bake for 50 minutes.

3 Drain off any fat, turn the duck over and pour the reserved stock into the pan. Bake for 40 minutes, or until the breast is golden brown. Remove the duck from the pan and leave in a warm place for 15 minutes before carving. Reserve any pan juices for making gravy or orange sauce.

4 For the orange sauce, skim any fat off the reserved pan juices. Place in a saucepan with the rind, juice and Cointreau and bring to the boil. Reduce the heat and simmer for 5 minutes. Blend the cornflour with 1 tablespoon water, add to the sauce and stir over heat until the mixture boils and thickens.

NOTE: You may need to order your duck in advance from a game specialist or poulterer.

ABOVE: Roast duck with orange sauce

ROAST GOOSE

Preparation time: 15 minutes
Total cooking time: 1 hour 30 minutes
Serves 6

★★

3 kg (6 lb) fresh or frozen goose
1 tablespoon plain (all-purpose) flour
2 tablespoons brandy
1 1/2 cups (375 ml/12 fl oz) chicken stock
bread sauce (see page 231), to serve

1 If using a frozen goose, thaw in the refrigerator—it may take 1–2 days. Preheat the oven to moderate 180°C (350°F/Gas 4). Remove any excess fat from inside the cavity of the goose. Place the goose in a large pan, cover with boiling water, then drain. Dry thoroughly with paper towels.

2 Place the goose breast-side-down on a rack in a very large baking dish. (Make sure the goose doesn't sit directly on the dish or it will be very greasy.) Using a fine skewer, prick the skin of the goose all over, being careful to pierce only the skin, not the flesh.

3 Bake the goose for 1 hour, then remove from the oven and drain off any excess fat. Turn the goose over and bake for another 30 minutes, or until the outside is golden and crisp. Remove from the baking dish, cover loosely with foil and leave for 5–10 minutes.

4 For gravy, drain all except 2 tablespoons of fat from the baking dish and place the dish on the stove over low heat. Add the flour and stir to incorporate all the sediment. Stir constantly over medium heat until well browned, without burning. Remove from the heat and gradually stir in the brandy and chicken stock. Return to the heat and stir constantly, until the gravy boils and thickens. Season with salt and pepper, and serve with bread sauce.

NOTE: This cooking time will produce a well-done goose. If you prefer it a little less cooked, reduce the initial cooking time by 20 minutes. You may need to order the goose in advance from a poultry store or butcher as fresh geese are very hard to find.

BELOW: Roast goose

CHICKEN BALLOTTINE

Cut through the skin of the chicken down the centre back with a sharp knife.

Separate the flesh from the bone down one side to the breast.

Gradually ease the meat away from the thigh, drumstick and wing.

Roll the chicken up to enclose the filling, then secure with toothpicks.

ABOVE: Chicken ballottine

CHICKEN BALLOTTINE

Preparation time: 40 minutes + refrigeration
Total cooking time: 1 hour 45 minutes
Serves 8

★★★

1.6 kg (3¼ lb) chicken
2 red peppers (capsicums)
1 kg (2 lb) silverbeet (Swiss chard)
30 g (1 oz) butter
1 onion, finely chopped
1 clove garlic, crushed
½ cup (50 g/1¾ oz) grated Parmesan
1 cup (80 g/2¾ oz) fresh breadcrumbs
1 tablespoon chopped fresh oregano
200 g (6½ oz) ricotta

1 To bone the chicken, cut through the skin on the centre back with a sharp knife. Separate the flesh from the bone down one side to the breast, being careful not to pierce the skin. Follow along the bones closely with the knife, gradually easing the meat from the thigh, drumstick and wing. Cut through the thigh bone where it meets the drumstick and cut off the wing tip. Repeat on the other side, then lift the rib cage away, leaving the flesh in one piece and the drumsticks still attached to the flesh. Scrape all the meat from the drumstick and wings, discarding the bones. Turn the wing and drumstick flesh inside the chicken and lay the chicken out flat, skin-side-down. Refrigerate.
2 Preheat the oven to moderate 180°C (350°F/ Gas 4). Cut the peppers into large flattish pieces, discarding the membranes and seeds. Cook skin-side-up under a hot grill until the skins blister and blacken. Cool in a plastic bag, then peel.
3 Discard the stalks from the silverbeet and finely shred the leaves. Melt the butter in a large frying pan and cook the onion and garlic over medium heat for 5 minutes, or until soft. Add the silverbeet and stir until wilted and all the moisture has evaporated. Cool. In a food processor, process the silverbeet and onion mixture with the Parmesan, breadcrumbs, oregano and half the ricotta. Season with salt and freshly ground pepper.
4 Spread the silverbeet mixture over the chicken and lay the pepper pieces over the top. Form the remaining ricotta into a roll and place across the width of the chicken. Fold the sides of the chicken in over the filling so they overlap slightly. Tuck the ends in neatly. Secure with toothpicks, then tie with string at 3 cm (1¼ inch) intervals.
5 Grease a large piece of foil and place the chicken in the centre. Roll the chicken up

securely in the foil, sealing the ends well. Bake on a baking tray for 1¼–1½ hours, or until the juices run clear when a skewer is inserted in the centre of the meat. Cool, then refrigerate until cold before removing the foil, toothpicks and string. Cut into 1 cm (½ inch) slices to serve.
NOTE: You can ask the butcher or chicken specialist to bone the chicken.

ROAST TURKEY BREAST WITH PARSLEY CRUST

Preparation time: 10 minutes
Total cooking time: 45 minutes
Serves 8

Parsley crust
60 g (2 oz) butter
4 spring onions (scallions), finely chopped
2 garlic cloves, crushed
2 cups (160 g/5½ oz) fresh white breadcrumbs
2 tablespoons finely chopped fresh parsley

1 kg (2 lb) turkey breast supreme
1 egg, lightly beaten
raspberry and redcurrant sauce (see page 231) or beetroot relish (see page 232), to serve

1 To make the parsley crust, melt the butter in a small frying pan over medium heat. Add the spring onion and garlic and stir until softened. Add the breadcrumbs and parsley and stir until combined. Cool.
2 Preheat the oven to moderate 180°C (350°F/Gas 4). Place the turkey in a deep baking dish and pat the turkey dry with paper towels. Brush with egg.
3 Press the parsley crust firmly onto the turkey. Bake for 45 minutes, or until the crust is lightly golden. Serve sliced, with raspberry and redcurrant sauce, or beetroot relish, or your favourite accompaniment.
NOTE: The parsley crust can be made a day in advance. Turkey breast supreme is a boneless breast of the turkey with the skin on. It is available from chicken shops and supermarkets.

TURKEY
For centuries in England, the main course enjoyed for Christmas dinner consisted of boar's head and fattened goose. The turkey was imported from America to Europe, then to the United Kingdom in the early sixteenth century. Because of its succulent meat, it soon became an established part of the traditional English Christmas dinner and its popularity has spread to many other countries.

LEFT: Roast turkey breast with parsley crust (served with beetroot relish)

CACCIATORA

Cacciatora means 'in the style of the hunter'. Like many dishes throughout Italy, there are countless variations, with each region adding its own twist to the dish. Generally, the dish consists of a chicken or rabbit fricassee with tomato, onion and other vegetables.

ABOVE: Chicken cacciatora

CHICKEN CACCIATORA

Preparation time: 15 minutes
Total cooking time: 1 hour
Serves 4

1/4 cup (60 ml/2 fl oz) olive oil

1 large onion, finely chopped

3 cloves garlic, crushed

150 g (5 oz) pancetta, finely chopped

125 g (4 oz) button mushrooms, thickly sliced

1 large chicken (at least 1.6 kg/3 1/4 lb), cut into 8 pieces

1/3 cup (80 ml/2 3/4 fl oz) dry vermouth or dry white wine

2 x 400 g (13 oz) cans chopped good-quality tomatoes

1/4 teaspoon soft brown sugar

1/4 teaspoon cayenne pepper

1 sprig of fresh oregano

1 sprig of fresh thyme

1 bay leaf

1 Heat half the olive oil in a large heatproof casserole dish. Add the onion and garlic and cook for 6–8 minutes over low heat, stirring, until the onion is golden. Add the pancetta and mushrooms, increase the heat and cook, stirring, for 4–5 minutes. Transfer to a bowl.
2 Add the remaining oil to the casserole dish and brown the chicken pieces, a few at a time, over medium heat. Season with salt and black pepper as they brown. Spoon off the excess fat and return all the chicken to the casserole dish. Increase the heat, add the vermouth to the dish and cook until the liquid has almost evaporated.
3 Add the chopped tomato, brown sugar, cayenne pepper, oregano, thyme and bay leaf, and stir in 1/3 cup (80 ml/2 3/4 fl oz) water to the dish. Bring to the boil, then stir in the reserved onion mixture. Reduce the heat, cover and simmer for 25 minutes, or until the chicken is tender but not falling off the bone.
4 If the liquid is too thin, remove the chicken from the casserole dish, increase the heat and boil until the liquid has thickened. Discard the sprigs of herbs and adjust the seasoning. Can be garnished with fresh oregano or thyme sprigs and served with steamed rice.

CHICKEN PIE

Preparation time: 30 minutes
Total cooking time: 1 hour 10 minutes
Serves 6

1 kg (2 lb) boneless skinless chicken breasts

2 cups (500 ml/16 fl oz) chicken stock

60 g (2 oz) butter

2 spring onions (scallions), trimmed and finely chopped

1/2 cup (60 g/2 1/2 oz) plain (all-purpose) flour

1/2 cup (125 ml/4 fl oz) milk

8 sheets filo pastry (40 x 30 cm/16 x 12 inches)

60 g (2 oz) butter, extra, melted

200 g (7 oz) feta, crumbled

1 tablespoon chopped fresh dill

1 tablespoon chopped fresh chives

1/4 teaspoon ground nutmeg

1 egg, lightly beaten

1 Cut the chicken into bite-sized pieces. Pour the stock into a saucepan and bring to the boil over high heat. Reduce the heat to low, add the chicken and poach gently for 10–15 minutes, or until the chicken is cooked through. Drain, reserving the stock. Add water to the stock to bring the quantity up to 2 cups (500 ml/ 16 fl oz). Preheat the oven to moderate 180°C (350°F/Gas 4).

2 Melt the butter in a saucepan over low heat, add the spring onion and cook, stirring, for 5 minutes. Add the flour and stir for 30 seconds. Remove the pan from the heat and gradually add the chicken stock and milk, stirring after each addition. Return to the heat and gently bring to the boil, stirring. Simmer for a few minutes, or until the sauce thickens. Remove from the heat.

3 Line a baking dish measuring 25 x 18 x 4 cm (10 x 7 x 1 1/2 inches) with 4 sheets of filo pastry, brushing one side of each sheet with melted butter as you go. Place the buttered side down. The filo will overlap the edges of the dish. Cover the unused filo with a damp tea towel to prevent it drying out.

4 Stir the chicken, feta, dill, chives, nutmeg and egg into the sauce. Season to taste with salt and freshly ground black pepper. Pile the mixture on top of the filo pastry in the dish. Fold the overlapping filo over the filling and cover the top of the pie with the remaining 4 sheets of filo, brushing each sheet with melted butter as you go. Scrunch the edges of the filo so they fit in the dish. Brush the top with butter. Bake for 45–50 minutes, or until the pastry is golden brown and crisp.

VARIATION: If you prefer, you can use puff pastry instead of filo. If you do so, bake in a hot 220°C (425°F/Gas 7) oven for 15 minutes, then reduce the temperature to moderate 180°C (350°F/Gas 4) and cook for another 30 minutes, or until the pastry is golden.

ABOVE: Chicken pie

289

CIRCASSIAN CHICKEN

Preparation time: 25 minutes
Total cooking time: 1 hour
Serves 6

★★

2 teaspoons paprika

1/4 teaspoon cayenne pepper

1 tablespoon walnut oil

4 chicken breasts, on the bone

4 chicken wings

1 large onion, chopped

2 sticks celery, coarsely chopped

1 carrot, chopped

1 bay leaf

4 sprigs fresh parsley

1 sprig fresh thyme

6 peppercorns

1 teaspoon coriander seeds

250 g (8 oz) walnuts, toasted (see Note)

2 slices of white bread, crusts removed

1 tablespoon paprika, extra

4 cloves garlic, crushed

1   Place the paprika and the cayenne pepper in a small dry frying pan and heat over low heat for about 2 minutes, or until aromatic, then add the walnut oil to the pan and set aside until ready to use.

2   Put the chicken in a large saucepan with the onion, celery, carrot, bay leaf, parsley, thyme, peppercorns and coriander seeds. Add 1 litre (32 fl oz) of water and bring to the boil. Reduce the heat to low and simmer for 15–20 minutes, or until the chicken is tender. Remove from the heat and allow to cool in the stock. Remove the chicken and return the stock to the heat. Simmer it for 20–25 minutes, or until reduced by half. Strain, skim off the fat and reserve the stock. Remove the chicken skin and shred the flesh into bite-sized pieces. Season well and ladle some stock over it to moisten it. Set aside.

3   Reserve a few of the walnuts to use as a garnish and blend the rest in a food processor to form a rough paste. Combine the bread with 1/2 cup (125 ml/4 fl oz) stock, add to the food processor and mix in short bursts for several seconds. Add the extra paprika, the garlic and some salt and pepper and process until smooth. Gradually add 1 cup (250 ml/8 fl oz) warm chicken stock until the mixture is of a smooth pourable consistency, adding a little more stock if necessary.

4   Mix half the sauce with the chicken and place on a serving platter. Pour the rest over to cover, then sprinkle with spiced oil and the remaining walnuts. Serve at room temperature.

NOTE: Californian walnuts are best for this recipe as they are much less bitter than some.

CIRCASSIAN CHICKEN
Circassian chicken comes from the culinary legacy of the Circassian women who were part of the Sultan's harem during the days of the Ottoman Empire. Noted for their gastronomic skills as well as their beauty, the Circassians contributed this dish, which bears their name and has become a classic of Turkish cuisine.

RIGHT: Circassian chicken

CHICKEN AND BACON GOUGERE

Preparation time: 40 minutes
Total cooking time: 50 minutes
Serves 6

60 g (2 oz) butter

1–2 cloves garlic, crushed

1 red onion, chopped

3 rashers bacon, chopped

1/4 cup (30 g/1 oz) plain (all-purpose) flour

1 1/2 cups (375 ml/12 fl oz) milk

1/2 cup (125 ml/4 fl oz) cream

2 teaspoons wholegrain mustard

250 g (8 oz) cooked chicken, chopped

1/2 cup (30 g/1 oz) chopped fresh parsley

Choux pastry

1/2 cup (60 g/2 oz) plain (all-purpose) flour

60 g (2 oz) butter, chilled and cut into cubes

2 eggs, lightly beaten

35 g (1 1/4 oz) grated Parmesan

1 Melt the butter in a frying pan, add the garlic, onion and bacon and cook for 5–7 minutes, stirring occasionally, or until cooked but not brown. Stir in the flour and cook for 1 minute. Gradually add the milk and stir until thickened. Simmer for 2 minutes, then add the cream and mustard. Remove from the heat and fold in the chicken and parsley. Season with pepper.

2 For the choux pastry, sift the flour onto a piece of baking paper. Put the butter in a large saucepan with 1/2 cup (125 ml/4 fl oz) water and stir over medium heat until the mixture comes to the boil. Remove from the heat, add the flour in one go and quickly beat it into the water with a wooden spoon. Return to the heat and continue beating until the mixture forms a ball and leaves the side of the pan. Transfer to a large clean bowl and cool slightly. Beat the mixture to release any more heat. Gradually add the beaten eggs, about 3 teaspoons at a time. Beat well after each addition until all the egg has been added and the mixture is thick and glossy—a wooden spoon should stand up in it. If it is too runny, the egg has been added too quickly. If so, beat for several minutes more, or until thickened. Add the Parmesan.

3 Preheat the oven to hot 210°C (415°F/ Gas 6–7). Grease a deep 23 cm (9 inch) ovenproof dish, pour in the filling and spoon heaped tablespoons of choux around the outside. Bake for 10 minutes, then reduce the oven to moderate 180°C (350°F/Gas 4). Bake for 20 minutes, or until the choux is puffed and golden. Sprinkle with a little more grated Parmesan if you wish.

CHOUX PASTRY

This is most often used to make profiteroles, eclairs, gougères and the French wedding cake called 'coquembouche'. Choux pastry is easy to make but the process is different from pastries such as shortcrust that have the butter rubbed into the flour. Instead, you melt the butter and water together, then beat the flour into the mixture and cook the mixture until it is no longer sticky.

LEFT: Chicken and bacon gougère

CHICKEN AND LEEK PIE

Preparation time: 20 minutes
Total cooking time: 40 minutes
Serves 4

★★

50 g (1¾ oz) butter
2 large leeks, white part only, thinly sliced
4 spring onions (scallions), sliced
1 clove garlic, crushed
¼ cup (30 g/1 oz) plain (all-purpose) flour
1½ cups (375 ml/12 fl oz) chicken stock
½ cup (125 ml/4 fl oz) cream
2 cups (280 g/9 oz) chopped cooked chicken
2 sheets frozen puff pastry, thawed
¼ cup (60 ml/2 fl oz) milk

1 Melt the butter in a saucepan and add the leek, spring onion and garlic. Cook over low heat for 6 minutes, or until the leek is soft but not browned. Stir in the flour and cook for 1 minute, or until pale and foaming. Remove from the heat and gradually stir in the stock.

ABOVE: Chicken and leek pie

Return to the heat and stir constantly until the sauce boils and thickens. Stir in the cream and chicken, then spoon into a shallow 20 cm (8 inch) pie dish and set aside to cool. Preheat the oven to moderately hot 200°C (400°F/Gas 6).
2 Brush around the rim of the pie dish with a little milk. Put 1 sheet of pastry on top and seal around the edge firmly. Trim off any overhanging pastry with a sharp knife and decorate the edge with the back of a fork. Cut the other sheet into 1 cm (½ inch) strips and roll each strip up loosely like a snail. Arrange the spirals on top of the pie, starting from the middle and leaving a gap between each one. The spirals may not cover the whole pie. Make a few small holes between the spirals to let out any steam, and brush the top of the pie lightly with milk. Bake for 25–30 minutes, or until the top is crisp and golden. Make sure the spirals look well cooked and are not raw in the middle.
VARIATIONS: Chopped leftover turkey can also be used. You can also make small pies by placing the mixture into 4 greased 1¼ cup (315 ml/10 fl oz) round ovenproof dishes. Cut the pastry into 4 rounds to fit the tops. Bake for 15 minutes, or until the pastry is crisp.

CHICKEN AND ASPARAGUS GRATIN

Preparation time: 10 minutes
Total cooking time: 30 minutes
Serves 6

4 cups (540 g/1 lb 2 oz) chopped cooked
    chicken
425 g (14 oz) can asparagus spears, drained
420 g (14 oz) can creamy chicken and corn
    soup, or cream of mushroom soup
1/2 cup (125 g/4 oz) sour cream
2 spring onions (scallions), sliced on the
    diagonal
1 red pepper (capsicum), thinly sliced
1 cup (125 g/4 oz) grated Cheddar
1/2 cup (50 g/1 3/4 oz) grated Parmesan
1/2 teaspoon sweet paprika

1 Preheat the oven to moderate 180°C (350°F/
Gas 4). Cover the base of a large, shallow
ovenproof dish with the chicken and top with
half the asparagus spears.
2 Combine the soup, sour cream, spring onion
and red pepper in a bowl. Season to taste and
pour over the chicken.
3 Arrange the remaining asparagus spears on top
of the chicken and cover with the combined
cheeses. Sprinkle with paprika and bake for
30 minutes, or until golden brown and bubbling.
Serve immediately.

TURKEY JAFFLE

Butter a slice of bread and gently press,
butter-side-down, onto the base of a
lightly-greased, preheated jaffle maker.
Spread on some cranberry sauce and top
with a couple of slices of turkey, sliced
camembert and some lightly mashed leftover baked pumpkin. Top with a second
buttered slice of bread, butter-side-up, and
cook until golden brown. Makes 1.

*BELOW: Chicken
and asparagus gratin*

CORONATION CHICKEN

According to legend, this dish, consisting of cold chicken pieces served with a curried mayonnaise sauce, was devised for the coronation of Queen Elizabeth II in 1953. The unsophisticated dish was meant to appeal to as many tastes as possible. Since then, many chefs have included variations of it on the menu.

ABOVE: Coronation chicken

CORONATION CHICKEN

Preparation time: 15 minutes
Total cooking time: 10 minutes
Serves 4–6

500 g (1 lb) cooked chicken
1 tablespoon oil
1 onion, finely chopped
2 teaspoons curry powder
1 tablespoon tomato paste (tomato purée)
2 tablespoons red wine
1¹/₂ tablespoons fruit chutney
¹/₂ cup (125 g/4 oz) whole-egg mayonnaise
2 sticks celery, sliced
3 spring onions (scallions), thinly sliced

1 Remove all the skin and any fat from the chicken and cut the flesh into bite-sized pieces. Heat the oil in a saucepan and add the onion. Cover and cook, stirring occasionally, over low heat for 5–10 minutes, or until soft, but not browned. Add the curry powder and stir until fragrant. Add the tomato paste and red wine and stir for 1 minute. Set aside to cool, then mix in a bowl with the chutney and mayonnaise.

2 Put the chicken, celery and 2 of the spring onions into a large bowl. Add the mayonnaise mixture and toss lightly to coat. Spoon into a serving bowl and sprinkle with thinly sliced spring onion.

NOTE: Coronation chicken is often accompanied by apricots. The addition of sliced celery is not traditional in this salad but it gives a nice crunchy texture.

DUCK WITH PEARS

Preparation time: 20 minutes
Total cooking time: 1 hour 40 minutes
Serves 4

★ ★

2 tablespoons olive oil

4 duck breasts

2 red onions, finely diced

1 carrot, finely diced

2 teaspoons fresh thyme

1 cup (250 ml/8 fl oz) chicken stock

2 ripe tomatoes, peeled, deseeded
    and diced

4 green, firm pears, peeled, halved and cored
    (leaving the stems intact)

1 cinnamon stick

60 g (2 oz) blanched almonds, toasted, chopped

1 clove garlic

100 ml (3 fl oz) brandy

1 Heat the oil in a heavy-based frying pan and cook the duck, skin-side-down first, over medium heat until brown all over. Remove and set aside, reserving 4 tablespoons of the cooking fat.
2 Return 2 tablespoons of the fat to the pan.

Add the onion, carrot and thyme and cook over medium heat for 5 minutes, or until the onion has softened. Add the stock and tomato and bring to the boil. Reduce the heat and simmer for 30 minutes, with the lid slightly askew, or until the sauce has thickened and reduced. Cool slightly, then purée in a food processor until smooth. Return to the pan with the duck. Simmer gently over low heat for 30–40 minutes, or until the duck is tender.
3 While the duck is cooking, place the pears in a saucepan with the cinnamon and just cover with cold water. Bring to the boil, reduce the heat and simmer gently for 5 minutes or until the pears are tender but still firm to the bite. Remove the pears, cover to keep warm and add ½ cup (125 ml/4 fl oz) of the pear poaching liquid to the tomato sauce.
4 Remove the duck from the sauce and keep warm. Grind the almonds, garlic and brandy together in a mortar and pestle or blender to make a smooth paste. Add to the tomato sauce, season to taste and cook for another 10 minutes.
5 Arrange the duck pieces on a serving plate and pour the sauce over the top. Arrange the warmed pears around the duck and serve.
NOTE: The sauce adds an interesting finish to this Catalan dish, which is traditionally made with goose.

DUCK WITH PEARS

Put the duck back in the pan with the sauce.

Grind the almonds, garlic and brandy in a mortar and pestle or in a blender.

LEFT: Duck with pears

MUSHROOMS
Fresh button mushrooms are commonly used in cookery, although there are many other types of mushroom available. The flavour of button mushrooms is delicate and they are excellent for use in fillings and sauces or with pasta. You might find it necessary to wipe over fresh mushrooms with a damp cloth to remove any dirt. Don't wash them as this will make them go soggy during cooking. They are best stored in the refrigerator in a paper bag, not in a plastic bag or container, as they will sweat and deteriorate very quickly.

ABOVE: Turkey filo parcels

TURKEY FILO PARCELS

Preparation time: 35 minutes
Total cooking time: 40 minutes
Makes 24

★★

20 g (³/₄ oz) butter
200 g (6¹/₂ oz) button mushrooms, sliced
4 rashers bacon, diced
350 g (11 oz) cooked turkey, chopped
150 g (5 oz) ricotta
2 spring onions (scallions), sliced
3 tablespoons shredded fresh basil
24 sheets filo pastry
butter, melted, extra, for brushing
sesame seeds, for sprinkling

1 Melt the butter in a large saucepan and add the mushrooms and bacon. Cook over high heat for 5 minutes, or until the mushrooms are soft and there is no liquid left. Combine the turkey, ricotta, spring onion and basil in a bowl, add the mushroom mixture, then season to taste.
2 Preheat the oven to moderate 180°C (350°F/ Gas 4). Cover the pastry with a damp tea towel to prevent drying out. Working with 3 sheets at a time, brush each layer with melted butter. Cut into 3 strips. Place 1 tablespoon of filling at the end of each strip and fold the pastry over to form a triangle. Fold until you reach the end of the pastry. Repeat with the remaining pastry and filling. Place on a greased baking tray, brush with butter and sprinkle with sesame seeds. Bake for 30–35 minutes, or until golden.

TURKEY AND CORN SOUP

Melt 20 g (³/₄ oz) butter in a large saucepan, add 1 thinly sliced leek and stir over medium heat for 5 minutes, or until soft. Mix in 3¹/₂ cups (875 ml/28 fl oz) chicken stock and a 420 g (14 oz) can creamed corn. Season. Bring to the boil, then reduce the heat and simmer, covered, for 5 minutes. Add 250 g (8 oz) shredded cooked turkey to the pan and stir until heated through. Serves 4.

TURKEY, POTATO AND APPLE SALAD

Preparation time: 25 minutes
Total cooking time: 15 minutes
Serves 6

4 spring onions (scallions)
2 tablespoons oil
750 g (1 1/2 lb) new baby potatoes
1 red apple
1 tablespoon lemon juice
2 zucchini (courgettes), thickly sliced
400 g (13 oz) cooked turkey meat
2 tablespoons chopped fresh parsley

Dressing

1/2 cup (125 g/4 oz) whole-egg mayonnaise
3 teaspoons Dijon mustard
1 tablespoon wholegrain mustard
2 tablespoons lemon juice

1 Cut the spring onions into thin strips. Heat the oil in a small frying pan and shallow-fry the spring onion until crisp. Remove and drain on crumpled paper towels.
2 Steam or boil the potatoes for 10 minutes, or until just tender (pierce with the point of a small knife—if the potato comes away easily, it is ready). Drain and allow to cool, then cut in halves.
3 Cut the unpeeled apple into thin wedges and toss with the lemon juice in a bowl (this prevents the apple from discolouring).
4 Boil, steam or microwave the zucchini until tender, then drain and refresh in cold water.
5 For the dressing, stir the ingredients together in a small bowl, then season to taste.
6 Cut the leftover cooked turkey meat into thin strips and put in a large bowl. Add the potato, apple, zucchini and parsley to the turkey, drizzle the dressing over the top and gently toss until well combined. Serve topped with the crispy spring onion.

ABOVE: Turkey, potato and apple salad

STIR-FRIED DUCK WITH PLUM AND GINGER SAUCE

Preparation time: 10 minutes +
   3 hours marinating
Total cooking time: 10 minutes
Serves 4-6

1 tablespoon hoisin sauce
1/2 teaspoon sesame oil
1 teaspoon ground ginger
1 teaspoon five-spice powder
2 cloves garlic, crushed
3 teaspoons soy sauce
4 x 185 g (6 oz) skinless, boneless duck breasts,
   trimmed and thinly sliced across the grain
1/4 cup (60 ml/2 fl oz) chicken stock
1/4 cup (60 ml/2 fl oz) plum sauce
2 teaspoons orange juice
1/2 teaspoon cornflour (cornstarch)
2 teaspoons vegetable oil
1 tablespoon julienned fresh ginger
5 spring onions (scallions), thinly sliced
   on the diagonal

1 Combine the hoisin sauce, sesame oil, ground ginger, five-spice powder, garlic and 2 teaspoons of the soy sauce in a large non-metallic bowl. Add the duck, cover with plastic wrap and marinate in the refrigerator for 3 hours.
2 To make the stir-fry sauce, combine the stock, plum sauce, orange juice and cornflour in a small jug or bowl. Whisk together with a fork.
3 Heat a wok over high heat, add 1 teaspoon of the vegetable oil and swirl to coat the side of the wok. Stir-fry the duck in batches for 30 seconds per batch, or until browned. Take care not to overcook the duck as it will turn tough and rubbery. Remove the duck from the wok.
4 Heat the remaining oil in the wok, then add the fresh ginger and most of the spring onion and stir-fry for 1 minute, or until softened and fragrant. Pour in the stir-fry sauce and bring to a simmer, stirring, for 1 minute, or until the sauce thickens. Return the duck meat to the wok and toss very briefly until mixed through. Season well, garnish with the remaining spring onion and serve immediately.

KUNG PAO CHICKEN

Preparation time: 15 minutes +
   30 minutes marinating
Total cooking time: 15 minutes
Serves 4

1 egg white
2 teaspoons cornflour (cornstarch)
1/2 teaspoon sesame oil
2 teaspoons Chinese rice wine
1 1/2 tablespoons soy sauce
600 g (1 1/4 lb) chicken thigh fillets, cut into
   2 cm (3/4 inch) cubes
1/4 cup (60 ml/2 fl oz) chicken stock
2 teaspoons Chinese black vinegar
1 teaspoon soft brown sugar
2 tablespoons vegetable oil
3 long dried red chillies, cut in half lengthways
3 cloves garlic, finely chopped
2 teaspoons finely grated fresh ginger
2 spring onions (scallions), thinly sliced on
   the diagonal
1/3 cup (50 g/1 3/4 oz) shelled unsalted raw
   peanuts, roughly crushed

1 Lightly whisk together the egg white, cornflour, sesame oil, Chinese rice wine and 2 teaspoons of the soy sauce in a large non-metallic bowl. Add the chicken and coat it in the marinade. Cover with plastic wrap and marinate in the fridge for 30 minutes.
2 To make the stir-fry sauce, combine the stock, vinegar, sugar and the remaining soy sauce in a small jug or bowl.
3 Heat a wok over high heat, add 1 tablespoon of the vegetable oil and swirl to coat the wok. Stir-fry the chicken in batches for 3 minutes, or until browned. Remove from the wok.
4 Heat the remaining oil in the wok, then add the chilli and cook for 15 seconds, or until it starts to change colour. Add the garlic, ginger, spring onion and peanuts, and stir-fry for 1 minute. Return the chicken to the wok, along with the stir-fry sauce, and stir-fry for 3 minutes, or until heated through and the sauce thickens slightly. Serve immediately.
NOTE: This dish is said to have been created for an important court official called Kung Pao who was stationed in the Sichuan province of China. It is characterised by the flavours of the long, dried red chillies and the crunchiness of peanuts.

OPPOSITE PAGE, FROM TOP: Stir-fried duck with plum and ginger sauce; Kung Pao chicken

Basil is often associated
with the Mediterranean,
but it has an important
place in the cuisine of
Southeast Asia, which is
not surprising considering
that it is native to India. In
Asia, Thai is often used
instead of the regular basil.
It has smaller and darker
leaves than regular basil
and a stronger aniseed and
clove flavour and aroma.
The stems and younger
leaves have a purplish
colour. The leaves are
prone to wilting quite
quickly, so use them as
soon as possible after
purchase. If unavailable,
substitute any variety of
fresh basil.

*ABOVE: Chicken with
Thai basil*

CHICKEN WITH THAI BASIL

Preparation time: 15 minutes
Total cooking time: 15 minutes
Serves 4

1/4 cup (60 ml/12 fl oz) peanut oil
500 g (1 lb) chicken breast fillets, cut into
    thin strips
1 clove garlic, crushed
4 spring onions (scallions), thinly sliced
150 g (5 oz) snake beans, trimmed and cut
    into 5 cm (2 inch) lengths
2 small fresh red chillies, thinly sliced
3/4 cup (35 g/1 1/4 oz) tightly packed fresh
    Thai basil
2 tablespoons chopped fresh mint
1 tablespoon fish sauce
1 tablespoon oyster sauce
2 teaspoons lime juice
1 tablespoon grated palm sugar
fresh Thai basil, extra, to garnish

1 Heat a wok over high heat, add 1 tablespoon
of the oil and swirl to coat. Cook the chicken
in batches for 3–5 minutes each batch, or until
lightly browned and almost cooked—add more
oil if needed. Remove from the wok.
2 Heat the remaining oil. Add the garlic, onion,
snake beans and chilli, and stir-fry for 1 minute,
or until the onion is tender. Return the chicken
to the wok.
3 Toss in the basil and mint, then add the
combined fish sauce, oyster sauce, lime juice,
palm sugar and 2 tablespoons water and cook for
1 minute. Garnish with the extra basil and serve
with jasmine rice.

CHICKEN AND ASPARAGUS STIR-FRY

Preparation time: 15 minutes
Total cooking time: 10 minutes
Serves 4

2 tablespoons vegetable oil
1 clove garlic, crushed
10 cm (4 inch) piece fresh ginger, thinly sliced
3 chicken breast fillets, sliced
4 spring onions (scallions), sliced
200 g (6 1/2 oz) fresh asparagus, cut into 1 cm
    (1/2 inch) diagonal pieces
2 tablespoons soy sauce
1/3 cup (40 g/1 1/4 oz) slivered almonds, roasted

1 Heat a wok over high heat, add the oil and
swirl to coat the side of the wok. Add the garlic,
ginger and chicken and stir-fry for 1–2 minutes,
or until the chicken changes colour.
2 Add the spring onion and asparagus and

stir-fry for a further 2 minutes, or until the spring onion is soft.

3 Stir in the soy sauce and ¼ cup (60 ml/ 2 fl oz) water, cover and simmer for 2 minutes, or until the chicken is tender and the vegetables are slightly crisp. Sprinkle with the almonds and serve over steamed rice or egg noodles.

CHICKEN CHOW MEIN

Preparation time: 15 minutes +
  1 hour standing
Total cooking time: 40 minutes
Serves 4

250 g (8 oz) fresh thin egg noodles

2 teaspoons sesame oil

½ cup (125 ml/4 fl oz) peanut oil

1 tablespoon Chinese rice wine

1½ tablespoons light soy sauce

3 teaspoons cornflour (cornstarch)

400 g (13 oz) chicken breast fillets, cut into
  thin strips

1 clove garlic, crushed

1 tablespoon finely chopped fresh ginger

100 g (3½ oz) sugar snap peas, trimmed

250 g (8 oz) wom bok (Chinese cabbage),
  finely shredded

4 spring onions (scallions) , cut into 2 cm
  (¾ inch) lengths

100 ml (3½ fl oz) chicken stock

1½ tablespoons oyster sauce

100 g (3½ oz) bean sprouts, tailed

1 small fresh red chilli, seeded and julienned,
  to garnish (optional)

1 Cook the noodles in a saucepan of boiling water for 1 minute, or until tender. Drain well. Add the sesame oil and 1 tablespoon of the peanut oil and toss well. Place on a baking tray and spread out in a thin layer. Leave in a dry place for at least 1 hour.

2 Meanwhile, combine the rice wine, 1 tablespoon of the soy sauce and 1 teaspoon of the cornflour in a large non-metallic bowl. Add the chicken and toss well. Cover with plastic wrap and marinate for 10 minutes.

3 Heat 1 tablespoon of the peanut oil in a small non-stick frying pan over high heat. Add one quarter of the noodles, shaping into a pancake. Reduce the heat to medium and cook for

4 minutes on each side, or until crisp and golden. Drain on crumpled paper towels and keep warm. Repeat with 3 tablespoons of the oil and the remaining noodles to make four noodle cakes in total.

4 Heat a wok over high heat, add the remaining peanut oil and swirl to coat the side of the wok. Stir-fry the garlic and ginger for 30 seconds. Add the chicken and stir-fry for 3–4 minutes, or until golden and tender. Add the sugar snap peas, shredded wom bok and spring onion and stir-fry for 2 minutes, or until the cabbage has wilted. Stir in the chicken stock, oyster sauce and bean sprouts and bring to the boil.

5 Combine the remaining cornflour with 1–2 teaspoons cold water. Stir it into the wok with the remaining soy sauce and cook for 1–2 minutes, or until the sauce thickens.

6 To assemble, place a noodle cake on each serving plate, then spoon the chicken and vegetable mixture on top. Serve immediately, garnished with chilli, if desired.

BELOW: Chicken chow mein

CHINESE ROAST DUCK
WITH RICE NOODLES

Using your fingers, remove the skin and fat from the duck.

Carefully separate the flesh from the bones with your fingers.

CHINESE ROAST DUCK WITH RICE NOODLES

Preparation time: 25 minutes
Total cooking time: 15 minutes
Serves 4

★★

1.5 kg (3 lb) Chinese roast duck (see Note)
500 g (1 lb) fresh flat rice noodles
    (1 cm/¹/₂ inch) wide)
3¹/₂ tablespoons peanut oil
3 small slender eggplants (aubergines), cut into
    1 cm (¹/₂ inch) thick slices
1 tablespoon thinly sliced fresh ginger
2 small fresh red chillies, finely chopped
4 spring onions (scallions), thinly sliced on
    the diagonal
3 tablespoons torn fresh basil
¹/₄ cup (60 ml/2 fl oz) Chinese barbecue sauce

1 Remove the crispy skin and meat from the duck, discarding the carcass and fat. Thinly slice the meat and skin and place it in a bowl—there should be at least 350 g (11 oz) of meat.
2 Put the noodles in a heatproof bowl, cover with boiling water and soak briefly. Gently separate the noodles. Rinse under cold water and drain well.
3 Heat a wok over high heat, add 2¹/₂ tablespoons of the peanut oil and swirl to coat the side of the wok. Add the eggplant and stir-fry for 3–4 minutes, or until softened. Transfer to a bowl.
4 Heat the remaining oil in the wok over high heat. Cook the ginger, chilli and spring onion for 30 seconds, stirring constantly. Return the eggplant to the wok along with the duck, basil and barbecue sauce, and gently toss together for 1–2 minutes, or until heated through. Add the noodles and stir-fry for 1–2 minutes, or until well combined and heated through, taking care not to break up the noodles. Serve immediately.
NOTE: Chinese roast duck is a crisp, dark, glossy-skinned duck that can be bought ready to eat from Asian barbecue shops or restaurants. Some Chinese people will only buy Chinese roast duck if the weather has been fine for at least 12 hours before purchase—humid weather is said to prevent the skin from becoming crisp.

ABOVE: Chinese roast duck with rice noodles

SATAY CHICKEN STIR-FRY

Preparation time: 10 minutes
Total cooking time: 20 minutes
Serves 4

1½ tablespoons peanut oil

6 spring onions (scallions), cut into 3 cm
(1¼ inch) lengths

800 g (1 lb 10 oz) chicken breast fillets, thinly
sliced on the diagonal

1–1½ tablespoons Thai red curry paste
(see page 256)

⅓ cup (90 g/3 oz) crunchy peanut butter

270 ml (9 fl oz) coconut milk

2 teaspoons soft brown sugar

1½ tablespoons lime juice

1 Heat a wok over high heat, add 1 teaspoon of
the peanut oil and swirl to coat. Add the spring
onion and stir-fry for 30 seconds, or until
softened slightly. Remove from the wok.
2 Add a little extra oil to the wok as needed and
stir-fry the chicken in three batches for about
1 minute per batch, or until the meat just
changes colour. Remove from the wok.
3 Add a little more oil to the wok, add the curry
paste and stir-fry for 1 minute, or until fragrant.
Add the peanut butter, coconut milk, sugar and
1 cup (250 ml/8 fl oz) water and stir well. Bring
to the boil and boil for 3–4 minutes, or until
thickened and the oil starts to separate. Return
the chicken and the spring onion to the wok,
stir well and cook for 2 minutes, or until heated
through. Stir in the lime juice, season and serve.

BAKED LEMON CHICKENS

Cut four baby chickens in half along the
backbone. Flatten slightly. Combine
2 chopped onions, 1 chopped spring onion
(scallion), 2 chopped red chillies, 2 crushed
garlic cloves and ¼ cup (60 ml/2 fl oz) each
peanut oil and lemon juice in a food
processor and process until smooth. Spoon
the mixture over the chickens. Marinate for
1 hour, then lift out of the marinade. Cook
in a baking dish in a moderate (180°C/
350°F/Gas 4) oven for 40 minutes, brushing
occasionally with the marinade. Serves 4.

THAI CURRY PASTES
Ready-made curry pastes
are available in Asian
grocery stores or the
Asian section of large
supermarkets. Red curry
pastes are classified as
red because they are made
using a high proportion
of dried red chillies,
which gives them their
characteristic colour. In
contrast, green curry
pastes use fresh green
chillies to give the vibrant
green colour. Different
brands vary in strength,
flavour and heat, so
experiment until you find
your favourite.
Alternatively, they are
easy to make at home (see
pages 256–259), and the
taste is far superior. The
process of making curry
pastes can be quite
engaging and rewarding.
Many curry paste
aficionados swear by the
mortar and pestle for
making curry pastes,
believing that the grinding
method garners better
results than if a food
processor is used.

LEFT: Satay
chicken stir-fry

GENERAL TSO'S CHICKEN

Preparation time: 10 minutes +
  1 hour marinating + 20 minutes soaking
Total cooking time: 10 minutes
Serves 4-6

2 tablespoons Chinese rice wine
1 tablespoon cornflour (cornstarch)
1/3 cup (80 ml/2 3/4 fl oz) dark soy sauce
3 teaspoons sesame oil
900 g (1 lb 13 oz) chicken thigh fillets, cut into
  3 cm (1 1/4 inch) cubes
2 pieces dried citrus peel (2 x 3 cm/
  3/4 x 1 1/4 inch)
1/2 cup (125 ml/4 fl oz) peanut oil
1 1/2–2 teaspoons chilli flakes
2 tablespoons finely chopped fresh ginger
1 cup (120 g/4 oz) thinly sliced spring onions
  (scallions)
2 teaspoons sugar
thinly sliced spring onion (scallion), to garnish

1 Combine the Chinese rice wine, cornflour, 2 tablespoons of the dark soy sauce and 2 teaspoons of the sesame oil in a large non-metallic bowl. Toss the chicken, cover and marinate in the fridge for 1 hour.
2 Meanwhile, soak the dried citrus peel in warm water for 20 minutes. Remove from the water and finely chop—you will need 1 1/2 teaspoons chopped peel.
3 Heat the oil in the wok over high heat. Drain the chicken from the marinade using a slotted spoon and stir-fry the chicken in batches for 2 minutes, or until browned and just cooked through. Remove from the oil with a slotted spoon and leave to drain in a colander or sieve.
4 Drain all the oil except 1 tablespoon from the wok. Reheat the wok over high heat, then add the chilli flakes and ginger. Stir-fry for 10 seconds, then return the chicken to the wok. Add the spring onion, sugar, soaked citrus peel, remaining soy sauce and sesame oil and 1/2 teaspoon salt and stir-fry for a further 2–3 minutes, or until well combined and warmed through. Garnish with spring onion, then serve with rice.
NOTE: This dish is named after a 19th century Chinese general from Yunnan province.

RIGHT: General Tso's chicken

THAI MINCED CHICKEN SALAD
(Larb gai)

Preparation time: 25 minutes
Total cooking time: 20 minutes
Serves 6

1 tablespoon jasmine rice

2 teaspoons vegetable oil

400 g (13 oz) minced (ground) chicken

2 tablespoons fish sauce

1 stem lemon grass, white part only, chopped

1/3 cup (80 ml/2 3/4 fl oz) chicken stock

1/4 cup (60 ml/2 fl oz) lime juice

4 spring onions (scallions), thinly sliced

4 red Asian shallots, sliced

1/2 cup (25 g/3/4 oz) finely chopped fresh
    coriander (cilantro) leaves

1/2 cup (25 g/3/4 oz) shredded fresh mint

200 g (6 1/2 oz) lettuce leaves, shredded

1/4 cup (40 g/1 1/4 oz) chopped roasted unsalted
    peanuts

1 small fresh red chilli, sliced

lime wedges, to serve

1 Heat a frying pan over low heat. Add the rice and dry-fry for 3 minutes, or until lightly golden. Transfer the rice to a mortar and pestle and then grind to a fine powder.

2 Heat a wok over medium heat. Add the oil and swirl to coat. Add the mince and cook for 4 minutes, or until it changes colour, breaking up any lumps with the back of a wooden spoon. Add the fish sauce, lemon grass and stock and cook for a further 10 minutes. Remove the wok from the heat and allow to cool.

3 Stir in the lime juice, spring onion, shallots, coriander, mint and ground rice and mix together thoroughly.

4 To serve, arrange the lettuce on a serving platter and top with the chicken mixture. Sprinkle with the nuts and chilli, and serve with lime wedges.

LARB
Popular in the north and northeast of Thailand, larb, or dressed salad, originated in neighbouring Laos. The predominant flavours of chilli and lime juice combined with fresh herbs and salad ingredients reflect the emphasis on freshness and raw ingredients that is characterised in Laotian food. In fact, many Laotian larb are entirely raw, using raw fish or meat, such as beef or buffalo. Because Laos is a landlocked country that has historically been quite isolated, Laotian cuisine is based on locally grown ingredients.

ABOVE: Thai minced chicken salad

MILD VIETNAMESE
CHICKEN CURRY

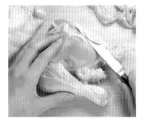

Remove the skin and any excess fat from the chicken.

Cut each chicken quarter into three even pieces.

MILD VIETNAMESE CHICKEN CURRY

Preparation time: 30 minutes +
  overnight refrigeration
Total cooking time: 1 hour 10 minutes
Serves 6

4 large chicken quarters (leg and thigh), skin
  and excess fat removed, cut into thirds
1 tablespoon good-quality curry powder
1 teaspoon caster (superfine) sugar
1/3 cup (80 ml/2 3/4 fl oz) vegetable oil
500 g (1 lb) orange sweet potato, peeled, cut
  into 3 cm (1 1/4 inch) cubes
1 large onion, cut into thin wedges
4 cloves garlic, chopped
1 stem lemon grass, white part only, finely
  chopped
2 bay leaves
1 large carrot, cut into 1 cm (1/2 inch) pieces
  on the diagonal
400 ml (13 fl oz) coconut milk

1 Pat the chicken dry with paper towels. Put the curry powder, sugar, 1/2 teaspoon black pepper and 2 teaspoons salt in a bowl, and mix together well. Rub the curry mixture onto the chicken pieces, then place the chicken on a plate, cover with plastic wrap and refrigerate overnight.

2 Heat a wok over high heat, add the oil and swirl to coat. Add the sweet potato and cook over medium heat for 3 minutes, or until lightly golden. Remove with a slotted spoon.

3 Remove all but 2 tablespoons of the oil from the wok. Add the onion and cook, stirring, for 5 minutes. Add the garlic, lemon grass and bay leaves, and cook for 2 minutes.

4 Add the chicken and cook, stirring, over medium heat for 5 minutes, or until well coated in the mixture and starting to change colour. Add 1 cup (250 ml/8 fl oz) water and simmer, covered, over low heat for 20 minutes, stirring once or twice.

5 Stir in the carrot, sweet potato and coconut milk, and simmer, uncovered, stirring occasionally, for 30 minutes, or until the chicken is cooked and tender. Be careful not to break up the sweet potato cubes. Serve with steamed rice or dried rice noodle sticks.

*ABOVE: Mild Vietnamese
chicken curry*

SALTY MALAYSIAN CHICKEN CURRY

(Ayam kapitan)

Preparation time: 35 minutes
Total cooking time: 1 hour 20 minutes
Serves 4-6

1¹/2 teaspoons dried shrimp

6–8 fresh red chillies, seeded and finely chopped

4 cloves garlic, finely chopped

3 stems lemon grass, white part only, finely chopped

2 teaspoons ground turmeric

10 candlenuts

¹/3 cup (80 ml/2³/4 fl oz) vegetable oil

2 large onions, chopped

1 cup (250 ml/8 fl oz) coconut milk

1.5 kg (3 lb) chicken, cut into 8 pieces

¹/2 cup (125 ml/4 fl oz) coconut cream

2 tablespoons lime juice

1 Put the shrimp in a frying pan and dry-fry over low heat, shaking the pan regularly, for 3 minutes, or until dark orange and aromatic. Transfer to a food processor and finely grind.
2 Put the chilli, garlic, lemon grass, turmeric, candlenuts and 2 tablespoons of the oil in a food processor and process in short bursts until very finely chopped, regularly scraping down the side of the bowl with a rubber spatula.
3 Heat a wok over high heat, add the remaining oil and swirl. Add the onion and ¹/4 teaspoon salt, and cook, stirring regularly, over low heat for 8 minutes, or until golden. Add the processed spice mixture and ground shrimp, and stir for 5 minutes, or until the mixture is cooked thoroughly. If it begins to stick to the bottom of the wok, add 2 tablespoons coconut milk.
4 Add the chicken to the wok and cook, stirring, for 5 minutes, or until beginning to brown. Stir in the remaining coconut milk and 1¹/2 cups (375 ml/12 fl oz) water, and bring to the boil. Reduce the heat to very low and simmer, covered, for 45 minutes. Remove the lid and skim off any excess oil with a spoon. Simmer, uncovered, for 25 minutes, or until the chicken is cooked and the sauce has thickened slightly. Skim off any excess oil. Add the coconut cream and bring the mixture back to the boil, stirring constantly, until combined. Stir in the lime juice, then serve with rice.

NONYA COOKING
Incorporating the saltiness of dried shrimps with the heat of chillies and fragrance of lemon grass, Ayam kapitan is a classic example of Malaysia's tradition of Nonya cooking. Nonya cooking developed from combining Chinese and Malaysian ingredients and cooking techniques when Malaysia was settled by Chinese immigrants from the 15th century onwards. The subsequent marriage between Chinese immigrants and the native Malaysian population led to the creation of a distinct cuisine referred to as Nonya cooking. Nonya is the label for the Malaysian wives of Chinese men (the husbands were called 'Baba'). Chillies, shrimp paste, coconut milk and aromatic herbs and spices are combined with Chinese staples such as pork and noodles.

LEFT: Salty Malaysian chicken curry

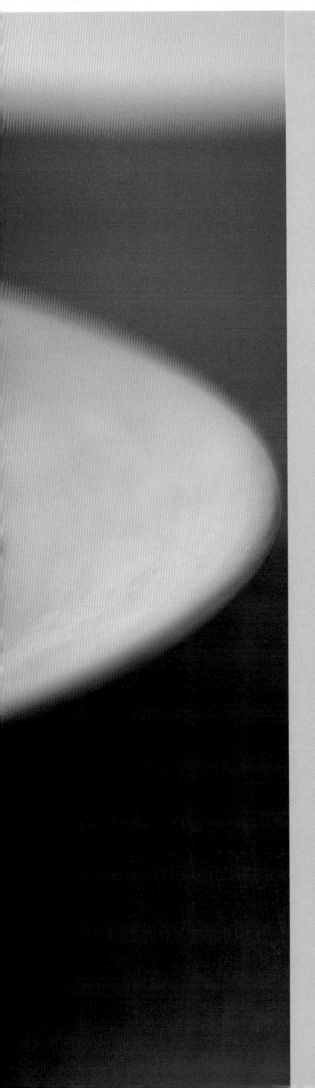

RICE&NOODLES

ARANCINI

When cooking the meat, break up any lumps with a wooden spoon.

Place 2 heaped teaspoons of the filling into the centre of each rice ball.

Enclose the rice around the filling, pressing the rice back into a ball shape.

Roll each ball in flour, then dip in egg before coating in the breadcrumbs.

ARANCINI
(Fried stuffed rice balls)

Preparation time: 30 minutes + 30 minutes
  cooling + 30 minutes refrigeration
Total cooking time: 45 minutes
Makes 12

2¼ cups (500 g/1 lb) short-grain
  white rice
¼ teaspoon saffron threads
2 eggs, beaten
1 cup (100 g/3½ oz) freshly grated Parmesan
plain (all-purpose) flour, for coating
2 eggs, beaten, extra
1 cup (100 g/3½ oz) dry breadcrumbs
oil, for deep-frying

Filling
1 tablespoon olive oil
1 small onion, finely chopped
150 g (5 oz) minced (ground) pork and veal
  or beef
⅔ cup (170 ml/5½ fl oz) white wine
1 tablespoon tomato paste (tomato purée)
2 teaspoons fresh thyme leaves

1 Bring 1 litre (32 fl oz) water to the boil in a large saucepan and add the rice and saffron threads. Bring slowly back to the boil, then reduce the heat and simmer. Cover and cook over low heat for 20 minutes, or until tender. Transfer to a large bowl and cool to room temperature. Stir in the egg and grated Parmesan.
2 For the filling, heat the oil in a small frying pan over medium heat. Add the onion and cook for 2–3 minutes, or until soft. Add the meat and cook for 2 minutes, or until it changes colour, pressing out any lumps. Add the wine and tomato paste. Reduce the heat and simmer for 3–4 minutes, or until the wine has evaporated. Stir in the thyme and set aside to cool.
3 With wet hands, divide the rice mixture into 12 balls. Flatten each slightly, make an indent in the centre of each and place 2 heaped teaspoons of the filling into each ball. Close the rice around the filling.
4 Roll each ball in the flour, dip in the extra egg, then roll in the breadcrumbs. Refrigerate for 30 minutes.
5 Fill a deep heavy-based saucepan one third full of oil and heat to 180°C (350°F), or until a cube of bread dropped into the oil browns in 15 seconds. Deep-fry the balls in four batches for 2–3 minutes each, or until golden brown. Drain on crumpled paper towels. Serve warm or at room temperature.

RIGHT: Arancini

LAMB PILAF

Preparation time: 25 minutes
  + 1 hour standing
Total cooking time: 40 minutes
Serves 4–6

★★

1 large eggplant (aubergine), about 500 g (1 lb),
  cut into 1 cm (1/2 inch) cubes
1/2 cup (125 ml/4 fl oz) olive oil
1 large onion, finely chopped
2 teaspoons ground cumin
1 teaspoon ground cinnamon
1 teaspoon ground coriander
300 g (10 oz) long-grain rice
2 cups (500 ml/16 fl oz) chicken or
  vegetable stock
500 g (1 lb) minced (ground) lamb
1/2 teaspoon allspice
2 tablespoons olive oil, extra
2 vine-ripened tomatoes, cut into wedges
3 tablespoons toasted pistachios
2 tablespoons currants
2 tablespoons chopped fresh coriander
  (cilantro) leaves, to garnish

1 Place the eggplant in a colander, sprinkle generously with salt and leave for 1 hour. Rinse well and squeeze dry in a clean tea towel. Heat 2 tablespoons oil in a large, deep frying pan with a lid, add the eggplant and cook over medium heat for 8–10 minutes, or until golden and cooked through. Drain on paper towels.
2 Heat the remaining oil, add the onion and cook for 4–5 minutes, or until soft but not brown. Stir in half of each of the cumin, cinnamon and ground coriander. Add the rice and stir to coat, then add the stock, season and bring to the boil. Reduce the heat and simmer, covered, for 15 minutes, adding a little more water if the pilaf starts to dry out.
3 Meanwhile, place the lamb in a bowl with the allspice and the remaining cumin, cinnamon and coriander. Season and mix well. Roll into balls the size of macadamia nuts. Heat the extra oil in the frying pan and cook the meatballs in batches over medium heat for 5 minutes each batch, or until lightly browned and cooked through. Drain on paper towels. Add the tomato to the pan and cook, turning, for 3–5 minutes, or until lightly golden. Remove from the pan.
4 Stir the eggplant, pistachios, currants and meatballs through the rice (this should be quite dry by now). Serve surrounded by the cooked tomato and garnished with the coriander leaves.

PISTACHIOS
These nuts have a hard, pale shell enclosing a green nut which is much prized around the world. As these nuts mature, the shells open slightly, revealing nuts with a delicate flavour. They are eaten roasted and salted, or used in cooking in both sweet and savoury dishes.

ABOVE: Lamb pilaf

311

¹/₃ cup (50 g/1³/₄ oz) toasted pine nuts

2 tablespoons chopped fresh mint

2 tablespoons chopped fresh flat-leaf (Italian) parsley

1 tablespoon chopped currants

1 cup (250 ml/8 fl oz) olive oil, extra

¹/₃ cup (80 ml/2³/₄ fl oz) lemon juice

extra virgin olive oil, to drizzle

lemon wedges, to serve

1 Heat the oil in a saucepan, add the onion and cook over medium heat for 10 minutes, or until golden. Add the allspice, cumin and nutmeg, and cook for 2 minutes, or until fragrant. Remove from the pan.

2 Bring a very large saucepan of water to the boil and add the bay leaves. Cut the tough outer leaves and about 5 cm (2 inches) of the core from the cabbage, then carefully add the cabbage to the boiling water. Cook it for 5 minutes, then carefully loosen a whole leaf with tongs and remove. Continue to cook and remove the leaves until you reach the core. Drain, reserving the cooking liquid and set aside to cool.

3 Take 12 leaves of equal size and cut a small 'V' from the core end of each to remove the thickest part. Trim the firm central veins so the leaf is as flat as possible. Place three-quarters of the remaining leaves on the base of a very large saucepan to prevent the rolls catching.

4 Combine the lamb, onion mixture, rice, garlic, pine nuts, mint, parsley and currants in a bowl and season well. With the core end of the leaf closest to you, form 2 tablespoons of the mixture into an oval and place in the centre of the leaf. Roll up, tucking in the sides. Repeat with the remaining 11 leaves and filling. Place tightly, in a single layer, in the lined saucepan, seam-side-down.

5 Combine 2¹/₂ cups (625 ml/20 fl oz) of the cooking liquid with the extra olive oil, lemon juice and 1 teaspoon salt, and pour over the rolls (the liquid should just come to the top of the rolls). Lay the remaining cabbage leaves over the top. Cover and bring to the boil over high heat, then reduce the heat and simmer for 1 hour 15 minutes, or until the meat and rice are cooked. Carefully remove from the pan with a slotted spoon, then drizzle with extra virgin olive oil. Serve with lemon wedges.

NOTE: Cabbage rolls are also delicious served with Avgolemono sauce from page 101. You can use the cooking liquid from the cooked rolls instead of the chicken stock to make the sauce.

CABBAGE ROLLS

Preparation time: 30 minutes
Total cooking time: 1 hour 35 minutes
Makes 12 large rolls

★★★

1 tablespoon olive oil

1 onion, finely chopped

large pinch of allspice

1 teaspoon ground cumin

large pinch of ground nutmeg

2 bay leaves

1 large head of cabbage

500 g (1 lb) minced (ground) lamb

1 cup (250 g/8 oz) short-grain white rice

4 cloves garlic, crushed

ABOVE: Cabbage rolls

STUFFED PEPPERS

Preparation time: 25 minutes
Total cooking time: 1 hour 15 minutes
Serves 6

175 g (4¹/2 oz) long-grain white rice
1¹/4 cups (315 ml/10 fl oz) chicken stock
6 medium-sized red, yellow or orange
  peppers (capsicums)
60 g (2 oz) pine nuts
¹/3 cup (80 ml/2³/4 fl oz) olive oil
1 large onion, chopped
¹/2 cup (125 g/4 oz) tomato passata
60 g (2 oz) currants
2¹/2 tablespoons chopped fresh flat-leaf
  (Italian) parsley
2¹/2 tablespoons chopped fresh mint leaves
¹/2 teaspoon ground cinnamon

1 Put the rice and stock in a saucepan and bring to the boil over medium heat. Reduce the heat to medium-low, cover tightly and cook for 15 minutes, or until tender. Remove from the heat and set aside, covered.
2 Bring a large saucepan of water to the boil. Cut off the tops of the peppers, reserving the lids. Remove the seeds and membrane from the peppers and discard. Blanch the peppers in the boiling water (not the lids) for 2 minutes, then drain and leave upturned to dry on paper towels.
3 Preheat the oven to moderate 180°C (350°F/ Gas 4). Toast the pine nuts in a small frying pan over low heat until golden brown, then remove from the pan and set aside. Increase the heat to medium and heat 2 tablespoons of oil. Add the onion and cook for 10 minutes or until soft, stirring occasionally.
4 Add the tomato passata, currants, parsley, mint, cinnamon, cooked rice and toasted pine nuts to the pan. Stir for 2 minutes, then season to taste with salt and pepper.
5 Stand the peppers in a baking dish in which they fit snugly. Divide the rice mixture among the pepper cavities. Replace the lids.
6 Pour 100 ml (3¹/2 fl oz) boiling water into the dish and drizzle the remaining oil over the top of the peppers. Bake for 40 minutes, or until the peppers are just tender when tested with the point of a small knife. Serve warm or cold.

SEMI-DRIED TOMATOES
To make semi-dried (sun-blushed) tomatoes, preheat the oven to warm 160°C (315°F/Gas 2–3). Cut 16 Roma (plum) tomatoes into quarters lengthways and lay them skin-side-down on a wire rack in a baking dish. Stir together 1 teaspoon each of salt and black pepper and 3 tablespoons chopped fresh thyme. Sprinkle over the tomatoes. Bake for 2¹/2 hours, checking occasionally to make sure they don't burn. Put them in a bowl and toss with 2 tablespoons olive oil. Cool before transferring to an airtight container. Refrigerate for 24 hours before using. Eat within 3–4 days.

LEFT: Stuffed peppers

PEA AND
HAM RISOTTO

Add half the wine to the frying pan and simmer, uncovered, until almost all the liquid has evaporated.

Gradually ladle in the hot stock mixture, waiting after each addition until the liquid is absorbed before adding more.

Stir constantly over low heat until all the stock has been absorbed and the rice is creamy and tender.

ABOVE: Pea and ham risotto

PEA AND HAM RISOTTO

Preparation time: 25 minutes
Total cooking time: 45 minutes
Serves 4

★★

1 tablespoon olive oil

1 celery stick, chopped

2 tablespoons chopped fresh flat-leaf (Italian)
  parsley

75 g (2 1/2 oz) sliced ham, coarsely
  chopped

1 2/3 cups (250 g/8 oz) frozen green peas

1/2 cup (125 ml/4 fl oz) dry white wine

3 cups (750 ml/24 fl oz) chicken stock

60 g (2 oz) butter

1 onion, chopped

2 cups (440 g/14 oz) arborio rice

1/3 cup (35 g/1 1/4 oz) grated Parmesan

shaved Parmesan, to serve

1 Heat the oil in a frying pan, add the celery, parsley and some freshly ground black pepper and cook, stirring, over medium heat for 2–3 minutes to soften the celery. Add the ham and stir well. Add the peas and half the wine, bring to the boil, then reduce the heat and simmer, uncovered, until almost all the liquid has evaporated. Set aside.

2 Put the stock, remaining wine and 3 cups (750 ml/24 fl oz) water in a separate pan and keep at simmering point.

3 Melt the butter in a large heavy-based saucepan. Add the onion and stir until softened. Add the rice and stir well. Gradually stir in the hot stock mixture, 1/2 cup (125 ml/4 oz) at a time, making sure the liquid has been absorbed before adding more. Stir constantly over low heat with a wooden spoon, until all the stock has been absorbed and the rice is creamy and tender (this will take about 25–30 minutes altogether). Season to taste.

4 Add the pea mixture and grated Parmesan to the rice and serve with Parmesan shavings and black pepper.

SALMON AND RICE PIE

When the salmon has cooled slightly, add the egg, dill and parsley and season to taste.

Roll out the pastry and trim to a neat shape. Reserve the trimmings to decorate.

Spread the remaining rice over the other layers of filling.

Roll out the remaining pastry and place over the filling. Seal with beaten egg.

SALMON AND RICE PIE

Preparation time: 25 minutes
+ 30 minutes refrigeration
Total cooking time: 1 hour 40 minutes
Serves 4–6

★ ★

1/3 cup (65 g/2 1/4 oz) brown rice

60 g (2 oz) butter

1 onion, finely chopped

200 g (6 1/2 oz) button mushrooms, sliced

2 tablespoons lemon juice

200 g (6 1/2 oz) salmon fillet, boned and cut into small pieces, or 220 g (7 oz) can red salmon

2 hard-boiled eggs, chopped

2 tablespoons chopped fresh dill

3 tablespoons chopped fresh parsley

1/4 cup (60 ml/2 fl oz) cream

500 g (1 lb) home-made or bought puff pastry (see page 488)

1 egg, lightly beaten

1 Bring a large saucepan of water to a rapid boil. Add the brown rice and cook, uncovered, for 30–40 minutes, stirring occasionally. Drain.
2 Grease a baking tray. Melt half the butter in a frying pan, add the onion and cook for 5 minutes until soft but not browned. Add the mushrooms and cook for 5 minutes, or until softened. Add the lemon juice, then remove from the pan.
3 Heat the remaining butter in the pan, add the salmon, stir and cook for 2 minutes. Remove from the heat, cool slightly and mix in the egg, dill, parsley and salt and pepper, to taste. Mix the rice and cream in a small bowl.
4 Roll out half the pastry to a 15 x 25 cm (6 x 10 inch) rectangle. Trim the pastry, saving the trimmings, and put on a greased baking tray.
5 Layer the filling onto the pastry, leaving a 3 cm (1 1/4 inch) border. Put half the rice on the pastry, then the salmon and egg, followed by the mushroom mixture. Top with the remaining rice. Brush the border with egg.
6 Roll out the remaining pastry to 20 x 30 cm (8 x 12 inches) and place over the filling. Seal the edges. Knock up the pastry by using the blunt edge of a floured knife to push into the edge at 2 cm (3/4 inch) intervals, leaving a scallop pattern. Make two slits in the top. Decorate with the pastry trimmings and chill for 30 minutes.
7 Preheat the oven to moderately hot 200°C (400°F/Gas 6). Lightly brush the pie with egg and bake for 15 minutes. Reduce the oven to moderate 180°C (350°F/Gas 4) and bake for 25–30 minutes, or until golden brown. Serve with sour cream.

ABOVE: Salmon and rice pie

SEAFOOD RISOTTO

Add the prawns to the pan and cook them until pink.

Gradually stir in the hot liquid until it is all absorbed.

SEAFOOD RISOTTO

Preparation time: 25 minutes
Total cooking time: 45 minutes
Serves 4

2 ripe tomatoes
500 g (1 lb) black mussels
1¼ cups (315 ml/10 fl oz) white wine
1.25 litres (40 fl oz) fish stock
pinch of saffron threads
2 tablespoons olive oil
30 g (1 oz) butter
500 g (1 lb) raw prawns (shrimp), peeled
    and deveined
225 g (7 oz) squid hoods, sliced into thin rings
200 g (6½ oz) scallops
3 cloves garlic, crushed
1 onion, finely chopped
2 cups (370 g/12 oz) risotto rice (arborio,
    vialone nano or carnaroli)
2 tablespoons chopped fresh parsley

1 Score a cross in the base of each tomato. Place in a bowl of boiling water for 10 seconds, then plunge into cold water and peel the skin away from the cross. Chop the tomato flesh.
2 Scrub the mussels with a stiff brush and remove the hairy beards. Discard any broken mussels or any that do not close when tapped. Pour the wine into a large saucepan and bring to the boil. Add the mussels and cook, covered, over medium heat for 3–5 minutes, or until the mussels open. Discard any that do not open. Strain, reserving the liquid. Remove the mussels from their shells.
3 Combine the mussel liquid, stock and saffron in a saucepan, cover and keep at a low simmer.
4 Heat the oil and butter in a large saucepan over medium heat. Add the prawns and cook until pink. Remove. Add the squid and scallops and cook for about 1–2 minutes, until white. Remove. Add the garlic and onion and cook for 3 minutes, or until golden. Add the rice and stir until coated.
5 Add ½ cup (125 ml/4 fl oz) of the hot liquid, stirring constantly until it is all absorbed. Continue adding liquid, ½ cup (125 ml/4 fl oz) at a time, stirring constantly, for 25 minutes, or until the liquid is absorbed. Stir in the tomato, seafood and parsley and heat through. Season, to taste.
VARIATION: You can use almost any combination of seafood for this risotto. Try using small pieces of firm, white fish, clams (vongole) or octopus.

ABOVE: Seafood risotto

MUSHROOM RISOTTO

Preparation time: 10 minutes
  + 30 minutes soaking
Total cooking time: 1 hour
Serves 4–6

★ ★

20 g (³/4 oz) dried porcini mushrooms

1 litre (32 fl oz) chicken or vegetable stock

2 tablespoons olive oil

100 g (3¹/2 oz) butter, chopped

650 g (1 lb 5 oz) small cap or Swiss brown
  mushrooms, stems trimmed, sliced

3 cloves garlic, crushed

¹/3 cup (80 ml/2³/4 fl oz) dry white
  vermouth

1 onion, finely chopped

2 cups (440 g/14 oz) risotto rice
  (arborio, vialone nano or carnaroli)

1¹/2 cups (150 g/5 oz) grated Parmesan

1 Soak the porcini mushrooms in 2 cups (500 ml/16 fl oz) warm water for 30 minutes. Drain, retaining the liquid. Chop them and pour the liquid through a fine sieve lined with a paper towel.

2 Put the stock and the mushroom liquid together in a saucepan, bring to the boil, then reduce the heat, cover and keep at a low simmer.

3 Heat half the oil and 40 g (1¹/4 oz) of the butter in a large frying pan over high heat. Add all the mushrooms and the garlic to the pan and cook, stirring, for 10 minutes, or until soft and all the mushroom juices have been released. Reduce the heat to low and cook for another 5 minutes, or until all the juices have evaporated. Increase the heat, add the vermouth and cook for 2–3 minutes, until evaporated. Set aside.

4 Heat the remaining olive oil and 20 g (³/4 oz) butter in a large saucepan over medium heat. Add the onion and cook for 10 minutes, or until soft. Add the rice and stir for 1–2 minutes, or until well coated. Add ¹/2 cup (125 ml/4 fl oz) stock to the pan and stir constantly over medium heat until all the liquid is absorbed. Continue adding more stock, ¹/2 cup (125 ml/4 fl oz) at a time, stirring constantly for 20–25 minutes, or until tender and creamy.

5 Remove from the heat and stir in the mushrooms, Parmesan and the remaining butter. Season to taste with salt and freshly ground black pepper.

NOTE: It is important to make sure that the porcini mushrooms are soaked for at least 30 minutes in warm water and that the soaking liquid is passed through a fine sieve lined with a paper towel to ensure that all the grit has been removed. If stored in a tightly sealed container, porcini mushrooms will keep indefinitely.

RISOTTO
A common misconception surrounding risotto is that it should be eaten piping hot, straight from the stove. However, unlike pasta, risotto benefits from resting on your plate for a minute or so to allow the flavours to settle and the steam to disperse. Italians often spread the risotto on their plate from the centre out and then eat from the rim to the centre.

LEFT: Mushroom risotto

BLACK MUSSELS
Sometimes referred to as 'poor man's oyster' or 'blue mussel', the mussel is full of flavour. Mussels attach themselves to rocks or, if farmed, onto bags or ropes, with the tough brown fibres we call the 'beard'. Farmed mussels take 18 months to 2 years to mature. When buying mussels, avoid any with broken shells. Use soon after purchasing, or keep in a very cool place in a small amount of water, covered with a damp hessian bag. When you come to cook the mussels, if any of them have open shells, tap them on the bench and if they don't close, they are dead and should be thrown away. When mussels are cooked, the shells should open. Any that haven't opened by the end of cooking time (usually 3–5 minutes) should be thrown away.

ABOVE: Paella

PAELLA

Preparation time: 30 minutes
    + 2 hours soaking
Total cooking time: 45 minutes
Serves 4

12 raw medium prawns (shrimp)
12–16 black mussels
$^{1}/_{2}$ cup (125 ml/4 fl oz) white wine
1 small red onion, chopped
$^{1}/_{2}$ cup (125 ml/4 fl oz) olive oil
1 small chicken breast fillet, cut into
    bite-sized cubes
100 g (3$^{1}/_{2}$ oz) squid rings
100 g (3$^{1}/_{2}$ oz) skinless white fish fillet
    (eg. cod, ling, mahi mahi, blue-eye, monkfish),
    cut into bite-sized cubes
$^{1}/_{2}$ small red onion, extra, finely chopped
1 rasher bacon, finely chopped
4 cloves garlic, crushed
1 small red pepper (capsicum), finely chopped

1 ripe tomato, peeled and chopped
90 g (3 oz) chorizo or pepperoni, thinly sliced
pinch of cayenne pepper
1 cup (200 g/6$^{1}/_{2}$ oz) long-grain rice
$^{1}/_{4}$ teaspoon saffron threads
2 cups (500 ml/16 fl oz) chicken stock, heated
$^{1}/_{2}$ cup (80 g/2$^{3}/_{4}$ oz) fresh or frozen peas
2 tablespoons finely chopped fresh parsley

1 Peel the prawns and pull out the dark vein from each prawn back, starting at the head end.
2 Scrub the mussels with a stiff brush and pull out the hairy beards. Discard any broken mussels, or open ones that don't close when tapped on the bench.
3 Heat the wine and onion in a large pan. Add the mussels, cover and gently shake the pan for 4–5 minutes over high heat. After 3 minutes, start removing opened mussels and set aside. At the end of 5 minutes, discard any unopened mussels. Reserve the cooking liquid.
4 Heat half the oil in a large frying pan. Pat the chicken dry with paper towels, then cook the chicken for 5 minutes, or until golden brown. Remove from the pan and set aside. Add the

prawns, squid and fish to the pan and cook for 1 minute. Remove from the pan; set aside.

5 Heat the remaining oil in the pan, add the extra onion, bacon, garlic and red pepper and cook for 5 minutes, or until the onion is soft. Add the tomato, chorizo and cayenne. Season to taste. Stir in the reserved cooking liquid, then add the rice and mix well.

6 Blend the saffron with ½ cup (125 ml/4 fl oz) of stock, then add with the remaining stock to the rice and mix well. Bring slowly to the boil. Reduce the heat to low and simmer, uncovered, for 15 minutes, without stirring.

7 Place the peas, chicken, prawns, squid and fish on top of the rice. Using a wooden spoon, push pieces into the rice, cover and cook over low heat for 10–15 minutes, or until the rice is tender and the seafood cooked. Add the mussels for the last 2 minutes to heat. If the rice is not quite cooked, add a little extra stock and cook for a few more minutes. Serve sprinkled with parsley.

LEMONY HERB AND FISH RISOTTO

Preparation time: 20 minutes
Total cooking time: 30 minutes
Serves 4

★★

60 g (2 oz) butter
400 g (13 oz) skinless white fish fillets
   (eg. coley, cod, blue-eye, ling), cut
   into 3 cm (1¼ inch) cubes
1.25 litres (40 fl oz) fish stock
1 onion, finely chopped
1 clove garlic, crushed
1 teaspoon ground turmeric
1½ cups (330 g/11 oz) arborio rice
2 tablespoons lemon juice
1 tablespoon chopped fresh parsley
1 tablespoon chopped fresh chives
1 tablespoon chopped fresh dill

1 Melt half the butter in a pan. Add the fish in batches and fry over medium–high heat for 3 minutes, or until the fish is just cooked through. Remove from the pan and set aside.

2 Pour the fish stock into another pan, bring to the boil, cover and keep at simmering point.

3 To the first pan, add the remaining butter, onion and garlic and cook over medium heat for 3 minutes, or until the onion is tender. Add the turmeric and stir for 1 minute. Add the rice and stir to coat, then add ½ cup (125 ml/4 fl oz) of the fish stock and cook, stirring constantly, over low heat until all the stock has been absorbed. Continue adding ½ cup (125 ml/4 fl oz) of stock at a time until all the stock has been added and the rice is translucent, tender and creamy.

4 Stir in the lemon juice, parsley, chives and dill. Add the fish and stir gently. Serve, maybe garnished with slices of lemon or lime and fresh herb sprigs.

NOTE: The rice must absorb the stock between each addition—the whole process will take about 20 minutes. If you don't have time to make your own stock, you can buy fresh or frozen fish stock from delicatessens, some seafood outlets and most supermarkets.

BELOW: Lemony herb and fish risotto

FRIED RICE

To make fried rice, you need cold, cooked rice. Either use leftover rice or cook the rice a day ahead and refrigerate. To calculate the amount of raw rice you need, divide the cooked rice amount by three. For example, 3 cups cooked rice is equivalent to 1 cup raw rice.

THAI VEGETARIAN FRIED RICE
Heat a wok over high heat, add 2 tablespoons vegetable oil and swirl. Stir-fry 3 sliced red Asian shallots, 1 clove finely chopped garlic and 1 finely chopped small fresh red chilli for 2 minutes, or until the shallots start to brown. Add 100 g (3½ oz) sliced snake beans, 1 thinly sliced small red pepper (capsicum) (cut into 5 cm/2 inch lengths) and 90 g (3 oz) halved button mushrooms. Stir-fry for 3 minutes, or until cooked, then stir in 3 cups (555 g/1 lb 2 oz) cold, cooked jasmine rice until heated through.

Dissolve 1 teaspoon grated palm sugar in ¼ cup (60 ml/2 fl oz) light soy sauce and pour over the rice. Stir in 3 tablespoons shredded fresh Thai basil and 1 tablespoon chopped fresh coriander (cilantro). Serves 4.

INDONESIAN FRIED RICE
Cook 150 g (5 oz) finely chopped snake beans in boiling water for 3 minutes. Drain, rinse and set aside.

Blend 3 roughly chopped cloves garlic, 1 chopped onion and 1 small fresh bird's eye chilli in a food processor into a rough paste. Heat 2 tablespoons vegetable oil in a wok, swirl to coat the side of the wok, and cook the paste for 1 minute, or until fragrant. Add 200 g (6½ oz) peeled and deveined baby prawns (shrimp) and 250 g (8 oz) thinly sliced chicken breast, and stir-fry for 3 minutes, or until the prawns turn pink. Add the beans and 2 tablespoons water and season with salt and pepper. Add 4 cups (740 g/1½ lb) cold, cooked long-grain rice, 4 thinly sliced spring onions (scallions), 1 tablespoon kecap manis and 1–2 tablespoons light soy sauce, stirring continuously until heated. Serves 4–6.

NOTE: Nasi goreng is usually served with shredded omelette and prawn (shrimp) crackers (*krupuk udang* in Indonesia and Malaysia) on the top.

PINEAPPLE BEEF FRIED RICE

Heat a wok over high heat, add 1 tablespoon peanut oil and a few drops of sesame oil and swirl to coat. Add 2 teaspoons finely chopped fresh ginger, 1 finely chopped small fresh red chilli and 2 cloves crushed garlic and stir-fry for a few seconds, then add 250 g (8 oz) minced (ground) beef and stir-fry, breaking up any lumps, for 4–5 minutes, or until the beef is cooked through. Add 1/2 cup (80 g/2 3/4 oz) cooked frozen peas and 4 finely chopped spring onions (scallions) and stir-fry for 1 minute, or until the spring onion is soft. Add 4 cups (740 g/1 1/2 lb) cold, cooked long-grain rice, 1/4 cup (60 g/2 oz) finely diced bamboo shoots, 2/3 cup (175 g/6 oz) very well drained crushed pineapple and toss, then stir-fry for 2–3 minutes, or until the rice is heated through. Add 1 1/2 tablespoons soy sauce, 1 1/2 tablespoons fish sauce and 1 tablespoon rice vinegar and stir-fry for a minute, or until combined. Stir in 2 tablespoons finely chopped fresh coriander (cilantro) leaves and serve. Serves 4–6.

CHINESE FRIED RICE

Soak 2 tablespoons dried shrimp in boiling water for 20 minutes. Drain and finely chop. Heat a wok over high heat, add 1 tablespoon vegetable oil and swirl to coat the side of the wok. Add 3 lightly beaten eggs and stir until they start to scramble. When almost cooked, cut into small strips, then remove from the wok.

Heat 1 tablespoon vegetable oil in the wok, add 250 g (8 oz) finely diced Chinese barbecued pork and stir-fry for 1 minute, or until heated through. Add 50 g (1 3/4 oz) drained, rinsed and finely diced straw mushrooms and the shrimp, and stir-fry for 1–2 minutes. Add 1 tablespoon oil, then gradually add 4 cups (740 g/1 1/2 lb) cold, cooked long-grain rice, tossing for 2 minutes, or until heated through. Reduce the heat to medium, add 2 tablespoons light soy sauce, 3 finely chopped spring onions (scallions) and 2 1/2 tablespoons finely chopped garlic chives, and stir-fry until mixed and the soy sauce coats the rice. Season with white pepper and a drizzle of sesame oil, and serve topped with the omelette strips. Serves 4.

FROM LEFT: Thai vegetarian fried rice; Indonesian fried rice; Pineapple beef fried rice; Chinese fried rice.

321

THAI FRIED NOODLES WITH PRAWNS

Preparation time: 25 minutes +
 8 minutes standing
Total cooking time: 10 minutes
Serves 4

200 g (6½ oz) dried thick rice stick noodles

1 tablespoon oil

2 cloves garlic, crushed

2 fresh red chillies, seeded and finely chopped

1 chicken breast fillet, thinly sliced

150 g (5 oz) raw prawn (shrimp) meat, chopped

¼ cup (30 g/1 oz) chopped fresh garlic chives

2 tablespoons fish sauce

1 tablespoon soft brown sugar

2 tablespoons lemon juice

1 egg, lightly beaten

50 g (1¾ oz) deep-fried tofu, cut into strips

3 tablespoons fresh coriander (cilantro) leaves

¼ cup (25 g/¾ oz) bean sprouts

¼ cup (40 g/1¼ oz) roasted peanuts, chopped

1 lemon, cut into wedges, to serve

1 Put the noodles in a heatproof bowl. Cover with boiling water and leave for 5–8 minutes, or until the noodles are soft and tender. Drain and set aside.

2 Heat the wok until very hot, add the oil and swirl it around to coat the side. Stir-fry the garlic, chilli and sliced chicken over high heat for 2–3 minutes, or until the chicken is browned.

3 Add the prawn meat to the wok and cook for 2 minutes, or until the prawn meat turns pink. Add the drained noodles and garlic chives, and toss until thoroughly combined.

4 Add the fish sauce, brown sugar, lemon juice, egg and tofu, and toss gently to combine, using a pair of tongs or two wooden spoons. Serve sprinkled with the coriander leaves, bean sprouts and peanuts. Serve with lemon wedges.

NOTE: Deep-fried tofu is available from Asian grocery stores and some supermarkets.

ABOVE: Thai fried noodles with prawns

NASI GORENG

Preparation time: 25 minutes
Total cooking time: 15 minutes
Serves 6

★ ★

350 g (11 oz) raw medium prawns (shrimp)

5–8 long red chillies, seeded and chopped

2 teaspoons shrimp paste

8 cloves garlic, finely chopped

4 tablespoons oil

2 eggs, lightly beaten

350 g (11 oz) chicken thigh fillets, cut into
   thin strips

8 cups (1.5 kg/3 lb) cold, cooked rice

1/3 cup (80 ml/2¾ fl oz) kecap manis

1/3 cup (80 ml/2¾ fl oz) soy sauce

2 small Lebanese (short) cucumbers, chopped

1 large ripe tomato, seeded, finely chopped

lime halves, to serve

1 Peel the prawns and pull out the dark vein from each prawn back, starting at the head end.
2 Mix the chilli, shrimp paste and garlic in a food processor to form a paste.

3 Heat the wok until very hot, add 1 tablespoon of the oil and swirl it around to coat the side. Add the beaten eggs and, using a wok chan or metal spatula, push the egg up the edges of the wok to form a large omelette. Cook for 1 minute over medium heat, or until the egg is set, then flip it over and cook the other side for 1 minute. Remove from the wok and cool before slicing into strips.
4 Reheat the wok, add 1 tablespoon of the oil and stir-fry the chicken and half the chilli paste over high heat until the chicken is just cooked. Remove the chicken from the wok.
5 Reheat the wok, add 1 tablespoon of the oil and stir-fry the prawns and the remaining chilli paste until the prawns are cooked. Remove from the wok and set aside.
6 Reheat the wok, add 1 tablespoon of oil and the cold cooked rice, and toss constantly over medium heat for 4–5 minutes, or until the rice is heated through. Add the kecap manis and soy sauce, and toss constantly until all the rice is coated in the sauces. Return the chicken and prawns to the wok, and toss until well combined and heated through. Season well with freshly ground pepper and salt. Transfer to a large deep serving bowl and top with the omelette strips, chopped cucumber and tomato. Serve with the lime halves.

NASI GORENG

Remove the seeds from the red chillies and finely chop the flesh.

Process the chilli, shrimp paste and garlic until it forms a paste.

LEFT: Nasi goreng

YUM WOON SEN
Literally meaning
'assembled' or 'mixed
together', yums are a
type of Thai salad that
incorporate lightly cooked
meat or seafood. Dressed
with lime juice, fish sauce,
sugar and chilli, they are an
important feature of Thai
cuisine, showcasing the
Thai palate's emphasis on
freshness and the balance
between sour, salty, sweet
and hot flavours.

THAI PORK NOODLE SALAD
(Yum woon sen)

Preparation time: 20 minutes
Total cooking time: 35 minutes
Serves 4-6

Broth

1 cup (250 ml/8 fl oz) chicken stock
3 coriander (cilantro) roots
2 fresh makrut (kaffir) lime leaves
3 x 3 cm (1¼ x 1¼ inch) piece fresh ginger, sliced

30 g (1 oz) fresh black fungus
100 g (3½ oz) cellophane noodles or dried
   rice vermicelli
1 small fresh red chilli, seeded and thinly sliced
2 red Asian shallots, thinly sliced
2 spring onions (scallions), thinly sliced
2 cloves garlic, crushed
1 tablespoon vegetable oil
250 g (8 oz) minced (ground) pork
2½ tablespoons lime juice
2½ tablespoons fish sauce
1½ tablespoons grated palm sugar
¼ teaspoon ground white pepper
½ cup (15 g/½ oz) fresh coriander (cilantro)
   leaves, chopped

oakleaf or coral lettuce, torn or shredded
lime wedges, to garnish
fresh red chilli, extra, cut into strips, to garnish
fresh coriander (cilantro) leaves, extra, to
   garnish (optional)

1 To make the broth, put the chicken stock,
coriander roots, lime leaves, ginger and 1 cup
(250 ml/8 fl oz) water in a wok. Simmer for
25 minutes, or until it has reduced to ³/4 cup
(185 ml/6 fl oz). Strain.
2 Discard the woody stems from the fungus,
then thinly slice. Soak the noodles in boiling
water for 3–4 minutes, or until pliable. Rinse,
drain, then cut into 3 cm (1¼ inch) lengths.
Combine the noodles, fungus, chilli, shallots,
spring onion and garlic.
3 Heat a clean, dry wok over high heat, add
the oil and swirl to coat. Add the pork and
stir-fry, breaking up any lumps, for 1–2 minutes,
or until the pork changes colour and is cooked.
Add the broth and bring the mixture to the boil
over high heat. Boil for 1 minute, then drain,
and add the pork to the noodle mixture.
4 Combine the lime juice, fish sauce, palm sugar
and white pepper, stirring until the sugar is
dissolved. Add to the pork mixture with the
coriander and mix well. Season to taste with salt.
5 Arrange the lettuce on a serving dish, spoon
on the pork and noodle mixture and garnish
with the lime, chilli and, if desired, fresh
coriander leaves.

*RIGHT: Thai pork noodle
salad*

PORK AND HOKKIEN NOODLE STIR-FRY

Preparation time: 15 minutes +
10 minutes marinating
Total cooking time: 15 minutes
Serves 4

^{1}/3 cup (80 ml/2^3/4 fl oz) soy sauce

^{1}/4 cup (60 ml/2 fl oz) mirin

2 teaspoons grated fresh ginger

2 cloves garlic, crushed

1^1/2 tablespoons soft brown sugar

350 g (11 oz) pork loin fillet, thinly sliced
across the grain

500 g (1 lb) Hokkien (egg) noodles

2 tablespoons peanut oil

1 onion, cut into thin wedges

1 red pepper (capsicum), cut into thin strips

2 carrots, thinly sliced on the diagonal

4 spring onions (scallions), thinly sliced on
the diagonal

200 g (6^1/2 oz) fresh shiitake mushrooms, sliced

1 Combine the soy sauce, mirin, ginger, garlic and sugar in a large non-metallic bowl. Add the pork and toss to coat. Cover with plastic wrap and marinate in the refrigerator for at least 10 minutes.

2 Meanwhile, put the noodles in a heatproof bowl, cover with boiling water and soak for 1 minute to separate and soften. Drain well, then rinse under running water.

3 Heat a large wok over high heat, add 1 tablespoon of the oil and swirl it around to coat the side of the wok. Lift the pork out of the marinade with tongs or a slotted spoon, reserving the marinade. Stir-fry the pork in batches for 3 minutes each batch, or until nicely browned. Remove from the wok.

4 Reheat the wok over high heat, add the remaining oil and swirl to coat. Add the onion, pepper and carrot, and stir-fry for 2–3 minutes, or until just tender. Add the spring onion and shiitake mushrooms and cook for another 2 minutes. Return the pork to the wok along with the noodles and the reserved marinade. Toss together thoroughly until combined and heated through, then serve.

SOUTHEAST ASIAN STICKY RICE

Place 1^1/2 cups (300 g/10 oz) sticky rice in a sieve and wash until the water runs clear. Transfer to a large bowl, cover well with water and set aside for 8 hours, or overnight if time permits. Drain the rice thoroughly and place in a bamboo steamer lined with muslin and cover with the steamer lid. Sit the steamer over a wok of simmering water, making sure that the base of the steamer doesn't touch the water. Cook for 45–55 minutes, or until the rice is very soft. Add extra water to the wok if necessary. Fluff with a fork and serve immediately.
NOTE: Sticky rice can also be served at room temperature or rolled into balls and eaten as a snack. As a variation, try sprinkling it with toasted sesame seeds or ready made fried red Asian shallots.

ABOVE: Pork and hokkien noodle stir-fry

INDONESIAN-STYLE FRIED NOODLES
(Bahmi goreng)

Preparation time: 25 minutes
Total cooking time: 20 minutes
Serves 4

400 g (13 oz) fresh flat egg noodles
    (5 mm/^{1}/$_4$ inch wide)
2 tomatoes
2 tablespoons peanut oil
4 red Asian shallots, thinly sliced
2 cloves garlic, chopped
1 small fresh red chilli, finely diced
100 g (3^1/$_2$ oz) pork loin fillet, thinly sliced
    across the grain

300 g (10 oz) chicken breast fillet, thinly sliced
200 g (6^1/$_2$ oz) small raw prawns (shrimp),
    peeled and deveined, with tails intact
2 wom bok (Chinese cabbage) leaves, shredded
2 carrots, halved lengthways and thinly sliced
100 g (3^1/$_2$ oz) snake beans, cut into 3 cm
    (1^1/$_4$ inch) lengths
^{1}/$_4$ cup (60 ml/2 fl oz) kecap manis
1 tablespoon light soy sauce
4 spring onions (scallions), sliced on the
    diagonal
1 tablespoon crisp fried onion
fresh flat-leaf (Italian) parsley, to garnish

1 Cook the noodles in a saucepan of boiling water for 1 minute, or until tender. Drain, then rinse under cold water.
2 Score a cross in the base of each tomato. Put the tomatoes in a bowl of boiling water for 30 seconds, then plunge into cold water and peel the skin away from the cross. Cut the tomatoes in half crossways, scoop out the seeds with a teaspoon, then chop the flesh.
3 Heat a wok over high heat, add the peanut oil and swirl to coat. Add the red Asian shallots and stir-fry for 1 minute. Add the garlic, chilli and pork and stir-fry for 2 minutes, then add the chicken and cook for a further 2 minutes. Add the prawns and stir-fry for a further 2 minutes, or until they are pink and cooked.
4 Stir in the wom bok, carrot and beans and cook for 3 minutes, then add the cooked noodles and stir-fry for another 4 minutes, or until everything is heated through.
5 Add the kecap manis, soy sauce, spring onion and tomato. Toss for 2 minutes. Season, then garnish with crisp fried onion and parsley. Serve.

STEAMED RICE

Rinse 1^1/$_2$ cups (300 g/10 oz) jasmine rice in a sieve until the water runs clear. Place in a large saucepan with 1^3/$_4$ cups (440 ml/ 14 fl oz) water. Bring to the boil and boil for 1 minute. Cover tightly, reduce the heat to as low as possible and cook for 10 minutes. Remove from the heat and leave to stand, covered, for 10 minutes. Fluff with a fork before serving. Serve with stir-fries, curries and steamed dishes. Serves 4.

BELOW: Indonesian-style fried noodles

SINGAPORE NOODLES

Preparation time: 35 minutes
Total cooking time: 15 minutes
Serves 2–4

300 g (10 oz) dried rice vermicelli

300 g (10 oz) raw medium prawns (shrimp)

2 tablespoons oil

2 cloves garlic, finely chopped

350 g (11 oz) pork loin, cut into strips

1 large onion, cut into thin wedges

1–2 tablespoons Asian curry powder (see Note)

150 g (5 oz) green beans, cut into
    short lengths

1 large carrot, sliced

1 teaspoon sugar

1 tablespoon soy sauce

200 g (6½ oz) bean sprouts

1 spring onion (scallion), cut into fine strips,
    to garnish

1 Soak the vermicelli in boiling water for about 5 minutes, or until soft. Drain well. Cut into short lengths.

2 Peel the prawns and pull out the dark vein from each prawn back, starting at the head end.

3 Heat half the oil in a wok over high heat and add the garlic, pork and prawns in batches. Stir-fry for 2 minutes, or until the mixture is just cooked. Remove from the wok and set aside.

4 Reduce the heat to medium. Add the remaining oil and stir-fry the onion and curry powder for 2–3 minutes. Add the beans, carrot, sugar and 1 teaspoon salt, sprinkle with a little water and stir-fry for 2 minutes.

5 Toss the vermicelli and soy sauce through the mixture. Add the bean sprouts, prawn and pork mixture to the wok. Season to taste with salt and pepper. Toss well and garnish with the spring onion.

NOTE: There are many varieties of Asian curry powder, each with a blend of spices designed to match the meat, chicken or seafood it is cooked with. Here we have used Asian fish curry powder, available from Asian food speciality stores. Commercial brands are not suitable for this recipe.

RICE VERMICELLI
Commonly used fresh in rice-growing areas in southern China, rice vermicelli (or rice noodles) are usually sold elsewhere in dried bundles. Before using in recipes, they need to be soaked in boiling water to soften them. They can be deep-fried in hot oil instead of soaking, to create crispy noodles.

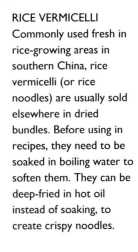

LEFT: Singapore noodles

CHILLI SALT AND PEPPER SQUID AND CELLOPHANE NOODLE SALAD

Preparation time: 30 minutes +
  10 minutes soaking + 15 minutes marinating
Total cooking time: 10 minutes
Serves 4

★★★

1 tablespoon dried shrimp
2 tablespoons Chinese rice wine
2 tablespoons light soy sauce
1 tablespoon Chinese black vinegar
2 teaspoons finely chopped fresh ginger
2 spring onions (scallions), thinly sliced
1 teaspoon chilli garlic sauce
1 teaspoon sesame oil

ABOVE: Chilli salt and pepper squid and cellophane noodle salad

Salad

600 g (1 1/4 lb) cleaned squid hoods
1/2 cup (125 ml/4 fl oz) lemon juice
250 g (8 oz) cellophane noodles
1 small Lebanese (short) cucumber, seeded and
  cut into batons
1 cup (90 g/3 oz) bean sprouts, tops and
  tails removed
2 tablespoons chopped fresh coriander
  (cilantro) leaves, plus extra, to garnish
1 tablespoon Sichuan peppercorns, dry-roasted
2 teaspoons sea salt
1 teaspoon ground white pepper
1 teaspoon freshly ground black pepper
1/4 teaspoon chilli flakes
1/2 cup (60 g/2 oz) plain (all-purpose) flour
1/4 cup (45 g/1 1/2 oz) rice flour
peanut oil, for deep-frying
2 egg whites, lightly beaten

1 Put the dried shrimp in a small heatproof bowl, cover with boiling water and soak for 10 minutes. Drain and finely chop. Return the shrimp to the bowl, cover with the rice wine and leave to soak until needed.
2 To make the dressing, put the soy sauce, black vinegar, ginger, spring onion, chilli garlic sauce and sesame oil in a small bowl. Mix together well, then set aside until needed.
3 Open out the squid hoods, then wash and thoroughly pat dry with paper towels. With the soft inside flesh facing upwards, score a diamond pattern in the squid, taking care not to cut all the way through. Cut the squid into 2.5 x 4 cm (1 x 1 1/2 inch) pieces. Put the pieces in a flat, non-metallic dish, then pour the lemon juice on top. Cover and refrigerate for 15 minutes.
4 Meanwhile, put the noodles in a heatproof bowl, cover with boiling water and soak for 3–4 minutes, or until softened. Drain and rinse under cold running water. Drain again, then transfer to a serving bowl. Add the cucumber, bean sprouts and chopped coriander to the bowl.
5 Combine the dry-roasted Sichuan peppercorns, sea salt, white pepper, black pepper and chilli flakes in a mortar and pestle or spice grinder and grind to a fine powder. Transfer to a bowl with the plain and rice flours and combine. Drain the squid and pat dry with paper towels.
6 Fill a wok one-third full of oil and heat to 180°C (350°F), or until a cube of bread dropped in the oil browns in 15 seconds. Dip the squid pieces in the egg white, then coat well in the seasoned flour. Deep-fry in batches of five or six

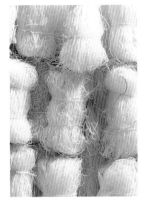

for about 1 minute each batch, or until lightly golden and cooked through—do not overcrowd the wok. Drain on crumpled paper towels and sprinkle with a little salt to soak up the oil.

7 Add the dressing and shrimp mixture to the bowl with the noodles and gently toss together. Place the squid on top of the noodles, garnish with coriander leaves, then serve immediately.

CRISPY NOODLES
(Mee grob)

Preparation time: 30 minutes + soaking
Total cooking time: 15 minutes
Serves 4-6

★ ★

4 dried shiitake mushrooms

oil, for deep-frying

100 g (3 1/2 oz) dried rice vermicelli

100 g (3 1/2 oz) fried tofu puffs, julienned

4 cloves garlic, crushed

1 onion, chopped

1 chicken breast fillet, thinly sliced

8 green beans, sliced on the diagonal

6 spring onions (scallions), thinly sliced

8 raw medium prawns (shrimp), peeled and deveined, with tails intact

30 g (1 oz) bean sprouts, tailed

fresh coriander (cilantro) leaves, to garnish

Sauce

1/4 cup (60 ml/2 fl oz) white vinegar

1/4 cup (60 ml/2 fl oz) fish sauce

5 tablespoons sugar

1 tablespoon soy sauce

1 tablespoon sweet chilli sauce

1 Soak the mushrooms in boiling water for 20 minutes. Squeeze dry, discard the stems and thinly slice the caps.

2 Fill a wok one-third full of oil and heat to 180°C (350°F), or until a cube of bread dropped into the oil browns in 15 seconds. Cook the noodles in small batches for 5 seconds, or until puffed and crispy. Drain well on crumpled paper towels.

3 Add the tofu to the wok in batches and deep-fry for 1 minute, or until crisp. Drain. Carefully remove all but 2 tablespoons of oil.

4 Reheat the wok until very hot. Add the garlic and onion, and stir-fry for 1 minute. Add the chicken, mushrooms, beans and half the spring onion. Stir-fry for 2 minutes, or until the chicken has almost cooked through. Add the prawns and stir-fry for a further 2 minutes, or until they just turn pink.

5 Combine all the sauce ingredients in a bowl, then add to the wok. Stir-fry for 2 minutes, or until the chicken and prawns are tender and the sauce is syrupy.

6 Remove from the heat and stir in the noodles, tofu and bean sprouts. Garnish with the coriander (cilantro) and remaining spring onion.

MEE GROB
Mee grob was created by the chef at a restaurant near the royal palace in Bangkok. One day the king returned from a journey and noticed a crowd gathered near the palace. Curious, he enquired why and was informed that the crowds were there to try a new noodle dish called mee grob. The king himself became a big fan of the crispy fried noodle dish. Mee grob is still available from descendants of the creator, but it has spread much further. Throughout Thailand, mee grob is served as a snack or an accompaniment to curry. It is an example of Thailand's fusion cuisine, as it combines traditional Chinese cooking methods with Thai flavours and ingredients.

ABOVE: Crispy noodles

FLAVOURED RICE

INDONESIAN COCONUT RICE
(Nasi lemak)

Wash 1½ cups (300 g/10 oz) medium-grain rice in a sieve until the water runs clear. Set aside for 30 minutes.

Put the rice, 1 cup (250 ml/8 fl oz) water, 1 cup (250 ml/8 fl oz) coconut milk and 1 pandanus leaf, tied in a knot, in a large saucepan. Bring to the boil, cover, reduce the heat to very low and simmer for 12 minutes. Remove from the heat and set aside for 10 minutes. Take out the pandanus leaf. Fluff the rice with a fork and serve garnished with spring onion (scallion), if desired. An excellent accompaniment to both Indonesian and Malaysian dishes. Serves 4.

INDIAN SPICED GHEE RICE

Wash 1½ cups (300 g/10 oz) basmati rice in a sieve until the water runs clear. Set aside for 30 minutes.

Heat 25 g (¾ oz) ghee or clarified butter in a large saucepan. Add 4 bruised cardamom pods, 1 cinnamon stick, 3 dried curry leaves, 1 chopped clove garlic, 2 teaspoons grated fresh ginger and 1 teaspoon cumin seeds and stir-fry until fragrant. Add the rice, stirring to coat well, then pour in 2 cups (500 ml/16 fl oz) water. Bring to the boil, cover, reduce the heat to very low and simmer for 12 minutes. Remove from the heat and set aside for 10 minutes, covered. Remove the lid, stir in 2 tablespoons

sultanas, and an extra teaspoon of ghee, then serve with curries. Serves 4.

SAFFRON RICE

Wash 1½ cups (300 g/10 oz) long-grain rice in a sieve until the water runs clear, then set aside for 30 minutes.

Meanwhile, put ¼ teaspoon saffron threads in a small bowl, cover with 2 tablespoons hot water and stand for 2–3 minutes.

Thinly slice 1 onion. Heat 1 tablespoon olive oil in a large saucepan, add the onion and sauté for 7–8 minutes over medium heat, or until golden brown. Remove the onion from the pan and keep warm.

Add the rice to the saucepan, and stir to coat with the remaining oil. Add 1 cup (250 ml/8 fl oz) chicken stock and 1 cup (250 ml/8 fl oz) water, bring to the boil then add the saffron threads and the soaking water. Simmer for 2–3 minutes before covering with a tight-fitting lid. Reduce the heat to very low and cook for 10 minutes. Remove from the heat and set aside, covered, for 10 minutes, before stirring in the onion. Serve immediately. An excellent accompaniment to curries. Serves 4.

LEMON GRASS AND LIME RICE

Wash 2 cups (400 g/13 oz) long-grain rice in a sieve until the water runs clear, then set aside for 30 minutes.

Put in a saucepan with 1 cup (250 ml/8 fl oz) water, 2 cups (500 ml/ 16 fl oz) coconut cream, 1 bruised lemon grass stem, 2 fresh makrut (kaffir) lime leaves and 1 teaspoon salt. Bring to the boil over high heat, stir well, then reduce the heat to very low. Cover with a tight-fitting lid and cook for 15 minutes. Remove from the heat and leave to stand, covered, for 5 minutes. Lightly stir the rice with a fork to incorporate any coconut cream that has not been absorbed. Remove the lemon grass and lime leaves. Great with stir-fries. Serves 4–6.

GINGER AND SPRING ONION RICE

Wash 1¼ cups (250 g/8 oz) jasmine rice in a sieve until the water runs clear, then set aside for 30 minutes.

Transfer the rice to a large saucepan. Add 1¾ cups (440 ml/14 fl oz) water and bring to the boil. Reduce the heat to very low and cook, covered, for 10 minutes. Remove the pan from the heat and stand, covered, for 10 minutes.

Heat 1 tablespoon vegetable oil in a small saucepan over medium–low heat. When the oil is warm but not smoking, remove the pan from the heat and add 2 teaspoons grated fresh ginger and 3 finely chopped spring onions (scallions). Season with ¼ teaspoon salt, stirring quickly to combine, taking care not to brown. Stir this mixture through the rice and add 1 tablespoon soy sauce. Great with stir-fries. Serves 4.

FROM LEFT: Indonesian coconut rice; Indian spiced ghee rice; Saffron rice; Lemon grass and lime rice; Ginger and spring onion rice

PASTA & GNOCCHI

MAKING PASTA

FRESH OR DRIED?

Fresh pasta, unlike dried, has eggs added to the dough and a softer wheat flour is used rather than the hard durum wheat semolina that gives dried pasta its *al dente* texture. Fresh pasta is ideal for lasagne sheets, pasta lengths and filled pastas.

BEFORE YOU START

Making pasta isn't difficult but there are a few tips that will help. A well-ventilated kitchen and good-quality ingredients brought to room temperature are a good starting point. A large work area with a hard, even surface, ideally wood or marble, dusted with flour, makes the process easier. Kneading is critical as it

works the flour's gluten content, resulting in a firm yet tender dough. This is especially important if you are rolling and cutting the dough by hand, as the more elastic the dough, the easier it will be to roll. The dough should be kneaded until pliable, gradually adding small amounts of flour if it is too soft or sticky. Rolling is equally important as it makes the pasta more porous, enabling it to absorb a maximum amount of sauce, while the thinness ensures it is tender after cooking.

BASIC PLAIN PASTA DOUGH

To make enough to serve six as a first course or four as a main course, you will need 300 g (10 oz) of plain (all-purpose)

flour, 3 large (60 g/2 oz) eggs, 30 ml (1 fl oz) of olive oil and a pinch of salt.

1 Mound the flour on a work surface or in a large bowl and make a well in the centre. Break the eggs into the well and add the oil and a large pinch of salt. Using a fork, begin to whisk the eggs and oil together, incorporating a little of the flour as you go. Gradually blend the flour with the eggs, working from the centre out.

2 Knead the dough on a lightly floured surface for 6 minutes, or until you have a soft, smooth elastic dough which is dry to touch. If it is sticky, knead in a little flour. Cover with plastic wrap and allow to rest for 30 minutes.

ROLLING BY HAND

1 Divide the dough into four even portions and cover with a cloth. Lightly flour a large work surface and using a floured long rolling pin, roll out one portion from the centre to the edge. Continue, always rolling from in front of you outwards. Rotate the dough often.

2 When a well-shaped circle has formed, fold the dough in half and roll it out again. Continue this process seven or eight times to make a smooth circle of pasta about 5 mm (¼ inch) thick. Roll this sheet quickly and smoothly to a thickness of 2.5 mm (⅛ inch).

3 As each sheet is done, transfer it to a dry tea towel. Keep the pasta sheets covered if making filled pasta, or leave uncovered to dry slightly if cutting the pasta sheets into lengths or shapes.

4 To make lasagne sheets, cut the pasta into the required sizes.

5 For cutting lengths such as fettucine, roll each pasta sheet up like a swiss roll, then cut into uniform lengths with a long, sharp knife. Allow the lengths to dry in a single layer on a tea towel for a maximum of 10 minutes or hang on broom handles between two chairs.

6 To make farfalle (bow-ties), roll pasta sheets to a thickness of 2.5 mm (⅛ inch). Using a zigzag pastry wheel against a ruler, cut 2.5 x 5.5 cm (1 x 2¼ inch) rectangles and pinch the centres together to form bow-tie shapes. Lay them on a tea towel to dry for 10–12 minutes.

USING A MACHINE

1 Divide the pasta dough into four even portions. Keep the unworked portions covered so they don't dry out. Take one portion and flatten it with a rolling pin, forming rectangles roughly the same width as the machine. Lightly dust the dough and the pasta machine rollers with flour.

2 With the machine rollers set to the widest setting, crank the dough through the machine two or three times. Fold the dough into thirds, turn it by 90 degrees and feed it through again, repeating this process eight to ten times, until the pasta dough is smooth and elastic and has a velvety appearance.

3 Reduce the roller width by one setting and pass the dough through. Repeat this process with the roller setting one notch closer each time until the dough is rolled to the required thickness. If using the cutting attachment on the machine, pass the lengths through immediately after rolling, then allow them to dry for 10 minutes. Cover them if they are to be filled.

20 black mussels

200 g (6¹/₂ oz) raw medium prawns (shrimp)

¹/₄ cup (60 ml/2 fl oz) white wine

¹/₄ cup (60 ml/2 fl oz) fish stock

I clove garlic, crushed

375 g (12 oz) spaghetti

30 g (I oz) butter

125 g (4 oz) squid rings

125 g (4 oz) skinless fish fillets
  (eg. blue-eye, groper, striped marlin), cubed

¹/₂ cup (10 g/¹/₄ oz) fresh parsley, chopped

200 g (6¹/₂ oz) can clams (vongole), drained

1 For the tomato sauce, heat the olive oil in a pan, add the onion and carrot and stir over medium heat for 10 minutes, or until the vegetables are lightly browned. Add the garlic, tomato, white wine and sugar, bring to the boil, reduce the heat and gently simmer for 30 minutes, stirring occasionally.

2 Scrub the mussels with a stiff brush and pull out the hairy beards. Discard any broken mussels, or open ones that don't close when tapped on the bench. Rinse well.

3 Peel the prawns and gently pull out the dark vein from each prawn back, starting at the head end.

4 Heat the wine together with the stock and garlic in a large pan. Add the unopened mussels. Cover the pan and shake it over high heat for 4–5 minutes. After 3 minutes, start removing any opened mussels and set them aside. After 5 minutes, discard any unopened mussels and reserve the liquid.

5 Cook the spaghetti in a large pan of rapidly boiling salted water until *al dente*. Drain and keep warm.

6 Meanwhile, melt the butter in a frying pan, add the squid rings, fish and prawns in batches and stir-fry for 2 minutes, or until just cooked through. Remove from the heat and add the reserved liquid, mussels, squid, fish, prawns, parsley and clams to the tomato sauce and stir gently until heated through. Gently combine the sauce with the pasta and serve at once.

SPAGHETTI MARINARA

Preparation time: 40 minutes
Total cooking time: 50 minutes
Serves 6

★★

Tomato sauce

2 tablespoons olive oil

I onion, finely chopped

I carrot, sliced

2 cloves garlic, crushed

425 g (14 oz) can crushed tomatoes

¹/₂ cup (125 ml/4 fl oz) white wine

I teaspoon sugar

ABOVE: Spaghetti marinara

SPAGHETTI CARBONARA

Preparation time: 10 minutes
Total cooking time: 20 minutes
Serves 6

☆

500 g (1 lb) spaghetti
8 bacon rashers, cut into thin strips
4 eggs
1/2 cup (50 g/1 3/4 oz) freshly grated Parmesan
1 1/4 cups (315 ml/10 fl oz) cream

1 Cook the spaghetti in a large pan of rapidly boiling salted water until *al dente*. Drain and return to the pan.
2 Meanwhile, cook the bacon in a heavy-based pan over medium heat until crisp. Remove and drain on paper towels.
3 Beat the eggs, Parmesan and cream in a bowl until well combined. Add the bacon and pour the sauce over the warm pasta. Toss gently until pasta is well coated.
4 Return the pan to very low heat and cook for 1/2–1 minute, or until slightly thickened.

PASTA POMODORO

Cook 500 g (1 lb) pasta in a large pan of rapidly salted water until *al dente*. Drain and return to the pan. Heat 1 1/2 tablespoons olive oil in a large frying pan. Add 1 very finely chopped onion and cook over medium heat until softened. Stir in two 400 g (13 oz) cans of chopped tomatoes and simmer for 5 minutes, or until the sauce has reduced and thickened. Season. Stir in 3 tablespoons fresh basil leaves and cook for another minute. Pour over the pasta and gently toss. Serves 4.

CARBONARA

There is some mystery surrounding the invention and naming of this simple sauce. Some say that Carbonara is relatively new, having appeared in Rome during the Second World War, when American GIs combined their rations of bacon and eggs with the local spaghetti. It is likely that the dish has been around a lot longer than that. Was it simply that it was a quick and easy meal whipped up by the coal vendors, *carbonari*, over street charcoal burners, or was it so named because the flecks of black pepper spotting the creamy sauce looked like coal dust? However it came about, the concept of using egg to thicken and flavour a simple bacon and cream sauce was truly inventive.

ABOVE: Spaghetti carbonara

337

LINGUINE PESTO

Preparation time: 15 minutes
Total cooking time: 15 minutes
Serves 4–6

2 cups (100 g/3 1/2 oz) fresh basil leaves
2 cloves garlic, crushed
1/4 cup (40 g/1 1/4 oz) pine nuts, toasted
3/4 cup (185 ml/6 fl oz) olive oil
1/2 cup (50 g/1 3/4 oz) grated Parmesan
500 g (1 lb) linguine
shaved or grated Parmesan, extra, to serve

ORECCHIETTE WITH BROCCOLI

Preparation time: 5 minutes
Total cooking time: 15 minutes
Serves 6

750 g (1 1/2 lb) broccoli, cut into florets
450 g (14 oz) orecchiette
1/4 cup (60 ml/2 fl oz) extra virgin olive oil
8 anchovy fillets
1/2 teaspoon dried chilli flakes
1/3 cup (30 g/1 oz) grated Pecorino or Parmesan

SUN-DRIED TOMATO PESTO

To make sun-dried tomato pesto, put a 200 g (6 1/2 oz) jar sun-dried tomatoes in oil, 4 tablespoons fresh basil leaves, 4 tablespoons fresh flat-leaf (Italian) parsley leaves, 2 chopped cloves garlic, 2 teaspoons rinsed and drained capers, 1 anchovy fillet and 4 tablespoons lightly toasted pine nuts in a food processor or blender. Process until finely minced. With the motor running, pour in 2 tablespoons red wine vinegar and 1/2 cup (125 ml/4 fl oz) extra virgin olive oil. When blended, add 2 tablespoons freshly grated Parmesan and freshly ground black pepper. Makes about 1 1/4 cups (310 g/10 oz).

1 Finely chop the basil, garlic and pine nuts together in a food processor. With the motor running, add the oil in a steady stream until mixed to a smooth paste. Transfer to a bowl, stir in the Parmesan and season to taste.
2 Cook the pasta in a large saucepan of rapidly boiling salted water until *al dente*. Drain and return to the pan. Toss enough of the pesto through the pasta to coat it well. Serve sprinkled with Parmesan.
NOTE: Refrigerate any leftover pesto in an airtight jar for up to a week. Cover the surface with a layer of oil. Freeze for up to a month.

1 Blanch the broccoli in a large saucepan of boiling salted water for 5 minutes, or until just tender. Remove with a slotted spoon, drain well and return the water to the boil. Cook the pasta in the boiling water until *al dente*, then drain well and return to the pan.
2 Meanwhile, heat the oil in a heavy-based frying pan and cook the anchovies over very low heat for 1 minute. Add the chilli flakes and broccoli. Increase the heat to medium and cook, stirring, for 5 minutes, or until the broccoli is well-coated and beginning to break apart. Season. Add to the pasta, add the cheese and toss.

RIGHT: Linguine pesto

338

PENNE ALLA NAPOLITANA

Preparation time: 20 minutes
Total cooking time: 25 minutes
Serves 4–6

2 tablespoons olive oil
1 onion, finely chopped
2–3 cloves garlic, finely chopped
1 small carrot, finely diced
1 celery stick, finely diced
2 x 400 g (13 oz) cans peeled, chopped
    tomatoes, or 1 kg (2 lb) ripe tomatoes,
    peeled and chopped
1 tablespoon tomato paste (tomato purée)
1/4 cup (15 g/1/2 oz) shredded fresh basil leaves
500 g (1 lb) penne
Parmesan, to serve

1 Heat the oil in a large frying pan, add the onion and garlic and cook for 2 minutes, or until golden. Add the carrot and celery and cook for another 2 minutes.
2 Add the tomato and tomato paste. Simmer for 20 minutes, or until the sauce thickens, stirring occasionally. Stir in the shredded basil and season to taste with salt and freshly ground black pepper.
3 While the sauce is cooking, cook the pasta in a large saucepan of rapidly boiling salted water until *al dente*. Drain well and return to the pan. Add the sauce to the pasta and mix well. This dish is delicious served with freshly grated or shaved Parmesan.

BUCATINI AMATRICIANA

Place 1 finely chopped onion in a heavy-based frying pan with 2 tablespoons olive oil and cook over medium heat until golden. Add 150 g (5 oz) chopped pancetta to the pan and stir for 1 minute. Add a 400 g (13 oz) can crushed tomatoes, salt and pepper and 1/2 teaspoon chilli flakes. Simmer for 20–25 minutes. Meanwhile, cook 450 g (14 oz) bucatini in a large pan of boiling water until *al dente*. Drain and add to the sauce with 3 tablespoons of freshly grated Parmesan. Toss well and serve immediately. Serves 4.

TOMATOES
Unless tomatoes have been allowed to ripen on the vine, they are, more often than not, tasteless and watery and impart very little to cooking apart from acid. Outside the summer months, most tomatoes available to the consumer are very poor in quality. For this reason it is important to consider the season when planning a meal which calls for fresh tomatoes. If you are unable to get good-quality fresh tomatoes, it is better to use canned tomatoes, preferably whole peeled Roma (plum) tomatoes from Italy.

*ABOVE: Penne
alla Napolitana*

PUTTANESCA

The name puttanesca is a derivation of the word puttana which in Italian means whore. There are many stories surrounding this dish but according to one story, the name comes from the fact that the intense flavours of the sauce were like a siren call to the men who visited such 'ladies of pleasure'. Another story claims that the dish got its name because these wayward women were forbidden to shop for groceries during regular hours like the gentile ladies and were left to rely upon the pantry staples such as olives, capers and anchovies.

ABOVE: Spaghetti puttanesca

SPAGHETTI PUTTANESCA

Preparation time: 15 minutes
Total cooking time: 20 minutes
Serves 6

★

1/3 cup (80 ml/2³/4 fl oz) olive oil
2 onions, finely chopped
3 cloves garlic, finely chopped
1/2 teaspoon chilli flakes
6 large ripe tomatoes, diced
4 tablespoons capers, rinsed
8 anchovies in oil, drained, chopped
150 g (5 oz) Kalamata olives
3 tablespoons chopped fresh flat-leaf (Italian) parsley
375 g (12 oz) spaghetti

1 Heat the olive oil in a saucepan, add the onion and cook over medium heat for 5 minutes. Add the garlic and chilli flakes to the saucepan and cook for 30 seconds. Add the tomato, capers and anchovies. Simmer over low heat for 10–15 minutes, or until the sauce is thick and pulpy. Stir the olives and parsley through the sauce.

2 While the sauce is cooking, cook the spaghetti in a large saucepan of rapidly boiling salted water until *al dente*. Drain and return to the pan.

3 Add the sauce to the pasta and stir it through. Season with salt and freshly ground black pepper, to taste, and serve immediately.

SPAGHETTINI WITH GARLIC AND CHILLI

Cook 500 g (1 lb) spaghettini in a large saucepan of rapidly boiling salted water until *al dente*. Drain and return to the pan. Meanwhile, heat 1/2 cup (125 ml/4 fl oz) of extra virgin olive oil in a large frying pan. Add 2–3 finely chopped cloves of garlic and 1–2 seeded, finely chopped, fresh red chillies, and cook over very low heat for 2–3 minutes, or until the garlic is golden. Take care not to burn the garlic or chillies as this will make the sauce bitter. Toss 3 tablespoons chopped fresh flat-leaf (Italian) parsley and the warmed oil, garlic and chilli mixture through the pasta. Season with salt and freshly ground black pepper. Serve with grated Parmesan. Serves 4–6.

SPAGHETTI WITH SARDINES, FENNEL AND TOMATO

Preparation time: 30 minutes
Total cooking time: 45 minutes
Serves 4–6

3 Roma (plum) tomatoes, peeled, seeded and chopped
¹/₃ cup (80 ml/2³/₄ fl oz) olive oil
3 cloves garlic, crushed
1 cup (80 g/2³/₄ oz) fresh white breadcrumbs
1 red onion, thinly sliced
1 fennel bulb, quartered and thinly sliced
¹/₄ cup (40 g/1¹/₄ oz) raisins
¹/₄ cup (40 g/1¹/₄ oz) pine nuts, toasted
4 anchovy fillets, chopped
¹/₂ cup (125 ml/4 fl oz) white wine
1 tablespoon tomato paste (tomato purée)
4 tablespoons finely chopped fresh
    flat-leaf (Italian) parsley
350 g (11 oz) butterflied sardine fillets
500 g (1 lb) spaghetti

1 Score a cross in the base of each tomato. Place the tomatoes in a bowl of boiling water for 10 seconds, then plunge into cold water and peel the skin away from the cross. Cut the tomatoes in half and scoop out the seeds with a teaspoon. Roughly chop the tomato flesh.

2 Heat 1 tablespoon of the oil in a large frying pan over medium heat. Add 1 clove of the garlic and the breadcrumbs and stir for about 5 minutes, until golden and crisp. Transfer to a plate.

3 Heat the remaining oil in the same pan and cook the onion, fennel and remaining garlic for 8 minutes, or until soft. Add the tomato, raisins, pine nuts and anchovies and cook for another 3 minutes. Add the wine, tomato paste and ¹/₂ cup (125 ml/4 fl oz) water. Simmer for 10 minutes, or until the mixture thickens slightly. Stir in the parsley and set aside.

4 Pat the sardines dry with paper towels. Cook the sardines in batches in a lightly greased frying pan over medium heat for 1 minute, or until cooked through. Take care not to overcook or they will break up. Set aside.

5 Cook the pasta in a large saucepan of rapidly boiling salted water until *al dente*. Drain and return to the pan.

6 Stir the sauce through the pasta until the pasta is well coated and the sauce evenly distributed. Add the sardines and half the breadcrumbs and toss gently. Sprinkle the remaining breadcrumbs over the top and serve immediately.

SARDINES
These small fish have an oily, soft flesh with a fine texture. The backbone is easy to remove and the small remaining bones are edible. Sardines are sold whole, butterflied and filleted. They have a strong distinctive flavour and are suitable for baking, grilling, pan-frying and barbecuing.

LEFT: Spaghetti with sardines, fennel and tomato

HERB-FILLED RAVIOLI
WITH SAGE BUTTER

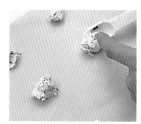

Place heaped teaspoons of filling at intervals along the pasta sheets.

Use a pastry wheel or sharp knife to cut the ravioli.

HERB-FILLED RAVIOLI WITH SAGE BUTTER

Preparation time: 1 hour
+ 30 minutes standing
Total cooking time: 10 minutes
Serves 4

★ ★ ★

Pasta
300 g (10 oz) plain (all-purpose) flour
3 eggs, beaten
3 tablespoons oil

1 cup (250 g/8 oz) ricotta
2 tablespoons grated Parmesan, plus extra, shaved, to garnish
2 teaspoons chopped fresh chives
1 tablespoon chopped flat-leaf (Italian) parsley
2 teaspoons chopped fresh basil
1 teaspoon chopped fresh thyme

Sage butter
200 g (6¹/₂ oz) butter
12 fresh sage leaves

1 Sift the flour into a bowl and make a well in the centre. Gradually mix in the eggs and oil.

Turn out onto a lightly floured surface and knead for 6 minutes, or until smooth. Cover with plastic wrap and leave for 30 minutes.
2 Mix the ricotta, Parmesan and herbs. Season.
3 Follow the pasta rolling instructions on page 335 to make 4 sheets of pasta, two slightly larger than the others. Cover with a tea towel.
4 Spread 1 of the smaller sheets out on a work surface and place heaped teaspoons of filling at 5 cm (2 inch) intervals. Brush a little water between the filling along the cutting lines. Place a larger sheet on top and firmly press the sheets together along the cutting lines. Cut the ravioli with a pastry wheel or knife and transfer to a lightly floured baking tray. Repeat with the remaining dough and filling.
5 For the sage butter, melt the butter over low heat in a small heavy-based saucepan, without stirring or shaking. Carefully pour the clear butter into another container and discard the remaining white sediment. Return the clarified butter to a clean pan and heat gently over medium heat. Add the sage leaves and cook until crisp but not brown. Remove and drain on paper towels. Reserve the warm butter.
6 Cook the ravioli in batches in a large pan of salted simmering water for 5–6 minutes, or until tender. Top with warm sage butter and leaves and garnish with shaved Parmesan.
NOTE: Don't cook the ravioli in rapidly boiling water or the squares will split and lose the filling.

RIGHT: Herb-filled ravioli with sage butter

BASIL
Perhaps one of the most useful tips for cooking with basil is the fact that the less it cooks the better. So when adding basil to a pasta sauce it is best to add it at the last moment when it is being tossed with the pasta. Occasionally however, one might cook basil in a soup or stew in order that the flavour marries with the other ingredients but if in doubt, add it at the last moment. Use only the freshest basil, never blackened or drooping leaves. Unless the recipe calls for julienned basil, it is preferable to tear the basil leaves with your hands rather than cut them with a knife which tends to bruise the basil and cause it to go brown.

BUCATINI ALLA NORMA

Preparation time: 15 minutes
Total cooking time: 40 minutes
Serves 4–6

3/4 cup (185 ml/6 fl oz) olive oil
1 brown onion, finely chopped
2 cloves garlic, crushed
2 x 400 g (13 oz) cans crushed good-quality
   tomatoes
1 large eggplant (aubergine), about 500 g (1 lb)
1/2 cup (30 g/1 oz) fresh basil leaves, torn
400 g (13 oz) bucatini
1/2 cup (60 g/2 oz) ricotta salata (see Note),
   crumbled
1/2 cup (50 g/1 3/4 oz) grated Pecorino or
   Parmesan
1 tablespoon extra virgin olive oil

1 Heat 2 tablespoons of the oil in a heavy-based frying pan and cook the onion over moderate heat for 5 minutes, or until softened. Add the garlic to the pan and cook for another 30 seconds. Add the tomato and salt and pepper, to taste, and reduce the heat. Cook for 20–25 minutes, or until the sauce has thickened and reduced.

2 While the sauce is cooking, cut the eggplant lengthways into 5 mm (1/4 inch) thick slices. Heat the remaining olive oil in a large heavy-based frying pan. When the oil is hot but not smoking, add the eggplant slices a few at a time and cook for 3–5 minutes, or until lightly browned on both sides. Remove from the pan and drain well on crumpled paper towels.

3 Cut each slice of eggplant into 3 pieces and add to the tomato sauce with the torn basil. Stir and keep warm over very low heat.

4 Cook the bucatini in a large saucepan of rapidly boiling, salted water until *al dente*. Drain well and add to the tomato sauce with half each of the ricotta and pecorino. Toss well and serve immediately sprinkled with the remaining cheeses. Drizzle with the extra virgin olive oil.
NOTE: Ricotta salata is a lightly salted, pressed ricotta. If unavailable, use a mild feta.

ABOVE: Bucatini alla Norma

SPAGHETTI BOLOGNESE

Preparation time: 20 minutes
Total cooking time: 1 hour 40 minutes
Serves 4–6

★

2 tablespoons olive oil

2 cloves garlic, crushed

1 large onion, chopped

1 carrot, chopped

1 celery stick, chopped

500 g (1 lb) minced (ground) beef

2 cups (500 ml/16 fl oz) beef stock

1 1/2 cups (375 ml/12 fl oz) red wine

2 x 425 g (14 oz) cans crushed tomatoes

1 teaspoon sugar

1/4 cup (7 g/1/4 oz) fresh parsley, chopped

500 g (1 lb) spaghetti

freshly grated Parmesan, to serve

ABOVE: Spaghetti bolognese

1 Heat the olive oil in a large deep pan. Add the garlic, onion, carrot and celery and stir for 5 minutes over low heat until the vegetables are golden.

2 Increase the heat, add the beef and brown well, stirring and breaking up any lumps with a fork as it cooks. Add the stock, wine, tomato, sugar and parsley.

3 Bring the mixture to the boil, reduce the heat and simmer for 1 1/2 hours, stirring occasionally. Season to taste.

4 While the sauce is cooking and shortly before serving, cook the pasta in a large pan of rapidly boiling salted water until *al dente*. Drain and then divide among serving bowls. Serve the sauce over the top of the pasta and sprinkle with the freshly grated Parmesan.

TAGLIATELLE WITH VEAL, WINE AND CREAM

Preparation time: 15 minutes
Total cooking time: 20 minutes
Serves 4

500 g (1 lb) veal scaloppine or escalopes,
   cut into thin strips
plain (all-purpose) flour, seasoned
60 g (2 oz) butter
1 onion, sliced
1/2 cup (125 ml/4 fl oz) dry white wine
3–4 tablespoons beef stock or chicken stock
2/3 cup (170 ml/51/2 fl oz) cream
600 g (11/4 lb) fresh plain or spinach tagliatelle
   (or a mixture of both)
freshly grated Parmesan

1 Coat the veal strips with the seasoned flour. Melt the butter in a pan. Add the veal strips and fry quickly until browned. Remove with a slotted spoon and set aside.
2 Add the onion slices to the pan and stir until soft and golden, about 8–10 minutes. Pour in the wine and cook rapidly to reduce the liquid. Add the stock and cream and season with salt and pepper, to taste. Reduce the sauce again, and add the veal towards the end.
3 Meanwhile, cook the tagliatelle in a large pan of rapidly boiling salted water until *al dente*. Drain and transfer to a warm serving dish.
4 Stir 1 tablespoon of Parmesan through the sauce. Pour the sauce over the pasta. Serve with a sprinkle of Parmesan. Some chopped herbs can be used as an extra garnish and will add flavour.
NOTE: This dish is lovely served with a mixed salad. If you prefer a lighter sauce, you can omit the cream. The flavour is just as delicious.

PASTA ALFREDO

Preparation time: 10 minutes
Total cooking time: 15 minutes
Serves 4–6

500 g (1 lb) pasta
90 g (3 oz) butter
11/2 cups (150 g/5 oz) freshly grated Parmesan
11/4 cups (315 ml/10 fl oz) cream
3 tablespoons chopped fresh parsley

1 Cook the pasta in a large pan of rapidly boiling salted water until *al dente*. Drain and return to the pan.
2 While the pasta is cooking, melt the butter in a pan over low heat. Add the Parmesan and cream and bring to the boil, stirring constantly. Reduce the heat and simmer, stirring, until the sauce has thickened slightly. Add the chopped fresh parsley, salt and pepper, to taste, and stir until well combined.
3 Add the sauce to the pasta and toss well so the sauce coats the pasta. This dish can be garnished with chopped herbs or sprigs of fresh herbs such as thyme.
NOTE: Traditionally, plain fettucine is used with this sauce, but you can use any style of pasta. It is a very simple sauce to make and should be prepared just before the pasta is cooked.

WHITE WINE
White wine contributes a delicate body to dishes. The taste should never be discernible and only a small amount should be used, which must then be completely cooked off to dispel the alcohol. The wine should be the same quality as a good drinking wine. Non-fruity dry white wines are used in savoury cooking, particularly with seafood, and for sweet dishes fortified wines or liqueurs are chosen, but not sweet white wine.

ABOVE: Tagliatelle with veal, wine and cream

345

CINNAMON

The best quality cinnamon comes from the Sri Lankan cinnamon tree, *cinnamomum zeylanicum*, which has the most fragrant scent and a delicate and fresh flavour. It is made from the dried inner bark of young shoots where, once exposed, thin layers curl up into a cylinder as they dry. These are slipped together in rolls of ten, then cut into quills of equal length. It is more costly than Chinese cinnamon, *cassia,* where older, outer bark is collected for drying. Cinnamon is used whole, broken into pieces or ground to flavour sweet dishes and baked foods, and it is an ingredient of curry powder and garam masala.

ABOVE: Macaroni cheese

MACARONI CHEESE

Preparation time: 20 minutes
Total cooking time: 35 minutes
Serves 4

☆

2 cups (500 ml/16 fl oz) milk

1 cup (250 ml/8 fl oz) cream

1 bay leaf

1 whole clove

1/2 cinnamon stick

60 g (2 oz) butter

2 tablespoons plain (all-purpose) flour

2 cups (250 g/8 oz) freshly grated
   Cheddar cheese

1/2 cup (50 g/13/4 oz) freshly grated Parmesan

375 g (12 oz) elbow macaroni

1 cup (80 g/23/4 oz) fresh breadcrumbs

2 rashers rindless bacon, chopped and fried
   until crisp

1 Preheat the oven to moderate 180°C (350°F/Gas 4). Pour the milk and cream into a medium pan with the bay leaf, clove and cinnamon stick. Bring to the boil, then remove from the heat and set aside for 10 minutes. Strain into a jug; remove and discard the flavourings.

2 Melt the butter in a medium pan over low heat. Add the flour and stir for 1 minute. Remove from the heat and gradually add the milk and cream mixture, stirring until smooth. Return to the heat and stir constantly until the sauce boils and thickens. Simmer for 2 minutes, then remove from the heat and add half the Cheddar cheese, half the Parmesan and salt and pepper, to taste. Set aside.

3 Cook the macaroni in a large pan of rapidly boiling salted water until *al dente*. Drain and return to the pan. Add the sauce and mix well. Spoon into a deep casserole dish. Sprinkle with combined breadcrumbs, bacon and remaining cheeses. Bake for 15–20 minutes, or until golden. Serve.

VARIATION: You can add chopped cooked chicken to the white sauce before mixing with the pasta.

CONCHIGLIE WITH CHICKEN AND RICOTTA

Preparation time: 15 minutes
Total cooking time: 1 hour 10 minutes
Serves 4

500 g (1 lb) conchiglie (shell pasta)
2 tablespoons olive oil
1 onion, chopped
1 clove garlic, crushed
60 g (2 oz) prosciutto, sliced
125 g (4 oz) mushrooms, chopped
250 g (8 oz) minced (ground) chicken
2 tablespoons tomato paste (tomato purée)
425 g (14 oz) can crushed tomatoes
1/2 cup (125 ml/4 fl oz) dry white wine
1 teaspoon dried oregano
250 g (8 oz) ricotta cheese
1 cup (150 g/5 oz) grated mozzarella cheese
1 teaspoon snipped fresh chives
1 tablespoon chopped fresh parsley
3 tablespoons freshly grated Parmesan

1 Cook the conchiglie in a large pan of rapidly boiling salted water until *al dente*. Drain well.
2 Heat the oil in a large frying pan. Add the onion and garlic and stir over low heat until the onion is tender. Add the prosciutto and stir for 1 minute. Add the mushrooms and cook for 2 minutes. Add the chicken and brown well, breaking up with a fork as it cooks.
3 Stir in the tomato paste, tomato, wine, oregano and salt and pepper, to taste. Bring to the boil, reduce the heat and simmer for 20 minutes.
4 Preheat the oven to moderate 180°C (350°F/Gas 4). Combine the ricotta, mozzarella, chives, parsley and half the Parmesan. Spoon a little of the mixture into each shell. Spoon some of the chicken sauce into the base of a casserole dish. Arrange the conchiglie on top. Spoon the remaining sauce over the top. Sprinkle with the remaining Parmesan. Bake for 25–30 minutes, or until golden.
NOTE: Conchiglie (shell pasta) vary in size— medium or large shells are best for this dish.

PRIMAVERA SAUCE

Cook 1 cup (155 g/5 oz) frozen broad (fava) beans in a pan of boiling water for 2 minutes. Plunge into iced water, then drain. Remove and discard the skins from the broad beans. Trim the stalks from 200 g (6½ oz) sugar snap peas and break the woody ends from 155 g (5 oz) fresh asparagus spears. Cut the asparagus into short lengths. Melt 30 g (1 oz) butter in a frying pan. Add the vegetables, 1 cup (250 ml/8 fl oz) cream and 60 g (2 oz) freshly grated Parmesan. Simmer gently over medium heat for 3 minutes, or until the vegetables are just tender. Season. Toss with 500 g (1 lb) cooked pasta. Serves 4.

ABOVE: Conchiglie with chicken and ricotta

347

*ABOVE: Baked
spaghetti frittata*

BAKED SPAGHETTI FRITTATA

Preparation time: 30 minutes
Total cooking time: 35 minutes
Serves 4

★★

30 g (1 oz) butter
125 g (4 oz) mushrooms, sliced
1 green pepper (capsicum), seeded
  and chopped
125 g (4 oz) ham, sliced
1/2 cup (80 g/2³/4 oz) frozen peas
6 eggs
1 cup (250 ml/8 fl oz) cream or milk
100 g (3¹/2 oz) spaghetti, cooked and chopped
2 tablespoons chopped fresh parsley
1/4 cup (25 g/³/4 oz) freshly grated Parmesan

1 Preheat the oven to moderate 180°C (350°F/Gas 4). Lightly brush a 23 cm (9 inch) flan dish with oil or melted butter.
2 Melt the butter in a frying pan, add the mushrooms and cook over low heat for 2–3 minutes. Add the pepper and cook for 1 minute. Stir in the ham and peas. Remove the pan from the heat and allow the mixture to cool slightly.
3 In a small bowl, whisk the eggs, cream and salt and pepper, to taste. Stir in the spaghetti, parsley and mushroom mixture and pour into the prepared dish. Sprinkle with Parmesan and bake for 25–30 minutes.
NOTE: Serve with chargrilled vegetables and leafy salad greens.

BAKED CANNELLONI MILANESE

Preparation time: 40 minutes
Total cooking time: 1 hour 50 minutes
Serves 4

500 g (1 lb) minced (ground) pork and veal
1/2 cup (50 g/1 3/4 oz) dry breadcrumbs
1 cup (100 g/3 1/2 oz) freshly grated Parmesan
2 eggs, beaten
1 teaspoon dried oregano
12–15 cannelloni tubes
375 g (12 oz) fresh ricotta cheese
1/2 cup (60 g/2 oz) freshly grated Cheddar
    cheese

Tomato sauce

425 ml (14 fl oz) can tomato purée (passata)
425 g (14 oz) can crushed tomatoes
2 cloves garlic, crushed
3 tablespoons chopped fresh basil

1 Preheat the oven to moderate 180°C
(350°F/Gas 4). Lightly brush a rectangular
casserole dish with melted butter or oil.
2 In a bowl, combine the pork and veal,
breadcrumbs, half the Parmesan, egg, oregano
and salt and pepper, to taste. Use a teaspoon to
stuff the cannelloni tubes with the meat mixture.
Set aside.
3 To make the tomato sauce, bring the tomato
purée, tomato and garlic to the boil in a
medium pan. Reduce the heat and simmer
for 15 minutes. Add the basil and pepper, to
taste, and stir well.
4 Spoon half the tomato sauce over the base of
the prepared dish. Arrange the stuffed cannelloni
tubes on top. Cover with the remaining sauce.
Spread with ricotta cheese. Sprinkle with the
combined remaining Parmesan and Cheddar
cheeses. Bake, covered with foil, for 1 hour.
Uncover and bake for another 15 minutes, or
until golden. Cut into squares for serving.

NAPOLITANA

Heat 2 tablespoons olive oil in a pan. Add
1 finely chopped onion, carrot and celery
stick. Cover and cook for 10 minutes over
low heat, stirring occasionally. Add 500 g
(1 lb) chopped ripe tomatoes, 2 tablespoons
chopped fresh parsley, 2 teaspoons sugar
and 1/2 cup (125 ml/4 fl oz) water. Bring to
the boil, reduce the heat to low, cover and
simmer for 45 minutes, stirring occasionally.
Season. If necessary, add more water until
the required consistency is reached. About
15 minutes before serving, add 500 g (1 lb)
pasta to a large pan of rapidly boiling salted
water and cook until *al dente*. Drain and
return to the pan. Pour over the sauce, then
serve. Serves 4.

*ABOVE: Baked
cannelloni Milanese*

349

1 egg, beaten
1 tablespoon chopped fresh parsley
1 clove garlic, crushed
1/4 teaspoon mixed spice

Tomato sauce

2 tablespoons olive oil
1 onion, finely chopped
2 cloves garlic, crushed
2 x 425 g (14 oz) cans tomatoes, crushed
3 tablespoons chopped fresh basil
1/2 teaspoon mixed dried herbs
herb sprigs, optional

1 To make the pasta, sift the flour and a pinch of salt into a large bowl and make a well in the centre. Whisk together the eggs, oil and 1 tablespoon of water, add gradually to the flour and combine until the mixture forms a ball. Knead on a floured surface for 5 minutes, or until smooth and elastic. Transfer to an oiled bowl, cover with plastic wrap and set aside for 30 minutes.

2 To make the filling, mix all the filling ingredients with salt and pepper, to taste, in a food processor until finely chopped.

3 To make the tomato sauce, heat the oil in a pan, add the onion and garlic and stir over low heat until the onion is tender. Increase the heat, add the tomato, basil, herbs and salt and pepper, to taste. Bring to the boil, reduce the heat and simmer for 15 minutes. Remove from the heat.

4 Roll out half the pasta dough until 1 mm (1/25 inch) thick. Cut with a knife or fluted pastry wheel into 10 cm (4 inch) wide strips. Place teaspoons of filling at 5 cm (2 inch) intervals down one side of each strip. Whisk the extra egg yolk with 3 tablespoons of water and brush along one side of the dough and between the filling. Fold the dough over the filling to meet the other side. Repeat with remaining filling and dough. Press the edges of the dough together firmly to seal. Cut between the mounds with a knife or a fluted pastry wheel. Cook, in batches, in a large pan of rapidly boiling salted water for 10 minutes. Reheat the sauce in a large pan. Add the ravioli and stir until heated through. Garnish and serve.

RAVIOLI WITH CHICKEN FILLING

Preparation time: 1 hour
+ 30 minutes standing
Total cooking time: 35 minutes
Serves 4

★★

Pasta

2 cups (250 g/8 oz) plain (all-purpose) flour
3 eggs
1 tablespoon olive oil
1 egg yolk, extra

Filling

125 g (4 oz) minced (ground) chicken
75 g (2 1/2 oz) ricotta or cottage cheese
60 g (2 oz) chicken livers, trimmed and chopped
30 g (1 oz) prosciutto, chopped
1 slice salami, chopped
2 tablespoons freshly grated Parmesan

ABOVE: Ravioli with chicken filling

CHICKEN MEZZELUNE WITH CREAM SAUCE

Preparation time: 45 minutes
Total cooking time: 15 minutes
Serves 4–6 as a first course

250 g (8 oz) packet gow gee wrappers

Chicken and ham filling

250 g (8 oz) chicken breast fillet
1 egg, beaten
90 g (3 oz) cooked ham or prosciutto
2 teaspoons finely snipped chives
2 teaspoons chopped fresh marjoram

Cream sauce

30 g (1 oz) butter
2 spring onions (scallions), finely chopped
2 tablespoons white wine
1½ cups (375 ml/12 fl oz) cream

1 To make the filling, remove any excess fat and sinew from the chicken breast. Cut the flesh into pieces and chop in a food processor. Add the egg, ½ teaspoon of salt and a pinch of white pepper and process until finely chopped. Transfer to a bowl. Chop the ham or prosciutto finely and stir into the chicken with the herbs.

2 Lay the gow gee wrappers on a work surface, six at a time, and put a teaspoonful of chicken filling in the centre of each. Brush the edges with cold water, fold in half to form a half moon shape (mezzelune), and press the edges together firmly to seal. Place on a tea towel and continue with the remaining circles.

3 If making your own pasta, roll the dough as thinly as possible on a lightly floured surface, or use a pasta machine and pass the dough through 5 or 6 settings. Cut into circles with an 8 cm (3 inch) cutter, fill and seal as above.

4 To make the cream sauce, heat the butter in a small pan, add the spring onion and cook for 2–3 minutes. Add the wine and cream and simmer until reduced. Season to taste.

5 Cook the mezzelune in batches, in rapidly boiling salted water. Don't crowd the pan. Simmer for 2–3 minutes, until the chicken is cooked. Don't overcook or the chicken will be dry. Drain.

6 Serve the sauce immediately with the mezzelune. Garnish, if you like.

BELOW: Chicken mezzelune with cream sauce

RICOTTA CHEESE

Ricotta is an unsalted, unripened cheese made from the whey of ewe's or cow's milk. It has a limited shelf life and can only be used when fresh. When kept too long it sours and develops an acid flavour. It has a delicate, creamy flavour and a light, crumbly texture that blends well with other ingredients, especially other dairy produce. Ricotta, literally recooked, takes its name from the method by which it is made. In ordinary cheese-making there is left-over hot whey of milk. When this is heated again and the solid milk parts skimmed off and drained, ricotta results.

ABOVE: Spinach and ricotta shells

SPINACH AND RICOTTA SHELLS

Preparation time: 20 minutes
Total cooking time: 15 minutes
Serves 4

20 giant conchiglie (shell pasta)
1 tablespoon oil
2 bacon rashers, finely chopped
1 onion, finely chopped
500 g (1 lb) English spinach, chopped
750 g (1 1/2 lb) ricotta cheese
1/3 cup (35 g/1 1/4 oz) freshly grated Parmesan
1 cup (250 g/8 oz) bottled tomato
  pasta sauce

1 Cook the conchiglie in a large pan of rapidly boiling salted water until *al dente*; drain.
2 Heat the oil in a pan, add the bacon and onion and stir over medium heat for 3 minutes, or until lightly browned. Add the spinach and stir over low heat until wilted. Add the ricotta cheese and stir until combined.
3 Spoon the mixture into the pasta shells and sprinkle with Parmesan. Put the shells on a cold, lightly oiled grill tray. Cook under medium–high heat for 3 minutes, or until lightly browned and heated through.
4 Put the tomato pasta sauce in a small pan and stir over high heat for 1 minute, or until heated through. Spoon the sauce onto serving plates and top with the shells.

PRAWN TORTELLONI

Preparation time: 40 minutes
Total cooking time: 20–30 minutes
Serves 4

★ ★

300 g (10 oz) raw prawns (shrimp)
20 g (3/4 oz) butter
1 clove garlic, crushed
2 spring onions (scallions), chopped
125 g (4 oz) ricotta cheese
1 tablespoon chopped fresh basil
200 g (6 1/2 oz) packet gow gee wrappers

Sauce

5 tablespoons olive oil
shells and heads of prawns (shrimp)
1 clove garlic, crushed
2 spring onions (scallions), including green part,
    chopped
1 dried chilli, crumbled
1 firm tomato, finely diced, or
    1 tablespoon diced sun-dried tomato

1 Shell the prawns, reserving the heads and shells to flavour the sauce. With a sharp knife, slit down the back of each prawn and discard the vein. Chop the prawns roughly.
2 Heat the butter and gently cook the garlic and spring onion until soft and golden. Allow to cool, mix with the prawns, ricotta and basil and season to taste. Put a teaspoonful of the mixture on each gow gee wrapper, moisten the edges with water, fold over to form a semi-circle and press firmly to seal. Press the corners together to make a tortelloni shape. For a large circular shape, use more filling and cover with another circle of pasta.
3 To make the sauce, heat 3 tablespoons of the olive oil in a large frying pan. When hot, add the shells and heads of the prawns and toss over high heat until they turn red. Lower the heat and cook for a few minutes, pressing the heads to extract as much flavour as possible. Add 1/2 cup (125 ml/4 fl oz) of water, cover and cook over low heat for 5 minutes. Remove the shells and heads from the pan using a slotted spoon, pressing out as much of the flavoured oil as possible before discarding them.
4 In another pan, heat the remaining 2 tablespoons of olive oil, add the garlic, spring onion and dried chilli and stir over low

heat until the garlic is pale golden. Add the prawn stock and diced tomato and heat through.
5 Bring a large pan of salted water to the boil. Drop the tortelloni into the boiling water and cook for 3–4 minutes. Drain, then add to the sauce and toss so the pasta is well coated.
NOTE: Tortelloni are large tortellini.
VARIATION: You can use the same wrappers to encase a mushroom filling. Chop 1/2 cup (70 g/ 2 1/4 oz) toasted and skinned hazelnuts in a food processor. Heat 90 g (3 oz) unsalted butter in a pan over medium heat until it sizzles and turns nutty brown. Remove from the heat, stir in the chopped hazelnuts and season. Wipe 150 g (5 oz) mushrooms clean with a paper towel. Chop the stems and caps finely. Heat 1 tablespoon oil in a pan, add the mushrooms and stir until soft. Season, then cook until the liquid has evaporated. Allow to cool. Follow the instructions in the recipe for filling the pasta.

ABOVE: Prawn tortelloni

353

2 cups (500 ml/16 fl oz) milk

2 cups (500 ml/16 fl oz) dry white wine

125 g (4 oz) Cheddar, grated

1/2 cup (125 ml/4 fl oz) cream

60 g (2 oz) Parmesan, grated

2 tablespoons chopped fresh parsley

1 Preheat the oven to moderate 180°C (350°F/ Gas 4). Line a greased shallow ovenproof dish (about 30 cm/12 inches square) with lasagne sheets, gently breaking them to fill any gaps. Set aside.

2 Slice or pull off any vein, membrane or hard white muscle from the scallops, leaving any roe attached.

3 Peel the prawns and gently pull out the dark vein from each prawn back, starting at the head end. Chop the seafood into even-sized pieces.

4 Melt the butter in a large pan over low heat, add the leek and cook, stirring over medium heat for 1 minute, or until starting to soften. Stir in the flour and cook for 1 minute, or until pale and foaming. Remove from the heat and gradually stir in the combined milk and wine. Return to the heat and stir constantly over medium heat until the sauce boils and thickens. Reduce the heat and simmer for 2 minutes. Add the seafood and simmer for 1 minute. Remove from the heat and stir in the cheese and some salt and pepper.

5 Spoon half the seafood mixture over the lasagne sheets in the dish, then top with another layer of lasagne sheets. Spoon the remaining seafood mixture over the lasagne sheets, then cover with another layer of lasagne sheets.

6 Pour the cream over the top, then sprinkle with the combined Parmesan and parsley. Bake, uncovered, for 30 minutes, or until bubbling and golden brown.

SEAFOOD LASAGNE

Preparation time: 15 minutes
Total cooking time: 45 minutes
Serves 4-6

250 g (8 oz) instant lasagne sheets

125 g (4 oz) scallops

500 g (1 lb) raw medium prawns (shrimp)

500 g (1 lb) skinless white fish fillets (eg. hake, snapper, flake, gemfish, ling)

125 g (4 oz) butter

1 leek, white part only, thinly sliced

2/3 cup (85 g/3 oz) plain (all-purpose) flour

ABOVE: Seafood lasagne

SQUID INK SPAGHETTI

Preparation time: 20 minutes
Total cooking time: 20 minutes
Serves 4-6

500 g (1 lb) small squid hoods

375 g (12 oz) spaghetti

4 tablespoons extra virgin olive oil

3 cloves garlic, crushed

1 onion, finely chopped

1/3 cup (80 ml/2³/4 fl oz) white wine

3 x 4 g sachets squid ink

1 Cut the squid hoods in half and then cut into thin strips.

2 Cook the spaghetti in a large pan of rapidly boiling water until *al dente*. Drain; keep warm.

3 Heat 2 tablespoons of the oil in a large deep frying pan, add the garlic and onion and stir over medium heat until golden. Add the wine, bring to the boil and boil for 5 minutes, or until half the liquid has evaporated. Reduce the heat and stir in the squid ink. Add to the spaghetti and toss. Season well with salt and pepper. Divide among warmed serving bowls

4 Heat the remaining oil and stir-fry the squid in batches, over high heat, for 1 minute, or until white and tender. Serve over the pasta.

FARFALLE WITH TUNA, MUSHROOMS AND CREAM

Preparation time: 10 minutes
Total cooking time: 15 minutes
Serves 4

60 g (2 oz) butter
1 tablespoon olive oil
1 onion, chopped
1 clove garlic, crushed
125 g (4 oz) button mushrooms, sliced
1 cup (250 ml/8 fl oz) cream
450 g (14 oz) can tuna in brine, drained and flaked
1 tablespoon lemon juice
1 tablespoon chopped fresh parsley
500 g (1 lb) farfalle

1 Heat the butter and olive oil in a large frying pan. Add the onion and garlic to the pan and stir over low heat for 3–5 minutes, until the onion is soft.

2 Add the mushrooms to the pan and cook for 2 minutes. Pour in the cream, bring to the boil, then reduce the heat and simmer until the sauce begins to thicken. Add the tuna, lemon juice and parsley and stir until heated through. Add salt and pepper, to taste.

3 While the sauce is cooking, add the farfalle to a large pan of rapidly boiling water and cook until *al dente*. Drain thoroughly, then return to the pan. Add the sauce to the farfalle and toss to combine. Serve immediately.

VARIATION: You can use a can of salmon, drained and flaked, instead of tuna.

NOTE: Farfalle, attractive pasta made into the shape of a bow or butterfly, comes in various sizes, as well as flavours other than the plain, such as tomato or spinach.

SQUID INK
Squid and octopus use ink as a means of defence and escape from predators. The squid fires ink into the water, forming a cloud about the same size as its own body. It then speeds away, leaving this decoy behind to confuse the predator. Squid ink is today popular as a dye for pasta. However, sepia, the pigment extracted from the ink sacs, has been used as a drawing ink since ancient Roman times.

LEFT: Farfalle with tuna, mushrooms and cream

355

MAKING GNOCCHI

Today, our favourite gnocchi are potato-based but variations can be made using

other vegetables such as pumpkin or parsnip, or traditional semolina or cheese.

Gnocchi are little dumplings. No matter what they are based on, the consistency of the dough should be soft and light. When cooking vegetables to be used for gnocchi, ensure that the cooking process doesn't result in soggy vegetables, otherwise you will have to add more flour, thus making the dough too heavy. Work quickly so the dough doesn't become too sticky or soft.

Gnocchi are best eaten as soon after cooking as possible and you should have any accompanying sauce ready before you cook the dumplings.

TRADITIONAL
POTATO GNOCCHI
When making potato gnocchi, it is important to use floury potatoes, preferably old boiling potatoes, because

they have a low moisture content. Traditionally, the potatoes are prepared by baking in their skins, thus keeping the potato dry. However, as this is quite time-consuming, most people prefer to steam or boil them. If you do this, make sure you don't overcook the potatoes or they will break up and absorb too much moisture. Also, drain them thoroughly.

Many recipes for potato gnocchi include eggs, to make the gnocchi easier to handle. However, eggs also require the addition of more flour to absorb the extra moisture, thus making the gnocchi a little tougher. Experiment to find which way you prefer to work. The traditional method follows. To make enough for 4–6 people, you will need 1 kg (2 lb) of floury old potatoes, unpeeled, and about 200 g (6½ oz) of plain (all-purpose) flour.

1 Prick the unpeeled potatoes all over with a fork and bake in a moderately hot 200°C (400°F/Gas 6) oven for 1 hour, or until tender. Don't wrap in foil. When cool enough to handle but still hot, peel and mash in a bowl with a masher, or put through a ricer or food mill into a bowl.

2 Add three-quarters of the flour and gradually work it in with your hands. When a loose dough forms, transfer it to a lightly floured surface and knead gently. Work in the remaining flour as you knead, but only enough to give a soft, light dough that does not stick to your hands or the work surface, but is still damp to touch. Stop kneading at this stage. Lightly flour the work surface and dust the inside tines of a fork with flour. Take a portion of the dough, about one-fifth, and roll it with your hands on the floured surface to form a long, even rope the thickness of your ring finger. Cut it into 2 cm (¾ inch) pieces.

3 Put a piece on the tines of a fork and press down with your finger, flipping the gnocchi as you do so. It will be rounded into a concave shell shape, ridged on the outer surface. Form a good hollow in the centre, as this allows the gnocchi to cook evenly and hold the sauce more easily. Continue with the remaining dough.

4 Lower the gnocchi in batches, about 20 at a time, into a large pan of boiling salted water. The gnocchi are cooked when they all rise to the surface, after 2–3 minutes cooking. Remove each batch with a slotted spoon and keep them warm while cooking the remainder. Sauce, and serve.

Potato gnocchi can be frozen, shaped but uncooked, for up to two months. They will need to be first frozen in a single layer, not touching, before being stored in airtight containers. When you are ready to use them, lower them gently, in batches, into boiling water straight from the freezer.

357

GNOCCHI ROMANA
(Semolina gnocchi with rich cheese sauce)

Preparation time: 20 minutes
+ 1 hour refrigeration
Total cooking time: 40 minutes
Serves 4

3 cups (750 ml/24 fl oz) milk
1/2 teaspoon ground nutmeg
2/3 cup (85 g/3 oz) semolina
1 egg, beaten
1 1/2 cups (150 g/5 oz) freshly
    grated Parmesan
60 g (2 oz) butter, melted
1/2 cup (125 m/4 fl oz) cream
1/2 cup (75 g/2 1/2 oz) freshly grated
    mozzarella cheese

1 Line a deep Swiss roll tin with baking paper. Combine the milk, half the nutmeg, and salt and freshly ground pepper, to taste, in a medium pan. Bring to the boil, reduce the heat and gradually stir in the semolina. Cook, stirring occasionally, for 5–10 minutes, or until the semolina is very stiff.
2 Remove the pan from the heat, add the egg and 1 cup of the Parmesan. Stir to combine and then spread the mixture in the tin. Refrigerate for 1 hour, or until the mixture is firm.
3 Preheat the oven to moderate 180°C (350°F/Gas 4). Cut the semolina into rounds using a floured 4 cm (1 1/2 inch) cutter and arrange in a greased shallow casserole dish.
4 Pour the melted butter over the top, followed by the cream. Combine the remaining grated Parmesan with the mozzarella cheese and sprinkle them on the rounds. Sprinkle with the remaining nutmeg. Bake for 20–25 minutes, or until the mixture is golden. You can serve garnished with a sprig of fresh herbs.
NOTE: Some claim that this traditional dish from Rome can be traced as far back as Imperial Roman times. A crisp garden salad is the ideal accompaniment for this lovely rich recipe.

SEMOLINA
Semolina is a term that describes a particular meal milled from grain. Usually applied to wheat, it has a coarse, discernible bead, unlike flour which is fine and powdery. It is higher in protein than flour and has a firmer texture that gives 'bite' to the pasta or dough it goes into. Different grades are milled, with fine semolina preferred for the making of gnocchi and a medium grain for baked desserts and puddings.

ABOVE: Gnocchi Romana

ON THE SIDE

TURNIPS WITH TOMATO, WINE AND GARLIC Heat a little olive oil in a frying pan, add some chopped garlic, chilli and onion and cook over low heat until golden. Add a can of peeled, crushed Italian tomatoes in their juice and a little red wine, bring to the boil then reduce the heat to a simmer. Add some thickly sliced turnips and simmer until the sauce thickens and the turnips are tender. Do not overcook or the turnips will start to break up. Stir through some shredded fresh basil just before serving.

POTATO GNOCCHI WITH TOMATO AND BASIL SAUCE

Preparation time: 1 hour
Total cooking time: 45–50 minutes
Serves 4-6

Tomato sauce

1 tablespoon oil
1 onion, chopped
1 celery stick, chopped
2 carrots, chopped
2 x 425 g (14 oz) cans crushed tomatoes
1 teaspoon sugar
1/2 cup (30 g/1 oz) fresh basil, chopped

Potato gnocchi

1 kg (2 lb) old potatoes
30 g (1 oz) butter
2 cups (250 g/8 oz) plain (all-purpose) flour
2 eggs, beaten

freshly grated Parmesan, to serve

1 To make the tomato sauce, heat the oil in a large frying pan, add the onion, celery and carrot and cook for 5 minutes, stirring regularly. Add the tomato and sugar and season with salt and pepper, to taste. Bring to the boil, reduce the heat to very low and simmer for 20 minutes. Cool slightly and process, in batches, in a food processor until smooth. Add the basil; set aside.

2 To make the potato gnocchi, peel the potatoes, chop roughly and steam or boil until very tender. Drain thoroughly and mash until smooth. Using a wooden spoon, stir in the butter and flour, then beat in the eggs. Cool.

3 Turn onto a floured surface and divide into two. Roll each into a long sausage shape. Cut into short pieces and press each piece with the back of a fork.

4 Cook the gnocchi, in batches, in a large pan of boiling salted water for about 2 minutes, or until the gnocchi rise to the surface. Using a slotted spoon, drain the gnocchi, and transfer to serving bowls. Serve with the tomato sauce and freshly grated Parmesan. Garnish with fresh herbs if you like.

POTATO

The best potatoes for gnocchi are old, starchy ones that have a low water content. Their mealy flesh results in a gnocchi that is tender and light. If the potatoes hold a lot of moisture, more flour will be required for the dough, which in turn will cause the gnocchi to be rubbery. The potatoes are best baked, steamed or boiled, and they should not be puréed in a processor as this only results in a gluey texture that is unsuitable for gnocchi dough.

LEFT: Potato gnocchi with tomato and basil sauce

FONTINA CHEESE
A semi-hard cheese from the Italian Alps, fontina has a creamy texture and a sweet, nutty flavour. It is eaten as a table cheese, but is also ideal for cooking because it melts completely to give a thick, rich cream. It is used in sauces for pasta and vegetables, and is the star ingredient of the famous *fonduta*, the Piedmontese version of fondue.

ABOVE: Gnocchi with fontina sauce

GNOCCHI WITH FONTINA SAUCE

Preparation time: 10 minutes
Total cooking time: 15 minutes
Serves 4

200 g (6¹/2 oz) fontina cheese, finely chopped
¹/2 cup (125 ml/4 fl oz) cream
80 g (2³/4 oz) butter
2 tablespoons freshly grated Parmesan
400 g (13 oz) fresh potato gnocchi

1 Combine the fontina cheese, cream, butter and Parmesan in a bowl over a pan of simmering water. Heat, stirring occasionally, for 6–8 minutes, or until the cheese has melted and the sauce is smooth and hot.

2 When the sauce is halfway through cooking, lower the gnocchi, in batches, into a large pan of boiling salted water and cook for about 2 minutes, or until the gnocchi rise to the surface.
3 Drain the gnocchi, using a slotted spoon, and serve with sauce over the top. Can be garnished with fresh oregano leaves or other fresh herbs.

HERBED POTATO GNOCCHI WITH CHUNKY TOMATO

Preparation time: 1 hour
Total cooking time: 30 minutes
Serves 4

500 g (1 lb) floury potatoes, chopped

1 egg yolk

3 tablespoons grated Parmesan

3 tablespoons chopped fresh herbs
(parsley, basil and chives)

up to 1 cup (125 g/4 oz) plain (all-purpose)
flour

2 cloves garlic, crushed

1 onion, chopped

4 bacon rashers, roughly chopped

150 g (5 oz) sun-dried tomatoes,
roughly chopped

425 g (14 oz) can peeled tomatoes

1 teaspoon soft brown sugar

2 teaspoons balsamic vinegar

1 tablespoon shredded fresh basil

shaved Parmesan, to serve

1 To make the gnocchi, steam or boil the potatoes until just tender. Drain thoroughly, cool and mash. Transfer 2 cups of the potato to a large bowl. Add the egg yolk, grated Parmesan and herbs and mix until combined. Gradually add enough flour to form a slightly sticky dough. Knead gently for 5 minutes, adding more flour if necessary, until smooth.

2 Divide the dough into four. Roll each portion on a lightly floured surface to form a sausage 2 cm (¾ inch) thick and cut into 2.5 cm (1 inch) pieces. Roll each piece into an oval shape and roll carefully over lightly floured prongs on the back of a fork. Put on a lightly floured non-stick baking tray and cover until ready to use.

3 To make the sauce, heat a tablespoon of olive oil in a large frying pan, add the garlic and onion and cook over medium heat for 5 minutes, or until the onion is soft and golden.

4 Add the bacon and cook, stirring occasionally, for 5 minutes, or until the bacon has browned.

5 Stir in the sun-dried tomato, tomato, sugar and vinegar, bring to the boil, reduce the heat and simmer for 15 minutes, or until the sauce has thickened. Stir the shredded basil through just before serving.

6 Cook the gnocchi, in batches, in a large pan of boiling salted water for about 2 minutes, or until the gnocchi rise to the surface. Drain well and serve topped with the tomato sauce and Parmesan shavings.

BELOW: Herbed potato gnocchi with chunky tomato

VEGETABLES

ROSEMARY TEA
Rosemary makes a refreshing herbal tea that is used to relieve headaches, to improve the memory and as a bedtime drink. Simply infuse 3 teaspoons of fresh leaves in 1 cup (250 ml/8 fl oz) boiling water.

OPPOSITE PAGE, FROM TOP:
Basic potatoes; Orange sweet potato; Roast onions; Pancetta potatoes

ROAST VEGETABLES

For all these recipes, preheat the oven to moderate 180°C (350°F/Gas 4). Peel all the vegetables. The cooking time will vary, depending on the size and type of vegetable. Vegetables can be placed around the meat roast while it is cooking if oven space is tight. The caramelized meat juices add flavour to the vegetables. While the meat is resting, you can turn the oven up to moderately hot 200°C (400°F/Gas 6) to crisp the vegetables.

BASIC POTATOES

Preparation time: 15 minutes
Total cooking time: 55 minutes
Serves 4

4 large floury or all-purpose potatoes
  (eg. spunta, sebago, russet, desiree, pontiac)
20 g (³/4 oz) butter, melted
1 tablespoon oil

Cut the potatoes in half and simmer in a pan of water for 5 minutes. Drain, then cool on paper towels. Using a fork, scrape the rounded side of the potatoes to form a rough surface. Place on a greased baking dish and brush with the butter and oil. Roast for 50 minutes, or until golden, brushing halfway through the cooking time with a little more butter and oil.

ORANGE SWEET POTATO

Preparation time: 10 minutes
Total cooking time: 25 minutes
Serves 4

800 g (1 lb 10 oz) orange sweet potato
20 g (³/4 oz) butter, melted
2 teaspoons sesame seeds
¹/2 teaspoon cracked black pepper

Cut the orange sweet potato into 1 cm (¹/2 inch) thick slices. Combine with the butter, sesame seeds and pepper. Toss, then roast in a baking dish for 25 minutes, or until lightly browned and tender, turning once. Sprinkle with salt before serving.

ROAST ONIONS

Preparation time: 20 minutes
Total cooking time: 1 hour 10 minutes
Serves 6

6 onions
³/4 cup (60 g/2 oz) fresh breadcrumbs
¹/4 cup (25 g/³/4 oz) grated Romano or Parmesan
1 tablespoon chopped fresh basil
20 g (³/4 oz) butter, melted

Peel the onions, leaving the root ends intact. Place in a pan of water, bring to the boil and simmer gently for 20 minutes. Remove and cool. Cut off and discard the top quarter of each onion, and scoop out a third of the inside. Combine the breadcrumbs, cheese, basil and butter in a bowl and season. Spoon into the onions and roast in a lightly greased baking dish for 50 minutes, or until the onions are soft.

PANCETTA POTATOES

Preparation time: 20 minutes
Total cooking time: 50 minutes
Serves 4

8 medium floury or all-purpose potatoes
  (eg. sebago, spunta, russet, desiree, pontiac)
2 slices pancetta
8 sprigs of fresh rosemary
2 teaspoons butter, softened
oil, for brushing

Cut the potatoes and trim the bases so they sit flat. Cut each pancetta slice lengthways into 4 pieces. Roll a sprig of rosemary in each piece of pancetta. Cut a hole in the centre of the potatoes about halfway through and insert the pancetta. Place on a greased baking dish. Top each potato with ¹/4 teaspoon of the butter. Brush with oil and sprinkle with pepper. Roast for 40–50 minutes, or until golden.
NOTE: The texture of potatoes varies from waxy to floury or starchy and it is best to use the type stated in recipes. Sebago and pontiac are good all-rounders and are particularly good for baking. Russet and spunta have a floury texture and are also good baking varieties.

2 Combine the apricots, raisins and orange juice in a small pan. Cover and bring to the boil, then remove from the heat and leave for 5 minutes.

3 Combine the potato, orange sweet potato and undrained fruit in a shallow ovenproof dish. Dot with butter and bake for 45 minutes, or until lightly browned. Stir occasionally. Garnish with chives before serving.

IN ADVANCE: This dish can be prepared up to baking stage 4 hours ahead.

SWEET ROAST BEETROOT

Preparation time: 15 minutes
Total cooking time: 1 hour 30 minutes
Serves 6

12 small fresh beetroot
1¹/₂ tablespoons olive oil
20 g (³/₄ oz) butter
1¹/₂ teaspoons ground cumin
1 teaspoon coriander seeds, lightly crushed
¹/₂ teaspoon mixed spice
1 clove garlic, crushed, optional
3–4 teaspoons soft brown sugar
1 tablespoon balsamic vinegar

1 Preheat the oven to moderate 180°C (350°F/Gas 4) and brush a baking dish with melted butter or oil. Trim the leafy tops from the beetroot (cut about 3 cm/1¹/₄ inches above the pulp to prevent bleeding), wash the bulbs thoroughly and place on the tray. Bake for 1 hour 15 minutes, or until very tender. Set aside until the bulbs are cool enough to handle.

2 Peel the beetroot and trim the tops and tails to neaten. Heat the oil and butter in a frying pan, add the cumin, coriander seeds, mixed spice and garlic and cook over medium heat for 1 minute. Add the sugar and vinegar to the pan and stir for 2–3 minutes, or until the sugar dissolves. Add the beetroot, reduce the heat to low and turn the beetroot for 5 minutes, or until glazed all over. Serve warm or at room temperature.

NOTE: When handling beetroot, take care to prevent them from bleeding. Wash carefully to prevent the skin breaking and don't cut them before cooking.

VARIATION: These are also delicious with some natural yoghurt stirred through and served as a salad.

FRUITY POTATOES

Preparation time: 20 minutes
Total cooking time: 50 minutes
Serves 8

1 kg (2 lb) new potatoes
1 kg (2 lb) orange sweet potato
³/₄ cup (135 g/4¹/₂ oz) dried apricots
³/₄ cup (90 g/3 oz) raisins
²/₃ cup (170 ml/5¹/₂ fl oz) orange juice
60 g (2 oz) butter, cubed
2 tablespoons chopped fresh chives

1 Preheat the oven to moderate 180°C (350°F/Gas 4). Peel the potato and orange sweet potato and cut into 3 cm (1¹/₄ inch) pieces. Cook in simmering water for 5 minutes, or until tender, then drain.

ABOVE: Fruity potatoes

ZUCCHINI PATTIES

Preparation time: 20 minutes
Total cooking time: 15 minutes
Makes 16

 ★★

300 g (10 oz) zucchini (courgettes), grated
1 small onion, finely chopped
1/4 cup (30 g/1 oz) self-raising flour
1/3 cup (35 g/1 1/4 oz) grated kefalotyri or
    Parmesan
1 tablespoon chopped fresh mint
2 teaspoons chopped fresh flat-leaf (Italian)
    parsley
pinch of ground nutmeg
1/4 cup (25 g/3/4 oz) dry breadcrumbs
1 egg, lightly beaten
olive oil, for shallow-frying

1 Put the zucchini and onion in the centre of a clean tea towel, gather the corners together and twist as tightly as possible to remove all the juices. Combine the zucchini, onion, flour, cheese, mint, parsley, nutmeg, breadcrumbs and egg in a large bowl. Season well with salt and freshly ground black pepper, then mix with your hands to a stiff mixture that clumps together.
2 Heat the oil in a large frying pan over medium heat. When hot, drop level tablespoons of mixture into the pan and shallow-fry for 2–3 minutes, or until well browned all over. Drain well on crumpled paper towels and serve hot, with lemon wedges, or with Cucumber and yoghurt salad (page 69).

BEANS WITH TOMATOES

Trim 500 (1 lb) green beans, then cut them in half. Cook in boiling water for 3 minutes, then drain and rinse. Set aside. Heat 2 tablespoons olive oil in a pan, add 1 chopped onion and 1 crushed garlic clove and cook, stirring, until the onion starts to brown. Sprinkle 2 teaspoons sugar over the onion and cook until it caramelises. Add 2 tablespoons red wine vinegar and cook for 1 minute. Add a 440 g (14 oz) can of chopped tomatoes, 1 tablespoon chopped fresh basil, 3 tablespoons chopped olives and a little freshly ground black pepper. Simmer, uncovered, for 5 minutes. Add the beans and simmer until warmed through. Serve garnished with fresh basil leaves. Serves 6.

ABOVE: Zucchini patties

2 Mash with a potato masher, adding the butter, milk and cinnamon. Season to taste with salt and freshly ground pepper, then spoon into a shallow 1 litre (32 fl oz) capacity casserole dish and smooth the top.

3 For the crumble topping, remove the crusts from the bread, break the bread into smaller pieces and finely chop in a food processor. Mix in the Parmesan and thyme, then scatter over the mash and bake for 20 minutes, or until the crumble is golden and crispy.

BRAISED FENNEL

Preparation time: 15 minutes
Total cooking time: 30 minutes
Serves 8

4 small fennel bulbs
20 g (³/4 oz) butter
1 tablespoon sugar
¹/3 cup (80 ml/2³/4 fl oz) white wine
²/3 cup (160 ml/5 fl oz) chicken stock
1 tablespoon sour cream

1 Slice the fennel bulbs into quarters, reserving the fronds. Melt the butter in a frying pan and stir in the sugar. Add the fennel, and cook for 5–10 minutes, until lightly browned all over.

2 Pour in the wine and stock and bring to the boil, then reduce the heat and simmer, covered, for 10 minutes, or until tender.

3 Uncover and boil until most of the liquid has evaporated and the sauce has become sticky. Remove from the heat and stir in the sour cream. Garnish with the reserved fennel fronds.

ORANGE SWEET POTATO CRUMBLE

Preparation time: 25 minutes
Total cooking time: 40 minutes
Serves 6

1 kg (2 lb) orange sweet potato
50 g (1³/4 oz) butter
¹/3 cup (80 ml/2³/4 fl oz) milk or cream
¹/4 teaspoon ground cinnamon
480 g (15 oz) loaf sourdough bread
¹/2 cup (55 g/2 oz) grated Parmesan
1 teaspoon dried thyme leaves

1 Preheat the oven to moderate 180°C (350°F/ Gas 4). Cut the orange sweet potato into chunks, put in a saucepan and cook in lightly salted boiling water for 15 minutes, or until tender. Drain and return to the saucepan.

ABOVE: Orange sweet potato crumble

CABBAGE WITH HERBS

Finely shred 850 g (1 lb 12 oz) cabbage (green or red or a combination of both). Melt 60 g (2 oz) butter in a large pan with a lid, add the cabbage and toss to combine with the butter. Put the lid on the pan and 'steam' the cabbage over low heat for 5 minutes. Remove the lid and cook the cabbage over low heat for 3 minutes more, stirring so it cooks evenly. Stir through ²/3 cup (40 g/1¹/4 oz) finely shredded basil. Season with salt and freshly ground black pepper and serve immediately. Serves 4.

BROCCOLI WITH ALMONDS

Preparation time: 10 minutes
Total cooking time: 10 minutes
Serves 6

500 g (1 lb) broccoli, cut into small florets
2 teaspoons oil
20 g (³/4 oz) butter
1 clove garlic, crushed
1 tablespoon flaked almonds

1 Add the broccoli to a saucepan of boiling water and cook for 1–2 minutes, or until just tender. Drain thoroughly. Heat the oil and butter in a large frying pan, add the garlic and almonds and cook for 1–2 minutes, or until the almonds are golden. Remove from the pan and set aside.
2 Add the broccoli to the frying pan and toss over medium heat for 2–3 minutes, or until the broccoli is heated through. Return the almonds to the pan and stir until well distributed. Serve hot.

CELERIAC AND TARRAGON PUREE

Preparation time: 15 minutes
Total cooking time: 15 minutes
Serves 6

2 cups (500 ml/16 fl oz) vegetable stock
¹/4 cup (60 ml/2 fl oz) lemon juice
3 celeriacs, peeled and chopped
40 g (1¹/4 oz) butter
1 tablespoon cream
1 tablespoon finely chopped fresh tarragon

1 Put the vegetable stock, lemon juice and 2 cups (500 ml/16 fl oz) water in a saucepan and bring to the boil. Add the celeriac and cook for 10–15 minutes, or until tender. You may need to add extra water, depending on the size of the celeriac.
2 Drain and place in a food processor with the butter and cream. Season with salt and freshly ground pepper and process until smooth. Alternatively, mash until smooth. Stir in the chopped tarragon. If the mixture is too thick, add a little more cream.

MINTED PEAS

Preparation time: 5 minutes
Total cooking time: 6 minutes
Serves 6

4 cups (620 g/1¹/4 lb) fresh or frozen peas
4 sprigs fresh mint
30 g (1 oz) butter
2 tablespoons shredded fresh mint

1 Place the peas in a saucepan and pour in water to just cover the peas. Add the mint sprigs.
2 Bring to the boil and simmer for 5 minutes (only 2 minutes if frozen), or until the peas are just tender. Drain and discard the mint. Return to the saucepan, add the butter and shredded mint and stir over low heat until the butter has melted. Season with salt and pepper.

ABOVE: Broccoli with almonds

369

LEEKS

Leeks come from the same family as onions but, because they are milder with a sweeter flavour, they are used when a more delicate taste is desired. They can be cooked as a vegetable in their own right and are especially useful in soups and sauces that don't require a strong flavour. Like onions, they should be cooked slowly so they soften but don't burn. When buying leeks, choose smaller ones as they will be more tender than large leeks. If very young, the whole plant can be used as the green leaves will not be tough.

ABOVE: Steamed mixed bean bundles

STEAMED MIXED BEAN BUNDLES

Preparation time: 15 minutes
Total cooking time: 8 minutes
Serves 4

8 long chives
20 green beans
20 butter beans

1 Place the chives in a small bowl, cover with boiling water to soften, then drain. Trim the tops and tails from all the beans, divide into 8 bundles and tie them together with a chive. Place the bundles in a steamer over a medium pan half-filled with simmering water, or, alternatively, place them in a medium pan with 3 tablespoons of water.
2 Cover the steamer and steam the beans over medium heat for 5–8 minutes, or until just tender. Don't allow the water to completely evaporate—add more if necessary. Sprinkle the cooked beans with salt and ground black pepper and serve immediately.

ROAST LEEK WITH BACON

Preparation time: 15 minutes
Total cooking time: 25 minutes
Serves 6

3 leeks
2 rashers bacon
20 g (3/4 oz) butter, softened
1 teaspoon chopped fresh thyme

1 Preheat the oven to moderate 180°C (350°F/Gas 4). Discard most of the green part from the top section of the leeks, then cut each leek in half lengthways and wash well.
2 Cut each bacon rasher into 3 long strips and wrap a piece around the middle of each portion of leek.
3 Place the leeks, rounded-side-up, in a greased shallow baking dish. Combine the butter and thyme and spread over the leeks. Bake for 25 minutes, or until lightly browned and tender.
NOTE: Grit tends to stick between the tightly compacted layers of leeks, so rinse carefully.

ASPARAGUS WITH BUTTER AND PARMESAN

Preparation time: 15 minutes
Total cooking time: 3 minutes
Serves 4–6

300 g (10 oz) fresh asparagus
40 g (1½ oz) butter, melted
fresh Parmesan shavings

1 Snap any thick woody ends from the asparagus and discard. Peel the bottom half of each spear with a vegetable peeler if the skin is very thick.
2 Plunge the asparagus into a pan of boiling water and cook for 2–3 minutes, or until the asparagus is bright-green and just tender. Drain and place on serving plates. Drizzle with a little melted butter. Top with Parmesan shavings and sprinkle with freshly ground black pepper.
VARIATIONS: You can use green, purple or white asparagus for this recipe, or a combination. Lightly toasted, crushed hazelnuts or pecan nuts can be sprinkled over the top.

POTATOES WITH ROSEMARY

Preparation time: 10 minutes
Total cooking time: 20 minutes
Serves 6

750 g (1½ lb) baby new potatoes, halved
30 g (1 oz) butter
2 tablespoons olive oil
1 teaspoon cracked black pepper
2 cloves garlic, crushed
1 tablespoon finely chopped fresh rosemary
1 teaspoon sea salt

1 Lightly boil or steam the potatoes for about 5 minutes, or until just tender (pierce with the point of a small knife—the knife should come away easily). Drain and cool slightly.
2 Heat the butter and oil in a large heavy-based frying pan. When foaming, add the potatoes and season with half the pepper. Cook over medium heat for 5–10 minutes, or until golden and crisp, tossing to ensure the potatoes are evenly coloured.
3 Stir in the garlic, rosemary and salt and cook for another minute. Mix in the remaining cracked pepper.

ASPARAGUS

There are three types of cultivated asparagus, green, purple and white. Green is the one most commonly available in England, Australia and many other countries, while white is more popular in Belgium, Germany and parts of France. Green and white asparagus are the same variety but the white is harvested while the spear is still below the ground. White asparagus spears are usually thick with almost no scales, but only a short part of the length is young enough to be edible. Purple asparagus has a similar flavour to green asparagus but is less commonly available.

LEFT: Asparagus with butter and Parmesan

VEGETABLE CHIPS

Paper-thin or saw-toothed and chunky, chips are loved by everyone—and they don't

have to be made from potatoes, as these clever and surprising suggestions prove.

BEETROOT CHIPS

Using a sharp vegetable peeler or a knife, cut 500 g (1 lb) of peeled beetroot into paper-thin slices. Heat 3 cups (750 ml/ 24 fl oz) of oil in a pan and cook the beetroot chips in hot oil, in batches, until they are crisp and browned. Drain on paper towels and keep warm in a preheated moderate 180°C (350°F/Gas 4) oven while cooking the remainder. Serve beetroot chips with a blend of whole-egg mayonnaise and chopped fresh herbs of your choice.

CRISPY SWEET POTATO DISCS

Peel 500 g (1 lb) of orange sweet potato and cut into thin slices using a sharp vegetable peeler or a knife. Heat 3 cups (750 ml/24 fl oz) of oil in a pan and cook the sweet potato discs in batches until crisp and golden. Drain on paper towels and keep warm in a preheated moderate 180°C (350°F/ Gas 4) oven while cooking remainder. Serve with a mixture of mayonnaise, lime juice and curry powder.

ZUCCHINI RIBBONS

Using a sharp vegetable peeler, cut 500 g (1 lb) of large zucchinis (courgettes) into ribbons by running the peeler horizontally along the zucchinis. Dip the zucchini ribbons into a bowl of 4 lightly beaten eggs, then dip into a mixture of 1 cup (100 g/3½ oz) of dried breadcrumbs and 1 tablespoon of chopped fresh herbs. Cook the crumbed zucchini ribbons in batches in 3 cups (750 ml/24 fl oz) of hot oil until the ribbons are golden. Drain on paper towels and keep warm in a preheated moderate 180°C (350°F/ Gas 4) oven while cooking the remaining zucchini ribbons. Zucchini ribbons are delicious served with a dipping sauce made from chopped sun-dried tomatoes and natural yoghurt.

GOLDEN POTATO CHIPS

Cut 500 g (1 lb) washed old potatoes into thick country-style chips (wedges). Heat 3 cups (750 ml/24 fl oz) of oil in a pan and cook potatoes in batches until lightly golden; drain on paper towels. Repeat with remaining potatoes. Just before serving, re-fry the potatoes in batches until crisp and golden. Sprinkle with sea salt and malt vinegar, if desired.

PUMPKIN CRISPS

Peel 500 g (1 lb) butternut pumpkin (squash) and cut into crinkle-cut slices. Heat 3 cups (750 ml/24 fl oz) of oil in a pan and cook slices in batches until they are crisp and golden. Drain on paper towels and keep warm in a preheated moderate 180°C (350°F/Gas 4) oven while cooking the remaining pumpkin chips.

CARROT AND HERB RIBBONS

Peel 500 g (1 lb) carrots into ribbons by running a sharp peeler horizontally along the length of the carrot. Rinse and dry 1 cup (50 g/1¾ oz) of large basil leaves. Heat 3 cups (750 ml/24 fl oz) of oil in a pan and cook carrot ribbons and basil leaves in batches until crisp. Drain on paper towels and keep warm in a preheated moderate 180°C (350°F/ Gas 4) oven while cooking remaining carrot and basil. Serve with a dipping sauce of sweet chilli sauce, lime juice and chopped fresh coriander (cilantro).

CLOCKWISE, FROM TOP LEFT: Golden potato chips; Zucchini ribbons; Beetroot chips; Pumpkin crisps; Carrot and herb ribbons; Crispy sweet potato discs

CREAMY POTATO
GRATIN

Sprinkle a little of the grated Cheddar cheese over each layer.

Pour the cream mixture over the top of the potato and onion.

CREAMY POTATO GRATIN

Preparation time: 20 minutes
Total cooking time: 40 minutes
Serves 6

750 g (1 1/2 lb) waxy or all-purpose potatoes
1 onion
1 cup (125 g/4 oz) grated Cheddar
1 1/2 cups (375 ml/12 fl oz) cream
2 teaspoons chicken stock powder

1 Preheat the oven to moderate 180°C (350°F/ Gas 4). Thinly slice the potatoes and slice the onion into rings.
2 Arrange a layer of overlapping potato slices in a baking dish and top with a layer of onion rings. Divide the cheese in half and set aside one half for topping. Sprinkle a little of the remaining cheese over the onion. Continue layering in this order until all the potato and the onion have been used, finishing with a little cheese.

3 Pour the cream into a small jug, add the chicken stock powder and whisk gently until thoroughly combined. Pour the mixture over the layered potato and onion and sprinkle the top with the reserved cheese. Bake for 40 minutes, or until the potato is tender, the cheese has melted and the top is golden brown.
NOTES: A gratin is any dish topped with cheese and/or breadcrumbs and cooked until browned. There are many versions of potato gratin—some are creamy like this one, others less so.

If you have a mandolin, use it to cut the potatoes into thin slices. If not, make sure you use a very sharp knife. Peel the skin very thinly.

Waxy or all-purpose potatoes are best as they hold their shape better when cooked in this way.
VARIATION: If you prefer, you can use different types of stock, including vegetable, to vary the flavour.

ABOVE: Creamy
potato gratin

ORANGE POPPY SEED ROASTED VEGETABLES WITH ORANGE DRESSING

Preparation time: 20 minutes
Total cooking time: 50 minutes
Serves 8

500 g (1 lb) new potatoes, halved

6 parsnips, peeled and quartered lengthways

500 g (1 lb) orange sweet potato, cut into large chunks

330 g (11 oz) baby carrots, some with tops on

6 pickling onions, halved

1/3 cup (80 ml/2³/4 fl oz) oil

2 tablespoons poppy seeds

200 g (6¹/2 oz) triple cream Brie, thinly sliced

Orange dressing

1/2 cup (125 ml/4 fl oz) orange juice

2 cloves garlic, crushed

1 tablespoon Dijon mustard

1 teaspoon white wine vinegar

1 teaspoon sesame oil

1 Preheat the oven to moderately hot 200°C (400°F/Gas 6). Place all the vegetables and the oil in a large deep baking dish. Toss the vegetables to coat with the oil. Bake for 50 minutes, or until the vegetables are crisp and tender, tossing every 15 minutes. Remove from the oven and sprinkle with the poppy seeds.
2 For the orange dressing, whisk the ingredients together in a small jug.
3 Pour the dressing over the warm vegetables and toss. Transfer to a large bowl, top with the Brie and serve immediately while still warm.

ZUCCHINI WITH LEMON AND CAPER BUTTER

Rinse, drain and chop 2 tablespoons bottled capers and put in a small bowl with 100 g (3¹/2 oz) butter, 2 teaspoons grated lemon rind, 1 tablespoon lemon juice and some salt and freshly ground black pepper. Mix until combined. Thinly slice 8 small zucchini (courgettes) lengthways and steam in a saucepan for 3–5 minutes, or until tender. Toss with the caper butter and serve immediately. Serves 4.

ABOVE: Orange poppy seed roasted vegetables with orange dressing

HONEY-ROASTED VEGETABLES

Preparation time: 20 minutes
Total cooking time: 50 minutes
Serves 4

4 parsnips
2 carrots
2 small orange sweet potatoes
4 beetroot, cut into wedges
8 cloves garlic, unpeeled
1/4 cup (60 ml/2 fl oz) oil
1 tablespoon honey
1 teaspoon cumin seeds
1/2 teaspoon cracked black pepper
1/2 teaspoon rock salt

1 Preheat the oven to moderately hot 200°C (400°F/Gas 6). Cut the parsnips, carrots and sweet potatoes into 10 cm (4 inch) lengths. Place the vegetables and the unpeeled garlic in a large baking dish, and drizzle with the oil and honey. Sprinkle with the cumin seeds, pepper and salt. Toss to coat.
2 Bake the vegetables for 40–50 minutes, or until tender inside and golden brown outside.

DUCHESS POTATOES

Preparation time: 20 minutes + refrigeration
Total cooking time: 30 minutes
Serves 6

860 g (1 lb 12 oz) floury potatoes, quartered
2 eggs
1/4 cup (60 ml/2 fl oz) cream
2 tablespoons freshly grated Parmesan
1/4 teaspoon grated nutmeg
1 egg yolk, for glazing

1 Boil or steam the potato for 10 minutes, or until just tender (pierce with the point of a small knife—if the potato comes away easily, it is ready). Drain and return to the pan. Turn the heat to very low and shake the pan for 1–2 minutes to dry out the potato. Transfer to a bowl and mash well until smooth.
2 Beat together the eggs, cream, Parmesan,

nutmeg and some salt and black pepper. Add to the potato and mash to combine. Taste for seasoning and adjust if necessary. Cover and leave for 20 minutes to cool slightly. Preheat the oven to moderate 180°C (350°F/Gas 4).
3 Put the just warm potato mixture in a piping bag with a 1.5 cm (5/8 inch) star nozzle. Pipe the mixture in swirls, not too close together, onto greased baking trays. Brush lightly all over with the extra egg yolk, to give a golden, crisp finish. Bake for 15–20 minutes, or until golden. Serve hot, sprinkled with a little paprika if desired.
IN ADVANCE: These can be prepared in advance and refrigerated, covered with plastic. Just before serving, brush with egg yolk and bake.

RISOTTO-STUFFED ONIONS

Preparation time: 15 minutes
Total cooking time: 1 hour 40 minutes
Serves 8

8 onions (about 200 g/6 1/2 oz each)
1 tablespoon oil
20 g (3/4 oz) butter
70 g (2 1/4 oz) mushrooms, chopped
20 g (3/4 oz) prosciutto, chopped
1/2 cup (110 g/3 1/2 oz) arborio rice
2 1/2 cups (600 ml/20 fl oz) hot chicken stock
2 tablespoons grated Parmesan
2 tablespoons chopped fresh parsley

1 Preheat the oven to moderately hot 200°C (400°F/Gas 6). Trim the bases of the onions so they sit flat and cut the tops off, leaving a wide opening. Place in a baking dish, drizzle with the oil and bake for 1–1 1/2 hours, or until golden.
2 Meanwhile, melt the butter in a pan, add the mushrooms and prosciutto and cook for 5 minutes, or until the mushrooms have softened. Add the rice and stir until well coated with the butter. Gradually stir in the hot chicken stock, about 1/2 cup (125 ml/4 fl oz) at a time, making sure the liquid has been absorbed before adding more. When all the stock has been absorbed, stir in the Parmesan and parsley.
3 Scoop out the flesh from the middle of each onion, leaving at least 3 outside layers on each, to hold the filling. Chop the scooped flesh and stir through the risotto mixture. Spoon the filling into the onion shells, piling a little on top. Bake for 10 minutes to heat through, then serve.

*OPPOSITE PAGE,
CLOCKWISE FROM TOP:
Honey-roasted vegetables;
Risotto-stuffed onions;
Duchess potatoes*

377

CAULIFLOWER CHEESE

Preparation time: 15 minutes
Total cooking time: 20 minutes
Serves 4

500 g (1 lb) cauliflower, cut into
    small pieces
2 tablespoons fresh breadcrumbs
1/4 cup (30 g/1 oz) grated Cheddar

Cheese sauce

30 g (1 oz) butter
30 g (1 oz) plain (all-purpose) flour
1 1/4 cups (315 ml/10 fl oz) warm milk
1 teaspoon Dijon mustard
1/2 cup (60 g/2 oz) grated Cheddar
1/2 cup (50 g/1 3/4 oz) grated Parmesan

*ABOVE: Cauliflower
cheese*

1 Lightly grease a 1.5 litre (48 fl oz) heatproof
dish. Cook the cauliflower pieces in a saucepan
of lightly salted boiling water for 10 minutes, or
until just tender. Drain thoroughly, then transfer
to the prepared dish and keep warm.
2 For the cheese sauce, melt the butter in a pan
over low heat. Stir in the flour and cook for
1 minute, or until pale and foaming. Remove
from the heat and gradually stir in the milk and
mustard. Return to the heat and stir constantly
until the sauce boils and thickens. Reduce the
heat and simmer for 2 minutes, then remove
the pan from the heat. Add the Cheddar and
Parmesan and stir until melted. Do not reheat
or the oil will come out of the cheese. Season
with salt and white pepper, to taste, and pour
over the cauliflower.
3 Combine the breadcrumbs and Cheddar
and sprinkle over the sauce. Grill under
medium heat until the top is brown and
bubbling. Serve immediately.
NOTE: This cheese sauce is also delicious poured
over other vegetables such as broccoli, asparagus,
or a combination of vegetables.

TOMATO AND FENNEL IN ROASTED RED PEPPERS

Preparation time: 20 minutes
Total cooking time: 1 hour
Serves 6

2 small fennel bulbs
3 large red peppers (capsicums)
6 ripe Roma (plum) tomatoes
6 cloves garlic, sliced
3 teaspoons fennel seeds
1/4 cup (60 ml/2 fl oz) lemon juice
2 tablespoons olive oil

1 Preheat the oven to moderate 180°C (350°F/ Gas 4). Brush a large baking dish with oil.
2 Cut each fennel bulb in half, then cut into thick slices. Place in a pan of boiling salted water, cook for 1 minute, then drain and cool.
3 Cut the red peppers in half lengthways, leaving the stalk attached. Remove the seeds and membrane.
4 Cut the tomatoes in half lengthways and

arrange in the pepper halves with the fennel slices. (The amount of fennel used will depend on the size of the peppers and the fennel, but the vegetables should fit firmly inside the peppers.) Add garlic slices to each pepper half and sprinkle with fennel seeds. Season with salt and freshly ground black pepper. Sprinkle the lemon juice and half the oil over the peppers.
5 Bake for 1 hour, or until the peppers are tender, brushing with the remaining oil once or twice during cooking. Serve hot.

TOMATOES STUFFED WITH FETA

Cut a deep cross in the tops of 6 ripe tomatoes. Combine 150 g (5 oz) crumbled Greek feta in a bowl with 2 teaspoons chopped fresh oregano and 1 tablespoon freshly grated Parmesan. Season with pepper. Stuff each tomato with about 1 tablespoon of the feta mixture. Bake in a moderately hot 200°C (400°F/Gas 6) oven for 20 minutes, or until the skins split and soften. Makes 6.

FETA
This famous salty Greek cheese, often found in Greek salads, is now made in other places such as Australia, America and Denmark. Traditionally made from the milk from sheep or goats, it is now often made using milk from cows. Large blocks are salted, then sliced and salted again. It is packed and left to mature for a month in the salty whey.

LEFT: Tomato and fennel in roasted red peppers

VEGETARIAN

VEGETABLE TART WITH SALSA VERDE

Preparation time: 30 minutes +
30 minutes refrigeration
Total cooking time: 50 minutes
Serves 6

★★★

Pastry

1³/4 cups (215 g/7 oz) plain (all-purpose) flour
120 g (4 oz) butter, chilled and cubed
1/4 cup (60 ml/2 fl oz) cream

Salsa verde

1 clove garlic
2 cups (40 g/1 1/4 oz) fresh flat-leaf (Italian)
  parsley leaves
1/3 cup (80 ml/2³/4 fl oz) extra virgin olive oil
3 tablespoons chopped fresh dill
1 1/2 tablespoons Dijon mustard
1 tablespoon red wine vinegar
1 tablespoon drained bottled baby capers

Filling

1 large all-purpose potato
1 tablespoon olive oil
2 cloves garlic, crushed

1 red pepper (capsicum), chopped
1 red onion, sliced into rings
2 zucchini (courgettes), sliced
2 tablespoons chopped fresh dill
1 tablespoon chopped fresh thyme
1 tablespoon drained bottled baby capers
150 g (5 oz) marinated artichoke hearts, drained
2/3 cup (30 g/1 oz) baby English spinach leaves

1 Sift the flour and 1/2 teaspoon salt into a large bowl and rub in the butter with your fingertips until the mixture resembles fine breadcrumbs. Add the cream and 1–2 tablespoons iced water and mix with a flat-bladed knife until the mixture comes together in small beads. Gather into a ball and turn out onto a lightly floured work surface. Flatten into a disc, cover with plastic wrap, and refrigerate for 30 minutes.
2 Preheat the oven to moderately hot 200°C (400°F/Gas 6). Lightly grease a 27 cm (11 inch) shallow fluted flan tin with a removable base.
3 Roll the dough out between 2 sheets of baking paper until large enough to line the flan tin. Remove the paper and carefully lift the pastry into the flan tin, pressing it gently into the fluted sides. Roll the rolling pin over the tin, cutting off any excess. Line the pastry with crumpled baking paper large enough to cover the base and side. Fill with baking beads or uncooked rice. Place the flan tin on a baking tray

ABOVE: Vegetable tart with salsa verde

and bake for 15–20 minutes. Remove the beads and paper, reduce the oven to moderate 180°C (350°F/Gas 4) and bake for another 20 minutes, or until the pastry case is dry and golden.

4 For the salsa verde, blend all the ingredients together in a food processor until almost smooth.

5 For the filling, boil, steam or microwave the potato until just tender (the point of a sharp knife will come away easily when the potato is ready), but do not overcook. Drain.

6 Heat the oil in a large frying pan and add the garlic, pepper and onion. Cook over medium-high heat for 3 minutes, stirring frequently. Add the zucchini, dill, thyme and capers and cook for another 3 minutes, stirring often. Add the potato and artichokes, reduce the heat to low and cook for another 3–4 minutes, or until the potato and artichokes are heated through. Season to taste.

7 To assemble the tart, spread ¼ cup (60 ml/ 2 fl oz) of the salsa verde over the base of the pastry case. Spoon the vegetable mixture into the case and drizzle with half the remaining salsa verde. Pile the spinach in the centre, drizzle with the remaining salsa verde and serve immediately.

MUSHROOM NUT ROAST WITH TOMATO SAUCE

Preparation time: 30 minutes
Total cooking time: 1 hour
Serves 6

2 tablespoons olive oil

1 large onion, diced

2 cloves garlic, crushed

300 g (10 oz) cap mushrooms, finely chopped

200 g (6½ oz) raw cashews

200 g (6½ oz) brazil nuts

1 cup (125 g/4 oz) grated Cheddar

¼ cup (25 g/¾ oz) freshly grated Parmesan

1 egg, lightly beaten

2 tablespoons chopped fresh chives

1 cup (80 g/2¾ oz) fresh wholemeal breadcrumbs

Tomato sauce

1½ tablespoons olive oil

1 onion, finely chopped

1 clove garlic, crushed

400 g (13 oz) can chopped tomatoes

1 tablespoon tomato paste (tomato purée)

1 teaspoon caster (superfine) sugar

1 Grease a 14 x 21 cm (5½ x 8½ inch) loaf tin and line the base with baking paper.

2 Heat the oil in a frying pan and add the onion, garlic and mushrooms. Fry until soft, then cool.

3 Process the nuts in a food processor until finely chopped, but do not overprocess. Preheat the oven to moderate 180°C (350°F/Gas 4).

4 Combine the cooled mushrooms, chopped nuts, Cheddar and Parmesan, egg, chives and breadcrumbs in a bowl. Mix well and season, to taste. Press into the loaf tin and bake for 45 minutes, or until firm. Leave for 5 minutes, then turn out and cut into slices.

5 For the tomato sauce, heat the oil in a saucepan, add the onion and garlic and cook, stirring frequently, for 5 minutes, or until soft but not brown. Stir in the tomato, tomato paste, sugar and ⅓ cup (80 ml/2¾ fl oz) water. Simmer gently for 3–5 minutes, or until slightly thickened. Season with salt and pepper. Serve the tomato sauce with the sliced nut roast.

VARIATION: Use a different mixture of nuts and add some seeds. You can use nuts such as pecans, almonds, hazelnuts (without skins) and pine nuts. Suitable seeds to use include sesame, pumpkin or sunflower seeds.

ABOVE: Mushroom nut roast with tomato sauce

MUSHROOMS WITH BEAN PUREE, PUY LENTILS AND RED WINE SAUCE

Pull the stalks from the mushrooms, then very finely chop the stalks.

Simmer the lentil mixture until the lentils are cooked and the liquid is reduced.

Fry both sides of the mushroom caps in the butter and garlic until the mushrooms are tender.

ABOVE: Mushrooms with bean purée, puy lentils and red wine sauce

MUSHROOMS WITH BEAN PUREE, PUY LENTILS AND RED WINE SAUCE

Preparation time: 30 minutes
Total cooking time: 50 minutes
Serves 4

 ★ ★

4 large flat field mushrooms
1 tablespoon olive oil
1 red onion, cut into thin wedges
3 cloves garlic, crushed
1 cup (200 g/6¹/2 oz) puy green lentils
³/4 cup (185 ml/6 fl oz) red wine
1³/4 cups (440 ml/14 fl oz) vegetable stock
1 tablespoon finely chopped fresh parsley
30 g (1 oz) butter

Bean purée

1 large potato, cut into chunks
2 tablespoons extra virgin olive oil

400 g (13 oz) can cannellini beans, drained and rinsed
2 large cloves garlic, crushed
1 tablespoon vegetable stock

Red wine sauce

²/3 cup (170 ml/5¹/2 fl oz) red wine
2 tablespoons tomato paste (tomato purée)
1¹/2 cups (375 ml/12 fl oz) vegetable stock
1 tablespoon soft brown sugar

1 Wipe the mushrooms and finely chop the mushroom stalks. Heat the oil in a large saucepan, add the onion and cook over medium heat for 2–3 minutes, or until soft. Add 1 clove of the garlic and the mushroom stalks and cook for 1 minute. Stir in the lentils, red wine and vegetable stock and bring to the boil. Reduce the heat and simmer, covered, for 20–25 minutes, stirring occasionally, or until the liquid is reduced and the lentils are cooked. If the mixture is too wet, uncover and boil until slightly thick. Stir in the parsley. Keep warm.

2 For the bean purée, bring a small saucepan of water to the boil over high heat and cook the potato for 4–5 minutes, or until tender (pierce with the point of a sharp knife—if the knife comes away easily, the potato is cooked). Drain and mash with a potato masher or fork until smooth. Stir in half the extra virgin olive oil and set aside. Combine the cannellini beans and garlic in a food processor. Add the stock and remaining oil and process until smooth. Transfer to a bowl and fold the mashed potato through. Keep warm.

3 Melt the butter in a deep frying pan. Add the remaining garlic and the flat mushrooms and cook in batches over medium heat for 3–4 minutes each side, or until the mushrooms are tender. Set aside and keep warm.

4 For the sauce, add the red wine to the same frying pan, then scrape the bottom to release any sediment. Add the combined tomato paste, stock and sugar and bring to the boil. Cook for about 10 minutes, or until reduced and thick.

5 Place the mushrooms on individual serving plates and top with warm bean purée. Spoon some lentil mixture over the top and drizzle with the red wine sauce. Season and serve.

NOTE: The mushrooms will shrivel if kept warm in the oven.

PUMPKIN TARTS

Preparation time: 20 minutes
  + 30 minutes refrigeration
Total cooking time: 35 minutes
Serves 6

★ ★

2 cups (250 g/8 oz) plain (all-purpose) flour
125 g (4 oz) butter, chilled and cubed
1.2 kg (2 lb 6½ oz) pumpkin, cut into
  6 cm (2½ inch) pieces
6 tablespoons sour cream or cream
  cheese
sweet chilli sauce, to serve

 Sift the flour and a pinch of salt into a large bowl and rub in the chopped butter with your fingertips until the mixture resembles fine breadcrumbs. Make a well in the centre, add ⅓ cup (80 ml/2¾ fl oz) iced water and mix with a flat-bladed knife, using a cutting action until the mixture comes together in beads. Gently gather the dough together and lift out onto a lightly floured work surface. Press into a ball,

then flatten slightly into a disc, wrap in plastic wrap and refrigerate for 30 minutes.

2 Preheat the oven to moderately hot 200°C (400°F/Gas 6). Divide the pastry into six portions, roll each one out and fit into a 10 cm (4 inch) pie dish. Trim the edges and prick the bases all over. Bake on a baking tray for 15 minutes, or until lightly golden, pressing down any pastry that puffs up. Cool, then remove from the tins.

3 Meanwhile, steam the pumpkin for about 15 minutes, or until tender.

4 Place a tablespoon of sour cream in the middle of each pastry case and pile pumpkin pieces on top. Season with salt and cracked black pepper and drizzle with sweet chilli sauce, to taste. Return to the oven for a couple of minutes to heat through. Serve immediately.

ABOVE: Pumpkin tarts

3 marinated artichokes, drained and sliced

85 g (3 oz) semi-dried (sun-blushed) tomatoes, drained and chopped

100 g (3 1/2 oz) marinated mushrooms, drained and halved

1 Line a 23.5 x 13 x 6.5 cm (9 x 5 x 2 1/2 inch) loaf tin with plastic wrap, leaving a generous amount hanging over the sides. Place the ricotta and garlic in a bowl and beat until smooth. Season well and set aside.

2 Line the base of the tin with half the eggplant, cutting and fitting to cover the base. Top with a layer of half the red pepper, then all the zucchini slices. Spread evenly with the ricotta mixture and press down firmly. Place the rocket leaves on top of the ricotta. Arrange the artichoke, tomato and mushrooms in three rows lengthways on top of the ricotta.

3 Top with another layer of red pepper and finish with the remaining eggplant. Cover securely with the overlapping plastic wrap. Put a piece of cardboard on top and weigh it down with small food cans. Refrigerate overnight.

4 To serve, peel back the plastic wrap and turn the terrine out onto a plate. Remove the plastic wrap and cut into thick slices.

NOTE: Chargrilled vegetables and marinated mushrooms and artichokes are available at delicatessens.

CANDIED PUMPKIN

Preparation time: 20 minutes
Total cooking time: 35 minutes
Serves 4

500 g (1 lb) pumpkin

30 g (1 oz) butter

2 tablespoons cream

1 tablespoon soft brown sugar

fresh chives, chopped, to garnish

1 Preheat the oven to moderate 180°C (350°F/ Gas 4). Peel the pumpkin and remove the membrane and seeds. Cut the pumpkin into thin slices and place the slices, overlapping, in a 1 litre (32 fl oz) ovenproof dish. Put the butter, cream and sugar in a small pan over low heat. Stir until smooth, then pour the mixture over the pumpkin. Bake for 35 minutes, or until the pumpkin is tender. Sprinkle with chives.

CHARGRILLED VEGETABLE TERRINE

Preparation time: 30 minutes
+ overnight refrigeration
Total cooking time: Nil
Serves 8

☆☆

350 g (11 oz) ricotta

2 cloves garlic, crushed

8 large slices chargrilled eggplant (aubergine), drained

10 slices chargrilled red pepper (capsicum), drained

8 slices chargrilled zucchini (courgettes), drained

45 g (1 1/2 oz) rocket (arugula) leaves

ABOVE: Chargrilled vegetable terrine

Leave the yeast mixture to stand for 10 minutes, or until it is frothy.

Cut the pastry dough into two pieces and roll each into a circle.

Press the edges of the pastry together to seal and pinch to form a pattern.

FETA AND OLIVE HERB PIE

Preparation time: 40 minutes + rising of pastry
Total cooking time: 45 minutes
Serves 4–6

✿✿

2 teaspoons sugar
2 teaspoons (7 g/¼ oz) dried yeast
2 tablespoons olive oil
½ cup (60 g/2 oz) plain (all-purpose) flour
1 cup (125 g/4 oz) self-raising flour
1 onion, sliced
½ cup (15 g/½ oz) fresh flat-leaf (Italian) parsley, chopped
1 sprig fresh rosemary, chopped
3 sprigs fresh thyme, chopped
5 fresh basil leaves, torn
¼ cup (40 g/1¼ oz) pine nuts, toasted
1 clove garlic, crushed
175 g (5¾ oz) feta cheese, crumbled
¼ cup (35 g/1¼ oz) pitted olives, chopped

 Dissolve half the sugar in ½ cup (125 ml/ 4 fl oz) warm water and sprinkle the yeast over the top. Leave for 10 minutes, or until frothy (if it doesn't foam, the yeast is dead and you will need to start again), then mix with half the oil. Sift the flours and ½ teaspoon salt into a large bowl. Make a well in the centre and pour in the yeast mixture. Mix well and knead on a floured board until smooth. Cut in half, then roll each half into a 20 cm (8 inch) circle. Place one on a lightly greased baking tray, the other on a baking paper-covered baking tray. Cover the circles with a cloth and put in a warm place for 10–15 minutes, or until doubled in size.

2 Preheat the oven to moderately hot 200°C (400°F/Gas 6). Heat the remaining oil in a frying pan and cook the onion for 10 minutes, or until golden brown. Sprinkle with the remaining sugar and cook until caramelized. Transfer to a bowl and mix with the herbs, pine nuts, garlic, feta cheese and olives. Spread the mixture over the pastry on the greased tray. Brush the edge with water and put the second pastry circle on top, using the paper to help lift it over. Press the edges together to seal and pinch together to form a pattern. Cut a few slits in the top to allow steam to escape. Bake for 30–35 minutes, or until crisp and golden brown. Serve warm, cut into wedges.

NOTE: To toast pine nuts, you can dry-fry them in a frying pan, stirring and watching them constantly so they don't burn.

ABOVE: Feta and olive herb pie

EGGPLANT

The eggplant or aubergine is believed to have originated in India. However, an amazing variety of colours (from purple to white), shapes and sizes are now grown worldwide wherever the climate is suitable. The mild flavour and soft texture make eggplants suitable for all sorts of dishes in combination with other vegetables or meats. The first types to reach Europe from India were the shape of an egg, hence the name. Europeans did not accept it as an edible vegetable at first and grew it simply as a decoration. However, by the sixteenth century, it became popular and spread to America and gradually elsewhere.

ABOVE: Eggplant, tomato and goat's cheese stacks

EGGPLANT, TOMATO AND GOAT'S CHEESE STACKS

Preparation time: 15 minutes
Total cooking time: 10 minutes
Serves 4

★

1/2 cup (125 ml/4 fl oz) olive oil
2 large cloves garlic, crushed
2 small eggplants (aubergines)
2 ripe tomatoes
150 g (5 oz) goats cheese
8 large fresh basil leaves
small rocket (arugula) leaves, to garnish
extra virgin olive oil, to drizzle

Dressing

135 g (4 1/2 oz) sun-dried tomatoes in oil
1 clove garlic, crushed
1 tablespoon white wine vinegar
1/4 cup (60 g/2 oz) whole-egg mayonnaise

1 Mix the oil and garlic in a bowl and set aside. Cut each eggplant into six 1 cm (1/2 inch) slices and each tomato into four 1 cm (1/2 inch) slices. Use a sharp knife dipped in hot water to cut the cheese into eight 1 cm (1/2 inch) slices.

2 Brush both sides of the eggplant slices using half the oil. Heat a frying pan and cook the eggplant in batches over high heat for 3–4 minutes each side, or until golden. Remove and keep warm. Brush both sides of the tomatoes using the remaining oil and cook for 1 minute each side, or until sealed and warmed through.

3 For the dressing, drain the sun-dried tomatoes, reserving 1 tablespoon oil. Blend the tomatoes, oil and garlic in a food processor until smooth. Add the vinegar and process until combined. Stir in the mayonnaise and season to taste.

4 To assemble, place an eggplant slice on each plate. Top each with a slice of tomato, then a basil leaf and a slice of cheese. Repeat with the remaining ingredients to give two layers, finishing with a third piece of eggplant. Add a dollop of dressing and arrange the rocket around each stack. Drizzle a little of the extra virgin olive oil around the stacks. Serve immediately.

RATATOUILLE TARTE TATIN

Preparation time: 45 minutes
+ 20 minutes refrigeration
Total cooking time: 50 minutes
Serves 6

1¹/₂ cups (185 g/6 oz) plain (all-purpose) flour

90 g (3 oz) butter, chilled and chopped

1 egg, lightly beaten

1 tablespoon oil

20 g (³/₄ oz) butter, extra

2 zucchini (courgettes), halved lengthways and sliced

250 g (8 oz) eggplant (aubergine), cut into bite-sized cubes

1 large red onion, cut into bite-sized cubes

1 red pepper (capsicum), in bite-sized pieces

1 green pepper (capsicum), in bite-sized pieces

250 g (8 oz) cherry tomatoes, halved

2 tablespoons balsamic vinegar

¹/₂ cup (60 g/2 oz) grated Cheddar

300 g (10 oz) sour cream

¹/₄ cup (60 g/2 oz) good-quality ready-made pesto

1 Sift the flour into a large bowl and rub in the chopped butter with your fingertips until the mixture resembles fine breadcrumbs. Make a well and add the egg. Mix with a flat-bladed knife, using a cutting action, until the mixture comes together in beads, adding 1 tablespoon water if too dry. Gather together and lift onto a floured work surface. Press into a ball and flatten slightly into a disc. Chill in plastic wrap for 20 minutes.

2 Preheat the oven to moderately hot 200°C (400°F/Gas 6). Lightly grease a 25 cm (10 inch) springform tin and line the base with baking paper. Heat the oil and extra butter in a large frying pan, add the zucchini, eggplant, onion and peppers and cook over high heat for 8–10 minutes, or until just soft. Add the tomatoes and vinegar and cook for 3–4 minutes.

3 Place the tin on a baking tray, neatly lay the vegetables in the tin, then sprinkle with cheese. Roll the dough out between two sheets of baking paper to a 28 cm (11 inch) circle. Remove the paper and invert the pastry into the tin over the filling. Use a spoon handle to tuck the edges of the pastry down the side of the tin. Bake for 30–35 minutes (some liquid will leak out), then stand for 1–2 minutes. Remove from the tin and place on a serving plate, pastry-side down. Mix the sour cream and pesto in a small bowl and serve with the tarte tatin.

RATATOUILLE TARTE TATIN

Mix the combined flour and butter with the egg, using a flat-bladed knife, until it all comes together in beads.

Add the tomato halves and balsamic vinegar to the pan and cook for 3–4 minutes.

Tuck the edges of the pastry down the side of the tin with a spoon handle.

LEFT: Ratatouille tarte tatin

TAGINE
Tagine literally means 'stew' and is used in reference to many delicious dishes from Morocco. Common ingredients of the tagine are lamb or chicken, often with preserved lemon (available at delicatessens and speciality food stores). Traditionally, tagine recipes are cooked slowly over an open fire or a bed of coals in a special earthenware cooking vessel, or *tagine slaoui*. These vessels often have elaborate glazing and bright patterns. However, the recipes can also be cooked without using these special dishes.

ABOVE: Couscous with pear and vegetable tagine

COUSCOUS WITH PEAR AND VEGETABLE TAGINE

Preparation time: 20 minutes
Total cooking time: 1 hour
Serves 4–6

1/2 preserved lemon
3 tablespoons oil
2 onions, chopped
1 teaspoon ground ginger
2 teaspoons ground paprika
2 teaspoons ground cumin
1 cinnamon stick
pinch of saffron threads
1.5 kg (3 lb) vegetables (eg. carrot, eggplant/ aubergine, orange sweet potato, parsnip, potato, pumpkin), cut into large chunks
400 g (13 oz) can peeled tomatoes
1 cup (250 ml/8 fl oz) vegetable stock
100 g (3 1/2 oz) dried pears, halved
50 g (1 3/4 oz) pitted prunes
2 zucchini (courgettes), cut into large chunks

3 tablespoons chopped fresh parsley
300 g (10 oz) couscous
1/3 cup (30 g/1 oz) flaked or slivered almonds, toasted

1 Preheat the oven to moderate 180°C (350°F/ Gas 4). Remove the flesh from the preserved lemon and thinly slice the lemon rind.
2 Heat 2 tablespoons of the oil in a large saucepan or ovenproof dish, add the onion and cook over medium heat for 5 minutes, or until soft. Add the spices and cook for 3 minutes. Add all the vegetables, except the zucchini, and stir until coated with the spices and the outsides begin to soften. Add the lemon, tomatoes, stock, pears and prunes. Cover (if using a saucepan transfer to an ovenproof dish) and bake for 30 minutes. Add the zucchini and cook, uncovered, for 15 minutes, or until the vegetables are tender. Remove the cinnamon stick, then stir in the parsley.
3 Cover the couscous with the remaining oil and 2 cups (500 ml/16 fl oz) boiling water and stand until all the water has been absorbed. Fluff with a fork and serve around the outside of a platter, with the vegetables in the centre. Sprinkle with the toasted almonds.

COUSCOUS VEGETABLE LOAF

Preparation time: 20 minutes
 + overnight refrigeration
Total cooking time: 15 minutes
Serves 6–8

1 litre (32 fl oz) vegetable stock
500 g (1 lb) couscous
30 g (1 oz) butter
3 tablespoons olive oil
2 cloves garlic, crushed
1 onion, finely chopped
1 tablespoon ground coriander
1 teaspoon ground cinnamon
1 teaspoon garam marsala
250 g (8 oz) cherry tomatoes,
 quartered
1 zucchini (courgette), finely chopped
130 g (4½ oz) can corn kernels,
 drained
8 large fresh basil leaves
150 g (5 oz) sun-dried peppers (capsicums)
 in oil
1 cup (60 g/2 oz) chopped fresh basil, extra

Dressing
⅓ cup (80 ml/2¾ fl oz) orange juice
1 tablespoon lemon juice
3 tablespoons chopped fresh parsley
1 teaspoon honey
1 teaspoon ground cumin

1 Bring the stock to the boil in a saucepan. Place the couscous and butter in a large bowl, cover with the stock and set aside for 10 minutes.
2 Meanwhile, heat 1 tablespoon of the oil in a large frying pan and cook the garlic and onion over low heat for 5 minutes, or until the onion is soft. Add the spices and cook for 1 minute, or until fragrant. Remove from the pan.
3 Add the remaining oil to the pan and fry the tomatoes, zucchini and corn over high heat in batches until soft.
4 Line a 3 litre (96 fl oz) loaf tin with plastic wrap, allowing it to overhang the side. Arrange basil leaves over the base to form two flowers. Drain the peppers, reserving 2 tablespoons oil, then roughly chop. Add the onion, fried vegetables, sun-dried peppers and extra basil to the couscous and mix. Press into the tin and fold the plastic wrap over to cover. Weigh down with cans of food and refrigerate overnight.
5 For the dressing, place all the ingredients and the pepper oil in a jar with a lid and shake well.
6 Turn out the loaf, slice and serve with dressing.

ABOVE: Couscous vegetable loaf

VEGETABLE PIE

Prick the base of the pastry all over with a fork, then bake until dry and golden.

Cook the vegetables until they are soft and almost break up when tested with a knife.

OPPOSITE PAGE, FROM TOP: Vegetable pie; Vegetable frittata

VEGETABLE PIE

Preparation time: 25 minutes
  + 30 minutes refrigeration
Total cooking time: 1 hour 10 minutes
Serves 6

Pastry

1 cup (125 g/4 oz) plain (all-purpose) flour
60 g (2 oz) butter, chilled and chopped
1 egg yolk
2 teaspoons poppy seeds

30 g (1 oz) butter
2 tablespoons oil
1 onion, cut into thin wedges
1 leek, sliced
3 potatoes, cut into large chunks
300 g (10 oz) orange sweet potato (kumera), cut into large chunks
300 g (10 oz) pumpkin, cut into large chunks
200 g (6½ oz) swede (rutabaga), cut into large chunks
1 cup (250 ml/8 fl oz) vegetable stock
1 red pepper (capsicum), cut into large pieces
200 g (6½ oz) broccoli, cut into large florets
2 zucchini (courgettes), cut into large pieces
1 cup (125 g/4 oz) grated vintage peppercorn Cheddar

1 Preheat the oven to moderately hot 200°C (400°F/Gas 6). For the pastry, sift the flour into a large bowl and rub in the butter with your fingertips until the mixture resembles fine breadcrumbs. Make a well and add the egg yolk, poppy seeds and 1–2 tablespoons iced water and mix with a flat-bladed knife, using a cutting action, until the mixture comes together in beads. Gently gather together and lift out onto a lightly floured work surface. Press into a ball, flatten slightly into a disc, then wrap in plastic wrap and refrigerate for 30 minutes.
2 Roll the dough between two sheets of baking paper, then remove the top sheet and invert the pastry into a 23 cm (9 inch) pie plate. Use a small ball of pastry to press the pastry in, allowing excess to hang over the sides. Trim any excess pastry. Prick the base with a fork and bake for 15–20 minutes, or until dry and golden.
3 Meanwhile, for the filling, heat the butter and oil in a large saucepan, add the onion and leek and cook over medium heat for 5 minutes, or

until soft and golden. Add the potato, sweet potato, pumpkin and swede and cook, stirring occasionally, until the vegetables start to soften. Add the stock and cook for 30 minutes.
4 Add the remaining vegetables and cook, partially covered, for 20 minutes, or until the vegetables are soft—some may break up slightly. Season and cool a little. Spoon into the pie shell, sprinkle with cheese and cook under a medium grill for 5 minutes, or until the cheese is golden.

VEGETABLE FRITTATA

Preparation time: 35 minutes + cooling
Total cooking time: 35 minutes
Serves 6

1 large red pepper (capsicum)
¼ cup (60 ml/2 fl oz) olive oil
2 leeks, thinly sliced
2 cloves garlic, crushed
125 g (4 oz) zucchini (courgettes), thinly sliced
150 g (5 oz) eggplant (aubergine), thinly sliced
150 g (5 oz) orange sweet potato, thinly sliced
7 eggs, lightly beaten
2 tablespoons finely chopped fresh basil
1 cup (100 g/3½ oz) grated Parmesan

1 Cut the red pepper into large pieces, removing the seeds and membrane. Cook, skin-side-up, under a hot grill until the skin blackens and blisters. Cool in a plastic bag, then peel and cut into thin strips.
2 Heat 1 tablespoon oil in a deep round 23 cm (9 inch) frying pan, add the leek, garlic and zucchini and stir over medium heat for 5 minutes, or until soft. Remove from the pan and drain on paper towels.
3 Heat the remaining oil in the same pan and cook the eggplant in batches until golden on both sides. Cook the sweet potato in the pan and drain. Line the base of the pan with half the eggplant and spread with leek mixture. Cover with red pepper, eggplant and sweet potato.
4 Mix the eggs, basil, Parmesan and some pepper in a jug and pour over the vegetables. Cook over low heat for 15 minutes, or until almost set. Place the pan under a hot grill for 2–3 minutes, or until golden. Cool for about 30 minutes, then turn onto a board. Serve in wedges, cold or at room temperature (it falls apart if eaten hot).

ROAST VEGETABLE TART

Spread the onion mixture over the pastry, leaving a border all the way around.

Fold the edge of the pastry up and mould into shape to hold in the vegetables.

ABOVE: Roast vegetable tart

ROAST VEGETABLE TART

Preparation time: 30 minutes
  + 30 minutes refrigeration
Total cooking time: 1 hour 50 minutes
Serves 4–6

 ✷ ✷

1 eggplant (aubergine), cut into thick slices

350 g (11 oz) pumpkin, cut into large pieces

2 zucchini (courgettes), cut into thick slices

1–2 tablespoons olive oil

1 large red pepper (capsicum), chopped

1 teaspoon olive oil, extra

1 red onion, sliced

1 tablespoon Korma curry paste

natural yoghurt, to serve

Pastry

1½ cups (185 g/6 oz) plain (all-purpose) flour

125 g (4 oz) butter, chilled and chopped

²/₃ cup (100 g/3½ oz) roasted cashews,
  finely chopped

1 teaspoon cumin seeds

2–3 tablespoons chilled water

1 Preheat the oven to moderately hot 200°C (400°F/Gas 6). Put the eggplant, pumpkin and zucchini on a lined baking tray, then brush with oil and bake for 30 minutes. Remove from the oven, turn and add the pepper. Bake for another 30 minutes, then allow to cool.

2 To make the pastry, sift the flour into a large bowl and rub in the butter with your fingertips until the mixture resembles fine breadcrumbs. Stir in the cashews and cumin seeds. Make a well in the centre and add the water. Mix with a flat-bladed knife, using a cutting action, until the mixture comes together in small beads. Gently gather together and lift out onto a lightly floured work surface. Press together into a ball and flatten slightly into a disc, wrap in plastic wrap and refrigerate for 30 minutes. Roll out between two sheets of baking paper to a circle about 35 cm (14 inches) in diameter.

3 Heat the extra oil in a frying pan and cook the onion for 2–3 minutes, or until soft. Add the curry paste and cook, stirring, for 1 minute, or until fragrant and well combined. Allow to cool. Reduce the oven temperature to moderate 180°C (350°F/Gas 4).

4 Lift onto a lightly greased baking tray and spread the onion mixture over the pastry, leaving a 6 cm (2½ inch) border all around. Arrange the other vegetables over the onion, piling them slightly higher in the centre. Working your way around, fold the edge of the pastry in pleats over the vegetables. Bake for 45 minutes, or until the pastry is lightly golden and cooked. Serve immediately with a dollop of yoghurt.

BLUE CHEESE AND ONION FLAN

Preparation time: 40 minutes
  + 30 minutes refrigeration
Total cooking time: 1 hour 40 minutes
Serves 8

2 tablespoons olive oil
1 kg (2 lb) red onions, very thinly sliced
1 teaspoon soft brown sugar
1 1/2 cups (185 g/6 oz) plain (all-purpose) flour
100 g (3 1/2 oz) cold butter, cubed
3/4 cup (185 ml/6 fl oz) cream
3 eggs
100 g (3 1/2 oz) blue cheese, crumbled
1 teaspoon chopped fresh thyme leaves

1 Heat the oil in a heavy-based frying pan over low heat and cook the onion and sugar, stirring, for 45 minutes, or until the onion is caramelized.
2 Sift the flour into a large bowl and rub in the butter with your fingertips until the mixture resembles fine breadcrumbs. Make a well in the centre and add 3–4 tablespoons cold water. Mix with a flat-bladed knife, using a cutting action until the mixture comes together in beads. Gently gather together and lift onto a lightly floured work surface. Press into a ball, wrap in plastic wrap and refrigerate for 30 minutes.
3 Preheat the oven to moderate 180°C (350°F/ Gas 4). Roll out the pastry on a lightly floured surface to fit a lightly greased 22 cm (8 3/4 inch) round loose-based flan tin. Invert the pastry over the tin and press in with a small ball of pastry, allowing excess to hang over the side. Trim any excess pastry, then chill for 10 minutes. Line the pastry shell with baking paper and fill with baking beads or uncooked rice. Bake on a baking tray for 10 minutes. Remove the beads and paper, then bake for 10 minutes, or until lightly golden and dry.
4 Cool, then gently spread the onion over the base of the pastry. Whisk the cream in a bowl with the eggs, blue cheese, thyme and some pepper. Pour over the onion and bake for 35 minutes, or until firm.

BELOW: Blue cheese and onion flan

1/4 teaspoon cayenne pepper

2 teaspoons chopped fresh thyme

2 bay leaves

1 tablespoon red wine vinegar

1 teaspoon caster (superfine) sugar

3 tablespoons shredded fresh basil

1 Score a cross in the base of each tomato. Place in a bowl of boiling water for 10 seconds, then plunge into cold water and peel away from the cross. Roughly chop the flesh.

2 Heat 2 tablespoons of the oil in a large saucepan, add the eggplant and cook over medium heat for 4–5 minutes, or until softened but not browned. Remove. Add another 2 tablespoons oil to the pan, add the zucchini and cook for 3–4 minutes, or until softened. Remove. Add the green pepper, cook for 2 minutes and remove.

3 Heat the remaining oil, add the onion and cook for 2–3 minutes, or until softened. Add the garlic, cayenne, thyme and bay leaves, and cook, stirring, for 1 minute. Return the eggplant, zucchini and pepper to the pan and add the tomato, vinegar and sugar. Simmer for 20 minutes, stirring occasionally. Stir in the basil and season with salt and black pepper. Serve hot or at room temperature.

NOTE: You can serve ratatouille as a vegetable on the side or as a starter with bread.

RATATOUILLE
(French vegetable stew)

Preparation time: 25 minutes
Total cooking time: 40 minutes
Serves 4–6

6 vine-ripened tomatoes

5 tablespoons olive oil

500 g (1 lb) eggplants (aubergines), cut into 2 cm (3/4 inch) cubes

375 g (12 oz) zucchini (courgettes), cut into 2 cm (3/4 inch) slices

1 green pepper (capsicum), seeded, cut into 2 cm (3/4 inch) squares

1 red onion, cut into 2 cm (3/4 inch) wedges

3 cloves garlic, finely chopped

ABOVE: Ratatouille

ASPARAGUS VINAIGRETTE

To make the vinaigrette, combine 1/2 tablespoon Dijon mustard, 2 tablespoons sherry vinegar, 1/3 cup (80 ml/2 3/4 fl oz) good-quality olive oil and 1/2 teaspoon finely chopped chives in a small jug. Cook 24 asparagus spears, woody ends trimmed, in a large saucepan of boiling salted water over medium heat for 8–10 minutes, until tender. While the asparagus is cooking, heat 3 tablespoons olive oil in a medium frying pan, add 2 whole peeled cloves garlic and cook over low heat until the cloves are golden. Discard the garlic. Add 1 cup (80 g/2 3/4 oz) fresh breadcrumbs and increase the heat to medium. Cook until the breadcrumbs are crisp and golden. Season and drain on paper towels. Drain the asparagus and place on a platter. Drizzle with the vinaigrette and sprinkle with breadcrumbs. Serves 4.

VEGETABLE TIAN

Preparation time: 40 minutes
Total cooking time: 1 hour 20 minutes
Serves 6–8

☆

1 kg (2 lb) red peppers (capsicums)

1/2 cup (125 ml/4 fl oz) olive oil

800 g (1 lb 10 oz) silverbeet (Swiss chard),
   stalks removed and coarsely shredded

2 tablespoons pine nuts

ground nutmeg, to taste

1 onion, chopped

2 cloves garlic

2 teaspoons chopped thyme

750 g (1 1/2 lb) tomatoes, peeled, seeded, diced

1 large eggplant (aubergine), cut into 1 cm
   (1/2 inch) rounds

5 small zucchini (courgettes) (about 500 g/1 lb),
   thinly sliced diagonally

3 ripe tomatoes, cut into 1 cm (1/2 inch) slices

1 tablespoon fresh breadcrumbs

30 g (1 oz) Parmesan, grated

30 g (1 oz) butter

1 Preheat the oven to moderately hot 200°C (400°F/Gas 6). Preheat the grill to high.

2 Remove the seeds and membrane from the peppers and grill until black and blistered. Cool in a plastic bag, then peel and cut into 8 x 3 cm (3 x 1 inch) slices. Place in a lightly greased 25 x 20 x 5 cm (10 x 8 x 2 inch) ovenproof dish and season lightly.

3 Heat 2 tablespoons of the olive oil in a heavy-based frying pan and cook the silverbeet over medium heat for 8–10 minutes, or until softened. Add the pine nuts and season, to taste, with salt, pepper and nutmeg. Place the silverbeet over the pepper slices.

4 Heat another tablespoon of olive oil in a heavy-based frying pan. Add the onion and cook over medium heat for 7–8 minutes, or until soft and golden. Add the garlic and thyme, cook for 1 minute, then add the diced tomato and bring to the boil. Reduce the heat and simmer for 10 minutes. Spread the sauce evenly over the silverbeet.

5 Heat the remaining olive oil in a heavy-based frying pan and fry the eggplant slices over high heat for 8–10 minutes, or until golden on both sides. Drain on paper towels and place in a single layer over the tomato sauce. Season lightly.

6 Arrange the zucchini and tomato slices in alternating layers over the eggplant. Sprinkle the breadcrumbs and Parmesan over the top and then dot with the butter. Bake for 25–30 minutes or until golden. Serve warm or at room temperature.

TIAN
Tian is the name for a glazed earthenware dish which is used for baking. Now, tian has also come to mean the recipe itself.

ABOVE: Vegetable tian

FETA CHEESE
This Greek cheese is popular in Greek salads and savoury pastries. It is a soft, white cheese with a sharp, salty taste. It is made using the milk from sheep or goats and sometimes cows. The salty taste is intense because the cheese is ripened or pickled in a brine solution. It has a short ripening period of about one month. When buying feta, make sure it looks moist and is sitting in a briny solution. To store feta, place it in a container and cover with a salty solution. Change the solution each day and use the feta within four days. Feta cheese is made in many countries where it is quite popular, including Italy, Bulgaria, Denmark, Germany and Australia.

ABOVE: Sweet potato, feta and pine nut strudel

SWEET POTATO, FETA AND PINE NUT STRUDEL

Preparation time: 25 minutes
Total cooking time: 55 minutes
Serves 6

450 g (14 oz) sweet potato, cut into
  2 cm (³/4 inch) cubes
1 tablespoon olive oil
¹/2 cup (80 g/2³/4 oz) pine nuts, toasted
250 g (8 oz) feta, crumbled
2 tablespoons chopped fresh basil
4 spring onions (scallions), chopped
40 g (1¹/4 oz) butter, melted
2 tablespoons olive oil, extra, for brushing
7 sheets filo pastry
2–3 teaspoons sesame seeds

1 Preheat the oven to moderate 180°C (350°F/Gas 4). Brush the sweet potato with oil and bake for 20 minutes, or until softened and slightly coloured. Transfer to a bowl and cool slightly.
2 Add the pine nuts, feta, basil and spring onion to the bowl, mix gently and season to taste.
3 Mix the butter and extra oil. Remove one sheet of filo and cover the rest with a damp tea towel. Brush each sheet of filo with the butter mixture and layer them into a pile.
4 Spread the prepared filling in the centre of the filo, covering an area about 10 x 30 cm (4 x 12 inches). Fold the sides of the pastry into the centre, then tuck in the ends. Carefully turn the strudel over and place on a baking tray, seam-side down. Lightly brush the top with butter mix and sprinkle with sesame seeds. Bake for 35 minutes, or until the pastry is crisp and golden. Serve warm.
VARIATION: You can use 450 g (14 oz) of pumpkin instead of the sweet potato.

ONION TART

Preparation time: 40 minutes
+ 40 minutes refrigeration
Total cooking time: 1 hour 30 minutes
Serves 4– 6

Shortcrust pastry

1¼ cups (155 g/5 oz) plain (all-purpose) flour
90 g (3 oz) butter, chilled, cubed
2–3 tablespoons iced water

Filling

25 g (¾ oz) butter
7 onions, sliced
1 tablespoon Dijon mustard
3 eggs, lightly beaten
½ cup (125 g/4 oz) sour cream
¼ cup (25 g/¾ oz) grated Parmesan

1 Lightly grease a round 23 cm (9 inch) fluted tart plate. Sift the flour into a bowl and rub in the butter with your fingertips until the mixture looks like fine breadcrumbs. Make a well, add most of the water and mix with a flat-bladed knife, using a cutting action, until the mixture comes together in beads, adding more water if necessary.

2 Gather the dough together and lift out onto a lightly floured surface. Press together until smooth, cover with plastic wrap and chill for 20 minutes. Roll out between two sheets of baking paper to cover the base and side of the tart plate. Place the pastry in the tin and trim any excess pastry. Cover with plastic wrap and chill for 20 minutes.

3 Preheat the oven to moderate 180°C (350°F/ Gas 4). Line the pastry shell with a piece of crumpled baking paper and pour in some baking beads or uncooked rice. Bake for 10 minutes, remove the paper and beads and return to the oven for another 10 minutes, or until lightly golden. Cool completely.

4 For the filling, melt the butter in a large heavy-based frying pan. Add the onion, cover and cook over medium heat for 25 minutes. Uncover and cook for another 10 minutes, stirring often, until soft and golden. Cool.

5 Spread the mustard over the base of the pastry, then spread the onion over the mustard. Whisk together the eggs and sour cream and pour over the onion. Sprinkle with Parmesan and bake for 35 minutes, or until set and golden.

ONIONS

The common dry onion comes in a wide range of varieties, shapes, flavours and sizes. The most readily available are the white, brown and red (Spanish), all of which are inter-changeable in cooking. The red onion is milder in flavour and can be used raw in salads. High heat will burn onions and give them a bitter flavour so, as a general rule, the longer and slower the chopped or sliced onion is cooked in butter or oil, the sweeter it becomes. Do not buy onions if they have started to sprout. Always buy dry-skinned firm onions and store in a wire basket so air can circulate to keep them dry. They will keep for a month if stored this way.

LEFT: Onion tart

DASHI
Dashi is a distinctly Japanese-flavoured stock based on fish and seaweed. Other ingredients can be added to make the dashi (literally, stock) but good chefs keep these secret. Dashi takes the place of the widely used chicken, meat or fish stock used in other parts of the world. Used extensively in Japanese cuisine, it is made by steeping konbu, a form of kelp, in hot water, then adding shaved, dried bonito. Instant dashi is sold ready-to-use in powder, liquid and granule forms.

OPPOSITE PAGE, FROM TOP: Many mushroom noodles; Braised bok choy

MANY MUSHROOM NOODLES

Preparation time: 30 minutes + 20 minutes soaking
Total cooking time: 15 minutes
Serves 4-6

25 g (³/4 oz) dried shiitake mushrooms
500 g (1 lb) thin Hokkien (egg) noodles, separated
1 tablespoon vegetable oil
¹/2 teaspoon sesame oil
1 tablespoon finely chopped fresh ginger
4 cloves garlic, crushed
100 g (3¹/2 oz) fresh shiitake mushrooms, trimmed, sliced
150 g (5 oz) oyster mushrooms, sliced
150 g (5 oz) shimeji mushrooms, trimmed, pulled apart
1¹/2 teaspoons dashi granules dissolved in ³/4 cup (185 ml/6 fl oz) water
¹/4 cup (60 ml/2 fl oz) soy sauce
¹/4 cup (60 ml/2 fl oz) mirin
25 g (³/4 oz) butter
2 tablespoons lemon juice
100 g (3¹/2 oz) enoki mushrooms, trimmed, pulled apart
1 tablespoon chopped fresh chives

1 Soak the dried mushrooms in 1¹/2 cups (375 ml/12 fl oz) boiling water for 20 minutes, or until soft. Drain, reserving the liquid. Discard the woody stalks and slice the caps. Cover the noodles with boiling water for 1 minute, then drain and rinse.
2 Heat a wok over high heat, add the oils and swirl to coat the side. Add the ginger, garlic, fresh shiitake, oyster and shimeji mushrooms, and stir-fry for 1–2 minutes, or until the mushrooms have wilted. Remove from the wok.
3 Combine the dashi, soy, mirin, ¹/4 teaspoon white pepper and ³/4 cup (185 ml/6 fl oz) reserved liquid, add to the wok and cook for 3 minutes. Add the butter, lemon juice and 1 teaspoon salt and cook for 1 minute, or until the sauce thickens. Return the mushrooms to the wok, cook for 2 minutes, then stir in the enoki and shiitake mushrooms.
4 Add the noodles and stir for 3 minutes, or until heated through. Sprinkle with the chives and serve immediately.

BRAISED BOK CHOY

Preparation time: 10 minutes
Total cooking time: 5 minutes
Serves 4 (as a side dish)

2 tablespoons peanut oil
1 clove garlic, crushed
1 tablespoon julienned fresh ginger
500 g (1 lb) bok choy (pak choi), separated, cut into 8 cm (3 inch) lengths
1 teaspoon sugar
1 teaspoon sesame oil
1 tablespoon oyster sauce

1 Heat a wok over high heat, add the oil and swirl to coat. Add the garlic and ginger, and stir-fry for 1–2 minutes, then add the bok choy and stir-fry for 1 minute. Add the sugar, a pinch of salt and pepper and ¹/4 cup (60 ml/2 fl oz) water. Bring to the boil, then reduce the heat and simmer, covered, for 3 minutes, or until the stems are tender but crisp.
2 Stir in the sesame oil and oyster sauce and serve immediately.

MARINATED TOFU

Preparation time: 10 minutes + overnight marinating
Total cooking time: 15 minutes
Serves 4 (as a side dish)

¹/2 cup (125 ml/4 fl oz) peanut oil
2 cloves garlic, crushed
1 teaspoon grated fresh ginger
2 stems lemon grass, white part only, finely chopped
1 small fresh red chilli, finely chopped
2 tablespoons fish sauce
2 tablespoons lime juice
1 tablespoon soft brown sugar
500 g (1 lb) fried tofu puffs, halved on the diagonal

1 Combine all the ingredients in a flat non-metallic dish. Toss the tofu until coated in the marinade, then cover with plastic wrap and refrigerate overnight.
2 Heat a lightly oiled wok over high heat and stir-fry the tofu in batches for 1–2 minutes, or until browned. Serve hot.

1 cup (90 g/3 oz) bean sprouts, topped and
  tailed
40 g (1 1/4 oz) wom bok (Chinese cabbage),
  finely shredded
1 tablespoon julienned fresh ginger
2 tablespoons vegetarian oyster sauce
1 tablespoon mushroom soy sauce
1 tablespoon light soy sauce
1 tablespoon Chinese rice wine
1 teaspoon sesame oil
ground white pepper, to taste
fresh coriander (cilantro) leaves, to garnish

1 Cover the mushrooms in boiling water and soak for 20 minutes. Drain. Discard the woody stalks and thinly slice the caps.

2 Meanwhile, cook the noodles in a large saucepan of boiling water for 1 minute, stirring to separate. Drain. Rinse under cold, running water and drain again.

3 Heat a wok over high heat, add 1 tablespoon of the peanut oil and swirl to coat the side of the wok. Stir-fry the carrot and corn for 1–2 minutes, then add the bamboo shoots and stir-fry for a further 1–2 minutes, or until just cooked but still crisp. Remove the vegetables from the wok.

4 Reheat the wok (add 2 teaspoons peanut oil if necessary) and add the snow peas and red and green peppers. Stir-fry for 1–2 minutes, or until just cooked but still crisp. Add to the carrot and corn mixture. Reheat the wok (add another 2 teaspoons peanut oil if needed), then add the bean sprouts, wom bok and mushrooms and stir-fry for 30 seconds, or until wilted. Add the ginger and stir-fry for a further 1–2 minutes. Remove from the wok and add to the other vegetables.

5 Heat the remaining oil in the wok, and quickly stir-fry the noodles for 1–2 minutes, or until heated through, taking care not to let them break up. Stir in the vegetarian oyster sauce, mushroom soy sauce, light soy sauce and rice wine and stir thoroughly. Return all the vegetables to the wok and stir gently for 1–2 minutes, or until well combined with the noodles. Drizzle with the sesame oil, season with white pepper and garnish with the coriander leaves. Serve immediately.

NOTE: Garlic, onions, spring onions (scallions) and chillies have been omitted from this recipe because traditional Chinese vegetarians do not eat them.

BUDDHIST VEGETARIAN NOODLES

Preparation time: 25 minutes +
  20 minutes soaking
Total cooking time: 15 minutes
Serves

15 g (1/2 oz) dried shiitake mushrooms
400 g (13 oz) fresh flat egg noodles
2–3 tablespoons peanut or sunflower oil
1 small carrot, julienned
150 g (5 oz) fresh baby corn, quartered
  lengthways
227 g (7 oz) can bamboo shoots, drained and
  julienned
150 g (5 oz) snow peas (mangetout), julienned
1/2 small red pepper (capsicum), julienned
1 small green pepper (capsicum), julienned

*ABOVE: Buddhist
vegetarian noodles*

STIR-FRIED TOFU AND BOK CHOY

Preparation time: 20 minutes + marinating
Total cooking time: 10 minutes
Serves 4

600 g (1¼ lb) firm tofu, cubed
1 tablespoon finely chopped fresh ginger
2 tablespoons soy sauce
2 tablespoons peanut oil
1 red onion, thinly sliced
4 cloves garlic, crushed
500 g (1 lb) baby bok choy (pak choi), sliced
   lengthways
2 teaspoons sesame oil
2 tablespoons kecap manis
¼ cup (60 ml/2 fl oz) sweet chilli sauce
1 tablespoon toasted sesame seeds

1 Put the tofu and ginger in a bowl. Pour in the soy sauce and leave for 10 minutes. Drain.
2 Heat a wok over high heat, add half the oil and swirl to coat. Add the onion and stir-fry for 3 minutes, or until soft. Add the tofu and garlic, and stir-fry for 3 minutes. Remove from the wok.
3 Reheat the wok to very hot, add the remaining oil and the bok choy and stir-fry for 2 minutes, or until wilted. Return the tofu mixture to the wok and toss until heated through.
4 Stir in the sesame oil, kecap manis and chilli sauce. Scatter with the sesame seeds and serve.

TAMARI ROASTED ALMONDS WITH SPICY GREEN BEANS

Preparation time: 10 minutes
Total cooking time: 5 minutes
Serves 4-6

2 tablespoons sesame oil
1 long fresh red chilli, seeded and finely chopped
2 cm (¾ inch) piece fresh ginger, grated
2 cloves garlic, crushed
375 g (12 oz) green beans, cut into 5 cm
   (2 inch) lengths
½ cup (125 ml/4 fl oz) hoisin sauce
1 tablespoon soft brown sugar
2 tablespoons mirin
250 g (8 oz) tamari roasted almonds, roughly
   chopped (see Note)

1 Heat a wok over high heat, add the oil and swirl to coat. Add the chilli, ginger and garlic and stir-fry for 1 minute, or until lightly browned. Add the beans, hoisin sauce and sugar and stir-fry for 2 minutes. Stir in the mirin and cook for 1 minute, or until the beans are tender but still crunchy.
2 Remove from the heat and stir in the almonds just before serving. Serve on a bed of rice.
NOTE: Tamari roasted almonds are available from health-food stores. Tamari is a naturally brewed, thick Japanese soy sauce made with soy beans and rice.

BELOW: Tamari roasted almonds with spicy green beans

WOM BOK

Now cultivated year-round, wom bok (Chinese cabbage) is traditionally a winter vegetable, This versatile vegetable is commonly used in stir-fries, braises, soups and hotpots, and even appears in some salads. It is an excellent source of folic acid, vitamin A and potassium. Choose wom bok with tightly packed, green-tipped leaves that show no signs of wilting and that feel firm. To prepare the wom bok, trim the root end from the wom bok and slice it in half lengthways. Cut out the central core and discard.

ABOVE: Stir-fried vegetables

STIR-FRIED VEGETABLES

Preparation time: 20 minutes
Total cooking time: 5 minutes
Serves 6

2 tablespoons soy sauce
1 teaspoon fish sauce
1 tablespoon oyster sauce
1/4 cup (60 ml/2 fl oz) stock
1/2 teaspoon grated palm sugar
2 tablespoons vegetable oil
4 spring onions (scallions), cut into 3 cm
    (1 1/4 inch) lengths
3 cloves garlic, crushed
1 fresh red chilli, seeded and sliced
75 g (2 1/2 oz) button mushrooms, quartered
100 g (3 1/2 oz) wom bok (Chinese cabbage),
    roughly chopped
150 g (5 oz) snow peas (mangetout)
150 g (5 oz) cauliflower, cut into small florets
150 g (5 oz) broccoli, cut into small florets
chopped coriander (cilantro) leaves, to garnish

1 Combine the soy, fish and oyster sauces with the stock and palm sugar in a small bowl.
2 Heat a wok over high heat, add the oil and swirl to coat. Add the spring onion, garlic and chilli. Stir-fry for 20 seconds. Add the mushrooms and wom bok and stir-fry for 1 minute. Stir in the sauce and remaining vegetables. Cook for 2 minutes, or until tender. Garnish with coriander.

EGGPLANT WITH CHILLI BEAN PASTE

Preparation time: 20 minutes
Total cooking time: 15 minutes
Serves 4-6

1/2 cup (125 ml/4 fl oz) vegetable stock
1/4 cup (60 ml/2 fl oz) Chinese rice wine
2 tablespoons rice vinegar
1 tablespoon tomato paste (tomato purée)
2 teaspoons soft brown sugar
2 tablespoons soy sauce
1/4 cup (60 ml/2 fl oz) peanut oil
800 g (1 lb 10 oz) eggplant (aubergine), cut
    into 2 cm (3/4 inch) cubes
4 spring onions (scallions), chopped
3 cloves garlic, crushed
1 tablespoon finely chopped fresh ginger
1 tablespoon chilli bean paste
1 teaspoon cornflour (cornstarch) mixed with
    1 tablespoon water into a paste

1 Combine the stock, rice wine, rice vinegar, tomato paste, sugar and soy sauce in a bowl.
2 Heat a wok over high heat, add half the oil and swirl to coat. Stir-fry the eggplant in batches for 3 minutes each batch, or until brown. Remove.
3 Heat the remaining oil in the wok. Stir-fry the spring onion, garlic, ginger and bean paste for 30 seconds. Pour in the sauce and stir-fry for 1 minute. Add the cornflour paste and bring to the boil. Return the eggplant to the wok and stir-fry for 2–3 minutes, or until heated through.

ORANGE SWEET POTATO, SPINACH AND WATER CHESTNUT STIR-FRY

Preparation time: 15 minutes
Total cooking time: 20 minutes
Serves 4

500 g (1 lb) orange sweet potato, peeled and cut into 1.5 cm ($^5/_8$ inch) cubes
1 tablespoon vegetable oil
2 cloves garlic, crushed
2 teaspoons sambal oelek
227 g (7 oz) can water chestnuts, sliced
2 teaspoons grated palm sugar
390 g (13 oz) English spinach, stems removed
2 tablespoons soy sauce
2 tablespoons vegetable stock

1 Cook the sweet potato in a large saucepan of boiling water for 15 minutes, or until tender. Drain well.
2 Heat a wok over high heat, add the oil and swirl to coat the side of the wok. Stir-fry the garlic and sambal oelek for 1 minute, or until fragrant. Add the sweet potato and water chestnuts and stir-fry over medium–high heat for 2 minutes. Reduce the heat to medium, add the palm sugar and cook for a further 2 minutes, or until the sugar has melted. Add the spinach, soy sauce and stock and toss until the spinach has just wilted. Serve with steamed rice.

STIR-FRIED PEANUTS WITH CHILLI

Heat a wok over high heat, add 2 teaspoons peanut oil and a few drops of sesame oil and swirl to coat the side of the wok. Add 1$^1/_2$ cups (240 g/7$^1/_2$ oz) raw peanuts and stir-fry for 3–4 minutes, or until golden. Add 1 very finely chopped small fresh red chilli, 2 cloves crushed garlic and 1$^1/_2$ teaspoons salt and stir-fry for a further 1–2 minutes, taking care that the nuts don't burn. Sprinkle with 1$^1/_2$ teaspoons caster (superfine) sugar and toss well. Remove from the wok and cool before serving. Serve as a snack. Makes 1$^1/_2$ cups.

LEFT: Orange sweet potato, spinach and water chestnut stir-fry

405

SESAME OIL
Extensively used in
Chinese cuisine, sesame oil
adds fragrance to a dish. It
is usually used in small
quantities as it is highly
aromatic, and its flavour
can overwhelm those of
other ingredients if not
used with caution. Sesame
oil is made by pressing
toasted sesame seeds,
which give it the
characteristic amber
colour. A paler version of
sesame oil is pressed from
raw sesame seeds, but it is
not an acceptable
substitute as it lacks the
nutty fragrance of normal
sesame oil.

TEMPEH STIR-FRY

Preparation time: 15 minutes
Total cooking time: 15 minutes
Serves 4

1 teaspoon sesame oil
1 tablespoon peanut oil
2 cloves garlic, crushed
1 tablespoon grated fresh ginger
1 fresh red chilli, thinly sliced
4 spring onions (scallions), sliced on the diagonal
300 g (10 oz) tempeh, cut into 2 cm (3/4 inch)
  cubes
500 g (1 lb) baby bok choy (pak choi) leaves
800 g (1 lb 10 oz) gai larn (Chinese broccoli),
  chopped
1/2 cup (125 ml/4 fl oz) vegetarian oyster sauce
2 tablespoons rice vinegar
2 tablespoons fresh coriander (cilantro) leaves
1/4 cup (40 g/1 1/4 oz) toasted cashew nuts

1 Heat a wok over high heat, add the oils and
swirl to coat. Add the garlic, ginger, chilli and
spring onion and cook for 1–2 minutes, or until
the onion is soft. Add the tempeh and cook for
5 minutes. Remove from the wok.
2 Add half the greens and 1 tablespoon water to
the wok and cook, covered, for 3–4 minutes, or

until the greens have wilted. Remove from the
wok and repeat with the remaining greens and a
little more water.
3 Return the greens and tempeh to the wok,
add the sauce and vinegar and warm through.
Top with the coriander and nuts. Serve with rice.

ASIAN MUSHROOM STIR-FRY

Preparation time: 10 minutes
Total cooking time: 5 minutes
Serves 4

1 teaspoon cornflour (cornstarch)
1/4 teaspoon five-spice powder
2 1/2 tablespoons Chinese rice wine
1 tablespoon oyster sauce
2 tablespoons peanut oil
1 teaspoon sesame oil
1/3 cup (20 g/3/4 oz) thinly sliced spring onion
  (scallions)
2 cloves garlic, finely chopped
1 tablespoon finely julienned fresh ginger
200 g (6 1/2 oz) fresh shiitake mushrooms, halved
100 g (3 1/2 oz) button mushrooms, halved
100 g (3 1/2 oz) oyster mushrooms
100 g (3 1/2 oz) enoki mushrooms, trimmed
1 tablespoon sesame seeds, toasted

ABOVE: Tempeh stir-fry

1 Put the cornflour and five-spice powder in a small bowl, and gradually blend in the rice wine and oyster sauce.

2 Heat a wok over medium heat, add the peanut and sesame oils and swirl to coat. Add the spring onion, garlic and ginger and stir-fry over medium heat for 2 minutes. Increase the heat to high, add the shiitake and button mushrooms and stir-fry until the mushrooms become moist and almost tender. Add the oyster and enoki mushrooms and stir-fry until tender.

3 Stir in the five-spice mixture and stir-fry for 30 seconds, or until the mushrooms are glazed, then sprinkle with the sesame seeds.

BRAISED VEGETABLES WITH CASHEWS

Preparation time: 15 minutes
Total cooking time: 10 minutes
Serves 4

★

1 tablespoon peanut oil

2 cloves garlic, crushed

2 teaspoons grated fresh ginger

300 g (10 oz) choy sum, cut into 10 cm (4 inch) lengths

150 g (5 oz) baby corn, sliced in half on the diagonal

3/4 cup (185 ml/6 fl oz) chicken or vegetable stock

200 g (6 1/2 oz) sliced bamboo shoots

150 g (5 oz) oyster mushrooms, sliced in half

2 teaspoons cornflour (cornstarch)

2 tablespoons oyster sauce

2 teaspoons sesame oil

1 cup (90 g/3 oz) bean sprouts, tailed

75 g (2 1/2 oz) roasted unsalted cashews

1 Heat a wok over medium heat, add the oil and swirl to coat. Add the garlic and ginger and stir-fry for 1 minute. Increase the heat to high, add the choy sum and baby corn and stir-fry for another minute.

2 Add the stock and cook for 3–4 minutes, or until the choy sum stems are just tender. Add the bamboo shoots and mushrooms, and cook for 1 minute.

3 Combine the cornflour and 1 tablespoon water in a small bowl and mix into a paste. Stir into the vegetables, along with the oyster sauce. Cook for 1–2 minutes, or until the sauce is slightly thickened. Stir in the sesame oil and bean sprouts and serve immediately on a bed of steamed rice sprinkled with the roasted cashews.

BABY CORN
Baby corn (also known as miniature corn) are small (up to 10 cm/4 inches), young cobs of corn. Noted for their crunchiness and sweet flavour, baby corn are eaten whole. These edible, miniature, pale yellow corn cobs are often added to stir-fries to add colour and texture to a dish. They are a particular favourite in Chinese and Thai cuisine.

LEFT: Braised vegetables with cashews

BREAD&PIZZA

ALL ABOUT BREAD

When you master the techniques described here, in no time you will be delighted

by the wonderful aroma of freshly baked bread all over the house.

PLAIN BREAD

Once you have an understanding of some of the important elements of bread making, such as working with yeast, and kneading techniques, you will find that delicious bread is simple to make. As with all cookery, first read the recipe thoroughly, carefully weigh all the ingredients and assemble the equipment you need.

MYSTERIES OF YEAST SOLVED

Working with yeast, probably the most important ingredient in bread, is not as difficult as you may think. Yeast is available dried or fresh. Dried yeast, available at supermarkets, generally comes in a box containing 7 g (1/4 oz) sachets, one of which is enough for a standard loaf. Fresh yeast, sometimes harder to obtain, is available at some health food

shops and bakeries. It has quite a short storage life. 15 g (1/2 oz) of fresh yeast is equivalent to a 7 g (1/4 oz) sachet of dried. We used dried yeast in our recipes as it is readily available, can be stored in the pantry and carries a use-by date.

TYPES OF FLOUR

The type and quality of flour you use is vital. The correct flour makes a big

difference to the quality of bread. Many of the recipes call for the use of flour that is labelled as bread flour. This is high in protein and will form gluten, which helps the bread rise well and bake into a light airy loaf with a good crust. For most breads, if you use a regular flour the loaf will not rise well, gluten will not form and the loaf will be heavy and dense.

TO MAKE YOUR LOAF

This basic recipe is an excellent starting point as similar techniques are used in all bread making. Put a 7 g (¼ oz) sachet of dried yeast, ½ cup (125 ml/4 fl oz) warm water and 1 teaspoon caster (superfine) sugar in a small bowl and stir well to combine. Leave in a warm, draught-free place for 10 minutes, or until bubbles appear on the surface. The mixture should be frothy and slightly increased in

volume. If it isn't, discard it and start again. Sift 4 cups (500 g/1 lb) white bread flour, 1 teaspoon salt, 2 tablespoons dried whole milk powder and 1 tablespoon caster (superfine) sugar into a large bowl. Make a well in the centre, add the yeast mixture, ¼ cup (60 ml/2 fl oz) vegetable oil and 1 cup (250 ml/8 fl oz) warm water. Mix to a soft dough using a large metal spoon. The moisture content of flour can vary greatly between brands and even between batches so add extra water or flour, 1 tablespoon at a time, if the dough is too dry or sticky. Do not add too much flour because the dough will absorb more flour during kneading.

KNEADING THE DOUGH

The dough is then formed into a ball on a lightly floured surface and kneaded. Don't be tempted to cut short the

kneading time as it affects the texture of the finished bread. Kneading firstly distributes the yeast evenly throughout the dough and, secondly, allows the flour's protein to develop into gluten. Gluten gives the dough elasticity, strength and the ability to expand, as it traps the carbon dioxide gas created by the yeast and this allows the bread to rise.

The kneading action is simple and it is quite easy to get into a rhythm. Hold one end of the dough down with one hand, and stretch it away from you with the other hand. Fold the dough back together, make a quarter turn and repeat the action. Knead for 10 minutes, or until smooth and elastic. When you have finished, gather the dough into a ball, then follow the instructions on the next page to complete the bread-making process.

PREPARE TO BAKE

PROVING THE BREAD

After kneading, put the dough into a lightly greased bowl to prevent it from sticking. Cover loosely with plastic wrap or a clean damp tea towel. This helps retain moisture and stop the formation of a skin. Leave the bowl in a warm place (around 30°C is ideal) to allow the dough to rise—this stage is called proving. Do not put the dough in a very hot environment in an attempt to speed up the rising process as it will give an unpleasant flavour to the bread, and may damage the yeast action. The dough will take longer to rise in a cooler environment, but with no adverse effect. When the dough is ready it should be doubled in volume and not spring back when touched with a

fingertip. This will take about an hour. Lightly grease a bread tin that measures 22 x 9 x 9 cm (9 x 3½ x 3½ inches) with melted butter or oil. Heavy-gauge baking tins and trays are best as they resist buckling at high temperatures and prevent the loaf from burning on the base.

PUNCHING DOWN

After proving, punch down the dough (literally—one punch) to expel the air, and knead again briefly for 1 minute, or until smooth. The dough is now ready for shaping. Handle the dough carefully and gently and avoid excessive reshaping. Shape the loaf to fit into the prepared tin, placing it in with any seam at the base. Cover with plastic wrap or a damp tea

towel and place the tin in a warm, draught-free place until the dough is well risen and doubled in size. This will take about 45–60 minutes. This is the final rise for the dough.

BAKING

Preheat the oven to hot 210°C (415°F/ Gas 6–7). To glaze, beat 1 egg with 1 tablespoon milk and brush over the top of the dough with a pastry brush. Place the bread in the middle of the hot oven and bake for 10 minutes. Don't open the oven during the first 10 minutes of baking as intense heat is needed during this time. Reduce the oven temperature to moderate 180°C (350°F/Gas 4) and bake for another 30–40 minutes. At the

end of cooking time, test for doneness by turning the loaf out of the tin and tapping the base with your knuckles. The bread will sound hollow when cooked. If it is not cooked, return it to the tin and bake for another 5–10 minutes. Remove from the tin and cool on a wire rack.

OTHER SHAPES

Bread dough can be made into many shapes and does not have to be baked in a bread or loaf tin. You will need to grease a baking tray, and, as an option, sprinkle the tray with fine cornmeal or polenta.

BLOOMER: At the shaping stage, roll out the dough on a lightly floured surface to a rectangle about 2.5 cm (1 inch) thick. Starting from the short end, roll up the dough like you would a swiss roll. Roll quite firmly to make a short, rather thick loaf. Place with the seam underneath on the baking tray. Cover the dough with a cloth and leave in a warm, draught-free place for an hour, or until doubled in size. Using a sharp knife, make 6 evenly-spaced slashes across the top of the dough. Spray the loaf with water and place in a hot 220°C (425°F/Gas 7) oven for 10 minutes. Reduce to moderately hot 200°C (400°F/Gas 6) and bake for 30 minutes, or until the loaf is golden brown and sounds hollow when tapped underneath. Cool on a wire rack.

PLAITED LOAF: After knocking back, divide the dough into three. Gently roll each portion into a 30 cm (12 inch) sausage, then transfer to a greased baking tray. Arrange next to one another on the tray, then join the strands at one end and start plaiting them together. Pinch and tuck under at both ends to seal the plait. Cover with a tea towel and set aside in a warm, draught-free place for 1 hour, or until doubled in size. Brush with milk and bake in a hot 220°C (425°F/Gas 7) oven for 10 minutes. Reduce the oven to moderately hot 200°C (400°F/Gas 6) and cook for 30 minutes, or until the loaf is golden brown and sounds hollow when tapped underneath. Cool on a wire rack.

STORAGE

Home-baked bread is best eaten on the day of baking, or otherwise used to make toast. Because it has no preservatives it doesn't keep as long as commercial bread, but it can be tightly wrapped and frozen for up to 3 months. When required, thaw at room temperature, then refresh in a moderate 180°C (350°F/Gas 4) oven for 10 minutes.

VARIATION: A good flavour can be made by substituting 1 cup (125 g/4 oz) of the bread flour with 1 cup (150 g/5 oz) wholemeal or stoneground bread flour. Follow the instructions for the white loaf.

413

COTTAGE LOAF

Preparation time: 30 minutes
  + 1 hour 25 minutes rising
Total cooking time: 40 minutes
Makes 1 large loaf

★★

7 g (¼ oz) sachet dried yeast
1 tablespoon soft brown sugar
2 cups (250 g/8 oz) white bread flour
2 cups (300 g/10 oz) wholemeal bread flour
1 teaspoon salt
1 tablespoon vegetable oil

1 Place the yeast, 1 teaspoon of the sugar and ½ cup (125 ml/4 fl oz) warm water in a small bowl and mix well. Leave in a warm, draught-free place for 10 minutes, or until bubbles appear on the surface. The mixture should be frothy and slightly increased in volume. If your yeast mixture doesn't foam it is dead, so you will have to discard it and start again.
2 Place the flours and salt in a large bowl. Make a well in the centre and add the yeast mixture, oil, the remaining sugar and 1 cup (250 ml/ 8 fl oz) warm water. Mix with a wooden spoon, then turn out onto a lightly floured surface. Knead for 10 minutes, or until smooth and elastic. Incorporate a little extra flour into the dough as you knead, to stop the dough from sticking.
3 Place the dough in an oiled bowl and lightly brush oil over the dough. Cover with plastic wrap or a damp tea towel and leave in a warm place for 45 minutes, or until doubled in size.
4 Punch down the dough, then turn out onto a lightly floured surface and knead the dough for 3–4 minutes. Pull away one third of the dough and knead both portions into a smooth ball. Place the large ball on a large floured baking tray and brush the top with water. Sit the smaller ball on top and, using two fingers, press down into the centre of the dough to join the two balls together. Cover with plastic wrap or a damp tea towel and set aside in a warm place for 40 minutes, or until well risen.
5 Preheat the oven to moderately hot 190°C (375°F/Gas 5). Sift some white flour over the top of the loaf and bake for 40 minutes, or until golden brown and cooked. Leave on the tray for 2–3 minutes to cool slightly, then turn out onto a wire rack to cool.

COTTAGE LOAF
This is a traditional English style of bread with a distinctive look. It has a large round free-form base topped with a smaller top-knot. The smaller loaf is pressed down in the centre with two fingers to attach it firmly to the base loaf. It can be made with both white or wholemeal flours or a combination of the two. The addition of a little oil to bread doughs aids in the keeping quality of the bread after baking. This basic dough can be formed into any shape you like, either free-form or placed in a bread tin. This type of loaf is also delicious cut into thick slices and toasted.

RIGHT: Cottage loaf

SOY AND LINSEED LOAF

Preparation time: 30 minutes
 + 1 hour 45 minutes rising
Total cooking time: 50 minutes
Makes 1 loaf

✢ ✢

1/2 cup (110 g/3 1/2 oz) pearl barley

7 g (1/4 oz) sachet dried yeast

1 teaspoon caster (superfine) sugar

1 teaspoon salt

1 tablespoon linseeds

2 tablespoons soy flour

2 tablespoons gluten flour

1 cup (150 g/5 oz) wholemeal bread flour

2 1/2 cups (310 g/10 oz) white bread flour

2 tablespoons olive oil

1 Brush a 26 x 10 cm (10 1/2 x 4 inch) bread tin with oil. Put the barley in a saucepan with 2 cups (500 ml/16 fl oz) water, bring to the boil and boil for 20 minutes, or until softened. Drain.
2 Place the yeast, sugar and 155 ml (5 fl oz) warm water in a small bowl and mix well. Leave in a warm, draught-free place for 10 minutes, or until bubbles appear on the surface. The mixture should be frothy and slightly increased in volume. If your yeast doesn't foam it is dead, so you will have to discard it and start again.
3 Place the barley, salt, linseeds, soy and gluten flours, wholemeal flour and 2 cups (250 g/8 oz) of the white flour in a large bowl. Make a well and add the yeast mixture, oil and 155 ml (5 fl oz) warm water. Mix with a wooden spoon to a soft dough. Turn out onto a floured surface and knead for 10 minutes, or until smooth and elastic. Incorporate enough of the remaining flour until the dough is no longer sticky.
4 Place in an oiled bowl and brush the dough with oil. Cover with plastic wrap or a damp tea towel and leave in a warm, draught-free place for 45 minutes, or until doubled in size. Punch down and knead for 2–3 minutes.
5 Pat the dough into a 24 x 20 cm (9 1/2 x 8 inch) rectangle. Roll up firmly from the long side and place, seam-side-down, in the bread tin. Cover with plastic wrap or a damp tea towel and set aside in a warm, draught-free place for 1 hour, or until risen to the top of the tin. Preheat the oven to moderately hot 200°C (400°F/Gas 6).
6 Brush the dough with water and make two slits on top. Bake for 30 minutes, or until golden. Remove from the tin and cool on a wire rack.

SOY BEANS
Soy beans have been cultivated in Asia for centuries and were introduced to Europe in the seventeenth century. America is now the largest producer of soy beans. They are used mostly to make soy bean oil, but the bean is also used whole and manufactured into a wide range of food products. Soy flour is a high-protein food, but lacks gluten, which is essential for the rising of breads. Soy flour is added to bread to give a different flavour and as it is high in fat, it enriches the bread. A high proportion of wheat flour and/or gluten flour is necessary to give a satisfactorily risen loaf.

*ABOVE: Soy
and linseed loaf*

OPPOSITE PAGE, FROM TOP: Light fruit bread; Dense fruit bread

LIGHT FRUIT BREAD

Preparation time: 25 minutes
+ 1 hour 30 minutes rising
Total cooking time: 35 minutes
Makes 1 loaf

★

1 cup (160 g/5 1/2 oz) raisins
1 tablespoon sherry
1 tablespoon grated orange rind
7 g (1/4 oz) sachet dried yeast
1 cup (250 ml/8 fl oz) warm milk
1/4 cup (60 g/2 oz) caster (superfine) sugar
3 cups (375 g/12 oz) white bread flour
1/2 teaspoon salt
30 g (1 oz) butter, cubed

Glaze

1 egg yolk
2 tablespoons cream

1 Combine the raisins, sherry and rind in a small bowl and set aside.
2 Place the yeast, milk and 1 teaspoon of the sugar in a small bowl and mix well. Leave in a warm, draught-free place for 10 minutes, or until bubbles appear on the surface. The mixture should be frothy and slightly increased in volume. If your yeast doesn't foam it is dead, so you will have to discard it and start again.
3 Place 2 3/4 cups (340 g/11 oz) of the bread flour and the salt in a large bowl. Rub in the butter and remaining sugar with your fingertips. Make a well, add the yeast mixture and mix to a soft dough. Turn out onto a floured surface and knead for 10 minutes, or until smooth and elastic, incorporating the remaining flour as necessary.
4 Place the dough in an oiled bowl and brush with oil. Cover with plastic wrap or a damp tea towel and leave for 1 hour, or until well risen. Punch down, knead for 2 minutes, then roll to a rectangle, 40 x 20 cm (16 x 8 inches). Scatter with raisins and roll up firmly from the long end.
5 Grease a loaf tin with a base measuring 21 x 8 cm (8 1/2 x 3 inches) and line the base with baking paper. Place the dough in the tin, cover with plastic wrap or a damp tea towel and leave for 30 minutes, or until well risen. Preheat the oven to moderate 180°C (350°F/Gas 4).
6 Combine the egg yolk and cream and brush a little over the loaf. Bake for 30 minutes, or until cooked and golden. Glaze again, bake for 5 minutes then glaze again. Cool on a wire rack.

DENSE FRUIT BREAD

Preparation time: 25 minutes
+ 1 hour 40 minutes rising
Total cooking time: 50 minutes
Makes 1 large loaf

★ ★

7 g (1/4 oz) sachet dried yeast
1/4 teaspoon sugar
450 g (14 oz) white bread flour
1/4 teaspoon salt
25 g (3/4 oz) butter
1/2 teaspoon ground ginger
1/4 teaspoon grated nutmeg
1/3 cup (90 g/3 oz) caster (superfine) sugar
2 cups (320 g/11 oz) sultanas
1 1/4 cups (185 g/6 oz) currants
1/4 cup (45 g/1 1/2 oz) mixed peel

1 Place the yeast, sugar and 1 1/4 cups (315 ml/ 10 fl oz) warm water in a small bowl and mix well. Leave in a warm, draught-free place for 10 minutes, or until bubbles appear on the surface. The mixture should be frothy and slightly increased in volume. If your yeast doesn't foam it is dead, so you will have to discard it and start again.
2 Place the flour and salt in a large bowl and rub in the butter with your fingertips until the mixture resembles coarse breadcrumbs. Stir in the spices and three quarters of the caster sugar. Make a well in the centre and stir in the yeast mixture. Mix well until the dough comes together and leaves the side of the bowl clean. Turn onto a lightly floured surface and knead for 10 minutes, or until elastic and smooth. Place in a clean bowl, cover with plastic wrap or a damp tea towel and leave in a warm, draught-free place for 1 hour, or until doubled in size.
3 Turn the dough onto a lightly floured surface, add the fruit and knead for a couple of minutes, or until the fruit is incorporated. Shape the dough into a large round and place on a greased baking tray. Cover with plastic wrap or a damp tea towel and leave in a warm, draught-free place for 30–40 minutes, or until doubled in size.
4 Preheat the oven to moderately hot 200°C (400°F/Gas 6). Bake on the middle shelf for 40–45 minutes, or until the loaf is nicely coloured and sounds hollow when tapped on the base. Transfer to a wire rack to cool slightly.
5 Dissolve the remaining caster sugar in 1 tablespoon hot water and brush over the loaf. Bake for 2–3 minutes, then cool on a wire rack.

DAMPER

Preparation time: 20 minutes
Total cooking time: 25 minutes
Makes 1 damper

3 cups (375 g/12 oz) self-raising flour
1–2 teaspoons salt
90 g (3 oz) butter, melted
1/2 cup (125 ml/4 fl oz) milk
milk, extra, to glaze
flour, extra, to dust

1 Preheat the oven to hot 210°C (415°F/ Gas 6–7). Grease a baking tray. Sift the flour and salt into a bowl and make a well. Combine the butter, milk and 1/2 cup (125 ml/4 fl oz) water and pour into the well. Stir with a knife until just combined. Turn the dough onto a lightly floured surface and knead for 20 seconds, or until smooth. Place the dough on the baking tray and press out to a 20 cm (8 inch) circle.
2 Using a sharp pointed knife, score the dough into 8 sections about 1 cm (1/2 inch) deep. Brush with milk, then dust with flour. Bake for 10 minutes.
3 Reduce the oven temperature to moderate 180°C (350°F/Gas 4) and bake the damper for another 15 minutes, or until the damper is golden and sounds hollow when the surface is tapped. Serve with butter.
NOTE: Damper is the Australian version of soda bread. It is traditionally served warm with slatherings of golden syrup. If you prefer, you can make four rounds instead of one large damper and slightly reduce the cooking time. Cut two slashes in the form of a cross on the top.

BELOW: Damper

BROWN SODA BREAD

Preparation time: 10 minutes
Total cooking time: 30 minutes
Makes 1 loaf

2 cups (250 g/8 oz) self-raising flour
2 cups (250 g/8 oz) unbleached self-raising flour
1 teaspoon bicarbonate of soda
3 cups (750 ml/24 fl oz) buttermilk

1 Preheat the oven to moderately hot 190°C (375°F/Gas 5). Lightly grease a baking tray. Sift the flours and bicarbonate of soda into a large bowl, add the husks to the bowl and make a well in the centre. Add 2 1/2 cups (625 ml/21 fl oz) of the buttermilk and mix with a knife to form a soft dough, adding some of the remaining buttermilk if required.
2 Turn the dough onto a floured surface and knead gently and briefly—don't knead too much as this will make it tough. Press the dough out to a 20 cm (8 inch) round and place on the baking tray. Score a deep cross with a floured knife one third the depth of the dough. Lightly brush with water and sprinkle with a little flour. Bake for 20–30 minutes, or until the bread sounds hollow when tapped.
VARIATIONS: You can use wholemeal self-raising flour instead of the plain self raising-flour to make a heavier bread. You can substitute natural yoghurt, or milk soured with a little lemon juice, for the buttermilk.

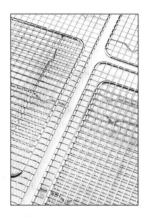

RYE BREAD

Preparation time: 40 minutes
 + 2 hours 30 minutes rising
Total cooking time: 45 minutes
Makes 1 loaf

★★

7 g (¼ oz) sachet dried yeast
1 teaspoon sugar
¾ cup (185 ml/6 fl oz) warm milk
2 cups (200 g/6½ oz) rye flour
1⅓ cups (165 g/5½ oz) white bread flour
1 teaspoon salt
rye flour, extra, to dust

1 Place the yeast, sugar and milk in a small bowl and mix well. Leave in a warm place for 10 minutes, or until bubbles appear on the surface. The mixture should be frothy and slightly increased in volume. If your yeast doesn't foam it is dead, so you will have to discard it and start again.
2 Sift the flours and salt into a large bowl and make a well in the centre. Add the yeast mixture and ¾ cup (185 ml/6 fl oz) warm water and, using your fingers, gradually incorporate the flour to form a dough.
3 Turn the dough onto a lightly floured surface and knead for 10 minutes, or until smooth and elastic. Place the dough in a large lightly oiled bowl and cover with plastic wrap or a damp tea towel. Leave in a warm place for up to 1½ hours, until doubled in size.
4 Lightly grease a baking tray and dust lightly with flour. Punch down the dough and turn onto a lightly floured surface. Knead for 1 minute, or until smooth. Shape into an 18 cm (7 inch) circle and, using a sharp knife, score a shallow criss-cross pattern on top of the loaf. Lightly dust the top with the extra rye flour.
5 Cover the dough with plastic wrap or a damp tea towel and leave in a warm place for 1 hour, or until doubled in size. Preheat the oven to moderate 180°C (350°F/Gas 4) and bake the bread for 40–45 minutes, or until golden brown and the bread sounds hollow when tapped. Transfer to a wire rack to cool completely before cutting.

RYE FLOUR

Rye is cultivated mainly in northern Europe, notably Scandinavia, and Eastern Europe, particularly Russia. Only a small proportion of the cereal is used for human consumption, the majority being produced to feed livestock. It grows well in these regions, as unlike most cereals, it is tolerant to poor soils and cold temperatures. A by-product of the cereal is rye flour which is used to make bread. Because it lacks the protein gluten, which is responsible for the elasticity of bread, rye bread is a much denser and more compact bread. It is also very strong in flavour and makes a distinctive-tasting bread that marries well with cheese, herrings and pickles. It is a moist bread so it keeps well.

ABOVE: Rye bread

419

CHEESE AND HERB PULL-APART

Preparation time: 30 minutes
  + 1 hour 30 minutes rising
Total cooking time: 30 minutes
Makes 1 loaf

★★

7 g (¹/4 oz) sachet dried yeast

1 teaspoon sugar

4 cups (500 g/1 lb) plain (all-purpose) flour

1¹/2 teaspoons salt

2 tablespoons chopped fresh parsley

2 tablespoons chopped fresh chives

1 tablespoon chopped fresh thyme

60 g (2 oz) Cheddar, grated

milk, to glaze

1 Place the yeast, sugar and ¹/2 cup (125 ml/ 4 fl oz) warm water in a small bowl and stir well. Leave in a warm place for 10 minutes, or until bubbles appear on the surface. The mixture should be frothy and slightly increased in volume. If your yeast doesn't foam it is dead, so you will have to discard it and start again.

2 Sift the flour and salt in a large bowl. Make a well in the centre and add the yeast mixture and 1 cup (250 ml/8 fl oz) warm water. Mix to a soft dough. Turn onto a lightly floured surface and knead for 10 minutes, or until smooth. Place the dough in an oiled bowl, cover with plastic wrap or a damp tea towel and leave for 1 hour, or until doubled in size.

3 Punch down the dough and knead for 1 minute. Divide the dough in half and shape each half into 10 flat discs, 6 cm (2¹/2 inches) in diameter. Mix the fresh herbs with the Cheddar and place 2 teaspoons of the mixture on one of the discs. Press another disc on top, then repeat with the remaining discs and herb mixture.

4 Grease a 21 x 10.5 x 6.5 cm (8¹/2 x 4¹/4 x 2¹/2 inch) loaf tin. Stand the filled discs upright in the prepared tin, squashing them together. Cover the tin with plastic wrap or a damp tea towel and leave in a warm place for 30 minutes, or until the dough is well risen. Preheat the oven to hot 210°C (415°F/Gas 6–7).

5 Lightly brush the loaf with a little milk and bake for 30 minutes, or until the bread is brown and crusty and sounds hollow when tapped on the base.

ROSETTAS

Preparation time: 40 minutes + 2 hours rising
Total cooking time: 25 minutes
Makes 10

★★★

7 g (¼ oz) sachet dried yeast
1 teaspoon sugar
4½ cups (560 g/1 lb 2 oz) unbleached plain
  (all-purpose) flour, sifted
1 teaspoon salt
50 g (1¾ oz) butter, softened
¼ cup (60 ml/2 fl oz) olive oil
¼ cup (60 g/2 oz) caster (superfine) sugar
milk, to glaze
plain (all-purpose) flour, extra, to dust

1 Grease two baking trays. Place the yeast, sugar and ½ cup (125 ml/4 fl oz) warm water in a small bowl and stir well. Leave in a warm, draught-free place for 10 minutes, or until bubbles appear on the surface. The mixture should be frothy and slightly increased in volume. If your yeast doesn't foam it is dead, so you will have to discard it and start again.
2 Set aside ¼ cup (30 g/1 oz) of the flour and put the rest in a large bowl with the salt. Make a well in the centre. Add the yeast mixture, butter, oil, sugar and 1¼ cups (315 ml/10 fl oz) warm water. Stir with a wooden spoon, until the dough leaves the side of the bowl and forms a rough, sticky ball. Turn out onto a floured surface. Knead for 10 minutes, or until the dough is smooth and elastic. Add enough of the reserved flour, if necessary, to make a smooth dough. Place in a large, lightly oiled bowl and brush the surface with melted butter or oil. Cover with plastic wrap and leave in a warm place for 1 hour, or until well risen.
3 Punch down the dough, then knead for 1 minute. Divide into 10 portions and shape each into a smooth ball. Place the balls 5 cm (2 inches) apart on the trays. Using a 3 cm (1¼ inch) round cutter, press a 1 cm (½ inch) deep indent into the centre of each ball. With a sharp knife, score five evenly-spaced, 1 cm (½ inch) deep cuts down the side of each roll. Cover with plastic wrap or a damp tea towel and leave in a warm place for 1 hour, or until well risen.
4 Preheat the oven to moderate 180°C (350°F/Gas 4). Brush the rolls with milk and sift a fine layer of the extra flour over them. Bake for 25 minutes, or until golden. Rotate the trays in the oven if one tray is browning faster than the other. Cool on a rack.
NOTE: These are best eaten on the day of cooking and can be frozen for up to 1 month.

ROSETTAS

Press a deep round indent into the centre of each ball of dough.

Sift a fine layer of plain flour over the tops of the rolls before baking.

BELOW: Rosettas

BEER BREAD

Preparation time: 15 minutes
Total cooking time: 40 minutes
Makes 1 loaf

3 1/4 cups (405 g/13 oz) white bread flour
3 teaspoons baking powder
1 teaspoon salt
1 tablespoon caster (superfine) sugar
2 teaspoons dill seeds
50 g (1 3/4 oz) butter, chilled and cubed
375 ml (12 fl oz) can beer
plain (all-purpose) flour, extra
dill seeds, extra
coarse sea salt

1 Preheat the oven to hot 210°C (415°F/ Gas 6–7). Lightly grease a baking tray. Sift the flour, baking powder and salt into a large bowl. Add the sugar and dill seeds and combine. Rub the butter into the dry ingredients using your fingers, until the mixture resembles breadcrumbs. Make a well in the centre and add the beer all at once. Using a wooden spoon, quickly mix to form a soft dough.
2 Turn out onto a floured surface, sprinkling extra flour on your hands and on the surface of the dough. Knead for 1–2 minutes, or until the dough forms a smooth ball. Elongate the ball slightly, flatten a little, and with the blunt end of a large knife press down 2 cm (3/4 inch) along the centre. Brush the surface with water, and sprinkle liberally with the extra dill seeds and sea salt.
3 Bake for 20 minutes, then reduce the oven to moderate 180°C (350°F/Gas 4) and bake for another 15–20 minutes, or until the bread sounds hollow when tapped. Remove from the oven, place on a wire rack and leave to cool.
NOTE: This bread is best eaten on the day of baking and it freezes well for up to a week.

CORN BREAD

Preparation time: 20 minutes
Total cooking time: 25 minutes
Makes 1 loaf

1 cup (125 g/4 oz) self-raising flour
1 cup (150 g/5 oz) fine cornmeal
1 teaspoon salt
1 egg
1 cup (250 ml/8 fl oz) buttermilk
1/4 cup (60 ml/2 fl oz) oil

1 Preheat the oven to hot 220°C (425°F/Gas 7). Generously grease a 20 cm (8 inch) cast iron frying pan with an ovenproof or screw off handle, or round cake tin, with oil. Place in the oven to heat while making the batter.
2 Sift the flour into a bowl, add the cornmeal and salt and make a well in the centre. Whisk together the egg, buttermilk and oil, add to the dry ingredients and stir until just combined. Do not overbeat.
3 Pour into the hot cast iron pan or cake tin and bake for 25 minutes, or until firm to the touch and golden brown. Serve, cut into wedges, warm or at room temperature.

QUICK MIX ONION AND BUTTERMILK BREAD

Preheat the oven to moderate 180°C (350°F/Gas 4). Sift 3 cups (375 g/12 oz) self-raising flour into a large bowl and stir in a 35 g (1 1/4 oz) packet of dried French onion soup and 2 tablespoons chopped chives. Mix in 1 3/4 cups (440 ml/14 fl oz) buttermilk with a knife, using a cutting action, until the mixture forms a soft dough. Add extra buttermilk if the mixture is too dry. Turn out onto a lightly floured surface and quickly knead into a smooth ball. Cut into 4 even-sized pieces and shape each into a ball. Place on a floured tray, allowing room for each to rise. Sift extra flour over the top and make a slash with a sharp knife across the top of each loaf. Bake the loaves for 25–30 minutes, or until cooked and golden. Makes 4 loaves.

CORNMEAL

Corn is the only native American cereal grain, believed to have originated in Mexico or Central America. Archeologists have discovered evidence of corn as far back as 7000 years ago. The first explorers to the New World found corn growing from Canada to Chile. The native Indians made great use of corn as did the early settlers. Corn has a large variety of culinary uses. It can be cooked fresh or processed into cornstarch, cornflour, hominy, corn germ, corn oil, corn flakes and cornmeal. Cornmeal is obtained by grinding dried corn kernels into a coarse white or yellow meal, and is ground into degrees of coarseness. It is used slightly coarse in the baking of corn bread and muffins. Polenta is more porridge-like. It is also used to make tortillas, corn chips and tamales.

OPPOSITE PAGE, FROM TOP: Corn bread; Beer bread

BREAD ROLLS

Create your own selection of delicious rolls using plain (page 410) or wholemeal bread dough and the following toppings and glazes.

SPIRAL ROLLS

Divide the dough into 16–24 even pieces. Roll each into a 30 cm (12 inch) long rope. Shape into tight spirals, tuck under the ends, then seal. Place 5 cm (2 inches) apart on lightly oiled baking trays. Cover with plastic wrap and leave in a warm place for 20 minutes, or until well risen. Brush with a glaze or topping. Bake in a moderate 180°C (350°F/Gas 4) oven for 15–20 minutes, or until risen and golden.

KNOT ROLLS

Divide the dough into 16–24 even pieces. Roll into 30 cm (12 inch) long ropes. Tie each rope into a loose knot. Place 5 cm (2 inches) apart on lightly oiled baking trays. Proceed as for spiral rolls.

CLOVER LEAF ROLLS

Divide the dough into 16–24 even pieces. Divide each piece into 3 even-sized balls. Place the trio of balls from each piece close together on lightly oiled baking trays and 5 cm (2 inches) apart. Proceed as for spiral rolls.

OVAL ROLLS

Divide the dough into 16–24 even pieces, and then shape into ovals. Leave plain or slash the tops once lengthways, or twice diagonally. Place 5 cm (2 inches) apart on lightly oiled baking trays. Proceed as for spiral rolls.

TOPPINGS AND GLAZES

Glazing dough and adding toppings will change the appearance as well as the taste of the bread. Glazing affects the result of the crust and is done before or after baking, depending on the result you are after. The high oven temperature used for baking bread may cause some toppings to brown too quickly. If you notice this happening, lower the oven temperature slightly or place a sheet of foil or double thickness of baking paper on top of the rolls to prevent them from burning.

TOPPINGS

Lightly sprinkle the dough with a topping such as flour, rolled oats, crushed rock salt, cracked wheat or grated Cheddar. You can also try seeds such as poppy, sesame, caraway, pumpkin, dill, fennel or sunflower. Cereals such as cornmeal (polenta), barley flakes, cracked wheat and rye flakes also make interesting toppings and add a little flavour.

GLAZES

Use a wide pastry brush to brush one of these glazes over the dough, choosing the appropriate glaze for your desired result.

AFTER BAKING

Soft crust: Brush the cooked, hot bread with melted butter and return to the oven for 2 minutes. Remove, brush again with melted butter and leave to cool.
Glossy crust: Whisk 1 egg white with 1 tablespoon water. Brush the cooked, hot bread with the glaze, then return to the oven for 5 minutes. Cool.
Sweet glossy crust: Combine 1 tablespoon sugar with 2 tablespoons milk and brush over the hot bread. Return to the oven for 5 minutes. Cool.

Sugar glaze: Dissolve 1/4 cup (60 g/2 oz) sugar in 2 tablespoons water over low heat. Boil for 2 minutes, or until the mixture is syrupy. Brush on the hot bread.

BEFORE BAKING

Deep colour in the crust: Beat 1 whole egg with 1 teaspoon water. For a very deep colour, beat 1 egg yolk with 1 teaspoon water.
Rich, dark gleam on savoury breads: Beat 1 egg with 1 teaspoon oil and some salt and pepper.
Crisp crust: Whisk together 1 egg white with 1 teaspoon water.
Light sheen: Brush with milk, cream or melted butter.

FROM LEFT: Spiral rolls; Knot rolls; Clover leaf rolls; Oval rolls; Knot rolls. Toppings (rack on right): Sesame seeds; Poppy seeds; Rock salt; Sunflower seeds

425

SOURDOUGH BREAD

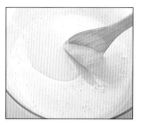

Gradually draw the flour into the yeast mixture and stir to form a thick paste.

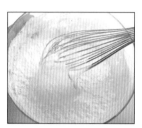

For the sponge, stir the flour into the starter mixture and whisk in warm water to form a smooth mixture.

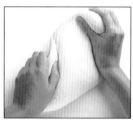

Knead the dough until it is smooth and elastic, incorporating more flour if necessary.

Use a sharp knife to make diagonal cuts along the loaves.

RIGHT: Sourdough bread

SOURDOUGH BREAD

Preparation time: 30 minutes +
  2 days standing + 1 hour 45 minutes rising
Total cooking time: 40 minutes
Makes two loaves

Starter

1 cup (125 g/4 oz) white bread flour
2 teaspoons fresh yeast

Sponge

1 cup (125 g/4 oz) white bread flour

Dough

3 cups (375 g/12 oz) white bread flour
1 teaspoon salt
2 teaspoons fresh yeast

1 To make the starter, sift the flour into a bowl and make a well in the centre. Cream the yeast and 1 cup (250 ml/8 fl oz) warm water together, pour into the flour and gradually draw the flour into the centre to form a thick smooth paste. Cover with plastic wrap or a damp tea towel and leave at room temperature for 24 hours. The starter will begin to ferment and bubble.
2 To make the sponge, stir the flour into the starter mixture and gradually whisk in 1/2 cup (125 ml/4 fl oz) warm water to form a smooth mixture. Cover with plastic wrap and leave for 24 hours.
3 To make the dough, sift the flour and salt into a large bowl and make a well in the centre. Cream the yeast and 1/3 cup (80 ml/2 3/4 fl oz) warm water together and add to the dry ingredients with the starter and sponge mixture. Gradually incorporate the flour into the well. Turn the dough onto a lightly floured surface and knead for 10 minutes, or until smooth and elastic, incorporating extra flour if needed.
4 Place the dough in a lightly oiled bowl, cover with plastic wrap or a damp tea towel and place in a warm place for 1 hour, or until doubled in size. Lightly grease two baking trays and dust lightly with flour. Punch the dough down and turn onto the work surface. Knead for 1 minute, or until smooth. Divide into two equal portions and shape each into a 20 cm (8 inch) round. Using a sharp knife, score diagonal cuts 1 cm (1/2 inch) deep along the loaves.
5 Place the loaves on the trays and cover with plastic wrap or a damp tea towel. Leave in a warm place for 45 minutes, or until doubled. Preheat the oven to moderately hot 190°C (375°F/Gas 5). Bake for 35–40 minutes, changing the breads around halfway through. Bake until the bread is golden and crusty and sounds hollow when tapped. Cool on a wire rack before cutting.

POTATO BREAD

Preparation time: 45 minutes
  + I hour 45 minutes rising
Total cooking time: 35 minutes
Makes I loaf

✳ ✳

7 g (¹/₄ oz) sachet dried yeast

4 cups (500 g/I lb) unbleached plain
  (all-purpose) flour

I teaspoon salt

2 tablespoons full-cream milk powder

I cup (230 g/7¹/₂ oz) warm cooked mashed
  potato

¹/₂ cup (25 g/³/₄ oz) chopped fresh chives

I egg white, to glaze

2 teaspoons cold water

sunflower or pumpkin (pepita) seeds

 Lightly grease a 25 cm (10 inch) round cake tin and line the base with baking paper. Place the yeast and ¹/₄ cup (60 ml/2 fl oz) warm water in a small bowl and stir well. Leave in a warm, draught-free place for 10 minutes, or until bubbles appear on the surface. The mixture should be frothy and slightly increased in volume. If your yeast doesn't foam it is dead, so you will have to discard it and start again.

2 Sift 3¹/₂ cups (435 g/14 oz) of the flour, the salt and milk powder into a large bowl. Using a fork, mix the potato and chives through the dry ingredients. Add the yeast mixture and 1 cup (250 ml/8 fl oz) warm water and mix until combined. Add enough of the remaining flour to make a soft dough.

3 Turn the dough onto a lightly floured surface. Knead for 10 minutes, or until the dough is smooth and elastic. Place in an oiled bowl, then brush the surface of the dough with oil. Cover with plastic wrap and leave in a warm place for 1 hour, or until well risen.

4 Punch down the dough, then knead for 1 minute. Divide into 12 equal pieces and form each piece into a smooth ball.

5 Place evenly spaced balls in a daisy pattern in the tin, piling 2 balls in the centre. Cover with plastic wrap and leave to rise for 45 minutes, or until the dough has risen to the top of the tin. Preheat the oven to hot 210°C (415°F/Gas 6–7).

6 Brush the top with the combined egg white and water and sprinkle the seeds onto the centre ball. Bake for 15 minutes. Reduce the oven to moderate 180°C (350°F/Gas 4) and bake for another 20 minutes, or until a skewer inserted in the centre comes out clean. Leave for 10 minutes, then turn out onto a wire rack.

NOTE: Depending on the moisture content of the potato, extra flour may have to be added. The bread keeps for three days in an airtight container.

POTATO BREAD

The addition of cooked mashed potato to bread results in a moist, springy crumb and a dense bread, due to the moisture in the potatoes. Potato also adds interest, flavour and keeping qualities to the bread. The best potatoes to use for mashing are the floury varieties such as King Edward and pontiac, rather than the waxy potatoes. To prepare the potatoes, cut the peeled potatoes into even-sized pieces and boil or steam until softened. Drain well and mash while hot.

ABOVE: Potato bread

GLUTEN-FREE BREAD

Preparation time: 25 minutes
+ 1 hour rising
Total cooking time: 45 minutes
Makes 1 loaf

7 g (1/4 oz) sachet dried yeast

2 teaspoons sugar

2 1/4 cups (400 g/13 oz) gluten-free plain
(all-purpose) flour (see Note)

1/2 teaspoon salt

1/2 cup (50 g/1 3/4 oz) milk powder

1 tablespoon xanthan gum (see Note)

2 eggs, lightly beaten

1/4 cup (60 ml/2 fl oz) oil

1 tablespoon sesame seeds

1 Lightly grease a loaf tin with a base measuring 22 x 9 x 5.5 cm (9 x 3 1/2 x 2 1/4 inches). Place the yeast, sugar and 1 3/4 cups (440 ml/14 fl oz) warm water in a small bowl and stir well. Leave in a warm, draught-free place for 10 minutes, or until bubbles appear on the surface. The mixture should be frothy and slightly increased in volume. If your yeast doesn't foam it is dead, so you will have to discard it and start again.

2 Sift the flour, salt, milk powder and xanthan gum into a large bowl. Make a well in the centre and add the yeast mixture, egg and oil. Using a wooden spoon, stir together well until it forms a soft moist mixture. Beat with the spoon for 1 minute.

3 Spoon the mixture into the loaf tin and smooth the surface with moist hands. Sprinkle the sesame seeds over the top. Cover with lightly greased plastic wrap and leave in a warm, draught-free place for 1 hour, or until the mixture has nearly risen to the top of the tin. Preheat the oven to moderately hot 190°C (375°F/Gas 5). Bake the bread for 40–45 minutes, or until it is golden and sounds hollow when tapped. Leave in the tin for 5 minutes before transferring to a wire rack to cool. Allow the bread to cool completely before cutting.

NOTE: You can buy gluten-free plain (all-purpose) flour in the health food section of the supermarket. Xanthan gum is used as a gluten substitute as it gives structure to the bread. It is available from health food shops.

WALNUT BREAD

Preparation time: 45 minutes
+ 2 hours 30 minutes rising
Total cooking time: 50 minutes
Makes 1 loaf

2 1/2 teaspoons dried yeast

1/4 cup (90 g/3 oz) liquid malt

2 tablespoons olive oil

3 cups (300 g/10 oz) walnut halves, lightly
toasted

4 1/4 cups (530 g/1 lb 1 oz) white bread flour

1 1/2 teaspoons salt

1 egg, lightly beaten

1 Grease a baking tray. Place the yeast, liquid malt and 1 1/3 cups (350 ml/11 fl oz) warm water in a small bowl and stir well. Leave in a warm, draught-free place for 10 minutes, or until bubbles appear on the surface. The mixture should be frothy and slightly increased in volume. If your yeast doesn't foam it is dead, so you will have to discard it and start again. Stir in the oil.

2 Process 2 cups (200 g/6 1/2 oz) of the walnuts in a food processor to a coarse meal. Combine 4 cups (500 g/1 lb) of the flour and the salt in a large bowl and stir in the walnut meal. Make a well and add the yeast mixture. Mix with a large metal spoon until a loose clump forms. Turn out onto a lightly floured surface and knead for 10 minutes, or until smooth, incorporating enough of the remaining flour to keep the dough from sticking—it should be soft and moist, but it won't become very springy. Shape the dough into a ball. Place in a lightly oiled bowl, cover with plastic wrap or a damp tea towel and leave in a warm place for up to 1 1/2 hours, or until doubled.

3 Punch down the dough and turn out onto a lightly floured surface. With very little kneading, shape the dough into a 25 x 20 cm (10 x 8 inch) rectangle. Spread with the remaining walnuts and roll up firmly from the short end. Place the loaf on the baking tray, cover with plastic wrap or a damp tea towel and leave to rise for 1 hour, or until well risen and doubled in size.

4 Preheat the oven to moderately hot 190°C (375°F/Gas 5). Glaze the loaf with the egg and bake for 45–50 minutes, or until golden and hollow sounding when tapped. Transfer to a wire rack to cool.

NOTE: Use good-quality pale and plump walnuts as cheaper varieties can be bitter.

WALNUT BREAD

Firmly roll the loaf from the short end and place on the greased baking tray.

When the dough has doubled in size, brush with the beaten egg.

OPPOSITE PAGE, FROM TOP: Walnut bread; Gluten-free bread

GRISSINI

Preparation time: 40 minutes
  + 1 hour rising
Total cooking time: 15 minutes
Makes 24

7 g (1/4 oz) sachet dried yeast
1 teaspoon sugar
4 cups (500 g/1 lb) white bread flour
1 teaspoon salt
1/4 cup (60 ml/2 fl oz) olive oil
1/4 cup (15 g/1/2 oz) chopped fresh basil
4 cloves garlic, crushed
1/2 cup (50 g/1 3/4 oz) finely grated Parmesan
2 teaspoons sea salt flakes
2 tablespoons finely grated Parmesan, extra

1 Place the yeast, sugar and 1 1/4 cups (315 ml/10 fl oz) warm water in a small bowl and stir well. Leave in a warm, draught-free place for 10 minutes, or until bubbles appear on the surface. The mixture should be frothy and slightly increased in volume. If your yeast doesn't foam it is dead, so you will have to discard it and start again.

2 Sift the flour and salt into a bowl and make a well in the centre. Add the yeast mixture and oil and mix to combine. Add more water if the dough is dry.

3 Gather the dough into a ball and turn out onto a lightly floured surface. Knead for 10 minutes, or until soft and elastic. Divide the dough into two portions, add the basil and garlic to one portion, and the Parmesan to the other. The best way to do this is to flatten the dough into a rectangle and place the filling on top. Fold the dough to enclose the filling, then knead for a few minutes to incorporate the filling evenly.

4 Place each dough in a lightly oiled bowl and cover with plastic wrap or a damp tea towel. Leave in a warm, draught-free place for 1 hour, or until doubled in volume. Preheat the oven to very hot 230°C (450°F/Gas 8). Lightly grease two baking trays.

5 Punch down the doughs and knead each again for 1 minute. Divide each piece of dough into 12 portions, and roll each portion into a stick about 30 cm (12 inches) long and 5 mm (1/4 inch) across. Place on the trays and brush with water. Sprinkle the basil and garlic dough with the sea salt flakes, and the cheese dough with the extra Parmesan. Bake for 15 minutes, or until crisp and golden brown.

GRISSINI

These long thin sticks of crisp bread originated in the city of Turin. They can be pencil thin or as thick as a cigar and are always served at the Italian table as part of an antipasto platter to start a meal. They are a light starter designed so as not to curb one's appetite for the following courses. Toppings vary from coarse salt to seeds, cheese or dried herbs, either on their own or combined for interesting variations.

RIGHT: Grissini

CIABATTA

Preparation time: 30 minutes
 + 5 hours 15 minutes rising
Total cooking time: 30 minutes
Makes 1 freeform loaf

7 g (¼ oz) sachet dried yeast
1 teaspoon sugar
2 teaspoons salt
3 cups (750 g/1½ lb) white bread flour
50 ml (1¾ fl oz) olive oil
extra flour, to sprinkle

1 Place the yeast, sugar and 75 ml (2½ oz) warm water in a small bowl and stir well. Leave in a warm, draught-free place for 10 minutes, or until bubbles appear on the surface. The mixture should be frothy and slightly increased in volume. If your yeast doesn't foam it is dead, so you will have to discard it and start again.
2 Place the salt and 2 cups (250 g/8 oz) of the flour in a large bowl and make a well in the centre. Add the yeast mixture, oil and 225 ml (7 fl oz) water to the bowl and stir to combine.

Use a cupped hand to knead the wet dough, lifting and stirring for 5 minutes. The dough will be quite wet at this stage.
3 Shape the dough into a ball and place in a clean bowl. Cover with plastic wrap or a damp tea towel and leave in a warm place for 4 hours, or until doubled in size.
4 Stir in the remaining flour, using a cupped hand, and mix until the flour has been incorporated. Scrape down the side of the bowl. Cover with plastic wrap or a clean tea towel and leave in a warm place for 1–1¼ hours.
5 Liberally sprinkle a large baking tray with flour. Do not punch down the dough but carefully tip it out onto the tray. Use floured hands to spread the dough into an oval about 30 x 12 cm (12 x 4½ inches). Use heavily floured hands to spread evenly and tuck under the dough edges to plump up the dough. Sprinkle liberally with flour. Cover with plastic wrap and leave for 30 minutes.
6 Preheat the oven to hot 210°C (415°F/ Gas 6–7). Place a heatproof container of ice on the base of the oven. Bake the ciabatta for 30 minutes, or until puffed and golden. Remove the melted ice after about 20 minutes. The loaf is cooked when it sounds hollow when tapped.

CIABATTA
Now a popular bread baked all over the world, ciabatta originated in the Emilia Romagna region of Italy. Its name means 'slipper' bread as it is said to resemble a well-worn slipper. Its light airy texture is due to its long rising time and the use of a wet dough. It is an unusual process in that the dough is not punched down to eliminate the air bubbles as with other breads. It needs to be handled with great care so as not to lose the air bubbles that have formed after the long rising.

ABOVE: Ciabatta

BAGELS

Leave the yeast mixture until bubbles appear on the surface.

Knead the dough until smooth and quite stiff.

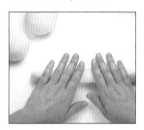

Roll each ball of dough into a long rope, the same thickness all the way along.

With the circle around the base of your fingers and the overlap under your palm, roll the rope several times. Apply firm pressure to seal the seam.

ABOVE: Bagels

BAGELS

Preparation time: 35 minutes
  + 12 hours refrigeration
Total cooking time: 16 minutes
Makes 8

✷ ✷

7 g (¹/4 oz) sachet dried yeast

1 teaspoon sugar

1 tablespoon barley malt syrup or honey

4 cups (500 g/1 lb) white bread flour

2 teaspoons salt

coarse polenta, to dust

1 Place the yeast, sugar and 1½ cups (375 ml/ 12 fl oz) warm water in a small bowl and stir until dissolved. Leave in a warm place for 10 minutes, or until bubbles appear on the surface. The mixture should be frothy and slightly increased in volume. If your yeast doesn't foam it is dead, so you will have to discard it and start again. Stir in the malt syrup.

2 Put 2 cups (250 g/8 oz) of the flour in a large bowl, make a well in the centre and add the yeast mixture and salt. Stir with a wooden spoon, adding flour as necessary to make the dough firm. Turn out onto a floured work surface and knead for 10–12 minutes, or until smooth and stiff. Add more flour if necessary to make the dough quite stiff, then divide into 8 portions and roll them into smooth balls. Cover with plastic wrap or a clean tea towel and leave for 5 minutes.

3 Roll each ball under your palms to form a rope 28 cm (11 inches) long. Do not taper the ends of the rope. Dampen the ends slightly, overlap by 4 cm (1½ inches) and pinch firmly together. Place one at a time around the base of your fingers and, with the overlap under your palm, roll the rope several times. Apply firm pressure to seal the seam. It should be the same thickness all the way around. Place them all on polenta-dusted baking trays, cover with plastic wrap and refrigerate for 12 hours.

4 Preheat the oven to very hot 240°C (475°F/ Gas 9). Line two baking trays with baking paper. Remove the bagels from the fridge 20 minutes before baking. Bring a large saucepan of water to the boil and drop the bagels, in batches of 3 or 4, into the water for 30 seconds. Remove and drain, base-down, on a wire rack.

5 Place the bagels on the trays and bake for 15 minutes, or until deep golden brown and crisp. Cool on a wire rack.

SCOTTISH BAPS

Preparation time: 40 minutes
  + 1 hour 15 minutes rising
Total cooking time: 30 minutes
Makes 12

7 g (1/4 oz) sachet dried yeast
1 teaspoon caster (superfine) sugar
3 1/2 cups (435 g/14 oz) white bread flour
1 cup (250 ml/8 fl oz) lukewarm milk
1 1/2 teaspoons salt
45 g (1 1/2 oz) butter, melted
1 tablespoon plain (all-purpose) flour, extra

1 Lightly dust two baking trays with flour. Place the yeast, sugar and 2 tablespoons flour in a small bowl. Gradually add the milk, blending until smooth and dissolved. Leave in a warm, draught-free place for 10 minutes, or until bubbles appear on the surface. The mixture should be frothy and slightly increased in volume. If your yeast doesn't foam it is dead, so you will have to discard it and start again.

2 Sift the salt and remaining flour into a large bowl. Make a well in the centre and add the yeast mixture and butter. Using a knife, mix to form a soft dough.

3 Turn the dough onto a lightly floured surface and knead for 3 minutes, or until smooth. Shape into a ball and place in a large oiled bowl. Cover with plastic wrap or a damp tea towel and leave in a warm place for 1 hour, or until well risen.

4 Preheat the oven to hot 210°C (415°F/ Gas 6–7). Punch down the dough with your fist. Knead the dough again for 2 minutes, or until smooth. Divide into 12 pieces. Knead one portion at a time on a lightly floured surface for 1 minute, roll into a ball and shape into a flat oval. Repeat with the remaining dough.

5 Place the ovals on the trays and dust with the extra flour. Cover with plastic wrap and leave in a warm place for 15 minutes, or until well risen. Make an indent in the centre of each oval with your finger. Bake for 30 minutes until browned and cooked through. Serve warm.

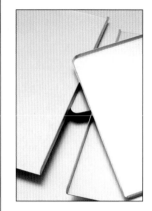

SCOTTISH BAPS

Baps are flattish soft bread rolls that are traditionally from Scotland but are now common all over Britain. Eaten at breakfast time, they are often called 'morning rolls'. They are best eaten warm straight from the oven. Baps are distinguished from other breads in that they are always dusted with white flour and made with milk, which gives the rolls a tender crumb and soft crust. The origins of the bread are not known but the word has been in use since late in the sixteenth century.

LEFT: Scottish baps

INDIAN BREADS From paper-

thin parathas to puffed-up naan, these Indian breads are traditionally cooked in a

clay oven and torn apart to mop up curries.

PARATHAS

Place 2¼ cups (280 g/9 oz) atta flour and a pinch of salt in a large bowl. Rub in 40 g (1¼ oz) ghee with your fingertips until fine and crumbly. Make a well in the centre and gradually add ¾ cup (185 ml/6 fl oz) cold water to form a firm dough. Turn onto a well-floured surface and knead until smooth. Cover with plastic wrap and set aside for 40 minutes. Divide into 10 portions. Roll each portion on a floured surface to a 13 cm (5 inch) circle. Brush lightly with melted ghee or oil. Cut through each round to the centre and roll tightly to form a cone shape, then press down on the pointed top. Re-roll into a 13 cm (5 inch) circle again. Cook one at a time in hot oil or ghee in a frying pan until puffed and lightly browned on both sides. Drain on crumpled paper towels. Makes 10.

NOTE: Atta flour, also known as chapatti flour, is a finely milled, low-gluten, soft-textured, wholemeal wheat flour used for making Indian flatbreads. Plain (all-purpose) whomeeal flour can be used instead—sift first and discard the bran—but may result in heavier, coarser bread.

NAAN

Preheat the oven to moderately hot, 200°C (400°F/Gas 6). Sift together 500 g (1 lb) plain (all-purpose) flour, 1 teaspoon baking powder, ½ teaspoon bicarbonate of soda and 1 teaspoon salt into a large bowl. Add 1 beaten egg, 1 tablespoon melted ghee or butter, ½ cup (125 g/4 oz) yoghurt and gradually add 1 cup (250 ml/8 fl oz) milk or enough to form a soft dough. Cover with a damp cloth and leave in a warm place for 2 hours. Lift onto a well-floured surface and knead for 2–3 minutes, or until you have a smooth dough. Divide the dough into eight portions and roll each one into an oval 15 cm (6 inch) long. Using a pastry brush, brush with water and place, wet-side-down, on lightly greased baking trays. Brush with melted ghee or butter and bake for 8–10 minutes, or until golden brown. Makes 8.

PURIS

Sift together 2½ cups (375 g/12 oz) wholemeal flour and a pinch of salt. With your fingertips, rub in 1 tablespoon ghee or oil. Gradually add 1 cup (250 ml/8 oz) water to form a firm dough. Knead on a lightly floured surface until smooth. Cover with plastic wrap and set aside for 50 minutes. Divide into 18 portions and roll each into a 14 cm (5½ inch) circle. Heat 3 cm (1¼ inches) oil in a deep frying pan until moderately hot; fry one at a time, spooning oil over until they puff up and swell. Cook on each side until golden brown. Drain on paper towels. Serve immediately. Makes 18.

CHAPATTIS

Place 2¼ cups (280 g/9 oz) atta flour and a pinch of salt in a large bowl. Gradually add 1 cup (250 ml/8 fl oz) water, or enough to form a firm dough. Knead on a lightly floured surface until smooth. Cover with plastic wrap and set aside for 50 minutes. Divide into 14 portions and roll into 14 cm (5½ inch) circles. Brush a heated frying pan with a little melted ghee or oil. Cook over medium heat, flattening the surface, until both sides are golden brown and bubbles appear. Makes 14.

POPPADOMS

Poppadoms are thin wafers made of lentil, rice or potato flour. Use tongs to slide them one at a time into 2 cm (¾ inches) very hot oil—they should puff at once. Turn over, remove quickly and drain on paper towels.

FROM LEFT: Parathas; Naan; Puris; Chapattis; Poppadoms

1 Place a third of the flour in a large bowl and stir in 1 teaspoon salt. Place the yeast, sugar and 1 cup (250 ml/8 fl oz) warm water in a small bowl and stir well. Set aside in a warm, draught-free place for 10 minutes, or until bubbles appear on the surface. The mixture should be frothy and slightly increased in volume. If your yeast doesn't foam, it is dead and you will have to start again.

2 Add the yeast mixture to the flour and salt mixture in the bowl and stir to make a thin, lumpy paste. Cover with a tea towel and set aside in a warm, draught-free place for 45 minutes, or until doubled in size.

3 Stir in the remaining flour and the oil and ½ cup (125 ml/4 fl oz) warm water. Mix with a wooden spoon until a rough dough forms. Transfer to a lightly floured work surface and knead for 10–12 minutes, incorporating as little extra flour as possible to keep the dough soft and moist, but not sticky. Form into a ball. Oil a clean large bowl and roll the dough around in it to lightly coat in the oil. Cut a cross on top, cover the bowl with a tea towel and set aside in a warm place for 1 hour, or until doubled in size.

4 Lightly grease a baking tray and dust with flour. Punch down the dough on a lightly floured surface. Roll out to 30 x 25 x 1 cm (12 x 10 x ½ inches). Squeeze any excess liquid from the olives and toss to coat in the extra flour. Scatter over the dough and top with the oregano. Roll up tightly lengthways, pressing firmly to expel any air pockets as you roll. Press the ends together to form an oval loaf 25 cm (10 inches) long. Transfer to the prepared tray, join-side-down. Make 3 shallow diagonal slashes across the top. Slide the tray into a large plastic bag and leave in a warm place for 45 minutes, or until doubled in bulk.

5 Preheat the oven to hot 220°C (425°F/Gas 7). Brush the top of the loaf with olive oil and bake for 30 minutes. Reduce the heat to moderate 180°C (350°F/Gas 4) and bake for another 5 minutes. Cool on a wire rack. Serve warm or cold.

VARIATION: Instead of the oregano you can use 2 teaspoons of finely chopped rosemary. Fold it through the dough and sprinkle whole leaves on the top after brushing with olive oil.

OLIVE BREAD

Preparation time: 30 minutes
   + 2 hours 30 minutes rising
Total cooking time: 35 minutes
Makes 1 loaf

3 cups (375 g/12 oz) plain (all-purpose) flour

7 g (¾ oz) sachet dry yeast

2 teaspoons sugar

2 tablespoons olive oil

110 g (3½ oz) Kalamata olives, pitted, halved

2 teaspoons plain (all-purpose) flour, extra

1 small sprig of fresh oregano, leaves removed and torn into small pieces, optional

olive oil, to glaze

ABOVE: Olive bread

FOCACCIA
(Italian flatbread)

Preparation time: 30 minutes
+ 3 hours 30 minutes rising
Total cooking time: 20 minutes per loaf
Makes two loaves

$^{1}/_{2}$ teaspoon caster (superfine) sugar
7 g ($^{3}/_{4}$ oz) sachet dry yeast
1 kg (2 lb) bread flour
$^{1}/_{4}$ cup (60 ml/2 fl oz) olive oil

1 Put the sugar, yeast and 2 tablespoons warm water in a small bowl, mix well and leave in a warm, draught-free place for 10 minutes, or until bubbles appear on the surface. The mixture should be frothy and slightly increased in volume. If your yeast doesn't foam it is dead and you will have to start again.
2 Put the flour and 2 teaspoons salt in a large bowl and mix. Add 2 tablespoons of the oil, the yeast mixture and 3 cups (750 ml/24 fl oz) warm water. Mix with a wooden spoon until the mixture comes together in a loose dough, then turn out onto a lightly floured surface. Start kneading to form a soft, moist, but non-sticky dough, adding a little extra flour or warm water as needed. Knead for 8 minutes, or until smooth, or until the impression made by a finger springs back out.
3 Lightly oil a large bowl. Place the dough in the bowl and roll around to coat. Cut a cross on top with a sharp knife. Cover the bowl with a clean tea towel and leave in a dry, warm place for 1 hour 30 minutes, or until doubled in size.
4 Punch down the dough on a lightly floured surface and divide in half. One or both portions can be frozen at this point. Roll one portion out to 28 x 20 cm (11 x 8 inches). Use the heels of your hands to work from the middle outwards and shape to measure 38 x 28 cm (15 x 11 inches).
5 Lightly oil a baking tray and dust with flour. Place the dough in the centre and slide the tray inside a large plastic bag. Leave in a dry, warm place for 2 hours, or until doubled in size.
6 Preheat the oven to hot 220°C (425°F/ Gas 7). Brush the surface of the dough with some of the remaining olive oil and bake for 20 minutes, or until golden. Transfer to a wire rack to cool. Allow plenty of air to circulate under the loaf to keep the crust crisp. Repeat with the remaining dough. Best eaten within 6 hours of baking.
NOTES: When bread flour is unavailable and plain (all-purpose) flour must be used, start by adding 1 cup (250 ml/8 fl oz) of the water in step 2, then gradually adding more to give a soft but non-sticky dough. Plain flour requires less water in a dough, and will give a denser textured bread.
VARIATIONS: For a simple variation, try the simple toppings given below. Add them when the dough has risen a second time.

Brush the top with olive oil, scatter 200 g (6$^{1}/_{2}$ oz) green olives over the dough and press them down firmly. Sprinkle with sea salt and rosemary sprigs and bake.

Brush the top with olive oil, scatter 100 g (3$^{1}/_{2}$ oz) diced pancetta over the dough and press it down firmly. Sprinkle with 2 tablespoons grated Parmesan and bake.

BELOW: Focaccia

PIZZA

The idea of cooking a flat piece of dough with a savoury topping was known to the ancient Greeks and Romans even though the Armenians claim to have invented the pizza. In more modern times, the world was introduced to the pizza via Naples in Italy, although every region in Italy has its own variations. The classic Naples version is basically a very thin dough with a simple tomato and mozzarella cheese sauce, maybe with a few herbs, anchovies and black olives added for extra flavour. It was the Americans, though, who transformed pizza into the ultimate fast food item with its many variations. It is now usually made with a thick bready crust topped with a variety of ingredients.

RIGHT: Pizza dough (with classic topping)

PIZZA DOUGH

Preparation time: 30 minutes
+ 1 hour 30 minutes rising
Total cooking time: 30 minutes
Makes two 30 cm (12 inch) or one 42 cm (17 inch) pizza

7 g (1/4 oz) sachet dried yeast
3 teaspoons caster (superfine) sugar
3 1/2 cups (435 g/14 oz) white bread flour
1/2 teaspoon salt
1/4 cup (60 ml/2 fl oz) olive oil

1 Place the yeast, sugar and 1/3 cup (80 ml/ 2 3/4 oz) warm water in a small bowl and stir well. Leave in a warm, draught-free place for 5 minutes, or until bubbles appear on the surface. The mixture should be frothy and slightly increased in volume. If your yeast doesn't foam it is dead, so you will have to discard it and start again.
2 Sift the flour and salt into a bowl and make a well in the centre. Add the yeast mixture, oil and 1/2 cup (125 ml/4 fl oz) warm water and mix together. Add more water if the dough is dry.
3 Gather the dough into a ball and turn out onto a lightly floured surface. Knead for 12 minutes, or until soft and elastic.
4 Place the dough in a lightly oiled bowl and brush over the surface with oil. Cover with plastic wrap or a damp tea towel and leave in a warm place for 1–1 1/2 hours, or until doubled in volume.
5 Punch down the dough. Divide the dough and gently knead on a lightly floured surface into the desired size and shape.

TOPPING: To make a classic topping, using a half quantity of pizza dough, roll out to a 30 cm (12 inch) circle. Spread 3/4 cup (185 ml/6 fl oz) bottled tomato pasta sauce over the base. Top with 125 g (4 oz) sliced Italian salami, cut into strips. Follow with 2 tablespoons chopped fresh basil, 125 g (4 oz) sliced small cap mushrooms, 1 onion, cut into thin wedges, 1/2 green pepper (capsicum), sliced, and 12 pitted black olives. Place 6 anchovy fillets over the top and sprinkle with 150 g (5 oz) grated mozzarella and 30 g (1 oz) grated Parmesan. Bake in a moderately hot 190°C (375°F/Gas 5) oven for 30 minutes.

POTATO AND ONION PIZZA

Preparation time: 40 minutes
  + 1 hour 30 minutes rising
Total cooking time: 45 minutes
Serves 4

7 g (¹/4 oz) sachet dry yeast

¹/2 teaspoon sugar

1¹/2 cups (185 g/6 oz) white bread flour

1 cup (150 g/5 oz) wholemeal
  plain (all-purpose) flour

1 tablespoon olive oil

Topping

1 large red pepper (capsicum)

1 potato

1 large onion, sliced

125 g (4 oz) soft goat's cheese,
  crumbled into small pieces

3 tablespoons capers

1 tablespoon dried oregano

1 teaspoon olive oil

1 Mix the yeast, sugar, a pinch of salt and 1 cup (250 ml/8 fl oz) warm water in a bowl. Leave in a warm, draught-free place for 10 minutes, or until foamy. Sift both flours into a bowl. Make a well, add the yeast mixture and mix to a firm dough. Knead on a lightly floured surface for 5 minutes, or until smooth. Place in a lightly oiled bowl, cover with plastic wrap or a damp tea towel and leave in a warm, draught-free place for 1–1¹/2 hours, or until doubled in size.
2 Preheat the oven to moderately hot 200°C (400°F/Gas 6). Brush a 30 cm (12 inch) pizza tray with oil. Punch down the dough and knead for 2 minutes. Roll out to a 35 cm (14 inch) round. Put the dough on the tray and tuck the edge over to form a rim.
3 For the topping, cut the red pepper into large flat pieces and remove the membrane and seeds. Place, skin-side-up, under a hot grill until blackened. Cool in a plastic bag, then peel away the skin and cut the flesh into narrow strips.
4 Slice the potato paper-thin and arrange over the base with the red pepper, onion and half the cheese. Sprinkle with capers, oregano and black pepper and drizzle with oil. Brush the crust edge with oil and bake for 20 minutes. Add the remaining cheese and bake for 15–20 minutes, or until the crust has browned. Serve in wedges.

*ABOVE: Potato
and onion pizza*

TURKISH BREAD

Preparation time: 30 minutes + rising
Total cooking time: 30 minutes
Makes 6

2 x 7 g (¹/₄ oz) sachets dry yeast
¹/₂ teaspoon sugar
¹/₂ cup (60 g/2 oz) plain (all-purpose) flour
3¹/₂ cups (435 g/14 oz) bread flour
  (see Note)
¹/₄ cup (60 ml/2 fl oz) olive oil
1 egg
nigella or sesame seeds, to sprinkle

1 Mix the yeast, sugar and ¹/₂ cup (125 ml/ 4 fl oz) warm water in a bowl. Add the plain flour and mix until smooth. Cover with a plate and leave for 30 minutes, or until frothy and trebled in size.
2 Place the bread flour in a large bowl with 1 teaspoon salt. Add the oil, yeast mixture and 270 ml (8¹/₂ fl oz) warm water. Mix to a loose dough, then turn out onto a lightly floured surface and knead for 15 minutes. Add minimal flour as the dough needs to be soft and moist.
3 Shape into a ball and place in a large oiled bowl. Cover with a tea towel and leave in a warm place for 1 hour, or until doubled in size. Punch down once, to expel the air, then divide into 6 portions and shape into smooth balls, kneading as little as possible. Place apart on a tray and place the tray in a plastic bag for 10 minutes.
4 Sprinkle a large baking tray with flour. Roll out two balls of dough, each to a 15 cm (6 inch) circle and place on the baking tray, leaving room for spreading. Cover with a tea towel and set aside for 20 minutes. Preheat the oven to very hot 230°C (450°F/Gas 8) and place another baking tray on the centre rack to heat.
5 Indent the surface of the dough with your finger. Lightly beat the egg with ¹/₄ cup (60 ml/ 2 fl oz) water and brush over the surface, then sprinkle with the seeds. Place the tray on top of the hot tray and bake for 8–10 minutes, or until puffed and golden. Wrap in a clean tea towel to soften the crusts while cooling. Meanwhile, repeat with the remaining dough.
NOTE: Bread flour requires more water so if you have to use all plain (all-purpose) flour, start by adding only half the water in step 2, then gradually adding the rest until a loose, soft dough forms. The texture will differ if using all plain flour.

TURKISH PIZZA

Preparation time: 25 minutes + rising
Total cooking time: 45 minutes
Makes 8

1 teaspoon dried yeast
¹/₂ teaspoon sugar
225 g (7 oz) plain (all-purpose) flour
4 tablespoons olive oil
250 g (8 oz) onions, finely chopped
500 g (1 lb) minced (ground) lamb
2 cloves garlic
1 teaspoon ground cinnamon
1¹/₂ teaspoons ground cumin
¹/₂ teaspoon cayenne pepper
3 tablespoons tomato paste (tomato purée)
400 g (13 oz) can good-quality crushed tomatoes
¹/₃ cup (50 g/1³/₄ oz) pine nuts
3 tablespoons chopped fresh coriander (cilantro)
Greek-style natural yoghurt, to serve

1 Mix the yeast, sugar and ¹/₄ cup (60 ml/2 fl oz) warm water in a bowl. Leave in a warm place for 20 minutes, or until bubbles appear on the surface. The mixture should be frothy and increased in volume.
2 Sift the flour and 1 teaspoon salt into a bowl, stir in the yeast mixture, 1 tablespoon oil and 100 ml (3 fl oz) warm water. Mix to form a soft dough, then turn onto a floured board and knead for 10 minutes, or until smooth. Place in an oiled bowl, cover and leave in a warm place for 1 hour, or until doubled in size.
3 Heat 2 tablespoons oil in a frying pan over low heat and cook the onion for 5 minutes, or until soft but not golden. Add the lamb and cook for 10 minutes, or until brown. Add the garlic and spices, tomato paste and tomato. Cook for 15 minutes, until quite dry. Add half the pine nuts and 2 tablespoons coriander. Season, then leave to cool. Preheat the oven to hot 210°C (415°F/Gas 6–7). Grease two baking trays.
4 Knock down the dough, then turn out onto a floured surface. Form into 8 portions and roll each into an 18 x 12 cm (7 x 5 inch) oval. Place on the trays. Divide the lamb among them and spread, leaving a small border. Sprinkle with pine nuts. Brush the edges with oil. Roll the uncovered dough over to cover the outer edges of the filling. Pinch the sides together at each end. Brush with oil. Bake for 15 minutes, or until golden. Sprinkle with coriander and serve with yoghurt.

TURKISH PIZZA

Knock down the dough, then turn onto a floured surface.

Divide the lamb among the ovals of dough and sprinkle pine nuts over the top.

OPPOSITE PAGE, FROM TOP: Turkish bread; Turkish pizza

441

SOUR CREAM TOMATO PIZZA

Preparation time: 30 minutes
  + 1 hour 30 minutes standing
Total cooking time: 40 minutes
Serves 4

★ ★

1 teaspoon dried yeast
1 teaspoon caster (superfine) sugar
2/3 cup (170 ml/5 1/2 fl oz) warm water
2 cups (250 g/8 oz) plain (all-purpose) flour
pinch of salt
1/2 cup (125 ml/4 fl oz) olive oil

Topping

1/2 cup (125 g/4 oz) sour cream
90 g (3 oz) ricotta cheese
2 tablespoons chopped fresh herbs
   (basil, lemon thyme, sage)
2 tablespoons oil
2 medium onions, thinly sliced
5 ripe tomatoes, sliced
2 cloves garlic, thinly sliced
45 g (1 1/2 oz) marinated Niçoise olives
10 sprigs fresh lemon thyme

1 Preheat the oven to moderately hot 200°C (400°F/Gas 6). To make the base, place the yeast, sugar and warm water into a bowl and mix to dissolve the sugar. Set aside in a warm draught-free area for 5 minutes or until the mixture is foamy.
2 Place the flour and salt into a food processor, add the olive oil and the yeast mixture with the motor running and process until it forms a rough dough. Turn out onto a lightly floured surface and knead until smooth. Place into a lightly oiled bowl, cover and allow to rest in a warm area for 1 1/2 hours or until doubled in volume. Punch down the dough and remove from the bowl. Knead and roll out to a 30 cm (12 inch) circle, or four 14 cm (about 5 1/2 inch) circles and place on a non-stick baking tray.
3 Combine the sour cream, ricotta and herbs. Spread over the base, leaving a 1 cm (1/2 inch) border.
4 Heat the oil in a frying pan, add the onions and cook for 10 minutes or until the onions are caramelized. Cool slightly, spoon over the ricotta mixture, top with the sliced tomatoes and the garlic, olives, lemon thyme and a little

freshly ground black pepper. Bake for 15–30 minutes, depending on the size, until the base is crisp and golden.

SANTA FE PIZZETTA WITH GUACAMOLE

Preparation time: 15 minutes
Total cooking time: 15 minutes
Serves 6

★

6 ready-made small pizza bases
3/4 cup (185 g/6 oz) ready-made spicy
   tomato salsa
4 spring onions (scallions), sliced
1 red pepper (capsicum), sliced
440 g (14 oz) canned red kidney beans,
   drained and washed
2 tablespoons chopped fresh basil
1/2 cup (75 g/2 1/2 oz) grated mozzarella cheese
1/4 cup (30 g/1 oz) grated Cheddar cheese
1/2 cup (125 g/4 oz) sour cream
125 g (4 oz) corn chips

Guacamole

1 clove garlic, crushed
1 small red onion, finely chopped
1 large avocado, mashed
1 teaspoon lemon juice
1 tablespoon ready-made tomato salsa
2 tablespoons sour cream

1 Preheat the oven to moderately hot 200°C (400°F/Gas 6). Spread the pizza bases with the spicy tomato salsa.
2 Top with the spring onions, red pepper, kidney beans and basil.
3 Sprinkle with the grated mozzarella and Cheddar cheese. Bake for 15 minutes or until the pizza bases are crisp and the cheese is golden brown. Serve topped with corn chips, guacamole and sour cream.
4 To make the guacamole, place the garlic, onion, avocado, lemon juice, salsa and sour cream in a bowl and stir to combine.

OPPOSITE PAGE, FROM TOP: Sour cream tomato pizza; Santa Fe pizzetta with guacamole

442

PISSALADIERE

Preparation time: 30 minutes
  + 15 minutes standing
  + 1 hour 30 minutes rising
Total cooking time: 1 hour 25 minutes
Serves 4–6

7 g (1/4 oz) sachet dry yeast
1 1/2 cups (185 g/6 oz) plain (all-purpose) flour
1 egg, beaten
1 tablespoon olive oil

Filling

1/4 cup (60 ml/2 fl oz) olive oil
2 cloves garlic
1 sprig of fresh thyme
4 large onions, thinly sliced
pinch of ground nutmeg
30 g (1 oz) drained anchovy fillets,
  halved lengthways
16 pitted black olives

BELOW: Pissaladière

1 Place the yeast in a small bowl with 2 tablespoons lukewarm water. Leave in a warm, draught-free place for 15 minutes, or until foamy. If your yeast doesn't froth, it is dead and you will have to start again.
2 Sift the flour and 1/4 teaspoon salt into a large bowl, make a well in the centre and add the yeast mixture, egg, oil and 2 tablespoons warm water. Bring the ingredients together with a wooden spoon and when clumped together, transfer to a lightly floured surface. Knead to a soft, pliable dough, adding a little more water or flour as needed. Continue kneading for 6–8 minutes, or until smooth and elastic. Lightly oil a clean large bowl and place the dough in it. Roll the dough around to coat with oil, cover the bowl with a dry tea towel and place in a warm place for 1 hour, or until doubled in size.
3 For the filling, heat the oil in a large, heavy-based frying pan, add the garlic, thyme and onion and cook, stirring occasionally, over very low heat for 1 hour, or until the onion is soft and buttery but not brown. Discard the garlic and thyme, add the nutmeg and season well.
4 Brush a 30 cm (12 inch) pizza tray with oil. Punch down the dough and lightly knead into a ball. Roll out to a 30 cm (12 inch) circle and place on the oiled tray. Spread the onions over the surface leaving a 1 cm (1/2 inch) border. Make a diamond cross-hatch pattern on top with the anchovies. Intersperse with the olives. Slide the tray into a large plastic bag and leave to rise again for 30 minutes. Preheat the oven to moderately hot 200°C (400°F/Gas 6).
5 Bake for 20–25 minutes, or until the dough is cooked and golden. Reduce the heat to 190°C (375°F/Gas 5) if the crust starts to overbrown. Cut into wedges for serving.

GOAT'S CHEESE GALETTE

Preparation time: 20 minutes + refrigeration
Total cooking time: 1 hour 15 minutes
Serves 6

Pastry

1 cup (125 g/4 oz) plain (all-purpose) flour
1/4 cup (60 ml/2 fl oz) olive oil
3–4 tablespoons chilled water

Filling

1 tablespoon olive oil
2 onions, thinly sliced

1 teaspoon fresh thyme leaves

125 g (4 oz) ricotta

100 g (3½ oz) goat's cheese

2 tablespoons pitted Niçoise olives

1 egg, lightly beaten

¼ cup (60 ml/2 fl oz) cream

1 For the pastry, sift the flour and a pinch of salt into a large bowl and make a well. Add the olive oil and mix with a flat-bladed knife until crumbly. Gradually add the water until the mixture comes together. Remove and pat together to form a disc. Refrigerate for 30 minutes.

2 For the filling, heat the olive oil in a frying pan. Add the onion, cover and cook over low heat for 30 minutes. Season and stir in half the thyme. Cool slightly.

3 Preheat the oven to moderate 180° C (350°F/ Gas 4). Lightly flour the work bench and roll out the pastry to a 30 cm (12 inch) circle. Evenly spread the onion over the pastry leaving a 2 cm (¾ inch) border. Sprinkle the ricotta and the goat's cheese evenly over the onion. Place the olives over the cheeses, then sprinkle with the remaining thyme. Fold the pastry border in to the edge of the filling, gently pleating as you go.

4 Combine the egg and cream in a small jug, then carefully pour over the filling. Bake on a heated baking tray on the lower half of the oven for 45 minutes, or until the pastry is golden. Serve warm or at room temperature.

MINI VEGETABLE PIZZAS

Preheat the oven to hot 210°C (415°F/ Gas 6–7). Lightly grease 2 baking trays. Cut 1 green pepper (capsicum) into short, thin strips. Heat 1 tablespoon oil in a frying pan and add the pepper strips, 150 g (5 oz) thinly sliced mushrooms and 1 thinly sliced zucchini (courgette). Stir over medium heat for 3 minutes, or until soft, then allow to cool. Spread 4 mini pizza bases with ready-made napoletana pasta sauce. Top with the cooked vegetables, 410 g (13 oz) drained and quartered canned artichokes, 130 g (4½ oz) drained canned corn kernls. Sprinkle with 1 cup (150 g/5 oz) grated mozzarella cheese. Bake for 15–20 minutes, or until the cheese has melted and the pizza bases are crisp. Serve immediately. Serves 4.

BELOW: Goat's cheese galette

DESSERTS

HOT CHOCOLATE
Chocolate was originally taken as a drink or used in recipes. It was sold as a paste or in solid bars and was very expensive. Milk was added to chocolate in England, but it was the Swiss who made the first commercial milk chocolate. Cocoa beans were known to Europeans from the time of Colombus, but it wasn't until 1519 when Hernando Cortes tasted chocolate drink, given to him by the Aztecs, that the Europeans knew how to use them. Chocolate drink was thought to be energy-giving and was used as a restorative. To make truly decadent hot chocolate, roughly chop 60 g (2 oz) dark chocolate and place in a small saucepan. Add 2 tablespoons water and stir over low heat until the chocolate has melted. Add 2 cups (500 ml/16 fl oz) hot milk, whisking until smooth and slightly frothy. Don't allow to boil. Pour into two mugs and float marshmallows on top.

*ABOVE: Petits
pots au chocolat*

PETITS POTS AU CHOCOLAT

Preparation time: 20 minutes + chilling
Total cooking time: 1 hour
Serves 8

 ✷ ✷

²/₃ cup (170 ml/5¹/₂ fl oz) thick (double/heavy) cream
¹/₂ vanilla bean, split lengthways
150 g (5 oz) good-quality dark bittersweet chocolate, chopped
¹/₃ cup (80 ml/2³/₄ fl oz) milk
2 egg yolks
¹/₄ cup (60 g/2 oz) caster (superfine) sugar
whipped cream and cocoa powder, to serve

1 Lightly brush eight 80 ml (2¾ fl oz) moulds or ramekins with melted butter and put them in a deep baking dish. Preheat the oven to very slow 140°C (275°F/Gas 1). Heat the cream in a small pan with the vanilla bean until the cream is warm, then leave to infuse.

2 Combine the chocolate and milk in a small pan. Stir constantly over low heat until the chocolate has just melted.

3 Place the egg yolks in a small bowl, and slowly whisk in the sugar. Continue whisking until the sugar has dissolved and the mixture is light and creamy. Scrape the seeds out of the vanilla bean into the cream, and discard the empty bean. Add the vanilla cream and the melted chocolate mixture to the beaten egg yolks, and mix until well combined.

4 Pour the mixture into the ramekins, filling approximately two-thirds of the way. Fill the baking dish with enough boiling water to come halfway up the pots. Bake for 45 minutes, or until the chocolate pots have puffed up slightly and feel spongy. Remove from the baking dish and cool completely. Cover with plastic wrap and refrigerate for 6 hours before serving. Serve with cream and a sprinkle of cocoa powder.
NOTE: The pots will have a slight crust on the top when they first come out of the oven.

CHOCOLATE BAVAROIS

Preparation time: 30 minutes + chilling
Total cooking time: 5 minutes
Serves 6

200 g (6¹/₂ oz) good-quality dark
   chocolate, chopped
1¹/₂ cups (375 ml/12 fl oz) milk
4 egg yolks
¹/₃ cup (90 g/3 oz) caster (superfine) sugar
1 tablespoon gelatine
1¹/₄ cups (315 ml/10 fl oz) cream

1 Combine the chocolate and milk in a small pan. Stir over low heat until the chocolate has melted and the milk just comes to the boil. Remove from the heat.
2 Beat the egg yolks and sugar until combined. Gradually add the hot chocolate milk, whisking until combined. Return to a clean pan and cook over low heat until the mixture thickens enough to coat the back of a wooden spoon. Do not allow to boil. Remove from the heat.
3 Put 2 tablespoons water in a small heatproof bowl, sprinkle the gelatine in an even layer over the surface and leave to go spongy. Stir into the hot chocolate mixture until dissolved.
4 Refrigerate until the mixture is cold but not set, stirring occasionally. Beat the cream until soft peaks form, then fold into the chocolate mixture in two batches. Pour into six 250 ml (8 fl oz) glasses and refrigerate for several hours or overnight, or until set.

BLANCMANGE

Preparation time: 40 minutes + chilling
Total cooking time: 10 minutes
Serves 6

100 g (3¹/₂ oz) blanched almonds
1 cup (250 ml/8 fl oz) milk
¹/₂ cup (125 g/4 oz) caster (superfine) sugar
3 teaspoons gelatine
1¹/₄ cups (315 ml/10 fl oz) cream

1 Grease six 125 ml (4 fl oz) fluted moulds or ramekins. Process the almonds and 3 tablespoons water in a small food processor until finely chopped and paste-like. With the motor running, gradually add the milk. Pour into a small

pan, add the sugar and stir over low heat until the sugar has completely dissolved. Allow to cool.
2 Strain the milk through a strainer lined with muslin. Twist the muslin tightly to extract as much milk as possible—you should have 1¹/₄ cups (315 ml/10 fl oz) of almond milk.
3 Place 3 tablespoons cold water in a small heatproof bowl, sprinkle the gelatine in an even layer over the surface and leave to go spongy. Do not stir. Bring a small pan filled with about 4 cm (1¹/₂ inches) water to the boil, remove from the heat and place the bowl into the pan. The water should come halfway up the side of the bowl. Stir the gelatine until clear and dissolved, then stir it through the almond milk. Allow to cool completely.
4 Whip the cream into firm peaks, then fold the almond mixture through. Pour into the moulds and refrigerate for 6–8 hours, or until set. To unmould, loosen the edge with your fingertip and turn out onto a plate. If the blancmange do not unmould easily, wipe the outside of the moulds with a cloth dipped in hot water.

CREAMY CHOCOLATE THICKSHAKE
Pour 1 cup (250 ml/8 fl oz) milk and 1 tablespoon chocolate syrup in a blender and process briefly to combine. Add 2 scoops of chocolate ice cream and blend until the mixture is smooth but not runny. Pour into a large glass and serve with a wide straw.

ABOVE: Chocolate bavarois

449

and chill for 2 hours, or until set. Unmould by wiping a cloth dipped in hot water over the mould and upending it onto a plate.

3 To make the ruby sauce, stir the sugar with 1 cup (250 ml/8 fl oz) water in a pan over medium heat until the sugar has completely dissolved (do not allow to boil). Add the cinnamon stick and simmer for 5 minutes. Add the raspberries and wine and boil rapidly for 5 minutes. Remove the cinnamon stick and push the sauce through a sieve; discard the seeds. Cool, then chill before serving with the panna cotta. Can be garnished with fruit.

NOTE: Translated from the Italian 'cooked cream', panna cotta takes its name from the cream being cooked over heat before being set with gelatine as a thick creamy custard. If you wish, you can split the vanilla bean and add the seeds to the custard.

BAKED CUSTARD

Preparation time: 5 minutes
Total cooking time: 35 minutes
Serves 4

3 eggs
1/2 cup (95 g/3 oz) soft brown sugar
1 1/2 cups (375 ml/12 fl oz) milk
1/2 cup (125 ml/4 fl oz) cream
1 teaspoon vanilla essence
ground nutmeg, to dust

1 Preheat the oven to moderate 180°C (350°F/Gas 4). Brush a 1 litre (32 fl oz) ovenproof dish with melted butter.

2 Whisk the eggs, sugar, milk, cream and vanilla essence in a bowl for 1 minute. Pour into the dish and place the dish in a shallow baking dish. Pour enough boiling water into the baking dish to come halfway up the side of the ovenproof dish. Place on the oven shelf, sprinkle the top of the custard with nutmeg and bake for 15 minutes.

3 Reduce the heat to warm 160°C (315°F/Gas 2–3) and bake for another 20 minutes, or until the custard is set. It should no longer be liquid but should wobble slightly when the dish is shaken lightly. Remove the dish from the water bath immediately. Serve warm or cold.

PANNA COTTA WITH RUBY SAUCE

Preparation time: 20 minutes + chilling
Total cooking time: 20 minutes
Serves 6

3 cups (750 ml/24 fl oz) cream
3 teaspoons gelatine
1 vanilla bean
1/3 cup (90 g/3 oz) caster (superfine) sugar

Ruby sauce

1 cup (250 g/8 oz) caster (superfine) sugar
1 cinnamon stick
125 g (4 oz) fresh or frozen raspberries
1/2 cup (125 ml/4 fl oz) good-quality red wine

1 Lightly grease the inside of six 150 ml (5 fl oz) ramekins or moulds with flavourless oil. Place 3 tablespoons of the cream in a small bowl, sprinkle the gelatine in an even layer over the surface and leave to go spongy.

2 Put the remaining cream in a pan with the vanilla bean and sugar and heat gently while stirring, until almost boiling. Remove from the heat and whisk the gelatine into the cream mixture until dissolved. Pour into the moulds

ABOVE: Panna cotta with ruby sauce

DECADENT WHITE CHOCOLATE MOUSSE

Preparation time: 40 minutes + chilling
Total cooking time: 5 minutes
Serves 6

60 g (2 oz) good-quality dark chocolate, melted
4 egg yolks
1/2 cup (125 g/4 oz) caster (superfine) sugar
1 tablespoon honey
1 teaspoon instant coffee powder, optional
200 g (6 1/2 oz) white chocolate, melted
125 g (4 oz) unsalted butter
2/3 cup (170 ml/5 1/2 fl oz) thick (double/heavy) cream

Praline

80 g (2 3/4 oz) blanched almonds, lightly toasted
1/2 cup (125 g/4 oz) sugar

1 Place the chocolate in a small paper piping bag and pipe in a swirling pattern over the inside surface of six dessert glasses. Refrigerate until set.
2 To make the praline, line a baking tray with baking paper and spread the almonds over it. Combine the sugar with 1/3 cup (80 ml/2 3/4 fl oz) water in a small pan and stir over low heat, without boiling, until the sugar has dissolved. Brush the edges of the pan with water. Bring to the boil, reduce the heat and simmer, without stirring, until golden brown. Remove from the heat immediately and pour carefully over the almonds. Allow to set until hard. Break half into pieces for topping. Chop or process the remainder into fine crumbs.
3 Using electric beaters, beat the egg yolks, sugar, honey and the coffee blended with 1 teaspoon of hot water in a small bowl until very thick. Beat in the white chocolate until smooth. In a medium bowl, beat the butter with electric beaters until light and creamy. Add the egg yolk mixture and beat until smooth.
4 Beat the cream until soft peaks form. Using a metal spoon, gently fold the cream into the chocolate mixture. Fold in the finely chopped or processed praline. Spoon the mixture into dessert glasses. Refrigerate for 2–3 hours. Serve decorated with large praline pieces and perhaps whipped cream.

QUICK CHOCOLATE MOUSSE

This recipe is handy to use when you don't have much time. Break 175 g (6 oz) dark chocolate into pieces, place it in a heatproof bowl over a pan of steaming water and stir until the chocolate melts (buttons). Separate 5 eggs and put the whites in a large clean glass bowl. Cool the chocolate a little and gently stir in the egg yolks. Whisk the egg whites with a balloon whisk or electric beaters until they are stiff, add one tablespoon of the egg whites to the chocolate mixture and mix it in well. Add the chocolate mixture to the remaining egg whites and fold the whites into the chocolate, making sure you do not lose too much volume. Divide the mixture among six 150 ml (5 oz) ramekins. Chill in the refrigerator for 4 hours, or until set. Serve with cream. Serves 6.

BELOW: Decadent white chocolate mousse

CREME CARAMEL

Pour a little of the hot caramel mixture into each ramekin, covering the base.

BELOW: Crème caramel

CREME CARAMEL

Preparation time: 25 minutes + chilling
Total cooking time: 35 minutes
Serves 8

★★

³/4 cup (185 g/6 oz) sugar

Custard

3 cups (750 ml/24 fl oz) milk
¹/3 cup (90 g/3 oz) caster (superfine) sugar
4 eggs
1 teaspoon vanilla essence

1 Preheat the oven to warm 160°C (315°F/ Gas 2–3). Brush eight 125 ml (4 fl oz) ramekins or moulds with melted butter.
2 Place the sugar and ¹/4 cup (60 ml/2 fl oz) water in a pan. Stir over low heat until the sugar dissolves. Bring to the boil, reduce the heat and simmer until the mixture turns golden and starts to caramelize. Remove from the heat immediately and pour enough hot caramel into each ramekin to cover the base. The caramel will continue cooking in the pan so work quickly and be careful not to burn yourself.
3 To make the custard, heat the milk in a pan over low heat until almost boiling. Remove from the heat. Whisk together the sugar, eggs and vanilla essence for 2 minutes, then stir in the warm milk. Strain the mixture into a jug and pour into the ramekins.
4 Place the ramekins in a baking dish and pour in enough boiling water to come halfway up the sides of the ramekins. Bake for 30 minutes, or until the custard is set. The custards should be no longer liquid and should wobble slightly when the dish is shaken lightly. Allow to cool, then refrigerate for at least 2 hours, or until set. To unmould, run a knife carefully around the edge of each custard and gently upturn onto serving plates. Shake gently to assist removal, if necessary. Crème caramel can be served by itself or with fresh berries, whipped cream and wafers.
VARIATION: This recipe can be varied by flavouring the custard with spices such as cardamom, cinnamon and nutmeg, lemon or orange rind, or with a little of your favourite spirit or liqueur. Crème caramel appears in France as *crème renversée*, in Italy as *crema caramella* and in Spain, South America and Mexico as a flan.

BANANA CUSTARD

Preparation time: 15 minutes
Total cooking time: 5 minutes
Serves 4

★

1 egg, lightly beaten
2 tablespoons custard powder
2 tablespoons sugar
1 cup (250 ml/8 fl oz) milk
¹/2 cup (125 ml/4 fl oz) thick (double/heavy) cream
2 bananas, sliced diagonally

1 Combine the beaten egg, custard powder, sugar, milk and cream in a heatproof bowl and whisk until smooth.
2 Pour into a pan and stir constantly over low heat for 5 minutes, or until the custard thickens slightly and coats the back of a wooden spoon.
3 Remove the bowl from the heat and gently stir in the banana. Serve hot or cold.

CHERRY CLAFOUTIS

Preparation time: 15 minutes
Total cooking time: 35 minutes
Serves 6–8

500 g (1 lb) fresh cherries, or 800 g
  (1 lb 10 oz) can pitted cherries,
  well drained
1/2 cup (60 g/2 oz) plain (all-purpose) flour
1/3 cup (90 g/3 oz) sugar
4 eggs, lightly beaten
1 cup (250 ml/8 fl oz) milk
25 g (3/4 oz) unsalted butter, melted
icing (confectioners') sugar, to dust

1 Preheat the oven to moderate 180°C (350°F/
Gas 4). Brush a 23 cm (9 inch) glass or ceramic
shallow pie plate with melted butter.
2 Pit the cherries and spread onto the pie plate
in a single layer. If using canned cherries, drain
them thoroughly in a sieve before spreading in
the plate. If they are still wet, they will leak into
the batter.
3 Sift the flour into a bowl, add the sugar and
make a well in the centre. Gradually add the
combined eggs, milk and butter, whisking until
smooth and free of lumps.
4 Pour the batter over the cherries and bake for
30–35 minutes. The batter should be risen and
golden. Remove from the oven and dust
generously with icing sugar. Serve immediately.
NOTE: A clafoutis (pronounced 'clafootee') is a
classic French batter pudding, a speciality of the
Limousin region. Clafoutis comes from Clafir,
a dialect verb meaning 'to fill'. It is traditionally
made with cherries. Other berries such as
blueberries, blackberries, raspberries, or small
well-flavoured strawberries may be used. Use
a shallow pie plate or the top will not turn
golden brown.

ABOVE: Cherry clafoutis

ALMOND MASCARPONE CREPES WITH SUMMER FRUIT

Preparation time: 40 minutes + standing
Total cooking time: 35 minutes
Makes about 12 crepes

☆☆

Almond mascarpone

60 g (2 oz) slivered almonds
1/2 cup (125 g/4 oz) caster (superfine) sugar
500 g (1 lb) mascarpone

250 g (8 oz) fresh strawberries, sliced
1 tablespoon caster (superfine) sugar
1 cup (125 g/4 oz) plain (all-purpose) flour
2 eggs
1/2 cup (125 ml/4 fl oz) milk
30 g (1 oz) unsalted butter, melted
4 kiwi fruit, thinly sliced
200 g (6 1/2 oz) raspberries
250 g (8 oz) blueberries

1 To make the almond mascarpone, grill the almonds under a low heat until lightly golden, then place on an oiled baking tray. Put the caster sugar in a small heavy-based pan with 1/2 cup (125 ml/4 fl oz) water and stir, without boiling, until the sugar has dissolved. Bring to the boil, then reduce the heat and simmer, without stirring, for 15 minutes, or until the liquid turns golden brown. Quickly pour over the almonds and leave to set. Finely grind in a food processor, transfer to a bowl, then stir in the mascarpone, cover and refrigerate.
2 Place the strawberries in a large bowl and sprinkle with the caster sugar. Refrigerate.
3 Mix the flour, eggs and milk in a food processor for 10 seconds. Add 1/2 cup (125 ml/ 4 fl oz) water and the butter and process until smooth. Pour into a jug and set aside for 30 minutes.
4 Heat a small crepe pan or non-stick frying pan and brush lightly with melted butter. Pour 1/4 cup (60 ml/2 fl oz) batter into the pan, swirling to cover the base thinly. Cook for about 30 seconds, or until the edges just begin to curl, turn the crepe over and cook the other side until lightly browned. Transfer to a plate and cover with a tea towel while cooking the remaining batter.
5 Spread each warm crepe with almond mascarpone and fold into quarters. Serve with macerated strawberries and some kiwi fruit, raspberries and blueberries.

FILLINGS FOR CREPES

MIXED BERRY Macerate fresh berries in orange juice with a little icing (confectioners') sugar and grated orange rind for a few hours. They will be ready when they have given off a little syrupy juice.

APPLE Cook slices of peeled, cored apple in melted butter until golden and softened, but still in their shape. Sprinkle with sugar and keep cooking until they caramelize. Sprinkle with lemon juice or cinnamon.

ABOVE: Almond mascarpone crepes with summer fruit

Line a large baking tray with baking paper and draw a circle on the paper. Turn the paper over.

Beat the egg whites with electric beaters in a dry bowl until soft peaks form.

Spread the stiff mixture onto the paper on the tray inside the drawn circle.

Make furrows all the way round the outside of the meringue mixture by running a palette knife up the edge.

FRESH FRUIT PAVLOVA

Preparation time: 30 minutes
Total cooking time: 55 minutes
Serves 6–8

★★

6 egg whites
2 cups (500 g/1 lb) caster (superfine) sugar
1 1/2 tablespoons cornflour (cornstarch)
1 1/2 teaspoons vinegar
2 cups (500 ml/16 fl oz) cream, whipped
2 bananas, sliced
500 g (1 lb) strawberries, sliced
4 kiwi fruit, sliced
4 passionfruit, pulped

 Preheat the oven to slow 150°C (300°F/ Gas 2). Line a large baking tray with baking paper and draw a 26 cm (10 1/2 inch) circle on the paper. Turn the paper over and place on the tray. Beat the egg whites with electric beaters in a large dry bowl until soft peaks form. Gradually add all but 2 tablespoons of the sugar, beating well after each addition. Combine the cornflour and vinegar with the last of the sugar and beat for 1 minute before adding it to the bowl. Beat for 5–10 minutes, or until all the sugar has completely dissolved and the meringue is stiff and glossy. Spread onto the paper inside the circle.

2 Shape the meringue evenly, running the flat side of a palette knife along the edge and over the top. Run the palette knife up the edge of the meringue mixture all the way round, making furrows. This strengthens the pavlova and helps prevent the edge from crumbling, as well as being decorative.

3 Bake for 40 minutes, or until pale and crisp. Reduce the heat to very slow 120°C (250°F/ Gas 1/2) and bake for 15 minutes. Turn off the oven and cool the pavlova in the oven, using a wooden spoon to keep the door slightly ajar. When completely cooled, top with cream and fruit. Drizzle with passionfruit pulp and serve.

VARIATION: This can be made into individual pavlovas. Spoon 6 or 8 rounds of mixture onto two baking paper-covered trays. Alternate the trays halfway through cooking time.

ABOVE: Fresh
fruit pavlova

2 Melt the butter in a pan, add the flour and stir over low heat for 2 minutes, or until lightly golden. Add the milk gradually, stirring until smooth. Stir over medium heat until the mixture boils and thickens; boil for another minute, then remove from the heat. Transfer to a large bowl.
3 Dissolve the coffee in 1 tablespoon hot water, add to the milk with the remaining sugar, melted chocolate and egg yolks, then beat until smooth.
4 Beat the egg whites in a clean dry bowl until stiff peaks form and then fold a little into the chocolate mixture to loosen it slightly. Gently fold in the remaining egg white, then spoon the mixture into the soufflé dish and bake for 40 minutes, or until well risen and just firm. Remove the collar, dust the soufflé with icing sugar and serve immediately.

HOT CHOCOLATE SOUFFLE

Preparation time: 30 minutes
Total cooking time: 20 minutes
Serves 6

★★

175 g (6 oz) good-quality dark chocolate, chopped
5 egg yolks, lightly beaten
1/4 cup (60 g/2 oz) caster (superfine) sugar
7 egg whites
icing (confectioners') sugar, to dust

1 Preheat the oven to moderately hot 200°C (400°F/Gas 6). Wrap a double layer of baking paper around six 250 ml (8 fl oz) ramekins, to come 3 cm (1 1/4 inches) above the rim. Secure with string. Brush the insides with melted butter, sprinkle with caster sugar, shake to coat evenly, then tip out excess. Place on a baking tray.
2 Put the chocolate in a heatproof bowl. Half fill a saucepan with water and bring to the boil. Remove from the heat and place the bowl over the pan—don't let it touch the water. Stir occasionally until the chocolate has melted. Stir in the egg yolks and sugar. Transfer the mixture to a large bowl. Beat the egg whites in a large bowl until firm peaks form.
3 Fold a third of the beaten egg white through the chocolate mixture to loosen it. Using a metal spoon, fold through the remaining egg white until just combined. Spoon the mixture into the ramekins and bake for 12–15 minutes, or until well risen and just set. Cut the string and remove the collars. Serve immediately, dusted lightly with the sifted icing sugar.

HOT MOCHA SOUFFLE

Preparation time: 25 minutes
Total cooking time: 45 minutes
Serves 20

★★

3 tablespoons caster (superfine) sugar
40 g (1 1/4 oz) unsalted butter
2 tablespoons plain (all-purpose) flour
3/4 cup (185 ml/6 fl oz) milk
1 tablespoon instant espresso-style coffee powder
100 g (3 1/2 oz) good-quality dark chocolate, melted
4 eggs, separated
icing (confectioners') sugar, to dust

1 Preheat the oven to moderate 180°C (350°F/Gas 4). Wrap a double thickness of baking paper around a 1.25 litre (40 fl oz) soufflé dish extending 3 cm (1 1/4 inches) above the rim, then tie securely with string. Brush with oil or melted butter, sprinkle 1 tablespoon of the sugar into the dish, shake the dish to coat the base and side evenly, then shake out the excess.

ABOVE: Hot mocha soufflé

SLUMP

Preparation time: 30 minutes
Total cooking time: 30 minutes
Serves 6

500 g (1 lb) fresh or canned cherries, pitted
caster (superfine) sugar, to taste
1 1/2 cups (185 g/6 oz) self-raising flour
1 teaspoon baking powder
50 g (1 3/4 oz) unsalted butter, chilled and cubed
1/4 cup (55 g/2 oz) demerara sugar
150 ml (5 fl oz) cream

1 Cook the cherries in 1/4 cup (60 ml/2 fl oz) water in a large pan over moderate heat for 5 minutes, or until they have begun to soften. Add the sugar and transfer to a 1 litre (32 fl oz) ovenproof dish to cool. Preheat the oven to moderately hot 200°C (400°F/Gas 6).
2 Sift the flour, baking powder and a little salt into a large bowl, add the butter and demerara sugar and rub in, using just your fingertips, to form fine crumbs. Pour in the cream and stir well to mix everything together—you should have a spreadable mixture.
3 Cover the cooled cherries with blobs of the scone topping, leaving small gaps between the blobs. Bake for 25 minutes, or until the topping is puffed and golden. Slump can be served with cream or lightly whipped cream.

PLUM COBBLER

Preparation time: 15 minutes
Total cooking time: 45 minutes
Serves 6–8

750 g (1 1/2 lb) blood plums, or other plums
1/4 cup (60 g/2 oz) caster (superfine) sugar

Topping

1 cup (125 g/4 oz) self-raising flour
1/2 cup (60 g/2 oz) plain (all-purpose) flour
1/4 cup (60 g/2 oz) caster (superfine) sugar
125 g (4 oz) unsalted butter, chopped
1 egg
1/2 cup (125 ml/4 fl oz) milk
icing (confectioners') sugar, to dust

1 Preheat the oven to moderate 180°C (350°F/Gas 4). Lightly grease a 2 litre (64 fl oz) ovenproof dish. Cut the blood plums into quarters, discarding the stones.
2 Put the plums in a pan with the sugar and 1 tablespoon water. Stir over low heat for 5 minutes, or until the sugar dissolves and the fruit softens slightly. Spread the plum mixture in the prepared dish.
3 Sift the flours into a bowl, add the sugar and stir. Rub in the butter, using just your fingertips, until the mixture is fine and crumbly. Combine the egg and milk and whisk until smooth. Stir into the flour mixture.
4 Place large spoonfuls of mixture on top of the plums. Bake for 30–40 minutes, or until the top is golden and cooked through. Dust with icing sugar before serving.

BELOW: Plum cobbler

MERINGUE SECRETS

There are several types of meringue—ordinary, Italian, and meringue *cuite*.

To beat well, egg whites need to be fresh and at room temperature, as well as free from any oil or egg yolk. For ordinary meringue, the sugar is added in at least two batches and beaten until the sugar dissolves and stabilises the whites. Meringue should be thick and shiny and hold its shape when piped. It might not work on a humid day, when it may break down.

Italian meringue is made by adding boiling sugar syrup to beaten egg white. Meringue *cuite* is made by beating egg white and icing (confectioners') sugar over heat. Both these methods give a solid meringue which holds up well.

OPPOSITE PAGE, FILLED MERINGUE BASKETS, FROM TOP: Gingered custard and rhubarb; Rich chocolate mousse; Grilled fig and ricotta

MERINGUE BASKETS

Preparation time: 20 minutes
Total cooking time: 35 minutes + cooling
Makes 4

2 egg whites
¹/₂ cup (125 g/4 oz) caster (superfine) sugar

1 Preheat the oven to slow 150° (300°F/Gas 2). Line a baking tray with greaseproof paper. Mark out four 9 cm (3¹/₂ inch) circles. Put the egg whites in a large clean, dry bowl and leave for a few minutes to reach room temperature. Using electric beaters, whisk the egg whites until soft peaks form. Gradually add the sugar, beating well after each addition, until the mixture is thick and glossy. Do not overbeat.
2 Spread 1 tablespoon of the mixture evenly over each of the circles to a thickness of 5 mm (¹/₄ inch). Put the remaining mixture in a piping bag fitted with a 1 cm (¹/₂ inch) star nozzle. Pipe the mixture on the edge of the meringue circles to make a basket 1–2 cm (¹/₂–³/₄ inches) high.
3 Bake for 30–35 minutes, or until lightly golden, then turn the oven off and leave the meringues to cool completely in the oven. Once cooled, carefully remove from the trays. Transfer to an airtight container until required.

GINGERED CUSTARD AND RHUBARB FILLING

In a bowl, whisk 4 egg yolks and ¹/₂ cup (125 g/4 oz) sugar together until creamy, then stir in 1 tablespoon cornflour (cornstarch). In a small pan, combine 1 cup (250 ml/4 fl oz) milk with 2 teaspoons grated fresh ginger and bring to the boil. Remove from the heat, strain and allow to cool slightly, then gradually whisk into the egg mixture. Return to the pan and stir over low heat for 5 minutes, or until the mixture thickens. Remove from the heat and allow to cool. Cut 2 stalks of rhubarb in half lengthways, then cut into 3 cm (1¹/₄ inch) pieces. Combine 1 tablespoon caster (superfine) sugar and ¹/₄ cup (60 ml/2 fl oz) water in a small pan and stir over low heat until the sugar dissolves. Add the rhubarb and cook gently for 3–5 minutes, or until the rhubarb softens but still holds its shape. Spoon the cooled custard into the baskets, arrange the rhubarb over it and serve immediately. Garnish with a dusting of icing (confectioners') sugar or fine strips of preserved ginger. Serves 4.

RASPBERRY MASCARPONE FILLING

Combine 250 g (8 oz) mascarpone with the finely grated rind of 1 lime. Stir in 60 g (2 oz) raspberries, mixing well so that some of the raspberry juices are released into the mascarpone. Divide the mixture evenly among the four baskets and garnish, using about 60 g (2 oz) raspberries. Serve garnished with fresh mint leaves or a dusting of icing (confectioners') sugar. Serves 4.

RICH CHOCOLATE MOUSSE FILLING

Bring a pan filled with about 4 cm (1¹/₂ inches) water to the boil, then remove it from the heat. Put 60 g (1 oz) roughly chopped dark chocolate in a heatproof bowl and set over the pan, making sure the bowl is not touching the water. Stir until the chocolate has melted. Allow to cool. Using electric beaters, whip 1 cup (250 ml/8 fl oz) cream with ¹/₄ cup (60 g/2 oz) caster (superfine) sugar until soft peaks form. Mix one-third of the cream into the melted chocolate, stirring until the chocolate and cream are well combined. Fold in the remaining cream mixture, cover and refrigerate for 2 hours. Once firm, spoon into the meringue baskets and garnish with chocolate curls. A quick way to make chocolate curls is to run a vegetable peeler down the length of a block of chocolate. Serve immediately, dusted with icing (confectioners') sugar. Serves 4.

GRILLED FIG AND RICOTTA FILLING

Blend 500 g (1 lb) ricotta, 2 tablespoons honey, 2–3 tablespoons orange juice, 2 teaspoons soft brown sugar, ¹/₂ teaspoon cinnamon and ¹/₄ teaspoon vanilla essence together in a food processor until smooth. Transfer to a bowl and stir in 50 g (1³/₄ oz) sultanas. Quarter 4 firm, purple figs lengthways, place on a baking tray and sprinkle with 1 tablespoon soft brown sugar. Grill for 5–6 minutes, or until the sugar has begun to caramelize. Spoon the ricotta mixture into the baskets, top with the grilled figs, sprinkle with finely chopped pistachios and serve immediately. Any remaining fig can be served separately. Serves 4.

BAKED ALASKA

Preparation time: 40 minutes + freezing
Total cooking time: 8 minutes
Serves 6–8

2 litres good-quality vanilla ice cream
250 g (8 oz) mixed glacé fruit,
    finely chopped
1/4 cup (125 ml/4 fl oz) Grand Marnier
    or Cointreau
2 teaspoons grated orange rind
60 g (2 oz) toasted almonds,
    finely chopped
60 g (2 oz) dark chocolate,
    finely chopped
1 sponge or butter cake, cut into
    3 cm (1 1/4 inch) slices
3 egg whites
3/4 cup (185 g/6 oz) caster (superfine) sugar

BAKED ALASKA
Baking ice cream inside an insulating hot layer is an idea probably invented by the Chinese, who baked ice cream wrapped in pastry. The French used the same idea to make *omelette Norvegienne,* using meringue instead of pastry. The Americans coined the name Baked Alaska.

ABOVE: Baked Alaska

1 Line a 2 litre (64 fl oz) pudding basin with damp muslin. Soften 1 litre (4 cups) of ice cream enough to enable the glacé fruit to be folded in with 2 tablespoons liqueur and 1 teaspoon orange rind. Spoon into the basin, smooth over the base and up the sides, then freeze. Soften the remaining ice cream and fold in the almonds, chocolate, remaining liqueur and orange rind. Spoon into the frozen shell and level the surface.
2 Work quickly to evenly cover the ice cream with a 3 cm (1 1/4 inch) thick layer of cake. Cover with foil and freeze for at least 2 hours. Preheat the oven to hot 220°C (425°F/Gas 7). Using electric beaters, beat the egg whites in a dry bowl until soft peaks form. Gradually add the sugar, beating well after each addition. Beat for 4–5 minutes, until thick and glossy.
3 Unmould the ice cream onto an ovenproof dish and remove the muslin. Quickly spread the meringue over the top to cover the ice cream completely. Bake for 5–8 minutes, or until lightly browned. Cut into wedges and serve at once.
NOTE: Partly bury an upturned half egg shell in the top of the meringue before baking. Fill with warmed brandy and set alight to serve.

TIRAMISU

Preparation time: 30 minutes
  + overnight refrigeration
Total cooking time: Nil
Serves 6

✫✫

2 cups (500 ml/16 fl oz) strong black coffee,
  cooled
¼ cup (60 ml/2 fl oz) Marsala or
  coffee-flavoured liqueur
2 eggs, separated
¼ cup (60 g/2 oz) caster (superfine) sugar
250 g (8 oz) mascarpone
1 cup (250 ml/8 fl oz) cream
16 large sponge finger (savoiardi) biscuits
2 tablespoons dark cocoa powder

 Combine the coffee and Marsala in a bowl and set aside. Beat the egg yolks and sugar in a bowl with electric beaters for 3 minutes, or until thick and pale. Add the mascarpone and mix until just combined. Transfer to a large bowl. Beat the cream in a separate bowl, with electric beaters, until soft peaks form, then fold into the mascarpone mixture.

2 Place the egg whites in a small, clean, dry bowl and beat with electric beaters until soft peaks form. Fold quickly and lightly into the cream mixture.

3 Dip half the biscuits into the coffee mixture, drain off any excess and arrange in the base of a 2.5 litre (80 fl oz) ceramic or glass serving dish. Spread half the cream mixture over the biscuits.

4 Dip the remaining biscuits into the remaining coffee mixture and repeat the layers. Smooth the surface and dust liberally with the cocoa powder. Refrigerate overnight.

NOTE: This delicious rich dessert originated in Venice. Tiramisu translates as 'pick-me-up'. It is best made a day in advance to let the flavours develop but if you don't have time, refrigerate it for at least 2 hours before serving, by which time it should be firm.

ABOVE: Tiramisu

461

BERRIES IN CHAMPAGNE JELLY

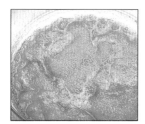

Sprinkle the gelatine over the Champagne in an even layer and leave until spongy.

Slowly pour the jelly into the wine glasses, covering the berries.

SUMMER BERRIES IN CHAMPAGNE JELLY

Preparation time: 10 minutes + refrigeration
Total cooking time: 5 minutes
Serves 8

★

1 litre (32 fl oz) Champagne
1 1/2 tablespoons powdered gelatine
1 cup (250 g/8 oz) sugar
4 strips lemon rind
4 strips orange rind
250 g (8 oz) small strawberries, hulled
250 g (8 oz) blueberries

1 Pour half the Champagne into a bowl and let the bubbles subside. Sprinkle the gelatine over the top in an even layer. Leave until the gelatine is spongy—do not stir. Pour the remaining Champagne into a large saucepan, add the sugar and rinds and heat gently, stirring constantly, until all the sugar has dissolved.

2 Remove the saucepan from the heat, add the gelatine mixture and stir until thoroughly dissolved. Cool completely, then remove the rind.

3 Divide the berries among eight 1/2 cup (125 ml/ 4 fl oz) stemmed wine glasses and gently pour the jelly over them. Refrigerate until set. Remove from the fridge 15 minutes before serving.

FRUIT GRATIN

Slice some fresh peaches and strawberries and layer them evenly in four small gratin dishes. Sprinkle with a few raspberries, making the surface of the fruit reasonably flat. Coat the fruit with an even thick layer of zabaglione and place the dishes under a preheated grill. Grill under low heat until the surface turns golden brown, then serve immediately. Serves 4.

ABOVE: Summer berries in Champagne jelly

PROFITEROLES WITH DARK CHOCOLATE SAUCE

Preparation time: 40 minutes + cooling
Total cooking time: 50 minutes
Serves 4–6

60 g (2 oz) butter, chopped
3/4 cup (90 g/3 oz) plain (all-purpose) flour
3 eggs, lightly beaten

White chocolate filling

1/4 cup (30 g/1 oz) custard powder
1 tablespoon caster (superfine) sugar
1 1/2 cups (375 ml/12 fl oz) milk
150 g (5 oz) white chocolate melts (buttons),
  chopped
1 tablespoon Grand Marnier

Dark chocolate sauce

125 g (4 oz) dark chocolate, chopped
1/2 cup (125 ml/4 fl oz) cream

1 Preheat the oven to hot 210°C (415°F/ Gas 6–7). Line a baking tray with baking paper. Put the butter and 3/4 cup (185 ml/6 fl oz) water in a pan. Bring to the boil, then remove from the heat. Add the flour all at once. Return to the heat and stir until the mixture forms a smooth ball. Set aside to cool slightly. Transfer to a bowl and, while beating with electric beaters, gradually add the eggs a little at a time, beating well after each addition, to form a thick, smooth, glossy paste.
2 Spoon 2 heaped teaspoons of the mixture onto the tray at 5 cm (2 inch) intervals. Sprinkle lightly with water and bake for 12–15 minutes, or until the dough is puffed. Turn off the oven. Pierce a small hole in the base of each profiterole with the point of a knife and return the profiteroles to the oven. Leave them to dry in the oven for 5 minutes.
3 For the filling, combine the custard powder and sugar in a pan. Gradually add the milk, stirring until smooth, then continue to stir over low heat until the mixture boils and thickens. Remove from the heat and add the white chocolate and Grand Marnier. Stir until the chocolate is melted. Cover the surface with plastic wrap and allow to cool. Stir the custard until smooth, then spoon into a piping bag fitted with a 1 cm (1/2 inch) plain nozzle. Pipe the filling into each profiterole. Serve with the warm chocolate sauce.
4 For the dark chocolate sauce, combine the chocolate and cream in a small saucepan. Stir over low heat until the chocolate is melted and the mixture is smooth. Serve warm.
IN ADVANCE: The profiteroles can be made a day ahead. Fill just before serving.
VARIATION: You can also make miniature profiteroles, using 1 teaspoon of the mixture. Dip the tops of the cooked profiteroles in melted chocolate. When set, fill them with whipped cream.

ABOVE: Profiteroles with dark chocolate sauce

PUDDING TOPPINGS

These custards, butters and sauces will complement your rich Christmas pudding,

whether you prefer classic toppings or something different.

VANILLA CUSTARD

Combine 1 cup (250 ml/8 fl oz) milk and
1/4 cup (60 ml/2 fl oz) cream in a pan. Bring
to the boil, then remove from the heat
immediately. In a bowl, whisk 3 egg yolks,
1/2 cup (125 g/4 oz) caster (superfine)
sugar and 2 teaspoons cornflour (cornstarch).
Slowly pour the hot milk and cream into
the egg mixture, whisking continuously.
Return to the pan and stir over low heat

for 5 minutes, or until thickened—do not
boil. Remove from the heat and stir in
1/2 teaspoon vanilla essence. Serve. Makes
1 1/2 cups (375 ml/12 fl oz).

WHISKY SAUCE

Melt 2 tablespoons butter in a saucepan
over low heat. Remove from the heat, add
1/3 cup (40 g/1 1/4 oz) plain (all-purpose)
flour and stir well. Gradually whisk in

2 cups (500 ml/16 fl oz) milk and
2 tablespoons caster (superfine) sugar.
Return to medium heat. Stir until it boils
and thickens. Reduce the heat and simmer
for 10 minutes, stirring occasionally.
Remove from the heat and stir in 1/3 cup
(80 ml/2 3/4 fl oz) whisky, 2 teaspoons
butter and 1 tablespoon thick (double)
cream. Cover with plastic wrap until ready
to serve. Makes 2 1/2 cups (600 ml/20 fl oz).

CREME A L'ANGLAISE

Whisk 3 egg yolks and 2 tablespoons caster (superfine) sugar together in a heatproof bowl for 2 minutes, or until light and creamy. Heat 1½ cups (375 ml/ 12 fl oz) milk until almost boiling, then pour into the bowl, whisking constantly. Return to the clean pan and stir over low heat for 5 minutes, or until thick enough to coat the back of a spoon. Don't let the mixture boil or it will scramble. Remove from the heat. Stir in ½ teaspoon vanilla essence. Transfer to a jug. Makes 2 cups (500 ml/16 fl oz).

GRAND MARNIER WHIPPED BUTTER

Remove the rind from an orange with a vegetable peeler, avoiding any white pith. Cut the rind into long thin strips, place in a pan of cold water and bring to

the boil. Drain and repeat. Return to the pan with ⅓ cup (80 ml/2¾ fl oz) water and 2 tablespoons caster (superfine) sugar. Stir over low heat until the sugar has dissolved, then boil for 2 minutes until thick and syrupy. Beat 250 g (4 oz) softened unsalted butter in a bowl with electric beaters until light and fluffy. Beat in ⅓ cup (40 g/1¼ oz) icing (confectioners') sugar, ¼ cup (60 ml/2 fl oz) orange juice and 2–3 tablespoons Grand Marnier, to taste, then fold in the orange rind syrup. Dollop on Christmas pudding. Makes 1 cup (250 g/8 oz).

BRANDY BUTTER

Beat 250 g (8 oz) softened unsalted butter and 1½ cups (185 g/6 oz) sifted icing (confectioners') sugar with electric beaters until smooth and creamy. Gradually add ¼ cup (60 ml/2 fl oz)

brandy, beating thoroughly. Refrigerate until required. Makes 1 cup (250 g/4 oz).

RICH CHOCOLATE SAUCE

Put 150 g (5 oz) chopped dark chocolate in a bowl. Bring 1¼ cups (315 ml/ 10 fl oz) cream to the boil in a pan. Stir in 2 tablespoons caster (superfine) sugar, then pour it over the chocolate. Leave for 2 minutes, then stir until smooth. Add a spoonful of any liqueur. Serve warm. Makes 1½ cups (375 ml/ 12 fl oz).

FROM LEFT: Vanilla custard; Whisky sauce; Crème à l'Anglaise; Grand Marnier whipped butter; Brandy butter; Rich chocolate sauce; Vanilla custard (on pudding)

465

CHRISTMAS PUDDING

According to research by Britain's largest producer of Christmas puddings, the Christmas pudding originated as a fourteenth century 'porridge' called frumenty made by boiling beef and mutton with raisins, currants, prunes, wines and spices. It was often more like soup and was eaten as a fasting dish before the festivities. By 1595 the frumenty was evolving into plum pudding, having been thickened with eggs, breadcrumbs and dried fruit and flavoured with ale and spirits. It became the Christmas dessert but the Puritans in 1664 banned it. However, George I tasted and enjoyed it and re-established it as part of Christmas in 1714, despite objections by Quakers. By Victorian times Christmas puddings had evolved into something similar to the ones enjoyed today.

ABOVE: Steamed pudding

STEAMED PUDDING

Preparation time: 40 minutes + overnight standing
Total cooking time: 8 hours
Serves 10–12

4 cups (640 g/1¼ lb) sultanas, currants and raisins
1²/₃ cups (330 g/11 oz) mixed dried fruit, chopped
¼ cup (45 g/1½ oz) mixed peel
½ cup (125 ml/4 fl oz) brown ale
2 tablespoons rum or brandy
⅓ cup (80 ml/2¾ fl oz) orange juice
⅓ cup (80 ml/2¾ fl oz) lemon juice
1 teaspoon finely grated orange rind
1 teaspoon finely grated lemon rind
225 g (7 oz) suet, grated (from your butcher)
1¹/₃ cups (245 g/8 oz) soft brown sugar
3 eggs, lightly beaten
2½ cups (200 g/6½ oz) fresh white breadcrumbs
¾ cup (90 g/3 oz) self-raising flour
1 teaspoon mixed spice
¼ teaspoon grated nutmeg
²/₃ cup (100 g/3½ oz) blanched almonds, roughly chopped

1 Put the sultanas, currants, raisins, mixed dried fruit, mixed peel, brown ale, rum, orange and lemon juices and rinds into a large bowl and stir together. Cover and leave overnight.
2 Add the suet, brown sugar, eggs, breadcrumbs, flour, spices, almonds and a pinch of salt to the bowl and mix well. The mixture should fall from the spoon—if it is too stiff, add a little more ale.
3 Put a 2 litre (64 fl oz) pudding basin on a trivet or upturned saucer in a large saucepan with a lid, and pour in enough water to come halfway up the side of the basin. Remove the basin and put the water on to boil.
4 Brush the basin with melted butter and line the base with baking paper. Fill with the pudding mixture, then cover by placing a sheet of foil on a bench, top with a piece of baking paper the same size and brush the paper with melted butter. Fold a pleat across the centre of the foil and paper. Place the paper and foil, foil-side-up, over the basin and smooth it down the side of the basin. Tie a double length of string around the rim of the basin, then tie another double length of string onto that string to form a handle. Steam the pudding for 8 hours, replenishing with boiling water when necessary. If you want to keep your pudding and reheat it later, then steam it for 6 hours and steam it for 2 hours on the day you want to eat it.

466

SUMMER PUDDING

Preparation time: 30 minutes
 + overnight refrigeration
Total cooking time: 5 minutes
Serves 6

150 g (5 oz) blackcurrants

150 g (5 oz) redcurrants

150 g (5 oz) raspberries

150 g (5 oz) blackberries

200 g (6¹/₂ oz) strawberries, hulled and
 quartered or halved

¹/₂ cup (125 g/4 oz) caster (superfine) sugar,
 or to taste

6–8 slices good-quality sliced white bread,
 crusts removed

1 Put all the berries, except the strawberries, in a large saucepan with ¹/₂ cup (125 ml/4 fl oz) water and heat gently for 5 minutes, or until the berries begin to collapse. Add the strawberries and remove from the heat. Add the sugar, to taste (this will depend on how sweet the fruit is). Allow to cool.
2 Line a 1 litre (32 fl oz) pudding basin or six ²/₃ cup (170 ml/5¹/₂ oz) moulds with the bread. For the large mould, cut a large circle out of one slice for the base and cut the rest of the bread into wide fingers. For the small moulds, use one slice of bread for each, cutting a small circle to fit the base and strips to fit snugly around the sides. Drain a little of the juice off the fruit mixture. Dip one side of each piece of bread in the juice before fitting it, juice-side-down, into the basin, leaving no gaps. Do not squeeze or flatten the bread or it will not absorb the juices.
3 Fill the centre of the basin with the fruit and add a little juice. Any fruit that doesn't fit in can be served with the pudding. Cover the top with the remaining dipped bread, juice-side-up, trimmed to fit. Cover with plastic wrap. Place a small plate which fits inside the dish onto the plastic wrap, then weigh it down with heavy cans or a glass bowl. Place on a baking tray to catch any juices. For the small moulds, cover with plastic and sit a small can, or a similar weight, on top of each. Refrigerate overnight. Turn out the pudding/s and serve with any leftover fruit mixture. This is delicious served with dollops of cream.

MANGO SORBET

Preparation time: 20 minutes + freezing
Total cooking time: 4 minutes
Serve 4–6

1 cup (250 g/8 oz) caster (superfine) sugar

2 tablespoons lemon juice

2 cups (500 ml/16 fl oz) mango purée,
 or 3 medium mangoes, puréed

1 Combine the sugar and 1¹/₄ cups (315 ml/ 10 fl oz) water in a saucepan and stir over low heat to dissolve the sugar. Bring to the boil and boil for 2 minutes without stirring. Set aside to cool to room temperature.
2 Add the lemon juice to the mango purée and slowly pour on the sugar syrup. Mix well. Pour into a shallow metal tray, cover with plastic wrap and freeze for 4–6 hours, or until firm.
3 Break up the mixture with a fork and process in a food processor until soft and smooth (it will be pale). Spoon into an airtight container and freeze for 4–6 hours, or until firm.

ABOVE: Summer pudding

SPOTTED DICK

Preparation time: 15 minutes + standing
Total cooking time: 1 hour 30 minutes
Serves 4

★ ★

SPOTTED DICK
This traditional suet pudding is usually made in the shape of a cylinder. It was also once known as Spotted Dog and Plum Bolster.

1½ cups (185 g/6 oz) plain (all-purpose) flour
1½ teaspoons baking powder
½ cup (125 g/4 oz) sugar
1½ teaspoons ground ginger
2 cups (160 g/5½ oz) fresh
   breadcrumbs
60 g (2 oz) sultanas
110 g (3½ oz) currants
125 g (4 oz) suet, grated
2 teaspoons finely grated lemon rind
2 eggs, lightly beaten
⅔ cup (170 ml/5½ fl oz) milk

BELOW: Spotted dick

1 Sift the flour, baking powder, sugar and ginger into a large bowl. Add the breadcrumbs, sultanas, currants, suet and lemon rind. Mix thoroughly with a wooden spoon.
2 Combine the egg and milk, add to the dry ingredients and mix well. Add a little more milk if necessary, then set aside for 5 minutes.
3 Lay a sheet of baking paper on a work surface and form the mixture into a roll shape about 20 cm (8 inches) long. Roll the pudding in the paper and fold up the ends—do not wrap it too tight as it has to expand as it cooks. Wrap the roll in a tea towel, put it in the top of a bamboo or metal steamer, cover and steam for 1 hour 30 minutes. Do not let the pudding boil dry—replenish with boiling water as the pudding cooks. Unmould the pudding onto a plate and slice. Can be served with custard or cream.

UPSIDE-DOWN BANANA CAKE

Preparation time: 20 minutes
Total cooking time: 45 minutes
Serves 8

★

50 g (1¾ oz) butter, melted
⅓ cup (60 g/2 oz) soft brown sugar
6 ripe large bananas, halved lengthways
125 g (4 oz) butter, softened
1¼ cups (230 g/7½ oz) soft brown
   sugar, extra
2 eggs, lightly beaten
1½ cups (185 g/6 oz) self-raising flour
1 teaspoon baking powder
2 large bananas, extra, mashed

1 Preheat the oven to moderate 180°C (350°/Gas 4). Grease and line a 20 cm (8 inch) square cake tin, pour the melted butter over the base of the tin and sprinkle with the sugar. Arrange the bananas cut-side-down over the brown sugar.
2 Cream the butter and extra brown sugar until light and fluffy. Add the eggs gradually, beating well after each addition.
3 Sift the flour and baking powder into a bowl, then fold into the cake mixture with the mashed banana. Carefully spread into the tin. Bake for 45 minutes, or until a skewer comes out clean when inserted in the centre of the cake. Turn out while still warm.
NOTE: The bananas must be very ripe or they will not be tender and squashy when cooked.

BANANA PUDDING WITH RICH BUTTERSCOTCH SAUCE

Preparation time: 30 minutes
Total cooking time: 1 hour 40 minutes
Serves 6–8

150 g (5 oz) unsalted butter

3/4 cup (140 g/4 1/2 oz) soft brown sugar

1 1/2 cups (185 g/6 oz) self-raising flour

1/2 cup (60 g/2 oz) plain (all-purpose) flour

1/2 teaspoon bicarbonate of soda

1/2 teaspoon ground nutmeg

1 teaspoon vanilla essence

2 eggs, lightly beaten

3/4 cup (185 ml/6 fl oz) buttermilk

2 small ripe bananas, mashed

Rich butterscotch sauce

125 g (4 oz) unsalted butter

2/3 cup (125 g/4 oz) soft brown sugar

1 cup (315 g/10 oz) condensed milk

1 1/3 cups (350 ml/11 fl oz) cream

1 Grease a 2 litre (64 fl oz) pudding basin and line the base with baking paper. Place the empty basin in a saucepan, on a trivet, and pour in enough water to come halfway up the side of the basin. Remove the basin and put the water on to boil. Place a sheet of foil on a work surface and put a sheet of baking paper on top. Grease the paper. Make a large pleat in the centre.
2 Stir the butter and sugar over low heat until dissolved. Remove from the heat. Sift the combined flours, soda and nutmeg into a bowl and make a well. Add the butter mixture, vanilla, egg and buttermilk. Stir with a wooden spoon until smooth. Stir in the banana. Spoon into the basin. Place the foil and paper over the basin, foil-side-up. Cover if your basin has a lid. If not, tie a double piece of string around the rim, knot tightly and, using another double piece of string, tie a handle onto the string. Lower the basin into the boiling water, reduce to a fast simmer, cover the pan and boil for 1 hour 30 minutes, or until a skewer comes out clean. Top up the water if necessary. Leave for 5 minutes then turn out.
3 To make the sauce, combine the ingredients in a pan and stir over low heat until the sugar is dissolved. Bring to the boil, reduce the heat and simmer for 3–5 minutes. Serve hot.

ABOVE: Banana pudding with rich butterscotch sauce

SWEET SAUCES What a marriage

made in heaven... deliciously sweet sauces poured over sponge puddings that soak

up their syrup and soften into irresistible gooeyness.

BUTTERSCOTCH SAUCE

Stir 75 g (2½ oz) butter, 1 cup (185 g/ 6 oz) soft brown sugar and ¾ cup (185 ml/6 fl oz) cream in a small pan over low heat until the butter has melted and the sugar dissolved. Bring to the boil, reduce the heat and simmer for 2 minutes. Makes 1⅔ cups (410 ml/13 fl oz).

CARAMEL BAR SAUCE

Chop four Snickers® bars. Put in a pan with ¼ cup (60 ml/2 fl oz) milk and ¾ cup (185 ml/6 fl oz) cream and stir over low heat until melted. Add 100 g (3½ oz) chopped milk chocolate and stir until melted. Cool to room temperature. Makes 2¼ cups (560 ml/18 fl oz).

DARK CHOCOLATE SAUCE

Put 150 g (5 oz) chopped dark chocolate in a bowl. Bring 300 ml (10 fl oz) cream to the boil in a pan. Stir in 2 tablespoons caster (superfine) sugar, then pour over the chocolate. Leave for 2 minutes, then stir until smooth. Add a spoonful of liqueur. Serve warm. Makes 2 cups (500 ml/16 fl oz).

CHOCOLATE FUDGE SAUCE

Put 1 cup (250 ml/8 fl oz) cream, 30 g (1 oz) butter, 1 tablespoon golden syrup and 200 g (6½ oz) chopped dark chocolate in a pan. Stir over low heat until melted and smooth. Serve hot or warm. Makes 2 cups (500 ml/16 fl oz).

LIQUEUR TOKAY SYRUP

Put 250 g (8 oz) sugar and 250 ml (8 fl oz) water in a medium pan. Slowly bring to the boil, stirring to dissolve the sugar. Add half a vanilla bean and boil, without stirring for 5 minutes. Add 250 ml (8 fl oz) liqueur tokay, liqueur muscat or sauterne and stir. Bring back to the boil and cook for 15 minutes, depending on the thickness desired. Makes 2 cups (500 ml/16 fl oz).

VANILLA HAZELNUT SAUCE

Pour 300 ml (10 fl oz) cream into a small pan. Split 1 vanilla bean and scrape the seeds into the cream. Add the pod and bring to the boil. Remove from the heat, cover and leave for 10 minutes, then strain. Put 200 g (6½ oz) chopped white chocolate in a bowl, reheat the cream and pour over the chocolate. Leave for 2 minutes, then stir until melted. Stir in 30 g (1 oz) chopped roasted hazelnuts. Makes 2 cups (500 ml/16 fl oz).

RICH BRANDY SAUCE

Bring 2 cups (500 ml/16 fl oz) cream to the boil in a heavy-based pan. Whisk 4 egg yolks with ½ cup (125 g/4 oz) caster (superfine) sugar until creamy. Slowly pour the hot cream in, stirring. Return to the pan and stir over low heat for 5–6 minutes, until slightly thickened; do not boil. Stir in 3 tablespoons brandy before serving. Makes 3¼ cups (810 ml/26 fl oz).

CITRUS SYRUP

Cut the rind from an orange, a lemon and a lime. Remove the pith. Cut the rind into fine strips. Put in a pan with the juice from the lime and half the juice from the lemon and orange. Add 125 g (4 oz) sugar and 125 ml (4 fl oz) water. Stir over low heat to dissolve. Add half a vanilla bean. Simmer for 10 minutes; do not stir. Makes 1 cup (250 ml/8 fl oz).

FROM LEFT: Butterscotch; Caramel bar; Dark chocolate; Liqueur Tokay; Chocolate fudge; Vanilla hazelnut; Rich brandy; Citrus syrup

471

TRIFLES and
ZUPPA INGLESE
Trifles were originally
flavoured creams eaten by
the Elizabethans. They
changed gradually: the
cream was thickened,
biscuits and other
ingredients were added
and decorations were
used. In 1755, Hannah
Glasse had a recipe for a
'Grand Trifle', described
as 'fit to go on a King's
table'. It contained
biscuits and ratafias
soaked in alcohol, a layer
of custard, then syllabub
on top. Trifle means 'a
thing of little importance'
and this is where the dish
got its name.
    Zuppa inglese means
'English soup' in Italian,
presumably because the
dish resembles the English
trifle. Originally it was
baked but modern
versions are not cooked.

*OPPOSITE PAGE, FROM
TOP: English trifle; Zuppa
inglese*

ENGLISH TRIFLE

Preparation time: 25 minutes + chilling
Total cooking time: 10 minutes
Serves 6

4 slices Madeira (pound) cake or trifle sponges
1/4 cup (60 ml/2 fl oz) sweet sherry or Madeira
250 g (8 oz) raspberries
4 eggs
2 tablespoons caster (superfine) sugar
2 tablespoons plain (all-purpose) flour
2 cups (500 ml/16 fl oz) milk
1/4 teaspoon vanilla essence
1/2 cup (125 ml/4 fl oz) cream
1/4 cup (25 g/3/4 oz) flaked almonds, to decorate
raspberries, to decorate

1 Put the cake in a decorative bowl and sprinkle with the sherry. Scatter the raspberries over the top and crush them gently into the sponge with the back of a spoon, leaving some of them whole.
2 Mix the eggs, sugar and plain flour together in a bowl. Heat the milk in a pan, pour it over the egg mixture, stir well and pour back into a clean pan. Cook over medium heat until the custard boils and thickens and coats the back of a spoon. Stir in the vanilla, cover the surface with plastic wrap and leave to cool.
3 Pour the cooled custard over the raspberries and leave to set in the fridge, it will firm up but not become solid. Whip the cream and spoon it over the custard. Decorate with almonds and raspberries and refrigerate until needed.

TIPSY TRIFLE

Preparation time: 25 minutes + chilling
Total cooking time: Nil
Serves 6

20 cm (8 inch) sponge cake
1/2 cup (160 g/51/2 oz) apricot jam
1/2 cup (125 ml/4 fl oz) brandy
85 g (3 oz) packet apricot jelly crystals
2 sliced bananas, sprinkled with a little
    lemon juice
2 cups (500 ml/16 fl oz) prepared custard
1 cup (250 ml/8 fl oz) cream, whipped
60 g (2 oz) toasted almonds, chopped
pulp of 2 passionfruit

1 Cut the sponge into small cubes and put in a large serving bowl, or layer the trifle in individual parfait glasses. Combine the jam, brandy and 1/2 cup (60 ml/2 fl oz) water and sprinkle over the sponge.
2 Add the jelly crystals to 2 cups (500 ml/ 16 fl oz) boiling water and stir until dissolved. Pour into a 27 x 18 cm (11 x 7 inch) rectangular tin. Refrigerate until set, then cut into cubes with a rubber spatula.
3 Put the jelly cubes over the sponge and top with the bananas and custard. Decorate with whipped cream, almonds and passionfruit. Refrigerate until required.

ZUPPA INGLESE

Preparation time: 35 minutes + chilling
Total cooking time: 10 minutes
Serves 6

2 cups (500 ml/16 fl oz) milk
1 vanilla bean, split lengthways
4 egg yolks
1/2 cup (125 g/4 oz) caster (superfine) sugar
2 tablespoons plain (all-purpose) flour
300 g (10 oz) Madeira (pound) cake, cut into
    1 cm (1/2 inch) slices
1/3 cup (80 ml/23/4 fl oz) rum
30 g (1 oz) chocolate, grated or shaved
50 g (13/4 oz) flaked almonds, toasted

1 Grease a 1.5 litre (48 fl oz) serving dish with flavourless oil or melted butter. Place the milk and vanilla bean in a pan and slowly heat until bubbles appear around the edge of the pan. Whisk the egg yolks, sugar and flour together in a bowl, until thick and pale.
2 Discard the vanilla bean, whisk the warm milk slowly into the egg mixture and blend well. Return the custard mixture to a clean pan and stir over medium heat until the custard boils and thickens.
3 Line the base of the prepared dish with one-third of the cake slices and brush well with the rum combined with 1 tablespoon of water. Spread one-third of the custard over the cake, top with cake slices and brush with rum mixture. Repeat this process, finishing with a layer of custard. Cover and refrigerate for at least 3 hours. Sprinkle with grated or shaved chocolate and toasted flaked almonds just before serving.

SORBETS, SHERBETS AND SPOOMS

Sorbets are water-based ices which traditionally do not contain dairy products or eggs, although it is now common for beaten egg whites to be added. Sorbets are served as palate cleansers between courses as well as refreshing desserts. Escoffier mentions that sorbets should be eaten when they are almost a drinkable consistency. Sorbets are called 'water ices' in America and *sorbetto* in Italy. They can be churned or still frozen.

Sherbets are water ices which contain some milk or cream. The word is derived from the Arabic word *sharab/sharbah*, which means 'sweetened, cold drink'. In America, sorbets are often called sherbets. Sherbets can be churned or still frozen.

Spooms are sorbets which have an equal volume of Italian meringue mixed into them and are then refrozen without any further mixing or beating. Spooms can be churned or still frozen before having the meringue added.

ABOVE: Lemon lime sorbet

LEMON LIME SORBET

Preparation time: 25 minutes + freezing
Total cooking time: 10 minutes
Serves 4

1 cup (250 g/8 oz) sugar
3/4 cup (185 ml/6 fl oz) lemon juice
3/4 cup (185 ml/6 fl oz) lime juice
2 egg whites, lightly beaten

1 Stir 2 cups (500 ml/16 fl oz) water with the sugar in a pan, over low heat, until the sugar has dissolved. Bring to the boil, reduce the heat to low, simmer for 5 minutes, then cool.
2 Add the lemon and lime juice to the syrup and pour into a metal tray. Cover with a piece of greaseproof paper and freeze for 2 hours. Transfer the icy mixture to a food processor or bowl and process or beat with electric beaters to a slush, then return to the freezer. Repeat the beating and freezing twice more.
3 Transfer to a bowl or food processor. With the electric beaters or processor motor running, add the egg whites and blend. Return to the freezer container, cover with a piece of greaseproof paper and freeze until firm.
4 If you are using an ice cream machine, add the egg white when the sorbet is almost churned and the machine is still running.

PINEAPPLE SORBET

Preparation time: 25 minutes + freezing
Total cooking time: 15 minutes
Serves 4

850 ml (27 fl oz) can unsweetened pineapple juice
1 1/2 cups (375 g/12 fl oz) sugar
3 tablespoons lemon juice, strained
1 egg white, lightly beaten

1 Stir the juice and sugar in a large pan over low heat until the sugar has dissolved. Bring to the boil, reduce the heat and simmer for 5 minutes. Skim off any scum.
2 Stir in the lemon juice and pour into a metal tray. Cover with a sheet of greaseproof and freeze for 2 hours. Transfer the icy mixture to a bowl or food processor and beat with electric beaters, or process, to a slush, then return to the freezer. Repeat the beating and freezing twice more, then process or beat for a final time adding the egg white until it is all incorporated. Beat or process until smooth. Return to the freezer container, cover with a piece of greaseproof paper and freeze until firm.
3 If you are using an ice cream machine, add the egg white when the sorbet is almost churned and the machine is still running.

RASPBERRY MOUSSE

Preparation time: 30 minutes + chilling
Total cooking time: Nil
Serves 4

3 teaspoons gelatine
I cup (250 g/8 oz) low-fat vanilla yoghurt
2 x 200 g (6½ oz) tubs light vanilla frûche or
   fromage frais
4 egg whites
150 g (5 oz) fresh raspberries, mashed, or
   frozen, thawed
fresh raspberries and mint leaves, to serve

1 Put 1 tablespoon hot water in a small heatproof bowl, sprinkle the gelatine over the top and leave to go spongy. Bring a small pan of water to the boil, remove from the heat and place the bowl into the pan. The water should come halfway up the side of the bowl. Stir the gelatine until dissolved. In a large bowl, stir the vanilla yoghurt and frûche together to combine, then add the cooled gelatine and mix well.
2 Using electric beaters, beat the egg whites until stiff peaks form, then fold through the yoghurt mixture until just combined. Transfer half the mixture to a separate bowl and fold the mashed raspberries through.
3 Divide the raspberry mixture among four long glasses, then top with the vanilla mixture. Refrigerate for several hours, or until set. Decorate with fresh raspberries and mint leaves.

CHOCOLATE MOUSSE

Preparation time: 20 minutes + chilling
Total cooking time: Nil
Serves 6

2 tablespoons cocoa
I teaspoon gelatine
300 g (10 oz) silken tofu
I tablespoon brandy
2 egg whites
¼ cup (60 g/2 oz) caster (superfine) sugar

1 Stir the cocoa with ¼ cup (60 ml/2 fl oz) hot water until dissolved. Sprinkle the gelatine in an even layer onto 1 tablespoon water in a small bowl and leave to go spongy. Bring a small pan of water to the boil, remove from the heat and place the bowl into the pan. The water should come halfway up the side of the bowl. Stir the gelatine until dissolved.
2 Drain the tofu and place in a blender. Add the cocoa mixture and brandy and blend until smooth, scraping down the sides. Transfer to a bowl and stir in the gelatine mixture.
3 Whisk the egg whites in a clean dry bowl until soft peaks form. Gradually add the sugar, beating well between each addition, until stiff and glossy peaks form. Fold into the chocolate mixture and spoon into six ½ cup (125 ml/4 fl oz) dishes. Refrigerate for several hours or until set.

ABOVE: Raspberry mousse

475

PARFAITS
These are American style parfaits with layers of ice cream, fruit and sauces made to classic 'soda fountain' formulae. The original French parfait was a type of ice cream made with eggs, sugar and cream.

VANILLA AND CARAMEL PARFAIT

Heat 90 g (3 oz) unsalted butter in a heavy-based pan. Add ¾ cup (140 g/ 4½ oz) soft brown sugar and stir over low heat, without boiling, until the sugar is dissolved. Increase the heat and simmer, without boiling, for 3 minutes, or until golden. Remove from the heat and cool slightly. Stir in ⅔ cup (170 ml/ 5½ fl oz) cream, allow to cool, then whisk until smooth. Layer 500 g (1 lb) vanilla ice cream, halved chocolate-coated malt balls and the caramel sauce into four parfait glasses and top with some more halved malt balls. Serve immediately.
Serves 4.

STRAWBERRY AND RASPBERRY PARFAIT

Stir an 85 g (3 oz) packet strawberry-flavoured jelly crystals in 2 cups boiling water until the crystals have dissolved, then refrigerate until set. Process 125 g (4 oz) chopped strawberries in a food processor for 30 seconds. Layer 500 g (1 lb) vanilla ice cream, the jelly, 125 g

(4 oz) chopped strawberries, 100 g (3½ oz) raspberries and the strawberry purée in six parfait glasses. Serve immediately. Serves 6.

SPICED CHERRY BRANDY PARFAIT

Place 3 tablespoons sugar, 2 tablespoons soft brown sugar, 1 teaspoon mixed spice and 3 tablespoons brandy in a pan with 1 cup of water and stir without boiling until all the sugar has dissolved, then bring to the boil. Add 500 g (1 lb) pitted cherries and reduce the heat, simmer for 10 minutes, remove from the heat and cool. Layer the cherries with 1 litre (32 fl oz) vanilla ice cream in tall glasses and top with some of the cherry syrup. Serve with brandy snaps.
Serves 6.

CHOCOLATE KAHLUA PARFAIT

Combine 125 g (4 oz) chopped chocolate and vanilla cream biscuits with 2 tablespoons Kahlua in a bowl. Set aside for 5 minutes. Layer 500 g (1 lb) chocolate ice cream, the biscuit mixture, 1 cup (250 ml/8 fl oz) cream, whipped, and 60 g (2 oz) choc-chips, alternately, in four parfait glasses. Finish with whipped cream, sprinkle with choc-chips. Serves 4.

CARAMEL NUT PARFAIT

Put 100 g (3½ oz) butter, 2 tablespoons golden syrup, ½ cup (95 g/3 oz) soft brown sugar and 1 cup (250 ml/8 fl oz) cream in a pan and stir over low heat until dissolved. Do not boil. Cool slightly. Layer 1 litre (32 fl oz) of vanilla ice cream and the warm sauce in parfait glasses. Sprinkle with chopped nuts. Serves 4–6.

BANANA SPLIT

Put 200 g (6½ oz) good-quality dark chocolate, ¾ cup (185 ml/6 fl oz) cream and 30 g (1 oz) butter in a pan and stir over low heat until smooth. Cool slightly. Split 4 ripe bananas lengthways, and place one half on each side of a glass dish. Place 3 scoops of ice cream between the bananas and pour the chocolate sauce over the top. Sprinkle chopped nuts over the banana splits. Serves 4.

FROM LEFT: Vanilla and caramel parfait; Strawberry and raspberry parfait; Spiced cherry brandy parfait; Chocolate Kahlua parfait; Caramel nut parfait; Banana split

PAPAYA AND PAWPAW
Papaya and pawpaw, from the same family, are the fruit of a large tropical softwood tree. Their size bears no relation to maturity. Papaya skins range from yellowy-green to pinky-red. The flesh also varies in colour. Some are yellow and some pinky-red or orange. Ripen at room temperature until the skin loses most of its green tinge and the fruit has a pleasant aroma, then store in the refrigerator. Cut in half lengthways and spoon out the seeds. Peel, then slice or chop. Papaya makes good fools and creamy desserts. It does not work well with gelatine as it contains an enzyme, papain, which inhibits setting.

*OPPOSITE PAGE,
CLOCKWISE FROM TOP:
Eastern fruit platter;
Melon medley;
Summer citrus salad*

SUMMER CITRUS SALAD

Preparation time: 15 minutes
Total cooking time: 5 minutes
Serves 4–6

3 ruby grapefruits, peeled and pith removed
3 large oranges, peeled and pith removed
1 tablespoon caster (superfine) sugar
1 cinnamon stick
3 tablespoons whole mint leaves

1 Cut the grapefruit and orange into segments and mix in a bowl.
2 Put the sugar, cinnamon and mint in a small pan with 3 tablespoons water and stir over low heat until the sugar has dissolved. Remove the cinnamon stick and mint leaves and drizzle the syrup over the fruit.

EASTERN FRUIT PLATTER

Preparation time: 15 minutes
Total cooking time: 5 minutes
Serves 4–6

1 stem lemon grass, white part only, chopped
2 cm (³/4 inch) piece ginger, roughly chopped
1 teaspoon soft brown sugar
¹/2 cup (125 ml/4 fl oz) coconut milk
2 mangoes
1 nashi pear, quartered
6 lychees or rambutans, halved and
    stones removed
¹/2 pawpaw, seeded and cut into wedges
¹/2 red papaya, seeded and cut into wedges
2 star fruit, thickly sliced
1 lime, quartered

1 Simmer the lemon grass, ginger, sugar and coconut milk in a small pan over low heat for 5 minutes. Strain and set aside.
2 Cut down both sides of the mangoes close to the stones. Score a crisscross pattern into each half, without cutting through the skin. Fold the outer edges under, pushing the centre up from underneath. Arrange with the rest of the fruit on a platter. Add the lime, for squeezing on the fruit.
3 Serve the coconut dressing on the side as a dipping sauce or drizzle over just before serving.

MELON MEDLEY

Preparation time: 10 minutes + chilling
Total cooking time: Nil
Serves 4

¹/2 rockmelon
¹/2 honeydew melon
¹/4 watermelon
pulp from 2 passionfruit

1 Cut the melons into bite-sized pieces or use a melon baller to cut them into balls. Chill, covered, for 30 minutes. Drizzle with passionfruit.

RED FRUIT SALAD

Preparation time: 10 minutes + soaking
Total cooking time: 5 minutes
Serves 4

250 g (8 oz) strawberries, halved
125 g (4 oz) raspberries
250 g (8 oz) cherries, pitted
1 tablespoon Cointreau
1 tablespoon soft brown sugar

1 Put the fruit in a bowl, drizzle with Cointreau, cover and set aside for 20 minutes.
2 Stir the sugar with 2 tablespoons water in a small pan over gentle heat for 3 minutes, or until dissolved. Cool, pour over the fruit and serve.

STONE FRUITS

Preparation time: 15 minutes
Total cooking time: Nil
Serves 4

4 apricots, halved and thinly sliced
4 peaches, halved and thinly sliced
4 nectarines, halved and thinly sliced
4 plums, halved and thinly sliced
2 tablespoons apricot juice
125 g (4 oz) mascarpone
1 teaspoon soft brown sugar

1 Mix the fruit together and drizzle with apricot juice. Combine the mascarpone and sugar and serve with the fruit salad.

to the boil and then taken off the heat—make sure the base of the bowl is not touching the water. Serve from the bowl or fondue with marshmallows and fresh fruit.

NOTE: Fruits which work well in fondues include strawberries, pear, cherries and bananas.

WHITE CHOCOLATE FONDUE WITH FRUIT

Preparation time: 30 minutes
Total cooking time: 20 minutes
Serves 6–8

1/2 cup (125 ml/4 fl oz) light corn syrup
2/3 cup (170 ml/5 1/2 fl oz) thick (double/heavy) cream
1/4 cup (60 ml/2 fl oz) Cointreau
250 g (8 oz) white chocolate, chopped
marshmallows and chopped fruit, to serve

1 Combine the corn syrup and cream in a small pan or fondue. Bring to the boil, then remove from the heat.
2 Add the Cointreau and white chocolate and stir until melted. Serve with marshmallows and fresh fruit.

GRILLED APPLE STACK

Preparation time: 10 minutes
Total cooking time: 5–10 minutes
Serves 4

3–4 large apples, cores removed
30 g (1 oz) butter
lime marmalade, or any jam
cream, ice cream or custard, to serve

1 Cut the apples into thin slices across the core and place on a lightly greased grill tray. Top each slice with a small piece of butter and 1/2 teaspoon of marmalade.
2 Cook under a hot grill until the butter has melted and the apple is golden brown. Serve 4–5 slices stacked on top of one another with a spoonful of cream, ice cream or custard.
NOTE: It is best to use apples such as Golden Delicious which will not break up too much when cooked.

DARK CHOCOLATE FONDUE WITH FRUIT

Preparation time: 30 minutes
Total cooking time: 20 minutes
Serves 6–8

250 g (8 oz) good-quality dark chocolate, chopped
1/2 cup (125 ml/4 fl oz) thick (double/heavy) cream
marshmallows and chopped fruit, to serve

1 Place the chocolate and cream in a fondue or a heatproof bowl and either heat it gently in the fondue, stirring until it is smooth, or place the bowl over a pan of water which has been brought

ABOVE, FROM TOP:
White chocolate fondue with fruit and dark chocolate fondue with fruit

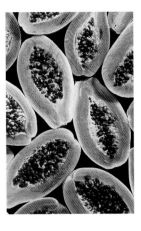

PAPAYA LIME FOOL

Preparation time: 15 minutes + chilling
Total cooking time: Nil
Serves 4

2 red pawpaw or papaya, about 1 kg
1–2 tablespoons lime juice
3 tablespoons vanilla sugar
1¼ cups (315 ml/10 fl oz) cream

1 Peel the pawpaw, remove the seeds and mash the flesh until smooth. Do not do this in a food processor or the fruit will be too runny.
2 Add the lime juice and vanilla sugar, to taste—the amount will vary according to the sweetness of the fruit.
3 Whisk the cream until soft peaks form, then fold through the mashed pawpaw. Spoon into serving glasses and chill until ready to serve.
VARIATION: 500 g (1 lb) stewed rhubarb can be substituted for the pawpaw.

MANGO FOOL

Preparation time: 20 minutes + chilling
Total cooking time: Nil
Serves 6

3 large mangoes
1 cup (250 ml/8 fl oz) custard
1⅔ cups (410 ml/13 fl oz) cream

1 Peel and stone the mangoes and purée the flesh in a food processor. Add the custard and blend to combine.
2 Whip the cream until soft peaks form, then gently fold into the mango mixture until just combined—do not overmix as you want to end up with a decorative marbled effect.
3 Pour the mixture into a serving dish or individual glasses. Gently smooth the top or tops, then refrigerate for at least 1 hour before serving.
NOTE: Fresh fruit can be served with fool.

BELOW: Papaya lime fool

STRAWBERRIES ROMANOFF

Preparation time: 20 minutes + chilling
Total cooking time: Nil
Serves 4

750 g (1 1/2 lb) strawberries, quartered
2 tablespoons Cointreau
1/4 teaspoon finely grated orange rind
1 tablespoon caster (superfine) sugar
1/2 cup (125 ml/4 fl oz) cream
2 tablespoons icing (confectioners') sugar

1 Combine the strawberries, liqueur, rind and the caster sugar in a large bowl, cover and refrigerate for 1 hour. Drain the strawberries, reserving any juices. Purée about one-quarter of the berries with the reserved juices.
2 Divide the remaining berries among four glasses. Beat the cream and icing sugar until soft peaks form, then fold the berry purée through the whipped cream. Spoon the mixture over the top of the strawberries, then cover and refrigerate until required.

COINTREAU GLAZED PEACHES

Preparation time: 10 minutes
Total cooking time: 8 minutes
Serves 6

6 peaches
1–2 tablespoons soft brown sugar
1/3 cup (80 ml/2 3/4 fl oz) Cointreau
250 g (8 oz) mascarpone
ground nutmeg, to dust

1 Line a grill tray with foil and lightly grease the foil. Preheat the grill to medium. Cut the peaches in half, remove the stones and place the peaches, cut-side-up, on the tray.
2 Sprinkle the peaches with the sugar and Cointreau and grill for 5–8 minutes, or until the peaches are soft and a golden glaze has formed on top.
3 Serve immediately with dollops of mascarpone. Dust lightly with ground nutmeg.

PEACH MELBA

Preparation time: 25 minutes
Total cooking time: 10 minutes
Serves 4

300 g (10 oz) fresh raspberries, or frozen, thawed
2 tablespoons icing (confectioners') sugar
1 1/2 cups (375 g/12 oz) sugar
1 vanilla bean, split lengthways
4 firm, ripe peaches
vanilla ice cream, to serve

1 Purée the raspberries and icing sugar together in a food processor. Pass through a strainer and discard the seeds. Stir the sugar, vanilla bean and 2 1/2 cups (600 ml/20 fl oz) water in a pan over low heat until the sugar has completely dissolved.
2 Bring the sugar syrup to the boil and add the peaches, ensuring they are covered with the syrup. Simmer for 5 minutes, or until tender, then remove the peaches with a slotted spoon and carefully remove the skin.
3 Put a scoop of vanilla ice cream on a plate, add a peach, then spoon the purée over the top.

PEARS BELLE HELENE

Preparation time: 15 minutes
Total cooking time: 15 minutes
Serves 6

1 1/2 cups (375 g/12 oz) sugar
2 cinnamon sticks
2 cloves
6 pears, peeled and cored
6 scoops vanilla ice cream
1 cup (250 ml/8 fl oz) dark chocolate sauce (see page 470)

1 Combine the sugar, cinnamon and cloves in a large pan with 3 cups (750 ml/24 fl oz) water, stir over low heat until the sugar dissolves, then bring the syrup to the boil. Add the pears and simmer for 10 minutes, or until tender. Remove the pears with a slotted spoon and leave to cool.
2 Put a scoop of ice cream on each plate and make a hollow in each scoop with the back of a spoon. Stand the pears in the hollow and coat with the chocolate sauce.

PEACH MELBA
Created by Escoffier at the Carlton hotel in 1892, Peach Melba consisted of vanilla ice cream with peaches, set between the wings of a swan carved from ice and covered in spun sugar. In 1900, he came up with an easier version of the pudding, in which raspberry sauce is used rather than the swan. Escoffier served the dish to Dame Nellie Melba and asked if he could name his creation after her.

OPPOSITE PAGE, FROM TOP: Strawberries romanoff and Peach Melba

CREPES SUZETTE

Cook the first side of the crepe until the edges just begin to curl.

Add the crepes to the pan one at a time, folding each finished one into quarters and pushing to one side.

ABOVE: Crepes with sugar, lemon and cream

CREPES WITH SUGAR, LEMON AND CREAM

Preparation time: 10 minutes + standing
Total cooking time: 25 minutes
Makes about 14 crepes

★ ★

1 cup (125 g/4 oz) plain (all-purpose) flour
1 egg
1¼ cups (315 ml/10 fl oz) milk
30 g (1 oz) unsalted butter, melted
sugar, lemon juice and thick (double/heavy)
    cream, to serve

1 Sift the flour and a pinch of salt into a large bowl and make a well in the centre. Gradually whisk in the combined egg and milk until the batter is smooth and free of lumps. Cover and set aside for 30 minutes.
2 Transfer the batter to a jug for easy pouring. Heat a small crepe or non-stick frying pan and brush lightly with melted butter. Pour a little batter into the pan, swirling to thinly cover the base, and pour any excess back into the jug. If the batter is too thick, add 2–3 teaspoons milk. Cook for about 20 seconds, or until the edges just begin to curl, then toss or turn over and lightly brown the other side. Transfer to a plate and cover with a tea towel while cooking the

remaining batter, greasing the pan when necessary. Stack the crepes between greaseproof paper to prevent them sticking together.
3 Sprinkle the crepes with sugar and a little lemon juice and fold into quarters. Put two or three on each plate and top with cream.

CREPES SUZETTE

Preparation time: 10 minutes + standing
Total cooking time: 45 minutes
Serves 4–6

★ ★

Crepes

2 cups (250 g/8 oz) plain (all-purpose) flour
3 eggs, lightly beaten
200 ml (6½ fl oz) milk
50 g (1¾ oz) unsalted butter, melted

125 g (4 oz) unsalted butter
½ cup (125 g/4 oz) caster (superfine) sugar
grated rind of 1 orange
¾ cup (185 ml/6 fl oz) orange juice
3 tablespoons orange liqueur
2 tablespoons brandy
rind of 1 orange, cut into
    thin strips

1 To make the crepes, sift the flour into a large bowl and make a well in the centre. Gradually whisk in the beaten egg, drawing the flour in from the edges. As the mixture becomes thicker, add the milk combined with 1 cup (250 ml/ 8 fl oz) water and whisk until smooth and free of lumps. Pour in the melted butter and stir to combine. Transfer to a jug for easy pouring, cover and set aside for 30 minutes.

2 Heat a 20 cm (8 inch) crepe pan or non-stick frying pan and brush lightly with melted butter. Pour in a little batter, swirling to thinly cover the base, and pour any excess back into the jug. Cook until the edges just begin to curl, then turn and brown the other side. Transfer to a plate and cover with a tea towel while cooking the remaining batter, greasing the pan when necessary. Stack the crepes between greaseproof paper to prevent them sticking together.

3 Put the butter, sugar, orange rind, juice and liqueur in a large frying pan and simmer for 2 minutes. Add the crepes one at a time to the pan, adding each one flat and then folding into quarters and pushing to one side.

4 Pour the brandy over the crepes and with care, ignite the crepes, either with a gas flame or a match. (Keep a lid large enough to cover the pan beside you in case you need to smother the flame.) Serve on warmed plates with the orange rind scattered over the top.

LEMON SYRUP PEARS WITH PANCAKES

Preparation time: 40 minutes + standing
Total cooking time: 1 hour 10 minutes
Serves 6

★★

1 cup (125 g/4 oz) plain (all-purpose) flour
2/3 cup (85 g/3 oz) self-raising flour
2 tablespoons caster (superfine) sugar
3 eggs, lightly beaten
1 1/2 cups (375 ml/12 fl oz) milk
60 g (2 oz) unsalted butter, melted

Lemon syrup pears

5 firm pears such as beurre bosc
1 lemon
3/4 cup (185 g/6 oz) caster (superfine) sugar
2 tablespoons honey
1/2 cup (125 ml/4 fl oz) lemon juice
1 cup (250 g/8 oz) sour cream

1 Sift the flours into a large bowl, add the sugar, make a well and whisk in the combined eggs, milk and butter. Beat until smooth, then set aside for 30 minutes.

2 To make the lemon syrup pears, peel, halve and core the pears, then cut into wedges. Peel the lemon and cut the rind into thin strips. Combine the sugar, honey and 1 1/2 cups (375 ml/12 fl oz) water in a pan, stirring over low heat until the sugar dissolves. Add the lemon juice, bring to the boil, reduce the heat and simmer for 8 minutes. Skim any froth, add the pears and simmer for another 5 minutes, or until just tender. Remove from the heat, stir in the lemon rind and leave to cool slightly.

3 Pour 1/4 cup (60 ml/2 fl oz) pancake batter into a lightly greased 20 cm (8 inch) non-stick frying pan and cook over medium heat for 2 minutes each side. Continue with the rest of the batter, greasing the pan when necessary. Stack between greaseproof paper to prevent them sticking together. Strain 1/2 cup (125 ml/4 fl oz) of the lemon syrup and mix with the sour cream to make a sauce for the pancakes. Strain the pears to serve. Decorate with strips of rind.

IN ADVANCE: Poached pears can be left in the syrup, covered in the fridge for up to two days to allow the flavours to develop. Reheat to serve.

BELOW: Lemon syrup pears with pancakes

LIQUEUR FRUITS

These liqueur-infused fruits are luscious with cream or ice cream, waffles or crepes.

They are also great with brioche or panettone spread with ricotta or mascarpone.

PEARS IN MULLED WINE

Put 2 cups (500 g/1 lb) sugar and 3 cups (750 ml/24 fl oz) red wine in a large pan. Stir over low heat until the sugar has dissolved. Add 1.25 kg (2½ lb) peeled, halved and cored small pears, 1 cinnamon stick, 6 cloves, 6 whole allspice and 2 strips each of orange and lemon rind. Cover with a plate to keep the pears submerged. Bring to the boil (at least 90°C), then reduce the heat and simmer for 10 minutes. Arrange the pears in a heatproof, warm, sterilized 1 litre (32 fl oz) jar. Boil the syrup for 15 minutes, then mix ½ cup (125 ml/ 4 fl oz) syrup with ½ cup (125 ml/ 4 fl oz) brandy and 3 cloves. Pour over the pears to cover, seal and invert for 2 minutes. Store in a cool, dark place for up to a month before using. Refrigerate after opening. Fills a 1 litre (32 fl oz) jar.

DRUNKEN PRUNES

Put 750 g (1½ lb) pitted prunes in a heatproof, warm sterilized 1 litre (32 fl oz) jar. Cut a vanilla bean in half lengthways and add to the jar. Add 2 cups (500 ml/16 fl oz) tawny port to cover the prunes, seal and invert for 2 minutes. Leave for at least 1 month before using. Store for up to 6 months. Refrigerate after opening. Fills a 1 litre (32 fl oz) jar.

CLEMENTINES OR CUMQUATS IN LIQUEUR

Cut a cross in the tops of 500 g (1 lb) cumquats or clementines and pack into heatproof, warm sterilized jars. Place 1 cup (250 g/8 oz) sugar and ¾ cup (185 ml/6 fl oz) water in a saucepan and boil for 1 minute. Stir in ¼ cup (60 ml/2 fl oz) orange liqueur, then pour over the fruit. Screw on the lids loosely—do not tighten. Place layers of cloth on the base of a deep, heavy-based saucepan. Put the jars on top and cover with hot water to reach the shoulders of the jars. Bring the water slowly to simmering point, then reduce the heat and simmer for 20 minutes, or until the fruit starts to look clear. Remove the jars. Immediately tighten the lids fully with a tea towel. Cool, label and date. Store in a cool, dark place for 2 months before using, turning the jars upside-down every 2 weeks.

Will keep for 6 months. Refrigerate after opening. Fills a 750 ml (24 fl oz) jar.

PEACHES IN SPICED SAUTERNES

Cut 4–6 kg (8–12 lb) ripe freestone peaches in half, discard the stones and pack the peaches, with 1 cinnamon stick and 1 star anise into a heatproof, warm sterilized 2 litre (64 fl oz) jar. Place 2 cups (500 g/1 lb) sugar in a large saucepan, add 2 cups (500 ml/16 fl oz) water and stir over low heat until all the sugar has dissolved. Bring to the boil (at least 90°C) and boil for 5 minutes, then pour the hot syrup over the peaches and top with 1 cup (250 ml/4 fl oz) Sauternes. Following the cumquat instructions, simmer in the jar for 10 minutes, or until the peach syrup reaches 90° (check with a thermometer). Keep in a cool, dark place for at least 2 weeks before using. Will keep for

6 months. Refrigerate after opening. Fills a 2 litre (64 fl oz) jar.

CHERRIES IN VANILLA BRANDY

Prick the skins of 750 g (1½ lb) cherries with a fine skewer. Heat 1½ cups (375 g/ 12 oz) sugar with ½ cup (125 ml/4 fl oz) each of brandy and water in a pan, stirring until all the sugar has dissolved. Add the cherries and a vanilla bean and heat until boiling (90°C). Place the cherries and syrup in a heatproof, warm, sterilized jar, seal while hot and invert for 2 minutes. Store in a cool place for 6 weeks, turning every couple of days for the first 2 weeks. Serve the cherries in the liqueur. Refrigerate after opening. Fills a 1 litre (32 fl oz) jar.

FROM LEFT: Pears in mulled wine; Drunken prunes; Clementines in liqueur; Peaches in spiced Sauternes; Cherries in vanilla brandy

487

PUFF PASTRY Made by layering dough

with butter and folding to create hundreds of layers. The butter melts, the dough

produces steam, forcing the layers apart and making the pastry rise to great heights.

For perfect pastry which rises evenly, the edges must be cut cleanly with a sharp knife or cutter, not torn. Egg glazes give a shine but must be applied carefully—any drips down the side may glue the layers together and stop them rising evenly. The pastry should be chilled for at least 30 minutes before baking to relax it.

Always bake puff pastry at a very high temperature—it should rise evenly so, if

your oven has areas of uneven heat, turn the pastry around when it has set. If you have an oven with a bottom element, cook your pastry on the bottom shelf. When puff pastry is cooked, the top and base should be browned, with only a small amount of underbaked dough inside, and the layers should be visible. Puff pastry is not always perfect—it may fall over or not rise to quite the heights

you had imagined—but provided you don't burn it and it is well cooked it will still be delicious.

MAKING PUFF PASTRY
We've given a range of fat quantities—if you've never made puff pastry before, you'll find it easier to use the lower amount. This recipe makes about 500 g (1 lb) pastry. You will need 200–250 g

(6½–8 oz) unsalted butter, 2 cups (250 g/ 8 oz) plain (all-purpose) flour, ½ teaspoon salt and ⅔ cup (170 ml/5½ fl oz) cold water.

1 Melt 30 g (1 oz) butter in a pan. Sift the flour and salt onto a work surface and make a well in the centre. Add the butter and water to the centre and blend with your fingertips, gradually drawing in the flour. You should end up with a crumb mixture—if it seems a little dry, add extra drops of water before bringing it all together to form a dough.

2 Cut the dough with a pastry scraper, using a downward cutting action, then turn the dough and repeat in the opposite direction. The dough should now come together to form a soft ball. Score a cross in the top to prevent shrinkage, wrap and refrigerate for 15–20 minutes.

3 Soften the remaining butter by pounding it between 2 sheets of baking

paper with a rolling pin. Then, still between the sheets of baking paper, roll it into a 10 cm (4 inch) square. The butter must be the same consistency as the dough or they will not roll out the same amount and the layers will not be even. If the butter is too soft, it will squeeze out of the sides. Too hard and it will break through the dough and disturb the layers.

4 Put the pastry on a well floured surface. Roll it out to form a cross, leaving the centre slightly thicker than the arms. Place the butter in the centre of the cross and fold over each of the arms to make a parcel. Turn the dough so that it looks like a book with the hinge side to the left. Tap and roll out the dough to form a 15 x 45 cm (6 x 18 inch) rectangle. Make this as neat as possible, squaring off the corners—otherwise, every time you fold, the edges will become less neat and the layers will not be even.

5 Fold the dough like a letter, the top third down and the bottom third up, to form another square, brushing off any excess flour between the layers. Turn the dough 90° to bring the hinge side to your left and press the seam sides down with the rolling pin to seal them. Re-roll and fold as before to complete two turns and mark the dough by gently pressing into the corner with your fingertip for each turn—this will remind you where you're up to. Wrap the dough and chill again.

6 Re-roll and fold twice more and then chill, and then again to complete 6 turns. If it is a very hot day, you may need to chill between each turn. The pastry should now be an even yellow and is ready to use—if it looks a little streaky, roll and fold once more. Refrigerate until required.

SHORTCRUST TIPS The

secret of good pastry is to work quickly and lightly, with cool ingredients, in a cool

room and, preferably, not on a hot day. A cold marble slab is the ideal work surface.

If you don't have a marble slab, rest a tray of iced water on the work surface for a while before you start. Use *real* unsalted butter for pastry, not margarine or softened butter blends.

Unsweetened pastry works well with sweet fillings, giving a good contrast of flavours. Add two tablespoons of caster (superfine) sugar to the flour for a sweet pastry. Some recipes contain egg yolks to enrich the pastry and give good colour.

SHORTCRUST PASTRY

To make enough to line a 23 cm (9 inch) tin, use 1½ cups (185 g/6 oz) plain (all-purpose) flour, 100 g (3½ oz) chopped chilled unsalted butter, and about 3 tablespoons chilled water.

1 Sift the flour into a large bowl and add the butter. Using just your fingertips, rub the butter into the flour until the mixture resembles fine breadcrumbs.

2 Make a well in the centre, then add 2–4 tablespoons water and mix with a flat-bladed knife. Use a cutting action and turn the bowl with your free hand. The mixture will come together in small beads of dough. To test if you need more water, pinch a little dough between your fingers. If it doesn't hold together, add a little more water. If the pastry is too dry, it will fall apart when you roll it; if too wet it will be sticky and shrink when baked.

3 Gently gather the dough together with your hand and lift out onto a sheet of baking paper or a floured work surface.
4 Press, don't knead, the dough together into a ball. Handle gently, keeping your actions light and to a minimum.
5 Press the dough into a flat disc, wrap and refrigerate for 20 minutes. Roll out between 2 sheets of baking paper or plastic wrap, or on a lightly floured surface. Always roll from the centre outwards, rotating the dough, rather than rolling backwards and forwards.
6 If you used baking paper to roll out the pastry, remove the top sheet, carefully invert the pastry over the tin (make sure you centre the pastry, as it can't be moved once in place), and then peel away the paper. If you rolled out on a lightly floured surface, roll the pastry back over the rolling pin so it is hanging, and ease it into the tin.

7 Once the pastry is in the tin, quickly lift up the sides so they don't break over the edges of the tin, which can be sharp, particularly in metal flan tins. Use a small ball of excess dough to help ease and press the pastry shell into the side of the tin. Allow the excess to hang over the side and, if using a flan tin, roll the rolling pin over the top of the tin, to cut off the excess pastry. If you are using a glass or ceramic pie dish, use a small sharp knife to cut away the excess pastry.
8 However gently you handle dough, it is bound to shrink a little, so let it sit a little above the sides of the tin. If you rolled off the excess pastry with a rolling pin, you may find it has 'bunched' down the sides. Gently press the sides of the pastry with your thumbs to flatten and lift it a little. Refrigerate the pastry in the tin for 15 minutes to relax it and prevent or minimise shrinkage. Preheat the oven.

BLIND BAKING
If pastry is to have a moist filling, it will probably require partial blind baking to prevent the base becoming soggy. If it is not cooked again after filling, it will need to be fully blind baked. This means baking the pastry without the filling, but with some weight to prevent it rising. Line the shell with crumpled greaseproof or baking paper. Pour in some baking beads, dried beans or uncooked rice (these can be used again). Bake the pastry for the given time, then lift out the filled paper. Return the pastry to the oven. When cooked, it should look dry with no greasy patches. Small pastry shells can just be pricked with a fork to prevent them rising or bubbling, but only do this if specified, as the filling may run through.

Cool pastry completely before filling. Cooked filling should also be cooled before adding, to prevent soggy pastry.

491

JALOUSIE

Preparation time: 40 minutes
Total cooking time: 45 minutes
Serves 4–6

30 g (1 oz) unsalted butter

¼ cup (45 g/1½ oz) soft brown sugar

500 g (1 lb) apples, peeled, cored and cubed

1 teaspoon grated lemon rind

1 tablespoon lemon juice

¼ teaspoon nutmeg

¼ teaspoon cinnamon

30 g (1 oz) sultanas

375 g (12 oz) puff pastry

1 egg, lightly beaten, to glaze

1 Preheat the oven to hot 220°C (425°F/Gas 7). Lightly grease a baking tray and line with baking paper. Melt the butter and sugar in a frying pan. Add the apple, lemon rind and lemon juice. Cook over medium heat for 10 minutes, stirring occasionally, until the apples are cooked and the mixture is thick and syrupy. Stir in the nutmeg, cinnamon and sultanas. Cool completely.

2 Cut the block of puff pastry in half. On a lightly floured surface roll out one half of the pastry to a 24 x 18 cm (10 x 7 inch) rectangle. Spread the fruit mixture onto the pastry, leaving a 2.5 cm (1 inch) border. Brush the edges lightly with the beaten egg.

3 Roll the second half of the pastry on a lightly floured surface to a 25 x 18 cm (10 x 7 inch) rectangle. Using a sharp knife, cut slashes in the pastry across its width, leaving a 2 cm (¾ inch) border around the edge. The slashes should open slightly and look like a venetian blind (*jalousie* in French). Place over the fruit and press the edges together. Trim away any extra pastry. Knock up the puff pastry (brush the sides upwards) with a knife to ensure rising during cooking. Glaze the top with egg. Bake for 25–30 minutes, or until puffed and golden.

PUFF PASTRY

Commercially made puff pastry can be bought in different forms. Blocks of puff pastry are available frozen or fresh and sheets are available frozen flat or as a roll, sometimes fresh. You do not need to roll out sheets of puff but they benefit from having their edges trimmed. Commercial puff pastries use vegetable or canola (rapeseed) oil or butter as their fat. If you are using a pastry with vegetable fat as its base, you can add a buttery flavour by brushing the pastry with melted butter and chilling it before glazing.

RIGHT: Jalousie

MILLE FEUILLE

Preparation time: 30 minutes
Total cooking time: I hour 30 minutes
Serves 6–8

600 g (1¼ lb) puff pastry or 3 sheets
   ready-rolled
2½ cups (600 ml/20 fl oz) thick (double/heavy)
   cream
500 g (1 lb) small strawberries, halved
70 g (2¼ oz) blueberries, optional

I Preheat the oven to hot 220°C (425°F/Gas 7).
Line a baking tray with baking paper. If using a
block of puff pastry, cut the pastry into three and
roll out to 25 cm (10 inch) squares. Place one
sheet of puff pastry on the tray, prick all over
and top with another piece of baking paper and
another baking tray and bake for 15 minutes.
Turn the trays over and bake on the other side
for 10–15 minutes, or until golden brown. Allow
to cool and repeat with the remaining pastry.
2 Trim the edges of each pastry sheet and cut
each one in half. Pour the cream into a large
bowl and whisk to firm peaks. Place two of the
pastry pieces on a serving dish and spoon some
of the cream on top. Carefully arrange some of
the strawberries and blueberries over the cream,
pressing them well down. Top each one with
another pastry sheet and repeat with the berries.
Top with a final layer of pastry and dust with
icing (confectioners') sugar.

APPLE GALETTES

Preparation time: 45 minutes + chilling
Total cooking time: 30 minutes
Serves 8

2 cups (250 g/8 oz) plain (all-purpose) flour
250 g (8 oz) unsalted butter, chopped
8 apples
¾ cup (185 g/6 oz) caster (superfine) sugar
125 g (4 oz) unsalted butter, chopped

I Place the flour and butter in a bowl and cut
the butter into the flour with two knives until it
resembles large crumbs. Gradually add about
½ cup (125 ml/4 fl oz) chilled water, stirring
with a knife and pressing together, until a rough
dough forms. Turn onto a lightly floured board
and roll into a rectangle. The dough will be
crumbly and hard to manage at this point. Fold
the pastry into thirds; turn it so the hinge is on
your left and roll into a large rectangle. Always
turn the pastry the same way so the hinge is on
the left. Refrigerate in plastic wrap for 30 minutes.
2 Complete two more turns and folds before
refrigerating the pastry for another 30 minutes.
Repeat the process so that you have completed
6 folds and turns. Wrap the pastry in plastic wrap
and refrigerate before use. The pastry can be
stored in the refrigerator for 2 days or in the
freezer for up to 3 months.
3 Preheat the oven to moderately hot 190°C
(375°F/Gas 5). Roll the pastry out on a lightly
floured surface until 3 mm (⅛ inch) thick. Cut
into eight 10 cm (4 inch) rounds. Peel and core
the apples and slice thinly. Arrange the apples in
a spiral on the pastry. Sprinkle well with sugar
and dot with unsalted butter. Bake on greased
baking trays for 20–30 minutes, until the pastry is
crisp and golden. Serve warm.

ABOVE: Apple galettes

4–5 tablespoons iced water

2 tablespoons marmalade

I egg, lightly beaten

I tablespoon sugar

I Lightly grease a 23 cm (9 inch) pie plate. Peel, core and cut the apples into wedges. Place in a saucepan with the sugar, lemon rind, cloves and 2 tablespoons water. Cover and cook over low heat for 8 minutes, or until the apples are just tender, shaking the pan occasionally. Drain and cool completely.

2 Sift the flours into a bowl and rub in the butter, using your fingertips, until the mixture resembles fine breadcrumbs. Stir in the sugar, then make a well in the centre. Add almost all the water and mix with a flat-bladed knife, using a cutting action, until the mixture comes together in beads. Add more water if the dough is too dry. Gather together and lift out onto a lightly floured surface. Press into a ball and divide into two, making one half a little bigger. Cover with plastic wrap and refrigerate for 20 minutes.

3 Preheat the oven to moderately hot 200°C (400°F/Gas 6). Roll out the larger piece of pastry between two sheets of baking paper to line the base and side of the pie plate. Line the pie plate with the pastry. Use a small sharp knife to trim away any excess pastry. Brush the marmalade over the base and spoon the apple into the shell. Roll out the other pastry between the baking paper until large enough to cover the pie. Brush water around the rim, then place the top on. Trim off any excess pastry, pinch the edges and cut a round hole or a couple of steam slits in the top.

4 Re-roll the pastry scraps and cut into leaves for decoration. Lightly brush the top with egg, then sprinkle with sugar. Bake for 20 minutes, then reduce the oven temperature to moderate 180°C (350°F/Gas 4) and bake for another 15–20 minutes, or until golden.

APPLE PIE

Preparation time: 45 minutes
  + 20 minutes refrigeration
Total cooking time: 50 minutes
Serves 6

★ ★

Filling

6 large Granny Smith apples

2 tablespoons caster (superfine) sugar

I teaspoon finely grated lemon rind

pinch of ground cloves

2 cups (250 g/8 oz) plain (all-purpose) flour

¼ cup (30 g/1 oz) self-raising flour

150 g (5 oz) unsalted butter, chilled, cubed

2 tablespoons caster (superfine) sugar

ABOVE: Apple pie

LEMON MERINGUE PIE

Preparation time: I hour
  + 15 minutes refrigeration
Total cooking time: 45 minutes
Serves 6

★ ★

1½ cups (185 g/6 oz) plain (all-purpose) flour

125 g (4 oz) unsalted butter, chilled, cubed

2 tablespoons icing (confectioners') sugar

2–3 tablespoons iced water

Lemon filling

¹/4 cup (30 g/1 oz) cornflour (cornstarch)

¹/4 cup (30 g/1 oz) plain (all-purpose) flour

1 cup (250 g/8 oz) caster (superfine) sugar

³/4 cup (185 ml/6 fl oz) lemon juice

3 teaspoons grated lemon rind

40 g (1¹/4 oz) unsalted butter

6 egg yolks

Meringue topping

6 egg whites

1¹/2 cups (375 g/12 oz) caster (superfine) sugar

¹/2 teaspoon cornflour (cornstarch)

1 Lightly grease a deep 23 cm (9 inch) pie plate. Sift the flour into a bowl and rub in the butter, using your fingertips, until the mixture resembles fine breadcrumbs. Stir in the icing sugar, then make a well in the centre. Add 2 tablespoons water and mix with a flat-bladed knife, using a cutting action, until the mixture comes together in beads. Add the remaining water if the dough is too dry.

2 Gather the dough together and roll between two sheets of baking paper until large enough to line the base and side of the pie plate. Line the plate with the pastry. Trim off any excess pastry. Fork the edge and refrigerate for 15 minutes.

3 Preheat the oven to moderate 180°C (350°F/Gas 4). Line the pastry shell with crumpled baking paper and pour in some baking beads or uncooked rice. Bake for 10–15 minutes, then remove the paper and beads. Return the pastry to the oven for 10 minutes, or until cooked through. Cool completely. Increase the oven temperature to hot 220°C (425°F/Gas 7).

4 For the lemon filling, put the flours and sugar in a saucepan. Whisk in the lemon juice, rind and 1¹/2 cups (375 ml/12 fl oz) water. Whisk continually over medium heat until the mixture boils and thickens, then reduce the heat and cook for 1 minute. Remove from the heat, then whisk in the butter, then egg yolks, one at a time. Cover the surface with plastic wrap and cool. Spread the filling into the pastry shell.

5 For the meringue topping, put the egg whites and sugar in a clean, dry bowl. Beat with electric beaters on high for 10 minutes, or until the sugar is almost completely dissolved and the meringue is thick and glossy. Beat in the cornflour. Spread the meringue over the top, making peaks by drawing the meringue up with a knife, piling it high towards the centre. Bake for 5–10 minutes, or until lightly browned. Cool before serving.

SOFT MERINGUES
A soft meringue is a mixture of stiffly beaten egg white and sugar, usually in a proportion of 1 egg white to 60 g (2 oz) sugar. The sugar is gradually added to the beaten egg white until the sugar is dissolved and the mixture is smooth and glossy. Soft meringues are used as swirled topping on various sweet pies such as lemon meringue pie and fruit pies. The meringue is piled high onto the pie filling, then lightly browned in the oven. The pie should be eaten soon after browning as the meringue topping will start to 'weep' and lose volume if it stands too long.

LEFT: Lemon meringue pie

CUSTARD TARTS

Preparation time: 30 minutes
 + 20 minutes refrigeration
Total cooking time: 45 minutes
Makes 12

2 cups (250 g/8 oz) plain (all-purpose) flour
1/3 cup (60 g/2 oz) rice flour
1/4 cup (30 g/1 oz) icing (confectioners') sugar
120 g (4 oz) unsalted butter, chilled, cubed
1 egg yolk
3 tablespoons iced water
1 egg white, lightly beaten

Custard filling

3 eggs
1 1/2 cups (375 ml/12 fl oz) milk
1/4 cup (60 g/2 oz) caster (superfine) sugar
1 teaspoon vanilla essence
1/2 teaspoon ground nutmeg

1 Sift the flours and icing sugar into a large bowl and rub in the butter, using your fingertips, until the mixture resembles fine breadcrumbs. Make a well and add the egg yolk and almost all the water. Mix with a flat-bladed knife, using a cutting action, until the mixture comes together in small beads, adding more water if the dough is too dry. Gather together and roll out between two sheets of baking paper. Divide the dough into 12 equal portions and roll each portion out to fit the base and side of a 10 cm (4 inch) loose-based fluted tart tin. Line the tins with the pastry and roll the rolling pin over the tins to cut off any excess pastry. Refrigerate for 20 minutes.
2 Preheat the oven to moderate 180°C (350°F/Gas 4). Line each pastry-lined tin with crumpled baking paper. Fill with baking beads or uncooked rice. Place the tins on two large baking trays and bake for 10 minutes. Remove the baking paper and beads and return the trays to the oven. Bake for 10 minutes, or until the pastry is lightly golden. Cool. Brush the base and side of each pastry case with beaten egg white. Reduce the oven temperature to slow 150°C (300°F/Gas 2).
3 For the filling, whisk the eggs and milk in a bowl to combine. Add the sugar gradually, whisking to dissolve completely. Stir in the vanilla essence. Strain into a jug, then pour into the cooled pastry cases. Sprinkle with nutmeg and bake for 25 minutes, or until the filling is just set. Serve at room temperature.

APPLE TARTE TATIN

Preparation time: 30 minutes
 + 30 minutes refrigeration
Total cooking time: 50 minutes
Serves 6

1 2/3 cups (210 g/7 oz) plain (all-purpose) flour
125 g (4 oz) unsalted butter, chilled, cubed
2 tablespoons caster (superfine) sugar
1 egg, lightly beaten
2 drops vanilla essence
8 medium Granny Smith apples
1/2 cup (125 g/4 oz) sugar
40 g (1 1/4 oz) unsalted butter, chopped, extra

1 Sift the flour into a bowl and rub in the butter, using your fingertips, until the mixture resembles fine breadcrumbs. Stir in the caster sugar, then make a well in the centre. Add the egg and vanilla essence and mix with a flat-bladed knife, using a cutting action, until the mixture comes together in beads. Gather the dough together, then turn out onto a lightly floured surface and shape into a disc. Wrap in plastic wrap and refrigerate for at least 30 minutes, to firm.
2 Peel and core the apples and cut each into eight slices. Place the sugar and 1 tablespoon water in a heavy-based 25 cm (10 inch) frying pan that has a metal or removable handle, so that it can safely be placed in the oven. Stir over low heat for 1 minute, or until the sugar has dissolved. Increase the heat to medium and cook for 4–5 minutes, or until the caramel turns golden. Add the extra butter and stir to incorporate. Remove from the heat.
3 Place the apple slices in neat circles to cover the base of the frying pan. Return the pan to low heat and cook for 10–12 minutes, until the apples are tender and caramelized. Remove the pan from the heat and leave to cool for 10 minutes.
4 Preheat the oven to hot 220°C (425°F/Gas 7). Roll the pastry out on a lightly floured surface to a circle 1 cm (1/2 inch) larger than the frying pan. Place the pastry over the apples to cover them completely, tucking it down firmly at the edges. Bake for 30–35 minutes, or until the pastry is cooked. Leave for 15 minutes before turning out onto a plate. Serve warm or cold with cream or ice cream.
NOTE: Special high-sided tatin tins are available for making this dessert. Look for them at speciality kitchenware shops.

TARTE TATIN
This is traditionally an upside-down apple, or sometimes pear, tart. The fruit is cooked in an ovenproof dish or tin and the rolled pastry cooked on top in the oven. The pie is then inverted to show off the caramelized, juicy cooked fruit. The name commemorates the Tatin sisters who lived in the Loire Valley in the early twentieth century and made their living selling it. The French call it *tarte des demoiselles Tatin* or 'the tart of two unmarried women named Tatin'.

OPPOSITE PAGE, FROM TOP: Custard tarts; Apple tarte tatin

PUMPKIN PIE

Preparation time: 20 minutes
 + 20 minutes refrigeration
Total cooking time: 1 hour 10 minutes
Serves 8

Filling

500 g (1 lb) pumpkin
2 eggs, lightly beaten
3/4 cup (140 g/4 1/2 oz) soft brown sugar
1/3 cup (80 ml/2 3/4 fl oz) cream
1 tablespoon sweet sherry
1 teaspoon ground cinnamon
1/2 teaspoon ground nutmeg
1/2 teaspoon ground ginger

Pastry

1 1/4 cups (155 g/5 oz) plain (all-purpose) flour
100 g (3 1/2 oz) unsalted butter, cubed
2 teaspoons caster (superfine) sugar
1/3 cup (80 ml/2 3/4 fl oz) iced water
1 egg yolk, lightly beaten, to glaze
1 tablespoon milk, to glaze

1 Lightly grease a 23 cm (9 inch) round pie plate. Chop the pumpkin for the filling into small chunks and steam or boil for 10 minutes, or until the pumpkin is just tender. Drain the pumpkin thoroughly, then mash and set aside to cool.

2 For the pastry, sift the flour into a large bowl and rub in the butter, using your fingertips, until the mixture resembles fine breadcrumbs. Stir in the caster sugar. Make a well in the centre, add almost all the water and mix with a flat-bladed knife, using a cutting action, until the mixture comes together in beads, adding the remaining water if the dough is too dry.

3 Gather the dough together and roll out between two sheets of baking paper until large enough to cover the base and side of the pie plate. Line the dish with pastry, trim away excess pastry and crimp the edges. Roll out the pastry trimmings to 2 mm (1/8 inch) thick. Using a sharp knife, cut out leaf shapes of different sizes and score vein markings onto the leaves. Refrigerate the pastry-lined dish and the leaf shapes for about 20 minutes.

4 Preheat the oven to moderate 180°C (350°F/ Gas 4). Cut baking paper to cover the pastry-lined dish. Spread baking beads or uncooked rice over the paper. Bake for 10 minutes, then remove the paper and beads. Return the pastry to the oven for 10 minutes, or until lightly golden. Meanwhile, place the leaves on a baking tray lined with baking paper, brush with the combined egg yolk and milk and bake for 10–15 minutes, or until lightly golden. Set aside to cool.

5 For the filling, whisk the eggs and brown sugar in a large bowl. Add the cooled mashed pumpkin, cream, sherry, cinnamon, nutmeg and ginger to the bowl and stir to combine thoroughly. Pour the filling into the pastry shell, smooth the surface with the back of a spoon, then bake for 40 minutes, or until set. If the pastry edges begin to brown too much during cooking, cover the edges with foil. Allow the pie to cool to room temperature and then decorate the top with the leaves. Pumpkin pie can be served with ice cream or whipped cream.

BELOW: Pumpkin pie

FREE-FORM BLUEBERRY PIE

Preparation time: 20 minutes
+ 10 minutes refrigeration
Total cooking time: 35 minutes
Serves 4

1 1/2 cups (185 g/6 oz) plain (all-purpose) flour

1/2 cup (60 g/2 oz) icing (confectioners') sugar,
   plus extra, to dust

125 g (4 oz) unsalted butter, chilled and
   cut into cubes

1/4 cup (60 ml/2 fl oz) lemon juice

500 g (1 lb) blueberries

1/4 cup (30 g/1 oz) icing (confectioners') sugar

1 teaspoon finely grated lemon rind

1/2 teaspoon ground cinnamon

1 egg white, lightly beaten

1 Preheat the oven to moderate 180°C (350°F/ Gas 4). Sift the flour and icing sugar into a bowl and rub in the butter, using your fingertips, until the mixture resembles fine breadcrumbs. Make a well in the centre and add almost all the juice. Mix together with a flat-bladed knife, using a cutting action, until the mixture comes together in beads, adding the remaining juice if necessary.
2 Gently gather the dough together and lift onto a sheet of baking paper. Roll out to a circle about 30 cm (12 inches) in diameter. Cover with plastic wrap and refrigerate for 10 minutes.
3 Place the blueberries in a bowl and sprinkle them with icing sugar, rind and cinnamon.
4 Place the pastry (still on baking paper) on a baking tray. Brush the centre of the pastry lightly with egg white. Pile the blueberry mixture onto the pastry in a 20 cm (8 inch) diameter circle, then fold the edges of the pastry over the filling, leaving the centre uncovered. Bake for 30–35 minutes. Dust with icing sugar before serving. Cut into wedges and serve warm with whipped cream or ice cream.

BLUEBERRIES
These are native to North America but are now grown all over the world. However, America, where blueberry is called huckleberry, is still the major producer. They are available in the warmer months. The small purplish-blue berry is grown on an evergreen shrub related to heather. Purchase firm, dry and unblemished blueberries with their natural whitish 'bloom' still evident. Store them unwashed and in their container. They can be refrigerated for up to two days and can be used for pies, tarts and muffins, as well as for jam and in berry fruit salads.

ABOVE: Free-form blueberry pie

499

DEEP DISH APPLE PIE

Preparation time: I hour
  + 40 minutes refrigeration
Total cooking time: I hour
Serves 8

★★

2 cups (250 g/8 oz) plain (all-purpose) flour
1/4 cup (30 g/1 oz) self-raising flour
150 g (5 oz) unsalted butter, chilled, cubed
2 tablespoons caster (superfine) sugar
4–5 tablespoons iced water
I egg, extra, lightly beaten, to glaze

Filling

8 large Granny Smith apples
2 thick strips lemon rind
6 whole cloves
I cinnamon stick
1/2 cup (125 g/4 oz) sugar

BELOW: Deep dish apple pie

1 Lightly grease a deep 20 cm (8 inch) diameter springform tin. Line the base with baking paper and grease the paper, then dust lightly with flour and shake off the excess.
2 Sift the flours into a bowl and rub in the butter with your fingertips until the mixture resembles fine breadcrumbs. Mix in the sugar, then make a well in the centre. Add almost all the water and mix with a flat-bladed knife, using a cutting action, until the mixture comes together in beads. Add more water if necessary. Gather together on a floured surface. Wrap in plastic wrap and refrigerate for 20 minutes.
3 Roll two thirds of the pastry between two sheets of baking paper until large enough to cover the base and side of the tin. Line the tin with the pastry. Roll out the remaining pastry between the baking paper sheets to fit the top of the tin. Refrigerate the pastry for 20 minutes.
4 Peel and core the apples and cut each apple into 12 wedges. Combine with the lemon rind, cloves, cinnamon, sugar and 2 cups (500 ml/16 fl oz) water in a large saucepan. Cover and simmer for 10 minutes, or until tender. Drain well and set aside until cold. Discard the rind, cloves and cinnamon.
5 Preheat the oven to moderate 180°C (350°F/Gas 4). Spoon the apple into the pastry shell. Cover with the pastry top. Brush the pastry edges with beaten egg and trim with a sharp knife, crimping the edges to seal. Prick the top with a fork and brush with beaten egg. Bake for 50 minutes, or until the pastry is cooked. Leave in the tin for 10 minutes before removing.

LINZERTORTE

Preparation time: 30 minutes
  + 40 minutes refrigeration
Total cooking time: 30 minutes
Makes I

★★

2/3 cup (100 g/3 1/2 oz) blanched almonds
1 1/2 cups (185 g/6 oz) plain (all-purpose) flour
1/2 teaspoon ground cinnamon
90 g (3 oz) unsalted butter, chilled, cubed
1/4 cup (60 g/2 oz) caster (superfine) sugar
I egg yolk
2–3 tablespoons lemon juice or water
I cup (315 g/10 oz) raspberry jam
I egg yolk, extra
1/4 cup (80 g/2 3/4 oz) apricot jam

LINZERTORTE
This beautiful tart originally came from Linz in Austria but is now well known all over the world. Mrs Beeton's famous *Book of Household Management* mentions the tart as far back as 1906. The pastry is rich and contains ground almonds and spices. The base is traditionally spread with jam, always raspberry, and the top is decoratively latticed with pastry and glazed with egg yolk to give it a rich dark crust.

1 Grind the almonds in a food processor until they are the consistency of a medium coarse meal. Place the flour and cinnamon in a bowl and rub in the butter with your fingertips until the mixture resembles fine breadcrumbs. Stir in the caster sugar and almonds.

2 Make a well in the centre and add the egg yolk and lemon juice. Mix with a flat-bladed knife, using a cutting action until the mixture comes together in beads. Turn onto a lightly floured surface and knead briefly until smooth. Wrap in plastic wrap and refrigerate for at least 20 minutes to firm.

3 Roll two thirds of the pastry out between two sheets of baking paper into a circle to fit a 20 cm (8 inch) round, loose-based, fluted tart tin. Press into the tin and trim away any excess pastry. Spread the raspberry jam over the base.

4 Roll out the remaining pastry, including any scraps, to a thickness of 3 mm (⅛ inch). Cut it into 2 cm (¾ inch) strips with a fluted cutter.

Lay half the strips on a sheet of baking paper, leaving a 1 cm (½ inch) gap between each strip. Interweave the remaining strips to form a lattice pattern. Place on top of the tart and trim the edges with a sharp knife. Cover with plastic wrap and refrigerate for 20 minutes.

5 Preheat the oven to moderate 180°C (350°F/ Gas 4). Place a baking tray in the oven to heat. Combine the extra egg yolk with 1 teaspoon water and brush over the tart. Place the tin on the heated tray and bake for 25–30 minutes, or until the pastry is golden brown.

6 Meanwhile, heat the apricot jam with 1 tablespoon of water, then strain the jam and brush over the tart while hot. Leave to cool in the tin, then remove and cut into wedges.

NOTE: Fluted cutters or special lattice cutters are available from speciality kitchenware stores. If you cannot obtain these, simply cut straight lines instead.

ABOVE: Linzertorte

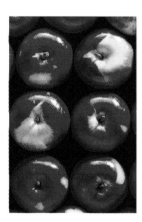

*OPPOSITE PAGE, FROM
TOP: Tart au citron;
Apple tart*

TART AU CITRON

Preparation time: 1 hour + chilling
Total cooking time: 1 hour 40 minutes
Serves 6–8

Pastry

1 cup (125 g/4 oz) plain (all-purpose) flour
75 g (2½ oz) unsalted butter, softened
1 egg yolk
2 tablespoons icing (confectioners') sugar, sifted

3 eggs
2 egg yolks
¾ cup (185 g/6 oz) caster (superfine) sugar
½ cup (125 ml/4 fl oz) cream
¾ cup (185 ml/6 fl oz) lemon juice
1½ tablespoons finely grated lemon rind
2 small lemons
⅔ cup (160 g/5½ oz) sugar

1 To make the pastry, sift the flour and a pinch
of salt into a large bowl. Make a well and add
the butter, egg yolk and icing sugar. Work
together the butter, yolk and sugar with your
fingertips, then slowly incorporate the flour. Bring
together into a ball—you may need to add a few
drops of cold water. Flatten the ball slightly, cover
with plastic wrap and refrigerate for 20 minutes.
2 Preheat the oven to moderately hot 200°C
(400°F/Gas 6). Lightly grease a shallow loose-
bottomed flan tin, about 2 cm (¾ inch) deep and
21 cm (8½ inches) across the base.
3 Roll out the pastry between two sheets of
baking paper until it is 3 mm (⅛ inch) thick, to
fit the base and side of the tin. Trim the edge.
Chill for 10 minutes. Line the pastry with
crumpled baking paper, fill with baking beads or
rice and bake for 10 minutes, or until cooked.
Remove the paper and beads and bake for
another 6–8 minutes, or until the pastry looks dry
all over. Cool the pastry and reduce the oven
temperature to slow 150°C (300°F/Gas 2).
4 Whisk the eggs, yolks and sugar together, add
the cream and juice and mix well. Strain into a
jug and then add the rind. Place the flan tin on a
baking sheet on the middle shelf of the oven and
carefully pour in the filling right up to the top.
Bake for 40 minutes or until it is just set—it
should wobble in the middle when the tin is
firmly tapped. Cool the tart before removing
from its tin.
5 Wash and scrub the lemons well. Slice very
thinly (about 2 mm/⅛ inch thick). Combine the

sugar and 200 ml (6½ fl oz) water in a small
frying pan and stir over low heat until the sugar
has dissolved. Add the lemon slices and simmer
over low heat for 40 minutes, or until the peel is
very tender and the pith looks transparent. Lift
out of the syrup and drain on baking paper. If
serving the tart immediately, cover the surface
with the lemon slices. If not, keep the slices
covered and decorate the tart when ready to
serve. Serve warm or chilled, with a little cream.

APPLE TART

Preparation time: 30 minutes + chilling
Total cooking time: 1 hour 15 minutes
Serves 6–8

Pastry

1½ cups (185 g/6 oz) plain (all-purpose) flour
100 g (3½ oz) chilled unsalted butter, chopped
2–3 tablespoons chilled water

2 cooking apples
3 tablespoons sugar
1 egg
⅓ cup (80 ml/2¾ fl oz) cream
1 tablespoon Calvados or Kirsch

1 Sift the flour into a bowl, then, using just your
fingertips, rub the butter into the flour until the
mixture resembles breadcrumbs. Make a well in
the centre and add almost all the water. Using a
knife, mix to a dough, adding more water if
necessary. Gather together and turn out onto a
sheet of baking paper. Press together gently until
smooth, wrap and chill for 15 minutes. Roll out
to fit a 23 cm (9 inch) loose-bottomed, fluted
flan tin. Line the tin with the pastry, trimming
any excess. Chill for 20 minutes. Preheat the
oven to moderately hot 190°C (375°F/Gas 5).
2 Line the pastry with a sheet of crumpled
baking paper and fill with baking beads or rice.
Bake for 10 minutes, remove the paper and
beads and bake for 15 minutes, until cooked on
the base and golden around the edge; cool.
3 Peel, core and thinly slice the apples. Arrange
in the pastry shell with the slices overlapping,
sprinkle with 2 tablespoons sugar and bake for
15 minutes. Meanwhile, whisk together the egg,
remaining sugar and the cream. Stir in the
liqueur, then pour carefully over the apples. Bake
for 35 minutes, or until the cream mixture has
set and is puffed and golden (it will sink down as
it cools). Serve hot or at room temperature.

FRUIT SAUCES Fresh fruits, herbs

and spices can be used to make sublime sauces that transform a bowl of ice cream

or simple dessert into something quite out of the ordinary.

RHUBARB SAUCE

Chop 350 g (11 oz) rhubarb and place in a pan with ½ cup (95 g/3 oz) soft brown sugar, 1 cup (250 ml/8 fl oz) water and ¼ teaspoon ground mixed spice. Slowly bring to the boil, stirring to dissolve the sugar. Simmer for 10 minutes, stirring often. Push through a sieve and serve hot or cold. Makes 1½ cups (375 ml/12 fl oz).

LEMON GRASS, LIME AND CORIANDER SYRUP

Finely grate 250 g (8 oz) palm sugar and place in a small pan with 1 cup (250 ml/ 8 fl oz) water. Stir over low heat until the sugar has dissolved. Add 2 thinly sliced stems lemon grass (white part only), 1 teaspoon lightly crushed coriander seeds, 1 teaspoon lime rind and 2 teaspoons lime juice. Bring to the boil

and simmer for 15–20 minutes, or until syrupy. Strain, if you like, and serve with tropical fruits, ice cream or pancakes. Makes 1 cup (250 ml/8 fl oz).

MANGO COULIS

Chop 2 small mangoes. Blend in a food processor with 3 tablespoons orange juice and 2 teaspoons Cointreau (optional), until smooth. Makes 1⅓ cups (350 ml/11 fl oz).

PASSIONFRUIT COULIS

Put ½ cup (125 ml/4 fl oz) fresh passionfruit pulp (canned is not suitable for this recipe), ½ cup (125 ml/4 fl oz) water and 2 tablespoons caster (superfine) sugar in a small pan. Slowly bring to the boil, stirring to dissolve the sugar. Simmer, without stirring, for 5 minutes. Makes 1 cup (250 ml/8 fl oz).

HOT BLUEBERRY SAUCE

In a non-metallic bowl, combine 500 g (1 lb) blueberries, ¼ cup (60 g/2 oz) sugar and 1 tablespoon balsamic vinegar. Set aside for 30 minutes. Place in a pan with 2 tablespoons water and stir over low heat to dissolve the sugar. Bring to the boil and simmer for 5 minutes. Serve warm. Delicious on ice cream and good with fresh ricotta or warm chocolate cake. Makes 2 cups (500 ml/16 fl oz).

STRAWBERRY COULIS

Hull 250 g (8 oz) strawberries and place in a food processor with 2 tablespoons icing (confectioners') sugar, 2 teaspoons lemon juice and 1–2 teaspoons Grand Marnier (optional). Process until smooth and strain through a fine sieve, if desired. Makes 1 cup (250 ml/8 fl oz).

BUMBLEBERRY COULIS

Place 300 g (10 oz) fresh or thawed frozen berries (use a combination of raspberry, strawberry, blueberry and blackberry) and 2 tablespoons icing (confectioners') sugar in a food processor. Blend in short bursts until smooth and glossy. Strain in a fine sieve to remove the seeds. Add 2 teaspoons lemon juice and 3 teaspoons Cassis liqueur (optional) and mix well. Makes 1 cup (250 ml/8 fl oz).

SPICY PEACH SAUCE

Put 500 g (1 lb) peaches in a bowl, cover with boiling water and leave for 20 seconds. Drain, peel and chop, then put in a pan with 1 cup (250 ml/8 fl oz) water, ½ vanilla bean, 2 cloves and a cinnamon stick. Bring to the boil, reduce the heat and simmer for 15–20 minutes, or until tender. Add 3 tablespoons sugar and stir over low heat until dissolved. Increase the heat and simmer for 5 minutes. Remove the vanilla and spices and cool slightly. Blend in a food processor. Push through a fine sieve before serving. Makes 1¾ cups (440 ml/14 fl oz).

CLOKWISE, FROM TOP LEFT: Lemon grass, lime and coriander syrup; Mango coulis; Passionfruit coulis; Bumbleberry coulis; Spicy peach sauce; Strawberry coulis; Hot blueberry sauce; Rhubarb sauce

PECANS

Native to North America, pecans are grown across America, as well as in Australia and South Africa. Pecans look like long versions of walnuts but have a smooth, very hard, brown-red shell. The trees can grow to 50 metres and the nuts have to be harvested by shaking the trees, sometimes with mechanical tree shakers. The nuts are usually sold shelled—the hard shells have to be cracked carefully to extract the nuts intact. Pecan pie is a popular dessert that appears on tables around the world but always seems American.

 ABOVE: Pecan pie

PECAN PIE

Preparation time: 30 minutes + chilling
Total cooking time: 1 hour 15 minutes
Serves 6

★ ★

Shortcrust pastry

1 1/2 cups (185 g/6 oz) plain (all-purpose) flour
125 g (4 oz) chilled unsalted butter, chopped
2–3 tablespoons chilled water

Filling

200 g (6 1/2 oz) pecans
3 eggs, lightly beaten
50 g (1 3/4 oz) unsalted butter, melted and cooled
3/4 cup (140 g/4 1/2 oz) soft brown sugar
2/3 cup (170 ml/5 1/2 fl oz) light corn syrup
1 teaspoon vanilla essence

1 Preheat the oven to moderate 180°C (350°F/ Gas 4). Sift the flour into a large bowl, then rub in the butter, using just your fingertips, until the mixture resembles breadcrumbs. Add almost all the water and mix until the mixture comes together, adding more water if necessary. Turn out onto a lightly floured surface and gather together into a ball.

2 Roll out the pastry to a 35 cm (14 inch) round. Line a 23 cm (9 inch) flan tin with pastry, trim the edges and refrigerate for 20 minutes. Pile the pastry trimmings together, roll out on baking paper to a rectangle about 2 mm (1/8 inch) thick, then refrigerate.

3 Line the pastry-lined tin with a sheet of crumpled baking paper and spread a layer of baking beads or rice evenly over the paper. Bake for 15 minutes, remove the paper and beads and bake for another 15 minutes, or until lightly golden. Cool completely.

4 To make the filling, spread the pecans over the pastry base. In a large jug, whisk together the eggs, butter, sugar, corn syrup, vanilla essence and a pinch of salt until well combined, then pour over the nuts.

5 Using a fluted pastry wheel or small sharp knife, cut narrow strips from half the pastry. Cut out small stars with a biscuit cutter from the remaining pastry. Arrange decoratively over the filling. Bake the pie for 45 minutes, or until firm. Allow to cool completely and serve at room temperature.

CHERRY PIE

Preparation time: 25 minutes
  + chilling
Total cooking time: 40 minutes
Serves 6–8

★ ★

Almond pastry

1 1/4 cups (155 g/5 oz) plain (all-purpose) flour
1/4 cup (30 g/1 oz) icing (confectioners') sugar
100 g (3 1/2 oz) chilled unsalted butter,
  chopped
60 g (2 oz) ground almonds
3 tablespoons chilled water

2 x 700 g (1 lb 7 oz) jars pitted
  morello cherries, drained
1 egg, lightly beaten
caster (superfine) sugar, to decorate
cream or ice cream, optional,
  to serve

1 Sift the flour and icing sugar into a bowl. Add the butter and rub in with just your fingertips until the mixture is fine and crumbly. Stir in the ground almonds, then add almost all the water and stir into the flour mixture with a flat-bladed knife until the mixture forms a dough, adding the remaining water if necessary.
2 Turn the dough onto a lightly floured surface and gather together into a ball. Roll out on a sheet of baking paper into a circle about 26 cm (10 1/2 inches) in diameter. Flatten slightly, cover with plastic wrap and refrigerate for 20 minutes. Spread the cherries into a 23 cm (9 inch) round pie dish.
3 Preheat the oven to moderately hot 200°C (400°F/Gas 6). Cover the pie dish with the pastry and trim the overhanging edge. Roll out the remaining scraps of pastry and use a small sharp knife to cut out decorations. Brush the pastry top all over with beaten egg and arrange the decorations on top. Brush these with beaten egg as well, and then sprinkle lightly with caster sugar. Place the pie dish on a baking tray (the cherry juice may overflow a little) and cook for 35–40 minutes, or until golden brown. Serve warm or at room temperature, with cream or ice cream, if you like.

ALMONDS IN COOKING

Almonds are the seeds of a tree related to the apricot and peach trees. Almonds are native to the Middle East and have a tough, oval, pale brown outer shell which is pointed at one end. In Europe, almonds are also picked when the shell is still covered by a velvety green outer coating. The inner shell has a dark brown skin which can be removed by blanching. Almonds are available whole in shells, shelled with their skins on, blanched, flaked, chopped and ground. Ground almonds are the basis of many biscuits and cakes, as well as being used in pastries and desserts.

ABOVE: Cherry pie

Gas 4) and grease a 2 litre (64 fl oz) ovenproof dish. Sift the flour and 2 tablespoons of the cocoa into a large bowl. Stir in ½ cup (125 g/ 4 oz) of the sugar and make a well in the centre.

2 Pour in the combined milk, egg, butter and vanilla. Stir until smooth, but do not overbeat. Pour into the dish and dissolve the remaining cocoa and sugar in 2½ cups (600 ml/20 fl oz) boiling water. Pour gently over the back of a spoon over the pudding mixture.

3 Bake for 40 minutes, or until a skewer comes out clean when inserted into the centre.

4 To make the orange cream, beat the cream, orange rind, icing sugar and Grand Marnier with electric beaters until soft peaks form.

5 Dust the pudding with sifted icing sugar and serve immediately with the orange cream.

EVE'S PUDDING

Preparation time: 25 minutes
Total cooking time: 55 minutes
Serves 4–6

500 g (1 lb) cooking apples
2 tablespoons sugar
125 g (4 oz) unsalted butter
½ cup (125 g/4 oz) caster (superfine) sugar
2 eggs
1 teaspoon vanilla essence
½ cup (125 ml/4 fl oz) milk
1½ cups (185 g/6 oz) self-raising flour

1 Preheat the oven to moderate 180°C (350°F/Gas 4). Grease a deep, 1.5 litre (48 fl oz) ovenproof dish with oil or melted butter. Line the base with baking paper.

2 Peel, core and thickly slice the apples. Place the apple slices, sugar and 1 tablespoon water into a pan. Cover and cook over medium heat for 12 minutes, or until the apples are soft but still hold together. Using a slotted spoon, spoon the apples into the base of the prepared dish. Allow to cool.

3 Using electric beaters, beat the butter and sugar until light and creamy. Add the eggs, one at a time, beating well after each addition. Using a large metal spoon, fold in the combined essence and milk alternately with the sifted flour.

4 Spoon the mixture over the apples and smooth the surface. Bake for 40–45 minutes, or until the pudding is cooked when tested with a skewer.

SELF-SAUCING CHOCOLATE PUDDING WITH ORANGE CREAM

Preparation time: 25 minutes
Total cooking time: 40 minutes
Serves 4–6

1 cup (125 g/4 oz) self-raising flour
⅓ cup (40 g/1¼ oz) cocoa powder
1¼ cups (310 g/10 oz) caster (superfine) sugar
½ cup (125 ml/4 fl oz) milk
1 egg
60 g (2 oz) unsalted butter, melted
1 teaspoon vanilla essence
icing (confectioners') sugar, to dust

Orange cream

1¼ cups (315 ml/10 fl oz) cream
1 teaspoon grated orange rind
1 tablespoon icing (confectioners') sugar
1 tablespoon Grand Marnier

1 Preheat the oven to moderate 180°C (350°F/

ABOVE: Self-saucing chocolate pudding with orange cream

LEMON TIPS
When buying lemons, select fruit that are heavy for their size and feel firm. Thinner-skinned lemons such as *Lisbon* and *Meyer* are juicier than thick-skinned ones such as *Eureka*. *Lisbon* and *Eureka* have more acidity and are tarter than *Meyer* lemons.

The juice of one lemon is usually about three tablespoons. Lemons at room temperature, or those warmed in the microwave for a few seconds, juice more easily than cold ones.

To grate rind easily, cover the fine side of a grater with a piece of baking paper and grate through the paper. Pull the paper off the grater and scrape off the rind.

The essential oils contained in lemon rind (zest) give a perfume rather than flavour. The flavour comes mainly from the juice.

Discard any lemons which have soft patches or look as if they are about to go mouldy. Lemons will go mouldy more quickly if stored with other fruit, so store separately.

LEMON DELICIOUS

Preparation time: 20 minutes
Total cooking time: 40 minutes
Serves 4

★★

60 g (2 oz) unsalted butter
3/4 cup (185 g/6 oz) caster (superfine) sugar
3 eggs, separated
1 teaspoon grated lemon rind
1/3 cup (40 g/1 1/4 oz) self-raising flour, sifted
1/4 cup (60 ml/2 fl oz) lemon juice
3/4 cup (185 ml/6 fl oz) milk
icing (confectioners') sugar, to dust

1 Preheat the oven to moderate 180°C (350°F/Gas 4). Brush a 1 litre (32 fl oz) ovenproof dish with oil. Using electric beaters, beat the butter, sugar, egg yolks and rind in a small bowl until the mixture is light and creamy. Transfer to a medium bowl.
2 Add the flour and stir with a wooden spoon until just combined. Add the juice and milk and stir to combine.
3 Place the egg whites in a small, dry bowl. Using electric beaters, beat until firm peaks form. Fold in the pudding mixture with a metal spoon until just combined.
4 Spoon into the ovenproof dish and place the dish in a deep baking dish. Pour in boiling water to come one-third of the way up the side of the pudding dish. Bake for 40 minutes. Dust with icing sugar. Spoon some sauce on each serving.

ABOVE: Lemon delicious

APPLE BETTY

Preparation time: 15 minutes
Total cooking time: 50 minutes
Serves 4–6

5 cooking apples, peeled, cored and chopped
100 g (3½ oz) unsalted butter
½ cup (95 g/3 oz) soft brown sugar,
  plus 1 tablespoon
grated rind of 1 lemon
¼ teaspoon ground cinnamon
pinch of ground nutmeg
3 cups (240 g/7½ oz) fresh breadcrumbs

1 Cook the apples with 1 tablespoon of the butter, 1 tablespoon brown sugar and the rind, cinnamon and nutmeg, for 10–15 minutes, until the apples are soft enough to beat to a purée.
2 Preheat the oven to moderate 180°C (350°F/ Gas 4). Melt the remaining butter in a frying pan over low heat and add the breadcrumbs and the remaining brown sugar. Toss everything together until all the crumbs are coated, and continue tossing while you fry the crumbs until golden brown.
3 Spread one-third of the crumbs in a 1 litre (32 fl oz) ovenproof dish and add half the apple purée in an even layer. Repeat with another one-third of the crumbs and the remaining apple, then finish with a layer of crumbs. Bake for 20 minutes, or until crisp and golden on top.

APPLE CRUMBLE

Preparation time: 20 minutes
Total cooking time: 45 minutes
Serves 4–6

8 cooking apples (about 1.4 kg)
2 tablespoons caster (superfine) sugar
1 cup (125 g/4 oz) plain (all-purpose) flour
½ cup (95 g/3 oz) soft brown sugar
¾ teaspoon ground cinnamon
100 g (3½ oz) butter, chopped

1 Preheat the oven to moderate 180°C (350°F/ Gas 4). Peel and core the apples and cut each one into 8 wedges. Place in a saucepan with ¼ cup (60 ml/2 fl oz) water, bring to the boil, then reduce the heat to low and cover. Cook for about 15 minutes, or until the apples are just

soft. Remove from the heat, drain and then stir in the sugar. Spoon the apple into a 1.5 litre (48 fl oz) ovenproof dish.
2 Place the flour in a bowl and stir in the brown sugar and cinnamon. Add the butter and rub with just your fingertips until the mixture resembles coarse breadcrumbs. Sprinkle evenly over the top of the apple mixture to cover completely. Bake for 25–30 minutes, or until crisp and golden brown. Serve immediately with cream or ice cream.

RHUBARB CRUMBLE WITH CRUNCHY MAPLE CREAM

Preparation time: 15 minutes
Total cooking time: 25 minutes
Serves 4–6

1 kg (2 lb) rhubarb
⅔ cup (160 g/5½ oz) sugar
100 g (3½ oz) unsalted butter
¾ cup (90 g/3 oz) plain (all-purpose) flour
⅓ cup (75 g/2½ oz) demerara sugar
10 Amaretti biscuits, crushed

Crunchy maple cream

200 ml (6½ fl oz) thick (double/heavy) cream
2 tablespoons golden syrup or pure
  maple syrup
3 Amaretti biscuits, crushed

1 Preheat the oven to moderately hot 200°C (400°F/Gas 6). Trim the rhubarb, cut into short lengths and put in a pan with the sugar. Stir over low heat until the sugar has dissolved, then cover and simmer for 8–10 minutes, or until the rhubarb is soft but still chunky. Spoon into a deep 1.5 litre (48 fl oz) ovenproof dish.
2 Rub the butter into the flour until the mixture resembles fine breadcrumbs, then stir in the demerara sugar and biscuits.
3 Sprinkle the crumble over the stewed rhubarb and bake for 15 minutes, or until the topping is golden brown. Serve with the crunchy maple cream.
4 To make the crunchy maple cream, place the cream in a bowl, carefully swirl the golden syrup through, then the crushed biscuits. Do not overmix—there should be rich veins of the crunchy syrup through the cream.
NOTE: Taste the rhubarb, as you may need to add a little more sugar.

*ABOVE: Bread and
butter pudding*

BREAD AND BUTTER PUDDING

Preparation time: 20 minutes + soaking + chilling
Total cooking time: 40 minutes
Serves 4

60 g (2 oz) mixed raisins and sultanas

2 tablespoons brandy or rum

30 g (1 oz) unsalted butter

4 slices good-quality white bread or
   brioche loaf

3 eggs

3 tablespoons caster (superfine) sugar

3 cups (750 ml/24 fl oz) milk

1/4 cup (60 ml/2 fl oz) cream

1/4 teaspoon vanilla essence

1/4 teaspoon ground cinnamon

1 tablespoon demerara sugar

1 Soak the raisins and sultanas in the brandy
or rum for about 30 minutes. Butter the slices
of bread or brioche and cut each piece into
8 triangles. Arrange the bread in a 1 litre
(32 fl oz) ovenproof dish.
2 Mix the eggs with the sugar, add the milk,
cream, vanilla and cinnamon and mix well.
Drain the raisins and sultanas and add any liquid
to the custard.
3 Scatter the soaked raisins and sultanas over the
bread and pour the custard over the top. Cover
with plastic wrap and refrigerate for 1 hour.
4 Preheat the oven to moderate 180°C (350°F/
Gas 4). Remove the pudding from the
refrigerator and sprinkle with the demerara
sugar. Bake for 35–40 minutes, or until the
custard is set and the top crunchy and golden.
NOTE: It is very important that you use good-
quality bread for this recipe. Ordinary sliced
white bread will tend to go a bit claggy when
it soaks up the milk.

CARAMEL BREAD PUDDING

Preparation time: 40 minutes + standing
  + chilling
Total cooking time: 1 hour
Serves 6–8

2/3 cup (160 g/5 1/2 oz) caster (superfine) sugar

500 g (1 lb) panettone or brioche

1/2 cup (125 g/4 oz) caster (superfine) sugar,
  extra

2 cups (500 ml/16 fl oz) milk

2 wide strips lemon rind, white pith removed

3 eggs, lightly beaten

fresh fruit and cream, optional, to serve

1 Preheat the oven to moderate 180°C (350°F/
Gas 4). Lightly brush a 23 x 13 x 7 cm
(9 x 5 x 2¾ inch), 1.25 litre (40 fl oz) loaf tin
with oil or melted butter.
2 Place the caster sugar with 2 tablespoons water
in a small pan over medium heat and stir,
without boiling, until the sugar has completely
dissolved. Bring to the boil, reduce the heat
slightly and simmer, without stirring, for about
10 minutes, until the syrup becomes a rich
golden colour. Watch carefully towards the end
of cooking to prevent burning. As soon as it
reaches the colour you desire, pour into the loaf
tin and leave to cool.
3 Using a large serrated knife, cut the panettone
or brioche into 2 cm (¾ inch) thick slices and
remove the crusts. Trim into large pieces to fit
the tin in three layers, filling any gaps with
panettone cut to size.
4 Stir the extra caster sugar, milk and lemon
rind in a pan over low heat until the sugar has
dissolved. Bring just to the boil, remove from
the heat and transfer to a jug to allow the lemon
flavour to be absorbed and the mixture to cool.
Remove the lemon rind and whisk in the beaten
eggs. Pour the mixture gradually into the tin,
allowing it to soak into the panettone after each
addition. Set aside for 20 minutes to let the
panettone soak up the liquid.
5 Place the loaf tin into a large baking dish and
pour in enough hot water to come halfway up
the sides of the tin. Bake the pudding for
50 minutes, until just set. Carefully remove
the tin from the baking dish and set aside to
cool. Refrigerate the pudding overnight.
6 When ready to serve, turn out onto a plate
and cut into slices. Serve with fresh fruit and
cream, if desired.

BREAD AND BUTTER PUDDING VARIATIONS

Bread and butter pudding can be made with
all sorts of bread or cake leftovers.
Croissants, Danish pastries, panettone,
brioche and any kind of fruit loaf and buns
make luscious bread and butter puddings. A
sprinkling of demerara sugar or crushed
sugar cubes will give a lovely crunchy
topping. For a shiny top, glaze the hot
pudding with apricot jam.

*ABOVE: Caramel
bread pudding*

513

VANILLA ICE CREAM

To test the custard, run a finger through the mixture, across the back of a wooden spoon. It should leave a clear line.

Cover the surface of the custard with plastic wrap and freeze for 2 hours.

Beat the semi-frozen ice cream with electric beaters to break up any large ice crystals. Each time you beat the mixture, the ice crystals will get smaller and the mixture smoother.

OPPOSITE PAGE, FROM TOP: Vanilla ice cream; Premium chocolate and cinnamon ice cream

VANILLA ICE CREAM

Preparation time: 30 minutes + chilling + freezing
Total cooking time: 15 minutes
Serves 4

1 cup (250 ml/8 fl oz) milk
1 cup (250 ml/8 fl oz) cream
1 vanilla bean, split lengthways
6 egg yolks
1/2 cup (125 g/4 oz) caster (superfine) sugar

1 Combine the milk and cream in a pan and add the vanilla bean. Bring to the boil, then remove from the heat and set aside for 10 minutes.
2 Using a wire whisk, beat the yolks and sugar together in a bowl for 2–3 minutes, until thick and pale, then whisk in the warm milk mixture. Scrape the seeds from the vanilla bean into the mixture. Discard the bean.
3 Wash the pan, and pour the mixture into it. Stir over very low heat until thickened. This will take about 5–10 minutes. To test, run a finger through the mixture across the back of the wooden spoon—if it leaves a clear line, the custard is ready.
4 Pour the custard into a bowl and cool to room temperature, stirring frequently to hasten cooling.
5 Pour into a shallow metal container, cover the surface of the custard with plastic wrap or baking paper and freeze for about 2 hours, until almost frozen. Scoop into a chilled bowl and beat with electric beaters until smooth, then return to the tray and freeze again. Repeat this step twice more before transferring to a storage container. Cover the surface with baking paper or plastic wrap to stop ice crystals forming on the surface, then a lid.
6 To serve, transfer the ice cream to the refrigerator for about 30 minutes, to soften slightly. Ice cream will keep, well sealed, in the freezer for up to 1 month.
NOTE: This recipe can also be made using an ice cream machine.
VARIATIONS: To make strawberry ice cream, chop 250 g (8 oz) strawberries in a food processor just until smooth. Stir into the custard mixture when it is well chilled (end of step 4). Freeze the ice cream as directed.

To make banana ice cream, thoroughly mash 3 ripe bananas (or for a finer texture, purée in a food processor). Stir into the custard mixture when it is well chilled, along with 1 tablespoon lemon juice. Freeze as directed. Makes 1.5 litres (48 fl oz).

PREMIUM CHOCOLATE AND CINNAMON ICE CREAM

Preparation time: 20 minutes + chilling + freezing
Total cooking time: 30 minutes
Serves 6–8

2 cups (500 ml/16 fl oz) milk
200 g (6 1/2 oz) good-quality dark chocolate, chopped
4 cinnamon sticks
3/4 cup (185 g/6 oz) caster (superfine) sugar
1 1/2 teaspoons ground cinnamon
4 egg yolks
2 cups (500 ml/16 fl oz) cream

1 Heat the milk, chocolate and cinnamon sticks in a heavy-based pan, stirring occasionally, over low heat for 15 minutes, or until the chocolate has melted and the mixture is well mixed. Do not allow to boil. Remove the cinnamon sticks.
2 Mix the sugar and cinnamon in a large heatproof bowl. Add the egg yolks and place the bowl over a pan of simmering water. Whisk until the mixture is thick and pale.
3 Gradually whisk the chocolate mixture into the eggs and sugar. Cook, whisking all the time, for 5 minutes or until the mixture coats the back of a spoon.
4 Chill for 30 minutes in the refrigerator, strain and slowly stir in the cream. Pour into a shallow metal container. Freeze for 2 hours (the edges will be frozen and the centre soft). Transfer to a large bowl and beat with electric beaters until smooth. Repeat this step twice more. Freeze in a 2 litre (64 fl oz) plastic container, covered with a piece of baking paper or plastic wrap, then a lid, for 7–8 hours, or until solid.
NOTE: This recipe can also be made using an ice cream machine.

ICE CREAM TIPS

The temperature of your freezer should be -18°C/0°F to ensure proper freezing. The freezer should also be free from ice build-up and not too full. Cover the surface of your ice cream with baking paper or plastic wrap to stop ice crystals forming on the surface.

For full flavour, ice cream should not be eaten while rock hard, but slightly softened.

SUMMER FRUITS Fresh flowers

everywhere, long balmy days, the first swim of the year, plus the promise of rich, ripe

stone fruit and berries just around the corner—what better time of year than summer?

RASPBERRY FOOL

Beat 1¼ cups (315 ml/10 fl oz) cream until soft peaks form, add ⅓ cup (40 g/ 1¼ oz) sifted icing (confectioners') sugar and beat until just combined. Lightly crush 250 g (8 oz) fresh raspberries with a fork. Fold the crushed berries through the cream; refrigerate for up to 2 hours. To serve, spoon into dessert glasses and accompany with brandy snaps or wafers.

MANGO ICE CREAM

Heat 1¼ cups (315 ml/10 fl oz) cream until it just comes to the boil; remove from the heat. Whisk 4 egg yolks in a heatproof bowl with ¾ cup (185 g/ 6 oz) caster (superfine) sugar until thick and pale. Gradually add the hot cream to the egg mixture, whisking constantly. Return all this to the pan and stir over low heat for about 5 minutes until the

mixture thickens slightly. Be careful not to let it boil or it will curdle. Pour the mixture into a clean bowl and set aside to cool, stirring occasionally. Purée the flesh of 2 large mangoes in a blender. Stir into the cooled custard, then pour into a shallow metal tray. Cover, then freeze until firm. Transfer to a bowl, beat with electric beaters until smooth. Return to the tray and freeze until firm.

NECTARINE TARTS

Preheat the oven to moderately hot 200°C (400°F/Gas 6) and brush a flat oven tray with melted butter. Cut a sheet of thawed frozen puff pastry into four squares. Brush all over with melted butter and dust generously with icing (confectioners') sugar. Arrange thick slices of nectarine diagonally across the pastry, then fold two corners over and seal in the centre. Brush the pastry parcels again with melted butter and place them on the prepared tray. Bake for 20 minutes or until golden. Dust with more icing sugar, and serve warm with cream.

FRESH FRUIT WITH BUTTERSCOTCH MASCARPONE

Combine 60 g (2 oz) butter, ½ cup (95 g/3 oz) soft brown sugar and 1 cup (250 ml/8 fl oz) cream in a small pan. Stir over low heat until the mixture is melted and smooth and bring to the boil. Reduce the heat and simmer for about 3 minutes. Choose a selection of seasonal fruits such as berries, figs, plums, apricots, peaches or starfruit and serve with dollops of mascarpone or cream. (Also delicious with fresh ricotta.) Drizzle the butterscotch over the fruit or mascarpone. Serve immediately.

CHERRY GRATIN

Remove the stems and stones from 500 g (1 lb) cherries and arrange the cherries in a shallow heatproof dish. Combine ½ cup (125 ml/4 fl oz) cream and ½ cup (125 ml/4 fl oz) thick (double/heavy) cream in a pan and heat the mixture until it just boils. Whisk 2 egg yolks together with 2 tablespoons caster (superfine) sugar in a medium heatproof bowl until thick and pale. Pour in the hot cream gradually, whisking until combined. Return the mixture to the pan and stir over very low heat for about 5 minutes, until it thickens. Make sure that the mixture does not boil. Cool slightly, then pour over the cherries. To prepare ahead of time, you can refrigerate the gratin for up to 4 hours at this stage. To serve, sprinkle 2 tablespoons soft brown sugar evenly over the surface and cook under a hot grill until the top is browned and just bubbling. Sprinkle with icing (confectioners') sugar just before serving.

CLOCKWISE, FROM TOP LEFT: Nectarine tarts; Fresh fruit with butterscotch mascarpone; Raspberry fool; Cherry gratin; Mango ice cream

TEA TIME

ABOVE: Sultana scones

SCONES

Scones are the most popular of the 'quick breads' as they can be mixed and baked in a short time, unlike yeasted breads. *Devonshire Tea,* known all over the world, consists of freshly baked scones with jam and cream served with a pot of tea. The name originally came from the beautiful thick rich cream of Devon, called clotted cream, but whipped cream is an adequate substitute. Sweet additions to a scone dough can include sugar, spices and dried fruits such as chopped pitted dates, raisins and mixed peel. Savoury flavours can include a variety of herbs, ham, pumpkin or cheese.

SULTANA SCONES

Preparation time: 10 minutes
Total cooking time: 15 minutes
Makes 12

2 cups (250 g/8 oz) self-raising flour
1 teaspoon baking powder
30 g (1 oz) unsalted butter, chilled and cubed
1/2 cup (80 g/2³/4 oz) sultanas
1 cup (250 ml/8 fl oz) milk, plus extra, to glaze

1 Preheat the oven to hot 220°C (425°F/Gas 7). Lightly grease a baking tray or line with baking paper. Sift the flour, baking powder and a pinch of salt into a bowl. Rub in the butter using your fingertips, then stir in the sultanas. Make a well.
2 Add almost all the milk and mix with a flat-bladed knife, using a cutting action, until the dough comes together in clumps. Use the remaining milk if necessary. With floured hands, gently gather the dough together, lift out onto a lightly floured surface and pat into a smooth ball. Do not knead or the scones will be tough.
3 Pat the dough out to 2 cm (³/4 inch) thick. Using a floured 5 cm (2 inch) cutter, cut into rounds. Gather the trimmings together, press out

as before and cut more rounds. Place close together on the tray and brush with milk. Bake for 15 minutes, or until risen and golden brown on top. Serve warm or at room temperature.

CHEESE SCONES

Preparation time: 15 minutes
Total cooking time: 15 minutes
Makes 12

2 cups (250 g/8 oz) self-raising flour
1 teaspoon baking powder
1/2 teaspoon dry mustard
30 g (1 oz) unsalted butter, chilled and cubed
1/4 cup (25 g/³/4 oz) grated Parmesan
3/4 cup (90 g/3 oz) finely grated Cheddar
1 cup (250 ml/8 fl oz) milk

1 Preheat the oven to hot 220°C (425°F/Gas 7). Lightly grease a baking tray. Sift the flour, baking powder, mustard and a pinch of salt into a bowl and rub in the butter with your fingertips. Stir in the Parmesan and 1/2 cup (60 g/2 oz) Cheddar, making sure they don't clump together. Make a

well in the centre. Add almost all the milk, and mix with a flat-bladed knife, using a cutting action, until the dough comes together in clumps. Use the remaining milk if necessary. With floured hands, gently gather the dough together, lift out onto a lightly floured surface and pat into a smooth ball. Do not knead or the scones will be tough. **2** Pat the dough out to 2 cm (³/4 inch) thick. Using a floured 5 cm (2 inch) cutter, cut into rounds. Gather the trimmings and, without over-handling, press out as before and cut more rounds. Place close together on the tray and sprinkle with the remaining cheese. Bake for 12–15 minutes, or until risen and golden brown. Serve warm or at room temperature.

PUMPKIN SCONES

Preparation time: 15 minutes + cooling
Total cooking time: 30 minutes
Makes 12

250 g (8 oz) butternut pumpkin (squash), cut into cubes
2 cups (250 g/8 oz) self-raising flour
1 teaspoon baking powder
pinch of ground nutmeg
30 g (1 oz) unsalted butter, chilled and cubed
2 tablespoons soft brown sugar
¹/2 cup (125 ml/4 fl oz) milk, plus extra, to glaze

1 Steam the pumpkin for 12 minutes, or until soft, then drain well and mash until smooth. Cool to room temperature. Preheat the oven to hot 220°C (425°F/Gas 7). Lightly grease a baking tray or line with baking paper.
2 Sift the flour, baking powder and a pinch of salt into a bowl and add the nutmeg and butter. Rub the butter into the flour with your fingertips, then stir in the sugar and make a well in the centre.
3 Mix the milk into the pumpkin, add to the well in the flour and mix with a flat-bladed knife, using a cutting action, until the dough comes together in clumps. With floured hands, gather the dough together (it will be very soft) and lift out onto a lightly floured surface. Do not knead or the scones will be tough.
4 Pat the dough out to 2 cm (³/4 inch) thick. Using a floured 5 cm (2 inch) cutter, cut into rounds. Gather the trimmings and, without handling too much, press out and cut out more rounds. Place close together on the tray and brush with milk. Bake for 12–15 minutes, or until well risen and lightly golden. Serve warm.

BELOW: Pumpkin scones

FLAVOURING MUFFINS

Using buttermilk instead of milk in muffins results in a softer texture and a good crust. It also adds to the flavour. To achieve the same effect, you can sour your own milk by adding a few drops of lemon juice or vinegar, just until it curdles the milk, or you can use milk that has gone sour. Muffins can be iced with a simple icing if you like. Make it by combining 1 cup (125 g/4 oz) sifted icing (confectioners') sugar with 10 g (1/4 oz) butter and about 1 tablespoon hot water to form a smooth paste. Flavour it with vanilla or grated citrus rind. To make a chocolate-flavoured icing, add 1 tablespoon cocoa powder to the sifted icing sugar. Use a small metal spatula to ice the muffins.

RIGHT: Chocolate muffins

CHOCOLATE MUFFINS

Preparation time: 15 minutes
Total cooking time: 25 minutes
Makes 12

2¹/2 cups (310 g/10 oz) self-raising flour
¹/3 cup (40 g/1¹/2 oz) cocoa powder
¹/2 teaspoon bicarbonate of soda
²/3 cup (180 g/6 oz) caster (superfine) sugar
1¹/2 cups (375 ml/12 fl oz) buttermilk
2 eggs
150 g (5 oz) unsalted butter, melted and cooled

1 Preheat the oven to moderately hot 200°C (400°F/Gas 6). Lightly grease twelve regular muffin holes. Sift the flour, cocoa powder and bicarbonate of soda into a bowl and add the sugar. Make a well in the centre.
2 In a jug, whisk the buttermilk and eggs together and pour into the well. Add the butter and fold gently with a metal spoon until just combined. Do not overmix—the mixture should still be lumpy.
3 Fill each hole about three-quarters full. Bake for 20–25 minutes, or until the muffins are risen and come away slightly from the side of the tin. Allow to cool for a couple of minutes, then loosen with a flat-bladed knife and transfer to a wire rack. Serve warm or at room temperature.

APPLE CINNAMON MUFFINS

Preparation time: 15 minutes
Total cooking time: 25 minutes
Makes 12

400 g (13 oz) can pie apple
2¹/2 cups (310 g/10 oz) self-raising flour
2 teaspoons ground cinnamon
²/3 cup (125 g/4 oz) soft brown sugar
1¹/3 cups (350 ml/11 fl oz) milk
2 eggs
1 teaspoon vanilla essence
150 g (5 oz) unsalted butter, melted and cooled
¹/2 cup (60 g/2 oz) walnuts, finely chopped

1 Preheat the oven to moderately hot 200°C (400°F/Gas 6). Lightly grease twelve regular muffin holes. Place the pie apple in a bowl and break up with a knife.
2 Sift the flour and cinnamon into a bowl and add the sugar. Make a well in the centre. Whisk together the milk, eggs and vanilla in a jug and pour into the well. Add the melted butter.
3 Fold the mixture gently with a metal spoon until just combined. Add the pie apple and gently stir through. Do not overmix—the batter should be lumpy. Overmixing will make the muffins tough.

4 Fill each muffin hole with the mixture (the holes will be quite full, but don't worry because these muffins don't rise as much as some) and sprinkle with walnuts. Bake for 20–25 minutes, or until the muffins are risen, golden and come away slightly from the tin. Allow to cool for a couple of minutes, then gently loosen each muffin with a flat-bladed knife and transfer to a wire rack. Serve warm or at room temperature.
NOTE: Completely cool the melted butter before adding it. It doesn't always combine well with other liquids so it is often added separately.

ORANGE POPPY SEED MUFFINS

Preparation time: 15 minutes
Total cooking time: 30 minutes
Makes 12

2¹/₂ cups (310 g/10 oz) self-raising flour
¹/₄ cup (40 g/1¹/₄ oz) poppy seeds
¹/₃ cup (90 g/3 oz) caster (superfine) sugar
125 g (4 oz) unsalted butter
1 cup (315 g/10 oz) orange marmalade
1 cup (250 ml/8 fl oz) milk
2 eggs
1 tablespoon finely grated orange rind

1 Preheat the oven to moderately hot 200°C (400°F/Gas 6). Lightly grease twelve regular muffin holes. Sift the flour into a bowl. Stir in the poppy seeds and sugar, and make a well in the centre. Put the butter and ²/₃ cup (210 g/7 oz) of the marmalade in a small saucepan and stir over low heat until the butter has melted and the mixture is combined. Cool slightly.
2 Whisk together the milk, eggs and rind in a jug and pour into the well. Add the butter and marmalade. Fold gently with a metal spoon until just combined. Do not overmix—the batter should still be lumpy. Overmixing will make them tough.
3 Fill each hole about three-quarters full and bake for 20–25 minutes, or until the muffins are risen, golden and come away slightly from the tin.
4 Heat the remaining marmalade and push it through a fine sieve. Brush generously over the top of the warm muffins. Leave them to cool in the tin for a couple of minutes, then gently loosen each muffin with a flat-bladed knife and transfer to a wire rack. Serve warm or at room temperature.
NOTE: Muffins are most delicious if eaten on the day they are made and served warm. If you want to store muffins for a couple of days, let them cool completely, then store them in an airtight container. Muffins are also suitable for freezing.
VARIATION: A variation of this muffin can be made using lime marmalade and finely grated lemon rind.

EGGS
Eggs quickly lose their quality so it is important to store them correctly. Check the use-by date when you buy them and look to make sure none of the eggs are broken. Store eggs in their cartons to protect them. They are commercially packed with the pointed end down to prevent damage to the air cell and to keep the yolk centred. Eggs should be refrigerated as this slows down moisture loss. For every day that an egg is left out of the refrigerator, as much as four days in quality can be lost.

LEFT: Orange poppy seed muffins

FRIANDS

Friands (pronounced *free-onds*) are small oval-shaped cakes baked in special-purpose oval tins called friand tins or barquette moulds. Sometimes the same mixture is baked in a rectangular tin and is then named *Financier*, meaning 'gold ingot', which the shape resembles. Both are very popular in cafés and come in a variety of flavours. The tins can be purchased from kitchenware shops. Traditional friands are made with almond meal.

OPPOSITE PAGE, FROM LEFT ON PLATE: Hazelnut and chocolate friands; Almond friands

ALMOND FRIANDS

Preparation time: 10 minutes
Total cooking time: 20 minutes
Makes 10

160 g (5½ oz) unsalted butter
1 cup (90 g/3 oz) flaked almonds
⅓ cup (40 g/1¼ oz) plain (all-purpose) flour
1⅓ cups (165 g/5½ oz) icing (confectioners') sugar
5 egg whites
icing (confectioners') sugar, extra, to dust

1 Preheat the oven to hot 210°C (415°F/ Gas 6–7). Lightly grease ten ½ cup (125 ml/ 4 fl oz) friand tins (barquette moulds).
2 Melt the butter in a small saucepan over medium heat, then cook for 3–4 minutes, or until the butter turns deep golden. Strain to remove any residue (the colour will deepen on standing). Remove from the heat and set aside to cool until just lukewarm.
3 Place the flaked almonds in a food processor and process until finely ground. Transfer to a bowl and sift the flour and icing sugar into the same bowl.
4 Place the egg whites in a separate bowl and lightly whisk with a fork until just combined. Add the butter to the flour mixture along with the egg whites. Mix gently with a metal spoon until all the ingredients are well combined.
5 Spoon some mixture into each friand tin to fill to three-quarters. Place the tins on a baking tray and bake in the centre of the oven for 10 minutes, then reduce the heat to moderate 180°C (350°F/Gas 4) and bake for another 5 minutes, or until a skewer comes out clean when inserted in the centre of a friand. Remove and leave to cool in the tins for 5 minutes before turning out onto a wire rack to cool completely. Dust with icing sugar before serving.
NOTE: These friands will keep well for up to three days in an airtight container.
VARIATIONS: To make berry friands, make the mixture as above and place a fresh or frozen raspberry or blueberry in the top of each friand before placing in the oven.

To make lemon friands, add 2 teaspoons grated lemon rind to the flour and sugar mixture and proceed as above.

HAZELNUT AND CHOCOLATE FRIANDS

Preparation time: 20 minutes
Total cooking time: 40 minutes
Makes 12

⭐⭐

200 g (6½ oz) whole hazelnuts
185 g (6 oz) unsalted butter
6 egg whites
1¼ cups (155 g/5 oz) plain (all-purpose) flour
¼ cup (30 g /1 oz) cocoa powder
2 cups (250 g/8 oz) icing (confectioners') sugar
icing (confectioners') sugar, extra, to dust

1 Preheat the oven to moderately hot 200°C (400°F/Gas 6). Lightly grease twelve ½ cup (125 ml/4 fl oz) friand tins (barquette moulds).
2 Spread the hazelnuts out on a baking tray and bake for 8–10 minutes, or until fragrant (take care not to burn). Wrap in a clean tea towel and rub vigorously to loosen the skins. Discard the skins. Cool, then process in a food processor until finely ground.
3 Melt the butter in a small saucepan over medium heat, then cook for 3–4 minutes, or until the butter turns deep golden. Strain to remove any residue (the colour will deepen on standing). Remove from the heat and set aside to cool to lukewarm.
4 Place the egg whites in a clean, dry bowl and lightly whisk until frothy but not firm. Sift the flour, cocoa powder and icing sugar into a large bowl and stir in the ground hazelnuts. Make a well in the flour, add the egg whites and butter and mix to combine.
5 Spoon some mixture into each friand tin to fill to three-quarters. Place the tins on a baking tray and bake in the centre of the oven for 20–25 minutes, or until a skewer comes out clean when inserted in the centre of a friand. Remove and leave to cool in the tins for 5 minutes before turning out onto a wire rack to cool completely. Dust with icing sugar before serving.
NOTE: These friands will keep for up to four days in an airtight container.

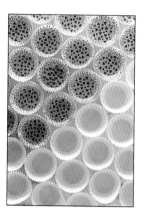

ROCK CAKES

Preparation time: 15 minutes
Total cooking time: 15 minutes
Makes about 20

2 cups (250 g/8 oz) self-raising flour
90 g (3 oz) unsalted butter, chilled, cubed
1/2 cup (125 g/4 oz) caster (superfine) sugar
1/2 cup (95 g/3 oz) mixed dried fruit
1/2 teaspoon ground ginger
1 egg
1/4 cup (60 ml/2 fl oz) milk

1 Preheat the oven to moderately hot 200°C (400°F/Gas 6). Grease two baking trays. Sift the flour into a large bowl and rub in the butter with your fingertips until the mixture resembles fine breadcrumbs. Stir in the sugar, fruit and ginger.
2 Whisk the egg into the milk in a bowl, add to the dry ingredients and mix to a stiff dough. Drop rough heaps of mixture, about 3 tablespoons at a time, onto the trays. Bake for 10–15 minutes, or until golden. Cool on a wire rack.

BUTTERFLY CAKES

Preparation time: 20 minutes
Total cooking time: 20 minutes
Makes 12

120 g (4 oz) unsalted butter, softened
2/3 cup (160 g/5 1/2 oz) caster (superfine) sugar
1 1/2 cups (185 g/6 oz) self-raising flour
1/2 cup (125 ml/4 fl oz) milk
2 teaspoons vanilla essence
2 eggs
1/2 cup (125 ml/4 fl oz) cream,
   whipped to soft peaks
1/3 cup (105 g/3 1/2 oz) strawberry jam
icing (confectioners') sugar, to dust

1 Preheat the oven to moderate 180°C (350°F/Gas 4). Line a 12-hole shallow patty tin with paper cases. Put the butter, sugar, flour, milk, vanilla and eggs in a bowl and beat with electric beaters on low speed for 2 minutes, or until well mixed. Increase the speed and beat for 2 minutes, or until smooth and pale.

2 Divide the mixture evenly among the cases and bake for 20 minutes, or until cooked and golden. Transfer to a wire rack to cool completely.
3 Using a small sharp knife, cut shallow rounds from the top of each cake. Cut these in half. Spoon a half tablespoon of cream into the cavity in each cake, then top with a teaspoon of jam. Position two halves of the cake tops in the jam in each cake to resemble butterfly wings. Dust the cakes with icing sugar before serving.
VARIATION: To make iced cup cakes, don't cut off the tops. Mix 1/2 cup (60 g/2 oz) sifted icing (confectioners') sugar, 1 teaspoon softened unsalted butter, 1/2 teaspoon vanilla essence and up to 3 teaspoons hot water to form a smooth paste, then spread icing on the cooled cakes.

ORANGE CUP CAKES

Preparation time: 15 minutes
Total cooking time: 20 minutes
Makes 12

120 g (4 oz) unsalted butter, softened
2/3 cup (160 g/5 1/2 oz) caster (superfine) sugar
1 1/2 cups (185 g/6 oz) self-raising flour
1/2 cup (125 ml/4 fl oz) orange juice
2 teaspoons vanilla essence
2 eggs
3 tablespoons grated orange rind
shredded orange rind, to decorate, optional

Icing

60 g (2 oz) unsalted butter, softened
3/4 cup (90 g/3 oz) icing (confectioners') sugar
1 tablespoon orange juice

1 Preheat the oven to moderate 180°C (350°F/Gas 4). Line a deep 12-hole shallow patty tin with paper cases. Place the butter, sugar, flour, juice, vanilla and eggs in a bowl and beat with electric beaters on low speed for 2 minutes, or until well mixed. Increase the speed and beat for 2 minutes, or until smooth and pale. Stir in the orange rind. Divide among the cases and bake for 20 minutes, or until golden. Transfer to a wire rack to cool.
2 For the icing, beat the butter in a bowl with electric beaters until pale. Beat in half the icing sugar, the juice, then the remaining icing sugar. Spread over the cakes, then decorate if you like.

BUTTER

Butter is made by churning cream until it solidifies. Unsalted butter is also known as sweet butter and is used in baking and desserts as it has a good flavour. Cultured butter, also called Danish butter, when available, can be used for sweet baking. It has a bacteria added to give extra flavour and interest. Prior to refrigeration, salt was added to butter to help preserve it, but today salt is added to please the palate. Butter should always be covered, or well wrapped, and stored in the refrigerator because it very readily takes on other flavours. It freezes well.

OPPOSITE PAGE, FROM TOP: Rock cakes; Butterfly cakes; Orange cup cakes

CHELSEA BUNS

Spread the creamed butter and sugar all over the dough, leaving a small border on one long edge.

Arrange the slices close together with the seams facing inward.

ABOVE: Chelsea buns

CHELSEA BUNS

Preparation time: 30 minutes
  + 1 hour 40 minutes rising
Total cooking time: 25 minutes
Makes 24

★ ★

7 g (¹/4 oz) sachet dried yeast

1 teaspoon sugar

2¹/2 cups (310 g/10 oz) plain (all-purpose) flour

¹/2 cup (125 ml/4 fl oz) milk, warmed

185 g (6 oz) unsalted butter, cubed

1 tablespoon sugar, extra

2 teaspoons grated lemon rind

1 teaspoon mixed spice

1 egg, lightly beaten

¹/4 cup (45 g/1¹/2 oz) soft brown sugar

1 cup (185 g/6 oz) mixed dried fruit

1 tablespoon milk, extra, for glazing

2 tablespoons sugar, extra, for glazing

Glacé icing

¹/2 cup (60 g/2 oz) icing (confectioners') sugar

1–2 tablespoons milk

1 Combine the yeast, sugar and 1 tablespoon of the flour in a small bowl. Add the milk and mix until smooth. Set aside in a warm place for 10 minutes, or until frothy. Sift the remaining flour into a large bowl and rub in 125 g (4 oz) of the butter with your fingertips. Stir in the extra sugar, rind and half the mixed spice. Make a well, add the yeast mixture and egg and mix. Gather together and turn out onto a lightly floured surface.

2 Knead for 2 minutes, or until smooth, then shape into a ball. Place in a large, lightly oiled bowl, cover with plastic wrap and set aside in a warm place for 1 hour, or until well risen. Punch down and knead for 2 minutes, or until smooth.

3 Preheat the oven to hot 210°C (415°F/ Gas 6–7). Lightly grease a baking tray. Beat the remaining butter with the brown sugar in a small bowl with electric beaters until light and creamy. Roll the dough out to a 40 x 25 cm (16 x 10 inch) rectangle. Spread the butter and sugar all over the dough to within 2 cm (³/4 inch) of the edge of one of the longer sides. Spread with the combined fruit and remaining spice. Roll the dough from the long side, firmly and evenly, to enclose the fruit. Use a sharp knife to cut the roll into eight slices about 5 cm (2 inches) wide. Arrange the slices, close together and with

the seams inwards, on the tray. Flatten slightly. Set aside, covered with plastic wrap, in a warm place for 30 minutes, or until well risen. Bake for 20 minutes, or until brown and cooked. When almost ready, stir the milk and sugar for glazing in a small saucepan over low heat until the sugar dissolves and the mixture is almost boiling. Brush over the hot buns. Cool.
4 Mix the icing sugar and milk, stir until smooth, then drizzle over the buns.

MADELEINES

Preparation time: 20 minutes
Total cooking time: 15 minutes
Makes 12

★

1 cup (125 g/4 oz) plain (all-purpose) flour
2 eggs
3/4 cup (185 g/6 oz) caster (superfine) sugar
185 g (6 oz) unsalted butter, melted and cooled
1 teaspoon finely grated orange rind
2 tablespoons icing (confectioners') sugar, to dust

1 Preheat the oven to moderate 180°C (350°F/ Gas 4). Lightly grease twelve madeleine holes in a madeleine tin (see Note). Lightly dust the madeleine tin with flour and shake off any excess.
2 Sift the flour three times onto baking paper. This process helps lighten the texture of the madeleines. Combine the eggs and sugar in a heatproof bowl. Place the bowl over a saucepan of simmering water and beat the mixture with a whisk or electric beaters until thick and pale yellow. Remove the bowl from the heat and continue to beat the mixture until cooled slightly and increased in volume.
3 Add the sifted flour, butter and orange rind to the bowl and fold in quickly and lightly with a metal spoon until just combined. Spoon the mixture carefully into the madeleine holes.
4 Bake for 10–12 minutes, or until lightly golden. Carefully remove from the tin and place on a wire rack until cold. Dust with icing sugar before serving. Madeleines are best eaten on the day of baking.
NOTE: Madeleine tins are available from kitchenware speciality shops. However, if you prefer, you can cook the mixture in shallow patty tins instead.

MADELEINES

Place the bowl over a saucepan of simmering water and beat the mixture until thick and pale yellow.

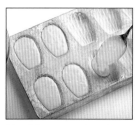

Carefully spoon the mixture into the lightly greased and floured madeleine holes.

LEFT: Madeleines

ECCLES CAKES

Preparation time: 20 minutes
Total cooking time: 20 minutes
Makes 27

1 cup (150 g/5 oz) currants
1/2 cup (95 g/3 oz) mixed peel
1 tablespoon brandy
1 tablespoon sugar
1/2 teaspoon ground cinnamon
500 g (1 lb) home-made or bought puff pastry
  (see page 488)
1 egg white
2 teaspoons sugar, extra

1 Preheat the oven to hot 210°C (415°F/ Gas 6–7). Lightly grease two baking trays. Combine the currants, peel, brandy, sugar and cinnamon in a bowl.
2 Divide the pastry into three and roll each piece out to a thickness of 3 mm (1/8 inch). Using an 8 cm (3 inch) scone cutter, cut nine circles from each sheet of pastry. (Any remaining pastry can be frozen.) Place 2 level teaspoons of filling on each circle. Bring the edges of the rounds up together and pinch to seal. Turn seam-side-down and roll out to 1 cm (1/2 inch) thick ovals.
3 Place on the trays. Brush the tops with egg white and sprinkle with extra sugar. Make three slashes across the top of each cake. Bake for 15–20 minutes, or until golden. Serve warm.

LAMINGTONS

Preparation time: 50 minutes
Total cooking time: 1 hour
Makes 16

1 1/2 cups (185 g/6 oz) self-raising flour
1/3 cup (40 g/1 1/4 oz) cornflour (cornstarch)
185 g (6 oz) unsalted butter, softened
1 cup (250 g/8 oz) caster (superfine) sugar
2 teaspoons vanilla essence
3 eggs, lightly beaten
1/2 cup (125 ml/4 fl oz) milk
3/4 cup (185 ml/6 fl oz) thick (double/heavy) cream

ECCLES CAKES
These spicy currant pastries originated in the British town of Eccles in Lancashire. They were traditionally made during the *Eccles Wakes* festival and today are still a favourite. The puff pastry round is rolled thinly so that the enclosed filling will show through when the pastry is cooked. They can be made with shortcrust pastry but whichever pastry is used they are always sprinkled with sugar before baking and are best eaten warm straight from the oven.

RIGHT: Eccles cakes

LAMINGTONS

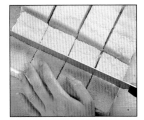

Using a serrated knife, carefully cut the filled cake into 16 squares.

Use two forks to lower each piece of cake into the icing and roll it around to cover all sides.

Roll the iced cake in coconut to thoroughly cover it, then place on a wire rack.

Icing

4 cups (500 g/1 lb) icing (confectioners') sugar

1/3 cup (40 g/1 1/4 oz) cocoa powder

30 g (1 oz) unsalted butter, melted

2/3 cup (170 ml/5 1/2 fl oz) milk

3 cups (270 g/9 oz) desiccated coconut

1 Preheat the oven to moderate 180°C (350°F/Gas 4). Lightly grease a shallow 23 cm (9 inch) square cake tin and line the base and sides with baking paper.

2 Sift the flour and cornflour into a large bowl. Add the butter, sugar, vanilla essence, eggs and milk. Using electric beaters, beat on low speed for 1 minute, or until the ingredients are just moistened. Increase the speed to high and beat for 3 minutes, or until free of lumps and increased in volume. Pour into the tin and smooth the surface. Bake for 50–55 minutes, or until a skewer comes out clean when inserted in the centre. Leave in the tin for 3 minutes before turning out onto a wire rack to cool.

3 Using a serrated knife, trim the top of the cake until flat. Trim the crusts from the sides, then cut the cake in half horizontally. Using electric beaters, beat the cream in a small bowl until stiff peaks form. Place the first layer of cake on a board and spread it evenly with cream. Place the remaining cake layer on top. Cut the cake into 16 squares.

4 For the icing, sift the icing sugar and cocoa into a heatproof bowl and add the butter and milk. Stand the bowl over a saucepan of simmering water, stirring, until the icing is smooth and glossy, then remove from the heat. Place 1 cup (90 g/3 oz) of the coconut on a sheet of baking paper. Using two forks, roll a piece of cake in chocolate icing, then hold the cake over a bowl and allow the excess to drain. (Add 1 tablespoon boiling water to the icing if it seems too thick.) Roll the cake in coconut, then place on a wire rack. Repeat with the remaining cake, adding extra coconut for rolling as needed.

NOTE: If you cook the cake a day ahead, it will be easier to cut and won't crumble as much. Lamingtons are not necessarily cream filled, so if you prefer, you can ice unfilled squares of cake.

ABOVE: Lamingtons

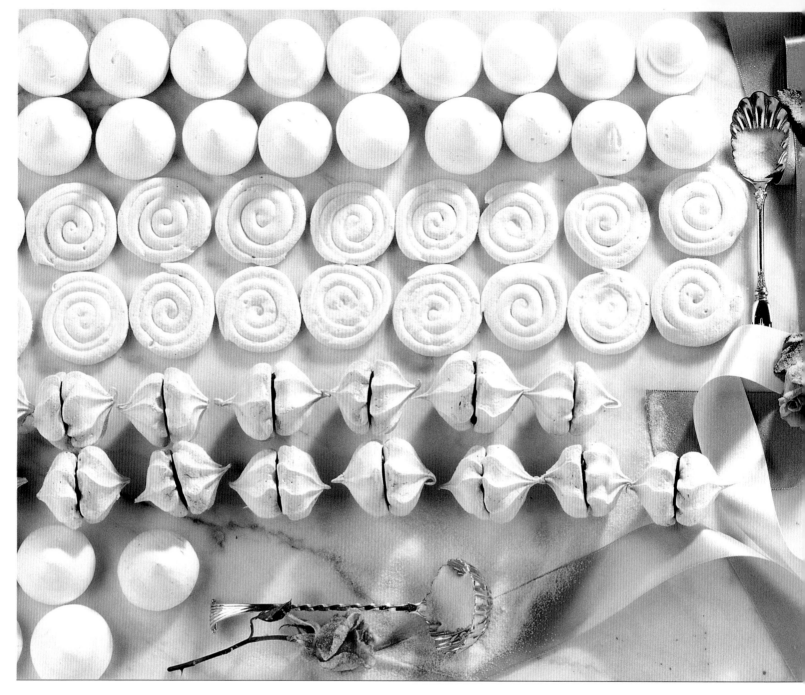

MERINGUES

Just two ingredients are all that you require to make a basic mixture for meringues. When egg white and sugar are beaten together, then baked, they miraculously turn into crunchy, delicate delights.

BASIC MERINGUE RECIPE

Preheat the oven to slow 150°C (300°F/ Gas 2) and line two baking trays with baking paper. Beat 2 egg whites into stiff peaks in a small dry bowl with electric beaters. Add ½ cup (125 g/4 oz) caster (superfine) sugar, 1 tablespoon at a time, beating well after each addition. Beat until the mixture is thick and glossy and the sugar has dissolved (this will take up to 10 minutes). Spoon into a piping bag and pipe small shapes onto the trays. Bake for 20–25 minutes, or until pale and dry. Turn off the oven, leave the door ajar and cool the meringues in the oven. When cold, store in an airtight jar. Makes 30.

CUSTARD DISCS

Make the basic meringue mixture until it is thick and glossy, then beat in 1 tablespoon custard powder. Spoon the mixture into a piping bag with a plain 5 mm (¼ inch) or 1 cm (½ inch) nozzle. Pipe spirals onto trays and bake as above. Dust with icing (confectioners') sugar. Makes 40.

COFFEE KISSES

Prepare the basic meringue mixture until it is thick and glossy, then beat in 2–3 teaspoons instant coffee powder. Spoon the mixture into a piping bag fitted with a small star nozzle and pipe onto the trays. Bake as for the basic recipe. Coffee kisses are delicious if served as is or sandwiched together with 60 g (2 oz) melted chocolate. Makes 30.

CHOCOLATE FINGERS

Prepare the basic meringue mixture until it is thick and glossy, then beat in 1 tablespoon sifted cocoa powder. Spoon the mixture into a piping bag fitted with a plain round nozzle and pipe fine 8 cm (3 inch) lengths onto

lined trays, allowing room for spreading. Bake as for the basic recipe and serve as they are, or drizzled with melted chocolate or lightly dusted with dark cocoa powder combined with a little icing (confectioners') sugar. Makes 40.

HAZELNUT SNAILS

Prepare the basic meringue mixture until it is thick and glossy. Gently beat in 2 tablespoons ground hazelnuts. Spoon the mixture into a piping bag fitted with a plain 1 cm (1/2 inch) nozzle and pipe in fine short zigzag lengths onto the trays. Bake as for the basic recipe. These can be served lightly dusted with a mixture of icing (confectioners') sugar and ground cinnamon, or drizzled with melted chocolate. Makes 30.

MERINGUE NESTS

Prepare the basic meringue mixture until it is thick and glossy. Spoon into a piping bag fitted with a star nozzle and pipe into nests on the trays. Bake as for the basic recipe. Meringue nests are delicious if filled with whipped cream flavoured with coffee or chocolate liqueur, topped with a chocolate-coated coffee bean. They can also be filled with a chocolate truffle mixture and topped with a slice of strawberry. Makes 40.

LEFT PAGE, FROM TOP: Basic meringues; Custard discs; Coffee kisses; Basic meringues
ABOVE PAGE, FROM LEFT: Chocolate fingers; Hazelnut snails; Meringue nests

1 Preheat the oven to moderate 180°C (350°F/ Gas 4). Lightly grease a 20 cm (8 inch) square cake tin and line with baking paper.
2 Cream the butter and sugars in a small bowl with electric beaters until light and fluffy. Add the eggs gradually, beating thoroughly after each addition. Beat in the vanilla and jam. Transfer to a large bowl. Using a metal spoon, gently fold in the combined sifted flour, cocoa and soda alternately with the milk. Stir until the mixture is just combined and almost smooth.
3 Pour into the tin and smooth the surface. Bake for 45 minutes, or until a skewer comes out clean. Leave in the tin for 15 minutes before turning onto a wire rack to cool completely.
4 For the buttercream, stir the ingredients in a small pan over low heat until smooth and glossy. Spread over the top with a flat-bladed knife.

CINNAMON TEACAKE

Preparation time: 20 minutes
Total cooking time: 30 minutes
Makes I

60 g (2 oz) unsalted butter, softened
1/2 cup (125 g/4 oz) caster (superfine) sugar
I egg, lightly beaten
I teaspoon vanilla essence
3/4 cup (90 g/3 oz) self-raising flour
1/4 cup (30 g/I oz) plain (all-purpose) flour
1/2 cup (125 ml/4 fl oz) milk

Topping

20 g (3/4 oz) unsalted butter, melted
I tablespoon caster (superfine) sugar
I teaspoon ground cinnamon

I Preheat the oven to moderate 180°C (350°F/ Gas 4). Grease a 20 cm (8 inch) round shallow cake tin and line the base with baking paper.
2 Cream the butter and sugar in a small bowl with electric beaters until light and fluffy. Gradually add the egg, beating well after each addition. Beat in the vanilla, then transfer to a large bowl. Using a metal spoon, fold in the sifted flours alternately with the milk. Stir until smooth. Spoon into the tin and bake for 30 minutes, or until a skewer comes out clean. Leave in the tin for 5 minutes before turning out onto a wire rack. Brush the warm cake with butter and sprinkle with sugar and cinnamon.

CHOCOLATE CAKE

Preparation time: 25 minutes
Total cooking time: 50 minutes
Makes I

125 g (4 oz) unsalted butter, softened
1/2 cup (125 g/4 oz) caster (superfine) sugar
1/3 cup (40 g/1 1/4 oz) icing (confectioners') sugar
2 eggs, lightly beaten
I teaspoon vanilla essence
1/4 cup (80 g/2 3/4 oz) blackberry jam
1 1/4 cups (155 g/5 oz) self-raising flour
1/2 cup (60 g/2 oz) cocoa powder
I teaspoon bicarbonate of soda
I cup (250 ml/8 fl oz) milk

Chocolate buttercream

50 g (1 3/4 oz) dark chocolate, finely chopped
25 g (3/4 oz) unsalted butter
3 teaspoons cream
3 tablespoons icing (confectioners') sugar, sifted

ABOVE: Chocolate cake

GINGER CAKE

Preparation time: 30 minutes
Total cooking time: I hour
Makes I

125 g (4 oz) unsalted butter
1/2 cup (175 g/6 oz) black treacle
1/2 cup (175 g/6 oz) golden syrup
1 1/2 cups (185 g/6 oz) plain (all-purpose) flour
1 cup (125 g/4 oz) self-raising flour
1 teaspoon bicarbonate of soda
3 teaspoons ground ginger
1 teaspoon mixed spice
1/4 teaspoon ground cinnamon
3/4 cup (165 g/5 1/2 oz) firmly packed
　 soft brown sugar
1 cup (250 ml/8 fl oz) milk
2 eggs, lightly beaten
glacé ginger, optional, to decorate

Lemon and ginger icing

2 cups (250 g/8 oz) icing (confectioners') sugar
1 teaspoon ground ginger
30 g (1 oz) unsalted butter, melted
3 teaspoons milk
3 teaspoons lemon juice
1 teaspoon lemon rind

1 Preheat the oven to moderate 180°C (350°F/ Gas 4). Lightly grease a deep 20 cm (8 inch) square cake tin and line the base with baking paper.
2 Combine the butter, treacle and golden syrup in a saucepan and stir over low heat until the butter has melted. Remove from the heat.
3 Sift the flours, bicarbonate of soda and spices into a large bowl, add the sugar and stir until well combined. Make a well in the centre. Add the butter mixture to the well, then pour in the combined milk and eggs. Stir with a wooden spoon until the mixture is smooth and well combined. Pour into the tin and smooth the surface. Bake for 45–60 minutes, or until a skewer comes out clean when inserted in the centre of the cake. Leave in the tin for 20 minutes before turning out onto a wire rack to cool.
4 For the lemon and ginger icing, sift the icing sugar into a small heatproof bowl and stir in the ground ginger, butter, milk, lemon juice and rind until the mixture forms a smooth paste.

Stand the bowl over a saucepan of simmering water, making sure the base of the bowl does not touch the water. Stir until smooth and glossy, then remove from the heat. Spread over the cake with a flat-bladed knife. Decorate the top with glacé ginger, if desired.
NOTES: If black treacle is unavailable, you can substitute the same amount of golden syrup.
　This delicious ginger cake can be served the day it is baked but it is best served two or three days after baking so the flavours have time to develop. It will store well for up to a week in an airtight container, or can be frozen, un-iced, for up to three months. It can also be served un-iced and decorated by lightly dusting the top with sifted icing sugar.

BELOW: Ginger cake

CARROT CAKE

Preparation time: 40 minutes
Total cooking time: 1 hour 30 minutes
Makes 1

1 cup (125 g/4 oz) self-raising flour
1 cup (125 g/4 oz) plain (all-purpose) flour
2 teaspoons ground cinnamon
1 teaspoon ground ginger
1/2 teaspoon ground nutmeg
1 teaspoon bicarbonate of soda
1 cup (250 ml/8 fl oz) oil
1 cup (185 g/6 oz) soft brown sugar
4 eggs
1/2 cup (175 g/6 oz) golden syrup
2 1/2 cups (400 g/13 oz) grated carrot
1/2 cup (60 g/2 oz) chopped pecans or walnuts

Lemon icing

175 g (6 oz) cream cheese, softened
60 g (2 oz) butter, softened
1 1/2 cups (185 g/6 oz) icing (confectioners') sugar
1 teaspoon vanilla essence
1–2 teaspoons lemon juice

1 Preheat the oven to warm 160°C (315°F/Gas 2–3). Lightly grease a 23 cm (9 inch) round cake tin and line the base and side with baking paper.
2 Sift the flours, spices and soda into a large bowl and make a well in the centre.
3 Whisk together the oil, sugar, eggs and golden syrup in a jug until combined. Add this mixture to the well in the flour and gradually stir into the dry ingredients with a metal spoon until smooth. Stir in the carrot and nuts, then spoon into the tin and smooth the surface. Bake for 1 hour 30 minutes, or until a skewer comes out clean when inserted into the centre of the cake.
4 Leave the cake in the tin for at least 15 minutes before turning out onto a wire rack to cool completely.
5 For the lemon icing, beat the cream cheese and butter with electric beaters until smooth. Gradually add the icing sugar alternately with the vanilla and lemon juice, beating until light and creamy. Spread the icing over the cooled cake using a flat-bladed knife. Can be sprinkled with freshly grated nutmeg.
NOTE: If you prefer, you can cut the cake in half horizontally, then sandwich the layers together with half the icing.

ORANGE CAKE

Preparation time: 15 minutes
Total cooking time: 50 minutes
Makes 1

2 cups (250 g/8 oz) self-raising flour
1/3 cup (40 g/1 1/4 oz) custard powder
1 1/3 cups (340 g/11 oz) caster (superfine) sugar
80 g (2 3/4 oz) unsalted butter, chopped
  and softened
3 eggs
2 teaspoons finely grated orange rind
1 cup (250 ml/8 fl oz) orange juice

Orange buttercream

3/4 cup (90 g/3 oz) icing (confectioners') sugar
125 g (4 oz) unsalted butter, softened
1 tablespoon orange juice
1 teaspoon finely grated orange rind

1 Preheat the oven to moderate 180°C (350°F/Gas 4). Lightly grease the base and side of a 23 cm (9 inch) round cake tin and line the base with baking paper.
2 Sift the flour and custard powder into a large bowl and add the sugar, butter, egg, orange rind and juice. Beat with electric beaters for 4 minutes, or until the mixture is smooth.
3 Spoon the mixture into the tin and smooth the surface. Bake for 50 minutes, or until a skewer comes out clean when inserted into the centre of the cake.
4 Leave the cake in the tin for 5 minutes before turning out onto a wire rack to cool completely.
5 For the orange buttercream, beat all the ingredients in a small bowl with electric beaters until smooth and creamy. Spread evenly over the cooled cake.
VARIATION: You can also make a cream cheese topping for this cake. Mix 125 g (4 oz) of softened cream cheese with 2 tablespoons icing (confectioners') sugar until well blended and spread over the top of the cake.

CITRUS RIND
The rind from any citrus fruit, including oranges, lemons and limes, is also known as the zest. It contains essential oils that impart an intense flavour. The rind is removed with a fine grater or zester. Remove the coloured area only as the white pith just under the rind has a bitter flavour. You can also extract the citrus oils by rubbing a sugar cube firmly over the fruit until the sugar cube becomes moist and coloured with the oils.

*OPPOSITE PAGE,
FROM TOP: Carrot cake;
Orange cake*

BANANA CAKE

Preparation time: 20 minutes
Total cooking time: 1 hour
Makes 1

★

125 g (4 oz) unsalted butter, softened
1/2 cup (125 g/4 oz) caster (superfine) sugar
2 eggs, lightly beaten
1 teaspoon vanilla essence
4 ripe medium bananas, mashed
1 teaspoon bicarbonate of soda
1/2 cup (125 ml/4 fl oz) milk
2 cups (250 g/8 oz) self-raising flour, sifted
1/2 teaspoon ground mixed spice

Butter frosting

125 g (4 oz) unsalted butter, softened
3/4 cup (90 g/3 oz) icing (confectioners') sugar
1 tablespoon lemon juice
1/4 cup (15 g/1/2 oz) flaked coconut, toasted

1 Preheat the oven to moderate 180°C (350°F/ Gas 4). Lightly grease a 20 cm (8 inch) round cake tin and line the base with baking paper.
2 Cream the butter and sugar in a small bowl with electric beaters until light and fluffy. Add the egg gradually, beating thoroughly after each addition. Add the vanilla and banana and beat until combined. Transfer to a large bowl.
3 Dissolve the soda in the milk. Using a metal spoon, gently fold the sifted flour and mixed spice alternately with the milk into the banana mixture. Stir until all the ingredients are just combined and the mixture is smooth. Spoon into the prepared tin and smooth the surface. Bake for 1 hour, or until a skewer comes out clean when inserted into the centre of the cake.
4 Leave the cake in the tin for 10 minutes before turning out onto a wire rack to cool completely.
5 For the frosting, beat the butter, icing sugar and lemon juice with electric beaters until smooth and creamy. Spread over the cooled cake using a flat-bladed knife and sprinkle with toasted coconut flakes.
NOTE: Very ripe bananas are best for this recipe as they have the most developed flavour.

BANANAS

Native to Southeast Asia, bananas are now grown in many other places that have a warm climate. There are many varieties but the most common are Cavendish and Lady Finger. Bananas can be purchased green and will slowly ripen. If you need to hurry up the ripening process, place the green bananas in a brown paper bag with a ripe banana or apple. For baking purposes a very ripe, or even an over-ripe banana, is very useful. An over-ripe banana adds an intense banana flavour to baked cakes, muffins and ice cream.

RIGHT: Banana cake

MADEIRA CAKE

Preparation time: 20 minutes
Total cooking time: 50 minutes
Makes 1

185 g (6 oz) unsalted butter, softened
3/4 cup (185 g/6 oz) caster (superfine) sugar
3 eggs, lightly beaten
2 teaspoons finely grated orange
   or lemon rind
1 1/4 cups (155 g/5 oz) self-raising flour,
   sifted
1 cup (125 g/4 oz) plain (all-purpose) flour
2 tablespoons milk

1 Preheat the oven to warm 160°C (315°F/ Gas 2–3). Lightly grease a loaf tin with a base measuring 20 x 10 x 7 cm (8 x 4 x 2¾ inches) and line the base and sides with baking paper.
2 Cream the butter and sugar in a small bowl with electric beaters until light and fluffy. Add the egg gradually, beating thoroughly after each addition. Add the rind and beat until combined. Transfer to a large bowl. Using a metal spoon, fold in the flour and milk. Stir until smooth.
3 Spoon into the loaf tin and smooth the surface. Bake for 50 minutes, or until a skewer comes out clean when inserted in the centre of the cake. Cool the cake in the tin for 10 minutes before turning out onto a wire rack to cool completely.
NOTE: This cake keeps well in an airtight container for up to a week.

MADEIRA CAKE
Also known as Pound cake. This rich butter cake was popular in Victorian England. It was often served with a glass of Madeira, hence the name. It is a moist tender cake due to the high butter content. Often, citrus rind is added, or a slice of candied citrus peel is placed on top as a decoration, but usually it is kept fairly plain so as not to mask the delicious buttery flavour.

ABOVE: Madeira cake

539

CHOCOLATE MUD CAKE

Preparation time: 30 minutes
Total cooking time: 2 hours
Makes 1

250 g (8 oz) unsalted butter
250 g (8 oz) dark chocolate, chopped
2 tablespoons instant coffee powder
150 g (5 oz) self-raising flour
150 g (5 oz) plain (all-purpose) flour
1/2 cup (60 g/2 oz) cocoa powder
1/2 teaspoon bicarbonate of soda
2 1/4 cups (550 g/1 lb 2 oz) caster (superfine) sugar
4 eggs, lightly beaten
2 tablespoons oil
1/2 cup (125 ml/4 fl oz) buttermilk

Icing

150 g (5 oz) unsalted butter, chopped
150 g (5 oz) dark chocolate, chopped

ABOVE: Chocolate mud cake

1 Preheat the oven to warm 160°C (315°F/ Gas 2–3). Lightly grease a deep 22 cm (9 inch) round cake tin and line with baking paper, making sure the paper around the side extends at least 5 cm (2 inches) above the top edge.
2 Put the butter, chocolate and coffee in a pan with 3/4 cup (185 ml/6 oz) hot water and stir over low heat until smooth. Remove from the heat.
3 Sift the flours, cocoa and bicarbonate of soda into a large bowl. Stir in the sugar and make a well in the centre. Add the combined eggs, oil and buttermilk and, using a large metal spoon, slowly stir into the dry ingredients. Gradually stir in the butter mixture.
4 Pour the mixture (it will be quite wet) into the tin and bake for 1 3/4 hours. Test the centre with a skewer—the skewer may be slightly wet. Remove the cake from the oven. If the top looks raw, bake for another 5–10 minutes, then remove. Leave in the tin until completely cold, then turn out and wrap in plastic wrap.
5 For the icing, combine the butter and chocolate in a saucepan and stir over low heat until the butter and chocolate are melted. Remove and cool slightly. Pour over the cake and allow it to run down the side.
NOTE: Refrigerate in an airtight container for up to three weeks or in a cool dry place for up to a week. Freeze for up to two months. For a 20 cm (8 inch) round cake, bake for 2 hours.

APPLE AND SPICE TEACAKE

Preparation time: 30 minutes
Total cooking time: 1 hour
Makes 1

★

180 g (6 oz) unsalted butter, softened
1/2 cup (95 g/3 oz) soft brown sugar
2 teaspoons finely grated lemon rind
3 eggs, lightly beaten
1 cup (125 g/4 oz) self-raising flour
1/2 cup (75 g/2 1/2 oz) wholemeal flour
1/2 teaspoon ground cinnamon
1/2 cup (125 ml/4 fl oz) milk
410 g (13 oz) can pie apple
1/4 teaspoon ground mixed spice
1 tablespoon soft brown sugar, extra
1/4 cup (25 g/3/4 oz) flaked almonds

1 Preheat the oven to moderate 180°C (350°F/Gas 4). Grease the base and side of a 20 cm (8 inch) springform pan, and line the base with baking paper.
2 Cream the butter and sugar in a small bowl with electric beaters until light and fluffy. Beat in the lemon rind. Add the eggs gradually, beating thoroughly after each addition.
3 Transfer the mixture to a large bowl. Using a metal spoon, fold in the sifted flours and cinnamon alternately with the milk. Stir until the mixture is just combined and almost smooth.
4 Spoon half the mixture into the tin, top with three-quarters of the pie apple, then the remaining cake mixture. Press the remaining pie apple around the edge of the top. Combine the mixed spice, extra sugar and flaked almonds and sprinkle over the cake.
5 Bake for 1 hour, or until a skewer comes out clean when inserted into the centre of the cake. Leave in the tin for 15 minutes before turning out onto a wire rack to cool.
NOTE: Pie apricots can be used instead of apples, if preferred.

APPLE AND SPICE TEACAKE

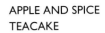
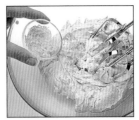

Cream the butter and sugar, then add the grated lemon rind.

Spoon apple onto half the batter and then top with the remaining batter.

The cake is cooked when a skewer inserted into the centre comes out clean.

LEFT: Apple and spice teacake

POUND CAKE

This fine-textured, buttery cake, dating back to the eighteenth century, is made in a loaf tin and was originally based on pound (pre-metric) measures of one pound each of butter, sugar, eggs and flour. The butter and sugar are well creamed before beating in the eggs and folding in the flour. Vanilla or grated citrus rind are added for extra flavour. Ground almonds and dried fruit such as sultanas are sometimes added but this is not traditional.

OPPOSITE PAGE, FROM LEFT: Lemon cake with crunchy topping; Pound cake

LEMON CAKE WITH CRUNCHY TOPPING

Preparation time: 25 minutes
Total cooking time: 1 hour 20 minutes
Makes 1

250 g (8 oz) unsalted butter, softened
200 g (6 1/2 oz) caster (superfine) sugar
2 teaspoons finely grated lemon rind
4 eggs, lightly beaten
2 cups (250 g/8 oz) self-raising flour
1 teaspoon baking powder
2 tablespoons lemon juice

Topping

1/2 cup (125 g/4 oz) sugar
1/4 cup (60 ml/2 3/4 fl oz) lemon juice

1 Preheat the oven to warm 170°C (325°F/ Gas 3). Lightly grease a 22 cm (9 inch) square tin and line the base with baking paper.
2 Cream the butter and sugar in a small bowl with electric beaters until the mixture is light and fluffy. Beat in the lemon rind, then add the egg gradually, beating thoroughly after each addition. Transfer the mixture to a large bowl. Using a large metal spoon, fold in the combined sifted flour, baking powder and 1/4 teaspoon salt, as well as the lemon juice. Stir until the mixture is just combined and almost smooth.
3 Spoon the mixture into the tin and smooth the surface. Bake for 1 hour 20 minutes, or until a skewer comes out clean when inserted into the centre of the cake. Remove from the tin and turn out onto a wire rack.
4 For the topping, mix together the sugar and lemon juice (do not dissolve the sugar), and quickly brush over the top of the warm cake. The juice will sink into the cake, and the sugar will form a crunchy topping. Leave to cool.

POUND CAKE

Preparation time: 25 minutes
Total cooking time: 1 hour
Makes 1

375 g (12 oz) unsalted butter, softened
1 1/2 cups (375 g/12 oz) caster (superfine) sugar
1 teaspoon vanilla essence
6 eggs, lightly beaten
3 cups (375 g/12 oz) plain (all-purpose) flour, sifted
1 teaspoon baking powder
1/4 cup (60 ml/4 fl oz) milk
icing (confectioners') sugar, to dust

1 Preheat the oven to moderate 180°C (350°F/ Gas 4). Lightly grease the base and side of a 22 cm (9 inch) round cake tin and line the base with baking paper.
2 Cream the butter and sugar in a small bowl with electric beaters until the mixture is light and fluffy. Beat in the vanilla essence, then add the eggs gradually, beating thoroughly after each addition. Transfer to a large bowl. Using a metal spoon, fold in the sifted flour and baking powder alternately with the milk. Do this in three or four lots. Stir until the mixture is just combined and almost smooth.
3 Spoon the mixture into the tin and smooth the surface. Bake for 1 hour, or until a skewer comes out clean when inserted into the centre of the cake. Leave in the tin for 10 minutes before turning out onto a wire rack to cool. Lightly dust the top with icing sugar just before serving.
VARIATIONS: This cake can be used as a base to make many variations in flavour.
   To make orange pound cake, add 2 tablespoons finely grated orange rind to the butter and use 1/4 cup (60 ml/2 fl oz) orange juice instead of the milk.
   To make coconut pound cake, add 1 cup (90 g/3 oz) desiccated coconut before folding in the flour and milk.
   To make hazelnut pound cake, add 125 g (4 oz) chopped toasted hazelnuts before folding in the flour. Dissolve 2 teaspoons instant coffee powder in the milk.

CREAM

Cream is used extensively in baking either as part of the baking mixture, or whipped to use as a decoration. It adds richness, moistness and flavour to the finished product. Cream needs to contain at least thirty per cent fat to be whipped successfully. When whipping cream, have the cream cold straight from the fridge. Ideally, pour it into a cold metal bowl and beat over a basin of cold water. Use ice cubes in the water in hot weather. Beat until stiff but take care not to overbeat or the cream will curdle. If you like, you can flavour beaten cream with a teaspoon each of icing (confectioners') sugar and vanilla.

ABOVE: Classic sponge

CLASSIC SPONGE

Preparation time: 20 minutes
Total cooking time: 25 minutes
Makes 1 layered sponge

75 g (2 1/2 oz) plain (all-purpose) flour
150 g (5 oz) self-raising flour
6 eggs
220 g (7 oz) caster (superfine) sugar
1/2 cup (160 g/5 1/2 oz) strawberry jam
1 cup (250 ml/8 fl oz) cream
icing (confectioners') sugar, to dust

1 Preheat the oven to moderate 180°C (350°F/ Gas 4). Lightly grease two 22 cm (9 inch) sandwich tins or round cake tins and line the bases with baking paper. Dust the tins with a little flour, shaking off any excess.
2 Sift the flours together three times onto a sheet of greaseproof paper. Beat the eggs in a large bowl with electric beaters for 7 minutes, or until thick and pale. Gradually add the sugar to the egg, beating well after each addition. Using a large metal spoon, quickly and gently fold in the sifted flour and 2 tablespoons boiling water.
3 Spread the mixture evenly into the tins and bake for 25 minutes, or until the sponges are lightly golden and shrink slightly from the sides of the tins. Leave the sponges in their tins for 5 minutes before turning out onto a wire rack to cool.
4 Spread jam over one of the sponges. Beat the cream in a small bowl until stiff, then spoon into a piping bag and pipe rosettes over the jam. Place the other sponge on top. Dust with icing sugar.
NOTES: The secret to making a perfect sponge lies in the folding technique. A beating action, or using a wooden spoon, will cause loss of volume in the egg mixture and result in a flat, heavy cake.

Unfilled sponges can be frozen for up to one month—freeze in separate freezer bags. Thaw at room temperature for about 20 minutes.

GENOISE SPONGE

Preparation time: 25 minutes
Total cooking time: 25 minutes
Makes 1

2¹/₃ cups (290 g/10 oz) plain (all-purpose) flour
8 eggs
220 g (7 oz) caster (superfine) sugar
100 g (3¹/₂ oz) unsalted butter, melted

1 Preheat the oven to moderate 180°C (350°F/ Gas 4). Lightly grease one 25 cm (10 inch) Genoise tin or two shallow 22 cm (9 inch) round cake tins with melted butter. Line the base with baking paper, then grease the paper. Dust the tin with a little flour, shaking off any excess.
2 Sift the flour three times onto baking paper.

Mix the eggs and sugar in a large heatproof bowl. Place the bowl over a pan of simmering water, making sure the base doesn't touch the water, and beat with electric beaters for 8 minutes, or until the mixture is thick and fluffy and a ribbon of mixture drawn in a figure of eight doesn't sink immediately. Remove from the heat and beat for 3 minutes, or until slightly cooled.
3 Add the cooled butter and sifted flour. Using a large metal spoon, fold in quickly and lightly until the mixture is just combined.
4 Spread the mixture evenly into the tin. Bake for 25 minutes, or until the sponge is lightly golden and has shrunk slightly from the side of the tin. Leave the cake in the tin for 5 minutes before turning out onto a wire rack to cool. The top can be lightly dusted with sifted icing (confectioners') sugar just before serving.

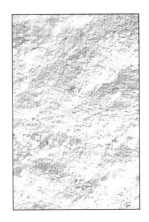

GENOISE SPONGE
The Genoise sponge is traditionally made in a tin with sloping sides and served dusted with icing (confectioners') sugar. However, it is often baked to be used for a decorated gateau or celebration cake, in which case it is generally baked in two sandwich tins. In this case, you can ensure you have exactly half the mixture in each tin by weighing each tin first, then dividing the mixture between the tins before weighing the tins again to make sure they are equal.

LEFT: Genoise sponge

CHOCOLATE SWISS ROLL

Preparation time: 25 minutes
+ 30 minutes chilling
Total cooking time: 12 minutes
Makes 1

★ ★

3 eggs

1/2 cup (125 g/4 oz) caster (superfine) sugar

1/4 cup (30 g/1 oz) plain (all-purpose) flour

2 tablespoons cocoa powder

1 cup (250 ml/8 fl oz) cream

1 tablespoon icing (confectioners') sugar, plus
extra, to dust

1/2 teaspoon vanilla essence

1 Preheat the oven to moderately hot 200°C (400°F/Gas 6). Lightly grease the base and sides of a 30 x 25 x 2 cm (12 x 10 x 3/4 inch) swiss roll tin. Line the base with baking paper, extending over the two long sides.

2 Beat the eggs and 1/3 cup (90 g/3 oz) caster sugar in a small bowl with electric beaters until thick and creamy. Using a metal spoon, gently fold in the combined sifted flour and cocoa.
3 Spread the mixture into the tin and smooth the surface. Bake for 10–12 minutes, or until the cake is just set. Meanwhile, place a clean tea towel on a work surface, cover with baking paper and sprinkle with the remaining caster sugar. When the cake is cooked, turn it out immediately onto the sugar. Roll the cake up from the short side, rolling the paper inside the roll and using the tea towel as a guide. Stand the rolled cake on a wire rack for 5 minutes, then carefully unroll and allow the cake to cool to room temperature. Trim the ends with a knife.
4 Beat the cream, icing sugar and vanilla essence until stiff peaks form. Spread the cream over the cooled cake, leaving a 1 cm (1/2 inch) border all around. Re-roll the cake, using the paper as a guide. Place the roll, seam-side-down, on a tray. Refrigerate, covered, for 30 minutes. Lightly dust the top of the swiss roll with icing sugar before cutting into slices to serve.

BELOW: Chocolate swiss roll

SWISS ROLL

Preparation time: 25 minutes
Total cooking time: 12 minutes
Makes 1

★

3/4 cup (90 g/3 oz) self-raising flour

3 eggs, lightly beaten

3/4 cup (185 g/6 oz) caster (superfine) sugar

1/2 cup (160 g/5 1/2 oz) strawberry jam

1 Preheat the oven to moderately hot 190°C (375°F/Gas 5). Lightly grease a shallow 30 x 25 x 2 cm (12 x 10 x 3/4 inch) swiss roll tin and line the base with baking paper, extending over the two long sides. Sift the flour three times onto baking paper.
2 Beat the eggs with electric beaters in a small bowl for 5 minutes, or until thick and pale. Add 1/2 cup (125 g/4 oz) of the sugar gradually, beating constantly until the mixture is pale and glossy.
3 Transfer to a large bowl. Using a metal spoon, fold in the flour quickly and lightly. Spread into the tin and smooth the surface. Bake for 10–12 minutes, or until lightly golden and springy to touch. Meanwhile, place a clean tea towel on a work surface, cover with baking paper and lightly sprinkle with the remaining caster sugar. When the cake is cooked, turn it

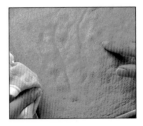

Add the sugar gradually to the eggs, beating until pale and glossy.

Bake the cake until lightly golden on top and springy to touch.

Roll up the cake with baking paper, using the tea towel as a guide.

out immediately onto the sugar.

4 Using the tea towel as a guide, carefully roll the cake up from the short side, rolling the paper inside the roll. Stand the rolled cake on a wire rack for 5 minutes, then carefully unroll and allow the cake to cool to room temperature. Spread with the jam and re-roll. Trim the ends with a knife.

NOTE: To make the jam easier to spread, beat it in a bowl with a fork for 30 seconds.

HONEY CREAM ROLL

Preparation time: 40 minutes
Total cooking time: 12 minutes
Makes 1

 ★ ★

3/4 cup (90 g/3 oz) self-raising flour

2 teaspoons mixed spice

3 eggs

2/3 cup (125 g/4 oz) soft brown sugar

1/4 cup (25 g/3/4 oz) desiccated coconut

Honey cream

125 g (4 oz) unsalted butter, softened

1/3 cup (40 g/1 1/4 oz) icing (confectioners') sugar

2 tablespoons honey

1 Preheat the oven to moderately hot 190°C (375°F/Gas 5). Lightly grease a 30 x 25 x 2 cm (12 x 10 x 3/4 inch) swiss roll tin and line the base with baking paper, extending over the two long sides. Sift the flour and mixed spice three times onto a sheet of baking paper.

2 Beat the eggs with electric beaters in a large bowl for 5 minutes, or until thick, frothy and pale. Add the sugar gradually, beating constantly until the sugar is dissolved and the mixture is pale and glossy. Using a metal spoon, fold in the flour quickly and lightly. Spread into the tin and smooth the surface. Bake for 10–12 minutes, or until the cake is lightly golden and springy to touch. Meanwhile, place a clean tea towel on a work surface, cover with baking paper and sprinkle the paper with coconut. Turn the cooked cake out onto the coconut.

3 Using the tea towel as a guide, carefully roll up the cake, along with the paper, from the short side. Leave until cool.

4 Beat the honey cream ingredients with electric beaters in a bowl until the mixture is light and creamy and the sugar has dissolved. Unroll the cake and discard the paper. Spread with the honey cream and re-roll. Trim the ends with a knife.

NOTE: Swiss roll cake mixtures contain little fat so they dry out quickly. They need a moist filling, which is usually made with cream or buttercream.

ABOVE: Honey cream roll

DEVIL'S FOOD CAKE

This is rich, moist and chocolaty, quite the opposite to the angel food cake. The dark colour contrasts with the white of the angel food cake. The devil's food cake is supposedly sinful because it is so rich. It is filled in the centre and coated, either on top or all over, with whipped cream or a white or chocolate icing. This cake always contains bicarbonate of soda which helps darken the cake.

ABOVE: Devil's food cake

DEVIL'S FOOD CAKE

Preparation time: 30 minutes
Total cooking time: 35 minutes
Makes 1 layered cake

1¹/2 cups (280 g/9 oz) soft brown sugar

¹/3 cup (40 g/1¹/4 oz) cocoa powder

1 cup (250 ml/8 fl oz) milk

90 g (3 oz) dark chocolate, chopped

125 g (4 oz) unsalted butter, softened

1 teaspoon vanilla essence

2 eggs, separated

1¹/2 cups (185 g/6 oz) plain (all-purpose) flour

1 teaspoon bicarbonate of soda

Rich chocolate icing

50 g (1³/4 oz) dark chocolate, chopped

30 g (1 oz) unsalted butter

1 tablespoon icing (confectioners') sugar

Filling

1 cup (250 ml/8 fl oz) cream

1 tablespoon icing (confectioners') sugar

1 teaspoon vanilla essence

1 Preheat the oven to warm 160°C (315°F/ Gas 2–3). Lightly grease two deep 20 cm (8 inch) round cake tins and line the bases with baking paper. Combine a third of the brown sugar with the cocoa and milk in a small saucepan. Stir over low heat until the sugar and cocoa have dissolved. Remove from the heat and stir in the chocolate, stirring until it is melted. Cool.
2 Cream the remaining brown sugar with the butter in a small bowl with electric beaters until light and fluffy. Beat in the vanilla and egg yolks and the cooled chocolate mixture. Transfer to a large bowl, and stir in the sifted flour and bicarbonate of soda.
3 Beat the egg whites in a small bowl until soft peaks form. Fold into the chocolate mixture. Divide the mixture evenly between the tins. Bake for 35 minutes, or until a skewer inserted in the centre of the cakes comes out clean.

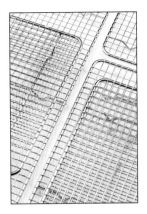

Leave in the tins for 5 minutes before turning out onto a wire rack to cool.

4 For the icing, put the chocolate and butter in a heatproof bowl. Place the bowl over a pan of simmering water, making sure it does not touch the water, and stir until the mixture is melted and smooth. Gradually add the sifted icing sugar and stir until smooth.

5 For the filling, whip the cream, icing sugar and vanilla in a small bowl with electric beaters until stiff peaks form. Spread over one of the cold cakes, top with the second cake and spread with icing, over the top or top and sides.

ANGEL FOOD CAKE

Preparation time: 30 minutes
Total cooking time: 40 minutes
Makes 1

1 cup (125 g/4 oz) self-raising flour
1 1/2 cups (375 g/12 oz) caster (superfine) sugar
12 egg whites
1 1/2 teaspoons cream of tartar
1/2 teaspoon vanilla essence
1/4 teaspoon almond essence
icing (confectioners') sugar, to dust
fresh fruit, sliced or chopped, to serve

1 Preheat the oven to moderate 180°C (350°F/ Gas 4). Have an ungreased angel food tin ready. Sift the flour and 3/4 cup (185 g/6 oz) sugar together four times.

2 Using electric beaters, beat the egg whites with the cream of tartar and 1/4 teaspoon salt until stiff peaks form. Beat in the remaining sugar, 1 tablespoon at a time. Fold in the vanilla and almond essences. Sift a quarter of the flour and sugar mixture onto the egg white and, using a spatula, gradually fold in. Repeat with the remaining flour and sugar.

3 Spoon the mixture into the angel food tin and bake for 35–40 minutes, or until puffed and golden, and a skewer inserted in the centre comes out clean. Turn upside-down on a wire rack and leave in the tin until cool. Gently shake to remove the cake. Lightly dust with icing sugar and serve with fruit.

NOTE: Angel food cake can be served with fresh fruit and whipped or thick (double/heavy) cream as a dessert cake.

ANGEL FOOD CAKE
This is a classic vanilla-flavoured sponge that was devised in America. It is made in a special high central-tubed tin, called an angel food tin, which is available at speciality kitchenware shops. Due to the high egg white content, the cake has a very light texture and is white. Traditionally, the cake is pulled apart with two forks into portions, rather than cutting. The cake is so light it is often difficult to cut neatly. The cake does not freeze well as it contains no fat and will therefore toughen on defrosting. The defrosted cake or leftover stale cake, however, is delicious sliced and toasted.

LEFT: Angel food cake

DARK CHOCOLATE
The seeds from the beans of the cacao tree, native to Central America, are fermented, dried, roasted and then formed into a solidified paste known as bitter unsweetened chocolate. The more bitter the chocolate, the more intense the flavour. Bitter-sweet and semi-sweet chocolates have some sugar added. Couverture chocolate, though very expensive, is considered the best baking chocolate as it is very high quality due to its high cocoa butter content.

OPPOSITE PAGE, FROM TOP: Black forest cake; Flourless chocolate cake

BLACK FOREST CAKE

Preparation time: 1 hour
Total cooking time: 1 hour
Makes 1

 ✿ ✿ ✿

200 g (6½ oz) unsalted butter, softened
¾ cup (185 g/6 oz) caster (superfine) sugar
3 eggs, lightly beaten
1 teaspoon vanilla essence
1²/₃ cups (210 g/7 oz) self-raising flour
¹/₃ cup (40 g/1¼ oz) plain (all-purpose) flour
¾ cup (90 g/3 oz) cocoa powder
1 tablespoon instant coffee powder
½ teaspoon bicarbonate of soda
½ cup (125 ml/4 fl oz) buttermilk
¹/₃ cup (80 ml/2¾ fl oz) milk
1¼ cups (315 ml/10 fl oz) cream, whipped
425 g (14 oz) can pitted cherries, drained
chocolate curls, for decoration

Chocolate topping

300 g (10 oz) dark chocolate, chopped
375 g (12 oz) unsalted butter, softened

1 Preheat the oven to moderate 180°C (350°F/Gas 4). Grease a 23 cm (9 inch) round cake tin and line the base and side with baking paper.
2 Cream the butter and sugar in a small bowl with electric beaters until light and fluffy. Add the egg gradually, beating thoroughly after each addition. Add the vanilla essence and beat until well combined.
3 Transfer the mixture to a large bowl. Using a metal spoon, fold in the sifted flours, cocoa, coffee and soda alternately with the combined buttermilk and milk. Stir until the mixture is just combined and almost smooth.
4 Pour the mixture into the tin and smooth the surface. Bake for 40–50 minutes, or until a skewer comes out clean when inserted into the centre of the cake. Leave the cake in the tin for 20 minutes before turning out onto a wire rack to cool.
5 For the chocolate topping, bring a saucepan of water to the boil and remove from the heat. Place the chocolate in a heatproof bowl and sit the bowl over the pan, making sure the bowl is not touching the water. Allow to stand, stirring occasionally, until the chocolate has melted. Beat the butter in a small bowl until light and creamy. Add the chocolate, beating for 1 minute, or until the mixture is glossy and smooth.

6 Turn the cake upside down and cut into three layers horizontally. Place the first layer on a serving plate. Spread evenly with half the whipped cream, then top with half the cherries. Continue layering with the remaining cake, cream and cherries, ending with the cake on the top. Spread the chocolate topping over the top and side, using a flat-bladed knife. Using a piping bag, pipe swirls with the remaining topping around the cake rim. Decorate with chocolate curls.
NOTE: This cake and its filling are best assembled and eaten on the day that it is made.

FLOURLESS CHOCOLATE CAKE

Preparation time: 20 minutes
Total cooking time: 1 hour 5 minutes
Makes 1

✿

250 g (8 oz) dark cooking chocolate, chopped
100 g (3½ oz) caster (superfine) sugar
100 g (3½ oz) unsalted butter, cubed
1 tablespoon coffee-flavoured liqueur
125 g (4 oz) ground hazelnuts
5 eggs, separated
icing (confectioners') sugar, to dust

1 Preheat the oven to moderate 180°C (350°F/Gas 4). Grease a 23 cm (9 inch) springform tin and line the base with baking paper.
2 Place the cooking chocolate, sugar, butter and liqueur in a heatproof bowl. Bring a small saucepan of water to the boil, then reduce the heat to a gentle simmer. Sit the bowl over the saucepan, making sure the base of the bowl does not touch the water. Stir occasionally to ensure even melting. When fully melted, remove from the heat and mix thoroughly.
3 Transfer the chocolate mixture to a large bowl. Stir in the hazelnuts, then beat in the egg yolks one at a time, mixing well after each addition. In a dry bowl, whisk the egg whites until they form medium stiff peaks. Stir a tablespoonful of the whisked whites into the chocolate, then gently fold in the rest using a large metal spoon or rubber spatula.
4 Pour the mixture into the tin and bake for 50–60 minutes, or until a skewer comes out clean when inserted into the centre of the cake. Leave to cool completely in the tin, before turning out and dusting with icing sugar.

ICINGS AND FROSTINGS

Sweet or piquant, cooked or uncooked, toppings like these help to convert an

unadorned home-made muffin or a simple sweet slice to an outstanding event.

EASY BUTTER CREAM

Using electric beaters, beat 80 g (2¾ oz) soft butter with ½ cup (60 g/2 oz) icing (confectioners') sugar. Flavourings, such as 2 teaspoons of finely grated orange rind, 60 g (2 oz) melted and cooled chocolate, or a few drops of your favourite flavoured essence and some complementary food colouring, can be added if you wish.

CHOCOLATE ICING

Combine 30 g (1 oz) melted butter, 2 tablespoons hot water and 2 tablespoons sifted cocoa powder in a bowl and stir the mixture until it forms a smooth paste. Add 1 cup (125 g/4 oz) sifted icing (confectioners') sugar and stir until the ingredients are well combined and the mixture is quite smooth.

HONEY MOCK CREAM

Using electric beaters, beat 125 g (4 oz) butter with ⅓ cup (90 g/3 oz) caster (superfine) sugar and 2 tablespoons honey until the mixture is light and creamy. Pour cold water onto the mixture, swirl around and pour off. Beat again for 2 minutes, then swirl water over the mixture and pour it off again. Repeat this process four more times until

the mixture is white and creamy and the sugar has completely dissolved. This cream is a delicious topping for spiced cakes or cupcakes.

CITRUS GLACE ICING

Combine 1 cup (125 g/4 oz) sifted icing (confectioners') sugar, 10 g (¼ oz) unsalted butter and 1 teaspoon finely grated citrus rind in a small heatproof bowl. Add about 1–2 tablespoons lemon juice to make a firm paste. Stand the bowl over a pan of simmering water and stir until the icing is smooth and glossy, then remove from the heat. Spread onto cake or biscuits with a long palette knife.

SOFT CITRUS ICING

Combine 1¼ cups (155 g/5 oz) sifted icing (confectioners') sugar, 30 g (1 oz) softened butter, a little grated citrus rind and enough hot water to mix to a thick, smooth paste. Spread over a cake. This mixture is easy to work with as it doesn't set quickly. The same mixture can also be heated in a small bowl over simmering water. Work quickly, using a hot, wet knife for spreading, as the icing will set very quickly.

CREAM CHEESE FROSTING

Chop 185 g (6 oz) cream cheese into small cubes and, using electric beaters, beat until smooth. Add ⅓ cup (40 g/1¼ oz) sifted icing (confectioners') sugar and a couple of teaspoons of lemon juice and beat until well combined. Add a little more juice, to taste, if you like but don't make the frosting too runny. This is an excellent topping for carrot or banana cakes.

CHOCOLATE GANACHE

Combine 100 g (3½ oz) chopped dark chocolate, 60 g (2 oz) unsalted butter and a tablespoon of cream in a heatproof bowl. Stand the bowl over a pan of simmering water; stir until the mixture is melted and smooth. This mixture can be cooled slightly and poured while still liquid over a very smooth cake. (If the top surface is rough, turn the cake upside down and use the base as the top.) Ganache can also be cooled until it is spreadable, or cooled and then beaten to make a lighter, fluffier topping.

CLOCKWISE, FROM TOP LEFT:
Citrus glacé icing; Chocolate ganache; Chocolate icing (with whipped cream and chocolate lattice); Honey mock cream; Soft citrus icing; Easy butter cream; Cream cheese frosting

FRUIT CAKES
Traditionally, rich fruit cakes are baked for celebrations such as Christmas, weddings and anniversaries. For special occasions, they are usually iced with a marzipan or almond paste covering the whole cake, then often decorated with piped and moulded icing. A good fruit cake should be made well in advance to give the flavour time to develop. The addition of sherry, rum or brandy adds to the flavour and helps to keep the cake moist.

BOILED FRUIT CAKE

Preparation time: 30 minutes
Total cooking time: 1 hour 30 minutes
Makes 1

★ ✸

250 g (8 oz) unsalted butter
1 cup (185 g/6 oz) soft brown sugar
1 kg (2 lb) mixed dried fruit
1/2 cup (125 ml/4 fl oz) sweet sherry
1/2 teaspoon bicarbonate of soda
1 1/2 cups (185 g/6 oz) self-raising flour
1 cup (125 g/4 oz) plain (all-purpose) flour
1 teaspoon mixed spice
4 eggs, lightly beaten

1 Preheat the oven to moderate 180°C (350°F/ Gas 4). Lightly grease and line a 22 cm (9 inch) round cake tin.
2 Put the butter, sugar, mixed fruit, sherry and 3/4 cup (185 ml/6 fl oz) water in a saucepan. Stir over low heat until the butter has melted and the sugar has dissolved. Bring to the boil, then reduce the heat and simmer for 10 minutes. Remove from the heat, stir in the bicarbonate of soda and cool.
3 Sift the flours and spice into a large bowl and make a well. Add the egg to the fruit, mix well, then pour into the well and mix thoroughly.

Pour into the tin and smooth the surface. Wrap the outside of the tin and sit the cake tin on several layers of newspaper in the oven. Bake for 1–1 1/4 hours, or until a skewer comes out clean when inserted into the centre of the cake. Leave in the tin for at least an hour before turning out. The flavour improves after standing for 3 days.
NOTE: This cake can be kept for up to 2 months. The cake colour will depend on the fruit. For a dark cake, use raisins, currants and sultanas. For a lighter colour, mix in chopped glacé fruit.

RICH FRUIT CAKE

Preparation time: 30 minutes
  + overnight soaking
Total cooking time: 3 hours 15 minutes
Makes 1

★ ✸

500 g (1 lb) sultanas
375 g (12 oz) raisins, chopped
250 g (8 oz) currants
250 g (8 oz) glacé cherries, quartered
1 cup (250 ml/8 fl oz) brandy or rum, plus
  1 tablespoon to glaze
250 g (8 oz) unsalted butter
230 g (7 1/2 oz) soft dark brown sugar

RIGHT: Boiled fruit cake

2 tablespoons apricot jam

2 tablespoons treacle or syrup

1 tablespoon grated lemon or orange rind

4 eggs

350 g (11 oz) plain (all-purpose) flour

1 teaspoon ground ginger

1 teaspoon mixed spice

1 teaspoon ground cinnamon

1 Put the fruit in a bowl with the brandy and soak overnight.

2 Preheat the oven to slow 150°C (300°F/Gas 2). Lightly grease and line a deep 22 cm (9 inch) round cake tin.

3 Beat the butter and sugar in a large bowl with electric beaters to just combine. Beat in the jam, treacle and rind. Add the eggs one at a time, beating after each addition.

4 Stir the fruit and the combined sifted flour and spices alternately into the mixture.

5 Spoon into the tin and smooth the surface. Tap the tin on the bench to remove any air bubbles. Level the surface with wet hands. Wrap the outside of the tin. Sit the cake tin on several layers of newspaper in the oven and bake for 3–3¼ hours, or until a skewer comes out clean when inserted into the centre. Brush with the extra tablespoon of brandy. Cover the top of the cake with paper and wrap in a tea towel. Cool completely in the tin.

NOTES: This cake can be kept, tightly wrapped in plastic wrap, in a cool dry place for up to eight months, or frozen for twelve months. You can cook the mixture in the following tins, changing the cooking time as stated:

For one 23 cm (9 inch) square cake, 3 hours.

For one 18 x 25 cm (7 x 10 inch) oval cake, 3½ hours.

For one 15 cm (6 inch) and one 30 cm (12 inch) round cake, use 2 quantities of mixture and bake for 2 hours 40 minutes and 3 hours 10 minutes respectively.

For one 12 cm (5 inch) and one 25 cm (10 inch) square cake, use 2 quantities of mixture and bake for 2 hours 50 minutes and 3½ hours respectively.

For one 16 cm (6½ inch) and one 30 cm (12 inch) square cake, use 3 quantities of mixture and bake for 3 hours and 4 hours 40 minutes respectively.

ABOVE: Rich fruit cake

555

**VANILLA BEANS
OR PODS**

These are the seed pod of a climbing orchid plant that is native to South America. The pods are dried and cured and are available at delicatessens. Pure vanilla extract is an aromatic, rich liquid made from the bean. It is very concentrated and should be used sparingly. Good-quality vanilla essence is is also extracted from the vanilla pod but is a thinner liquid. It has a strong flavour and is often used in cookery for convenience. Imitation vanilla essence is a much cheaper synthetic product.

*OPPOSITE PAGE, FROM
TOP: Refrigerator biscuits:
Plain; Spicy fruit; Mocha
spirals; Maple and pecan;
Macadamia; Marbled*

REFRIGERATOR BISCUITS

Preparation time: 30 minutes
  + 30 minutes refrigeration
Total cooking time: 15 minutes
Makes about 60

180 g (6 oz) unsalted butter, softened
1 cup (185 g/6 oz) soft brown sugar
1 teaspoon vanilla essence
1 egg
2¼ cups (280 g/9 oz) plain (all-purpose) flour
1 teaspoon baking powder

1 Cream the butter and sugar in a small bowl with electric beaters until light and fluffy. Add the vanilla essence and egg and beat until well combined. Transfer to a large bowl and add the sifted flour and baking powder. Using a knife, mix to a soft dough. Gather together, then divide the mixture into two portions.
2 Place one portion of the dough on a sheet of baking paper and press lightly until the dough is 30 cm (12 inches) long and 4 cm (1½ inches) thick. Fold the paper around the dough and roll neatly into a log shape. Twist the edges of the paper to seal. Repeat the process with the other portion. Refrigerate for 30 minutes, or until firm.
3 Preheat the oven to moderate 180°C (350°F/Gas 4). Line two baking trays with baking paper.
4 Cut the logs into slices about 1 cm (½ inch) thick. Place on the prepared trays, leaving 3 cm (1¼ inches) between each slice. Bake for 10–15 minutes, or until golden. Cool on the trays for 3 minutes before transferring to a wire rack to cool completely. When cold, store in an airtight container.
NOTE: Variations of the basic recipe can be made as suggested.

VARIATIONS:

SPICY FRUIT

Add 1 teaspoon mixed spice and ½ teaspoon ground ginger with the sifted flour. Divide the dough into two, roll one portion out on a sheet of baking paper to a rectangle about 2 mm (⅛ inch) thick and trim the edges. Refrigerate until just firm. Spread with ½ cup (95 g/3 oz) fruit mince (mincemeat), and then carefully roll up swiss-roll-style. Repeat the process with the other portion of dough. Refrigerate, slice and bake as above.

MOCHA SPIRALS

Divide the dough into two portions. Add 2 teaspoons of cocoa powder to one portion and 2 teaspoons of instant coffee powder to the other and knead each lightly. Divide both doughs in half again. Roll two of the different coloured portions separately to even rectangles about 2 mm (⅛ inch) thick, and then place one layer on top of the other on a sheet of baking paper. Trim the edges and roll up swiss-roll-style. Repeat with the remaining dough portions. Refrigerate and slice as above.

MAPLE AND PECAN

Add ¼ cup (60 ml/2 fl oz) maple syrup to the creamed butter and sugar mixture. Roll the logs in 1 cup (125 g/4 oz) finely chopped pecans before refrigerating. Press a whole nut into the top of each biscuit before baking as above.

MACADAMIA

Add ½ cup (45 g/1½ oz) desiccated coconut and ½ cup (70 g/2¼ oz) toasted chopped macadamia nuts with the flour. Using a ruler as a guide, shape the logs into a triangle shape. Refrigerate, slice and bake as above. When the log is cut, the biscuits will be in the shape of triangles.

MARBLED

Replace the brown sugar with caster (superfine) sugar. Divide the creamed butter and egg mixture into three bowls. Add a few drops of red food colouring to one and 50 g (1¾ oz) melted dark chocolate, 1 tablespoon cocoa powder and 2 teaspoons milk to another. Leave one plain. Add ¾ cup (90 g/3 oz) sifted flour and ¼ teaspoon baking powder to each bowl. Mix each to a soft dough, divide in half and roll into thin logs. Twist the 3 colours together to create a marbled effect, then shape the combined dough into 2 logs. Refrigerate, slice and bake as above.

ANZACS

These famous biscuits were developed at the time of the First World War and sent in food parcels to the ANZAC troops (Australia and New Zealand Army Corps). They are an economical, crisp, long-lasting biscuit made without eggs (which were in short supply at that time). The recipe is still popular, having been handed down through the generations.

BELOW: Anzac biscuits

ANZAC BISCUITS

Preparation time: 15 minutes
Total cooking time: 25 minutes
Makes 26

1 cup (125 g/4 oz) plain (all-purpose) flour
2/3 cup (160 g/5 1/2 oz) sugar
1 cup (100 g/3 1/2 oz) rolled oats
1 cup (90 g/3 oz) desiccated coconut
125 g (4 oz) unsalted butter, cubed
1/4 cup (90 g/3 oz) golden syrup
1/2 teaspoon bicarbonate of soda

1 Preheat the oven to moderate 180°C (350°F/ Gas 4). Line two baking trays with baking paper.
2 Sift the flour into a large bowl. Add the sugar, oats and coconut and make a well in the centre.
3 Put the butter and golden syrup together in a small saucepan and stir over low heat until the

butter has melted and the mixture is smooth. Remove from the heat. Dissolve the bicarbonate of soda in 1 tablespoon boiling water and add immediately to the butter mixture. It will foam up. Pour into the well in the dry ingredients and stir with a wooden spoon until mixed.
4 Drop level tablespoons of mixture onto the trays, allowing room for spreading. Gently flatten each biscuit with your fingertips. Bake for 20 minutes, or until just browned, leave on the tray to cool slightly, then transfer to a wire rack to cool completely. Store in an airtight container.

GINGERNUTS

Preparation time: 15 minutes
Total cooking time: 15 minutes
Makes 50

2 cups (250 g/8 oz) plain (all-purpose) flour
1/2 teaspoon bicarbonate of soda
1 tablespoon ground ginger
1/2 teaspoon mixed spice
125 g (4 oz) unsalted butter, chopped
1 cup (185 g/6 oz) soft brown sugar
1/4 cup (60 ml/2 fl oz) boiling water
1 tablespoon golden syrup

1 Preheat the oven to moderate 180°C (350°F/ Gas 4). Line two baking trays with baking paper.
2 Sift the flour, bicarbonate of soda, ginger and mixed spice into a large bowl. Add the butter and sugar and rub into the flour with your fingertips until the mixture resembles fine breadcrumbs.
3 Pour the boiling water into a small heatproof jug, add the golden syrup and stir until dissolved. Add to the flour and mix to a soft dough with a flat-bladed knife.
4 Roll into balls using 2 heaped teaspoons of mixture at a time. Place on the trays, allowing room for spreading, and flatten out slightly with your fingertips. Bake for 15 minutes, or until well-coloured and firm. Cool on the trays for 10 minutes before transferring to a wire rack to cool completely. Repeat with the remaining mixture. When cold, store in an airtight jar.
VARIATION: If you want to dress the biscuits up, make icing by combining 2–3 teaspoons lemon juice, 1/2 cup (60 g/2 oz) sifted icing (confectioners') sugar and 10 g(1/4 oz) melted butter in a bowl. Mix until smooth, then spread over the biscuits and allow to set.

CHOCOLATE CHOC CHIP COOKIES

Preparation time: 20 minutes
Total cooking time: 10 minutes
Makes 40

1¹/₂ cups (185 g/6 oz) plain (all-purpose) flour
³/₄ cup (90 g/3 oz) cocoa powder
1¹/₂ cups (280 g/9 oz) soft brown sugar
180 g (6 oz) unsalted butter, cubed
150 g (5 oz) dark chocolate, chopped
3 eggs, lightly beaten
1¹/₂ cups (265 g/8 oz) chocolate bits (chips)

1 Preheat the oven to moderate 180°C (350°F/ Gas 4). Line two baking trays with baking paper.
2 Sift the flour and cocoa powder into a large bowl, add the soft brown sugar and make a well in the centre.
3 Combine the butter and dark chocolate in a small heatproof bowl. Bring a saucepan of water to the boil, then remove the pan from the heat. Sit the heatproof bowl over the saucepan, making sure the base of the bowl does not sit in the water. Stir occasionally until the chocolate and butter have melted and are smooth. Mix well.
4 Add the butter and chocolate mixture and the eggs to the dry ingredients. Stir with a wooden spoon until well combined, but do not overbeat. Stir in the chocolate bits. Drop tablespoons of the mixture onto the trays, allowing room for spreading. Bake for 7–10 minutes, until firm to touch. Cool on the trays for 5 minutes before transferring to a wire rack to cool completely. When the cookies are completely cold, store in an airtight container.
NOTE: When dropping the dough onto the tray, it is easier and less messy to use two tablespoons, one to measure accurately and the other to push the dough off the spoon onto the tray.

COOKIES

This is an American term for 'biscuits'. Originally biscuits were small flat dry cakes, rather like rusks, that were baked twice to keep them crisp and long-lasting. Today the terms biscuit and cookie cover a wide range of small baked goods, from crispy to chewy, made in a variety of flavours and shapes. The basic ingredients usually include butter, sugar, eggs and flour. Flavours such as chocolate, nuts, dried fruits and essences are added, according to taste.

LEFT: Chocolate choc chip cookies

TOLLHOUSE COOKIES

Preparation time: 20 minutes
Total cooking time: 10 minutes
Makes 40

180 g (6 oz) unsalted butter, softened
3/4 cup (140 g/4 1/2 oz) soft brown
    sugar
1/2 cup (125 g/4 oz) sugar
2 eggs, lightly beaten
1 teaspoon vanilla essence
2 1/4 cups (310 g/10 oz) plain (all-purpose) flour
1 teaspoon bicarbonate of soda
2 cups (350 g/11 oz) dark chocolate bits (chips)
1 cup (100 g/3 1/2 oz) pecans,
    roughly chopped

BELOW: Tollhouse cookies

1 Preheat the oven to moderately hot 190°C (375°F/Gas 5). Line two baking trays with baking paper.
2 Cream the butter and sugars in a large bowl with electric beaters until light and fluffy. Gradually add the egg, beating well after each addition. Stir in the vanilla, then the sifted flour and bicarbonate of soda until just combined. Mix in the chocolate bits and pecans.
3 Drop tablespoons of mixture onto the trays, leaving room for spreading. Bake the cookies for 8–10 minutes, or until lightly golden. Cool slightly on the trays before transferring to a wire rack to cool completely. When completely cold, store in an airtight container.
VARIATION: You can use any nuts such as walnuts, almonds or hazelnuts.

PEANUT BISCUITS

Preparation time: 30 minutes
    + 15 minutes refrigeration
Total cooking time: 20 minutes
Makes 30

185 g (6 oz) unsalted butter, softened
2 cups (370 g/12 oz) soft brown sugar
1/2 cup (140 g/4 1/2 oz) smooth peanut butter
1 teaspoon vanilla essence
1 egg
1 1/2 cups (185 g/6 oz) plain (all-purpose) flour
1/2 teaspoon baking powder
1 1/4 cups (125 g/4 oz) rolled oats
3/4 cup (120 g/4 oz) raw peanuts

1 Preheat the oven to moderate 180°C (350°F/Gas 4). Line two baking trays with baking paper.
2 Cream the butter, sugar, peanut butter and vanilla essence in a small bowl with electric beaters until light and fluffy. Add the egg and beat until smooth. Transfer to a large bowl and mix in the combined sifted flour and baking powder. Fold in the oats and peanuts and mix until smooth. Chill for 15 minutes, or until firm.
3 Roll heaped tablespoons of the mixture into balls and place on the trays, leaving room for spreading. Press down gently with a floured fork to make a crisscross pattern. Bake for 15–20 minutes, or until golden. Cool slightly on the trays before transferring to a wire rack to cool completely. When cold, store in an airtight container.

FAMILY-STYLE GINGERBREAD PEOPLE

Preparation time: 40 minutes
  + 15 minutes refrigeration
Total cooking time: 10 minutes
Makes 16

125 g (4 oz) unsalted butter, softened
1/3 cup (60 g/2 oz) soft brown sugar
1/4 cup (90 g/3 oz) golden syrup
1 egg, lightly beaten
2 cups (250 g/8 oz) plain (all-purpose) flour
1/4 cup (30 g/1 oz) self-raising flour
1 tablespoon ground ginger
1 teaspoon bicarbonate of soda
1 tablespoon currants

Icing

1 egg white
1/2 teaspoon lemon juice
1 1/4 cups (155 g/5 oz) icing (confectioners')
  sugar, sifted
assorted food colourings

1 Preheat the oven to moderate 180°C (350°F/ Gas 4). Line two baking trays with baking paper.
2 Cream the butter, sugar and golden syrup in a small bowl with electric beaters until light and fluffy. Add the egg gradually, beating well after each addition. Transfer to a large bowl. Sift the dry ingredients onto the butter mixture and mix with a knife until just combined. Combine the dough with well-floured hands. Turn onto a well-floured surface and knead for 1–2 minutes, or until smooth. Roll out the dough on a chopping board, between two sheets of baking paper, to 5 mm (1/4 inch) thick. Refrigerate on the board for 15 minutes to firm.
3 Cut the dough into shapes with a 13 cm (5 inch) gingerbread person cutter. Press the remaining dough together and re-roll. Cut out shapes and place the biscuits on the trays. Place currants as eyes and noses. Bake for 10 minutes, or until lightly browned. Cool completely on the trays.
4 For the icing, beat the egg white with electric beaters in a small, clean, dry bowl until foamy. Gradually add the lemon juice and icing sugar and beat until thick and creamy. Divide the icing among several bowls. Tint the mixture with food colourings and spoon into small paper icing bags. Seal the open ends, snip the tips off the bags and pipe on faces and clothing.
NOTE: When the icing is completely dry, store the biscuits in an airtight container in a cool, dry place for up to three days.

FAMILY-STYLE GINGERBREAD PEOPLE

Mix the dry ingredients into the butter mixture with a knife until just combined.

Cut the dough into shapes with a gingerbread person cutter.

Snip the tip off the end of the piping bag and pipe on faces and clothing.

LEFT: Family-style gingerbread people

BISCOTTI

Preparation time: 25 minutes
Total cooking time: 50 minutes
Makes 45

★★

2 cups (250 g/8 oz) plain (all-purpose) flour
1 teaspoon baking powder
1 cup (250 g/8 oz) caster (superfine) sugar
3 eggs
1 egg yolk
1 teaspoon vanilla essence
1 teaspoon grated orange rind
3/4 cup (110 g/3 1/2 oz) pistachio nuts

ABOVE: Biscotti

1 Preheat the oven to moderate 180°C (350°F/ Gas 4). Line two baking trays with baking paper and lightly dust with flour.
2 Sift the flour and baking powder into a large bowl. Add the sugar and mix well. Make a well in the centre and add 2 whole eggs, the egg yolk, vanilla essence and orange rind. Using a large metal spoon, stir until just combined. Mix in the pistachios. Knead for 2–3 minutes on a lightly floured surface. The dough will be stiff at first. Sprinkle a little water onto the dough at this stage. Divide the mixture into two portions and roll each into a log about 25 cm (10 inches) long and 8 cm (3 inches) wide. Slightly flatten the tops.
3 Place the logs on the baking trays, allowing room for spreading. Beat the remaining egg and brush over the logs to glaze. Bake for 35 minutes, then remove from the oven.
4 Reduce the oven to slow 150°C (300°F/Gas 2). Allow the logs to cool slightly and cut each into 4 mm (1/4 inch) slices. Place them flat-side-down on the trays and bake for another 8 minutes. Turn them over and cook for 8 minutes, or until slightly coloured and crisp and dry. Transfer to a wire rack to cool. Store in an airtight container.
NOTE: You can make chocolate and macadamia nut biscotti using the same basic recipe. Remove the vanilla and pistachio nuts and replace 1/3 cup (40 g/1 1/4 oz) of the flour with 1/3 cup (40 g/ 1 1/4 oz) sifted cocoa (add to the flour). Stir 1/2 cup (70 g/2 1/4 oz) lightly toasted, roughly chopped macadamia nuts and 1/2 cup (90 g/3 oz) dark chocolate bits (chips) into the mixture until just combined. Divide into two portions and roll each into a log 25 x 8 cm (10 x 3 inches). Flatten the tops slightly. Bake and slice as above.

TRADITIONAL MINCE TARTS

Preparation time: 40 minutes + 35 minutes
  refrigeration + 3 weeks bottling
Total cooking time: 15 minutes
Makes 48

Fruit mince (mincemeat)

2 large green apples (about 440 g/14 oz),
  peeled, cored and finely chopped
250 g (8 oz) packet suet mix
1½ cups (345 g/11 oz) soft brown sugar
2⅓ cups (375 g/12 oz) raisins, chopped
1½ cups (240 g/8 oz) sultanas
1½ cups (225 g/7 oz) currants
¾ cup (140 g/5 oz) mixed peel
100 g (3½ oz) slivered almonds, chopped
1 tablespoon mixed spice
½ teaspoon ground nutmeg
½ teaspoon ground cinnamon
2 teaspoons grated orange rind
1 teaspoon grated lemon rind
1 cup (250 ml/8 fl oz) orange juice
½ cup (125 ml/4 fl oz) lemon juice
150 ml (5 fl oz) brandy

Pastry

800 g (1 lb 10 oz) plain (all-purpose) flour
1 teaspoon caster (superfine) sugar
400 g (13 oz) unsalted butter, chilled, chopped
4 eggs, lightly beaten
4 drops vanilla essence
1 egg white, lightly beaten, to glaze

1 Combine all the fruit mince ingredients with
½ cup (125 ml/4 fl oz) of the brandy in a large
bowl. Mix thoroughly. Spoon into sterilized,
warm jars. Use a skewer to remove air bubbles
and to pack the mixture in firmly. Leave a
1.5 cm (⅝ inch) space at the top of the jar and
wipe the jar clean with a cloth. Spoon a little
brandy over the surface of the mince and seal.
Label and date. Set aside for at least 3 weeks,
or up to 6 months, before using in pies and
tarts. Refrigerate the mince in hot weather.
2 For the pastry, in a large bowl, sift together
the flour, sugar and a large pinch of salt. Rub
the butter into the flour with your fingertips
until the mixture resembles fine breadcrumbs.
3 Make a well in the centre and pour in the
combined egg, vanilla and 2–3 teaspoons water.

4 Bring the mixture together with a flat-bladed
knife or pastry scraper to form a rough ball. If it
is slightly sticky, add a little more flour. Turn
out onto a lightly floured cool surface, gather
into a ball and flatten slightly. Wrap in plastic
wrap and chill for 20 minutes.
5 Separate one third of the pastry, re-wrap in
plastic and return to the fridge. Roll the remaining
pastry to 3 mm (⅛ inch) and cut out 48 rounds
using a 7 cm (2¾ inch) plain or fluted cutter.
6 Line four 12-hole, 7 cm (2¾ inch) diameter,
shallow tart tins. Fill each with 1 level tablespoon
fruit mince. Return to the fridge.
7 Preheat the oven to moderately hot 200°C
(400°F/Gas 6). Roll out the remaining pastry
and cut 48 round shapes for pastry lids using a
6 cm (2½ inch) round cutter. Cut shapes out of
the centre of some of the tops if you wish.
Gather the scraps and re-roll. Place one on top
of each pie and refrigerate for 15 minutes.
8 Brush with egg white, dust with sugar if you
wish, and bake for 12–15 minutes.

*ABOVE: Traditional
mince tarts*

GRAHAM CRACKERS

Preparation time: 25 minutes
  + 30 minutes refrigeration
Total cooking time: 10 minutes
Makes 12

2¹/3 cups (350 g/11 oz) wholemeal plain
  (all-purpose) flour
¹/2 cup (60 g/2 oz) cornflour (cornstarch)
¹/4 cup (60 g/2 oz) caster (superfine) sugar
150 g (5 oz) butter
³/4 cup (185 ml/6 fl oz) cream

1 Sift the flours into a bowl, stir in the sugar
and ¹/2 teaspoon salt. Rub in the butter with
your fingertips until the mixture resembles
breadcrumbs. Mix in the cream with a knife,
using a cutting motion, to make a pliable dough.
2 Gather the dough together and shape into a
disc. Wrap in plastic wrap and refrigerate for
30 minutes.
3 Preheat the oven to moderately hot 200°C
(400°F/Gas 6). Line two baking trays with
baking paper.
4 Roll out the dough to a rectangle measuring
30 x 24 cm (12 x 9 inches). Cut the dough
into 12 rectangles with a pastry wheel or sharp
knife. Place the rectangles on the baking trays,
allowing a little room for spreading.
5 Bake for 7–10 minutes, or until firm and
golden brown. Leave to cool on the trays for
2–3 minutes, then transfer to a wire rack to
cool completely. When the crackers are cold,
store in an airtight container.

SCOTTISH SHORTBREAD

Preparation time: 15 minutes
Total cooking time: 35 minutes
Makes one 28 cm (11 inch) round

250 g (8 oz) butter, softened
²/3 cup (160 g/5¹/2 oz) caster (superfine) sugar
1²/3 cups (210 g/7 oz) plain (all-purpose) flour
¹/2 cup (90 g/3 oz) rice flour
1 teaspoon sugar, for sprinkling

1 Preheat the oven to warm 160°C (315°F/
Gas 2–3). Brush a 28 cm (11 inch) round pizza
tray with melted butter or oil. Line with baking

paper. Beat the butter and sugar with electric
beaters in a small bowl until light and creamy.
Transfer to a large bowl and add the sifted flours.
Mix to a soft dough with a flat-bladed knife.
Lift onto a lightly floured surface and knead
for 30 seconds, or until smooth.
2 Transfer to the pizza tray and press into a
25 cm (10 inch) round (the tray must be larger
than the uncooked shortbread as the mixture
will spread during cooking). Pinch and flute
the edge decoratively with your fingers. Prick
the surface lightly with a fork and mark into
16 segments with a sharp knife. Sprinkle
with sugar and bake on the middle shelf for
35 minutes, or until firm and lightly golden.
Cool on the tray.

CHEESE BISCUITS

Preparation time: 10 minutes
  + 30 minutes freezing
Total cooking time: 10 minutes
Makes 45

125 g (4 oz) butter, chopped
125 g (4 oz) Cheddar, grated
2 tablespoons grated Parmesan
1 cup (125 g/4 oz) plain (all-purpose) flour
2 tablespoons self-raising flour
pinch of cayenne pepper
2 teaspoons lemon juice

1 Place the butter, cheeses, flours, cayenne
pepper, lemon juice and a pinch of salt in a
food processor. Process for 60 seconds, or
until the mixture comes together and forms
a ball.
2 Gently knead the mixture for 2 minutes on
a lightly floured surface. Form the dough into
a sausage shape about 3 cm (1¹/4 inches) in
diameter. Wrap in plastic wrap, then in foil
and freeze for 30 minutes. Remove and leave
at room temperature for 5 minutes.
3 Preheat the oven to moderate 180°C (350°F/
Gas 4). Line two baking trays with baking paper.
4 Slice the dough into thin slices, about 3 mm
(¹/8 inch) thick, and place on the trays, allowing
a little room for spreading. Bake the biscuits for
9–10 minutes, or until golden. Allow to cool on
the trays.
NOTE: Cheese biscuits are best eaten on the day
of baking. They are delicious served as an
accompaniment to drinks at a cocktail party.

GRAHAM CRACKERS
In the United States the
word 'graham' means any
bread, biscuit or cake that
is made from wholemeal
flour, including the
bran. Graham flour was
developed and promoted
by Dr Sylvester Graham in
the early nineteenth
century. He was an ardent
advocate of unrefined
foods and vegetarianism.
Graham bread, Graham
crackers and Graham
rusks all denote that the
baked products have been
made with wholemeal or
wholewheat flour.

*OPPOSITE PAGE, FROM
TOP: Cheese biscuits;
Graham crackers*

SANDWICHES

Sandwiches don't have to be ungainly chunks of bread filled with salmon paste or cheese spread. Welcome to the sophisticated party sandwich. It could just be the star of your show.

HAM AND CORN RELISH RIBBONS

Mix 1 cup (250 g/8 oz) sour cream with ½ cup (140 g/4½ oz) corn relish and spread on 8 slices of white bread. Top each with a slice of dark seed bread. Top that with sliced ham, then sandwich with a buttered slice of white bread. Remove the crusts and cut each sandwich into three. Makes 24.

VEGETABLE TRIANGLES

Cut 500 g (1 lb) butternut pumpkin (squash) into chunks, put in a baking dish, drizzle with oil and bake in a moderately hot 200°C (400°F/Gas 6) oven for 1 hour, or until tender. Cool, then mash. Spread 4 slices of bread with 1 tablespoon of tomato salsa. Top each with sliced marinated eggplant (aubergine), coriander (cilantro) leaves and sliced spring onion (scallion). Spread 4 more slices of bread with the pumpkin and place on top. Remove the crusts and cut into triangles. Makes 16.

CHICKEN AND GUACAMOLE SQUARES

Mash 2 avocados with 1 tablespoon mayonnaise, 1 teaspoon chopped chilli, 1 tablespoon lemon juice, 1 small chopped tomato and 1/2 finely chopped red onion. Spread over 8 slices of wholemeal bread and top with 250 g (8 oz) sliced smoked chicken breast. Add trimmed snow pea (mangetout) sprouts. Sandwich with more bread, remove the crusts and cut into squares. Makes 32.

TURKEY AND BRIE TRIANGLES

Trim the crusts from 8 slices bread. Spread 4 with cranberry sauce. Using 120 g (4 oz) turkey breast, 120 g (4 oz) sliced brie and 4 butter lettuce leaves, make into sandwiches. Cut into triangles. Makes 16.

ROAST BEEF, PATE AND ROCKET FINGERS

Trim the crusts from 16 slices of bread. Spread 160 g (5 1/2 oz) cracked pepper paté over half the bread. Make sandwiches using 250 g (8 oz) sliced rare roast beef, 160 g (5 1/2 oz) semi-dried (sun-blushed) tomatoes and rocket (arugula). Cut each into three fingers to serve. Makes 24.

LEMON SANDWICHES WITH PRAWNS

Wash and dry 1 1/2 thin-skinned lemons and slice finely. Make lemon sandwiches with 10 slices of multi-grain bread. Cut each sandwich into 8 triangles. Remove the crusts and serve with 500 g (1 lb) peeled and deveined cooked king prawns (shrimp), leaving the tails intact. Makes 40.

CHICKEN, ROCKET AND WALNUT SANDWICHES

Fry 250 g (8 oz) chicken breast fillets and 500 g (1 lb) chicken thigh fillets until cooked. Cool, then chop. Mix with 1 cup (250 g/8 oz) mayonnaise, some finely chopped celery and chopped walnuts. Season. Make into sandwiches with 20 slices bread, adding trimmed rocket (arugula) to each. Remove the crusts and cut the sandwiches into fingers. Makes 30.

CLOCKWISE, FROM BOTTOM LEFT: Chicken and guacamole squares; Vegetable triangles; Ham and corn relish ribbons; Turkey and brie triangles; Roast beef, pâté and rocket fingers; Chicken, rocket and walnut sandwiches; Lemon sandwiches with prawns

VANILLA SLICE

Preparation time: 40 minutes
Total cooking time: 15 minutes
Makes 9 pieces

500 g (1 lb) home-made or bought
   puff pastry (see page 488)
1 cup (250 g/8 oz) caster (superfine) sugar
3/4 cup (90 g/3 oz) cornflour (cornstarch)
1/2 cup (60 g/2 oz) custard powder
1 litre (32 fl oz) cream
60 g (2 oz) unsalted butter, cubed
2 teaspoons vanilla essence
3 egg yolks

Icing

1 1/2 cups (185 g/6 oz) icing (confectioners')
   sugar
1/4 cup (60 g/2 oz) passionfruit pulp
15 g (1/2 oz) unsalted butter, melted

1 Preheat the oven to hot 210°C (415°F/
Gas 6–7). Grease two baking trays with oil. Line
the base and side of a shallow 23 cm (9 inch)
square cake tin with foil, leaving the foil hanging
over on two opposite sides (the foil makes this
heavy slice easy to lift from the tin). Divide
the pastry in half, roll each piece to a 25 cm
(10 inch) square about 3 mm (1/8 inch) thick
and place each one on a prepared tray. Prick
all over with a fork and bake for 8 minutes,
or until golden. Trim each pastry sheet to a
23 cm (9 inch) square. Place one sheet top-side-
down in the cake tin.

2 Combine the sugar, cornflour and custard
powder in a saucepan. Gradually add the cream
and stir until smooth. Place over medium heat
and stir constantly for 2 minutes, or until the
mixture boils and thickens. Add the butter and
vanilla essence and stir until smooth. Remove
from the heat and whisk in the egg yolks until
combined. Spread the custard over the pastry
in the tin and cover with the remaining pastry,
top-side-down. Allow to cool.

3 For the icing, combine the icing sugar,
passionfruit pulp and butter in a small bowl
and stir together until smooth.

4 Lift the slice out, using the foil as handles,
spread the icing over the top and leave it to
set before carefully cutting into squares with
a serrated knife.

ABOVE: Vanilla slice

CHOCOLATE MINT SLICE

Preparation time: 25 minutes
+ 30 minutes refrigeration
Total cooking time: 20 minutes
Makes 24 pieces

2/3 cup (90 g/3 oz) self-raising flour

1/4 cup (30 g/1 oz) cocoa powder

1/2 cup (45 g/1 1/2 oz) desiccated coconut

1/4 cup (60 g/2 oz) sugar

140 g (4 1/2 oz) unsalted butter, melted

1 egg, lightly beaten

Peppermint filling

1 1/2 cups (185 g/6 oz) icing (confectioners')
sugar, sifted

30 g (1 oz) Copha (white vegetable shortening),
melted

2 tablespoons milk

1/2 teaspoon peppermint essence

Chocolate topping

185 g (6 oz) dark chocolate, chopped

30 g (1 oz) Copha (white vegetable shortening)

1 Preheat the oven to moderate 180°C (350°F/ Gas 4). Lightly grease a shallow tin measuring 18 x 28 cm (7 x 11 inches) and line with baking paper, leaving the paper hanging over on the two long sides. This makes it easy to lift the cooked slice out of the tin.

2 Sift the flour and cocoa into a bowl. Stir in the coconut and sugar, then add the butter and egg and mix well. Press the mixture firmly into the tin. Bake for 15 minutes, then press down with the back of a spoon and leave to cool.

3 For the peppermint filling, sift the icing sugar into a bowl. Stir in the Copha, milk and peppermint essence. Spread over the base and refrigerate for 5–10 minutes, or until firm.

4 For the chocolate topping, put the chocolate and Copha in a heatproof bowl. Half fill a saucepan with water, bring to the boil, then remove from the heat. Sit the bowl over the saucepan, making sure the base of the bowl does not touch the water. Stir occasionally until the chocolate and Copha have melted and combined. Spread evenly over the filling. Refrigerate the slice for 20 minutes, or until the chocolate topping is firm. Carefully lift the slice from the tin, using the paper as handles. Cut into pieces with a warm knife to give clean edges. Store in an airtight container in the refrigerator.

PEPPERMINT ESSENCE
Peppermint is a herb belonging to the mint family. The herb can be used fresh and as a herb tea. In baking, the oil that is extracted from the peppermint is used. This comes from its leaves and flowers and is sold as peppermint essence. Its concentrated flavour is added in small amounts to confectionery, chocolates, chocolate fillings and icings. The liqueur, crème de menthe, is flavoured with the oil.

ABOVE: Chocolate mint slice

CARAMEL SLICE

Preparation time: 30 minutes
 + 20 minutes refrigeration
Total cooking time: 30 minutes
Makes 20 pieces

1 cup (125 g/4 oz) self-raising flour
1 cup (90 g/3 oz) desiccated coconut
1/2 cup (125 g/4 oz) caster (superfine) sugar
125 g (4 oz) unsalted butter, melted

Caramel filling

400 g (13 oz) can sweetened condensed
 milk
20 g (3/4 oz) unsalted butter
2 tablespoons golden syrup

Chocolate topping

150 g (5 oz) dark chocolate, chopped
20 g (3/4 oz) Copha (white vegetable
 shortening)

1 Preheat the oven to moderate 180°C (350°F/ Gas 4). Lightly grease an 18 x 28 cm (7 x 11 inch) shallow tin and line with baking paper, leaving the paper hanging over on the two long sides.
2 Sift the flour into a bowl, then mix in the coconut and sugar. Add the melted butter to the bowl and stir through thoroughly. Press firmly into the tin and bake for 12–15 minutes, or until lightly coloured. Allow to cool.
3 For the caramel filling, place all the ingredients in a small saucepan over low heat. Slowly bring to the boil, stirring constantly, then boil gently, stirring, for 4–5 minutes, or until lightly caramelized. Quickly pour over the cooled base, spreading evenly. Bake for 10 minutes, then set aside to cool.
4 For the chocolate topping, place the dark chocolate and Copha in a heatproof bowl. Half fill a saucepan with water and bring to the boil. Remove from the heat and sit the bowl over the saucepan, making sure the bowl does not sit in the water. Stir occasionally until the chocolate and Copha have melted. Spread over the caramel. You can make a decorative effect with the side of a knife. Refrigerate for 20 minutes, or until set. Lift the slice from the tin, using the paper as handles. Cut into pieces with a hot, dry knife.

CONDENSED MILK
Condensed milk is sold canned or in a tube. It is a sweetened evaporated milk. The whole full-fat milk is evaporated by about forty per cent and then about forty per cent sugar is added. The high density of sugar acts as a preservative. Condensed milk will keep indefinitely but, after opening, it should be refrigerated. It is used to sweeten desserts, cakes, slices and sauces, and for making caramels.

RIGHT: Caramel slice

MUESLI SLICE

Preparation time: 20 minutes
 + 2 hours refrigeration
Total cooking time: 50 minutes
Makes 18 pieces

250 g (8 oz) unsalted butter, cubed

1 cup (250 g/8 oz) caster (superfine) sugar

2 tablespoons honey

2½ cups (250 g/8 oz) rolled oats

¾ cup (65 g/2¼ oz) desiccated coconut

1 cup (30 g/1 oz) cornflakes, lightly crushed

½ cup (45 g/1½ oz) flaked almonds

1 teaspoon mixed spice

½ cup (45 g/1½ oz) finely chopped dried apricots

1 cup (185 g/6 oz) dried mixed fruit

1 Preheat the oven to warm 160°C (315°F/ Gas 2–3). Lightly grease a shallow tin measuring 20 x 30 cm (8 x 12 inches) and line with baking paper, leaving the paper hanging over on the two long sides. This makes it easy to lift the cooked slice out of the tin.
2 Put the butter, sugar and honey in a small saucepan and stir over low heat for 5 minutes, or until the butter has melted and the sugar has dissolved.
3 Mix the remaining ingredients together in a bowl and make a well in the centre. Pour in the butter mixture and stir well, then press into the tin. Bake for 45 minutes, or until golden. Cool completely in the tin, then refrigerate for 2 hours, to firm.
4 Lift the slice from the tin, using the paper as handles, before cutting into pieces. This slice will keep for up to three days stored in an airtight container.

MIXED SPICE
This is a blend of freshly ground spices, usually including cloves, nutmeg, cinnamon and allspice, and sometimes ginger. It adds a lightly spiced flavour to puddings, spice cakes, biscuits and fruit cakes. It is often added when apples are being cooked as they seem to complement each other very well. As with all spices, mixed spice should be bought in small amounts and kept in an airtight container in a dark place. Spices can be frozen for up to six months.

ABOVE: Muesli slice

CHOCOLATE BROWNIES

Preparation time: 20 minutes
  + 2 hours refrigeration
Total cooking time: 50 minutes
Makes 24 pieces

1/3 cup (40 g/1 1/4 oz) plain (all-purpose) flour
1/2 cup (60 g/2 oz) cocoa powder
2 cups (500 g/1 lb) sugar
1 cup (125 g/4 oz) chopped pecans or walnuts
250 g (8 oz) good-quality dark chocolate,
  chopped into small pieces
250 g (8 oz) unsalted butter, melted
2 teaspoons vanilla essence
4 eggs, lightly beaten

1 Preheat the oven to moderate 180°C (350°F/ Gas 4). Lightly grease a 20 x 30 cm (8 x 12 inch) cake tin and line with baking paper, leaving the paper hanging over on the two long sides.
2 Sift the flour and cocoa into a bowl and add the sugar, nuts and chocolate. Mix together and make a well in the centre.
3 Pour the butter into the dry ingredients with the vanilla and eggs and mix well. Pour into the tin, smooth the surface and bake for 50 minutes (the mixture will still be a bit soft on the inside). Chill for at least 2 hours before lifting out, using the paper as handles, and cutting into pieces.

MACADAMIA BLONDIES

Preparation time: 20 minutes
Total cooking time: 45 minutes
Makes 25 pieces

100 g (3 1/2 oz) unsalted butter, cubed
100 g (3 1/2 oz) white chocolate, chopped
1/2 cup (125 g/4 oz) caster (superfine) sugar
2 eggs, lightly beaten
1 teaspoon vanilla essence
1 cup (125 g/4 oz) self-raising flour
1/2 cup (80 g/2 3/4 oz) macadamia nuts,
  roughly chopped

1 Preheat the oven to moderate 180°C (350°F/ Gas 4). Lightly grease a 20 cm (8 inch) square tin and line with baking paper, leaving the paper hanging over on two opposite sides.

2 Place the butter and white chocolate in a heatproof bowl. Half fill a saucepan with water and bring to the boil. Remove from the heat. Place the bowl over the saucepan, making sure the base of the bowl does not sit in the water. Stir occasionally until the butter and chocolate have melted and are smooth.
3 Add the caster sugar to the bowl and gradually stir in the eggs. Add the vanilla, fold in the flour and macadamia nuts, then pour into the tin. Bake for 35–40 minutes. If the top starts to brown too quickly, cover lightly with a sheet of foil. When cooked, cool in the tin before lifting out, using the paper as handles, and cutting into squares. Can be drizzled with melted white chocolate.

JAFFA TRIPLE-CHOC BROWNIES

Preparation time: 20 minutes
Total cooking time: 45 minutes
Makes 25 pieces

125 g (4 oz) unsalted butter, cubed
350 g (11 oz) dark chocolate, roughly chopped
1 cup (185 g/6 oz) soft brown sugar
3 eggs
2 teaspoons grated orange rind
1 cup (125 g/4 oz) plain (all-purpose) flour
1/4 cup (30 g/1 oz) cocoa powder
100 g (3 1/2 oz) milk chocolate bits (chips)
100 g (3 1/2 oz) white chocolate bits (chips)

1 Preheat the oven to moderate 180°C (350°F/ Gas 4). Lightly grease a 23 cm (9 inch) square shallow tin and line with baking paper, leaving the paper hanging over on two opposite sides.
2 Place the butter and 250 g (8 oz) of the dark chocolate in a heatproof bowl. Half fill a saucepan with water, bring to the boil, then remove from the heat. Sit the bowl over the saucepan, making sure the base of the bowl does not sit in the water. Stir occasionally until the butter and chocolate have melted. Cool.
3 Beat the sugar, eggs and rind in a bowl until thick and fluffy. Fold in the chocolate mixture.
4 Sift the flour and cocoa into a bowl, then stir into the chocolate mixture. Stir in the remaining dark chocolate and all the chocolate bits. Spread into the tin and bake for 40 minutes, or until just cooked. Cool in the tin before lifting out, using the paper as handles, and cutting into squares. Can be drizzled with melted dark chocolate.

MACADAMIAS

These are also called Queensland nuts because they are native to north-east Australia, although the Hawaiians cultivated the seeds and have become large producers of the nuts. The creamy nut is enclosed in an extremely hard shell, which needs to be cracked with a hammer or special-purpose clamp. The nut can be used raw or roasted and is usually chopped. It is used in the baking of brownies, cakes and biscuits. Buy unsalted nuts for cooking.

OPPOSITE PAGE, FROM LEFT: Chocolate brownies; Macadamia blondies; Jaffa triple-choc brownies

BERRIES
There are many berries which are wonderful to eat ripe off the vine but have multiple uses in baking. The most common varieties, depending on the region and climate, are sold from spring to early autumn. They include blackberries, raspberries, strawberries, blueberries, mulberries, cranberries, currants and gooseberries. Berries are used a lot in baking and are made into desserts such as pies, puddings and tarts, as well as being used to flavour slices, cakes, muffins, friands and biscuits.

ABOVE: Berry almond slice

BERRY ALMOND SLICE

Preparation time: 25 minutes
Total cooking time: 1 hour 15 minutes
Makes 15 pieces

★★

1 sheet ready-rolled puff pastry, thawed
150 g (5 oz) unsalted butter
3/4 cup (185 g/6 oz) caster (superfine) sugar
3 eggs, lightly beaten
2 tablespoons grated lemon rind
2/3 cup (125 g/4 oz) ground almonds
2 tablespoons plain (all-purpose) flour
150 g (5 oz) raspberries
150 g (5 oz) blackberries
icing (confectioners') sugar, to dust

1 Preheat the oven to moderately hot 200°C (400°F/Gas 6). Lightly grease a 23 cm (9 inch) square shallow tin and line with baking paper, leaving the paper hanging over on two opposite sides.
2 Place the pastry on a baking tray lined with baking paper. Prick the pastry all over with a fork and bake for 15 minutes, or until golden. Ease into the tin, trimming the edges if necessary. Reduce the oven to moderate 180°C (350°F/Gas 4).
3 Cream the butter and sugar in a small bowl with electric beaters until light and fluffy. Gradually add the egg, beating after every addition, then the lemon rind. Fold in the almonds and flour, then spread the mixture over the pastry.
4 Scatter the fruit on top and bake for 1 hour, or until lightly golden. Cool in the tin, then lift out, using the paper as handles. Cut into pieces and dust with icing sugar to serve.

ROCKY ROAD SLICE

Preparation time: 15 minutes
 + 30 minutes cooling
Total cooking time: 25 minutes
Makes 24 pieces

150 g (5 oz) unsalted butter, cubed, softened

1/2 cup (125 g/4 oz) sugar

1 egg, lightly beaten

50 g (1 3/4 oz) dark chocolate, melted

1 cup (125 g/4 oz) self-raising flour

2 tablespoons cocoa powder

250 g (8 oz) dark chocolate, chopped, extra

25 g (3/4 oz) unsalted butter, extra

1/2 cup (105 g/3 1/2 oz) glacé cherries, halved

50 g (1 3/4 oz) mini marshmallows

1/2 cup (80 g/2 3/4 oz) unsalted peanuts

1 Preheat the oven to moderate 180°C (350°F/ Gas 4). Lightly grease two 26 x 8 x 4.5 cm (10 1/2 x 3 x 1 3/4 inch) bar tins and line with baking paper, leaving the paper hanging over on the two long sides.

2 Cream the butter and sugar in a small bowl with electric beaters until light and fluffy. Beat in the egg and melted chocolate and transfer to a large bowl. Using a metal spoon, fold in the combined sifted flour and cocoa and mix well. Divide the mixture between the tins, smoothing the surface. Bake for 20–25 minutes. Gently press down the outer edges of the slice, using the back of a spoon, to make the surface level. Leave to cool in the tins for 30 minutes.

3 Place the extra chocolate and butter in a heatproof bowl. Half fill a saucepan with water, bring to the boil, then remove from the heat. Sit the bowl over the saucepan, making sure the base of the bowl does not sit in the water. Stir occasionally until the mixture has melted and is smooth. Spread melted chocolate over the bases, using about a third of the chocolate altogether. Top each randomly with cherries, marshmallows and peanuts, then spoon the remaining chocolate evenly over the tops. Tap the tins on a bench to distribute the chocolate evenly. Leave to set, lift out using the paper as handles, then cut into 2 cm (3/4 inch) wide fingers for serving. These will keep in an airtight container in a cool, dark place for up to four days.

FLOUR

Flour made from wheat is the most common type used for baking. It provides structure to bread doughs, cakes mixtures, pastries and batters. During manufacture, the whole grain is processed or milled until it is finely ground to a powder. Plain white flour is also known as all-purpose flour. Self-raising flour is the same product but with the addition of baking powder. The baking powder acts as a leavener or raising agent in baked products. Wholemeal plain and wholemeal self-raising flours are also available. They are less refined, so they have a coarser texture.

LEFT: Rocky road slice

slightly. Beat the mixture to release any remaining heat. Gradually add the egg, about 3 teaspoons at a time. Beat well after each addition until all the egg has been added and the mixture is glossy—a wooden spoon should stand upright. If it is too runny, the egg has been added too quickly. If this happens, beat for several more minutes, or until thickened.

3 Spoon the mixture into a piping bag fitted with a 1.5 cm (⅝ inch) plain nozzle. Sprinkle the baking trays lightly with water. Pipe 15 cm (6 inch) lengths onto the trays, leaving room for expansion. Bake for 10–15 minutes. Reduce the heat to moderate 180°C (350°F/Gas 4). Bake for another 15 minutes, or until golden and firm. Cool on a wire rack. Split each eclair, removing any uncooked dough. Fill the puffs with cream.

4 Put the chocolate in a heatproof bowl. Bring a saucepan of water to the boil and remove the pan from the heat. Sit the bowl over the pan, making sure the bowl is not touching the water. Allow to stand, stirring occasionally, until the chocolate has melted. Spread over the tops.

DANISH PASTRIES

Preparation time: 40 minutes
+ 1 hour 30 minutes rising
+ 4 hours 30 minutes refrigeration
Total cooking time: 25 minutes
Makes 12

★★★

7 g (¼ oz) sachet dried yeast
½ cup (125 ml/4 fl oz) warm milk
1 teaspoon caster (superfine) sugar
2 cups (250 g/8 oz) plain (all-purpose) flour
¼ cup (60 g/2 oz) caster (superfine) sugar, extra
1 egg, lightly beaten
1 teaspoon vanilla essence
250 g (8 oz) unsalted butter, chilled

Pastry cream
2 tablespoons caster (superfine) sugar
2 egg yolks
2 teaspoons plain (all-purpose) flour
2 teaspoons cornflour (cornstarch)
½ cup (125 ml/4 fl oz) hot milk

425 g (14 oz) can apricot halves, drained
1 egg, lightly beaten
40 g (1¼ oz) flaked almonds
¼ cup (80 g/2¾ oz) apricot jam, to glaze

CHOCOLATE ECLAIRS

Preparation time: 30 minutes
Total cooking time: 40 minutes
Makes 18

★★

125 g (4 oz) unsalted butter
1 cup (125 g/4 oz) plain (all-purpose) flour, sifted
4 eggs, lightly beaten
300 ml (10 fl oz) cream, whipped
150 g (5 oz) dark chocolate, chopped

1 Preheat the oven to hot 210°C (415°F/Gas 6–7). Grease two baking trays. Combine the butter and 1 cup (250 ml/8 fl oz) water in a large heavy-based saucepan. Stir over medium heat until the butter melts. Increase the heat, bring to the boil, then remove from the heat.

2 Add the flour to the saucepan all at once and quickly beat into the water with a wooden spoon. Return to the heat and continue beating until the mixture leaves the side of the pan and forms a ball. Transfer to a large bowl and cool

ABOVE: Chocolate eclairs

1 Stir the yeast, milk and sugar together in a small bowl until dissolved. Leave in a warm place for 10 minutes, or until bubbles appear on the surface. The mixture should be frothy and slightly increased in volume. If not, the yeast is dead and you should start again.

2 Sift the flour and ½ teaspoon salt into a large bowl and stir in the extra sugar. Make a well in the centre and add the yeast mixture, egg and vanilla essence all at once. Mix to a firm dough. Turn out onto a floured surface and knead for 10 minutes to form a smooth, elastic dough.

3 Place the dough in a lightly greased bowl, cover and set aside in a warm place for 1 hour, or until doubled in size. Meanwhile, roll the cold butter between two sheets of baking paper to a 15 x 20 cm (6 x 8 inch) rectangle and then refrigerate until required.

4 Punch down the dough (give it one good punch with your fist) and knead for 1 minute. Roll out to a rectangle measuring 25 x 30 cm (10 x 12 inches). Place the butter in the centre of the dough and fold up the bottom and top of the dough over the butter to join in the centre. Seal the edges with a rolling pin.

5 Give the dough a quarter turn clockwise then roll out to a 20 x 45 cm (8 x 18 inch) rectangle. Fold over the top third of the pastry, then the bottom third and then give another quarter turn clockwise. Cover and refrigerate for 30 minutes. Repeat the rolling, folding, turning and chilling four more times. Wrap in plastic wrap and chill for at least another 2 hours before using.

6 For the pastry cream, place the sugar, egg yolks and flours in a saucepan and whisk to combine. Pour the hot milk over the flour and whisk until smooth. Bring to the boil over moderate heat, stirring all the time, until the mixture boils and thickens. Cover and set aside.

7 Preheat the oven to moderately hot 200°C (400°F/Gas 6) and line two baking trays with baking paper. On a lightly floured surface, roll the dough into a rectangle or square 3 mm (⅛ inch) thick. Cut the dough into 10 cm (4 inch) squares and place on the baking trays.

8 Spoon a tablespoon of pastry cream into the centre of each square and top with 2 apricot halves. Brush one corner with the beaten egg and draw up that corner and the diagonally opposite one to touch in the middle between the apricots. Press firmly in the centre. Leave in a warm place to prove for 30 minutes. Brush each pastry with the egg and sprinkle with the flaked almonds. Bake for 15–20 minutes, or until golden. Cool on wire racks.

9 Melt the apricot jam with 1 tablespoon water and then strain. Brush the tops of the apricots with the hot glaze and serve.

PASTRY CREAM

'Crème patissiere' is the French term for pastry cream. It is a delicious, thick custard based on milk, eggs and sugar and is thickened with flour or cornflour (cornstarch). It becomes firm once cooked and left to stand and is mostly used to fill choux, shortcrust and puff pastry products. The custard often has a praline of crushed toffee and nuts folded through for a different flavour. It is used extensively by French pastry cooks, often to fill elaborate pastries.

BELOW: Danish pastries

BAKLAVA

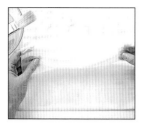

Mix the oil and melted butter and use to brush each filo sheet. Fold each sheet in half.

Place the oiled filo sheets in the greased tin.

Using a sharp knife, score the top of the baklava into four even strips.

Pour the cold syrup over the hot slice, then leave to soak in.

OPPOSITE PAGE, FROM TOP: Baklava; Apple turnovers

BAKLAVA

Preparation time: 50 minutes
Total cooking time: 40 minutes
Makes 16 pieces

3¹/₂ cups (375 g/12 oz) walnuts, finely chopped
1 cup (155 g/5¹/₂ oz) almonds, finely chopped
¹/₂ teaspoon ground cinnamon
¹/₂ teaspoon mixed spice
1 tablespoon caster (superfine) sugar
16 sheets filo pastry
1 tablespoon olive oil
200 g (6¹/₂ oz) unsalted butter, melted

Syrup

2 cups (500 g/1 lb) sugar
3 whole cloves
3 teaspoons lemon juice

1 Preheat the oven to moderate 180°C (350°F/ Gas 4). Lightly grease the base and sides of an 18 x 28 cm (7 x 11 inch) shallow tin.
2 Mix together the walnuts, almonds, spices and sugar, then divide into three portions.
3 Work with one sheet of filo at a time, keeping the rest covered with a damp tea towel to prevent drying out. Place a sheet of pastry on a work surface. Mix the oil and melted butter and brush liberally over the pastry sheet. Fold the sheet in half crossways. Trim the edges so the pastry fits the base of the tin. Repeat with another three sheets of pastry, brushing each layer liberally with the butter mixture.
4 Sprinkle one portion of the nut filling over the pastry. Continue buttering the pastry, four sheets at a time as before, and layering with the nuts. Finish with pastry on top.
5 Trim the edges and brush the top with the remaining butter and oil. Score the slice lengthways into four even portions and bake for 30 minutes, or until golden and crisp.
6 For the syrup, put the sugar, cloves, lemon juice and 1¹/₃ cups (330 ml/11 fl oz) water in a small saucepan and stir over low heat, without boiling, until the sugar has dissolved. Bring to the boil, then reduce the heat and simmer, without stirring, for 10 minutes, or until thickened. Remove from the heat and cool.
7 When the baklava is cooked, pour the cold syrup over the hot slice. The syrup should have the consistency of thick honey and will take a little while to soak in. Leave to cool and cut into diamonds when cold.

NOTES: The baklava can be stored for up to five days in an airtight container.

Filo pastry is a very fine pastry used in many sweet and savoury recipes from the Middle East and other parts of the world. It is available fresh or frozen.

APPLE TURNOVERS

Preparation time: 40 minutes
Total cooking time: 25 minutes
Makes 12 pieces

500 g (1 lb) home-made or bought
 puff pastry (see page 488)
1 egg white, lightly beaten
caster (superfine) sugar, to sprinkle

Filling

1 cup (220 g/7 oz) pie or stewed apple
1–2 tablespoons caster (superfine) sugar,
 to taste
¹/₄ cup (40 g/1¹/₄ oz) raisins, chopped
¹/₄ cup (30 g/1 oz) walnuts, chopped

1 Preheat the oven to hot 210°C (415°F/ Gas 6–7). Lightly grease a baking tray. Roll the pastry on a lightly floured surface to 45 x 35 cm (18 x 14 inches). Cut out twelve 10 cm (4 inch) rounds.
2 For the apple filling, mix together the apple, sugar, raisins and walnuts.
3 Divide the filling among the pastry rounds, then brush the edges with water. Fold in half and pinch firmly together to seal. Use the back of a knife to push up the pastry edge at intervals. Brush the tops with egg white and sprinkle with caster sugar. Make 2 small slits in the top of each turnover. Bake for 15 minutes, then lower the oven to moderately hot 190°C (375°F/Gas 5) and bake for 10 minutes, or until golden. Delicious served warm.
VARIATION: These delicious pastry treats are traditionally made as above using apple. However, you can make equally tasty turnovers by substituting the same quantity of cooked or canned pears or rhubarb for the apple. Fruit mince (mincemeat) of the same quantity also makes an interesting substitute for the raisins and walnuts.

GLOSSARY

AL DENTE Meaning 'to the tooth'. Pasta and risotto rice are cooked until they are *al dente*—the outside is tender but the centre still has a little resistance or 'bite'.

ARBORIO RICE A short-grained plump grain from Italy. Usually used in risottos.

BAKING POWDER This is a leavener used to aerate cakes, bread and buns. It is a mixture of bicarbonate of soda (baking soda), cream of tartar (an acid) and usually cornflour (cornstarch).

BASMATI RICE This is an aromatic, long, narrow-grained rice. The grains remain firm and separate when cooked. Basmati rice is commonly used as an accompaniment to Indian dishes.

BATTER An uncooked mixture of flour, liquid and sometimes a leavener such as baking powder.

BEAT To briskly combine ingredients, usually with electric beaters but sometimes with a wooden spoon, to introduce air into a mixture to make it smooth and light.

BOCCONCINI Small mozzarella balls are known as bocconcini or baby mozzarella. Keep refrigerated in the whey in which it is sold.

BOK CHOY Also called Chinese chard, Chinese white cabbage or pak choi. A member of the cabbage family with a slightly mustardy taste. It has fleshy white stems and dark green leaves. Separate the leaves and wash well before use. A smaller variety is called Shanghai or baby bok choy—use it in the same way.

BORLOTTI BEANS Slightly kidney shaped, this large bean is a beautifully marked pale, pinkish brown with burgundy specks.

BUTTERMILK Made by adding a culture to skim milk and leaving the mixture to sour and thicken. It has a tangy flavour.

Because of its acidic content it is used to act as a raising agent.

CANDLENUTS These are large cream-coloured nuts similar to macadamias in shape. They cannot be eaten raw as the oil is toxic unless cooked. Candlenuts are often roasted, then ground and used to thicken and enrich curries and sauces. You can substitute macadamias if you can't obtain them.

CAPERS The pickled flowers of the caper bush. Available preserved in brine, vinegar or salt, they should be rinsed well and squeezed dry before use.

CARDAMOM Available as pods, seeds or ground. The pods, each up to 1.5 cm (⁵/₈ inch) long, are tightly packed with brown or black seeds. Use to flavour Indian food. The fragrant seeds have a sweet, spicy flavour. Lightly bruise the pods before using.

CELLOPHANE NOODLES Also known as bean thread vermicelli, mung bean vermicelli or glass noodles. Made from mung bean and tapioca starch. Deep-fry from the packet or soak in boiling water for 3–4 minutes, then rinse and drain.

CHILLI FLAKES Made by crushing dried red chillies, usually with the seeds.

CHILLI PASTE AND JAM Chilli paste and jam are both available in Asian food stores. They are generally made with tomato, onion, chilli, oil, tamarind, garlic, sugar, salt, spices and vinegar. For vegetarian cooking, check the label to ensure the brand you buy does not contain shrimp paste. For our purposes, they are interchangeable.

CHILLI POWDER Made by finely grinding dried red chillies, chilli powder can vary in heat from mild to fiery. Chilli flakes can be substituted, but not Mexican chilli powder, which is mixed with cumin and has a quite different flavour.

CHINESE BARBECUED PORK Also known as char siu. A pork fillet that has been marinated in a mixture of soy sauce, five-spice powder and sugar, then barbecued over charcoal.

CHINESE CABBAGE Also called wom bok, napa cabbage or celery cabbage. Shaped like a cos lettuce with tightly packed leaves. It has a delicate flavour.

CHINESE RICE WINE Made from rice, millet, yeast and Shaoxing's local water, this is aged for at least three years, then bottled either in glass or decorative earthenware bottles. Several varieties are available. As a drink, rice wine is served warm in small cups. In cooking, dry sherry is the best substitute.

CHORIZO A highly seasoned minced (ground) pork sausage flavoured with garlic, chilli powder and other spices. It is widely used in both Mexican and Spanish cooking. Mexican chorizo is made with fresh pork, while the Spanish version uses smoked pork.

CINNAMON The dried aromatic bark from the laurel family of trees native to Asia. The paper-thin inner bark is rolled and dried to form quills or sticks. Also available ground.

CLAMS Also sold as vongole, these bivalves are slightly chewy and salty, and have a hard, ridged shell, measuring about 4 cm (1¹/₂ inches).

CLOVES These are the strongly scented flower buds of the clove tree which are sun-dried until hard. They contain essential oils and are used whole or ground.

COCONUT CREAM AND MILK Both are extracted from the flesh of fresh coconuts. The cream is pressed out first and is thicker than the milk.

COPHA Also called white vegetable shortening. Made from purified coconut oil that is processed into a white solid. It is generally used in making uncooked confections and slices or bar cookies.

CORIANDER Also called cilantro, coriander is an aromatic, green, leafy herb used as a flavouring and a garnish. The whole fresh plant is used—roots, stems and leaves. The seeds can also be roasted and are often ground to a powder.

CREAM To cream together means to beat one or more ingredients, usually butter and sugar, until light and fluffy. Electric beaters or a whisk can be used. The creaming process dissolves the sugar, resulting in a light texture.

CREME FRAICHE A naturally soured cream with a nutty, slightly sour taste. Available at delicatessens.

CRISP FRIED SHALLOTS Commonly used as a garnish in Southeast Asia, crisp fried shallots are thin slices of small red Asian shallots that are cut lengthways and deep-fried until light brown. They are available from Asian food stores in packets or tubs. Store them in the freezer to prevent the oil from going rancid.

CUMIN These small, pale brown, aromatic seeds have a warm, earthy flavour. In its ground form, cumin is an essential component of spice mixes.

CURRY LEAVES Small, pointed leaves with a spicy, toasty curry flavour. They are used widely in southern Indian and Malay cooking.

DASHI Made from dried kelp and dried fish, dashi is available as granules or as a powder. Dissolve in hot water to make the Japanese stock, dashi.

DRIED RICE NOODLES These dried rice-flour noodles come in varying widths; the wider they are, they longer they need to be soaked before use.

DRIED SHRIMP Small sun-dried prawns (shrimp) that are available whole or

shredded, but they are usually ground before use. Some require soaking and rinsing before use.

DUST This means to cover lightly, usually referring to icing sugar or cocoa powder that is sifted over the top of a cake or pie for presentation.

EGG NOODLES Made from wheat flour and eggs, these noodles are available fresh and dried in a variety of widths. Fresh egg noodles can be stored in the fridge for 1 week. Dried noodles will keep indefinitely.

ENOKI MUSHROOMS These are tiny white Japanese mushrooms on long, thin stalks growing in clumps. They need little cooking.

FETA CHEESE A soft, white cheese ripened in brine. Originally made from the milk of sheep or goats, but often now made with the more economical cow's milk. It has a sharp and salty taste.

FISH SAUCE A salty sauce with a strong fishy smell. Small fish are packed into wooden barrels, seasoned with salt and fermented for several months. The brown liquid run-off is fish sauce.

FIVE-SPICE POWDER This fragrant, ground spice blend is used extensively in Chinese cooking. It contains cloves, star anise, Sichuan peppercorns, fennel and cinnamon. Use it sparingly, as it can overpower more subtle flavours.

FLAT-LEAF PARSLEY Also known as Italian or continental parsley. Used as an ingredient rather than a garnish.

FRESH RICE NOODLES Made from a thin dough of rice flour, these are available uncut as fresh rice sheet noodles or pre-cut into different widths. Use the sheets within a few days as they shouldn't be stored in the fridge—they will go hard. Before use, soak in boiling water and gently separate. Drain and rinse.

GAI LARN Also called Chinese broccoli, this is a green vegetable with thick, green stalks, slightly leathery leaves and white flowers. It can be steamed whole, or the leaves and stems can be cut up and added to soups and stir-fries. Young, thinner stalks are crisp and mild; thicker stalks need to be peeled and halved.

GALANGAL A rhizome with brown skin and cream-coloured flesh. It is related to ginger but has a distinct flavour and perfume. Available fresh, as fresh slices in brine, dried slices in packets, and powdered.

GARAM MASALA Garam masala is a mixture of ground spices that usually includes cinnamon, black pepper, coriander (cilantro), cumin, cardamom, cloves and mace or nutmeg. It is often added towards the end cooking.

GHEE A highly clarified butter made from cow or water buffalo milk. Ghee can be heated to a high temperature without burning.

GINGER The rhizome of a tropical plant which is sometimes referred to as a 'root'. Fresh young ginger has a smooth, pinkish beige skin. As it ages, the skin toughens and the flesh becomes more fibrous. Choose pieces you can snap easily.

HALOUMI A salty Middle Eastern cheese made from ewe's milk. The curd is cooked, then matured in brine, often with herbs or spices.

HOISIN SAUCE Hoisin sauce is a thick, sweet-spicy Chinese sauce made from soy beans, garlic, sugar and spices. It is used both in cooking and as a dipping sauce. Once opened, store hoisin sauce in the refrigerator.

HOKKIEN NOODLES Thick, fresh egg noodles that have been cooked and lightly oiled before packaging. Most often found vacuum-packed. Cover with boiling water for 1 minute to separate before draining and rinsing.

JASMINE RICE A long-grain, fragrant, white rice used throughout Southeast Asia. Usually steamed or cooked using the absorption method and served as an accompaniment.

JULIENNE To cut a vegetable or citrus rind into short, thin 'julienne' strips.

KECAP MANIS A thick, dark, sweet, aromatic soy sauce used in Indonesian cooking. Traditionally it is flavoured with garlic, star anise and galangal, and sweetened with palm syrup.

LEMON GRASS A lemon-scented tropical grass with leaves and a central rib. Only the lower stalk is used in cooking. You can substitute one stalk of lemon grass for three thin strips of lemon zest. Dried lemon grass has little flavour.

MAKRUT (KAFFIR) LIME LEAVES The highly fragrant, dark green leaves of a citrus tree, which are available fresh, frozen or dried from greengrocers. Each leaf is shaped in a figure of eight—in our recipes, half of the eight represents one leaf.

MIRIN Sometimes incorrectly described as 'rice wine', this spirit-based sweetener from Japan is used for cooking, especially in marinades and glazes, and simmered dishes. It is sold in Asian food shops.

MARSALA A fortified wine from Marsala in Sicily. Dry Marsalas are used in savoury dishes and drunk as an aperitif; sweet ones are used in desserts.

MISO PASTE A paste made from fermented soy beans used as a staple in Japanese soups, sauces and marinades. Generally, the lighter the paste, the milder the flavour. It varies in colour from white, yellow, light brown to brown and red.

MOZZARELLA A smooth, fresh white cheese with a mild, slightly sweet flavour. It melts well.

NORI A seaweed which is pressed into sheets and dried. It is mostly used as a wrapper for sushi or is shredded and added to Japanese soups as a garnish.

MUSTARD SEEDS Black, brown, yellow and white mustard seeds are a common ingredient in many curries. Mustard seeds are fried before grinding to release essential oils and increase their flavour. Black and brown mustard seeds are the smallest and hottest, whereas yellow and white mustard seeds are larger and have a milder flavour.

OYSTER MUSHROOMS These are a fan or oyster-shell shaped mushroom, pale creamy grey or brown in colour with a slightly peppery flavour that becomes milder when cooked.

OYSTER SAUCE It is a rich, thick, salty sauce made from dried oysters, and it is used for both flavour and colour. Readily available in supermarkets.

PALM SUGAR A dark, unrefined sugar from the sap of sugar palm trees. The sap is collected from the trees, boiled until it turns into a thick syrup, then poured into moulds where it dries to form dense, heavy cakes. It is widely used in Southeast Asia. Shave the sugar off the cake with a sharp knife. Buy it in blocks or in jars from Asian shops. You can substitute soft brown sugar.

PANCETTA Cured belly of pork, somewhat like streaky bacon. Available in flat pieces or rolled up.

PANDANUS LEAF Also known as pandan leaf, this flavour enhancer is used in both savoury and sweet dishes of Sri Lanka, Malaysia, Indonesia and Thailand. It has a delicate, almost sweet taste. A strip may be added to rice on cooking or to simmering curries. It is also used to wrap ingredients, such as chicken and rice.

PARMESAN A hard cow's milk cheese widely used in Italian cooking, either grated and added to dishes or shaved to use as a garnish.

PICKLED DAIKON A yellow-coloured, firm and crunchy pickle made from daikon—a large white radish. It is usually pickled in dry rice bran after being hung to dry. It is available as whole pieces or presliced in supermarkets or Asian food stores.

PICKLED GINGER Whole, sliced or shredded peeled ginger root preserved in brine, rice wine or rice vinegar. It usually takes on a light pink colouring through chemical reaction. Thinly sliced pickled ginger is frequently used as a garnish in Japanese dishes.

PORCINI MUSHROOMS Used in Italian and French cooking, these have a brown cap and a thick white stem. Also known as cep mushrooms, they come fresh or dried. Soak dried ones in warm water, then rinse.

PRESERVED LEMONS Lemons that have been preserved in a salt–lemon juice mixture (sometimes with spices such as cinnamon, cloves and coriander) for about 30 days. Rinse and remove the white pith before using.

PROSCIUTTO An Italian ham that has been cured by salting then drying in the air. It doesn't require cooking.

PUY LENTILS This tiny, dark green lentil is considered a delicacy in France and is relatively expensive. Unlike most other lentils, they keep their shape and have a firm texture after cooking.

RAMEN NOODLES These Japanese wheat flour noodles are bound together with egg. Available fresh, dried and in instant form. They need to be boiled before use—2 minutes for fresh noodles, 4 minutes for dried, and for instant, just add boiling stock.

RED ASIAN SHALLOTS Small, red onions that grow in bulbs and are sold in segments that look like large cloves of pink garlic. They have a very concentrated flavour.

ROCKET This salad green, also known as *arugula* is native to the Mediterranean. The peppery flavour of the leaves increases with age.

SAFFRON The dried dark orange stigmas of a type of crocus flower, which are used to add aroma and flavour to food. Only a few threads are needed for each recipe as they are very pungent (and expensive).

SAKE is a Japanese alcoholic drink which is often called rice wine—a misnomer since it is brewed. It is often served warm in restaurants, but is also used as an ingredient to tenderize, tone down saltiness and to remove unwanted flavours and scents.

SALT COD Cod fillets that have been salted and dried. Needs to be soaked for at least two days before use. Available from speciality shops.

SAMBAL OELEK A hot paste made from fresh red chillies, chopped and mixed with sugar, salt and vinegar or tamarind. It is used like a relish or served as a side dish. It can also be used as a substitute for fresh chillies in most recipes. If covered, it will keep in the refrigerator for months.

SASHIMI Thinly sliced raw fish, typically served with grated horseradish or ginger and soy sauce. The preparation of the fish is a skill perfected with years of practice.

SESAME OIL An aromatic oil made from sesame seeds. It is best bought in small quantities as it loses its aroma quickly. Use sparingly as it has a very strong, rich flavour. The Asian variety is made from roasted sesame seeds; the Middle Eastern version from plain ones.

SHRIMP PASTE/SAUCE A pungent mixture made from fermented prawns. It can be pink, soft and with a liquidy consistency (available in jars) or dried and sold in dark, hard bricks. Cover in plastic wrap and store in an airtight container in the fridge. Usually fried or roasted before use.

SILVERBEET Also known as Swiss chard, silverbeet is often confused with spinach. The leaves are large and crinkly.

SNAKE BEANS Also called longbean, cowpea or yard-long beans. A long, green, stringless bean. Look for firm, deep green beans. Use as soon as possible after purchase.

SOY SAUCE Soy sauce is extracted from fermented and salted soy beans.

STAR ANISE A star-shaped Chinese fruit made up of eight segments. They are sun-dried until hard and brown, and they have a pronounced aniseed aroma and sweet aniseed flavour. Use them whole to infuse stocks, soups and sauces, then remove before serving.

SUN-DRIED TOMATOES Widely available either dry and loosely packed, or in jars in oil. The dry variety need to be rehydrated before use by soaking them in boiling water for 10 minutes.

SZECHWAN PEPPERCORNS A Chinese spice made from the red berries of the prickly ash tree and sold whole or ground. The flavour is woody and it has a strong, hot, numbing aftertaste. Often the powder is dry-fried to bring out the flavours. Also called Sichuan peppercorns.

TAHINI An oily paste made from ground sesame seeds, tahini adds a strong nutty flavour. It is popular in the eastern Mediterranean.

TAMARI A naturally fermented, thick, dark Japanese soy sauce with a stronger flavour than regular Japanese soy sauce (shoyu). Although true tamari is wheat-free, there are many lesser brands that have misapplied the name. Check the label on the bottle to be sure. It is often sold in health-food stores.

TAMARIND A large, brown, bean-like pod with a fruity, tart flavour. It is available as a dried shelled fruit, a block of compressed pulp, a purée or a concentrate. It adds a sweet–sour flavour.

THAI BASIL A member of the basil family with smaller and darker leaves than regular basil and a stronger aniseed and clove flavour and aroma. The stems and younger leaves have a purplish colour.

TOFU Tofu products are made from yellow soy beans that have been soaked, ground, combined with water and then cooked for a short time, until they solidify into a mass.

TOMATO PASSATA This is a bottled tomato sauce commonly used in Italian cooking. The sauce is made with fresh, ripe tomatoes which are peeled, seeded and slowly cooked down with basil, onion and garlic. The thickened sauce is then passed through a sieve before being bottled.

TURMERIC Dried turmeric, sold whole or ground, is a deep yellow colour, and has a slightly bitter flavour and pungent aroma. Turmeric is added to dishes for both colour and flavour.

UDON NOODLES These white Japanese noodles are made from wheat flour and are sold in a variety of widths, both fresh and dried. Boil for 1–2 minutes before use.

VANILLA Vanilla beans are the dried and cured beans or pods of a climbing orchid native to South America. The extract is made by using alcohol to extract the vanilla flavour from vanilla beans. Vanilla extract is strong and should be used sparingly. Avoid using artificial vanilla essence made with synthetic vanillin.

VIETNAMESE MINT This has narrow, pointed leaves with distinctive dark markings that vary from leaf to leaf. Its flavour resembles coriander.

VINE LEAVES Young leaves from the grape vine, blanched then preserved in brine. Available in packets, jars and cans.

WASABI PASTE A pungent Japanese flavouring resembling horseradish in taste. It comes from the herb *Wasabia japonica* and is turned into a powder or paste, both available from Asian food stores.

WATER CHESTNUTS Small, rounded, crisp vegetables, usually sold canned (if fresh, they need peeling). They give a crunchy texture to many Asian dishes. Any unused water chestnuts will keep fresh for 4 days if immersed in water in the fridge; change the water daily.

YEAST A naturally occurring raising agent. Dried yeast, available from supermarkets, can be added to liquid or mixed straight into dry ingredients.

INDEX

Page numbers in *italics* refer to photographs. Page numbers in **bold** type refer to margin notes.